Integrated Security Technologies and Solutions - Volume II

Cisco Security Solutions for Network Access Control, Segmentation, Context Sharing, Secure Connectivity, and Virtualization

Aaron Woland, CCIE® No. 20113

Vivek Santuka, CCIE® No. 17621

Jamie Sanbower, CCIE® No. 13637

Chad Mitchell, CCIE® No. 44090

Cisco Press

Integrated Security Technologies and Solutions - Volume II

Cisco Security Solutions for Network Access Control, Segmentation, Context Sharing, Secure Connectivity, and Virtualization

Aaron Woland, Vivek Santuka, Jamie Sanbower, Chad Mitchell

Published by:
Cisco Press
221 River St.
Hoboken, NJ 07030 USA

ScoutAutomatedPrintCode

Library of Congress Control Number: 2019931156

ISBN-13: 978-1-58714-707-4

ISBN-10: 1-58714-707-6

Warning and Disclaimer

Trademark Acknowledgments

Special Sales

For information about buying this title in bulk quantities, or for special sales opportunities (which may include electronic versions; custom cover designs; and content particular to your business, training goals, marketing focus, or branding interests), please contact our corporate sales department at corpsales@pearsoned.com or (800) 382-3419.

For government sales inquiries, please contact governmentsales@pearsoned.com.

For questions about sales outside the U.S., please contact intlcs@pearson.com.

Feedback Information

At Cisco Press, our goal is to create in-depth technical books of the highest quality and value. Each book is crafted with care and precision, undergoing rigorous development that involves the unique expertise of members from the professional technical community.

Readers' feedback is a natural continuation of this process. If you have any comments regarding how we could improve the quality of this book, or otherwise alter it to better suit your needs, you can contact us through email at feedback@ciscopress.com. Please make sure to include the book title and ISBN in your message.

We greatly appreciate your assistance.

Editor-in-Chief: Mark Taub	**Copy Editor:** Bill McManus
Alliances Manager, Cisco Press: Arezou Gol	**Technical Editor:** Chad Sullivan
Product Line Manager: Brett Bartow	**Editorial Assistant:** Cindy Teeters
Executive Editor: Mary Beth Ray	**Designer:** Chuti Prasertsith
Managing Editor: Sandra Schroeder	**Composition:** codeMantra
Development Editor: Christopher A. Cleveland	**Indexer:** Erika Millen
Project Editor: Mandie Frank	**Proofreader:** Jeanine Furino

CISCO.

Americas Headquarters	Asia Pacific Headquarters	Europe Headquarters
Cisco Systems, Inc.	Cisco Systems (USA) Pte. Ltd.	Cisco Systems International BV Amsterdam,
San Jose, CA	Singapore	The Netherlands

Cisco has more than 200 offices worldwide. Addresses, phone numbers, and fax numbers are listed on the Cisco Website at www.cisco.com/go/offices.

Cisco and the Cisco logo are trademarks or registered trademarks of Cisco and/or its affiliates in the U.S. and other countries. To view a list of Cisco trademarks, go to this URL: www.cisco.com/go/trademarks. Third party trademarks mentioned are the property of their respective owners. The use of the word partner does not imply a partnership relationship between Cisco and any other company. (1110R)

Credits

Figure 2-50   Hariprasad Holla

Table 1-1   Internet Assigned Numbers Authority

About the Authors

Aaron Woland, CCIE® No. 20113, is a principal engineer in Cisco's Advanced Threat Security group and works with Cisco's largest customers all over the world. His primary job responsibilities include security design, solution enhancements, standards development, advanced threat solution design, endpoint security, and futures.

Aaron joined Cisco in 2005 and is currently a member of numerous security advisory boards and standards body working groups. Prior to joining Cisco, Aaron spent 12 years as a consultant and technical trainer.

Aaron's other publications include *Integrated Security Technologies and Solutions - Volume I*; both editions of Cisco ISE for BYOD and Secure Unified Access; *Cisco Next-Generation Security Solutions: All-in-one Cisco ASA FirePOWER Services, NGIPS and AMP; CCNP Security SISAS 300-208 Official Cert Guide;* the *CCNA Security 210-260 Complete Video Course;* and many published white papers and design guides.

Aaron is one of only five inaugural members of the Hall of Fame Elite for Distinguished Speakers at Cisco Live, and he is a security columnist for *Network World*, where he blogs on all things related to security. His other certifications include GHIC, GCFE, GSEC, CEH, MCSE, VCP, CCSP, CCNP, and CCDP, among others.

You can follow Aaron on Twitter: @aaronwoland.

Vivek Santuka, CCIE® No. 17621, is a consulting systems engineer at Cisco and is a security consultant to some of Cisco's largest customers. He has over 13 years of experience in security, focusing on identity management and access control. Vivek is a member of multiple technical advisory groups.

Vivek holds two CCIE certifications: Security and Routing and Switching. In addition, he holds RHCE and CISSP certifications and is a Distinguished Speaker at Cisco Live.

Vivek is also the coauthor of the Cisco Press books *AAA Identity Management Security and Integrated Security Technologies and Solutions – Volume I.*

You can follow Vivek on Twitter: @vsantuka.

Jamie Sanbower, CCIE® No. 13637 (Routing and Switching, Security, and Wireless), is a principal systems engineer for Cisco's Global Security Architecture Team. Jamie has been with Cisco since 2010 and is currently a technical leader and member of numerous advisory and working groups.

With over 15 years of technical experience in the networking and security industry, Jamie has developed, designed, implemented, and operated enterprise network and security solutions for a wide variety of large clients. He is coauthor of the Cisco Press book *Integrated Security Technologies and Solutions - Volume I.*

Jamie is a dynamic presenter and is a Cisco Live Distinguished Speaker. Prior to Cisco, Jamie had various roles, including director of a cyber security practice, senior security consultant, and senior network engineer.

Chad Mitchell, CCIE® No. 44090, is a technical solutions architect at Cisco supporting the Department of Defense and supporting agencies. In his daily role, he supports the sales teams as a technical resource for all Cisco security products and serves as the Identity Services Engine subject matter expert for Cisco's US Public Sector team.

Chad has been with Cisco since 2013 supporting the DoD and other customers and is a contributing member to the Policy & Access Technical Advisors Group. Prior to joining Cisco, Chad spent 7 years as a deployment engineer and systems administrator implementing Cisco security products for customers.

While his primary area of expertise is enterprise network access control with ISE, Chad is well versed on all Cisco security solutions such as ASA firewalls, Firepower NGFW/IPS/IDS, and Stealthwatch, to name a few; he also has first-hand experience deploying these solutions in customer production environments.

Chad's other certifications include CCDA, CCNP, Network+, Security+, and many other industry certifications.

About the Technical Reviewer

Chad Sullivan (3xCCIE® No. 6493: Routing & Switching, Security, and SNA/IP) is the co-founder and President/CEO of Priveon, Inc., a security services-focused, Cisco Partner who globally implements and trains Cisco partners and customers on Cisco technologies. He has been working with Cisco Security and Networking products for decades and has even written and technical edited a handful of Cisco Press books around various endpoint and networking security technologies. You can often find him at an airport, or in front of an audience that is eager to learn from his vast experience in the security industry. When not working to help others secure global organizations, he spends his precious free time with his wife Jennifer and his six children (Avery, Brielle, Celine, Danae, Elliot, and Finley) in their Atlanta area home.

Dedications

First and foremost, this book is dedicated to my amazing best friend, fellow adventurer, and wife, Suzanne. Thank you for your continued support, encouragement, and patience and for putting up with all the long nights and weekends I had to be writing and for always believing in me and supporting me. You are beyond amazing.

To Mom and Pop. You have always believed in me, supported me in absolutely everything I've ever pursued, and showed pride in my accomplishments (no matter how small). I hope I can continue to fill your lives with pride, happiness, and "nachas"; and if I succeed, it will still only be a fraction of what you deserve.

To my four incredible daughters, Eden, Nyah, Netanya, and Cassandra. You girls are my inspiration, pride, and joy! I can only hope that one day you will look back at the ridiculous man that raised you and feel a level of pride.

—Aaron

To my beautiful wife. Thank you for your unconditional love and support. Your belief in me keeps me going. From my first CCIE to my third book, you have always encouraged me and have stood with me even when it took so much away from you. Thank you! I couldn't have done any of it without you.

To my son. Thank you for allowing me to miss all those gaming sessions to write this book. I promise to make it up to you. I know you will do much more than your dad and will make me proud. Love you.

—Vivek

This book is dedicated to my better half, my soulmate, my Christianna. From CCIEs to babies, we have accomplished so much together, blowing away the status quo. You always told me I could and should write a book, and I know without your support this book would not exist. The fact of the matter is you were as much a part of the writing process as I was. Thank you for putting up with all the late nights and weekends that I was writing and you didn't complain once (except for me being ADD about writing). Your companionship and love motivates me more than you will ever know.

To my amazing kids, Cayden and Lilianna. You are my inspiration and make me want to be a better version of myself. I know you both will amaze the world the way you amaze me each and every day! You make me smile and feel loved in ways that are indescribable.

To Mom and Dad for supporting my interests in technology from the start and certifications during grade school.

—Jamie

This book is dedicated to my loving family. To my wife, thank you for dealing with my time away from daily responsibilities, activities, and attention. Your unconditional love and support through the process of my CCIE studies, work travel, and writing this book let me know that I already found my one true love.

To my son, Caelin. You are my main man and the second love of my life. You impress me every day as you grow and always know how to make me smile. I can only hope to mentor and teach you, as others have for me, as you grow into an amazing gentleman.

Finally, to my mom and dad, Curtis and Cindy, for supporting me through my life journey. From multiple high schools to college dropout to trade school and back to college again, you have always been ready to help and guide me down the right path. Your support with watching Caelin while I was off writing this book is greatly appreciated as well. I couldn't have done it without all of your love and support and I am eternally grateful.

—*Chad*

Acknowledgments

There are so many to acknowledge, and I'm sorry that many will get left out.

Vivek Santuka, for not letting me give up and get out of writing this book and for keeping us all on time and on track.

Jamie Sanbower and Chad Mitchell for agreeing to coauthor this beast of a book with Vivek and I, and to Chad Sullivan for the painstaking job of tech-editing this beast. You guys are amazing!

I am honored to work with so many brilliant and talented people every day. Among those: Al Huger, Moses Frost, Steven Chimes, Andrew Benhase, Jeff Fanelli, Tim Snow, Andrew Ossipov, Mike Storm, Jason Frazier, Mo Sachedina, Eric Howard, Evgeny Mirolyubov, Matt Robertson, Brian McMahon, Adam O'Donnell, TK Keanini, Ben Greenbaum, Dean De Beer, Paul Carco, Karel Simek, Naasief Edross, Eric Hulse, and Craig Williams. You guys truly amaze me—seriously.

Last, but not least: to all those at Pearson, especially Mary Beth Ray, Chris Cleveland, and Mandie Frank, who have worked with me on nearly all of my publications. Thank you and your team of editors for making us look so good. Apparently, it takes an army of folks to do so. I'm sorry for all the times you had to correct our English, grammar, and CapItaLizaTioN.

—*Aaron*

Thank you to my wonderful coauthors, Aaron, Jamie, and Chad. Your efforts through professional and personal challenges are much appreciated. Thank you to our wonderful technical editor, Chad Sullivan, for all the hard work on this book.

To the wonderful people at Pearson—Mary Beth Ray, Chris Cleveland, Mandie Frank, and everyone else involved with this book—thank you for your tremendous work. Every time I opened an edited chapter, I couldn't help but be astonished at the attention to detail that you put into this.

Steven Bardsley and Gary McNiel, thank you for believing in me and for all the support and guidance.

Nirav Sheth, my first manager at Cisco, thank you for encouraging me to submit my first book proposal all those years ago. My professional achievements are rooted in your mentoring.

Finally, thank you to all the wonderful people I work with and learn from. There are too many to name, but you help me grow every day.

—*Vivek*

First and foremost, to the coauthors, Aaron, Vivek, Mason and Chad, together we conquered the two-volume set!

Thanks to our technical editor, Chad Sullivan, for keeping us straight and making Aaron split up his entirely too long chapter.

To Jamey Heary for encouraging me to write this book, and to the entire Global Security Architecture Team at Cisco, including Jeff Fanelli, Gary Halleen, Will Young, Mike Geller, Luc Billot, and, last but not least, the man who keeps the security experts in line, Randy Rivera. You all are inspiring, and together we cannot be beat. Seriously the best team at Cisco.

To Alex Golovin, my first mentor, who taught me what RTFM meant and how to keep learning and growing.

Lastly, to all those at Cisco Press, especially Mary Beth Ray, Chris Cleveland, and Mandie Frank. Thank you and your team of editors for producing a quality product and making the authors look good.

—*Jamie*

Throughout my career I have met many amazing people and I cannot list them all. I have learned so much from so many, and most don't even know it. If you have crossed my path, trust me, I have learned something from you even if you were there to learn something from me. I thank you all even if I don't mention you by name.

Thank you to my coauthors, Aaron, Vivek, and Jamie, for trusting in my technical aptitude to write this book and joining me on this next adventure of our careers.

Thank you to Chad Sullivan, our technical editor, for keeping us accurate and clear through our technical ramblings.

To Jamie Sanbower, for being a great friend and mentor. I wouldn't be where I am today in my career without your advice and where I am in life without your friendship. Your "Don't ask me questions until you have exhausted all resources or RTFM" method of teaching has helped me grow and learn more than I thought I ever would.

To Tony Pipta, for being a great friend and helping me keep my sanity with fishing trips in the Chesapeake Bay and hazy suds.

To Archie and TJ Guadalupe for being great friends who always go out of the way to help on anything and from time to time turning wrenches in the garage on my many projects.

To my dad, Curtis, for being my first mentor. I would not be the man, father, or engineer that I am today without you teaching me the way to learn from day one, literally.

Finally, to the folks at Cisco Press. I am glad that your editors paid attention during the punctuation and grammar classes, because I didn't. Your ability to take the ramblings of engineers and edit them into meaningful and readable content is unparalleled.

—*Chad*

Contents at a Glance

Contents

Reader Services

Register your copy at www.ciscopress.com/title/9781587147074 for convenient access to downloads, updates, and corrections as they become available. To start the registration process, go to www.ciscopress.com/register and log in or create an account.* Enter the product ISBN 9781587147074 and click Submit. When the process is complete, you will find any available bonus content under Registered Products.

*Be sure to check the box that you would like to hear from us to receive exclusive discounts on future editions of this product.

Command Syntax Conventions

The conventions used to present command syntax in this book are the same conventions used in the IOS Command Reference. The Command Reference describes these conventions as follows:

- **Boldface** indicates commands and keywords that are entered literally as shown. In actual configuration examples and output (not general command syntax), boldface indicates commands that are manually input by the user (such as a **show** command).

- *Italic* indicates arguments for which you supply actual values.

- Vertical bars (|) separate alternative, mutually exclusive elements.

- Square brackets ([ ]) indicate an optional element.

- Braces ({ }) indicate a required choice.

- Braces within brackets ([{ }]) indicate a required choice within an optional element.

Introduction

This book is the second and last volume of the *Integrated Security Technologies and Solutions* set in the Cisco CCIE Professional Development Series from Cisco Press. It offers expert-level instruction in security design, deployment, integration, and support methodologies to help security professionals manage complex solutions and prepare for the CCIE Security exams.

This book is an expert-level guide for Cisco security products and solutions, with a strong focus on inter-product integration. Its aim is to help security professionals in their day-to-day jobs as well as in preparing for CCIE written and lab exams.

This volume focuses on the Identity Services Engine, Context Sharing, TrustSec, Application Programming Interfaces (APIs), Secure Connectivity with VPNs, Virtualization, and Automation sections of the CCIE v5 blueprint.

Who Should Read This Book?

This book discusses expert-level topics on Cisco security products and solutions, with a focus on integration between these products. In particular, this volume covers ISE, context sharing, APIs, VPN, virtualization, and automation. The book has been designed with the CCIE Security v5 blueprint as a reference, making it a must-have for CCIE Security candidates.

This book presents real-world deployment scenarios, configuration examples, and troubleshooting steps, so it is invaluable to any network engineer, system administrator, security engineer, or security analyst who wants to configure or manage Cisco security products and solutions.

This book is very important for channel partners and managed security service providers who want to provide technical support to their own customers.

This book is also very useful for network administrators in classified environments, such as the U.S. government, who are not allowed to share their sensitive data and want to design, configure, and troubleshoot on their own.

How This Book Is Organized

This book consists of 11 chapters divided into 4 parts.

Part I, "Knock, Knock! Who's there?"

Chapter 1, "Who and What: AAA Basics"

The book begins with a discussion of the fundamentals of authentication, authorization, and accounting (AAA). This chapter discusses the two common protocols used for AAA: RADIUS and TACACS+.

Chapter 2, "Basic Network Access Control"

This chapter dives deeper into AAA with an introduction to Cisco Identity Services Engine (ISE). It discusses 802.1X, various EAP types, Machine Authentication Bypass (MAB), and how to configure ISE and network devices to use these authentication methods.

Chapter 3, "Beyond Basic Network Access Control"

This chapter discusses profiling features of ISE. It describes various methods available for profiling. It also covers ISE features such as EasyConnect and passive identity.

Chapter 4, "Extending Network Access with ISE"

This chapter discusses advanced ISE topics such as BYOD, mobile device management (MDM) integration, posture validation, and guest services. It describes the use of these features and how to configure ISE and network devices for them. This chapter also discusses components and configuration of TrustSec.

Chapter 5, "Device Administration Control with ISE"

This chapter discusses device administration AAA with ISE using TACACS+ and RADIUS. It describes various methods available to authenticate and authorize device administration requests across various Cisco devices with ISE.

Part II, "Spread the Love!"

Chapter 6, "Sharing the Context"

This chapter discusses context sharing with ISE. It describes ISE features and functions such as pxGrid and Rapid Threat Containment. It describes the various integrations and benefits of such integrations with other Cisco devices such as the Cisco Firepower Management Center (FMC) and Cisco Web Security Appliance (WSA). It also discusses the steps required to accomplish such integration.

Chapter 7, "APIs in Cisco Security"

This chapter describes various APIs available in Cisco security products and the benefits of using them. It also discusses specific examples of APIs available in Cisco security products.

Part III, "c2889775343d1ed91b"

Chapter 8, "Security Connectivity"

This chapter discusses fundamentals of virtual private networks (VPNs) and various types of VPNs available on Cisco products.

Chapter 9, "Infrastructure VPN"

This chapter discusses various types of infrastructure VPN such as site-to-site and Dynamic Multipoint VPN (DMVPN). It describes their features, functionality, and configuration required on various Cisco products.

Chapter 10, "Remote Access VPN"

This chapter discusses different types of remote access VPN solutions available on various Cisco devices. It describes their features, functionality, and configuration.

Part IV, "The Red Pill"

Chapter 11, "Security Virtualization and Automation"

This chapter discusses the virtualization of various Cisco security products. It also discusses the Cisco Virtual Security Gateway (VSG), Cisco Enterprise Network Functions Virtualization (NFV), and micro-segmentation with ACI.

Part I

Knock, Knock! Who's There?

Chapter 1

Who and What: AAA Basics

This chapter provides an overview of authentication, authorization, and accounting (AAA), enabling you to understand the fundamentals of the AAA security concept, and compares and contrasts the most common types of AAA.

Fundamentals of AAA

In the world of security, we can only be as secure as our controls permit us to be. There are laws in the United States defining what a passenger of an airplane is permitted to bring onboard. The Transportation Security Administration (TSA) is the enforcement body charged with travel security and enforcing those laws. If the TSA agents weren't operating the metal detectors and X-ray machines (and all the other things that slow us down when trying to reach our airplanes), then how would the Transport Security Administration (TSA) ever really enforce those laws?

With technology, we are faced with the same challenges. We need to have controls in place to ensure that only the correct entities are using our technological "gadgets." The same security concepts from the airport can be applied to many use cases, including human interaction with a computer, a computer's interaction with a network, and even an application's interaction with data.

This security principle of providing the correct level of access to the correct entity is known as authentication, authorization, and accounting (AAA), often referred to as *Triple-A*.

Before allowing an entity to perform an action, you must ensure you know who that entity actually is (authentication) and if that entity is authorized to perform that action (authorization). Additionally, you need to ensure that accurate records are maintained showing that the action has occurred, so you keep a security log of the events (accounting).

You can apply the concepts of AAA to many different aspects of a technology lifecycle; however, this book will focus on the two main aspects of AAA related to network security:

- **Device administration AAA:** Controlling access to who can log in to a network device console, Telnet session, Secure Shell (SSH) session, or other method is one form of AAA that you should be aware of. This is AAA for device administration, and although it can often seem similar to network access AAA, it has a completely different purpose and requires different policy constructs.

- **Network access AAA:** Securing network access can provide the identity of the endpoint, device, or user before permitting the entity to communicate with the network. This is AAA for network access and is the type of AAA that is most focused on in this book.

Understanding the Concept of Triple-A in the Real World

Authentication, simply put, is the validation of an identity, also known as a *credential*. It is a very important step in the process of performing any sort of secure access control, regardless of what you are controlling. Forget about information technology for a second, and consider paying for groceries with a credit card. As a credit card owner, you have the choice to sign the back of the card or to write "check ID" on the back. The more secure method is to force the validation of the credential (the ID) of the person using that card and ensure that credential matches the name on the front of the credit card.

Having a cashier check the identity of the card user to ensure the person in front of them matches the person shown on the ID itself is *authentication*. Ensuring that the identity matches the name printed on the credit card is *authorization*. Think about this scenario: Jamie Sanbower goes into a retail store and hands the cashier a credit card to pay for the $10,000 of electronics he is purchasing. He passes his driver's license to the cashier, who verified that the picture matches Jamie. It is certainly his identity. However, the name printed on the credit card is Vivek Santuka. Should the credit card transaction go through? Of course not (and he better not try).

Jamie's attempt to use Vivek's credit card is now in the log files of the point of sale system, the video monitoring system of the store, and other systems. This is the accounting portion of AAA. It's a critical piece that is required for reporting, audits, and more.

It will become paramount for you as a security professional to understand the difference and purpose of all three A's in the Triple-A security principal.

Compare and Select AAA Options

AAA itself often requires a specialized protocol that is designed to carry authentication requests and their corresponding responses, including authorization results and accounting logs. These specialized protocols are known as AAA protocols, and the two most common AAA protocols are Remote Authentication Dial-In User Service (RADIUS) and Terminal Access Controller Access Control System Plus (TACACS+), which we will define in more detail in this chapter. Each AAA protocol has its own set of pros and cons that makes it more appropriate for certain types of AAA.

Independent of the AAA protocol used, there are two uses of AAA that you will focus on in this book (as previously introduced): device administration and network access.

Device Administration

Device administration is a method of AAA for controlling access to a network device console, Telnet session, SSH session, or other method of accessing the device operating system itself where configuration of the device occurs. For example, imagine your company has an Active Directory group named Cisco Administrators, which should have full access (privilege level 15) to the Cisco switches in the company's network. Members of Cisco Administrators should therefore be able to make changes to virtual local-area networks (VLANs), see the entire running configuration of the device, and more.

There could be another group named Cisco Operators who should only be allowed to view the output of **show** commands, and not be allowed to configure anything in the device. Device administration AAA provides this capability.

However, device administration AAA can get much more granular. The Cisco Secure Access Control System (ACS) and the Cisco Identity Services Engine (ISE) both have the capability to provide *command sets*, which are lists of commands that are permitted or denied to be executed by an authenticated user. In other words, a user can authenticate to the Cisco IOS shell, and ISE can permit or deny the user's execution of individual commands, if you choose.

Figure 1-1 illustrates device administration.

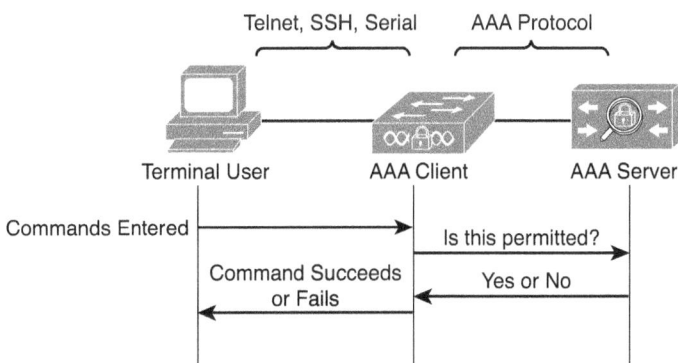

Figure 1-1   *Device Administration*

Device administration can be very interactive in nature, with the need to authenticate once but authorize many times during a single administrative session in the command line of a device. As such, it lends itself well to using the Terminal Access Controller Access Control System (TACACS) client/server protocol, more so than RADIUS.

As the name describes, TACACS was designed for device administration AAA, to authenticate and authorize users into mainframe and Unix terminals, and other terminals or consoles.

Both the TACACS and RADIUS protocols will be discussed in more depth within this chapter; however, because TACACS separates out the authorization portion of AAA, allowing for a single authentication and multiple authorizations within the same session, it lends itself to device administration more than RADIUS. RADIUS does not provide the capability to control which commands can be executed.

Network Access

Secure network access is essentially all about learning the identity of the user or endpoint before permitting that entity to communicate within the network. This type of AAA is the main focus in this book. Network access AAA really took a strong hold back in the day of modems and dial-up networking with plain old telephone service (POTS). Companies provided network access to workers from outside the physical boundaries of the company's buildings with the use of modems. People gained Internet access by using dial-up to an Internet service provider (ISP) over their modems, as well. Basically, all that was needed was a modem and a phone line.

Of course, allowing anyone to dial in to the company network just by dialing the modem's phone number was not a secure practice. The user needed to be authenticated and authorized before being allowed to connect. That is where the RADIUS AAA protocol came into play originally, as is evident in the name of the protocol (*Remote* Authentication *Dial-In* User Service). RADIUS was used between the network access device (NAD) and the authentication server. The authentication protocol was normally Password Authentication Protocol (PAP), Challenge/Handshake Authentication Protocol (CHAP), or Microsoft CHAP (MS-CHAP).

Figure 1-2 illustrates dial-up remote access.

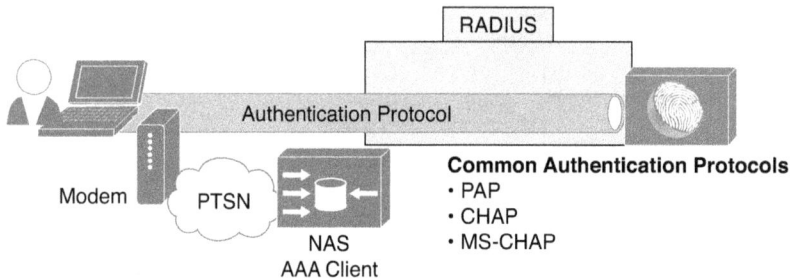

Figure 1-2 *Dial-Up Remote Access*

As technology continued to evolve and direct dial-in to a company was replaced by remote-access virtual private networks (RA-VPN), Wi-Fi became prevalent, and the Institute of Electrical and Electronics Engineers (IEEE) standardized on a method to use Extensible Authentication Protocol (EAP) over local-area networks (IEEE 802.1X), RADIUS was used as the protocol of choice to carry the authentication traffic. In fact, IEEE 802.1X cannot use TACACS. It must use RADIUS.

Note There is another AAA protocol similar to RADIUS, known as DIAMETER, that may also be used with 802.1X; however, it is mostly found in the service provider space and is out of scope for this book.

In today's world, RADIUS is the protocol used almost exclusively with network access AAA and is the main control plane in use between Cisco ISE and the network devices themselves. In retrospect, you could view the RADIUS control plane as the original software-defined network!

TACACS+

As previously introduced TACACS is a protocol set created and intended for controlling access to mainframe and Unix terminals. Cisco created a new protocol called TACACS+, which was released as an open standard in the early 1990s. TACACS+ may be derived from TACACS, but it is a completely separate and non-backward-compatible protocol designed for AAA. Although TACACS+ is mainly used for device administration AAA, it is possible to use it for some types of network access AAA.

TACACS+ became a supported protocol with Cisco ISE in version 2.0. Prior to ISE 2.0, the Cisco Secure Access Control Server (ACS) was the primary Cisco AAA server product for enterprises that needed to use TACACS+ for device administration AAA. However, starting with ISE 2.0, ISE has replaced ACS as Cisco's enterprise flagship AAA server for both RADIUS and TACACS+.

Note Other Cisco products support TACACS+, such as the Cisco Access Registrar solution. However, those solutions are geared toward service providers and are not germane to this book.

TACACS+ uses Transmission Control Protocol (TCP) port 49 to communicate between the TACACS+ client and the TACACS+ server. An example is a Cisco switch authenticating and authorizing administrative access to the switch's IOS CLI. The switch is the TACACS+ client, and the Cisco ISE is the TACACS+ server, as illustrated in Figure 1-3.

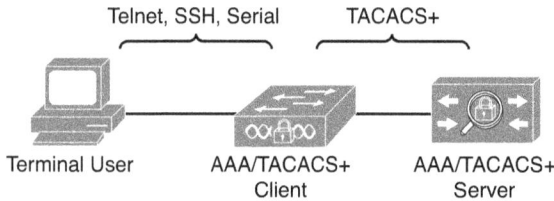

Figure 1-3 *TACACS+ Client–Server Communication*

One of the key differentiators of TACACS+ is its capability to separate authentication, authorization, and accounting as separate and independent functions. This is why TACACS+ is so commonly used for device administration, even though RADIUS is still certainly capable of providing device administration AAA.

Device administration can be very interactive in nature, with the need to authenticate once but authorize many times during a single administrative session in the command line of a device. A router or switch may need to authorize a user's activity on a per-command basis. TACACS+ is designed to accommodate that type of authorization need. As the name describes, TACACS+ was designed for device administration AAA to authenticate and authorize users into mainframe and Unix terminals and other terminals or consoles.

TACACS+ communication between the TACACS+ client and TACACS+ server uses different message types depending on the function. In other words, different messages may be used for authentication than are used for authorization and accounting. Another very interesting point to know is that TACACS+ communication will encrypt the entire packet.

TACACS+ Authentication Messages

When using TACACS+ for authentication, only three types of packets are exchanged between the client (the network device) and the server:

■ **START:** This packet is used to begin the authentication request between the AAA client and the AAA server.

■ **REPLY:** Messages sent from the AAA server to the AAA client.

■ **CONTINUE:** Messages from the AAA client used to respond to the AAA server requests for username and password.

The paragraphs that follow describe the authentication flow process and the messages used.

When an authentication request is sent from the client to the server, it begins with a START message from the network device (AAA client) to the AAA server. The START message tells the server that an authentication request is coming. All messages from the server to the network device will be a REPLY during authentication. The server sends a REPLY message asking for the client to retrieve the username. The username is sent to the server within a CONTINUE message.

After the server receives the username, it sends a REPLY message back to the client request-ing the password, which is sent back to the server in a CONTINUE message. The server sends a final REPLY message with the pass or fail status of the authentication request.

The possible values returned from the AAA server to the AAA client within the final REPLY message are as follows:

- **ACCEPT:** The user authentication succeeded and the authorization process may begin if the AAA client is configured for authorization.

- **REJECT:** The user authentication has failed. The login will be denied, or the end-user will be prompted to try again, depending on the configuration of the AAA client.

- **ERROR:** An error occurred at some point during the authentication. AAA clients will typically attempt to authenticate the user again, or attempt a different method of authenticating the user.

- **CONTINUE:** The user is prompted for additional information. This is not to be con-fused with the CONTINUE message sent from the AAA client to the AAA server. This value is one sent from the AAA server within a REPLY message, indicating that more information is required.

Figure 1-4 illustrates the authentication messages between the client and server.

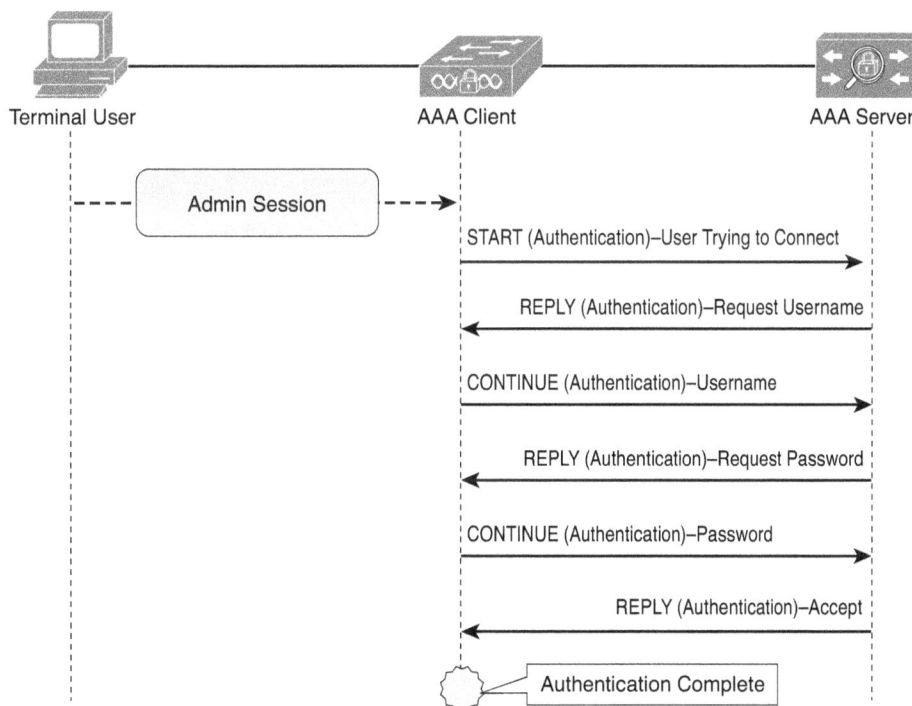

Figure 1-4 *TACACS+ Authentication Communication Flows*

TACACS+ Authorization and Accounting Messages

When using TACACS+ for authorization, only two messages are used between the AAA client and the AAA server:

- **REQUEST:** This message is sent from the AAA client to the AAA server to request an authorization. The authorization may be related to access to a CLI shell or possibly to authorize a specific command. The protocol communication does not discriminate. The function requested is known as a *service*. For example, the service would be "shell" for CLI access to a device running Cisco IOS. Each service may be communicated with attribute-value (AV) pairs. You can find more about specific TACACS+ AV pairs at http://bit.ly/1mF27aT.

- **RESPONSE:** This message is sent from the AAA server back to the AAA client with the result of the authorization request, including specific details, such as the privilege level assigned to the end user. RESPONSE messages may contain one of five replies:

  - **FAIL:** Indicates the user should be denied access to the requested service.

  - **PASS_ADD:** Indicates a successful authorization and that the information contained within the RESPONSE message should be used in addition to the requested information. If no additional arguments are returned by the AAA server within the RESPONSE message, then the request is simply authorized as is.

  - **PASS_REPL:** Indicates a successful authorization but the server has chosen to ignore the REQUEST and is replacing it with the information sent back in the RESPONSE.

  - **FOLLOW:** Indicates that the AAA server wants the AAA client to send the authorization request to a different server. The new server information will be listed in the RESPONSE packet. The AAA client can either use that new server or treat the response as a FAIL.

  - **ERROR:** Indicates a problem occurring on the AAA server and that further troubleshooting needs to occur.

A key function of AAA that cannot be overlooked is accounting. It is crucial to security to have a record of what has transpired. In addition to the authorization request being sent to the AAA server, there should be accounting records of the activities of the user.

Much like authorization messages, there are only two message types used in accounting:

- **REQUEST:** This message is sent from the AAA client to the AAA server to indicate a notification of activity. One of three values may be included with the REQUEST:

  - **START:** Indicates that a service has begun.

  - **STOP:** Indicates that the service has ended.

- **CONTINUE:** Indicates a service has already started and is in progress but there is updated information to provide in relation to the service; also sometimes referred to as a Watchdog or UPDATE record.

- **RESPONSE:** This message is sent from the AAA server back to the AAA client with the result of the accounting REQUEST, and may contain one of three replies:

  - **SUCCESS:** Indicates that the server received the record from the client.

  - **ERROR:** Indicates an error on the server and that the record was not stored.

  - **FOLLOW:** Indicates that the server wants the client to send the record to a different AAA server and includes that server's information in the RESPONSE.

Figure 1-5 illustrates an end user being authorized to access the IOS exec CLI. The figure is a direct continuation of the authentication sequence shown in Figure 1-4. In this illustration, the end user gets authorized to enter the IOS exec and is authorized to run the **show run** command.

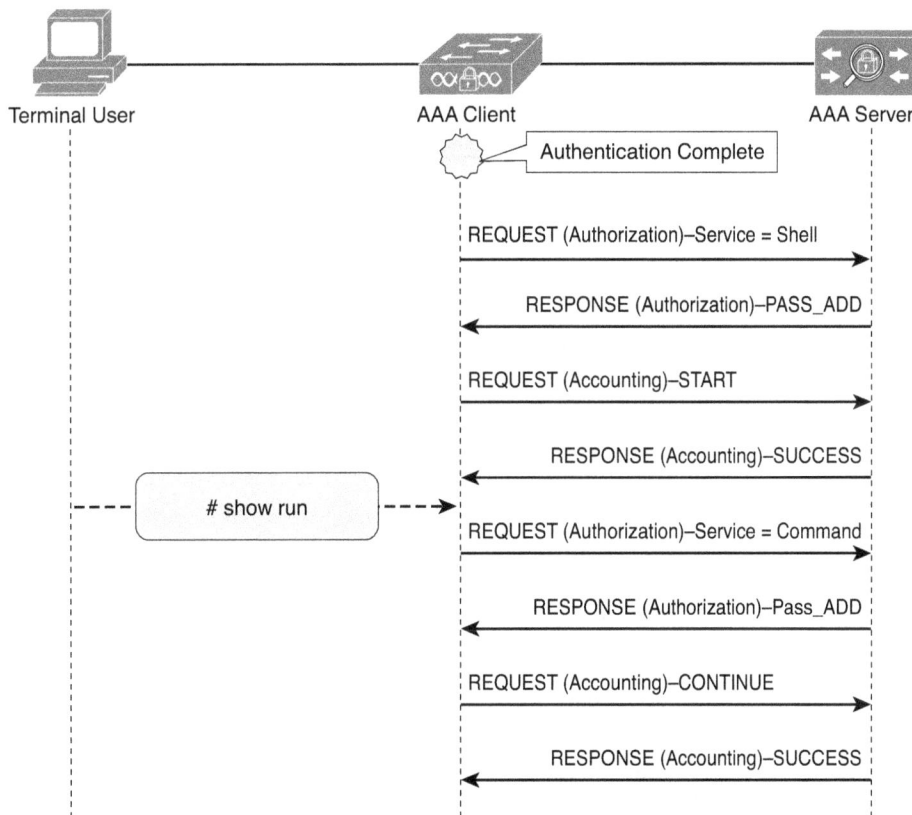

Figure 1-5 *TACACS+ Authorization and Accounting Communication Flows*

RADIUS

RADIUS is an IETF standard AAA protocol. As with TACACS+, it follows a client/server model where the client initiates the requests to the server. RADIUS is the AAA protocol of choice for network access AAA, and it's time to get very familiar with RADIUS. If you connect to a secure wireless network regularly, RADIUS is most likely being used between the wireless device and the AAA server. Why? Because RADIUS is the transport protocol for EAP, along with many other authentication protocols.

Originally, RADIUS was used to extend the authentications from the Layer 2 Point-to-Point Protocol (PPP) used between the end user and the network access server (NAS) and carry that authentication traffic from the NAS to the AAA server performing the authentication. This enabled a Layer 2 authentication protocol to be extended across Layer 3 boundaries to a centralized authentication server.

As described previously in this chapter, RADIUS has evolved far beyond just the dial-up networking use cases it was originally created for. Today it is still used in the same way, carrying the authentication traffic from the network device to the authentication server. With IEEE 802.1X, RADIUS is used to extend the Layer 2 EAP from the end user to the authentication server, as illustrated in Figure 1-6.

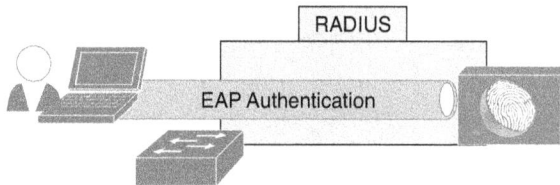

Figure 1-6   *RADIUS Carries the Layer 2 EAP Communication*

There are many differences between RADIUS and TACACS+. One such difference is that authentication and authorization are not separated in a RADIUS transaction. When the authentication request is sent to an AAA server, the AAA client expects to have the authorization result sent back in reply.

There are only a few message types with RADIUS authentication and authorization:

■ **Access-Request:** This message is sent from the AAA client to the AAA server to request an authentication and authorization. The request could be for network access or for device shell access; RADIUS does not discriminate. The function requested is known as a *service type*. For example, the service type may be Framed for an IEEE 802.1X authentication. Table 1-1 lists some common RADIUS service types. You can find a more complete listing of RADIUS service types at http://bit.ly/1CGDE8Y.

Table 1-1   *RADIUS Service Types*

Value	Service Type Name	Commonly Used For
1	Login	Login request; often used with web authentications with non-Cisco network equipment
2	Framed	IEEE 802.1X
5	Outbound	Local web authentication
10	Call-Check	MAC Authentication Bypass (MAB)

Access-Accept: Sent from the AAA server to the AAA client signaling a passed authentication. The authorization result will be included as AV pairs. The AV pairs may include items such as the assigned VLAN, a downloadable access control list (dACL), a security group tag (SGT), and much more.

- **Access-Reject:** Sent from the AAA server to the AAA client signaling the authentication failure. The failed authentication also signifies that no authorization has been granted.

- **Access-Challenge:** This optional message may be sent from the AAA server to the AAA client when additional information is needed, such as a second password for two-factor authentications.

Figure 1-7 illustrates a sample RADIUS flow.

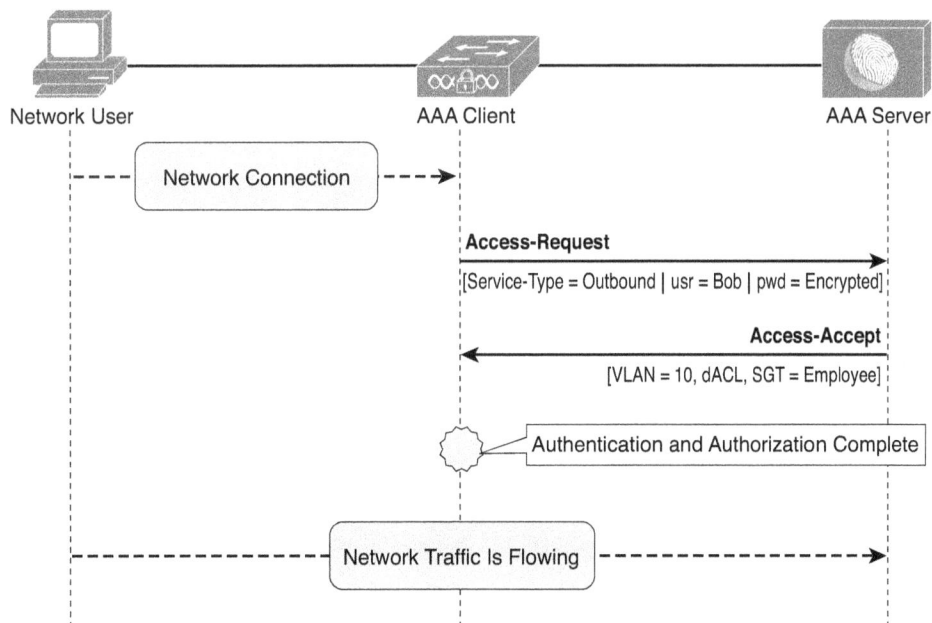

Figure 1-7   *RADIUS Authentication and Authorization Communication Flows*

When looking at Figure 1-7, keep in mind that authentication and authorization are combined with RADIUS. The Access-Accept message includes the AV pairs defining what the user is authorized to do.

A key function of AAA that cannot be overlooked is accounting. It is crucial to security to have a record of what has transpired. In addition to the authorization request being sent to the AAA server, there should be accounting records of the activities of the user.

Only two message types are used in accounting:

- **Accounting-Request:** This message is sent by the AAA client to the AAA server. It may include time, packets, Dynamic Host Configuration Protocol (DHCP) information, Cisco Discovery Protocol (CDP) information, and so on. The message may be a START message indicating that service has begun or a STOP message indicating the service has ended.

- **Accounting-Response:** This message acts like an acknowledgement of receipt, so the AAA client knows the accounting message was received by the AAA server.

Figure 1-8 illustrates a sample RADIUS accounting flow. The figure is a direct continuation of Figure 1-7 where the authentication and authorization occurred.

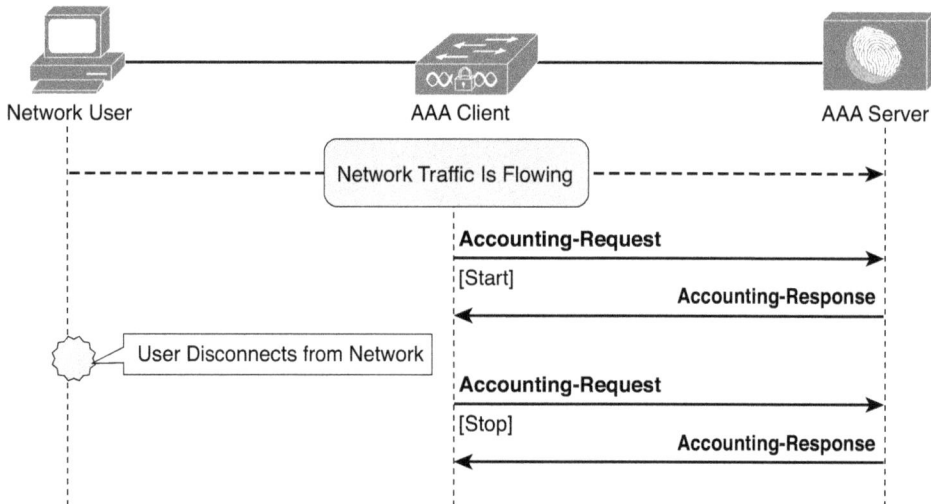

Figure 1-8 *RADIUS Authentication and Authorization Accounting Flows*

Unlike TACACS+, RADIUS uses UDP as the transmission protocol. The standard ports used by RADIUS are UDP/1812 for authentication and UDP/1813 for accounting. Cisco supported RADIUS before the standard was ratified and the ports used were UDP/1645 (authentication) and UDP/1646 (accounting). Most Cisco devices will support using either set of ports to ensure backward compatibility.

AV Pairs

As you noticed, attribute-value pair (AV pairs) were referenced all through the TACACS+ and RADIUS sections. When communicating with an AAA protocol, there are many attributes that can be referenced to clearly dictate answers or results. The RADIUS server may be assigning an attribute to the authentication session like a VLAN, for example. The VLAN placeholder is the attribute, and the actual assigned VLAN number is the value for that placeholder.

The placeholder in the AAA communication and its assigned value are paired together and referred to as AV pairs.

Change of Authorization (CoA)

Because RADIUS was always defined to be a client/server architecture, with the client always initiating the conversation, it became challenging for the AAA server to take action. As RADIUS was defined, the AAA server could only assign an authorization as a result to an authentication request.

As technology advanced, many new demands appeared, including the ability for the network to kick out misbehaving clients, to quarantine them, or basically to just change their access.

How can that happen when the network access is using a RADIUS control plane and the AAA client must always initiate the RADIUS conversations? That is where RFC 3576 and its successor RFC 5176 come in. These RFCs define a new enhancement to RADIUS known as Dynamic Authorization Extensions to RADIUS or, as it is more commonly called, Change of Authorization (CoA).

CoA is what allows a RADIUS server to initiate a conversation to the network device and disconnect a user's session, bounce the port (perform a shut/no-shut), or even tell the device to reauthenticate the user. As you learn more about Cisco ISE and the advanced functionality it brings to network access AAA, you will also see how critically important CoA is.

Comparing RADIUS and TACACS+

Table 1-2 summarizes the two main AAA protocols: RADIUS and TACACS+.

Table 1-2 *Comparison of RADIUS and TACACS+*

	RADIUS	**TACACS+**
Protocol and Port(s) Used	UDP: 1812 and 1813 -or- UDP: 1645 and 1646	TCP: 49
Encryption	Encrypts only the password field	Encrypts the entire payload
Authentication and Authorization	Combines authentication and authorization	Separates authentication and authorization
Primary Use	Network access	Device administration

Summary

This chapter examined the security principal of authentication, authorization, and accounting (AAA) and its importance in the security world. It introduced the different types of AAA relevant to networks, network access AAA and device administration AAA. This chapter compared and contrasted the two most common AAA protocols, RADIUS and TACACS+, revealing that TACACS+ is best suited for device administration while RADIUS is best suited for network access.

Chapter 2

Basic Network Access Control

This chapter focuses on network access authentication, authorization, and accounting (AAA), the process of validating who and what is allowed to access to the network before providing that access.

When you typically think about network access AAA, you might think about technologies like 802.1X or network access control (NAC) providing authentication and authorization before allowing a user or device onto a wired or wireless network. However, as a CCIE Security candidate, you must always remember that there are other tools in your toolbox for controlling access using identity.

Examples include the use of cut-through proxy functions to obtain a user's credentials before opening a path through a firewall or Cisco router, or even remote-access VPNs.

The method used for network access notwithstanding, the policy server that you will use to control that access will most likely be Cisco Identity Services Engine (ISE).

ISE can be used for network access AAA as well as device administration. However, device administration AAA will not be covered until Chapter 5, "Device Administration Control with ISE."

What Is Cisco ISE?

Given that this is a CCIE Security book, it is probably a good assumption that you already know (or think you know) what Cisco ISE is. Yes, ISE is Cisco's answer for network access control, but it does not use "proprietary magic" to communicate with the network infrastructure to control that access.

Cisco ISE is a RADIUS server at its core, but beyond that it is also:

- The premier policy server from Cisco, designed for the enterprise
- The solution for providing guest access to visitors

- The answer for providing visibility into the endpoints connecting to your enterprise network

- An information exchange broker for the sharing of security data between multiple systems

- An enterprise certificate authority (CA)

- The central identity source for the entire Cisco security ecosystem

As you can see, ISE is a central and critical component of the Cisco security architecture, serving many roles for many services.

An entire book could be written about ISE, and cover no other products at all. In fact, a few books have been written about ISE, such as *Cisco ISE for BYOD and Secure Unified Access, Second Edition* (Cisco Press, 2017). If you are attempting the CCIE Security exam, it's highly recommended to also read that book.

ISE Architecture for Network Access AAA

Given the many roles that Cisco ISE might play in an enterprise environment, it requires a distributed architecture to handle those responsibilities at scale, and the responsibilities are also known as *personas*.

Personas

ISE nodes are configured to run one or more of the three personas. A single node can be configured with just one persona, with multiple personas, and even with all personas in the case of a standalone or two-node deployment:

- **Policy admin:** The policy admin persona is responsible for synchronizing the database across all the nodes within an ISE deployment, commonly referred to as an "ISE cube." The policy admin persona is also responsible for providing the administrative user interface for the deployment. There can be only one or two nodes with the policy admin persona: a primary and secondary policy admin node (PAN) for redundancy. The PAN also acts as the root for the built-in certificate authority.

- **Monitoring:** The monitoring persona acts as the centralized logging server for the ISE cube. An ISE node with this persona enabled is referred to as a Monitoring and Troubleshooting (MnT) node. There can only be one or two MnT nodes in an ISE cube: a primary and secondary MnT for redundancy.

- **Policy services:** The policy services persona is a beast in and of itself. It serves so many functions and is often referred to as "the workhorse." A node running policy services is the RADIUS server for the ISE cube, handing the authentication requests, performing the identity lookups and policy evaluation, and issuing the resulting authorization result. A node running the policy service persona is referred to as a *Policy Services Node (PSN)*.

The PSN is also responsible for hosting the different web portals for guest access and sponsorship, as well as being the issuing CA for the built-in certificate authority. A PSN is also the ISE persona handling the profiling of endpoints, and it may also act as the connector for the Threat-Centric NAC (TC-NAC) service, an SGT eXchange Protocol (SXP) client and server, as well as a platform exchange Grid (pxGrid) controller.

There can be up to 50 PSNs per ISE cube for scalability and distribution of PSN functions and load.

Network Access AAA Architecture and ISE Personas

The basic architecture for network access AAA does not really change, regardless of scale. You have an endpoint that is attempting to connect to a network through an access layer network device, called a network access device (NAD), which sends the authentication request to an ISE policy services node (PSN) over RADIUS.

What does change is how many ISE nodes are deployed, which personas are running on each node, and where those nodes exist in the network design. ISE can be designed as standalone, two-node deployment, or distributed. As a CCIE Security candidate, you will need to be intimately familiar with ISE design options, what each persona does, and what all the ISE services are.

Figure 2-1 illustrates the standalone deployment, where a single ISE node is running the admin, monitoring, and policy services personas, so the NAD sends all access requests to the single ISE node. That single node is responsible for all the administrative functions, logging, profiling, certificate authority, hosting all web portals, and authentication. The other optional services such as pxGrid, device administration, and Threat-Centric NAC may also be run on the single node, but don't expect much scale.

Not only are you very limited in scale with a single-node deployment, the deployment does not provide any high availability either. If the ISE node were to become unreachable, then authentication services would be unavailable. For that reason, the standalone deployment is not very common. Most small deployments will typically deploy with a two-node model to add redundancy.

As illustrated in Figure 2-2, both nodes are still running all services and are exact mirrors of one another. This way, if one node should go down, the remaining node can still perform the authentications so that the end users attempting to access the network should not be affected.

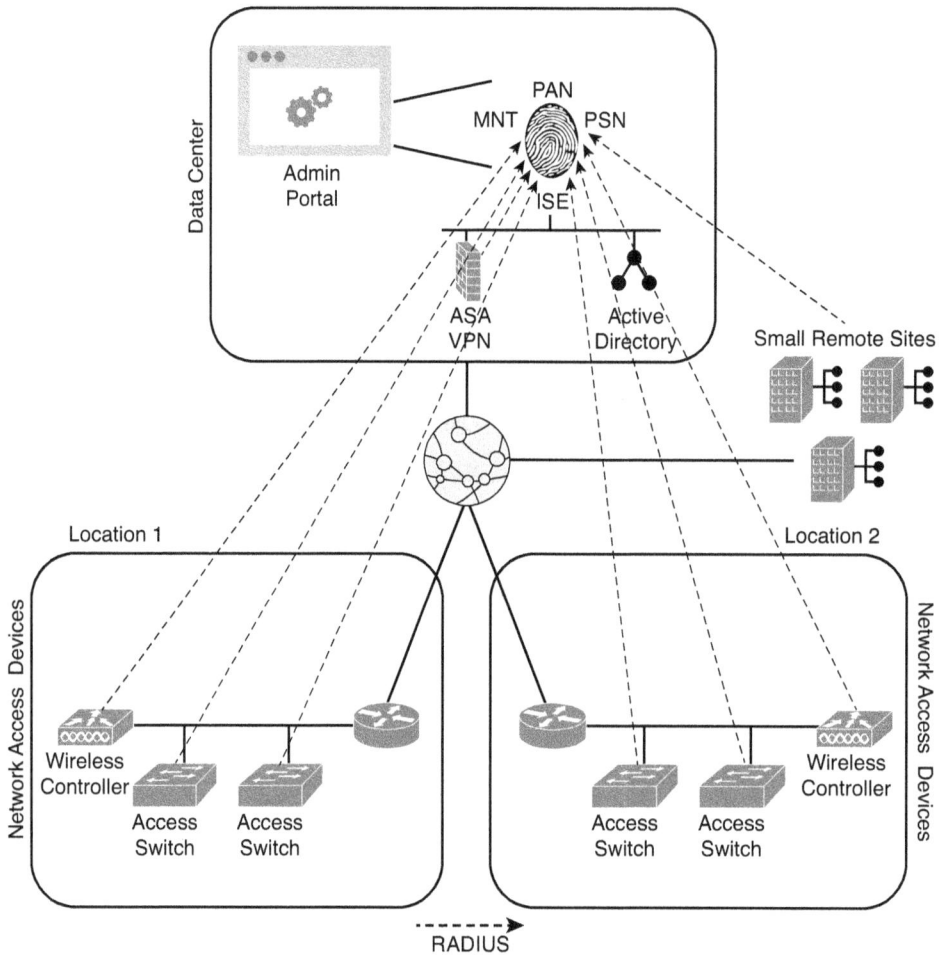

Figure 2-1   *ISE Standalone Deployment*

A standalone deployment and a two-node deployment maintain the exact same scale, which is up to 20,000 concurrent active sessions with ISE 2.4 when you leverage the larger physical appliance or an equivalent virtual machine.

As your deployment grows beyond two nodes running the policy services persona, you may choose to have dedicated PSNs. You can have no more than five PSNs in an ISE cube where the admin and monitoring personas are still running concurrently on a single node. This deployment model maintains a maximum concurrent session count of 20,000, but it allows you to distribute out the policy services functions for redundancy, round-trip time (getting the PSN closer to the NADs), and to dedicate PSNs for functions like TC-NAC, pxGrid, or SXP.

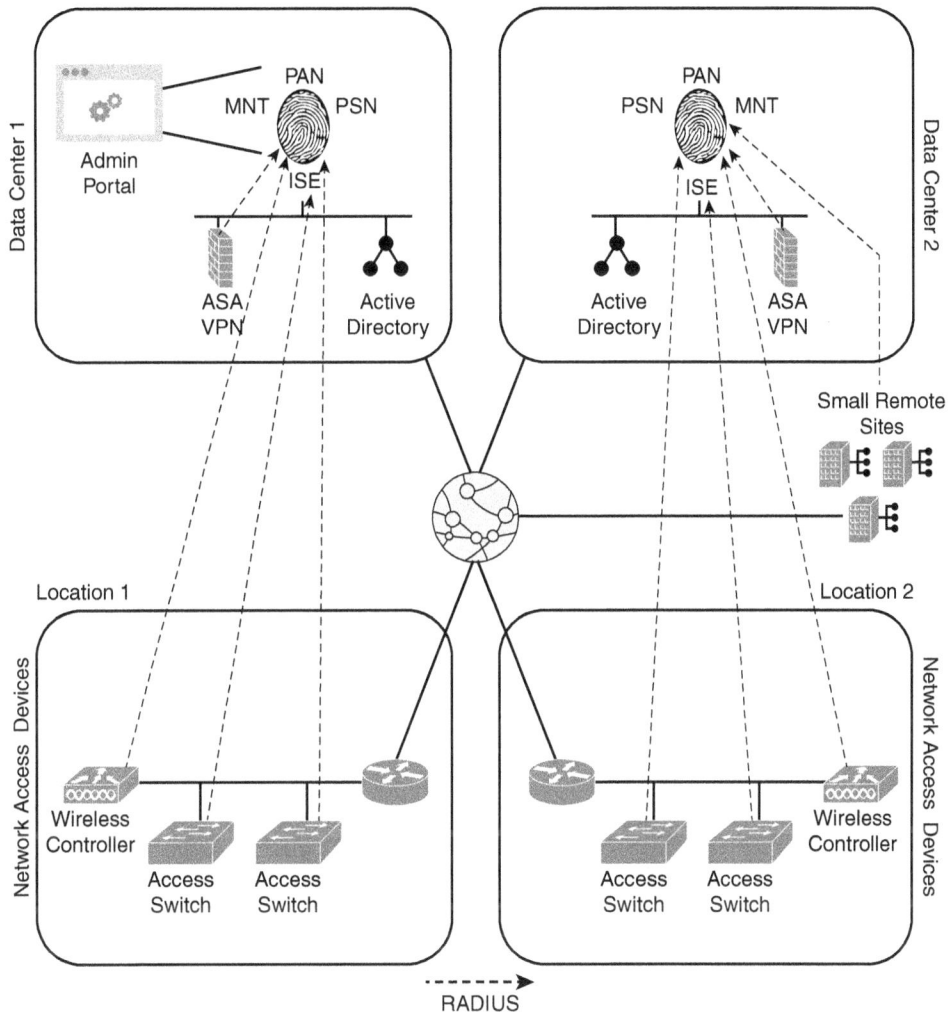

Figure 2-2   *Two-Node Deployment*

Figure 2-3 shows an ISE deployment where the admin and monitoring personas are still running together on the same node, with two of those nodes for redundancy; plus, it has five dedicated policy services nodes, one of which has been designated to run the pxGrid and TC-NAC functions.

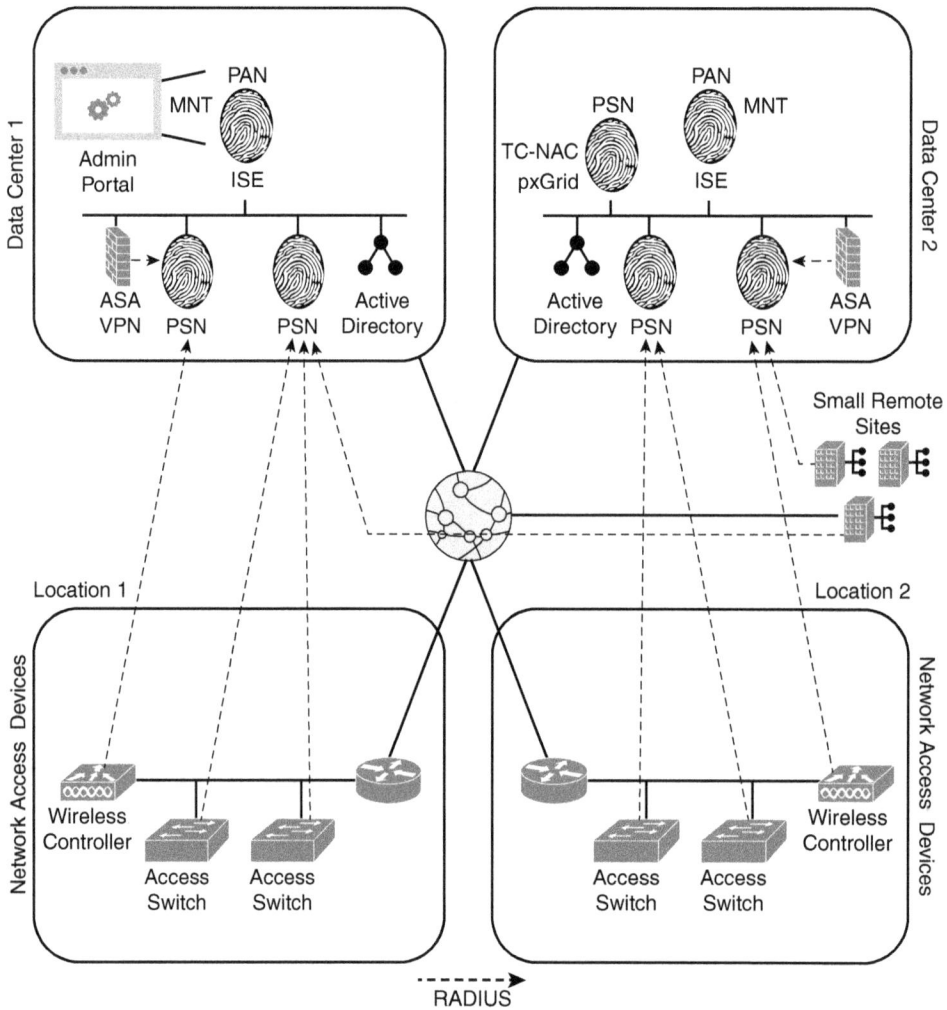

Figure 2-3   *Seven-Node Distributed Deployment*

To grow the scale beyond 20,000 concurrent active sessions or beyond five PSNs, the admin and monitoring personas must be running on dedicated nodes. Once all personas are divided up to dedicated nodes, the scale will reach 500,000 active concurrent sessions in ISE 2.4, with a maximum of 50 policy services nodes plus up to 4 dedicated pxGrid PSNs. Figure 2-4 depicts a fully distributed deployment.

Note   As of ISE version 2.4, only one node is able to run the TC-NAC function, regardless of the deployment size.

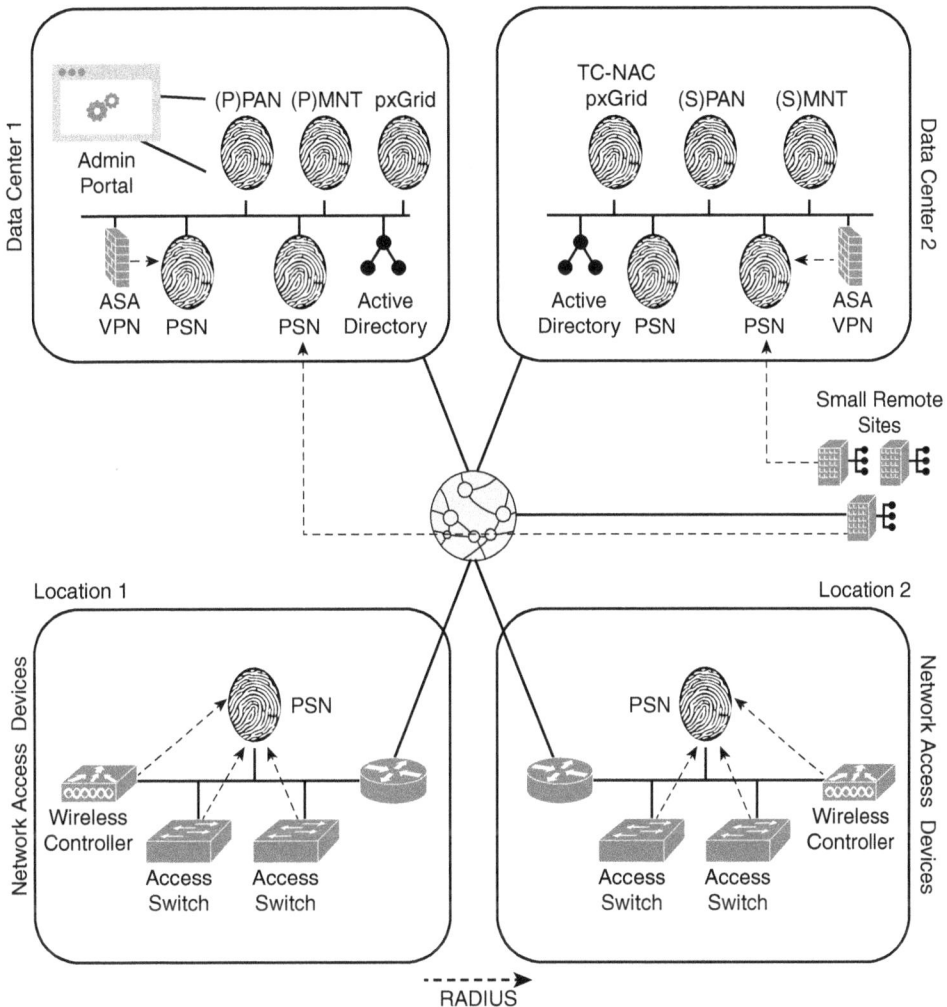

Figure 2-4 *Fully Distributed Deployment*

Configuring ISE for Single/Standalone and Multinode Deployments

All control over persona assignment, adding or removing nodes from deployments, and enabling or disabling of service is handled in the UI under the Deployment page. As a CCIE Security candidate, you will need to be intimately familiar with how to add nodes to an ISE cube and how to assign the different personas and services.

Standalone

The default state for any ISE node after ISE is installed is standalone. That means the node will be running the admin, monitoring, and policy services personas automatically.

All control over persona assignment, adding or removing nodes from deployments, and enabling or disabling of service is handled in the GUI under the Deployment page.

To see the ISE node configuration while in standalone mode:

Step 1.   Navigate to **Administration > System > Deployment.**

As shown in Figure 2-5, a pop-up warning appears, informing you that the node is currently in standalone mode, and that before you can add any other nodes to the ISE cube, you must first promote this node to primary.

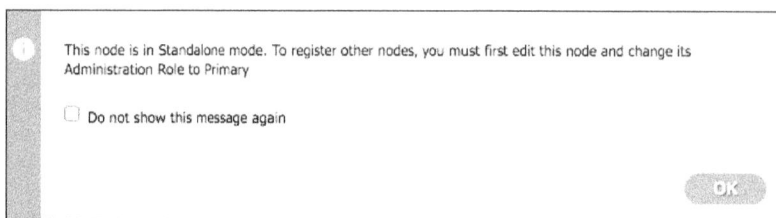

This node is in Standalone mode. To register other nodes, you must first edit this node and change its Administration Role to Primary

☐ Do not show this message again

OK

Figure 2-5   *Standalone Warning Message*

Step 2.   Click **OK** to close the warning.

You are now able to see a summary of the deployment, as shown in Figure 2-6.

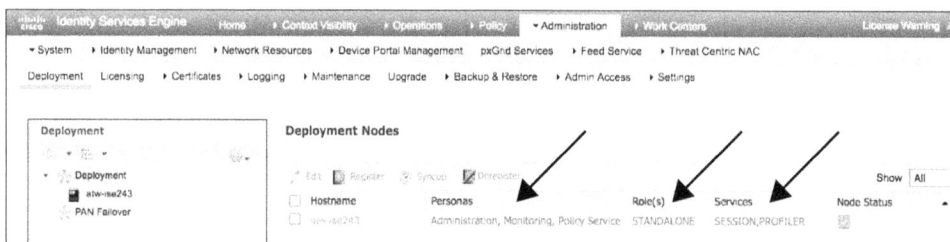

Figure 2-6   *Deployment Page for a Standalone ISE Node*

The role of the node is listed as standalone; the administration, monitoring, and policy service personas are listed for the node, and the session and profiler services are enabled by default.

The services refer to functions of a PSN. The session service is the name for the RADIUS server and access-control policy engine that are required for network access control, and the profiler service is used to try and identify the types of endpoints that are connecting to the network.

Dual Node

A few prerequisites must be met before you will be able to add another node to this ISE deployment (also called an ISE cube):

- Network connectivity must exist between the ISE nodes.

- Forward and reverse DNS entries must exist for each ISE node.

- The nodes must trust each other's admin certificate.

- The node whose GUI you are using must have been promoted to primary.

This is a CCIE-level book, and therefore we will not be going through the process of trusting each node's certificate. If this topic is at all confusing, Aaron Woland has presented at Cisco Live for many years on best practices for certificates with ISE, and those presentations are available for free within the on-demand library at https://ciscolive.cisco.com. There are also Cisco Press books on ISE that cover more of the basics, such as *Cisco ISE for BYOD and Secure Unified Access, Second Edition*.

To promote a standalone node to be primary:

Step 1.   Navigate to **Administration > System > Deployment**.

Step 2.   Click the name of the standalone ISE node (in this case, it is **atw-ise243**).

Step 3.   Click the **Make Primary** button, as shown in Figure 2-7.

Step 4.   Click **Save**.

You have now just made the ISE node into the primary PAN for an ISE cube that consists of only one node. Behind the scenes, this has enabled the database policy synchronization functions for which a PAN is responsible.

Within a few minutes, that node will be ready for you to add other nodes to the deployment. From this point forward, if all of the prerequisites for connectivity and certificate trust were met, you should only ever have to interact with the UI of this [primary] node for your deployment.

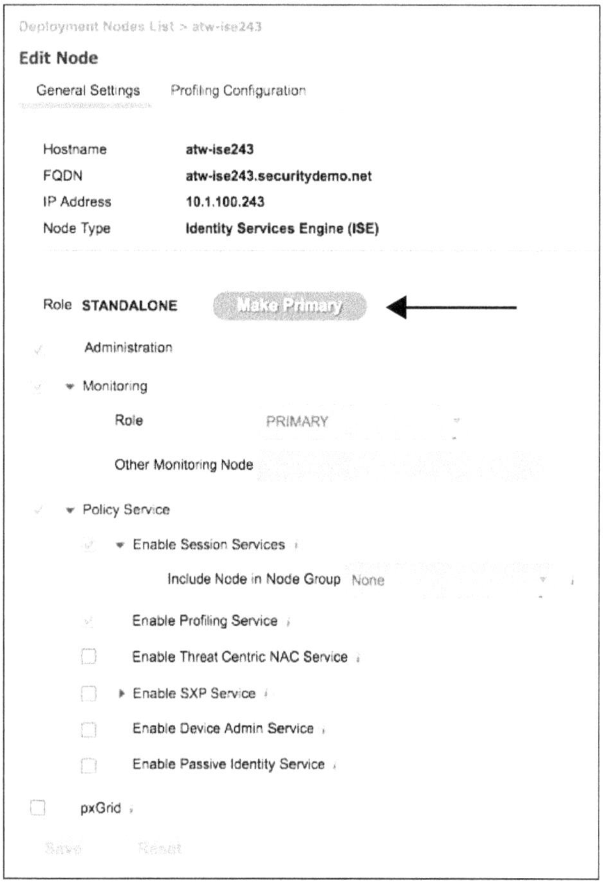

Figure 2-7 *Making a Standalone Node Primary*

To add the secondary node to the ISE cube:

Step 1.   Navigate to **Administration > System > Deployment**.

Step 2.   Click **Register**.

Step 3.   Enter the secondary node's fully qualified domain name (FQDN). Remember, forward and reverse lookup entries in DNS are required prerequisites.

Step 4.   Enter the administrative username and password.

Step 5.   Click **Next**. Figure 2-8 shows the node registration screen.

As shown in Figure 2-9, you can now select the roles for the secondary node that you are adding to the deployment. Because the goal is to create a two-node deployment, we will ensure the secondary node is configured for the administration, monitoring, and policy service personas.

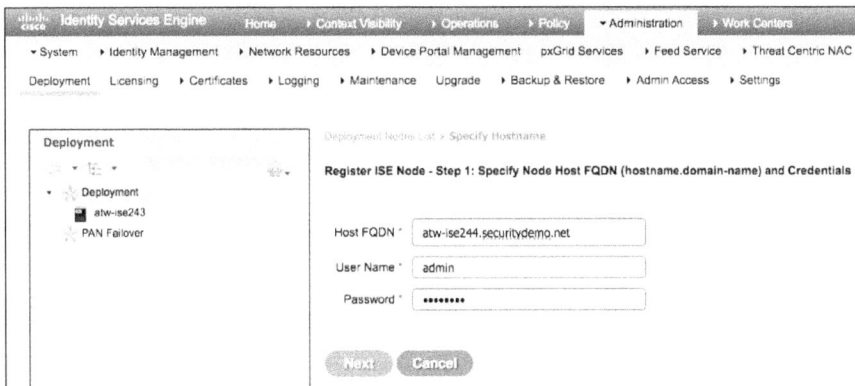

Figure 2-8   *Node Registration Screen*

Step 1.   Check the **Administration** check box.

Step 2.   Check the **Monitoring** check box and ensure that **SECONDARY** is selected in the Role field.

Step 3.   Check the **Policy Service** check box, along with the **Enable Session Services** and **Enable Profiling Service** check boxes.

Step 4.   Click **Submit**.

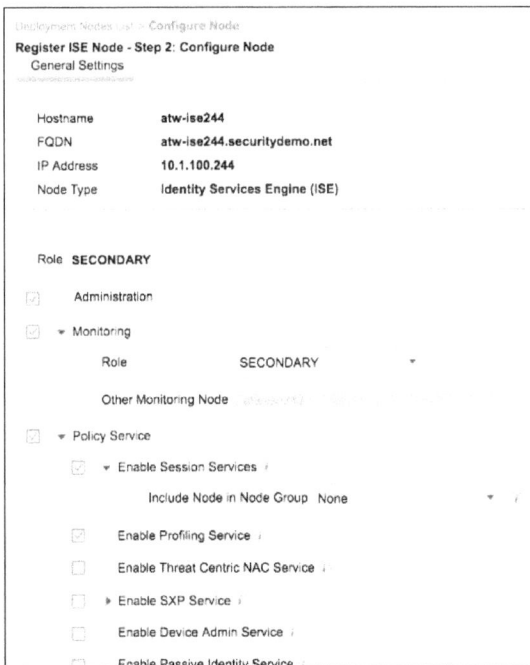

Figure 2-9   *Selecting the Personas and Services for the Secondary Node*

At this point, the databases from the primary node are being replicated to the secondary node, overwriting the existing ones and restarting the entire application server after the replication completes. Figure 2-10 shows the success message.

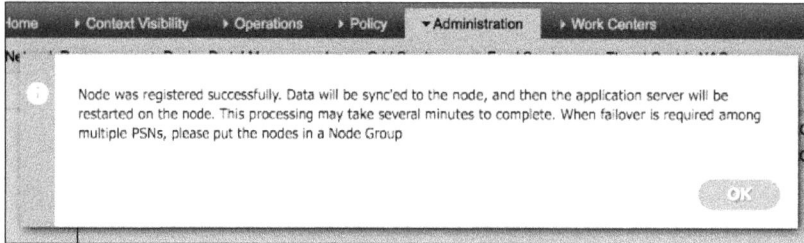

Figure 2-10   *Successfully Registered Secondary Node*

During the registration process, while the databases are being replicated, some of the certificates on each of the newly registered nodes are also replaced. The primary PAN is also the root of the ISE certificate authority, and any secondary nodes that join this PAN will replace their certificate authority certs with new ones that are signed by this root, becoming part of the same PKI tree. Additionally, the pxGrid certificate on all the nodes is also replaced with a certificate that is signed by this new PKI hierarchy.

Figure 2-11 illustrates our new two-node deployment.

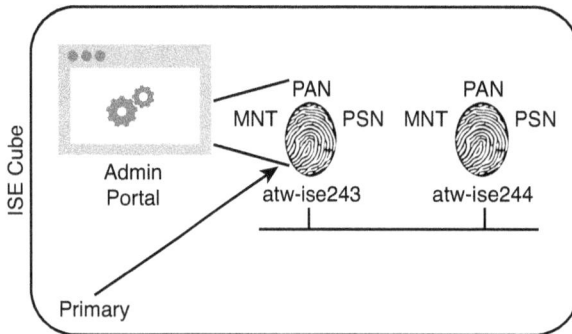

Figure 2-11   *Current Two-Node Deployment*

Note   A tip gained from performing countless real-world deployments is to wait until you have your primary and secondary administration nodes joined to the ISE cube before going through any of the licensing processes. This way you will have the serial number for both nodes, which is required for proper licensing, especially with failover configured.

Distributed Deployment

At this point, you have a two-node deployment, as illustrated in Figure 2-11, which is perfect for smaller organizations. All ISE services are running on one or both of these nodes, and that may be all you need.

As a CCIE Security candidate, however, you need to master the ability to describe, implement, and troubleshoot distributed ISE deployments. In that regard, you will now add three more nodes into the ISE cube, to bring the total node count up to five ISE nodes with distributed functions.

Figure 2-12 illustrates what the final deployment will look like. This final, distributed deployment is what we will use for any scenarios involving ISE for the remainder of the book.

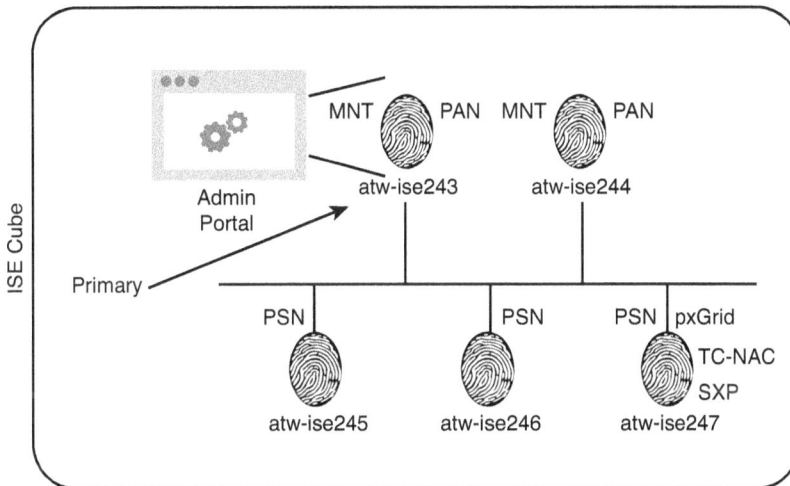

Figure 2-12   *Final Distributed Five-Node ISE Cube*

The ISE cube consists of five nodes. The ISE personas and services shall be divided as outlined in Table 2-1.

Table 2-1   *ISE Persona/Services Division*

Node	Personas	Services	Node Group
atw-ise243	(P)PAN, (P)MNT	—	—
atw-ise244	(S)PAN, (S)MNT	—	—
atw-ise245	PSN	Profiling	NodeGroup1
atw-ise246	PSN	Profiling	—
atw-ise247	pxGrid, PSN	TC-NAC, SXP	—

To add the remainder of the nodes to the ISE cube, click **Register** and follow the steps as before. Make sure to uncheck the Administration and Monitoring check boxes, or you will end up accidently removing those personas from the secondary PAN. Figures 2-13 and 2-14 show the two PSNs, while Figure 2-15 shows the dedicated pxGrid node.

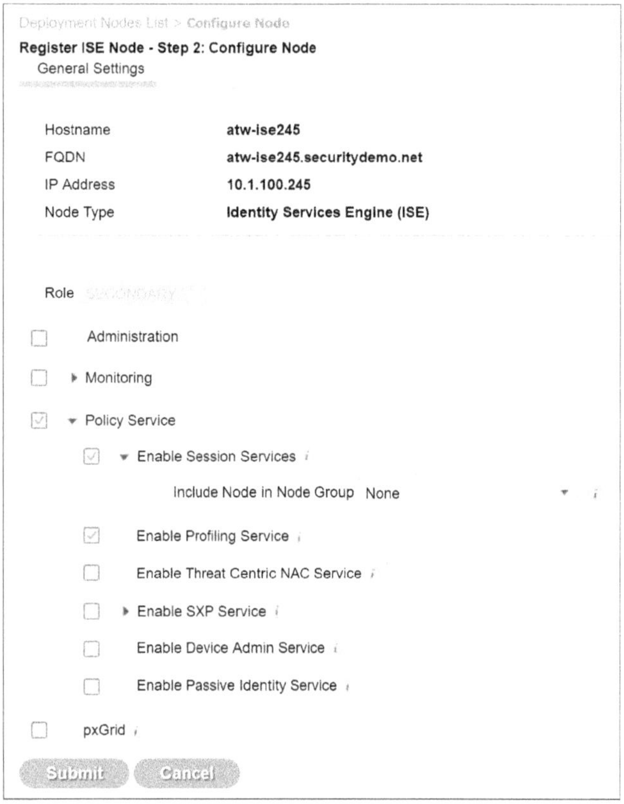

Figure 2-13   *Adding One of the Dedicated PSNs*

You'll notice in Figure 2-16 that the atw-ise247 node is configured a bit differently than the other PSNs. This is due to it being dedicated for pxGrid, SXP, and Threat-Centric NAC. Obviously, you do not need to deploy in this exact same fashion, but it is good for a CCIE Security candidate to see the variations.

Figure 2-16 shows the final deployment screen with all the nodes registered and in sync with the administrative node.

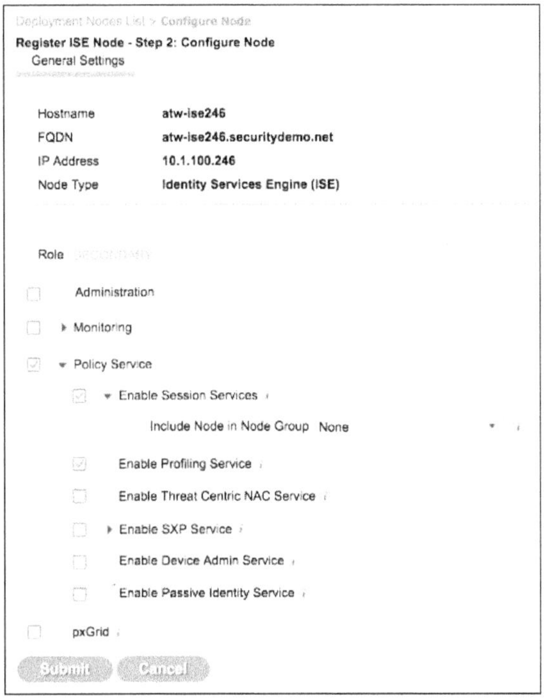

Figure 2-14   *Adding the Additional Dedicated PSNs*

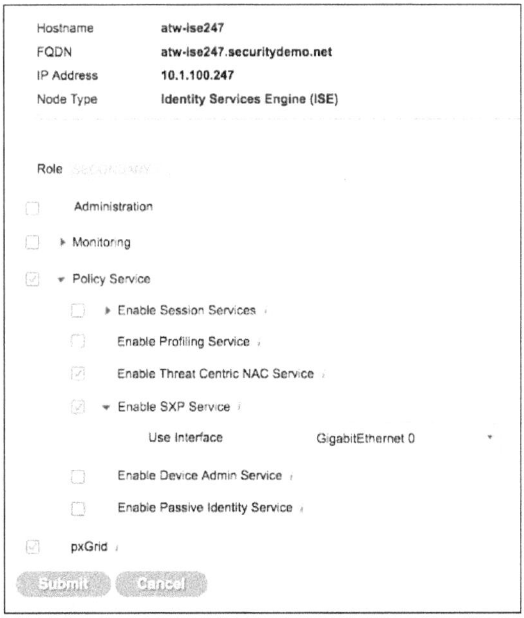

Figure 2-15   *Adding the Dedicated pxGrid, SXP, and TC-NAC Node*

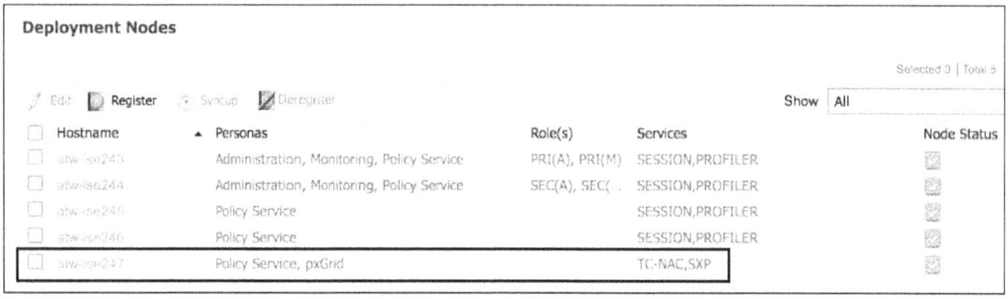

Deployment Nodes

Selected 0 | Total 5

/ Edit Register Syncup Deregister   Show All

	Hostname	▲ Personas	Role(s)	Services	Node Status
	atw-ise245	Administration, Monitoring, Policy Service	PRI(A), PRI(M)	SESSION,PROFILER	
	atw-ise244	Administration, Monitoring, Policy Service	SEC(A), SEC(...	SESSION,PROFILER	
	atw-ise245	Policy Service		SESSION,PROFILER	
	atw-ise246	Policy Service		SESSION,PROFILER	
	atw-ise247	Policy Service, pxGrid		TC-NAC,SXP	

Figure 2-16   *Final ISE Cube Deployment*

ISE Configuration for Network Access

One of ISE's most important functions is the way it determines the correct identity store to authenticate the user to. In other words, when a user or device is attempting to access a network, an authentication is sent to ISE containing the user's or device's identity (known as the credential). That credential needs to be checked for validity.

Identity Sources

ISE is rarely the "owner" of the credentials themselves, although there are certainly cases (such as guest access) where ISE does maintain the credential. However, for the normal use cases related to network access, the source of truth for the identity is most often external to ISE, and it is incumbent on ISE to find the correct source (sometimes referred to as an identity source, or an identity store).

The external identity store may be Microsoft Active Directory (90 percent or more of the time), a Lightweight Directory Access Protocol (LDAP) store, a token server (like a one-time password [OTP] service), or even another RADIUS server. In many ways, ISE acts like an identity router of sorts, finding the correct identity store to validate the user's or device's credential, or even checking with multiple identity stores in sequence or parallel.

Understanding the Available Identity Sources

The CCIE Security candidate must be able to describe, implement, verify, and trouble-shoot ISE integration with external identity sources such as LDAP, Active Directory, and external RADIUS services. You must also be able to describe the integration with RADIUS Token, RSA SecurID, and Security Assertion Markup Language (SAML) identity sources.

Microsoft Active Directory

The most common identity source for ISE deployments today is Active Directory (AD). It is very often the single source of truth for most organizations' user accounts, and their attributes. Although AD supports the LDAP standard for lookups, ISE employs a very advanced AD connector that emulates a native Windows connection to AD, instead of trying to use LDAP or Samba, which are very limited in their integration.

ISE may integrate with AD for active authentication lookups, where a user or machine is sending their credentials directly to ISE for validation in order to access the network; or AD may be leveraged for passive authentications, where the machine or user authenticates directly to AD and then ISE learns about it "second hand."

LDAP

LDAP is an open standard for accessing directory information services on an IP-based network. It is often considered the universal method for accessing identity stores and is supported by nearly all of the major players in the identity and access management (IAM) space. Examples of when you might use LDAP to connect to an identity store would be when the company leverages an identity management product such as NetIQ eDirectory (formerly known as Novell Directory Services [NDS]), Oracle Identity Manager (OIM), IBM Tivoli Identity Manager (TIM), or even Okta Universal Directory (UD).

The ISE user interfaces and policy engines both treat LDAP and AD very similarly, allowing the admin to preconfigure groups that should be considered "interesting," providing a major performance increase when a directory service might include hundreds or even thousands of groups.

ODBC

Open Database Connectivity (ODBC) is a standard application programming interface (API) used for accessing databases, such as directory services. ODBC seems to be losing ground to LDAP, SAML, and other identity protocols, but it is still in use by some organizations with legacy IAM solutions.

RADIUS Token

Multifactor authentication (MFA) systems are extremely commonplace in modern networking. The concept of MFA is to confirm that the authorized user is truly the one attempting to access the network. Example MFA systems include Duo Security MFA (acquired by Cisco), Google Authenticator, Yubico YubiKey USB two-factor tokens, PingID, and RSA SecurID.

These MFA systems add additional security by ensuring the user has something they know and something they have (known as two-step authentication). *Something they know* could be their username and password, while *something they have* could be a USB key that generates a token, or even an app that runs on the user's smartphone that requires the user to accept the authentication attempt.

These services will often integrate with NAC solutions through the RADIUS Token service. Using this method, ISE is able to send a RADIUS authentication request to the MFA solution and receive an Accept notification back if the user entered their second factor correctly to that MFA solution.

RSA SecurID

RSA SecurID is an MFA solution, and a very popular one; however, that product supports only its own, unique integration, and therefore is listed as its own identity store in ISE.

SAML ID Providers

SAML is an open standard for exchange authentication and authorization information between services. Specifically, the exchange occurs between a SAML identity provider (IdP) and a SAML service provider (SP).

SAML is most often used to provide single-sign on (SSO) through a web browser, allowing a user to authenticate to the IdP one time and then have that authentication shared to multiple SPs, such as web applications.

When the user attempts to authenticate to a web application (an SP) the first time, they are redirected to an authentication page for the IdP where their credentials are entered. Assuming the user is authenticated successfully, the IdP issues a SAML "assertion" that is passed from the IdP to the SP, to inform the SP of the user's identity and successful authentication. It is up to the SP to perform its own authorization.

Although you might think that ISE is a perfect product to be a SAML IdP, that is not how ISE interacts with SAML. Instead of ISE authenticating users and issuing SAML assertions to the web application SPs, ISE is merely an SP itself. There are many portal pages hosted by ISE, such as the Guest Sponsor portal, that can leverage SAML assertions for SSO of the sponsor; and that is the extent of SAML support in ISE today.

The Network Access Work Center

The ISE user interface is broken up into work centers where you perform tasks related to each specific work center. Because we are focused on network access in this chapter, we will perform the vast majority of tasks within the Network Access work center.

From the ISE interface, navigate to **Work Centers > Network Access**. All work centers are organized in a way that should allow you to complete all activities from the top down, left to right. As you see in Figure 2-17, the Network Access work center is grouped into the following sections:

- **Overview:** This section contains an Introduction page, which you most likely will read only once, if at all, and the RADIUS Live Log. The RADIUS Live Log is one of the most frequently visited pages within ISE, and it may behoove you to click the little lock icon that appears to the right side of the left navigation menu, which will set it as the default page to display when you visit the Overview section.

- **Identities:** This section contains the endpoint identities (each unique MAC address is one endpoint object), internal network access users (these are not guest users), and identity source sequences (ISSs). ISSs are something you will definitely get very familiar with in this window.

- **Id Groups:** Identity groups can be one of two types: endpoint ID groups or user ID groups. Endpoint ID groups may contain multiple MAC addresses, or even combine multiple device profiles into a group. User ID groups contain local user identities or guest user identities.

- **Ext Id Sources:** The majority of ISE deployments leverage external identity sources for authenticating users. Active Directory is used at over 90 percent of ISE deployments. Certificate authorities are used nearly as often thanks to the proliferation of mobile devices. LDAP, ODBC, RADIUS Token, RSA SecurID, and SAML are also all located within this section.

- **Network Resources:** Network devices are the switches, routers, and firewalls that send access requests to ISE. As previously mentioned, they are typically referred to as network access devices (NADs). Network Device Groups are sets of NADs and are critically important to smooth deployments of ISE. Other network resources are defined here, such as external RADIUS servers and RADIUS server sequences that are used for RADIUS proxy, and mobile device management (MDM) servers that ISE integrates with for onboarding and posture assessments.

- **Policy Elements:** These are the conditions and results that make up a rule entry in the policy table. Rules are designed to follow an "IF [conditions] THEN [results]" model.

  There are three types of conditions:

  - Library conditions are a mixture of conditions from Cisco and ones created by the admin.

  - Smart conditions are special and come directly from Cisco. They're used to define common use cases, such as MAC Authentication Bypass (MAB), and automatically translate that use case for the network device type in use. This enables the admin to choose a smart condition in the policy rule and leverage that exact same rule for any supported device type.

  - Time and date conditions.

  There are three types of results:

  - Allowed Protocols is the result type used in an authentication policy to determine which authentication types are permitted for that rule, and what the options should be for those authentication types.

  - Authorization profiles are the main result type used for network access. These include the RADIUS responses, VLAN attributes, interface templates, and so much more. They also contain a pointer to the third authorization type, the dACL.

  - A downloadable access control list (dACL) defines all the access control entries (ACEs) making up a full ACL that is sent to the NAD, providing a centralized location for access lists to be created, modified, and deleted.

■ **Policy Sets:** Policy sets are the heart and soul of what most organizations do with ISE. A policy set is a pair of authentication and authorization policies that work together. Always remember that the authentication comes first and leads to the authorization. The policy set will be chosen in a top-down, first-match manor based on the authentication conditions, and a successful authentication will pass the request from authentication to authorization.

■ **Troubleshoot:** This section of the work center is where the relevant tools related to network access have been brought together in one place. The tools are still in their original location within the Operations menu. The RADIUS Authentication Troubleshooting tool (also known as the Policy Trace tool) enables an administrator to simulate an authentication, including most of the possible attributes, in an attempt to determine which rules would be matched and why. The endpoint debug tool enables the debug level of all logs in ISE for the specified device and merges them all into a single text file to make troubleshooting easier and more concise. The TCP dump tool allows for packet captures to be taken on any node in the deployment, and the resulting PCAP file to be downloaded from the centralized console. The final tool in the Troubleshoot section is collection filters, which allow the administrator to disable the event suppression on a per-endpoint basis, to allow for more accurate troubleshooting.

■ **Reports:** This is another section of the work center where relevant reports have been brought together in one place. The reports still exist in their original location within the Operations menu.

■ **Settings:** This section brings together specific options from Administration > Settings that are related to network access. Settings related to client provisioning, authentication protocols, collection filters, and proxy settings are located here, as well as in their original location under the Administration menu.

■ **Dictionaries:** A dictionary is the most basic object making up a policy element. Administrators will only work directly with dictionary objects in very rare situations, or if TAC instructs them to.

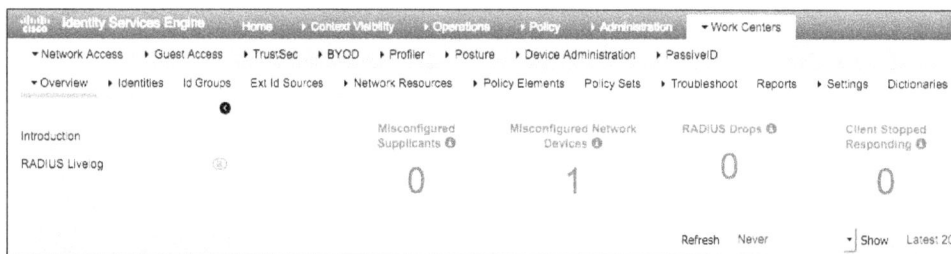

Figure 2-17   *Network Access Work Center*

Configuring Identity Sources

In this section we will focus mostly on Active Directory. ISE has an incredibly powerful AD connector that allows it to speak with AD as if it were a native Windows device, leveraging the same native Microsoft protocols. As a CCIE-level professional working with ISE, you will want to have a really strong understanding of how ISE and AD work together.

Joining AD

ISE can join up to 50 domains, referred to as *join points*. The domains can be part of a single AD forest or part of multiple forests; in the latter case ISE will perform identity disambiguation, learning the correct account even if there are two user accounts with the same name in different domains.

AD is often designed in a distributed nature, where the domain controllers are deployed at various locations, usually in an organized and regional fashion. The ISE AD connector is controlled at the administrative node, but each ISE node has its own connection to AD. You will join every PSN to AD, as well as the admin nodes. The PSNs are joined to AD, as each one will query AD directly during an authentication. This aids greatly in distributing the authentication load within ISE as well as with AD.

Active Directory includes a powerful configuration tool, *Active Directory Sites and Services*, that allows AD to understand the network segments that exist, and which network segment each domain controller belongs to. This allows AD to determine what the closest domain controller is to any given AD client, including ISE. All AD clients leverage the Domain Name System (DNS) to determine which servers to speak to for any specific AD function leveraging the SRV (server) record types. Because AD and DNS are linked together, the DNS response for those SRV record types will be crafted to include the address of the closest server based on the AD Sites and Services configuration.

ISE acts like any other AD client. It uses DNS to request the IP address of the domain controller that it "should" speak with. This means that each PSN will communicate with the domain controller closest to it, thanks to the smarts built into AD already.

It's important to note that this way of leveraging DNS and using native Windows protocols is in stark contrast to the way many other solutions "integrate" with AD. Most solutions leverage the open source Samba solution or LDAP and must connect with a specific domain controller. If that domain controller is offline or otherwise unavailable, the solution better possess a backup to reach out to directly or it will fail.

ISE does not choose which domain controller it communicates with. It allows AD to make that choice, which provides resiliency and scalability.

Note   Before joining AD, ensure that proper forward and reverse DNS entries exist for all the ISE nodes.

To join ISE to a domain:

Step 1.   Navigate to **Work Centers > Network Access > Ext Id Sources > Active Directory.**

Step 2.   Click **Add.**

Step 3.   Provide a name and the domain name for the join point. The author prefers to add an "AD-" prefix to all join point names, to make it easier when building policies; the example in Figure 2-18 shows a join point name of AD-SECDEMO for the securitydemo.net AD domain.

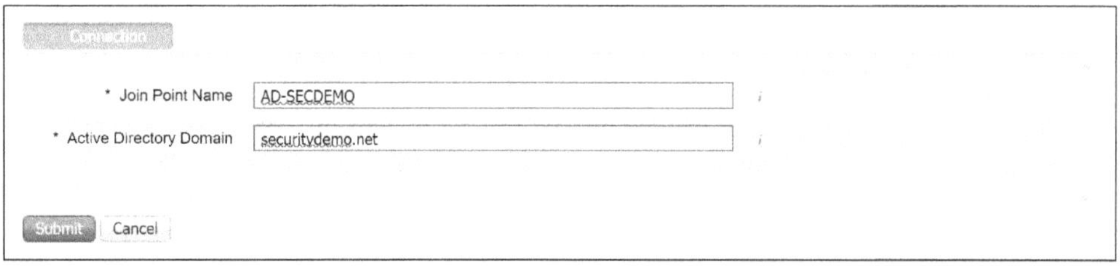

Figure 2-18   *Joining the securitydemo.net Domain*

Step 4.   Click **Submit.** As shown in Figure 2-19, ISE prompts you to click Yes to join all the nodes to the domain. In most cases, you will configure all nodes to join every domain, but there are certainly distributed designs where you may take a different approach.

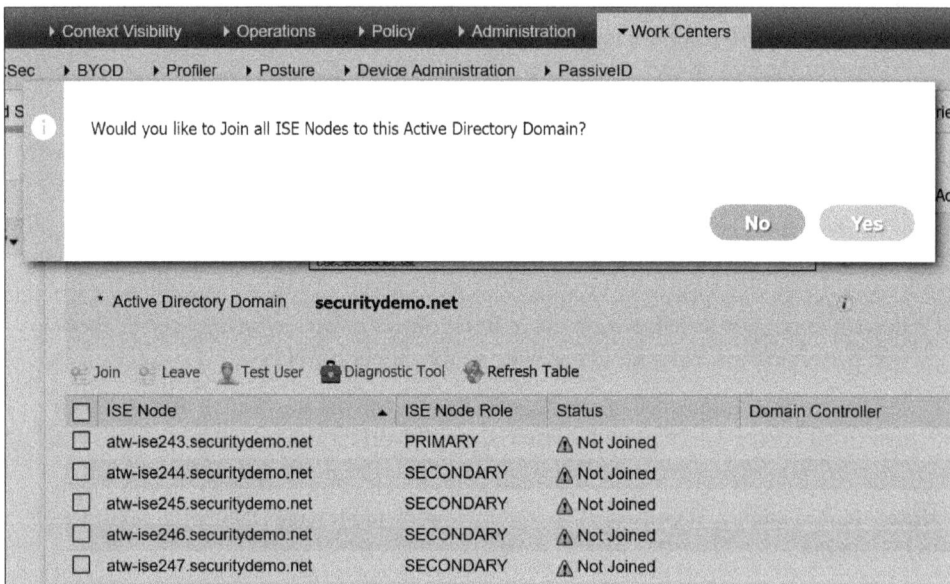

Figure 2-19   *Click Yes to Join All Nodes to the Domain*

Step 5.   Click **Yes** to join all nodes to the domain. The dialog box shown in Figure 2-20 will open to capture AD credentials required to join ISE to the domain and create its computer account within AD. There is a check box to **Store Credentials**, which is important for deployments that use EasyConnect or other passive identity integration options. Enter the AD username and password for an account with enough rights to join ISE to the domain and click **OK**.

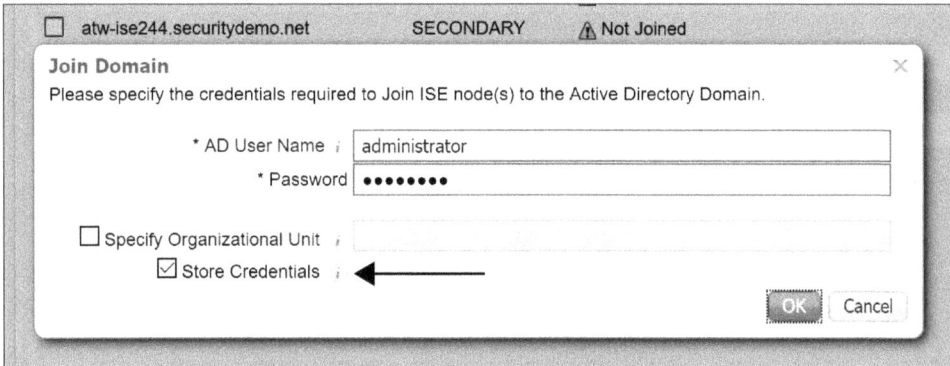

Figure 2-20   *Entering the AD Credentials*

Step 6.   In this particular instance, we received an error on one of the nodes when joining them all to the domain, which is perfect for the book so that you (the reader) can see an error and how it is remediated. As you can see in Figure 2-21, the atw-ise245 node received an error; clicking that error message displays the operation details, as shown in Figure 2-22.

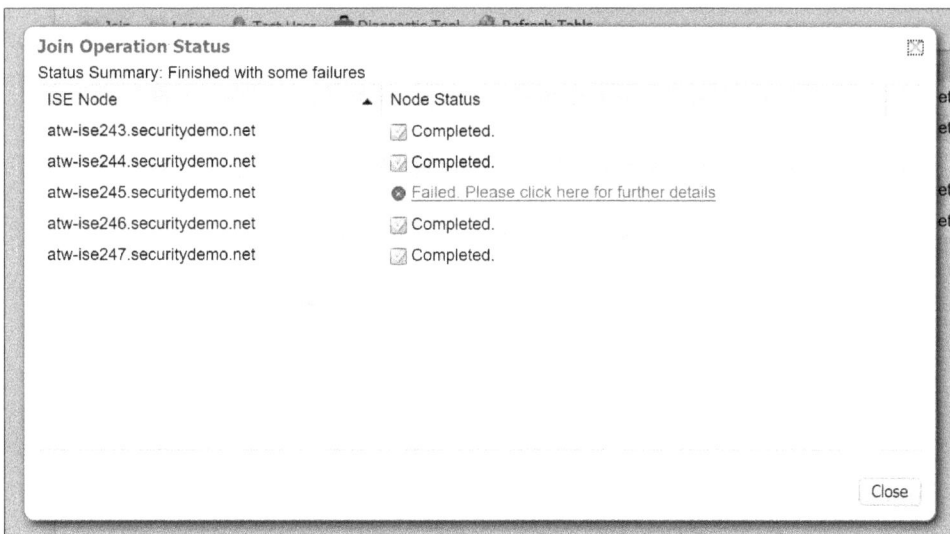

Figure 2-21   *Join Operation Status*

As you see in Figure 2-22, the error description shows that the clock skew is too great for the join operation to succeed. AD has very strict time sync requirements, and the use of reliable Network Time Protocol (NTP) servers is highly recommended.

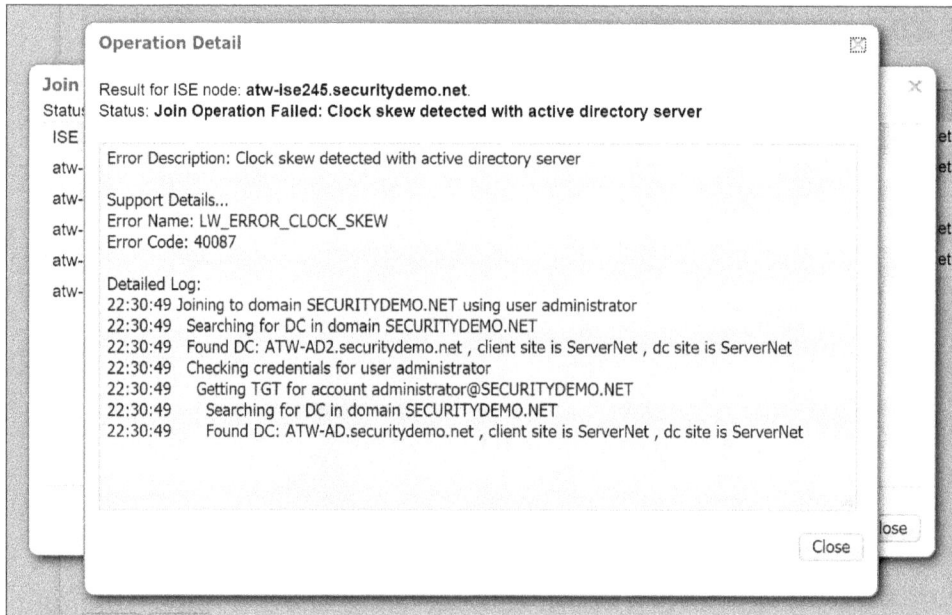

Figure 2-22   *Operation Details*

This is a very common issue that can occur when NTP is not set up correctly. Another possibility, if ISE is running as a virtual machine, is that the virtual machine may be configured to sync time from a hypervisor that is configured with the incorrect time. In our specific example, the latter issue was the culprit. After fixing the time on the VMware ESXi hypervisor, we rejoined the atw-esx245 node and it was successful, as shown in Figure 2-23.

That takes care of joining AD. Let's take a look at the other tabs to the right of the Connection tab at the top of ISE's AD configuration window: Whitelisted Domains, PassiveID, Groups, Attributes, and Advanced Settings. Also note the Test User and Diagnostic Tool buttons, which are both fantastic for troubleshooting AD connections.

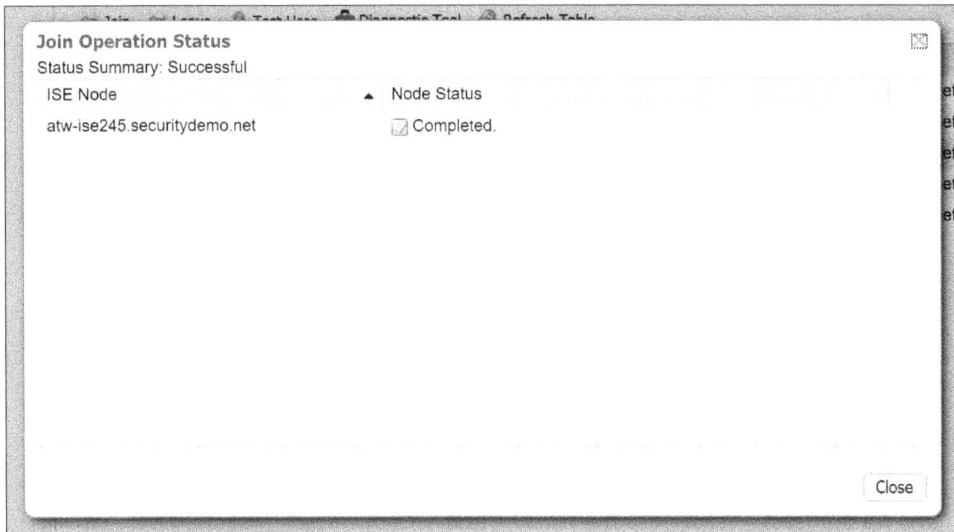

Figure 2-23 *Successful Join*

Whitelisted Domains

The Whitelisted Domains tab lists all the domains accessible through the selected join point. When the joined domain has connections to other domains (called *trust relationships*), there may be many domains available for ISE to search through. ISE can technically search through thousands of domains through these trust relationships, and not all of them should be searched through this connection. The Whitelisted Domains tab allows you to choose which domains should be searched through this particular join point.

PassiveID

The PassiveID tab is for working with passive identity. Using passive identity is a whole different world from the traditional network access AAA you've been exposed to thus far. In fact, there is a complete Work Center just for PassiveID, because there is that much to it.

To summarize it here, passive identity is the process of learning about an authentication from another source, in this case Active Directory. Instead of the end user's credentials being sent directly to ISE as part of an authentication, ISE learns about the authentication and the user's IP address by watching the AD authentications and reading the logs.

Groups

Given that Active Directory is usually the single source of truth for identity in most organizations, AD may have countless groups, sometimes hundreds or even thousands. Not only does that make the policy creation process within ISE much more difficult, it can also have a negative impact on ISE performance if ISE has to look through that many groups each time an authentication request comes to a PSN.

To use an AD group in an ISE authorization rule, it must be selected within the Groups tab. To select the groups that are applicable to your ISE deployment (also called "interesting groups"), choose **Add > Select Groups From Directory**, as shown in Figure 2-24.

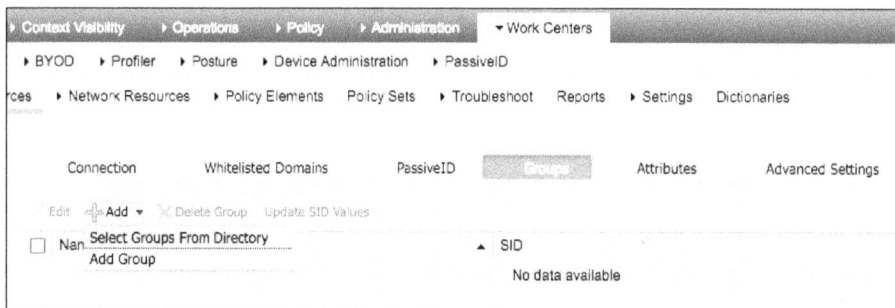

Figure 2-24   *Selecting Groups from Directory*

The Select Directory Groups window opens, which allows you to select the domain that you want to retrieve the groups from, and filter based on name, Microsoft security identifier (SID), or group type. AD has different types of groups, and different purposes. There are distribution groups that are used only for email distribution, and there are security groups that can be assigned permissions and rights. There are different types of security groups as well (Microsoft refers to it as the "scope" of the group), and the different scopes relate to the type of members each group can have.

The group types mostly only matter to AD itself, and external services leveraging those groups (such as ISE) will treat all the group types equally.

The types of AD security groups are as follows:

- **Global:** The group type you will use most, as it may contain user accounts that exist in the same domain only. These groups may also contain "nested groups"; that is, an admin may add other groups as members of this group. Domain Admins and Domain Users are examples of Global groups.

- **Universal:** The second group type that you might use often. Universal groups are just like Global groups, except they might contain members from other domains in the same AD forest. Enterprise Admins is an example of a Universal group.

■ **Domain Local:** These groups can contain groups from almost anywhere. Global groups, Universal groups, and other Domain Local groups (from the same domain) can all be members of these groups.

■ **Built-in:** Microsoft refers to these as the "default security groups." These groups are the ones created automatically when you install AD, and can be Global, Universal, and Domain Local. Examples include Domain Admins, Domain Users, Performance Log Users, Server Operators.

It is always easiest to use a filter when searching AD for groups that should be used with ISE. That way, you limit the results, which makes administering ISE that much easier.

Step 1.   From the Type Filter drop-down list, choose **Global**.

Step 2.   Click **Retrieve Groups**.

Step 3.   Check the check boxes for all the Global groups that should be used as part of the ISE deployment, as shown in Figure 2-25.

Step 4.   Click **OK**.

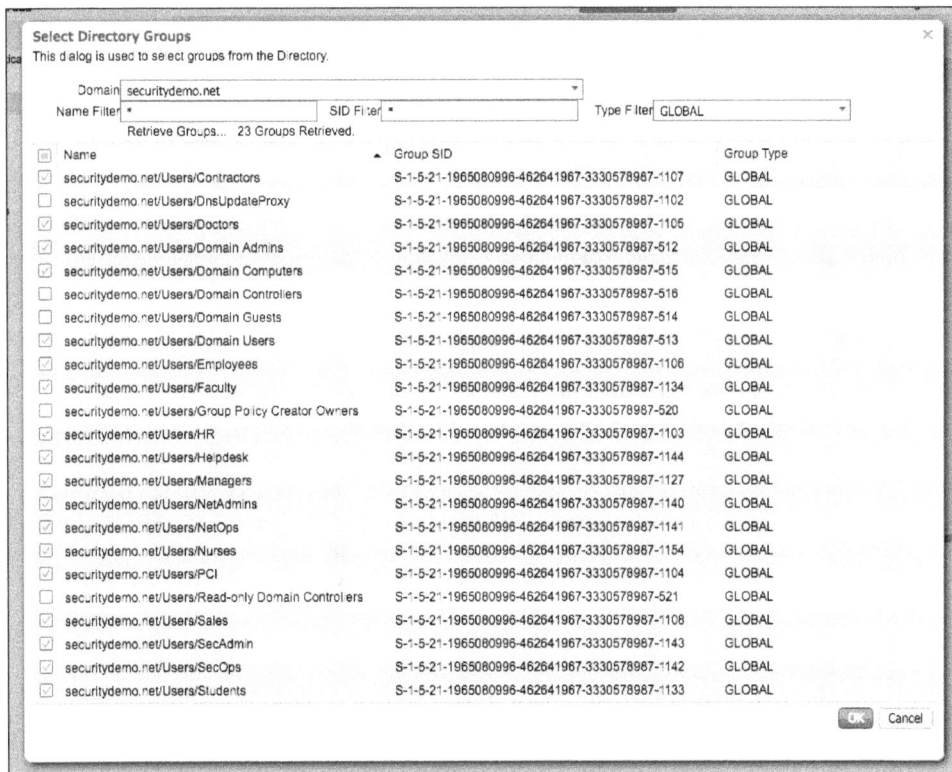

Figure 2-25 *Selecting Directory Groups*

Notice in Figure 2-25 how the AD SID is included with the groups added. This is because ISE leverages the unique SID of all groups instead of just the names, which can be changed and then duplicated in other domains. The SID will always be globally unique in the AD forest.

Step 5.   Click **Save** to finish adding the groups.

Attributes

Group membership is not the only important attribute that comes from Active Directory. Each AD object may have countless attributes associated to it. Examples of attributes that might be important to an access control solution are items such as department ID or even custom attributes that only matter to your organization, such as isManager.

As Chris Murray points out in his very thorough Cisco Live presentation on Active Directory integration, if you are going to use additional attributes, ensure that AD is indexing them in order to avoid performance issues with AD.

Note   Chris's presentation is available through the Cisco Live on-demand library at https://ciscolive.cisco.com. A direct link to the recorded session is https://tinyurl.com/ADIntMurray.

Advanced Settings

As you examine Figure 2-26, you will notice that the Advanced Settings tab has some interesting settings, such as those related to machine authentication, machine access restriction (MAR), and identity rewrite.

Let's call out a few of the important settings:

- **Enable Machine Authentication:** Windows endpoints are able to join Active Directory, creating a computer account. You read all about this in the context of how ISE joins the domain and creates a computer account for ISE itself. Those Windows computers must be able to authenticate and gain access to the network, to ensure proper communication with their management system: AD. The Enable Machine Authentication setting is enabled by default, allowing for those authentications to occur and Windows endpoints to gain network access using their computer credentials.

  To learn more about computer accounts, take a look at Aaron Woland's Network World blog: https://www.networkworld.com/article/2940463/it-skills-training/machine-authentication-and-user-authentication.html.

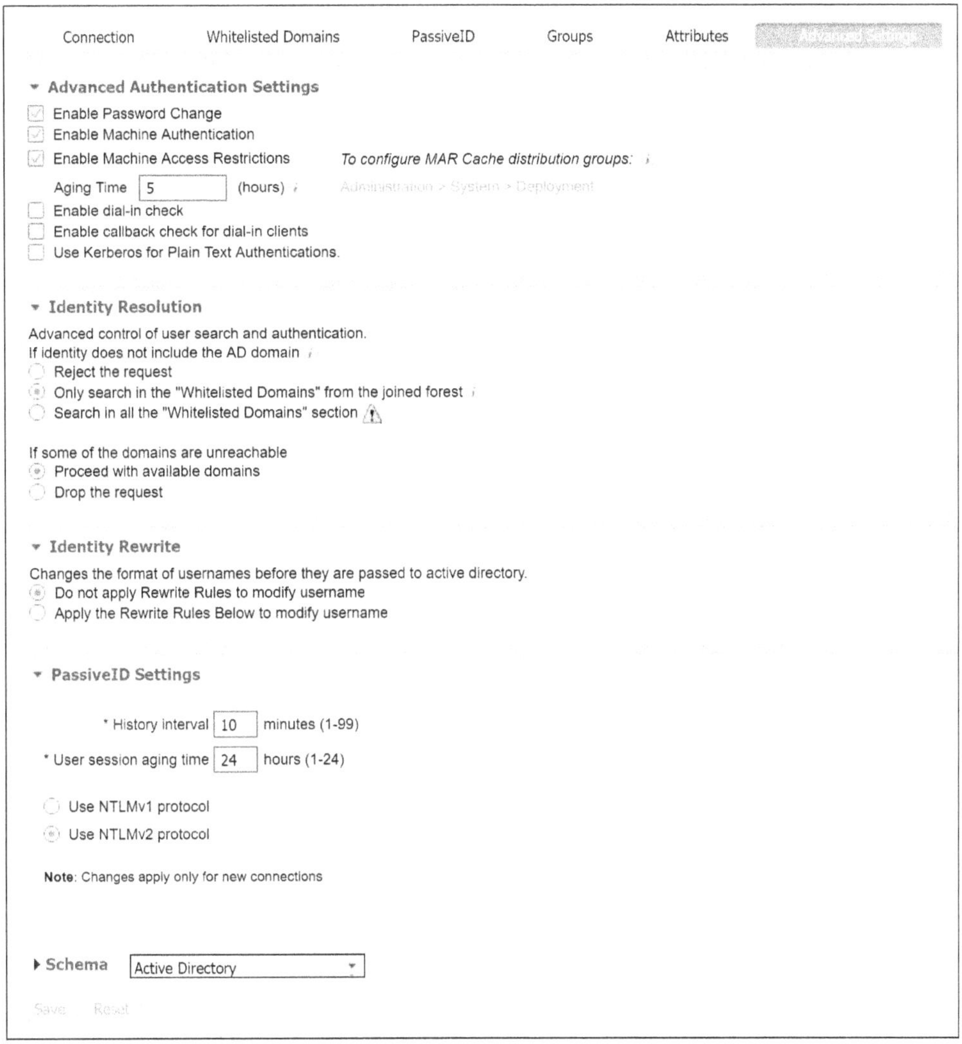

Connection	Whitelisted Domains	PassiveID	Groups	Attributes	Advanced Settings

▼ Advanced Authentication Settings

☑ Enable Password Change
☑ Enable Machine Authentication
☑ Enable Machine Access Restrictions   *To configure MAR Cache distribution groups:* ⅰ

   Aging Time [5]   (hours) ⅰ   Administration > System > Deployment
☐ Enable dial-in check
☐ Enable callback check for dial-in clients
☐ Use Kerberos for Plain Text Authentications.

▼ Identity Resolution

Advanced control of user search and authentication.
If identity does not include the AD domain ⅰ
◯ Reject the request
◉ Only search in the "Whitelisted Domains" from the joined forest ⅰ
◯ Search in all the "Whitelisted Domains" section ⚠

If some of the domains are unreachable
◉ Proceed with available domains
◯ Drop the request

▼ Identity Rewrite

Changes the format of usernames before they are passed to active directory.
◉ Do not apply Rewrite Rules to modify username
◯ Apply the Rewrite Rules Below to modify username

▼ PassiveID Settings

        * History interval [10]   minutes (1-99)

* User session aging time [24]   hours (1-24)

◯ Use NTLMv1 protocol
◉ Use NTLMv2 protocol

Note: Changes apply only for new connections

▶ **Schema**   [Active Directory   ▼]

Save   Reset

Figure 2-26 *Advanced Settings for AD Integration*

▪ **Enable Machine Access Restrictions:** Commonly referred to as MAR, this feature is used to combine two authentications together for authorization into the network. The authorization condition within the policy is named WasMachineAuthenticated and it allows an administrator to ensure that the computer and the user are both authorized to use the network, and that it is not (for example) an authorized user that is trying to access the network with their home computer.

MAR works by tracking the MAC address of the endpoint that passed machine authentication in a cache. When ISE is performing a user authentication and the configured authorization rule has the "WasMachineAuthenticated is True" condition set, then ISE compares the MAC address from the incoming user authentication request to the list of MAC addresses in the cache.

One of the original limitations of the MAR cache was that it was only in memory and therefore was cleared when a PSN rebooted. MAR cache persistence was added to ISE 2.1 where the cache is also written to disk and therefore survives a reboot. A second limitation to the original implementation of MAR is that the cache was local to the individual PSN, and therefore if the computer authentication and user authentications were sent to different PSNs, MAR was ineffective. ISE 2.3 added a feature known as *MAR cache distribution* that replicates the cache to other PSNs. Please note that the replication is restricted to PSNs that are members of the same node group.

Figure 2-27 shows the node group creation screen under **Administration > System > Deployment,** where you can see the MAR cache distribution settings.

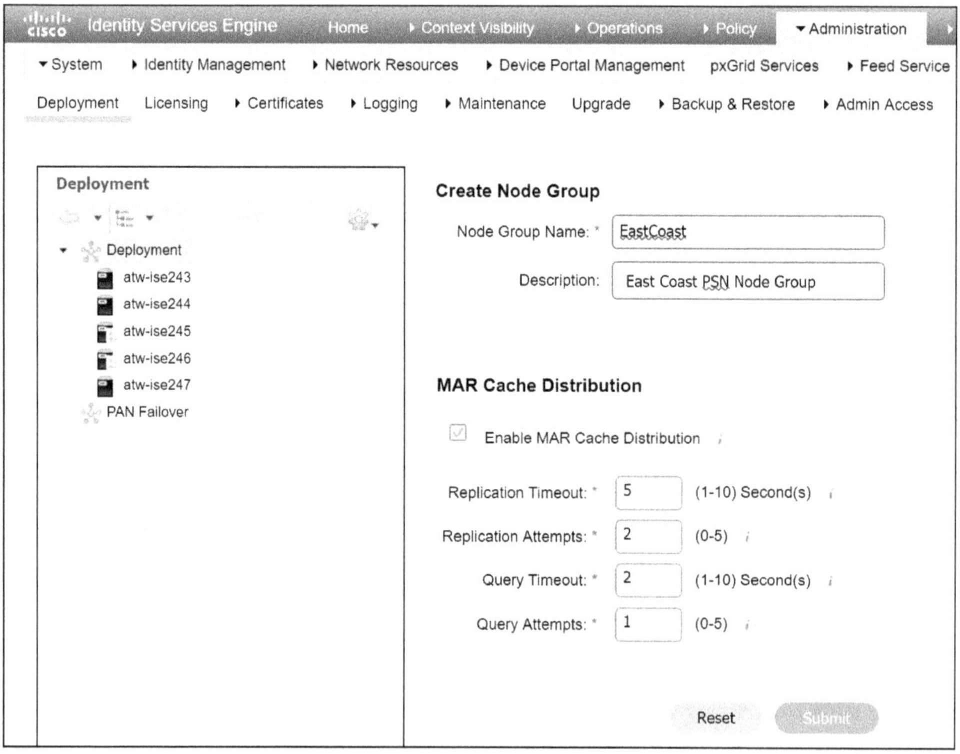

Figure 2-27   *MAR Cache Distribution*

To learn more about MAR and the use of multiple credentials for network access, take a look at Aaron Woland's blog: https://www.networkworld.com/article/2940463/it-skills-training/machine-authentication-and-user-authentication.html.

■ **Identity Resolution:** During an authentication, the user's credential may be sent in a common format such as DOMAIN\USER, where ISE is easily able to identify which of the many domains to query for validation of the user credentials. However, sometimes the identity might be sent as just USER and therefore ISE needs to figure out which domain the user belongs to. The choices for behavior when a credential arrives without a domain are to follow the domain whitelist (the default), drop the request, or search all domains.

■ **Identity Rewrite:** There are times when an incoming credential needs to be modified in order to authenticate against the correct identity store. Realm stripping is an example of when this type of rewrite functionality is required, and you can read about realm stripping on Aaron Woland's blog: https://www.networkworld.com/article/2226225/infrastructure-management/a-primer-on-support-for-realm-stripping.html.

■ **PassiveID Settings:** There are a few settings that can be configured for PassiveID. One of the most important settings is History Interval, which dictates how far into the past ISE will request information from the domain controller. This helps to ensure that no authentications are missed.

Other Identity Stores

Active Directory is not the only identity source. Certificate Authentication Profiles (CAPs) are another very common identity source; however, they work very differently than the other identity sources. A certificate is very similar to a document, like a driver's license or a passport, with fields that have text in them. The CAP is used to map those text fields from the certificate to attributes used for the authentication, such as a username or computer name. Figure 2-28 shows an example CAP, and the sections of the CAP are described after the figure.

The main component of a CAP is the Use Identity From option. The default setting is to leverage the common name portion of the certificate subject. Whatever text follows the CN= designation in the subject will be used as the identity for authorization. Clicking the drop-down arrow will display other certificate field options. The other radio button option, Any Subject or Alternative Name Attributes in the Certificate (for Active Directory Only), allows ISE to examine all the fields in the certificate and compare them to attributes of user and computer objects in Active Directory, to identify the correct identity.

Why would that be necessary? Well, not all certificates are created equal. Meaning, the administrator of the AD certificate authority might not have created the certificate template in a manor conducive to the needs of a network access solution. Okay, let's be honest. Most of the time the AD administrator doesn't actually have a full understanding of what they are doing with the certificate authority, and the security team is stuck dealing with the result.

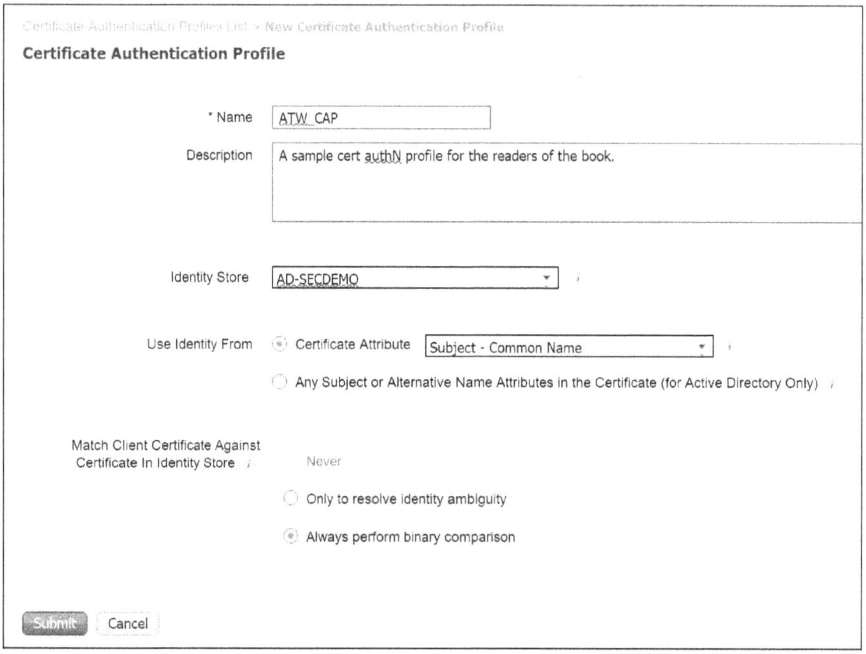

Figure 2-28   *Example Certificate Authentication Profile*

Another important field of the CAP is Identity Store. No identity store is selected by default, because it is not necessary for the CAP to function. It is, however, "nice to have" and it does add additional security. Originally, the identity store was used simply to perform a binary comparison of the public certificate from the supplicant device to a copy stored in the identity store, to ensure they are exactly the same. This functionality is still available by choosing the Always Perform Binary Comparison option. In later versions, the lookup into the directory was leveraged only to resolve identity ambiguity (the middle option), which refers to ISE comparing attributes in the certificate to attributes in AD to identify the specific identity when multiple similar identities exist—for example, multiple domains in a single AD forest that all contain a user named Joe.

Identity stores for the CAP are not limited to AD (for example, an LDAP store can also be used), but most deployments do not go through binary comparisons of certificates and instead simply trust the certificate based on the certificate signer.

Identity Source Sequences

Identity source sequences are brilliant and help to keep the policies of ISE more flexible and easier to work with. An ISS will check a series of identity sources from top to bottom (as configured), allowing a single authentication rule to check a number of identity sources, instead of just one.

There are a number of ISSs that come preconfigured when you install ISE, and are used in the policies by default to ensure an easy deployment. You view the preexisting ISSs and configure new ones in the ISE GUI under **Work Centers > Network Access > Identities > Identity Source Sequences.** Figure 2-29 shows the preexisting ISSs, and you can create more as needed.

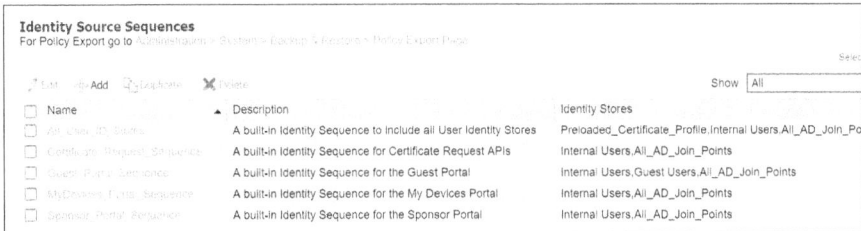

Figure 2-29   *Preconfigured Identity Source Sequences*

Examine the preconfigured ISS named All_User_ID_Stores by clicking on its name, as shown in Figure 2-30.

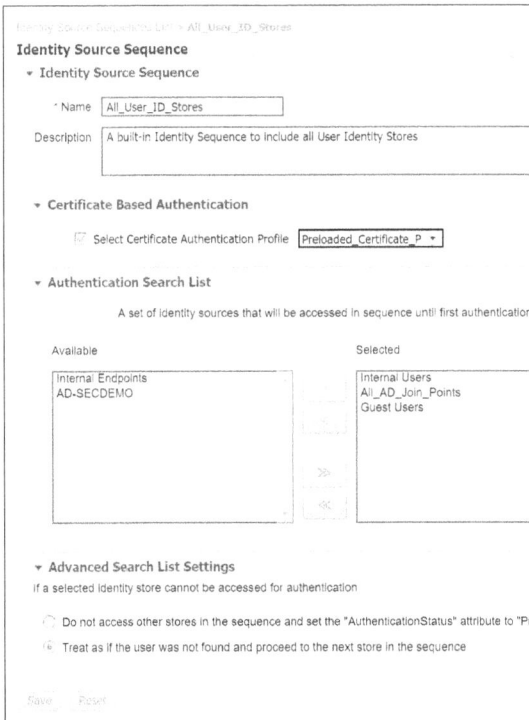

Figure 2-30   *All_User_ID_Stores ISS*

Notice in Figure 2-30 that a CAP is selected, to handle any certificate-based authentica-tions. Below that is the Authentication Search List, where you can see that identities will be checked in the Internal Users store, followed by the All_AD_Join_Points scope, and lastly in Guest Users.

It was not necessary to add AD-SECDEMO to the ISS because the All_AD_Join_Points will check that domain joint point already. If you join ISE to another domain, that domain will also be automatically searched as part of this ISS, without the administrator having to change any of the policies in ISE.

The Advanced Search List Settings determine how to handle an error with one of the sources in the ISS. So if that identity store times out or issues a process error, the ISS may keep processing the other stores in the list (default behavior) or the entire ISS can behave as if it had an error and stop processing the authentication request.

Network Resources

Following along the Network Access work center from left to right, the next section is Network Resources. This section contains the network devices and their groups, as well as external RADIUS and MDM servers for integration.

Much like user accounts and user groups, ISE has a concept of a network device and groups of network devices. Network devices are the authenticators of the hosts joining a network; they work in between the endpoint and the PSN, performing the authentication and the enforcement. As such they are commonly referred to as network access devices (NADs).

The NAD, and more specifically its capabilities, is a very critical part of any secure net-work access strategy. The more capabilities of the NAD (switch, wireless controller, wire-less access point, firewall, or VPN concentrator), the more flexibility and power the ISE admin will have to accomplish the business goals.

Device Groups

Before adding network access devices to ISE, it is highly recommended to create some logical Network Device Groups (NDGs).

Note   As previously mentioned, ISE work centers are designed to be followed from the top down, left to right. The Network Resources section deviates from that best practice, as Device Group is located below Network Devices in the navigation pane on the left. ISE's user experience (UX) team consciously decided to organize the work center this way because device groups are optional.

Device Groups are located under **Work Centers > Network Access > Network Resources > Device Groups**. The groups may be used as a very powerful tool when used correctly. With the use of NDGs, policy may be created based on the type of network device, its location, or any other logical grouping that an organization may want.

ISE is prebuilt with three top-level groups named "All Device Types," "All Locations," and "Is IPSEC Device." An ISE administrator may create other top-level groups as required. Examples of other top-level groups could be "Line of Business," "Deployment stage," etc. Basically, you can create anything that would be useful as an organizational unit for your business or deployment structure.

Figure 2-31 displays an example Network Device Group hierarchy.

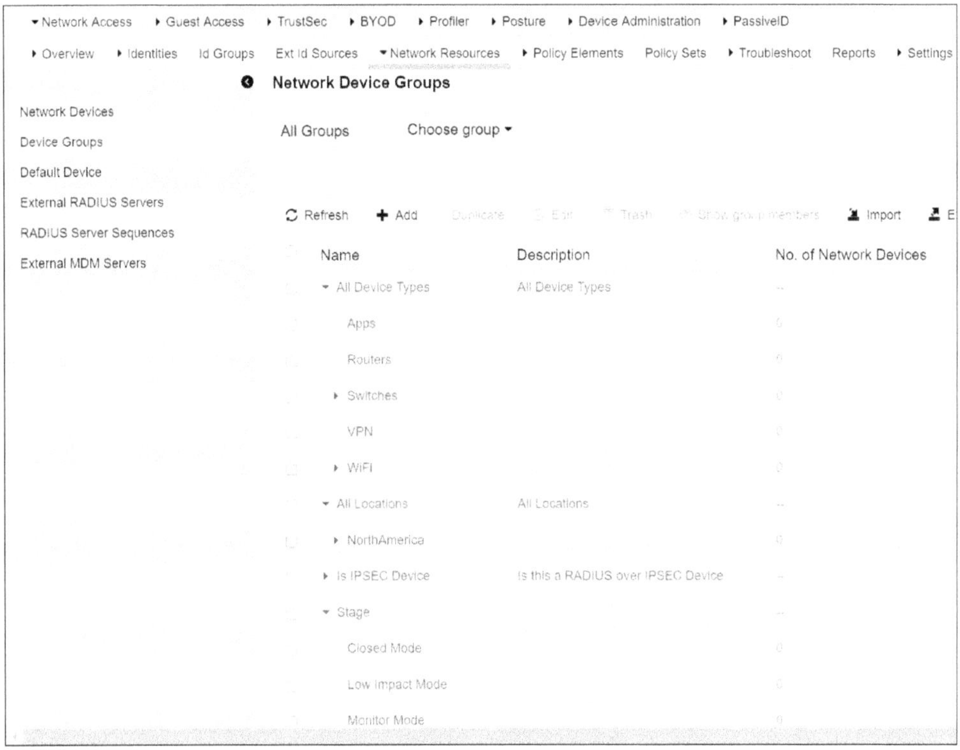

Figure 2-31 *Example Network Device Group Structure*

Network Access Devices

Now that the Network Device Group structure is in place, it is time to add the network access devices themselves. When you add a NAD (switch, wireless controller, VPN) to ISE, you are teaching ISE about its IP address, configuring a shared secret key for the RADIUS communication, and maybe even configuring some SNMP strings to pull data from that device (think profiling data). This process is what teaches ISE how to communicate to the device that will be doing all the enforcement of ISE policy.

To add a network access device to ISE, navigate to **Work Centers > Network Access > Network Resources > Network Devices,** and click **Add.** The network device is added to ISE as an object. That object has numerous important attributes that configure ISE to uniquely identify each NAD, as well as the shared secret key, SNMP community strings, and TrustSec configuration. The shared secret key must match the configured key on the NAD exactly.

Figure 2-32 shows an example network device being added to ISE.

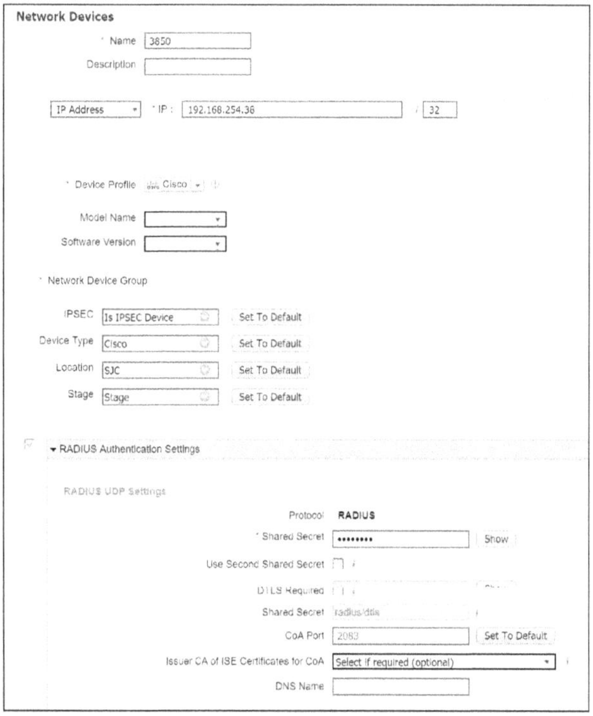

Figure 2-32 *Example Network Device*

As Figure 2-32 illustrates, each NAD object must be configured with one or more IP addresses that ISE will use to communicate with the NAD, as well as identify which NAD is the source of an incoming request. There are some environments where they will create a network device object that references a range of IP addresses, for example, an entire subnet of wireless access points. That type of configuration is usually left over from a migration from ACS, and is not typically recommended for ISE deployments due to the possibility of shared-secret misconfigurations, profiling data collection, and other more complex uses of network devices in ISE.

You assign a device profile to each NAD. The device profile defines common settings and configuration for NADs and allows the ISE admin to build a single policy that can work across Cisco and third-party network devices. While RADIUS and 802.1X are both certainly industry standards, not all devices are created equal in that realm. Each vendor may choose to implement a different set of Change of Authorization (CoA) capabilities or have a different mechanism to identity a MAB or 802.1X authentication. The device profile instructs ISE how to work with the network device, what attributes to match for the different authentication methods, and how to do web redirections and issue CoAs. You can examine device profiles in more details under **Administration > Network Resources > Network Device Profiles.**

This window is also where the NDGs will be selected. Each NAD may be assigned to one NDG of each type; in other words, one Location group, one Device Type group, and one of each manually created top-level NDG, such as Stage.

Very important is the RADIUS Authentication Settings section, which is where the RADIUS shared secret is configured, and you can select and configure the NAD to leverage RADSEC (RADIUS over Datagram Transport Layer Security [DTLS]).

Not shown in Figure 2-32 are the TACACS Authentication Settings, SNMP Settings, and Advanced TrustSec Settings sections. The TACACS Authentication Settings section will be covered in Chapter 5, "Device Administration Control with ISE."

The SNMP Settings section configures the SNMP community for the network device, which ISE will use for querying the NAD for profiling attributes such as Cisco Discovery Protocol (CDP) and Link Layer Discovery Protocol (LLDP) cache information. It's important to note: only configure the SNMP settings for devices that do not use the Device Sensor to send ISE profiling data within RADIUS accounting packets to avoid double-polling of the device and double entries for profiler.

The Advanced TrustSec Settings section is where Security Group Tag and Network Device Admission Control (NDAC) settings are configured.

Note   It is also possible and common to use a comma-separated values (CSV) file to do bulk imports of Network Device Groups and NADs.

Default Device

The next category below Device Groups in the navigation menu of the Network Resources section is Default Device. The purpose of the default device is to allow any non-defined NAD to authenticate to ISE as long as it uses the correct shared secret and/or RADSEC settings.

The use of a default device makes life easy for the uninformed; however, you should discourage the use of it and never enable it unless you have to. Using the default device breaks basic operational security (OPSEC) models and lowers the overall security and utility of the entire solution by allowing any device from anywhere to send RADIUS requests into ISE, and can also open you up to a possible denial of service (DoS) attack.

The best practice for network devices dictates that all NADs should be configured as individual objects, to ensure the best operational experience, stability, and security.

External RADIUS Servers and RADIUS Server Sequences

In the world of AAA, a term that comes up very frequently is RADIUS-Proxy. When a RADIUS server performs RADIUS-Proxy, it takes an incoming Access-Request message and, instead of performing that authentication, forwards the request on to another RADIUS server, unmolested.

External RADIUS servers in ISE are exactly what was described in the previous paragraph. These objects are RADIUS servers that are not part of this ISE cube, and when you use this object in an authentication policy, the ISE PSN will not perform any authentication of the incoming authentication request, but instead forwards the request to the external RADIUS server. The Access-Accept or Access-Reject from the external server is sent back to the ISE PSN, which can then manipulate the response or send it directly back to the NAD.

RADIUS server sequences are exactly like identity source sequences, except instead of identity stores, these objects contain a list of external RADIUS servers to try, in order.

External MDM Servers

For details about this final category in the Network Resources section, refer to Chapter 4, "Extending Network Access with ISE," which will cover external MDM servers in greater detail.

802.1X and Beyond

Back in 2001, the IEEE standardized on a solution for port-based network access control, known as 802.1X. It was predicted to revolutionize networking as we knew it, and no device would be able to plug in and communicate on a network without the user identifying themselves and being authorized again. Well, here we are, almost two decades later, and 802.1X on a wired network has just really started to catch on. 802.11, commonly known as Wi-Fi, really embraced 802.1X, and the adoption of 802X in the wireless world took off long before adoption in the wired world did.

Before diving into what 802.1X is or how it works, it's best to review the Extensible Authentication Protocol (EAP), an integral component of 802.1X. EAP is an authentication framework that defines the transport and usage of identity credentials. EAP encapsulates the usernames, passwords, certificates, tokens, one-time passwords, and so forth that a client sends for purposes of authentication.

EAP has become the de facto standard of authentication protocols. It is used for many different authentication methods including VPN, but most importantly the IEEE 802.1X standard defines the use of EAP over LAN (EAPoL).

IEEE 802.1X (commonly referred to as Dot1x) is defined as a standard for "port-based network access control" for local area networks and metropolitan area networks. The standardization of a network-based authentication framework was the catalyst for all identity-based networking that we see today. There are three main components to 802.1X: the supplicant, the authenticator, and the authentication server, as illustrated in Figure 2-33 and described in Table 2-2.

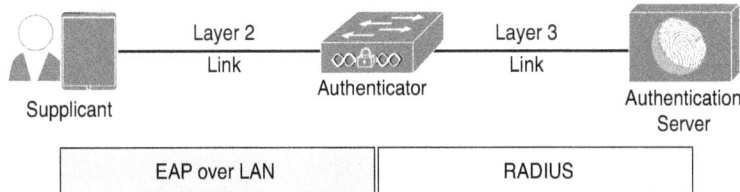

Figure 2-33 *Components of 802.1X EAP over LAN*

Table 2-2 *802.1X Components*

Component Name	Description
Supplicant	Software on the endpoint (also called a peer in the IETF RFC's, such as RFC 3748) that communicates with EAP at Layer 2. This software responds to the Authenticator and provides the identity credentials with the EAP communication.
Authenticator	The network device that controls physical access to the network based on the authentication status of the endpoint. The authenticator acts as the middleman, taking Layer 2 EAP communication from the supplicant, and encapsulating it in RADIUS directed at the active authentication server. The most common authenticators with a Cisco ISE deployment are LAN switches and Wireless LAN Controllers (WLCs). Cisco ISE will refer to these authenticators generically as network access devices.
Authentication server	The server that is performing the actual authentication of the client. The authentication server validates the identity of the endpoint and provides the authenticator with a result, such as accept or deny. Cisco Identity Services Engine is an authentication server.

While reviewing Figure 2-33 and Table 2-2, keep in mind that the authenticator (switch or WLC) acts as the middleman or proxy. The actual EAP identity exchange and authentication is occurring between the supplicant and the authentication server. The switch or WLC has no idea of what EAP type is in use, or if the user's credentials are valid; it simply takes the unmodified EAP frame and encapsulates it within the RADIUS packet sent to the authentication server and authorizes the port if the authentication server tells it to. Therefore, the EAP authentication itself is completely transparent to the authenticator.

Figure 2-34 displays the communication through a successful authentication.

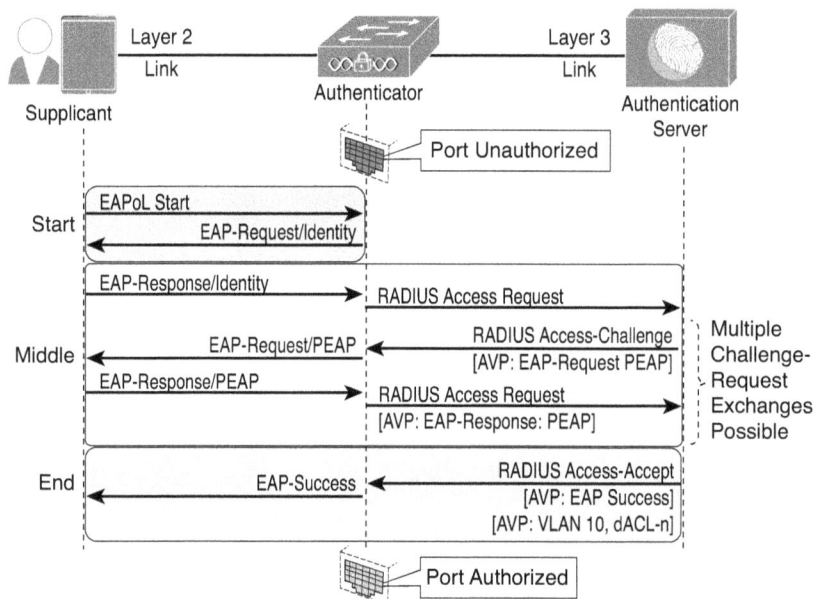

Figure 2-34   *Process Flow of a Successful 802.1X Authentication*

The authentication can be initiated by either the authenticator or the supplicant. The authenticator initiates authentication when the link state changes from down to up or periodically as long as the port remains up and unauthenticated. The switch sends an EAP-request/identity frame to the endpoint to request its identity. Upon receipt of the frame, the client's supplicant responds with an EAP-response/identity frame. However, enhancements were made to allow the supplicant to trigger the authenticator to request an identity by sending an EAPoL_Start message at any time. This enhancement provided for a much better end-user experience with 802.1X.

EAP Types

There are many different EAP types, each of which has its own benefit and downside. The EAP type defines the authentication mechanism to be used with EAP, which is usually self-evident in its name. Most of the numerous EAP types will not be discussed in this book due to lack of adoption or lack of inclusion in the exam blueprint, such as EAP-Kerberos.

The EAP types can be broken down into two categories: native EAP types and tunneled EAP types.

Native EAP Types

Native EAP types could also be thought of as pure EAP, where the communication is occurring exactly as intended in EAP. Figure 2-35 represents native EAP communications, described in the list that follows.

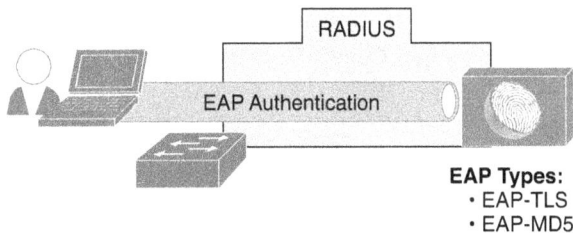

Figure 2-35   *Native EAP Methods*

■ **EAP-MD5:** Uses the MD5 message-digest algorithm to hide the credentials in a hash. The hash is sent to the server, where it is compared to a local hash to see if the credentials are accurate. However, EAP-MD5 does not have a mechanism for mutual authentication. That means the server validates the client but the client does not authenticate the server (i.e., it does not check whether it should trust the server). EAP-MD5 is common on Cisco IP Phones, and it is also possible that some switches will send MAB requests using EAP-MD5.

■ **EAP-TLS:** An EAP type that uses TLS to provide the secure identity transaction. This is very similar to SSL and the way encryption is formed between your web browser and a secure website. EAP-TLS has the benefit of being an open IETF standard, and is considered "universally supported."

EAP-TLS uses X.509 certificates and provides the ability to support mutual authentication, where the client must trust the server's certificate, and vice versa. It is considered among the most secure EAP types because password capture is not an option; the endpoint must still have the private key.

Note   EAP-TLS is quickly becoming the EAP type of choice when supporting BYOD in the enterprise.

■ **EAP-MSCHAPv2:** An EAP type where the client's credentials are sent to the server encrypted within an MSCHAPv2 session. This allows for the simple transmission of username and password, or even computer name and computer password, to the RADIUS server, which in turn will authenticate them to Active Directory.

Note   Cisco ISE does not currently support EAP-MSCHAPv2 as a native EAP type; support exists only within a tunneled EAP type.

■ **EAP-GTC**: EAP-Generic Token Card (GTC) was created by Cisco as an alternative to MSCHAPv2 to allow generic authentications to virtually any identity store, including OTP token servers, LDAP, NetIQ eDirectory (formerly Novell), and more.

Note   Cisco ISE does not currently support EAP-GTC as a native EAP type; support exists only when it is inside a tunneled EAP type.

Tunneled EAP Types

A tunneled EAP type simply uses a non-tunneled EAP type inside of a Transport Layer Security (TLS) tunnel between the supplicant and the authenticator. Whereas the native EAP types send their credentials immediately, tunneled EAP types form an encrypted tunnel first and then transmit the credentials with native EAP within that tunnel. Figure 2-36 represents the non-native, tunneled EAP communication, described in the list that follows.

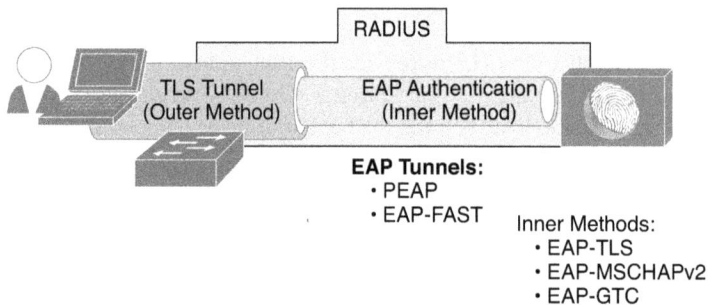

Figure 2-36   *Tunneled EAP Methods*

Note   It is important to understand that tunneled EAP methods work very similarly to the way a secure tunnel is formed between a web browser and a secure website (such as a banking site). The tunnel is formed first normally using only the certificate of the server (one-way trust), and then the user enters their banking login credentials within that secure tunnel.

■ **PEAP**: Protected EAP. Originally proposed by Microsoft, this EAP tunnel type has quickly become the most popular and widely deployed EAP method in the world. PEAP will form a potentially encrypted TLS tunnel between the client and server, using the X.509 certificate on the server in much the same way the SSL tunnel is established between a web browser and a secure website. After the tunnel has been formed, PEAP uses one of the following EAP types as an "inner method"—authenticating the client using EAP within the outer tunnel.

- **EAP-MSCHAPv2:** Using this inner method, the client's credentials are sent to the server encrypted within an MSCHAPv2 session. This is the most common inner method, as it allows for simple transmission of username and password, or even computer name and computer password, to the RADIUS server, which in turn will authenticate them to Active Directory.

- **EAP-GTC:** As previously described, this inner method was created by Cisco as an alternative to MSCHAPv2 to allow generic authentications to virtually any identity store, including OTP token servers, LDAP, NetIQ eDirectory, and more.

- **EAP-TLS:** While rarely used, and not widely known, PEAP is capable of using EAP-TLS as an inner method.

- **EAP-FAST:** Flexible Authentication via Secure Tunneling (FAST) is very similar to PEAP. FAST was created by Cisco Systems as an alternative to PEAP to allow for faster reauthentications and support faster wireless roaming. Just like PEAP, FAST forms a TLS outer tunnel and then transmits the client credentials within that TLS tunnel. Where FAST differs from the PEAP is the ability to use Protected Access Credentials (PACs). A PAC can be thought of like a secure "cookie," stored locally on the host as "proof" of a successful authentication.

  - **EAP-MSCHAPv2:** Using this inner method, the client's credentials are sent to the server encrypted within an MSCHAPv2 session. This is the most common inner method, as it allows for simple transmission of username and password, or even computer name and computer password, to the RADIUS server, which in turn will authenticate them to Active Directory.

  - **EAP-GTC:** This inner method was created by Cisco as an alternative to MSCHAPv2 to allow generic authentications to virtually any identity store, including OTP token servers, LDAP, NetIQ eDirectory, and more.

  - **EAP-TLS:** EAP-FAST is capable of using EAP-TLS as an inner method. This has become quite popular with EAP-Chaining.

With tunneled EAP types, there is a concept of *inner* and *outer* identities. The inner identity is easiest to explain. It is the user or device's actual identity credentials sent with the native EAP protocol. The outer identity is typically set to "anonymous." It's also the identity that is used between the supplicant and the authentication server for the initial TLS tunnel setup.

Cisco ISE is able to read that outer identity and use it to help make identity store selection decisions. Put simply, that outer identity might contain information (such as domain name) that tells Cisco ISE to submit the credentials to Active Directory or LDAP or some other identity store. Most supplicants will hide this option from the end user, and only administrators see the outer identity; however, one supplicant that does expose it to the end user is the native Android supplicant, as shown in Figure 2-37. One point of humor to this author is that the Android supplicant refers to the outer identity as the "Anonymous identity," which is an oxymoron.

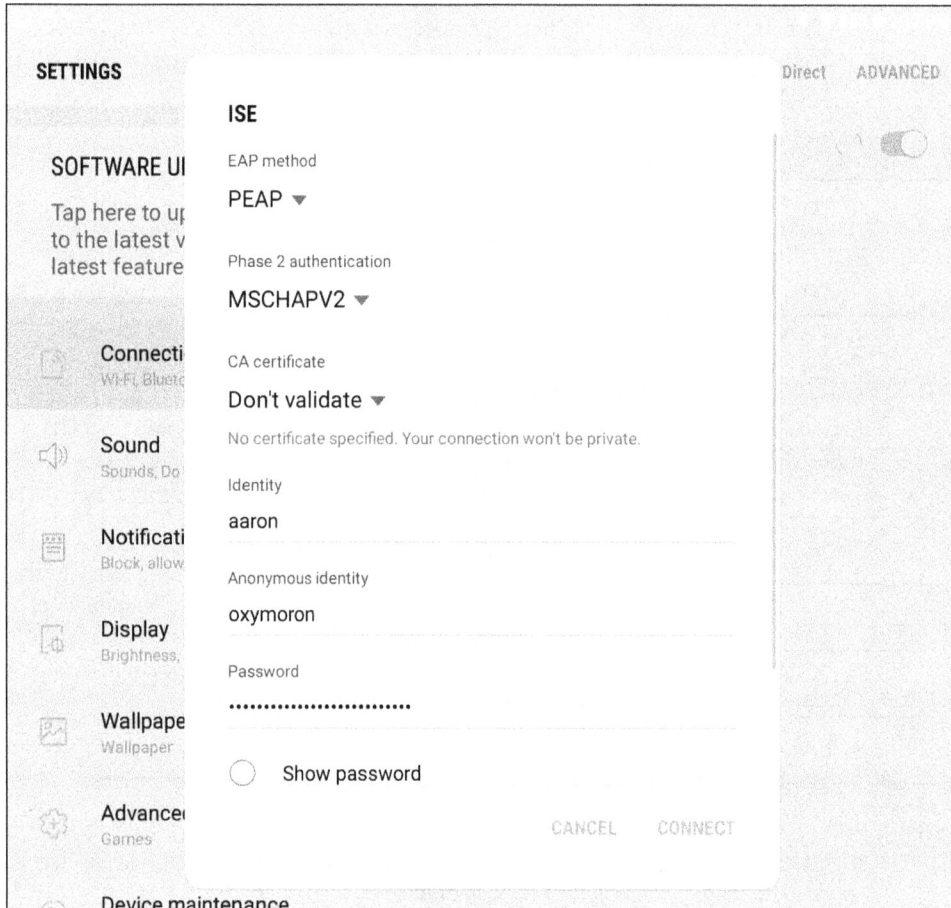

Figure 2-37   *Android Supplicant Exposes the Outer Identity*

Summary of EAP Authentication Types

Table 2-3 shows a comparison of common EAP authentication types.

Table 2-3   *EAP Comparison*

	EAP-PEAP	EAP-TLS	EAP-FAST
Client-side certs required	No	Yes	No
Server-side certs required	Yes	Yes	No
Security	High	High	High
	Protects EAP methods, including TLS tunnel creation for EAP packets, message authentication, message encryption, and authentication of server to client.	Authentication occurs automatically, with no intervention by user. No dependency on user password. Digital certs provide strong authentication. Message exchange is protected with public key encryption.	Crypto-binding between inner and outer methods prevents MITM attacks. Immunity to passive dictionary attacks. Uses pre-shared keys (PAC files) to construct tunnel through use of symmetric cryptography (optional).

EAP Authentication Type Identity Store Comparison Chart

Selecting the appropriate EAP type is dependent on the operating system, 802.1X supplicant, and supported back-end credential database or identity store. Table 2-4 outlines the comparison of EAP authentication type identity stores.

Table 2-4   *EAP Authentication Type Identity Store Comparison Table*

Identity Store	EAP/TLS	PEAP/ TLS	PEAP/ MSCHAPv2	PEAP/ GTC	EAP-FAST/ MSCHAPv2	EAP-FAST/ GTC	EAP-FAST/ TLS
MS-AD	Yes*	Yes*	Yes	Yes	Yes	Yes	Yes*
LDAP	Yes*	Yes*	No	Yes	No	Yes	Yes*
Token Server	No	No	No	Yes	No	No	No
RSA	No	No	No	Yes	No	Yes	No

*TLS authentication only validates the certificate, but the authorization function may use these identity stores.

Not Everything Has a (Configured) Supplicant

With 802.1X, a supplicant and an authenticator will exchange EAP messages, and if the endpoint connected to the authenticator (switch) did not have a supplicant, the EAP identity request messages would go unanswered. This would result in an authentication timeout, and with the original concept of identity networking and 802.1X, the endpoint would be denied access to the company network. In other words, only devices that can authenticate and have authenticated to the network will be allowed on the network.

When designing a secure network access solution, there is a tendency to only consider the managed desktops, laptops, and (more recently) tablet-type devices when thinking about network authentication. However, organizations tend to possess a plethora of devices beyond those. Think about the printers, IP cameras, IP phones, thin-client terminals, building automation, and other "headless" devices that exist in a modern day network.

Consider Cisco IP Phones, for an example. These devices do have a supplicant that can be configured individually at the keypad, which does not scale very well (imagine having to configure a supplicant on every phone in an organization with hundreds of thousands of phones). Cisco IP Phone supplicants can also be configured centrally from the Call Control Server (formerly named the Cisco Call Manager). What about the other devices? Do they also have a central management platform that is capable of configuring each supplicant across large numbers of devices deployed at scale?

One of the original "solutions" to deal with these non-authenticating devices was to not configure 802.1X on the individual switch ports where the nonauthenticating endpoint would be plugged into the network. Take a moment and think about that for a minute or two, as it would allow anyone to simply unplug the non-authenticating endpoint and plug their laptop into the port, and voila! The device has full network access without any challenge whatsoever.

What about when a device (like a printer) needs to be moved? That might require the network team to be involved for that move and enable 802.1X on the old switch port, while disabling 802.1X on the new switch port, which poses significant management burden on the IT department. It's just not a sustainable business model.

Next, what happens when an employee who should have network access has a misconfigured supplicant, or an expired credential, or is using a temporary device? What about guest users who only need access to the Internet?

All of these variations called for a series of "Band-Aids" to deal with them in a sustainable way (where possible).

MAC Authentication Bypass

The first "Band-Aid" to help with non-authenticating policies is for the authenticator to act on behalf of the endpoint that does not have a supplicant. In this scenario, the authenticator will craft a RADIUS Access-Request message and send it to the authentication server. The authenticator uses the endpoint's MAC address as the identity.

The authentication server (the RADIUS server) will perform an authentication lookup using that MAC address as the credential. If that MAC address is in a list of MAC addresses allowed to access the network, a RADIUS Access-Accept message will be sent back from the authentication server to the authenticator. This process is known as a MAC Authentication Bypass (MAB).

Figure 2-38 illustrates the process of MAC Authentication Bypass.

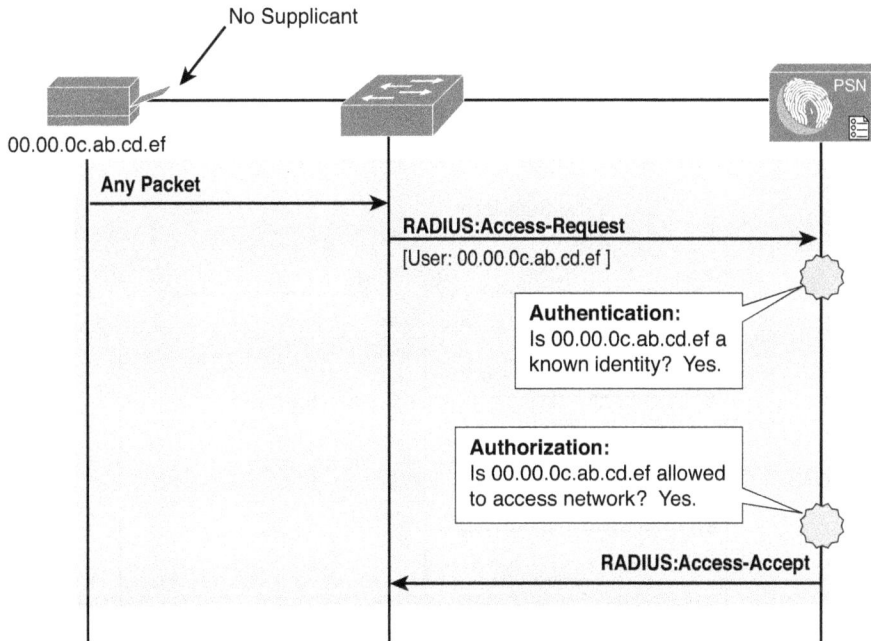

Figure 2-38   *MAC Authentication Bypass Process*

Examining Figure 2-38, there is a non-authenticating endpoint (a printer) with a MAC address of 00.00.0c.ab.cd.ef. There is also a switch, which is the authenticator, and an ISE server acting as the authentication server. Take a look at the steps that occur:

Step 1.   Because the printer does not have a supplicant, the authenticator crafts a RADIUS Access-Request message using the printer's MAC address as the identity.

Step 2.   The authentication server (ISE) receives the RADIUS Access-Request and performs an identity lookup, which determines if it is a known MAC address or not.

Step 3.   The authentication server (ISE) determines if the device should be granted access to the network and, if so, what level of access to provide.

Step 4.   The authentication server (ISE) sends the RADIUS response (Access-Accept) to the authenticator, allowing the printer to access the network.

It is also important to note that while 802.1X is a standard, MAB is not. MAB is something that each vendor could implement differently if they so choose, just as long as the RADIUS communication complies with the standard for RADIUS. With ISE, the network device profile takes care of normalizing MAB requests so that different policies do not need to be crafted for each vendor's implementation.

How does a switch (authenticator) know when the endpoint that is plugged into it does not have a supplicant? Following the 802.1X standard, the method is simply a timeout. The authenticator is meant to send EAP over LAN identity request (EAPoL-id-req) frames every 30 seconds by default. After three timeouts, a period of 90 seconds by default, it is accepted that the endpoint must not have a supplicant. As with most Cisco switch features, timers are adjustable. Figure 2-39 illustrates the timeouts occurring three times before MAB begins.

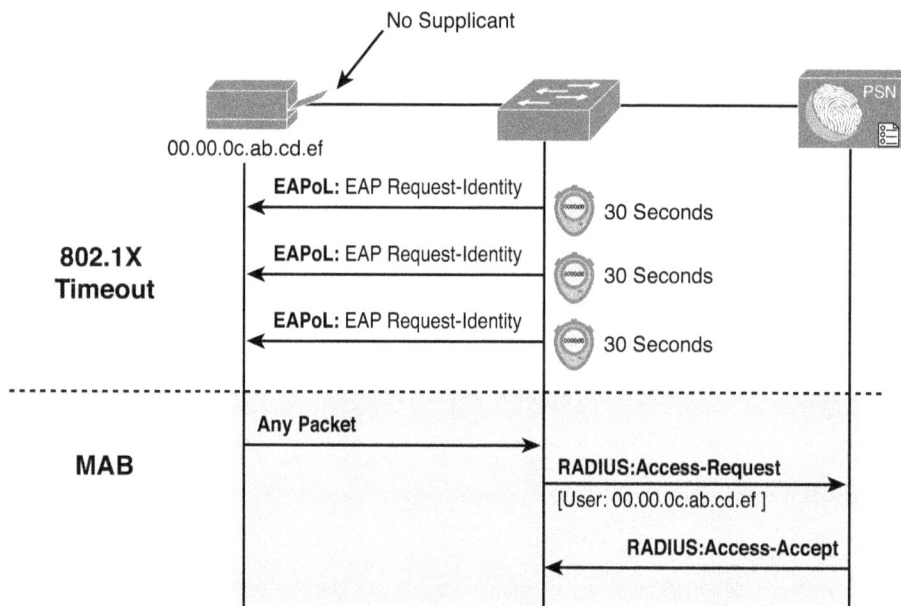

Figure 2-39   *MAC Authentication Bypass After Timeout*

Keep in mind that MAB is inherently not a secure technology. When implementing MAB, you are bypassing the stronger security of 802.1X by allowing specific MAC addresses to gain access without authentication. MAC addresses are easily spoofed, meaning it is easy to configure an endpoint to use a MAC address other than the one burned into the hardware. When using MAB, always follow a least-privilege and defense-in-depth approach. This means when authorizing a device for network access via MAB, the endpoint should be granted only enough access to communicate to the networks and services that device is required to speak to, and nothing else.

In other words: don't provide full access to devices that have been MAB'd; instead, provide them with an authorization that is more limited. Because MAB is a standard RADIUS authentication and the authorization decision is being sent from the authentication server (ISE), there really are no limitations to the type of authorization results that can be sent to the authenticator, especially if that NAD is a Cisco switch.

Some examples include, but are not in any way limited to:

- Downloadable ACLs (dACLs)

- Dynamic VLAN assignment (dVLAN)

- URL-redirection

- Security Group Tag (SGT)

- Smart port macros

Keep in mind that if an endpoint does not have a supplicant, it is not recommended to ever change its VLAN. When changing a VLAN assigned to an endpoint, that endpoint must know (somehow) to renew the DHCP lease. The best solution is to not use VLAN changes on open networks, because there is nothing on the client to detect the VLAN change and trigger the DHCP renewal. When the network uses 802.1X, there is a supplicant on the client to do the VLAN change detection (one common method is to periodically check if the default gateway is reachable) and trigger the DHCP renewal if the VLAN has changed.

If you still choose to change the VLAN on open networks, then you have only a few choices (none of which is considered a best practice). You can set the DHCP lease time to something *very* low, so it will renew the address frequently. There is also an option to use an ActiveX or Java applet on a web-authentication portal that will do the VLAN change detection in lieu of a supplicant.

Web Authentication

Just because there is no configured supplicant on an endpoint does not mean that the user of that endpoint does not need to authenticate. Consider the use cases of guests or visitors, or maybe just a misconfiguration or expired credential for the end user. Based on who the user is, they still may require network access and be granted some access to the network.

Enter the technology known as Web Authentication, commonly referred to as WebAuth. An authenticator would be able to send a user to a locally hosted web page, in other words a web page hosted on the local device itself: the switch, wireless controller, or even the firewall or VPN concentrator. It is a simple thing, really, just a very basic web page where a user may submit their username and password.

The username and password that are submitted to the web portal are then sent from the authenticator to the authentication server in a standard RADIUS Access-Request packet. So, in a very similar fashion to what occurs with MAB, the switch is sending the request for the endpoint because the endpoint is not authenticating to the switch. Figure 2-40 illustrates the WebAuth concept.

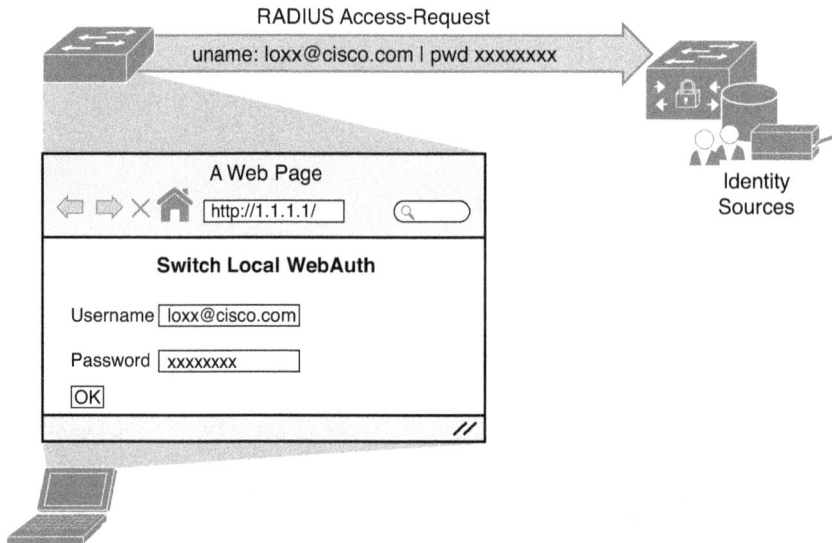

Figure 2-40   *Local WebAuth*

The credential that gets submitted through the WebAuth page could be Active Directory credentials of an employee. The credentials could be guest credentials for someone who is only temporarily allowed to have Internet access, and no other access. The use of WebAuth is really not limited to one type or another.

Keep in mind, WebAuth is only an effective authentication method for a device that is interactive. In other words, it would not make sense to try and use WebAuth for a printer. There is no user to interactively enter their credentials and click the submit button.

As with MAB, WebAuth is not a standard either. There are multiple ways to perform WebAuth, with benefits and downsides to each one.

Local Web Authentication

Local Web Authentication (LWA) is the original WebAuth. As described in the preceding paragraphs, the authenticator redirects web traffic (HTTP and/or HTTPS) to a locally hosted web portal where a user may enter their username and password.

The credentials are submitted through the web portal, and the authenticator (switch, wireless controller, etc.) sends the RADIUS Access-Request to the authentication server, using the username and password from the form. It is key to remember that any time the switch is sending the credentials for the user, it is considered Local Web Authentication.

Storing the web authentication portal on the local authenticator can often limit the customization capabilities of the web pages themselves. On a Cisco switch, the pages are not customizable at all. Some organizations not only prefer, but require that the web portals be customized to match the corporate branding. For those companies, traditional LWA is not usually an acceptable solution, at least not for wired WebAuth.

Additionally, when using LWA with Cisco switches, there is no native support for advanced services including acceptable use policy (AUP) acceptance pages, client provisioning, password changing capabilities, self-registration, or device registration. For those advanced capabilities, a company needs to consider using Centralized Web Authentication, discussed a bit later.

Cisco switches, as well as a variety of other 802.1X-compliant switches, have a configuration option that assigns a special VLAN to endpoints when the authentication timer expires, meaning they don't have a supplicant. This is known as the "Guest VLAN." It is an option that was available before the more powerful policy servers like Cisco ISE existed. There are still many production deployments of 802.1X today that use this Guest VLAN to provide wired guests access to the Internet; however, it is important to note that once the switch makes a local decision (such as assigning the Guest VLAN), LWA is no longer an option.

In addition to LWA and Guest VLAN being mutually exclusive, there are some other interesting bits of information about LWA. LWA does not support VLAN assignment, so you are basically limited to ACL assignment. LWA is also restricted from Change of Authorization (CoA) support; therefore, access policy cannot be changed based on posture or profiling state, or even an administrative change as a result of malware or other need to quarantine the endpoint.

Local Web Authentication with a Centralized Portal

There is an option with many modern authenticators to redirect the Local Web Authentication to a centralized web portal. Utilizing a centralized portal allows the organization to customize the portal with corporate branding and provide the right look and feel for the organization.

With Cisco switches, the locally stored web pages might contain the redirection string that sends the user web traffic to the centrally hosted portal. That hosted portal is configured to send the credentials entered into it to the source NAD through an HTTP POST method, or returned to the NAD through a hidden I-frame.

Figure 2-41 illustrates the process of the user entering their credentials into the centrally located portal (in this case, it's hosted on ISE), where the POST goes to the network device, while Figure 2-42 illustrates the RADIUS Access-Request being sourced from the switch, containing the credentials sent in the POST.

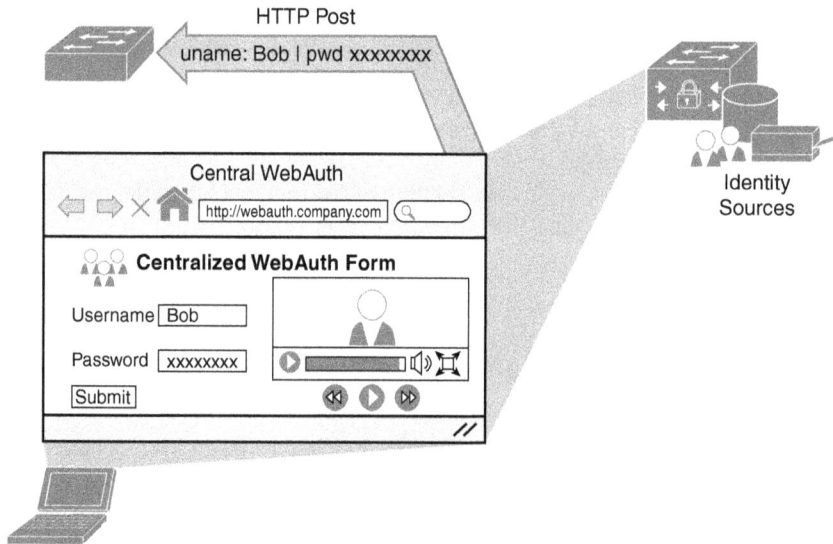

Figure 2-41   *Centrally Hosted Portal with Local Web Authentication*

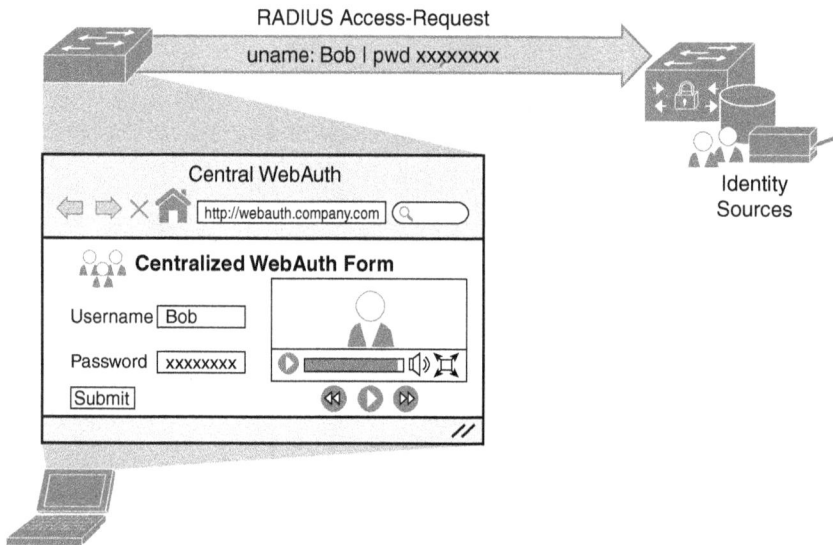

Figure 2-42   *NAD Sends POSTed Credentials via RADIUS Access-Request*

There are pros and cons to the POST method and the I-frame method. The I-frame method does not work with more recent browsers like Internet Explorer 9 and newer. The POST method does not work with some mobile browsers, and it is very insecure because the user's credentials are passed from the central portal through the network and back to the authenticator. The web portal needs to have the intelligence to determine which methods to use with each browser type, by examining the user-agent string from the browser.

Cisco Wireless LAN Controller (WLC) version 7.0 required the use of either the POST or I-frame method to support Local Web Authentication with a centralized portal on ISE. Traditional LWA would always still be available.

Even though the portal is centralized, the same restrictions associated with traditional LWA are still in effect. Change of Authorization will not function, nor will client provisioning and other advanced functionality.

Centralized Web Authentication

Centralized Web Authentication (CWA) is what a Cisco ISE solution typically uses almost exclusively. While Cisco ISE is still capable of supporting LWA methods, those methods are typically reserved for non-Cisco network devices (or deployments where people prefer to do things the hard way).

Just like LWA, CWA is only for interactive users that have a web browser, where the user will manually enter the username and password, and just as before, the WebAuth and Guest VLAN functions remain mutually exclusive.

CoA works fully with CWA, which leads to the support for all the authorization results, such as dACL and VLAN authorization. Keep in mind, any time you change VLANs on an endpoint, the endpoint must be able to detect the VLAN change and trigger an IP address renewal. With 802.1X, the supplicant takes care of the VLAN change detection and address renewal; however, when using CWA there normally is no supplicant on the endpoint. Therefore, the portal must use an ActiveX or Java applet to handle the renewal of the IP address after the VLAN assignment.

CWA also supports all the advanced services, such as client provisioning, posture assessments, acceptable use policies, password changing, self-registration, and device registration

Now that you've read all the things that CWA can do, you must be wondering how it works and what makes it different from the other WebAuth options. The authenticator only sees a MAB, and the rest is handled on the authentication server (ISE). Figure 2-43 shows the MAB occurring with a redirection to the centralized portal, and Figure 2-44 illustrates that the switch still only sees a MAB request while ISE is maintaining the user authentication.

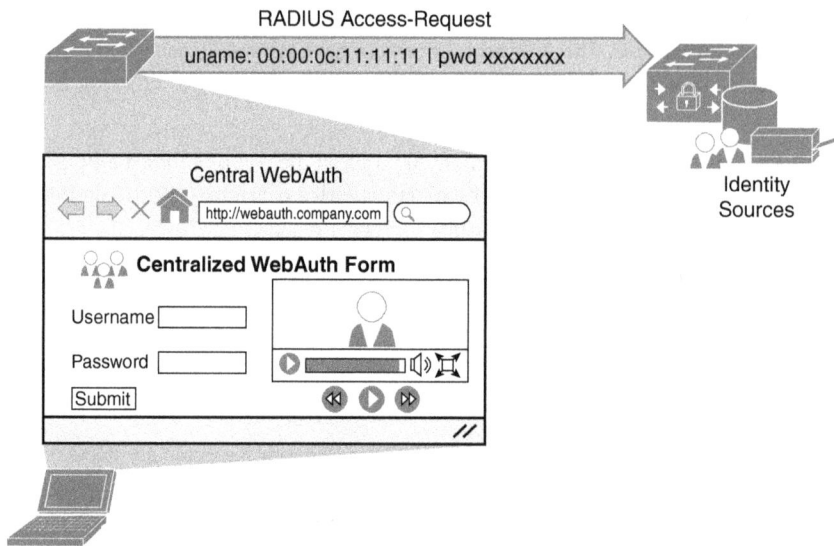

Figure 2-43   *URL-Redirected MACAuth Bypass*

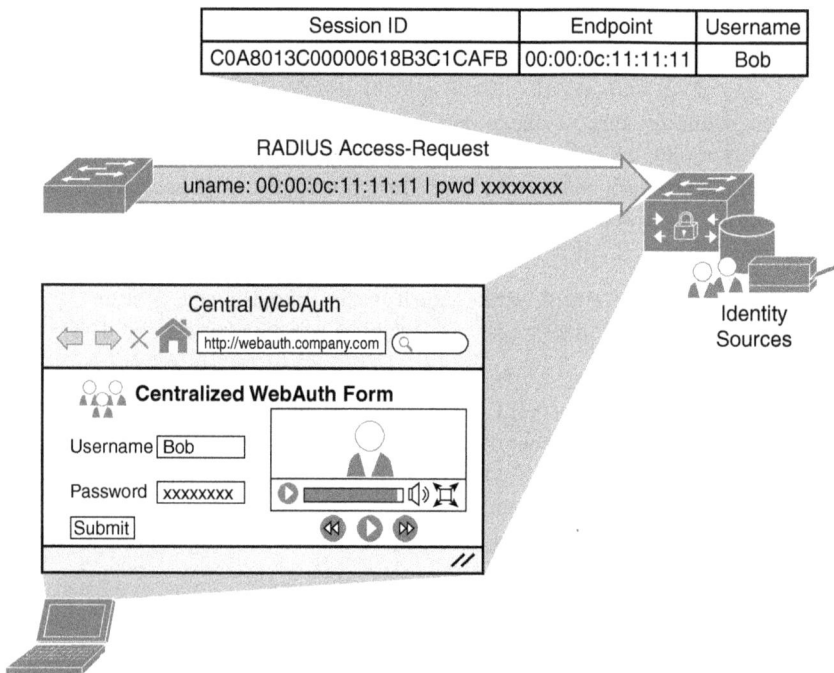

Figure 2-44   *Credentials Are Never Sent to the Authenticator*

The following steps detail what is occurring in Figures 2-43 and 2-44:

Step 1.   The endpoint entering the network does not have a configured supplicant.

Step 2.   The authenticator performs a MAB, sending the RADIUS Access-Request to Cisco ISE (the authentication server).

Step 3.   The authentication server (ISE) sends the RADIUS result including a URL-Redirection to the centralized portal on the ISE server itself.

Step 4.   The end user enters their credentials into the centralized portal. Unlike the LWA options, the credentials are never sent to the switch, but rather are stored within the ISE session directory and tied together with the MAB coming from the switch.

Step 5.   ISE sends a reauthentication Change of Authorization (CoA-reauth) to the switch. This causes the switch to send a new MAB request with the same session ID to ISE, which is processed.

Step 6.   ISE sends the final authorization result to the switch for the end user.

Configuring Wired Network Access with ISE

As you will recall from the previous section, CWA is ultimately an authorization result of a MAB; therefore, when configuring a Cisco Catalyst switch for secure network access, you simply configure it for Dot1x and MAB. All the other fancy parts of the ISE solution, such as guest access, onboarding, and profiling, will all happen through the RADIUS control plane.

You already added all the NADs to ISE earlier in the chapter. So, it's now time to configure those network devices to authenticate to the ISE PSNs.

Configuring Cisco Catalyst Switches

Cisco started as a networking company, taking the lead in the world for offering multi-protocol routers, and very shortly thereafter leading the world with network switching. It should come as no surprise, then, to learn that Cisco has the vast majority of market share for switching infrastructure.

Well, because of that long-standing market leadership position, some may think that Cisco should rest on its laurels and not innovate with switching anymore. Well, that's not Cisco's style. Even though Cisco has more ports configured for 802.1X in the world than any other vendor, they are still always making the authentication experience better and more feature rich.

With that comes a bit of confusion as to which version supports which new features, and so forth. Well, we are going to try and clear that up for you here, right now.

Cisco switches are undergoing an evolution when it comes to network access. Therefore, we should classify the switch capabilities into a few groupings to keep it easy. These are not official terms: these are "*Aaron-isms*".

- **Classic IOS:** This grouping encompasses IOS 12.2(55)SE versions. Think of it as the rock-solid workhorse, very stable and feature rich compared to non-Cisco switches—but still missing some of the newer advances in network authentication, profiling, and TrustSec. These are still the most common switch that we see during Secure Access deployments—they are tried and true and die-hard. Because they don't have the advanced profiling capabilities, such as the Device Sensor, we configure these for SNMP polling from ISE instead.

- **Newer IOS:** This grouping includes the IOS 15.x and 16.x flavors and their IOS-XE counterparts. These platforms add some incredible features and functions like the Device Sensor that enables large-scale profiling. With the Device Sensor capabilities, the switch will collect profiling attributes locally and send them to ISE in a RADIUS accounting packet. With this capability, we will not be configuring the switch for SNMP polling, and we must configure it to collect the profiling attributes. Overall, the configuration style on these switches is the same as the classic IOS switches, but there are some differences due to the more advanced capabilities.

- **C3PL:** There is an alternative configuration style on the newer IOS switches that follows the Cisco Common Classification Policy Language (C3PL) style of configuration. This provides some very intriguing and advanced authentication features, as well as a very different configuration style that is very powerful but can sometimes be confusing for those who aren't used to it yet. However, those who start to use this configuration style end up loving it and rarely want to go back to the classic methods of configuration. At the time of writing, this is the least common type of deployment, but it is gaining in popularity.

Global Configuration for All Catalyst Switches

This section covers the global configuration of all the non-C3PL switches participating with Cisco ISE. In other words, this section focuses on the configuration of both the Classic IOS and the Newer IOS groupings. C3PL switches will be covered in a separate section.

Configure Certificates on Switch

Within a secure access system, the switch performs the URL redirection for web authentication as well as redirecting the discovery traffic from the posture to the Policy Service Node.

Performing URL redirection at the Layer 2 access (edge) device is a vast improvement over previous NAC solutions that require an appliance to capture web traffic and perform redirection to a web authentication page, simplifying the deployment for both web authentication and the posture agent discovery process. The switch will need to be configured to redirect non-encrypted HTTP traffic as well as encrypted HTTP traffic (HTTPS).

From global configuration mode on the switch:

Step 1. Set the DNS domain name on the switch.

Cisco IOS does not allow for certificates, or even self-generated keys, to be created and installed without first defining a DNS domain name on the device.

Type **ip domain-name** *domain-name* at the global configuration prompt.

Step 2. Generate keys to be used for HTTPS.

Type **crypto key generate rsa general-keys mod 2048** at the global configuration prompt.

Enable the Switch HTTP/HTTPS server

The embedded HTTP/S server in Cisco IOS will be used to grab HTTP traffic from the user and redirect that user's browser to the Centralized Web Authentication portal, or a device registration portal, or even to the mobile device management onboarding portal. This same function is used for redirecting the posture agent's traffic to the Policy Service Node.

Step 1. Enable the HTTP server in global configuration mode.

Type **ip http server** at the global configuration prompt.

Step 2. Enable the HTTP secure server.

Type **ip http secure-server** at the global configuration prompt.

Many organizations will want to ensure that this redirection process that is using the switch's internal HTTP server is decoupled from the management of the switch itself. This may be accomplished by running the following two commands from global configuration mode:

```
ip http active-session-modules none
ip http secure-active-session-modules none
```

Global AAA Commands

There are a number of commands to enter at the global configuration level, such as enabling the AAA subsystem and adding the RADIUS servers to the switch.

Step 1. Enable AAA on the access switch(es).

By default, the AAA "subsystem" of the Cisco switch is disabled. Prior to enabling the AAA subsystem, none of the required commands will be available in the configuration.

```
C3560X(config)#aaa new-model
```

Step 2.   Create an authentication method for 802.1X.

An authentication method is required to instruct the switch on which group of RADIUS servers to use for 802.1X authentication requests.

```
C3560X(config)#aaa authentication dot1x default group radius
```

Step 3.   Create an authorization method for 802.1X.

The method created in Step 2 will enable the user/device identity (username/ password or certificate) to be validated by the RADIUS server; however, simply having valid credentials is not enough. There must be an authorization as well. The authorization is what defines that the user or device is actually allowed to access the network, and what level of access is actually permitted.

```
C3560X(config)#aaa authorization network default group radius
```

Step 4.   Create an accounting method for 802.1X.

RADIUS accounting packets are extremely useful, and in many cases are required. These types of packets will help ensure that the RADIUS server (Cisco ISE) knows the exact state of the switch port and endpoint. Without the accounting packets, Cisco ISE would have knowledge only of the authentication and authorization communication. Accounting packets provide information on when to terminate a live session, as well as local decisions made by the switch (such as AuthFail VLAN assignment, etc.).

If the switch supports the Device Sensor, the sensor data will be sent to ISE using the RADIUS accounting configuration.

```
C3560X(config)#aaa accounting dot1x default start-stop group
radius
```

Step 5.   Configure periodic RADIUS accounting updates.

Periodic RADIUS accounting packets allows Cisco ISE to track which sessions are still active on the network. This command sends periodic updates whenever there is new information. It will also send a periodic update once per 24 hours (1440 minutes) to show ISE that the session is still alive.

```
C3560X(config)#aaa accounting update newinfo periodic 1440
```

Global RADIUS Commands

Here we have a small difference between the Classic IOS and the IOS 15.x switches. The main difference exists because the Newer IOS grouping is gaining support for IPv6 infrastructure, while the Classic IOS grouping is limited to IPv4.

Classic IOS

We configure a proactive method to check the availability of the RADIUS server. With this practice, the switch will send periodic test authentication messages to the RADIUS server (Cisco ISE). It is looking for a RADIUS response from the server. A success message is not necessary—a failed authentication will suffice, because it shows that the server is alive.

Step 1. Within global configuration mode, add a username and password for the RADIUS keepalive.

The username we are creating here will be added to the local user database in Cisco ISE at a later step. This account will be used in a later step where we define the RADIUS server.

```
C3560X(config)#username radius-test password password
```

Step 2. Add the Cisco ISE servers to the RADIUS group.

In this step we will add each Cisco ISE PSN to the switch configuration, using the test account we created previously. The server will proactively be checked for responses one time per hour, in addition to any authentications or authorizations occurring through normal processes. Repeat for each PSN.

```
C3560X(config)#radius-server host ise_ip_address auth-port
1812 acct-port 1813 test username radius-test key
shared_secret
```

Step 3. Set the dead criteria.

The switch has been configured to proactively check the Cisco ISE server for RADIUS responses. Now configure the counters on the switch to determine if the server is alive or dead. Our settings will be to wait 5 seconds for a response from the RADIUS server and attempt the test three times before marking the server dead. If a Cisco ISE server doesn't have a valid response within 15 seconds, it will be marked as dead. We also set the value of how long the server will be marked dead, which we are setting to 15 minutes.

```
C3560X(config)#radius-server dead-criteria time 5 tries 3
C3560X(config)#radius-server deadtime 15
```

Step 4. Enable Change of Authorization.

Previously we defined the IP address of a RADIUS server to which the switch will send RADIUS messages; however, we define the servers that are allowed to perform Change of Authorization (RFC 5176) operations in a different listing, also within global configuration mode.

```
C3560X(config)#aaa server radius dynamic-author
C3560X(config-locsvr-da-radius)#client ise_ip_address
server-key shared_secret
```

Step 5.   Configure the switch to use the Cisco vendor-specific attributes (VSAs).

Here we configure the switch to send any defined VSAs to Cisco ISE PSNs during authentication requests and accounting updates.

```
C3560X(config)#radius-server vsa send authentication
C3560X(config)#radius-server vsa send accounting
```

Step 6.   Enable the VSAs:

```
C3560X(config)#radius-server attribute 6 on-for-login-auth
C3560X(config)#radius-server attribute 8 include-in-access-req
C3560X(config)#radius-server attribute 25 access-request
include
```

Step 7.   Ensure the switch always sends traffic from the correct interface.

Switches often have multiple IP addresses associated to them; therefore, it is a best practice to always force any management communications to occur through a specific interface. This interface IP address must match the IP address defined in the Cisco ISE Network Device object.

```
C3560X(config)#ip radius source-interface interface_name
C3560X(config)#snmp-server trap-source interface_name
C3560X(config)#snmp-server source-interface informs
interface_name
```

Newer IOS

Just as with the Classic IOS grouping, we configure a proactive method to check the availability of the RADIUS server in the Newer IOS grouping. With this practice, the switch will send periodic test authentication messages to the RADIUS server (Cisco ISE). It is looking for a RADIUS response from the server. A success message is not necessary—a failed authentication will suffice, because it shows that the server is alive.

Step 1.   Within global configuration mode, add a username and password for the RADIUS keepalive.

The username we are creating here will be added to the local user database in Cisco ISE at a later step. This account will be used in a later step where we define the RADIUS server.

```
Cat4503(config)#username radius-test password password
```

Step 2.   Add the Cisco ISE PSNs as RADIUS servers.

This is where things differ quite a bit from the Classic IOS configuration. We will actually create an object for the RADIUS server and then apply configuration to that object.

```
Cat4503onfig)#radius server server-name
Cat4503(config-radius-server)#address ipv4 address auth-port
1812 acct-port 1813
```

```
Cat4503(config-radius-server)#key Shared-Secret
Cat4503(config-radius-server)#automate-tester username
radius-test probe-on
```

Step 3.   Set the dead criteria.

The switch has been configured to proactively check the Cisco ISE server for RADIUS responses. Now configure the counters on the switch to determine if the server is alive or dead. Our settings will be to wait 5 seconds for a response from the RADIUS server and attempt the test three times before marking the server dead. If a Cisco ISE server doesn't have a valid response within 15 seconds, it will be marked as dead. We also set the value of how long the server will be marked dead, which we are setting to 15 minutes.

```
Cat4503(config)#radius-server dead-criteria time 5 tries 3
Cat4503(config)#radius-server deadtime 15
```

Step 4.   Enable Change of Authorization.

Previously we defined the IP address of a RADIUS server to which the switch will send RADIUS messages; however, we define the servers that are allowed to perform Change of Authorization (RFC 3576) operations in a different listing, also within global configuration mode.

```
Cat4503(config)#aaa server radius dynamic-author
Cat4503(config-locsvr-da-radius)#client ise_ip_address
server-key shared_secret
```

Step 5.   Configure the switch to use the Cisco VSAs.

Here we configure the switch to send any defined VSAs to Cisco ISE PDPs during authentication requests and accounting updates.

```
Cat4503(config)#radius-server vsa send authentication
Cat4503(config)#radius-server vsa send accounting
```

Step 6.   Enable the VSAs:

```
Cat4503(config)#radius-server attribute 6 on-for-login-auth
Cat4503(config)#radius-server attribute 8 include-in-access-req
Cat4503(config)#radius-server attribute 25 access-request
include
```

Step 7.   Ensure the switch always sends traffic from the correct interface.

Switches often have multiple IP addresses associated to them; therefore, it is a best practice to always force any management communications to occur through a specific interface. This interface IP address must match the IP address defined in the Cisco ISE Network Device object.

```
Cat4503(config)#ip radius source-interface interface_name
Cat4503(config)#snmp-server trap-source interface_name
Cat4503(config)#snmp-server source-interface informs
interface_name
```

Creating Local Access Control Lists for Classic and Newer IOS

Certain functions on the switch require the use of locally configured ACLs, such as URL redirection. Some of these ACLs created will be used immediately, and some might not be used until a much later phase of your deployment. The goal of this section is to prepare the switches for all possible deployment models at one time, and limit the operational expense of repeated switch configuration.

Step 1.   Add the following ACL to be used on switch ports in monitor mode:

```
C3560X(config)#ip access-list extended ACL-ALLOW
C3560X(config-ext-nacl)#permit ip any any
```

Step 2.   Add the following ACL to be used on switch ports in low-impact mode:

```
C3560X(config)#ip access-list ext ACL-DEFAULT
C3560X(config-ext-nacl)#remark DHCP
C3560X(config-ext-nacl)#permit udp any eq bootpc any eq
bootps
C3560X(config-ext-nacl)#remark DNS
C3560X(config-ext-nacl)#permit udp any any eq domain
C3560X(config-ext-nacl)#remark Ping
C3560X(config-ext-nacl)#permit icmp any any
C3560X(config-ext-nacl)#remark PXE / TFTP
C3560X(config-ext-nacl)#permit udp any any eq tftp
C3560X(config-ext-nacl)#remark Drop all the rest
C3560X(config-ext-nacl)#deny ip any any log
```

Step 3.   Add the following ACL to be used for URL redirection with Web Authentication:

```
C3560X(config)#ip access-list ext ACL-WEBAUTH-REDIRECT
C3560X(config-ext-nacl)#remark explicitly deny DNS from being
redirected to address a bug
C3560X(config-ext-nacl)#deny udp any any eq 53
C3560X(config-ext-nacl)#remark redirect all applicable traf-
fic to the ISE Server
C3560X(config-ext-nacl)#permit tcp any any eq 80
C3560X(config-ext-nacl)#permit tcp any any eq 443
C3560X(config-ext-nacl)#remark all other traffic will be
implicitly denied from the redirection
```

Step 4.   Add the following ACL to be used for URL redirection with the posture agent:

```
C3560X(config)#ip access-list ext ACL-AGENT-REDIRECT
C3560X(config-ext-nacl)#remark explicitly deny DNS and DHCP
from being redirected
```

```
C3560X(config-ext-nacl)#deny udp any any eq 53 bootps
C3560X(config-ext-nacl)#remark redirect HTTP traffic only
C3560X(config-ext-nacl)#permit tcp any any eq 80
C3560X(config-ext-nacl)#remark all other traffic will be
implicitly denied from the redirection
```

Global 802.1X Commands

There are a few more commands at the global level related to 802.1X and IP device tracking that we need to enable.

Step 1.   Enable 802.1X globally on the switch.

Enabling 802.1X globally on the switch does not actually enable authentication on any of the switch ports. Authentication will be configured, but it won't be enabled until the later sections where we configure monitor mode.

```
C3560X(config)#dot1x system-auth-control
```

Step 2.   Enable dACLs to function.

Downloadable ACLs are a very common enforcement mechanism in a Cisco TrustSec deployment. In order for dACLs to function properly on a switch, IP device tracking must be enabled globally.

```
C3560X(config)#ip device tracking
```

Global Logging Commands (Optional)

In addition to the authentication configuration commands that you've entered at the global level so far, you might wish to enable logging to be sent to ISE.

Step 1.   Enable syslog on the switch.

Syslog may be generated on Cisco IOS Software in many events. Some of the syslog messages can be sent to the ISE Monitoring Node (MNT) to be used for troubleshooting purposes. It is not recommended to enable this across all NADs all the time, but to enable it when beginning your project, and when troubleshooting.

To ensure Cisco ISE is able to compile appropriate syslog messages from the switch, use the following commands:

```
C3560X(config)#logging monitor informational
C3560X(config)#logging origin-id ip
C3560X(config)#logging source-interface <interface_id>
C3560X(config)#logging host <ISE_MNT_PERSONA_IP_Address_x>
transport udp port 20514
```

Step 2.   Set up standard logging functions on the switch to support possible trouble-shooting/recording for Cisco ISE functions.

The Cisco Enterprise Policy Manager (EPM) is a part of the Cisco IOS Software module responsible for features such as Web Authentication and dACLs. Enabling EPM logging generates a syslog related to dACL authorization, and part of the log can be correlated inside Cisco ISE when such logs are sent to Cisco ISE.

```
C3560X(config)#epm logging
```

Only the following NAD syslog messages are actually collected and used by Cisco ISE:

- AP-6-AUTH_PROXY_AUDIT_START
- AP-6-AUTH_PROXY_AUDIT_STOP
- AP-1-AUTH_PROXY_DOS_ATTACK
- AP-1-AUTH_PROXY_RETRIES_EXCEEDED
- AP-1-AUTH_PROXY_FALLBACK_REQ
- AP-1-AUTH_PROXY_AAA_DOWN
- AUTHMGR-5-MACMOVE
- AUTHMGR-5-MACREPLACE
- MKA-5-SESSION_START
- MKA-5-SESSION_STOP
- MKA-5-SESSION_REAUTH
- MKA-5-SESSION_UNSECURED
- MKA-5-SESSION_SECURED
- MKA-5-KEEPALIVE_TIMEOUT
- DOT1X-5-SUCCESS/FAIL
- MAB-5-SUCCESS/FAIL
- AUTHMGR-5-START/SUCCESS/FAIL
- AUTHMGR-SP-5-VLANASSIGN/VLANASSIGNERR
- EPM-6-POLICY_REQ
- EPM-6-POLICY_APP_SUCCESS/FAILURE
- EPM-6-IPEVENT:
- DOT1X_SWITCH-5-ERR_VLAN_NOT_FOUND
- RADIUS-4-RADIUS_DEAD

Global Profiling Commands

In this section, we are separating out the configuration of devices that support the Device Sensor and the configuration of those that must rely on SNMP for profiling.

Newer IOS Switches with Device Sensor Capabilities

The Cisco IOS Device Sensor requires a multipart configuration. The first part is to configure the Device Sensor filter lists. These lists inform the Device Sensor of which items to consider for the different protocols.

There are three protocols that the Device Sensor will support: DHCP, CDP, and LLDP. Therefore, we will create one list for each protocol.

Step 1.   Create a list for DHCP.

There are three options we need to configure for ISE: host-name, class-identifier, and client-identifier.

```
C3560X(config)#device-sensor filter-list dhcp list <dhcp_
list_name>
C3560X(config-sensor-dhcplist)#option name host-name
C3560X(config-sensor-dhcplist)#option name class-identifier
C3560X(config-sensor-dhcplist)#option name client-identifier
```

Step 2.   Create a list for CDP.

There are two CDP options we need to configure for ISE: device-name and platform-type.

```
C3560X(config)#device-sensor filter-list cdp list <cdp_list_
name>
C3560X(config-sensor-cdplist)#tlv name device-name
C3560X(config-sensor-cdplist)#tlv name platform-type
```

Step 3.   Create a list for LLDP.

There are three LLDP options we need to configure for ISE: port-id, system-name, and system-description.

```
C3560X(config)#device-sensor filter-list lldp list <lldp_
list_name>
C3560X(config-sensor-lldplist)#tlv name port-id
C3560X(config-sensor-lldplist)#tlv name system-name
C3560X(config-sensor-lldplist)#tlv name system-description
```

Step 4.   Include the lists created in Steps 1–3 in the Device Sensor.

In the preceding steps we defined which options the Device Sensor should store. At this point we configure the Device Sensor to use those lists.

```
C3560X(config)#device-sensor filter-spec dhcp include list
<dhcp_list_name>
```

```
C3560X(config)#device-sensor filter-spec lldp include list
<cdp_list_name>
C3560X(config)#device-sensor filter-spec cdp include list
<lldp_list_name>
```

Step 5.   Enable the Device Sensor.

The Device Sensor is now configured. Next we enable the Device Sensor service to run on the switch, and configure when it will send its updates.

```
C3560X(config)#device-sensor accounting
C3560X(config)#device-sensor notify all-changes
```

Classic IOS Switches Without Device Sensor Capability

The ISE PSN will use SNMP to query the switch for certain attributes to help identify the devices connected to the switch. As such, we will configure SNMP communities for Cisco ISE to query, as well as SNMP traps to be sent to Cisco ISE.

Step 1.   Configure a read-only SNMP community.

ISE only requires read-only SNMP access. Ensure this community string matches the one configured in the network device object in Cisco ISE.

```
C3560X(config)#snmp-server community community_string RO
```

Step 2.   Configure the switch to send traps.

We will now enable an SNMP trap to be sent with changes to the MAC address table. A trap that includes the device MAC address and interface identifier is sent to Cisco ISE whenever a new address is inserted, removed, or moved in the address table.

```
C3560X(config)#snmp-server enable traps mac-notification
change move threshold
```

Step 3.   Add Cisco ISE as an SNMP trap receiver (optional).

Here, a server is added as a trap receiver for the configured MAC notification. This is only needed if you will be using the SNMPTRAP probe. This is not needed in most cases, and you wouldn't want to send traps and use the RADIUS probe, as both will trigger the SNMPQUERY probe.

```
C3560X(config)#snmp-server host ise_ip_address version 2c
community_string mac-notification
```

Interface Configuration for Classic and Newer IOS Switches

We have just completed the global configuration settings of the access layer switches, including RADIUS, SNMP, profiling, and AAA methods.

This section focuses on building a single-port configuration that can be used across your entire Secure Unified Access deployment, regardless of the switch type, deployment stage, or deployment model you choose.

Configuring Interfaces as Switch Ports

One of the first things to do before configuring any of the authentication settings on the switch port is to ensure the switch port is configured as a Layer 2 port, not a Layer 3 port. This command is a simple, one-word command that we will run, and from that point the other commands we run will all take effect.

Step 1. Enter interface configuration mode for the switchport range:

```
C3560X(config)#interface range first_interface -
last_interface
```

Step 2. Ensure the ports are Layer 2 switch ports:

```
C3560X(config-if-range)#switchport
```

Step 3. Configure the port for layer 2 edge devices, using the host macro.

The host macro will automatically run three commands for you. It will configure the port to be an access port (nontrunk), disable channel groups, and configure the spanning tree to be in portfast mode.

```
C3560X(config-if-range)#switchport host
switchport mode will be set to access
spanning-tree portfast will be enabled
channel group will be disabled
```

Configuring Flexible Authentication and High Availability

The default behavior of 802.1X is to deny access to the network when an authentication fails. This behavior was discovered to be an undesirable behavior in many customer deployments, because it does not allow for guest access, nor does it allow employees to remediate their computer systems and gain full network access. The next phase in handling 802.1X authentication failures was to provide an "Auth-Fail VLAN" to allow a device/user that failed authentication to be granted access to a VLAN that provided limited resources.

This step was a step in the right direction, but was still missing some practicality, especially in environments that must use MAC Authentication Bypass for all the printers and other nonauthenticating devices. With the default behavior of 802.1X, an administrator would have to configure ports for printers and other devices that do not have supplicants differently from the ports where they planned to do authentication.

Therefore, Cisco created Flexible Authentication (FlexAuth). FlexAuth allows a network administrator to set an authentication order and priority on the switch port, thereby allowing the port to attempt 802.1X, MAB, and then WebAuth in order. All of these functions are provided while maintaining the same configuration on all access ports, thereby providing a much simpler operational model for customers than traditional 802.1X deployments.

As mentioned, there are multiple methods of authentication on a switch port: 802.1X (dot1x), MAB, and WebAuth. With 802.1X authentication, the switch sends an identity request (EAP-Identity-Request) periodically after the link state has changed to "up" (see the upcoming "Configuring Authentication Settings" section for recommended timer changes). Additionally, the endpoint supplicant should send a periodic EAP over LAN Start (EAPoL-Start) message into the switch port to speed up authentication. If a device is not able to authenticate, it merely has to wait until the dot1x timeout occurs, and MAB will occur. Assuming the device MAC address is in the correct database, it will then be authorized to access the network.

Figure 2-45 illustrates the FlexAuth flow concept.

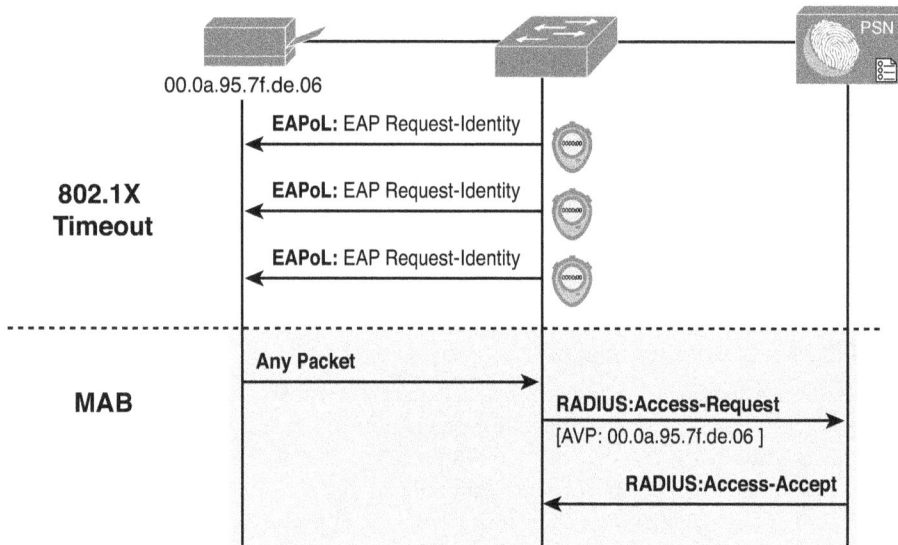

Figure 2-45   *Flexible Authentication*

The following steps will walk you through the configuration of FlexAuth and the configurable actions for authentication high availability.

Step 1.   Configure the authentication method priority on the switch ports.

The best practice is to always prefer the stronger authentication method (dot1x). The dot1x method is also the default of all Cisco switches.

```
C3560X (config-if-range)#authentication priority dot1x mab
```

Step 2.   Configure the authentication method order on the switch ports.

There are certain deployment methods where MAB should occur before 802.1X authentication. For those corner cases, Cisco switches do allow for a network administrator to set a user-definable authentication order; however, the best practice is to maintain the order of dot1x and then MAB.

```
C3560X(config-if-range)#authentication order dot1x mab
```

Step 3.   Configure the port to use FlexAuth:

```
C3560X(config-if-range)#authentication event fail action
next-method
```

Step 4.   Configure the port to use a local VLAN for voice and data when the RADIUS server is "dead" (when it stops responding).

In the "Global Configuration for All Catalyst Switches" section, we config-ured the RADIUS server entry to use a test account that will proactively alert the switch when Cisco ISE has stopped responding to RADIUS requests. Now we will configure the switch port to locally authorize the port when that server is found to be "dead" and reinitialize authentication when the server becomes "alive" again.

```
C3560X(config-if-range)#authentication event server dead
action authorize vlan vlan-id
C3560X(config-if-range)#authentication event server dead
action authorize voice
C3560X(config-if-range)#authentication event server alive
action reinitialize
```

Step 5.   Configure the port to use a local VLAN when the RADIUS server is "dead" and allow existing and new hosts.

This feature was introduced to resolve problems with multiple authenticating hosts on a single port when a portion of them already authenticate while the RADIUS server is operational, and others (new hosts) are trying to authenti-cate when the RADIUS server is down.

Before introducing this new feature, all authenticated hosts (when the RADIUS server is up) get full access to network and the others (the new hosts) do not get access to the network. With this new feature/CLI, when new hosts try to access to the network and the RADIUS server is down, that port is reinitialized immediately and all hosts (in this port) get the same VLAN.

```
C3560X(config-if-range)#authentication event server dead
action reinitialize vlan vlan-id
```

Step 6.   Set the host mode of the port.

The default behavior of an 802.1X-enabled port is to authorize only a single MAC address per port. There are other options, most notably Multidomain

Authentication (MDA) and Multiple Authentication (Multi-Auth) modes. During the initial phases of any Cisco TrustSec deployment, it is best practice to use Multi-Auth mode to ensure that there is no denial of service while deploying 802.1X.

Note   Port security is not compatible with 802.1X, because 802.1X handles this function natively.

Multi-Auth mode allows virtually unlimited MAC addresses per switch port, and requires an authenticated session for every MAC address. When the deployment moves into the late stages of the authenticated phase, or into the enforcement phase, it is then recommended to use Multi-Domain mode. Multi-Domain authentication will allow a single MAC address in the DATA domain and a single MAC address in the Voice domain per port.

```
C3560X(config-if-range)#authentication host-mode multi-auth
```

Step 7.   Configure the violation action.

When an authentication violation occurs, such as more MAC addresses than are allowed on the port, the default action is to put the port into an err-disabled state. Although this behavior may seem to be a nice, secure behavior, it can create an accidental denial of service, especially during the initial phases of deployment. Therefore, we will set the action to be **restrict**. This mode of operation will allow the first authenticated device to continue with its authorization and deny any additional devices.

```
C3560X(config-if-range)#authentication violation restrict
```

Configuring Authentication Settings

802.1X is designed to be binary by default. Successful authentication means the user is authorized to access the network. Unsuccessful authentication means the user has no access to the network. This paradigm does not lend itself very well to a modern organization. Most organizations need to do workstation imaging with Pre-Boot Execution Environments (PXE) or may have some thin clients that have to boot with DHCP and don't have any way to run a supplicant.

Additionally, when early adopters of 802.1X would deploy authentication companywide, there were repercussions. Many supplicants were misconfigured; there were unknown devices that could not authenticate because of a lack of supplicant, and other reasons.

Cisco created Open Authentication to aid with deployments. Open Authentication will allow all traffic to flow through the switch port, even without the port being authorized. This feature will allow authentication to be configured across the entire organization, but not deny access to any device.

Figure 2-46 depicts the difference between a port with the default behavior of 802.1X versus a port with Open Authentication configured. This is a key feature that enables the phased approach to deploying authentication.

Default 802.1X   **Authentication Open**

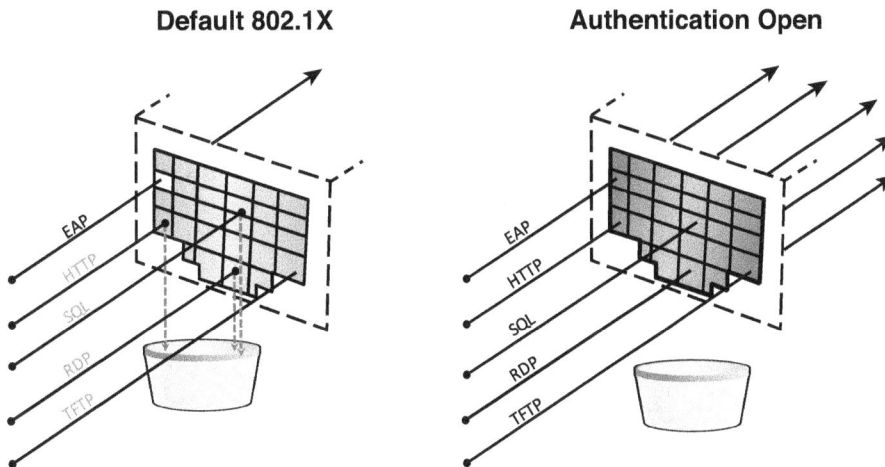

Figure 2-46   *Default 802.1X versus Open Authentication*

To begin configuring the port, ensure you are configuring the range of ports that you need to enable dot1x on, and then do the following:

Step 1.   Set the port for Open Authentication:

```
C3560X(config-if-range)#authentication open
```

Step 2.   Enable MAC Authentication Bypass on the port:

```
C3560X(config-if-range)#mab
```

Step 3.   Enable the port to do IEEE 802.1X authentication:

```
C3560X(config-if-range)#dot1x pae authenticator
```

Configuring Authentication Timers

Many timers can be modified as needed in a deployment. Unless you are experiencing a specific problem where adjusting the timer may correct unwanted behavior, it is recommended to leave all timers at their default values except for the 802.1X Transmit timer (tx-period).

The tx-period timer defaults to a value of 30 seconds. Leaving this value at 30 seconds provides a default wait of 90 seconds (3 × tx-period) before a switch port will begin the next method of authentication and begin the MAB process for non-authenticating devices.

Based on numerous deployments, we are recommending that you set the tx-period value to 10 seconds to provide the most optimal time for MAB devices:

```
C3560X(config-if-range)#dot1x timeout tx-period 10
```

Setting the value below 10 seconds can result in unwanted behavior, while setting the value greater than 10 seconds may result in DHCP timeouts.

Applying the Initial ACL to the Port and Enable Authentication

This step will prepare the port for monitor mode: applying a default ACL on the port without denying any traffic.

Step 1.   Apply the initial ACL (ACL-ALLOW):

```
C3560X(config-if-range)#ip access-group ACL-ALLOW in
```

Step 2.   (Optional) Turn authentication "on."

If you wish to enable authentication now, you may; however, we recommend you wait until after you configure your polices for monitor mode.

```
C3560X(config-if-range)#authentication port-control auto
```

Note   This command is required to enable authentication (802.1X, MAB, WebAuth). Without this command, everything will appear to be working, but no authentications will be sent to the RADIUS server.

Common Classification Policy Language Switches

This section reviews configuration for the newer 15.2.x and IOS-XE 3.6.x switches that follow the Cisco Common Classification Policy Language (C3PL) style of configuration. An interesting side note is that these types of switches are still able to accept the old style of commands. You actually must enable the C3PL style of commands with the global configuration command:

```
authentication display new-style
```

That command is a little misleading, because it is much more than just the display. It completely changes the way that you, the administrator, will interact with the switch and the available features. To change back to the classic model of configuring authentication and the classic features, use the **authentication display legacy** command.

It's very important to note that once you start configuring the C3PL policies themselves, you cannot revert to the legacy mode. You have to erase the switch configuration and reload, starting from scratch or restoring an older backup configuration.

Why Use C3PL?

There are many benefits to the new syntax, most of which are under the hood and not really noticeable to the end user, but it allows the configuration to exist in memory once and to be invoked multiple times. This is a processor and memory efficiency enhancement. Of the administrator-facing differences, most notable is the fact that 802.1X and MAB can run simultaneously without having to sequence the two distinctive authentication processes whereby 802.1X authentication has to be failed for MAB to start. Another notable difference is the use of service templates to control preconfigured ACLs on the interface in the event that RADIUS is not available. With the legacy methods (prior to C3PL), sequencing of 802.1X and MAB results in certain MAB endpoints not being able to get IP addresses in a timely manner. By processing 802.1X and MAB simultaneously, the endpoint can get a DHCP-assigned IP address in a timely manner. Also, with legacy methods, when a static ACL is applied on the interfaces to restrict network access for devices in the preauthentication stage, the ACL is applied to devices connecting while the RADIUS server is not available, resulting in denial of service until the RADIUS server is reachable again. This might seem desirable at first, but it actually makes life more difficult for the policy server administrator and is not recommended to be used.

Now that you've just been let down, let's build you back up. The new C3PL style does provide some very useful enhancements such as service templates. With the introduction of service templates, another ACL that would provide network access can be applied to the interface when a certain condition matches, such as the RADIUS server is not reachable. This is known as the *Critical ACL* functionality.

Next is a feature known as "differentiated authentication," which allows you to authenticate different methods with different servers. In other words, send MAB to ServerA and 802.1X authentications to ServerB. While this is a neat concept, it does not apply to Secure Access deployments with ISE, as it would not maintain state with a single policy server, which defeats the point of having a solution like ISE.

There is also a pretty cool feature in C3PL known as *Critical MAB*. This allows the switch to use a locally defined list of MAC addresses in the event that the centralized RADIUS server is unavailable.

Basically, the use of C3PL is only recommended in a Secure Access deployment with ISE in cases where you require the use of the Critical ACL, Critical MAB, or interface templates. Otherwise, just continue to use the old-fashioned, legacy method of authentication configuration and keep your configurations across all platforms similar.

Figure 2-47 illustrates the older method, where each interface has its own configuration associated to it.

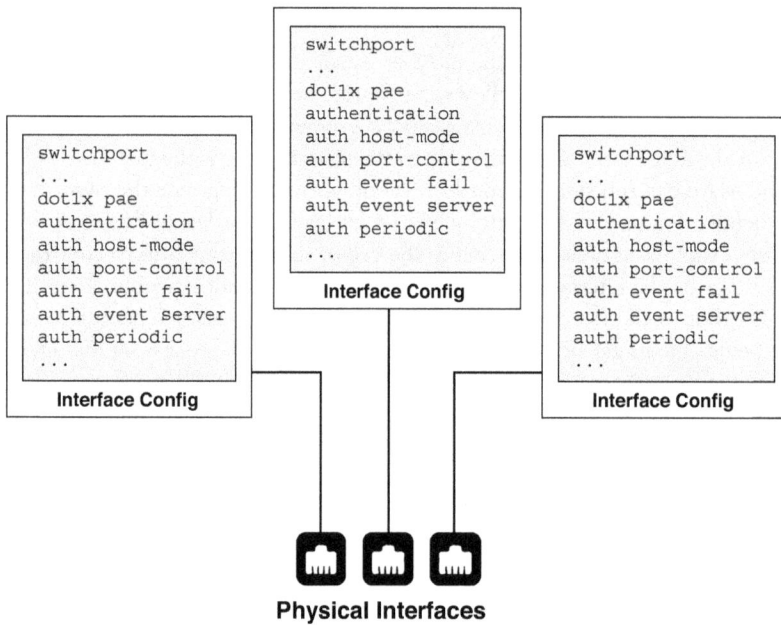

Figure 2-47   *Legacy Configuration*

In contrast, Figure 2-48 illustrates the C3PL method, where you have a bit more global configuration, but there is so much flexibility in what gets applied to the interface and when.

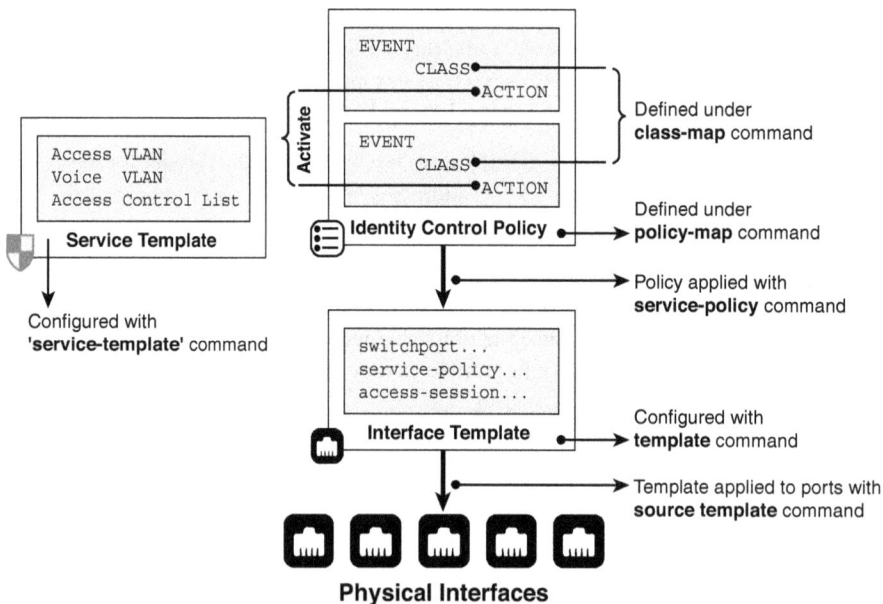

Figure 2-48   *C3PL Configuration*

Global Configuration for C3PL

Just like in the Classic IOS and IOS 15.x switches, we need to configure certificates for URL redirection.

From global configuration mode on the switch:

Step 1.   Set the DNS domain name on the switch.

Cisco IOS does not allow for certificates, or even self-generated keys, to be created and installed without first defining a DNS domain name on the device.

Type **ip domain-name** *domain-name* at the global configuration prompt.

Step 2.   Generate keys to be used for HTTPS.

Type **crypto key generate rsa general-keys mod 2048** at the global configuration prompt.

Step 3.   Enable the HTTP server in global configuration mode.

Type **ip http server** at the global configuration prompt.

Step 4.   Enable the HTTP secure server.

Type **ip http secure-server** at the global configuration prompt.

Many organizations will want to ensure that this redirection process that is using the switch's internal HTTP server is decoupled from the management of the switch itself. This can be accomplished by running the following two commands from global configuration mode:

```
ip http active-session-modules none
ip http secure-active-session-modules none
```

Now you will enable the C3PL configuration style. Remember that under the covers it is still the same authentication engine and IOS is doing the translation. However, you cannot use the C3PL-specific configurations without switching to the new style of configuration.

Step 5.   Within privileged EXEC mode, enable the new style of configuration:

```
C3850#authentication display new-style
```

Step 6.   Enable the AAA subsystem:

```
C3850(config)#aaa new-model
```

Step 7.   Ensure that any of the services that AAA network security services provide will use the same session ID:

```
C3850(config)#aaa session-id common
```

Step 8.   Create an authentication method for 802.1X.

An authentication method is required to instruct the switch on which group of RADIUS servers to use for 802.1X authentication requests.

```
C3850(config)#aaa authentication dot1x default group radius
```

Step 9.   Create an authorization method for 802.1X.

The authorization is what defines that the user or device is actually allowed to access the network, and what level of access is actually permitted.

```
C3850(config)#aaa authorization network default group radius
```

Step 10.   Create an accounting method for 802.1X.

RADIUS accounting packets are extremely useful, and in many cases are required. These types of packets will help ensure that the RADIUS server (Cisco ISE) knows the exact state of the switch port and endpoint. Without the accounting packets, Cisco ISE would have knowledge only of the authentication and authorization communication. Accounting packets provide information on when to terminate a live session, as well as local decisions made by the switch (such as AuthFail VLAN assignment, etc.).

```
C3850(config)#aaa accounting dot1x default start-stop group
radius
```

Step 11.   Configure periodic RADIUS accounting updates.

Periodic RADIUS accounting packets allows Cisco ISE to track which sessions are still active on the network. This command sends periodic updates whenever there is new information. It will also send a periodic update once per 24 hours (1440 minutes) to show ISE that the session is still alive.

```
C3850(config)#aaa accounting update newinfo periodic 1440
```

Global RADIUS Commands for C3PL

We configure a proactive method to check the availability of the RADIUS server. With this practice, the switch will send periodic test authentication messages to the RADIUS server (Cisco ISE). It is looking for a RADIUS response from the server. A success message is not necessary—a failed authentication will suffice, because it shows that the server is alive.

Step 1.   Within global configuration mode, add a username and password for the RADIUS keepalive.

The username we are creating here will be added to the local user database in Cisco ISE at a later step. This account will be used in a later step where we define the RADIUS server.

```
C3850(config)#username radius-test password password
```

Step 2. Add the Cisco ISE PSNs as RADIUS servers.

This is where things differ quite a bit from the Classic IOS configuration. You will actually create an object for the RADIUS server and then apply configuration to that object.

```
C3850(config)#radius server server-name
C3850(config-radius-server)#address ipv4 address auth-port
1812 acct-port 1813
C3850(config-radius-server)#key Shared-Secret
C3850(config-radius-server)#automate-tester username radius-
test probe-on
```

Step 3. Set the dead criteria.

The switch has been configured to proactively check the Cisco ISE server for RADIUS responses. Now configure the counters on the switch to determine if the server is alive or dead. Our settings will be to wait 5 seconds for a response from the RADIUS server and attempt the test three times before marking the server dead. If a Cisco ISE server doesn't have a valid response within 15 seconds, it will be marked as dead. We also set the value of how long the server will be marked dead, which we are setting to 15 minutes.

```
C3850(config)#radius-server dead-criteria time 5 tries 3
C3850(config)#radius-server deadtime 15
```

Step 4. Enable Change of Authorization.

Previously we defined the IP address of a RADIUS server that the switch will send RADIUS messages to. However, we define the servers that are allowed to perform Change of Authorization (RFC 3576) operations in a different listing, also within global configuration mode.

```
C3850(config)#aaa server radius dynamic-author
C3850(config-locsvr-da-radius)#client ise_ip_address server-
key shared_secret
```

Step 5. Configure the switch to use the Cisco vendor-specific attributes.

Here we configure the switch to send any defined VSAs to Cisco ISE PDPs during authentication requests and accounting updates.

```
C3850(config)#radius-server vsa send authentication
C3850(config)#radius-server vsa send accounting
```

Step 6. Enable the VSAs.

There are two additional entries here, compared to the non-C3PL switches. In the newer IOS-XE–based devices, attribute 31 is no longer on by default.

```
C3850(config)#radius-server attribute 6 on-for-login-auth
C3850(config)#radius-server attribute 8 include-in-access-req
```

```
C3850(config)#radius-server attribute 25 access-request
include
C3850(config)#radius-server attribute 31 mac format ietf
upper-case
C3850(config)#radius-server attribute 31 send nas-port-detail
mac-only
```

Step 7.   Ensure the switch always sends traffic from the correct interface.

Switches often have multiple IP addresses associated to them. Therefore, it is a best practice to always force any management communications to occur through a specific interface. This interface IP address must match the IP address defined in the Cisco ISE Network Device object.

```
Cat4503(config)#ip radius source-interface interface_name
Cat4503(config)#snmp-server trap-source interface_name
Cat4503(config)#snmp-server source-interface informs
interface_name
```

Configure Local ACLs and Local Service Templates

Just like the other switch type classifications, certain functions on the switch require the use of locally configured ACLs, such as URL redirection. Some of these ACLs created will be used immediately, and some might not be used until a much later phase of your deployment. The goal of this section is to prepare the switches for all possible deployment models at one time, and limit the operational expense of repeated switch configuration.

Step 1.   Add the following ACL to be used on switch ports in monitor mode:

```
C3850(config)#ip access-list extended ACL-ALLOW
C3850(config-ext-nacl)#permit ip any any
```

Step 2.   Add the following ACL to be used on switch ports in low-impact mode:

```
C3850(config)#ip access-list ext ACL-DEFAULT
C3850(config-ext-nacl)#remark DHCP
C3850(config-ext-nacl)#permit udp any eq bootpc any eq bootps
C3850(config-ext-nacl)#remark DNS
C3850(config-ext-nacl)#permit udp any any eq domain
C3850(config-ext-nacl)#remark Ping
C3850(config-ext-nacl)#permit icmp any any
C3850(config-ext-nacl)#remark PXE / TFTP
C3850(config-ext-nacl)#permit udp any any eq tftp
C3850(config-ext-nacl)#remark Drop all the rest
C3850(config-ext-nacl)#deny ip any any log
```

Step 3. Add the following ACL to be used for URL redirection with Web Authentication:

```
C3850(config)#ip access-list ext ACL-WEBAUTH-REDIRECT
C3850(config-ext-nacl)#remark explicitly deny DNS from being
redirected to address a bug
C3850(config-ext-nacl)#deny udp any any eq 53
C3850(config-ext-nacl)#remark redirect all applicable traffic
to the ISE Server
C3850(config-ext-nacl)#permit tcp any any eq 80
C3850(config-ext-nacl)#permit tcp any any eq 443
C3850(config-ext-nacl)#remark all other traffic will be
implicitly denied from the redirection
```

Step 4. Add the following ACL to be used for URL redirection with the posture agent:

```
C3850(config)#ip access-list ext ACL-AGENT-REDIRECT
C3850(config-ext-nacl)#remark explicitly deny DNS and DHCP
from being redirected
C3850(config-ext-nacl)#deny udp any any eq 53 bootps
C3850(config-ext-nacl)#remark redirect HTTP traffic only
C3850(config-ext-nacl)#permit tcp any any eq 80
C3850(config-ext-nacl)#remark all other traffic will be
implicitly denied from the redirection
```

Service templates are new to C3PL switches. They are similar to ISE authorization profiles, but can be locally present on the switch. A service template is a collection of VLAN, Named ACL, Timer, and URL Redirect string that can be applied based on the C3PL event. Just like dACLs, service templates can be centrally located on ISE and be downloaded during authorization. However, we are creating a service template local to the switch to apply when none of the configured RADIUS servers (ISE PSNs) are reachable to process 802.1X or MAB requests (known as the "critical-auth" state).

Add the following service template named CRITICAL to be used when no RADIUS servers are available (the critical-auth state):

```
C3850(config)#service-template CRITICAL
C3850(config-service-template)#description Apply for Critical Auth
C3850(config-service-template)#access-group ACL-ALLOW
```

Global 802.1X Commands

Step 1. Enable 802.1X globally on the switch.

Enabling 802.1X globally on the switch does not actually enable authentication on any of the switch ports. Authentication will be configured, but it won't be enabled until the later sections where we configure monitor mode.

```
C3560X(config)#dot1x system-auth-control
```

Step 2.   Enable dACLs to function.

Downloadable ACLs are a very common enforcement mechanism in a Cisco TrustSec deployment. In order for dACLs to function properly on a switch, IP device tracking must be enabled globally.

```
C3560X(config)#ip device tracking
```

Note   There are some uncommon cases with Windows 7 and some other devices that do not respond to ARPs. Windows will display *Duplicate IP Address Detected: 0.0.0.0*. In such instances, using the command **ip device tracking use SVI** may be required.

C3PL Fundamentals

The Cisco Common Classification Policy Language is used across a variety of Cisco solutions, including Catalyst switches, Cisco routers, Cisco ASA firewalls, and more. With these C3PL switches the configuration is made up of building blocks. Policies contain one or more events. Events contain one or more classes. Classes contain one or more conditions to be matched. Figure 2-49 illustrates this concept.

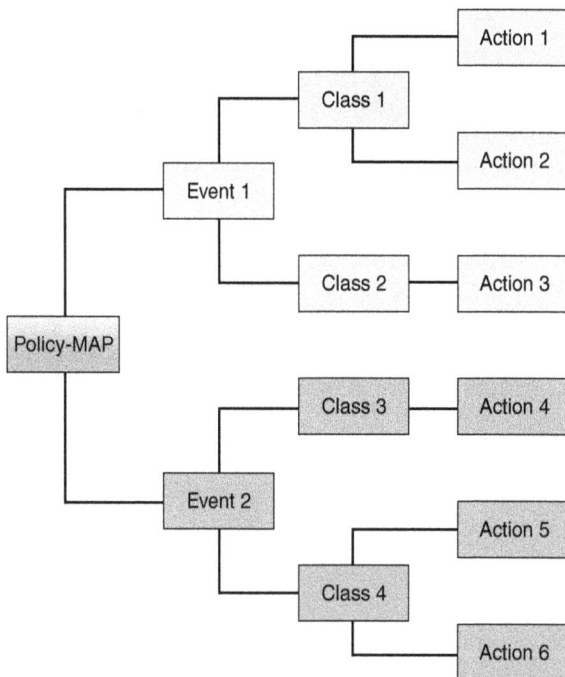

Figure 2-49   *C3PL Hierarchy*

Configure the C3PL Policies

The class is the base-level object and the first item you would configure for the C3PL policy. After you create the class, you create a policy with an event. That event will call the class that you created. Figure 2-50 is an illustration that was created by a truly gifted Technical Marketing Engineer at Cisco named Hariprasad Holla. Hari has presented on this topic countless times at Cisco Live and you can even watch recorded VoDs of those sessions for free at https://ciscolive.cisco.com; simply go there and search for sessions with Hariprasad Holla as the speaker.

Hari's figure illustrates the relationship of the event to one or more classes, as well as the class to one or more actions.

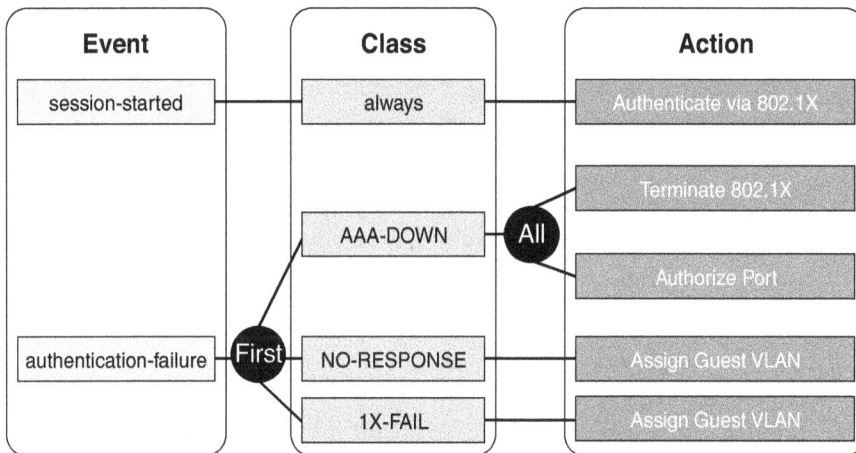

Figure 2-50   *Event, Class, and Action Relationships (by Hariprasad Holla)*

Configure Control Classes

A control class defines the conditions under which the actions of a control policy are executed. You define whether all, any, or none of the conditions must evaluate to true to execute the actions of the control policy. Control classes are evaluated based on the event specified in the control policy.

Note   If this is the first time C3PL-type commands are being used on this switch, it will present a warning that it cannot revert to legacy mode unless the switch configuration is cleared.

Step 1.   Configure a control class for when none of the RADIUS servers are available (the critical-auth state):

```
C3850(config)#class-map type control subscriber match-any
AAA-DOWN
C3850(config-filter-control-classmap)#match result-type aaa-
timeout
```

Step 2.   Configure a control class for when 802.1X authentication failed for the session:

```
C3850(config)#class-map type control subscriber match-all
DOT1X-FAILED
C3850(config-filter-control-classmap)#match method dot1x
C3850(config-filter-control-classmap)#match result-type
method dot1x authoritative
```

Configure Control Policies

Control policies are used to dictate which actions should be taken in response to the specified events. The policy contains one or more rules that associate a control class with one or more actions. The actions that you can configure in a rule are specific to the event itself. In other words, you wouldn't have a MAB action apply to a dot1x event. Control policies typically control the authentication of the end identity and the applying services to a session or to an interface. Figure 2-50 shows this hierarchy and the relationship between the components of the policy.

We will create a control policy leveraging the control classes created in the previous section and then apply the policy to a range of interfaces on the switch:

Step 1.   Configure a control policy that will be applied to all 802.1X/MAB-enabled interfaces:

```
C3850(config-service-template)#policy-map type control sub-
scriber DOT1X-DEFAULT
```

Step 2.   Configure actions for when session starts.

The following configuration will allow 802.1X and MAB to run simultaneously, assigning a higher priority for 802.1X over MAB. Keep in mind, this is just to illustrate the ability of running MAB and 802.1X at the same time; we do not recommend this for production environments.

```
C3850(config-event-control-policymap)#event session-started
match-all
C3850(config-class-control-policymap)#10 class always do-all
C3850(config-action-control-policymap)#10 authenticate using
dot1x priority 10
C3850(config-action-control-policymap)#20 authenticate using
mab priority 20
```

Step 3.   Configure actions for policy violations:

```
C3850(config-action-control-policymap)#event violation
match-all
C3850(config-class-control-policymap)#10 class always do-all
C3850(config-action-control-policymap)#10 restrict
```

Step 4.   Configure the switch to attempt to authenticate (using 802.1X) an endpoint when a supplicant is detected on the endpoint:

```
C3850(config-action-control-policymap)#event agent-found
match-all
C3850(config-class-control-policymap)#10 class always do-all
C3850(config-action-control-policymap)#10 authenticate using
dot1x
```

Step 5.   Configure the action for 802.1X authentication failures, or when there is a lack of ISE PSNs (RADIUS servers) available:

```
C3850(config-action-control-policymap)#event authentication-
failure match-all
C3850(config-class-control-policymap)#10 class AAA-DOWN
do-all
C3850(config-action-control-policymap)#10 authorize
C3850(config-action-control-policymap)#20 activate service-
template CRITICAL
C3850(config-action-control-policymap)#30 terminate dot1x
C3850(config-action-control-policymap)#40 terminate mab
C3850(config-action-control-policymap)#20 class DOT1X-FAILED
do-all
C3850(config-action-control-policymap)#10 authenticate
using mab
```

Note   Because we will be using Centralized Web Authentication (CWA), which sends Access-Accept even for unknown MAC addresses, there will be no failure for MAB, and thus a failure event for MAB is not defined in the previous configuration.

Applying Control Policy to the Interfaces

Now that the policy is created, it needs to be applied to the access layer interfaces, with the **service-policy** command. Not all aspects of the 802.1X configuration are completed in C3PL, so some configuration items will occur at the interfaces separately.

Step 1.   Apply control policy to the interface range:

```
C3850(config)#interface range GigabitEthernet 1/0/1 - 24
C3850(config-if-range)#description Dot1X Enabled Ports
C3850(config-if-range)#switchport host
C3850(config-if-range)#service-policy type control subscriber
DOT1X-DEFAULT
```

Step 2.   Apply the remaining interface configuration:

```
C3850(config-if-range)#authentication periodic
C3850(config-if-range)#authentication timer reauthenticate
server
```

```
C3850(config-if-range)#mab
C3850(config-if-range)#ip access-group DEFAULT-ACL in
C3850(config-if-range)#access-session host-mode multi-auth
C3850(config-if-range)#no access-session closed
C3850(config-if-range)#dot1x timeout tx-period 10
C3850(config-if-range)#access-session port-control auto
C3850(config-if-range)#no shutdown
```

Configuring ISE for Basic Wired Network Access Control

Beginning with ISE 2.3, a new user interface was introduced for the updated policy engine, and policy sets are automatically enabled. Katherine McNamara has a very nice blog entry on the changes in the policy engine experience: https://www.network-node.com/blog/2017/10/7/ise-23-new-policy-sets.

ISE comes with preconfigured policies that will allow network access for any successful 802.1X authentication sourced from a configured NAD, wired or wireless. We'll get started by taking a look at the preconfigured policy set.

A policy set is a collection of authentication and authorization policies that work together. When an authentication request enters ISE, the incoming attributes are compared to the authentication rules in a top-down fashion. Successful authentications will be passed to the authorization rules within the same policy set. The action taken if the authentication does not succeed is configurable within the authentication rule, under the Options section.

Figure 2-51 shows the list of policy sets, located at **Work Centers > Network Access > Policy Sets**. There is only a single policy set by default, but more can and should be added for a production deployment.

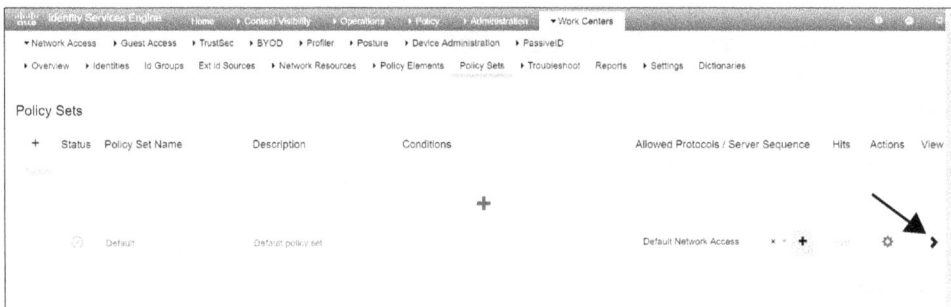

Figure 2-51   *Policy Sets*

Click the **>** symbol, as pointed out in Figure 2-51, to expand the policy set, as shown in Figure 2-52.

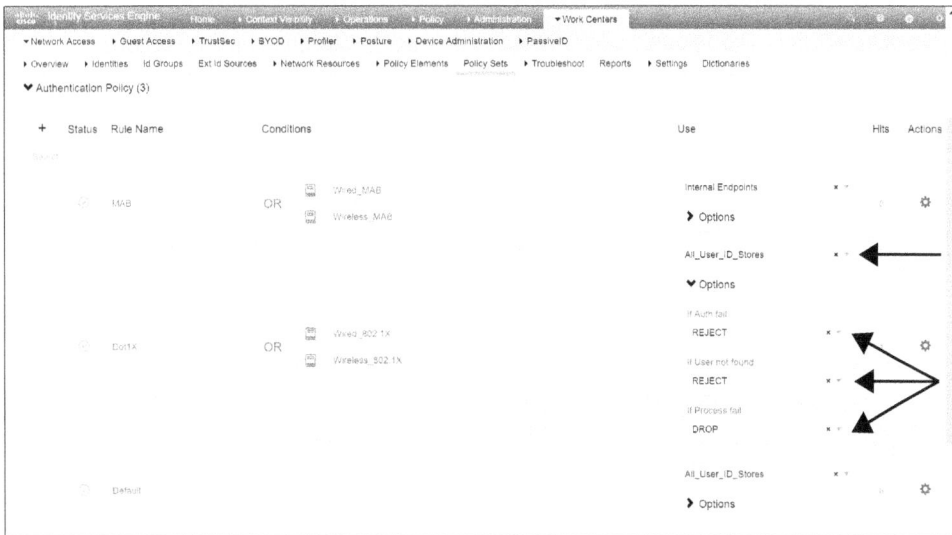

Figure 2-52 *Default Policy Set*

Examining Figure 2-52, the Default policy set includes a policy for MAB (wired and wireless) that will examine the Internal Endpoints store for MAC addresses. If the MAC address exists in the Internal Endpoints store, then the authentication (bypass) is deemed successful and the request is passed to the authorization rules. If the MAC address does not exist, the authentication will be treated as "user not found." By default, when a MAB ends up with "user not found," the authentication will CONTINUE on to the authorization rule.

Why would ISE want to let an unsuccessful MAB continue to the authorization rules? Because of profiling and Centralized Web Authentication. Both of those technologies need to allow some sort of limited network access to proceed.

Looking back at Figure 2-52, there is also an authentication policy labeled Dot1X that matches a condition for wired or wireless 802.1X and will check any incoming 802.1X requests and check the credentials against all user identity stores, leveraging the identity source sequence.

After a request passes the authentication policy, either through a successful authentication or via the CONTINUE option, it is compared to the rules in the authorization policy.

Figure 2-53 shows the default authorization policy, which contains a few preconfigured rules. Some of the rules are enabled out of the box and some of the rules are there to be leveraged as examples and enabled if and when the admin is ready.

Figure 2-53 *Default Authorization Policy Rules*

Examining some of the rules shown in Figure 2-53, you see two rules for IP phones: one for Cisco IP Phones and another for non-Cisco IP phones. Both of these rules leverage profiling policies as conditions for network access. There are rules for BYOD onboarding that are disabled until the admin enables them manually, rules for guest access, and a rule for leveraging the posture compliance status of the endpoint.

Creating a Policy for Differentiated Access

To better understand authorization policies, as well as to practice working with ISE policies and policy elements, we will create a policy that provides a different level of access for different types of users.

The goal is to create an authorization rule that permits access for members of the PCI group in Active Directory, and another rule for the rest of the employees. The rules should be representative of Table 2-5.

Table 2-5 *Least Privilege Access Rules Example*

User Type	Conditions	Results
PCI	Network authentication was successful. User is a member of the Employees and PCI groups in AD.	Apply a PCI specific dACL. Assign the user to VLAN 22. Encrypt the Layer 2 traffic. Assign TrustSec tag for PCI.
Employees	Network authentication was successful. User is a member of the Employees group in AD.	Apply a dACL for Employees. Assign the user to VLAN 44. Suggest encrypting the Layer 2 traffic. Assign the Employees TrustSec tag.

Before creating the authorization rule, we start by creating the authorization results and then the conditions.

Creating the Authorization Results

The authorization result will be made up of a standard authorization profile which also contains a dACL, and because we plan to assign a TrustSec tag, the result will also contain a Scalable Group Tag (SGT), also known as a Security Group Tag.

To begin this process, we should first create the dACL. dACLs are located within **Work Centers > Network Access > Policy Elements > Results > Downloadable ACLs,** and there are two dACLs that exist by default, as shown in Figure 2-54.

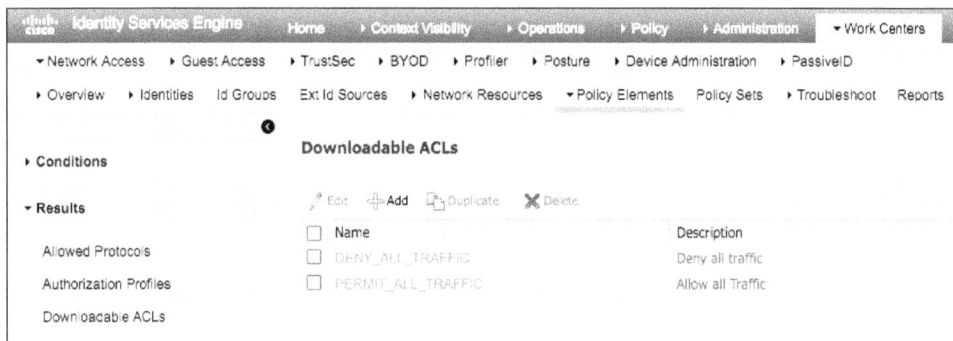

Figure 2-54   *Default Downloadable ACLs*

We will create a dACL that permits all traffic, as a placeholder. You can always come back later and make the dACL more specific for the specific environment.

Note   When you create a dACL, the syntax must always contain the keyword **any** in the source field of the access control entry (ACE), as the Cisco Catalyst switch will automatically replace that keyword with the source IP address of the endpoint.

Click **Add** to create a new dACL and name the dACL **PCI-dACL**. Enter a description, such as the one you see in Figure 2-55, type **permit ip any any** in the DACL Content text box, and click **Check DACL Syntax.** Click **Submit** to save the dACL.

Next, we will create an identical dACL for the Employees. It should look like the example in Figure 2-56.

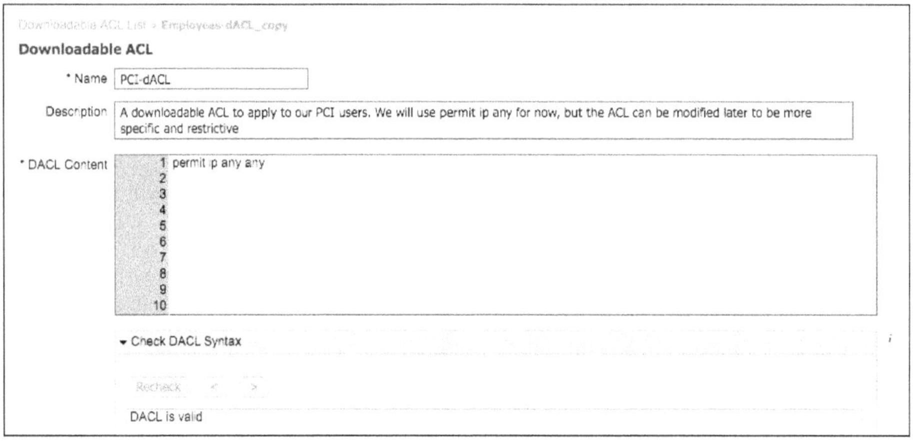

Figure 2-55 *PCI-dACL*

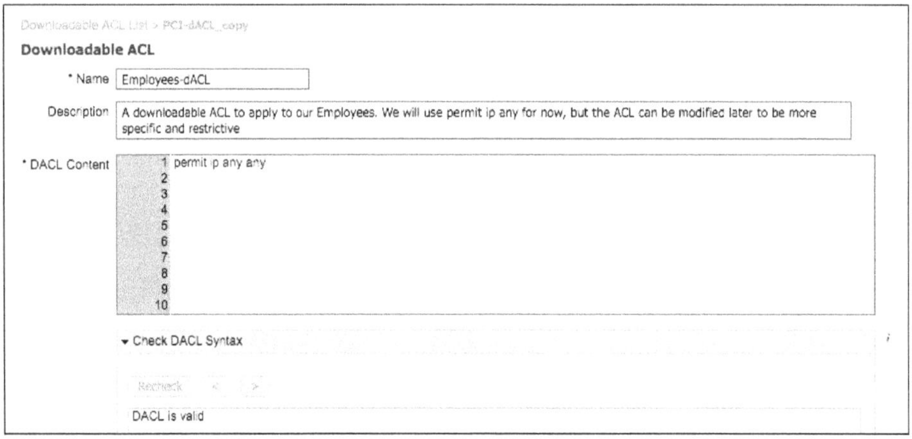

Figure 2-56 *Employees-dACL*

Now that the dACLs have been created, we will create our two authorization profiles. Navigate to **Work Centers > Network Access > Policy Elements > Results > Authorization Profiles.** Here you will notice the default profiles that are in use with the prebuilt authorization policies, as shown in Figure 2-57.

We will create an authorization profile for PCI users that allows network access and assigns VLAN 22 the network session.

Click **Add** to create a new authorization profile, name it **PCI Users**, and provide a description. Ensure that **ACCESS_ACCEPT** is set for the Access Type and the Network Device Profile is set to **Cisco**, as shown in Figure 2-58.

Under Common Tasks, check the **DACL Name** check box and choose **PCI-dACL** from the corresponding drop-down list. Check the **VLAN** check box and type **22** in the ID/Name text box.

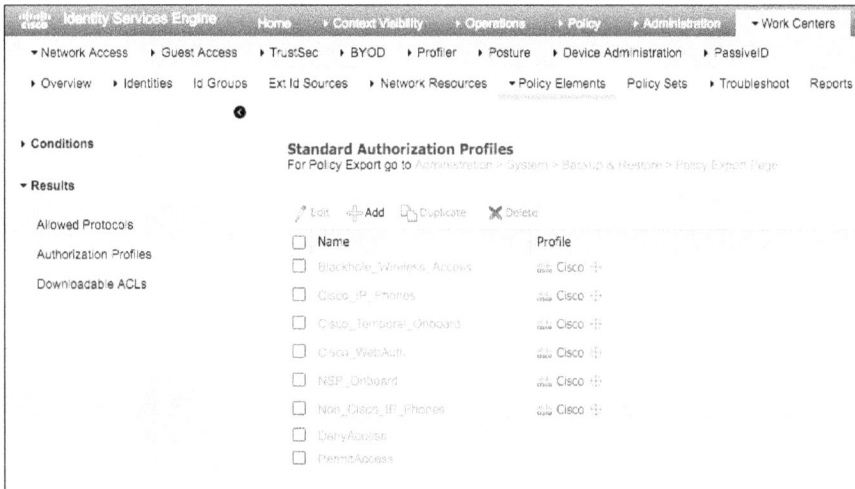

Figure 2-57 *Default Authorization Profiles*

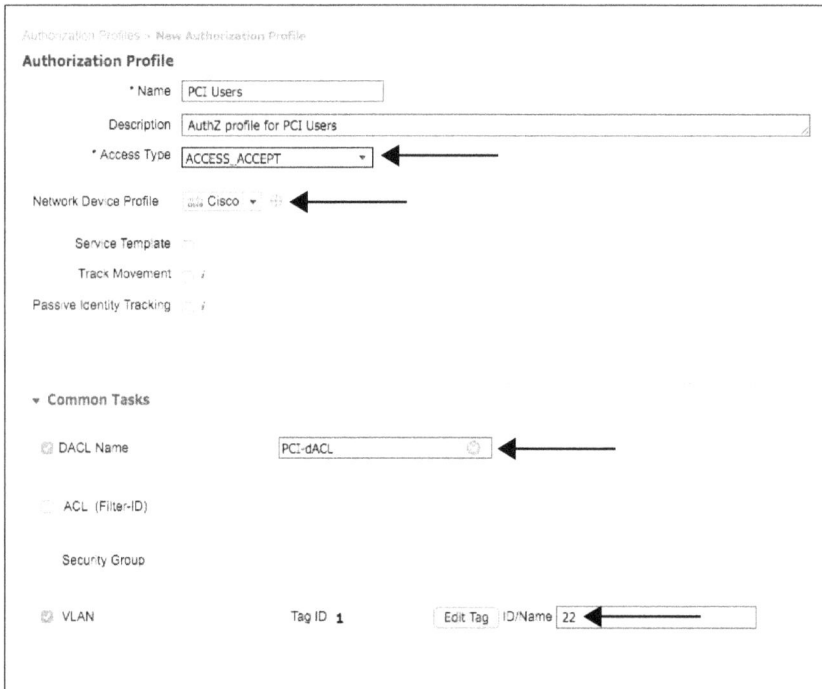

Figure 2-58 *PCI Users Authorization Profile*

Scroll further down the Common Tasks section, check the **MACSec Policy** check box, and select **must-secure** from the drop-down list, as shown in Figure 2-59. This forces the switch port to use 802.1AE (MACSec) encryption with the endpoint.

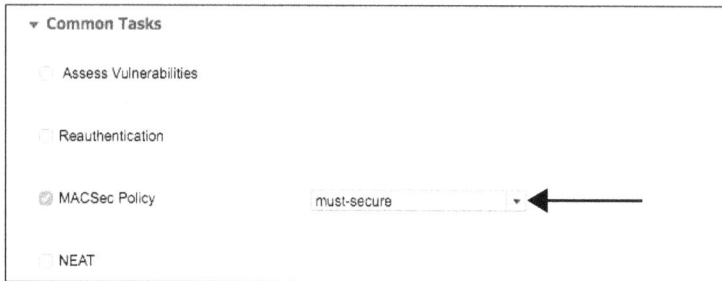

Figure 2-59   *MACSec Configuration in the PCI Users Authorization Profile*

There are a number of other check boxes and settings that can be leveraged in an authorization profile and we will review a few of the important ones now:

■ **Track Movement:** Check this check box to instruct ISE to monitor the physical location of the endpoint via the wireless Mobility Services Engine (MSE). Location tracking is used with wireless networks to enable authorization based on the physical location of a mobile client. For example, access to classified government servers may be restricted and only allowed for devices that are within *x* feet of a secure enclave within a government building.

■ **Passive Identity Tracking:** Check this check box when you are configuring EasyConnect. Enabling this setting causes ISE to monitor the logs from Active Directory for any AD authentications related to this endpoint and merge the user identity information from those logs into the ISE session for that endpoint. This concept will be covered more in the EasyConnect section of Chapter 3:"Beyond Basic Network Access Control."

■ **ACL (Filter-ID):** While Cisco switches are capable of receiving dACLS, the industry standard is to use an attribute named *Filter-ID*. Instead of downloading the contents of an ACL from the RADIUS server, checking this check box informs the switch to assign a preexisting ACL from the local switch configuration to the session.

■ **Security Group:** In previous versions of ISE, TrustSec tags were assigned separately in the authorization results section of an authorization policy. Security groups were added to authorization policies in ISE v2.4, but the user interface makes them mutually exclusive with the use of VLAN assignment.

■ **Voice Domain Permission:** Cisco switches are configured with a special VLAN known as the voice VLAN. When the voice domain permission attribute is sent as part of the authorization result, the switch will allow a phone to tag the incoming traffic with an 802.1Q VLAN tag, allowing the switch port to act as a pseudo-trunk, and permitting the IP phone to enter the voice VLAN instead of the default data VLAN. If you forget to assign this permission to an authorization result for an IP phone, that IP phone will most likely not work correctly in the network.

- **Web Redirection (CWA, MDM, NSP, CPP):** Web redirection is used for many of the advanced features between ISE and the Cisco Catalyst switch. Checking this check box leverages the built-in HTTP server within the switch to capture web traffic and redirect it to the specified URL.

- **Auto SmartPort:** Cisco switches have been software-defined network (SDN) capable since long before SDN was a "thing." SmartPort macros can be used to configure a switch port in a special way, and ISE has long had the ability to call those macros from a standard authorization profile.

- **Assess Vulnerabilities:** The tie-in for Threat-Centric NAC. ISE can be configured to work with Tenable, Qualys, and/or Rapid7 vulnerability scanning systems, and enabling this option in the authorization profile will cause ISE to trigger a vulnerability scan of the authenticating endpoint.

- **Airespace ACL Name:** Used with Cisco WLCs and invokes the locally configured ACL on that WLC.

- **ASA VPN:** A simplified name for RADIUS attribute 25, the CLASS attribute. That is a common attribute used with Cisco ASAs to assign the group policy for a user when authorizing a VPN connection.

- **AVC Profile Name:** A text field to specify the Application Visibility and Control (AVC) profile to assign to a session on a Cisco WLC.

- **Advanced Attribute Settings:** Allows the ISE admin to configure any RADIUS attribute at all, in case the admin needs to configure something that was not included in the Common Tasks area of the authorization profile.

- **Attribute Details:** Shows the raw RADIUS attributes that will be sent to the NAD. Figure 2-60 shows the attribute details for the PCI Users authorization profile.

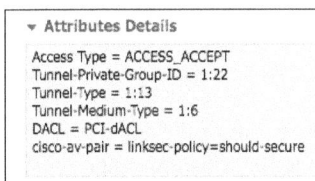

```
▼ Attributes Details

Access Type = ACCESS_ACCEPT
Tunnel-Private-Group-ID = 1:22
Tunnel-Type = 1:13
Tunnel-Medium-Type = 1:6
DACL = PCI-dACL
cisco-av-pair = linksec-policy=should-secure
```

Figure 2-60 *PCI Users Authorization Profile Attribute Details*

Note   We are not assigning the Security Group in the authorization profile because the UI in ISE version 2.4 does not allow both the security group and VLAN to be configured in the same authorization profile. We will add the security group to the authorization results when we build the authorization policy itself.

Click **Submit** to save the PCI Users authorization profile.

Add a second authorization profile named **Employee** that assigns the Employees-dACL, assigns the user to VLAN 44, and sets the MACSec Policy to **should-secure**, as shown in Figure 2-61.

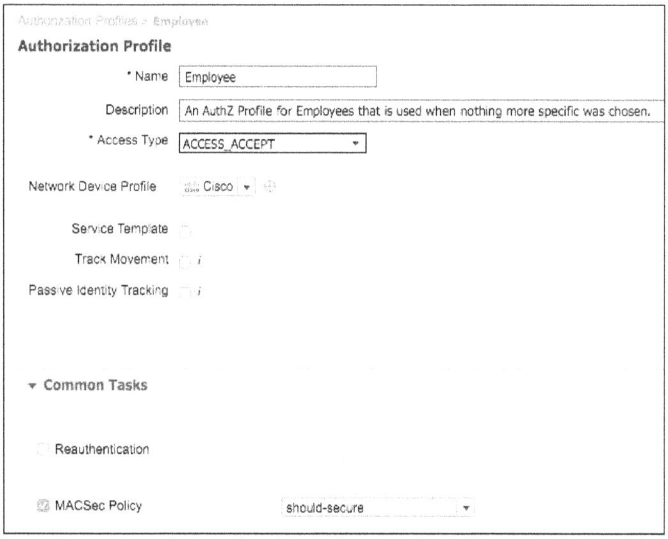

Figure 2-61   *Employee Authorization Profile with MACSec Policy Section*

The authorization policy is not the only result that we will be leveraging; we also need to assign a TrustSec tag to these authenticated sessions. A handful of security groups tags come preconfigured with ISE, which can be viewed under **Work Centers > TrustSec > Components > Security Groups**, as shown in Figure 2-62. We will be using the Employees and PCI_Servers tags in our policy.

Creating the Policy Conditions

We have created the authorization profiles, which are the end result of the authorization, but we have yet to define the policy conditions that will determine when to assign those profiles. You can create them while you create the policy itself, but it is often better to create them beforehand as defined policy objects, which also allows you to reuse those objects in multiple policies.

Begin by navigating to **Work Centers > Network Access > Policy Elements > Conditions > Library Conditions**. This brings up the condition studio user interface, shown in Figure 2-63, that was added to ISE in version 2.3 and allows for drag-and-drop creation of very complex conditions. On the left side is the Library of conditions that have been created already, either by the administrator or preconfigured conditions that come with ISE. You can search through the Library by name, or even filter it based on the classification of the condition represented by the "cute little icons" at the top (don't you miss the days of command-line configuration?). The first time you click the right side of the screen, the help overlay for the Editor will be displayed (see Figure 2-63).

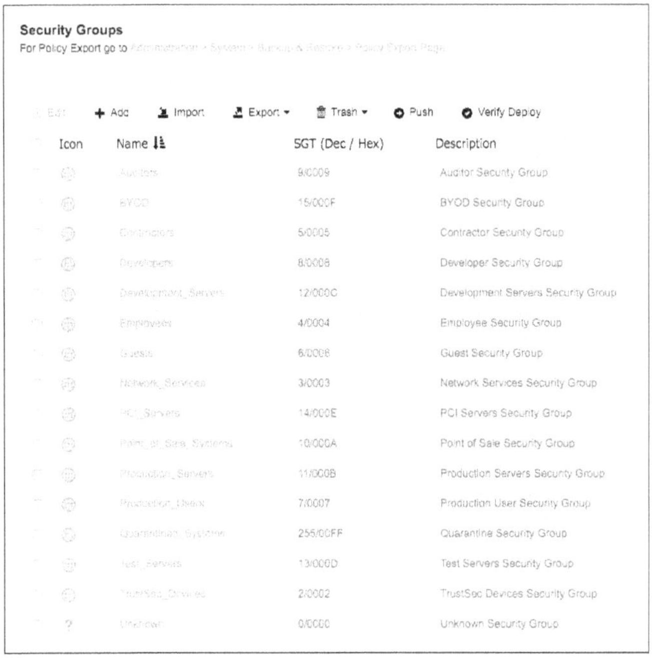

Figure 2-62 *Preconfigured Security Groups*

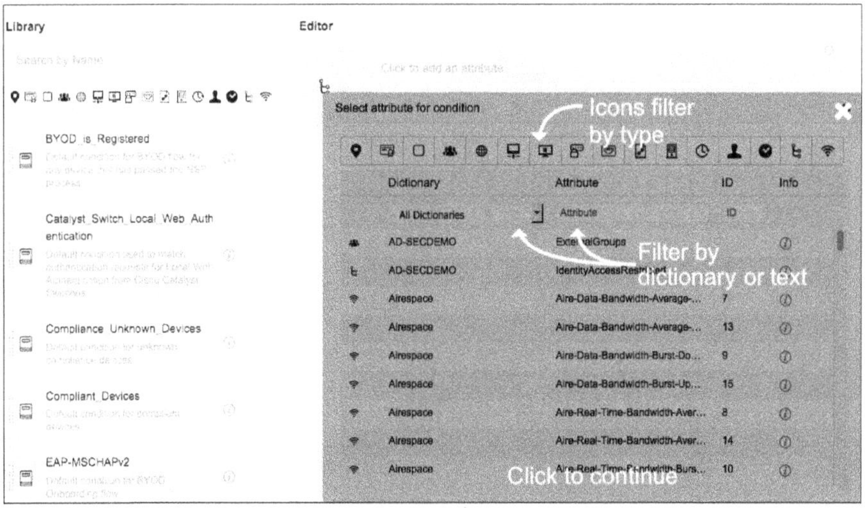

Figure 2-63 *Conditions Library and Editor with the Help Overlay*

We will now build a condition to match a user who is a member of the Employees group in Active Directory. In the Editor, click the **identities group** icon to filter the dictionaries, as shown in Figure 2-64, and select **AD-SECDEMO**, which is an ExternalGroups attribute.

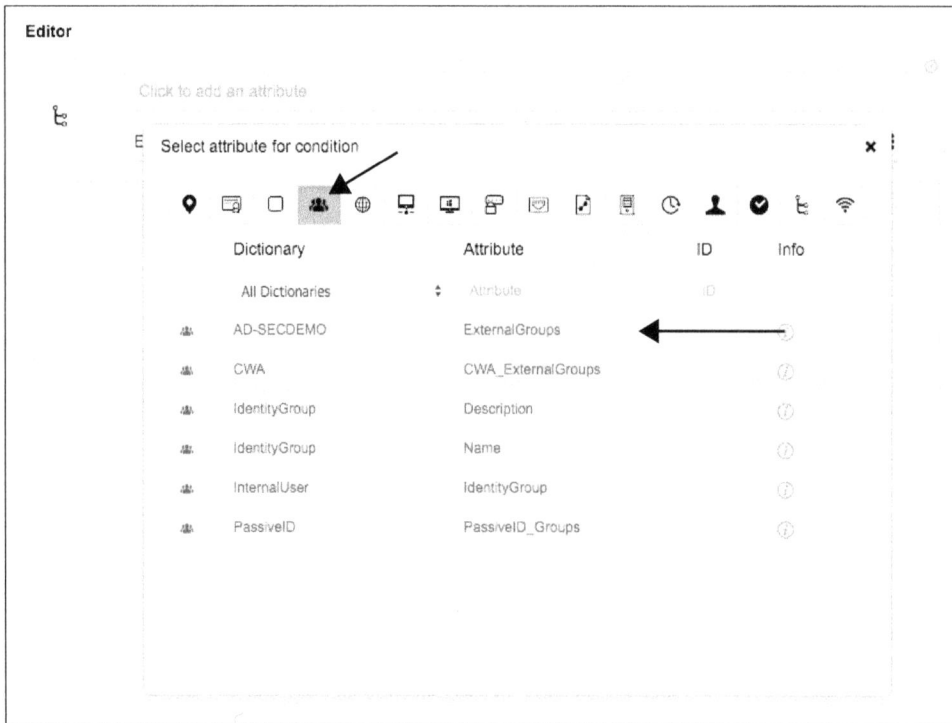

Figure 2-64   *Using the Identities Group Filter in the Condition Editor*

Ensure that the operator says **Equals,** and then select **securitydemo.net/Users/ Employees** from the drop-down list, as shown in Figure 2-65.

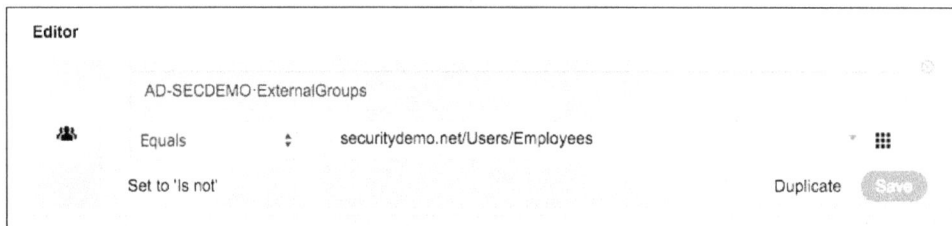

Figure 2-65   *Using the Identities Group Filter in the Condition Editor for Employees Group*

Click **Save**, save the condition as a new Library Condition named **AD-Employees**, as shown in Figure 2-66, and click **Save.**

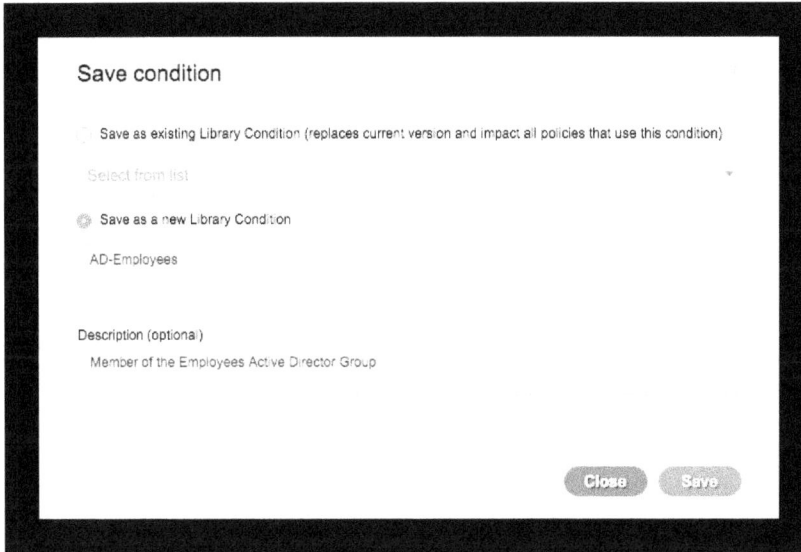

Save condition

Save as existing Library Condition (replaces current version and impact all policies that use this condition)

Select from list

Save as a new Library Condition

AD-Employees

Description (optional)

Member of the Employees Active Director Group

Close   Save

Figure 2-66 *Saving the AD-Employees Condition to the Library*

Repeat this process to create a new condition for the PCI group, and name the condition **AD-PCI.** After you create that condition, drag the AD-Employees condition from the library over to the AD-PCI condition so that you have a new condition that combines **AD-PCI AND AD-Employees,** as shown in Figure 2-67.

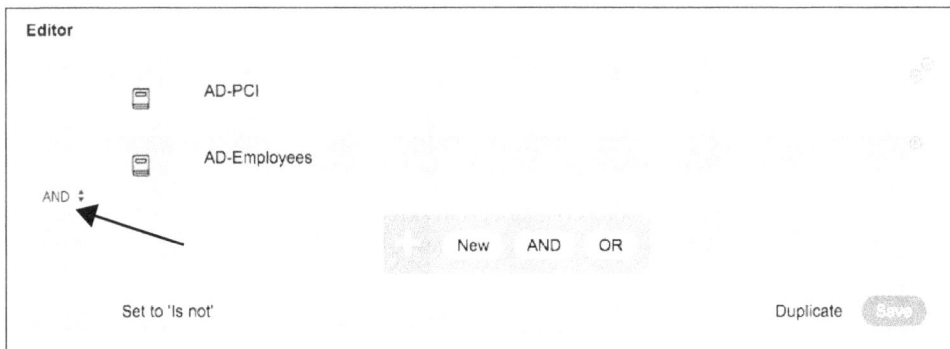

Editor

AD-PCI

AD-Employees

AND

New   AND   OR

Set to 'Is not'   Duplicate   Save

Figure 2-67 *Combining AD-PCI and AD-Employees*

Click **Save** and name the new compound condition **AD-Employee_PCI.** Your library now has three new conditions saved in it, as shown in Figure 2-68.

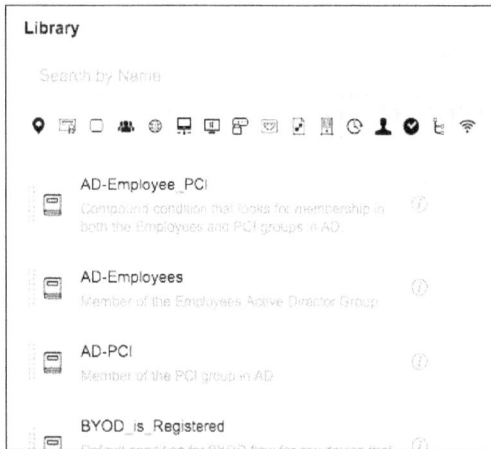

Figure 2-68   *All Three Conditions in the Library*

This new editor may take a little bit of time for you to get used to, but it sure is powerful, and once you are used to it, it really allows you to build very complex conditions—and do so very quickly.

Building the Policy for Differentiated Access

We now possess all the elements to build our policy, so let's create a brand-new policy set to use in our example.

Step 1.   Navigate to **Work Centers > Network Access > Policy Sets.**

Step 2.   Click the **+** sign to add a new policy set above the Default set.

Step 3.   Name the new set **Differentiated Access.**

Step 4.   Click the **+** sign to add a condition that differentiates this policy set from the default set.

Step 5.   Using the condition Editor, choose **Device > Device Type Starts with All Device Types#Switches**, as shown in Figure 2-69.

This means that all incoming RADIUS requests sourced from an NAD that is in the Switches NDG will use this new policy set.

Step 6.   Click **Save.**

Step 7.   Select **Default Network Access** from the Allowed Protocols/Server Sequence drop-down list, as shown in Figure 2-70, and then click **Save.**

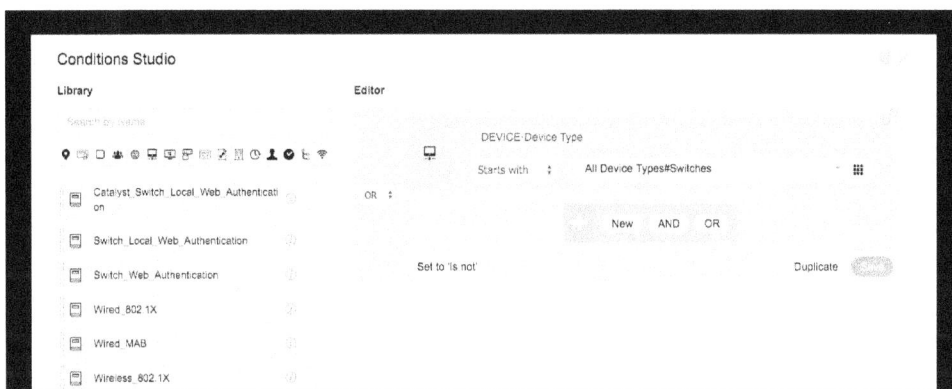

Figure 2-69 *Configuring the Device Type for the Policy Set*

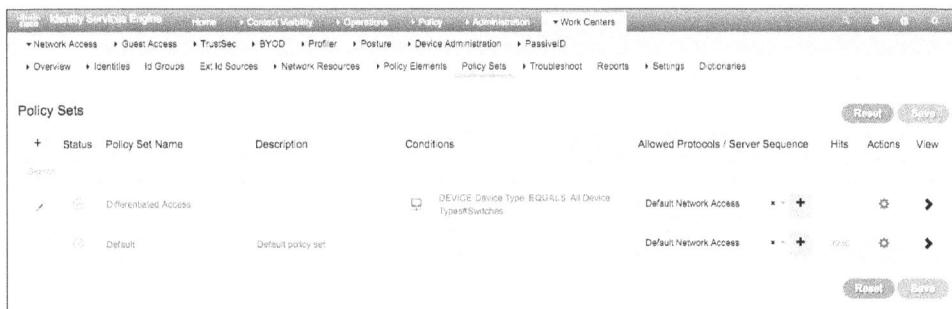

Figure 2-70 *New Policy Set Named Differentiated Access*

Step 8. Click the **>** symbol to expand the Differentiated Access policy set, and then expand the authentication policy.

Step 9. Create a new authentication policy for wired or wireless MAB that uses the Internal Endpoints identity store and is set to CONTINUE if the user is not found, as shown in Figure 2-71.

Step 10. Insert a new row below the MAB rule.

Step 11. Name the policy **Dot1X** and use Wired_802.1X OR Wireless_802.1X as the conditions, with **All_User_ID_Stores**.

Step 12. Change the default rule to **DenyAccess**, which limits this policy to MAB and 802.1X authentications only.

Figure 2-71 shows the completed authentication policy.

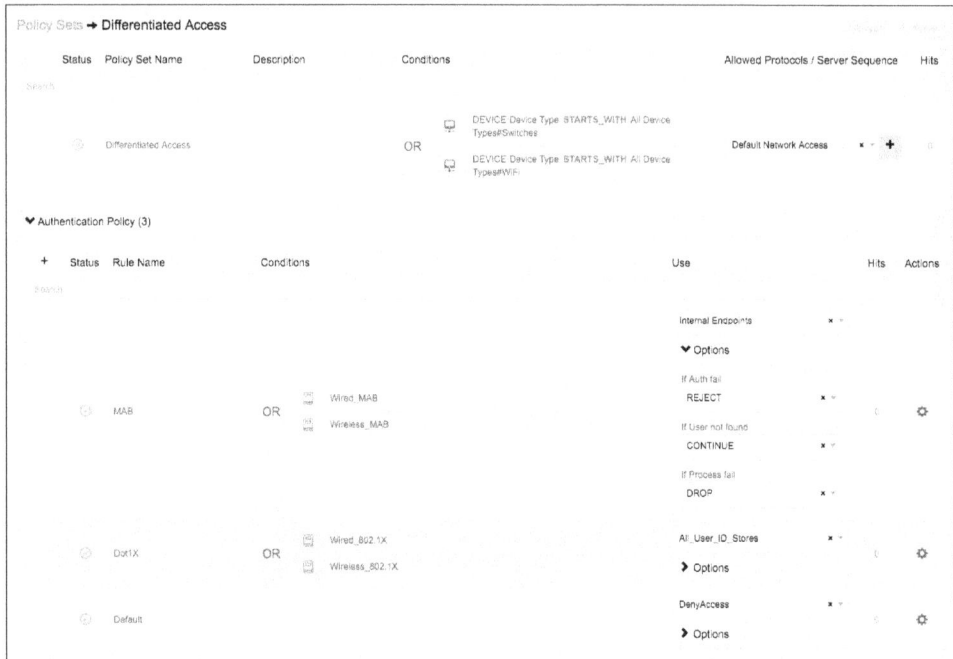

Figure 2-71   *The Authentication Policy*

Now expand the Authorization Policy section and add a rule above the default rule named **PCI Users**.

Step 13. Select the **AD-Employee_PCI** compound condition created earlier.

Step 14. Select the **PCI Users** authorization profile from the Profiles drop-down list.

Step 15. Select the **PCI_Servers** SGT from the Security Groups drop-down list, as shown in Figure 2-72.

Step 16. Insert a new rule below the PCI Users role named **Employees**.

Step 17. Select the **AD-Employees** condition that you created earlier, along with the **Employee** authorization profile and the **Employees** SGT, as shown in Figure 2-72.

Step 18. Click **Save**.

Congratulations, you just created a new policy set for all incoming authentications from NADs in the Switches NDG that authenticates 802.1X against all user identity stores; assigns a dACL, VLAN, and SGT to employees who are members of the PCI group, and enforces Layer 2 encryption on those same users. All other employees who are not members of the PCI group will be assigned a different dACL, VLAN, and SGT, and Layer 2 encryption will be suggested but not mandatory. Any other authentication requests will be denied.

There is one thing missing. What do we do with all those devices that are not authenticating and need to use MAB? To address those devices:

Step 1.   Insert one more authorization rules at the top of our authorization policy.

Step 2.   Name that rule **MAB Devices to Default VLAN**.

Step 3.   Add a condition for **Wired_MAB**, and authorization profile of **PermitAccess** and an SGT of **Unknown**.

This is not a good security policy, just something that will prevent an Access-Reject from being sent to devices for now. By allowing those devices onto the network, you are allowing profiling to work. As you build out more specific policies for the devices that are allowed in your network, you will also want to ensure that you limit unknown devices and where they can go, or even deny access to unknown devices once you enter the full enforcement phase of your deployment.

Step 4.   Click **Save**.

Figure 2-72 shows the authorization policy.

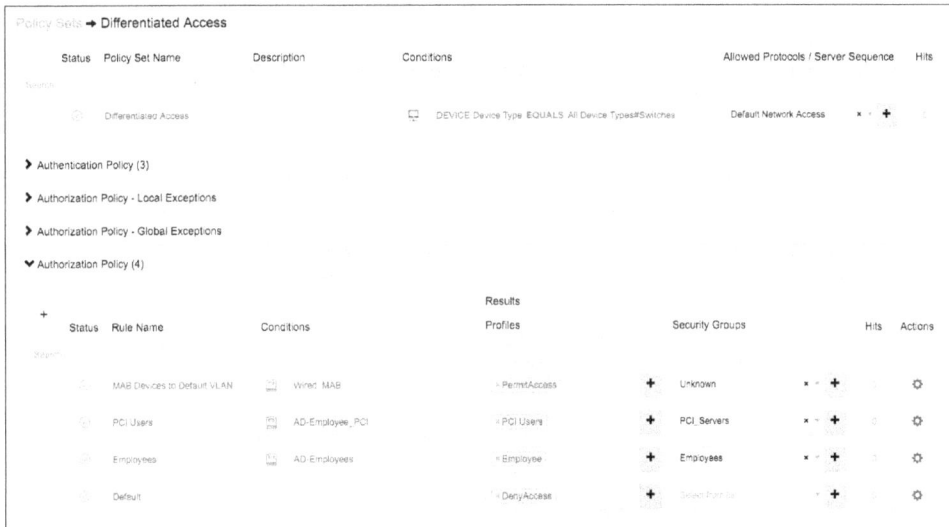

Figure 2-72   *The Authorization Policy*

Configuring Wireless Network Access with ISE

In the previous section you configured wired network access. The largest difference between wired and wireless access is, naturally, the physical medium used. Wired networks use electricity on copper wires, or light waves flowing through very thin strands of glass, whereas wireless networks use radio frequencies in the air.

What matters for this section of the chapter is that wired and wireless networks work very differently when it comes to authentications. Sure, both mediums are capable of performing 802.1X authentications. However, wired network configuration is capable of supporting authenticating and non-authenticating endpoints on the same physical switch port, and you configure a single port to support all of the possible authentication types.

That is where wireless works completely differently. Each wireless LAN (WLAN) gets configured to use 802.1X or to be open; but it cannot support both. Therefore, there is no fallback. If authentication fails, you can't get a different level of access; you get no access at all. The access point won't allow your radio to communicate with its radio and your device gets no connectivity.

Think about it. If you can't join a wireless network, you typically accept that it has a problem and go look for a wired port somewhere. Yet, if you plug into a wired port and it doesn't work...now the sky is falling.

As a CCIE Security candidate, or a CCIE Security certified professional, it is quite possible that you aren't overly familiar with wireless networking. On the other hand, you could be a wireless expert already and are currently chuckling to yourself about the previous sentence you just read.

If you are not familiar with the technical details of wireless, you may not be familiar with some of the terminology used in the wireless world, such as the concept of a WLAN also being referred to as a Service Set Identifier (SSID). A WLAN does not define a VLAN, and in fact, a single WLAN may map to multiple VLANs that can be assigned to the client by the authentication server.

With wired networks, the client has no idea what network it is trying to connect to; it is just whatever port you plug into. With wireless, the client itself must actually choose which network to try and associate with (connect to) by picking the SSID of the WLAN. There are more differences that will be pointed out to you along the way, as you read this section.

Introduction to AireOS and Its Versions

This section will review configuration for the Cisco WLCs. The focus will be on version 8.0 and higher, although all the WLC screenshots in this chapter are from WLC version 8.5, which includes many nice enhancements to the WLC, such as a single check box that ensures the timers and other values on the WLC are set to the recommended values for ISE.

Anytime you have questions or concerns as to which version of the WLC is the best, the most stable, and the most recommended, check out this website: https://supportforums. cisco.com/document/12481821/tac-recommended-aireos. That is where a team made up of Wireless TAC and the ISE TAC put their joint recommendations based on their experiences.

AireOS Features and Version History

Much like any other product, the WLC version you choose will need to be based on examining which features you want or need for your environment and weigh the benefit of those features against the older versions that may not have the features but are more of a known and proven entity. To help you a little with your version decision, Table 2-6 provides a brief rundown of some ISE-related features that have come into the WLC since version 7.0.

Table 2-6 *History of WLC ISE-Related Features*

Cisco WLC Version	Secure Access Features
AireOS 7.0	URL redirection, CoA, and ISE-NAC features are limited to 802.1X-enabled networks only.
	Open SSIDs must use Local WebAuth (LWA); no posture or onboarding capabilities.
AireOS 7.2	URL redirection, CoA, and ISE-NAC features enabled on open and Dot1X-enabled WLANs.
	Device Sensor functionality added.
AireOS 7.3	FlexConnect support for the ISE-NAC features added.
	CLI support for DNS snooping and URL-based ACLs.
	TrustSec support with SXP.
AireOS 7.4	mDNS snooping.
	Application Visibility and Control (AVC).
	NetFlow support .
AireOS 7.6	GUI configuration of DNS snooping and URL-based ACLs introduced.
AireOS 8.0	HTTPS redirection support added.
AireOS 8.3	True URL filtering provided.
	RADIUS-NAC renamed to ISE-NAC, RFC 3576 renamed to "Support for CoA."
AireOS 8.4	Captive portal bypass is enabled per-WLAN in the GUI.
	Check box is added for RADIUS server to apply best practice timers and settings for ISE with one click.
AireOS 8.5	Apple Fastlane support is added.

Now that you've examined the different versions, it is time to begin the configuration of the Wireless LAN Controller.

Authentication Configuration on WLCs

As with the Cisco Catalyst switches, this section assumes you have established basic connectivity with the NAD and are now to the point of bootstrapping the WLC for use with ISE. Similarly, there will be some configuration that is "globally" applicable, meaning it applies to the entire system, and other configuration that is per wireless LAN (per SSID), which is comparable to interface configurations on the wired NADs.

Configure the AAA Servers

The first step for the bootstrapping of the WLC is to add the ISE Policy Service Nodes to the WLC as RADIUS authentication and accounting servers.

Add the RADIUS Authentication Servers

From the WLC GUI:

Step 1.   Navigate to **Security > AAA > RADIUS > Authentication**.

Step 2.   Ensure that MAC Delimiter field is set to **Hyphen**.

This will ensure that the format of the MAC address is aa-bb-cc-dd-ee-ff, which is the way ISE expects it to be. Figure 2-73 shows the MAC Delimiter setting.

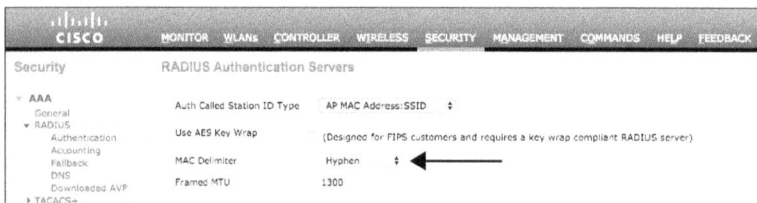

Figure 2-73   *Setting the MAC Delimiter to Hyphen*

Step 3.   Click **New** to add the ISE Policy Service Node as a new RADIUS authentication server.

Step 4.   In the Server IP Addresses(Ipv4/Ipv6) field, enter the IP address of the PSN (we are adding 10.1.100.245 in this example).

Step 5.   In the Shared Secret field, enter the shared secret, which *must* match what is configured in ISE for the network device.

Step 6.   If your WLC is version 8.4 or higher, check the **Apply Cisco ISE Default Settings** check box.

Step 7.   Set the Port Number field to **1812** for authentication.

Step 8.   Ensure that the Server Status field is set to **Enabled**.

Step 9.   Ensure that the Support for CoA field is set to **Enabled** (in older WLCs, this will be labeled as RFC 3576).

Step 10.   Change the Server Timeout field from the default value to **5** seconds, which should work nicely.

Step 11.   Ensure that the Network User **Enable** check box is checked. This simply indicates that the RADIUS server may be used for network authentications.

Step 12.   Click **Apply** in the upper-right corner.

Step 13.   Click **Save Configuration**.

Figure 2-74 shows a completed server configuration.

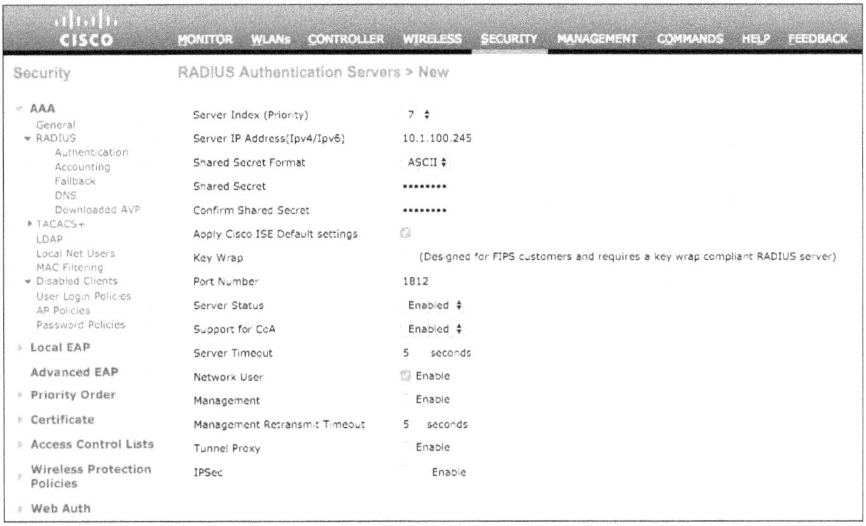

Figure 2-74   *RADIUS Authentication Server Configuration*

Repeat these steps for each PSN that you need to add. In our distributed ISE environment, you will only be adding two PSNs: 10.1.100.245 and 10.1.100.246.

Add the RADIUS Accounting Servers

The WLC does not have an option to leverage the same RADIUS authentication server for RADIUS accounting, so you will end up creating each RADIUS server in both locations.

From the WLC GUI:

Step 1.   Navigate to **Security > AAA > RADIUS > Accounting**.

Step 2.   Ensure the MAC Delimiter field is set to **Hyphen**.

Step 3.   Click **New** to add the ISE PSN.

Step 4.   Enter the IP address of the PSN.

Step 5.   Enter the shared secret to match what is configured on ISE.

Step 6.   Ensure the Port Number field is **1813**.

Step 7.   Ensure the Server Status field is set to **Enabled**.

Step 8.   Verify that the Network User **Enable** check box is checked.

Step 9.   Click **Apply** in the upper-right corner.

Step 10.   Click **Save Configuration**.

Figure 2-75 shows a completed server entry.

Figure 2-75 *RADIUS Accounting Server Configuration*

Repeat these steps for each PSN that you need to add.

Configure RADIUS Fallback (High Availability)

The primary RADIUS server (the server with the lowest server index) is assumed to be the most preferable server for the Cisco WLC. If the primary server becomes unresponsive, the controller switches to the next active server (the server with the next lowest server index). The controller continues to use this backup server, unless you configure the controller to fall back to the primary RADIUS server when it recovers and becomes responsive or to a more preferable server from the available backup servers.

From the WLC GUI:

Step 1. Navigate to **Security > AAA > RADIUS > Fallback**.

Step 2. Set the Fallback Mode field to **Active**.

Selecting Active causes the Cisco WLC to revert to a server with a lower priority from the available backup servers by using RADIUS probe messages to proactively determine whether a server that has been marked inactive is back online.

Step 3. In the Username field, enter the name to be sent in the inactive server probes.

We have been using radius-test as the username so far in the book. Technically, you do not need to enter a password for this test user account, because the system will simply look for a response from the RADIUS server; pass or fail does not matter.

Step 4. Enter a value in the Interval in Sec field or leave it at the default setting.

The interval states the inactive time in passive mode and probe interval in active mode. The valid range is 180 to 3600 seconds, and the default value is 300 seconds.

Figure 2-76 shows the fallback settings for RADIUS.

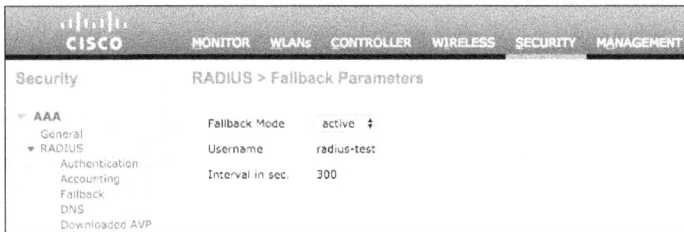

Figure 2-76 *Fallback Parameters*

Configure the Airespace ACLs

Just as we did with the Cisco Catalyst switches, we will prestage the Wireless LAN Controller with an access-list for a Web Authentication ACL named **ACL_WEBAUTH_REDIRECT.**

This ACL name is used specifically because it matches the preconfigured setting in ISE, and it may make your life a little easier if this is a greenfield deployment. Beginning with ISE 2.0, there was some smart-default configurations that ship with ISE to make unboxing ISE and setting it up very fast and easy. The smart-default configurations for Guest and BYOD include the use of the redirect ACL with this specific name.

Naturally, you can use whatever name you wish, and simply change the configuration built into ISE. However, for the purposes of this book, we will keep the same ACL name.

Create the Web Authentication Redirection ACL

As with the Catalyst switches, we will need a local ACL on the WLC that will redirect web traffic to the Centralized Web Authentication portal. However, with the Catalyst switch, a **permit** statement means that the traffic should be redirected, and a **deny** statement describes traffic that should not be redirected. With the Catalyst switch, we need two ACLs: one to define what gets redirected, and a second one to filter traffic (permit or deny traffic flow).

With the WLC, there is a single access list, and it pulls double-duty. It will permit and deny traffic flow, but at the same time the traffic that is denied will be redirected to the Centralized Web Authentication portal.

From the WLC GUI:

Step 1.   Navigate to **Security > Access Control Lists > Access Control Lists.**

Step 2.   Click **New** to add a new ACL.

Step 3.   Fill in the name as **ACL_WEBAUTH_REDIRECT.**

Step 4.   Click **Apply.**

You will be returned to the main Access Control List screen.

Step 5.   Click the new entry: **ACL_WEBAUTH_REDIRECT**.

Step 6.   Click **Add New Rule** in the upper-right corner.

A "rule" in the WLC is the equivalent of an access control entry in the switch. It is a line in the Access List.

Step 7.   Create a set of rules for this ACL that does the following:

- Permits all traffic outbound (toward the client).

- Permits DNS inbound and outbound.

- Permits TCP port 8443 inbound (from the client into the network) to the ISE servers. For simplicity, you may wish to permit all traffic to the ISE nodes. It will also allow you to reuse the same ACL for most use cases.

- Denies all other traffic, which will redirect the rest.

Figure 2-77 shows an example of a completed ACL.

General									
Access List Name	ACL_WEBAUTH_REDIRECT								
Deny Counters	0								
Seq	Action	Source IP/Mask	Destination IP/Mask	Protocol	Source Port	Dest Port	DSCP	Direction	Number of Hits
1	Permit	0.0.0.0 / 0.0.0.0	0.0.0.0 / 0.0.0.0	Any	Any	Any	Any	Outbound	0
2	Permit	0.0.0.0 / 0.0.0.0	0.0.0.0 / 0.0.0.0	UDP	Any	DNS	Any	Any	0
3	Permit	0.0.0.0 / 0.0.0.0	10.1.100.240 / 255.255.255.240	Any	Any	Any	Any	Inbound	0
4	Permit	0.0.0.0 / 0.0.0.0	10.1.100.224 / 255.255.255.240	Any	Any	Any	Any	Inbound	0
5	Permit	0.0.0.0 / 0.0.0.0	10.1.103.0 / 255.255.255.0	Any	Any	Any	Any	Inbound	0
6	Deny	0.0.0.0 / 0.0.0.0	0.0.0.0 / 0.0.0.0	Any	Any	Any	Any	Inbound	0

Figure 2-77   *Sample ACL_WEBAUTH_REDIRECT ACL*

Add Google URLs for ACL Bypass

This may come as a big surprise to you, but Android mobile devices need to communicate to the Google cloud. Now that you've heard that earth-shattering news, it shouldn't surprise you that when Android endpoints go through the BYOD onboarding process, they must have access to the Google cloud and at the very least have access to the Google Play store in order to download the Network Setup Assistant (NSA) app.

So, you can allow access out to Google in your ACL; however, it is not as simple as just putting in an IP address—there are thousands of addresses that may resolve to the DNS names needed for the Google Play store.

Beginning with WLC version 7.6, the ability to use DNS-based ACLs in the form of URL lists was added to the Airespace ACLs.

Begin by navigating to **Security > Access Control Lists > Access Control Lists**:

Step 1.   Hover the mouse pointer over the blue-and-white downward-facing arrow next to the ACL_WEBAUTH_REDIRECT access list that you created in the previous section.

Step 2.   Select **Add-Remove URL**, as shown in Figure 2-78.

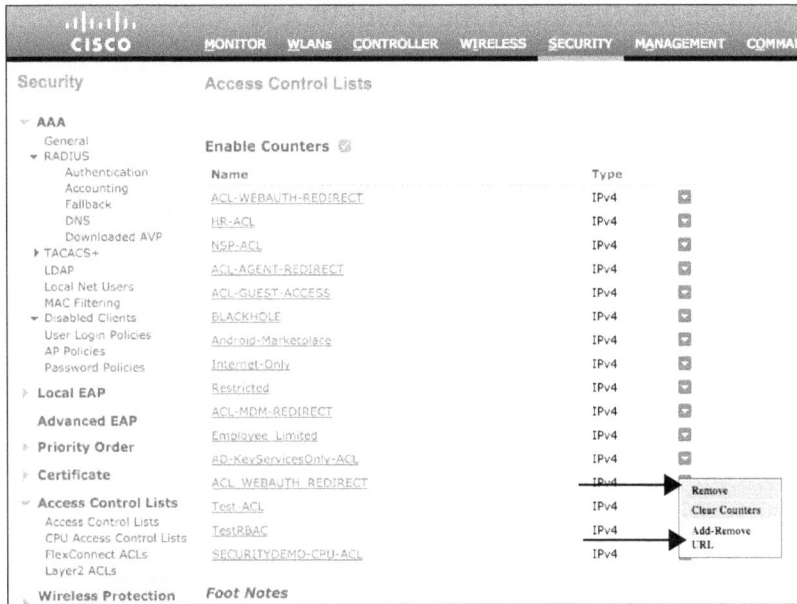

Figure 2-78 *Add-Remove URL*

You are now brought to the URL List section. The URLs that you enter here are configured with an implicit wildcard in the first portion of the FQDN. In other words, entering "google.com" will match *.google.com. Any matches to these URL entries will be permitted through the ACL.

Step 3.   In the URL String Name field, enter the URLs to be permitted through the ACL and click **Add**.

In the United States, entering "google.com" and "clients.google.com" typically does the trick. In other countries there may be other URLs required for the smooth operation of Android endpoints. One solution that has worked is to add "*.*" for the domain extensions. In other words, enter **google.*.*** instead of google.com and **android.clients.google.*.*** instead of adroid.clients.google.com.

Figure 2-79 shows an example URL List.

Figure 2-79 *URL List*

Create the Dynamic Interfaces for the Client VLANs

When we want to assign a user or device to a VLAN on a Catalyst switch, we just assign the VLAN to the port, and the entire switch port will now be assigned to that particular VLAN.

The Wireless LAN Controller has only a few physical connections to the wired network, and it must bridge all wireless users from their RF network (Wi-Fi) to the physical wired network, and also have the ability to assign a different VLAN per authenticated session (if necessary). You're thinking it just needs to be connected with a trunk, right? Well, yes that's true.

The WLC will be configured to use 802.1Q to tag traffic for a specific VLAN as that traffic exits the controller. However, the WLC will call this a "dynamic interface" because of the way it can assign a physical interface to traffic, or assign a tag.

We will create two dynamic interfaces in this section, one for employee traffic and one for guest traffic.

Create the Employee Dynamic Interface

The employee dynamic interface will be used for all successful authentications to the Corporate Wireless LAN, providing full access to the entire network.

From the WLC GUI:

Step 1.   Navigate to **Controller > Interfaces.**

Step 2.   Click **New.**

Step 3.   In the Interface Name field, name your interface. We will use the name **employee** in the example.

Step 4.   Provide the VLAN ID to be used in the 802.1Q tag (**44** in the example).

Step 5.   Click **Apply.**

Step 6.   Click on the new Interface named **employee.**

Note   You will most likely leave the settings at their defaults until you reach the Physical Information section.

Step 7.   In the Interface Address section, provide an IP address, netmask, and gateway for the VLAN in the corresponding fields.

Step 8.   In the DHCP Information section, provide the primary DHCP server address.

Step 9.   Click **Apply.**

Figure 2-80 shows an example employee dynamic interface configuration.

```
General Information

  Interface Name           employee

  MAC Address              d0:d0:fd:91:e2:65

Configuration

  Guest Lan

  Quarantine

  Quarantine Vlan Id       0

  NAS-ID                   none

Physical Information

  Port Number                      2

  Backup Port                      0

  Active Port                      2

  Enable Dynamic AP Management

Interface Address

  VLAN Identifier          44

  IP Address               10.1.44.2

  Netmask                  255.255.255.0

  Gateway                  10.1.44.1

  IPv6 Address             ::

  Prefix Length            128

  IPv6 Gateway             ::

  Link Local IPv6 Address  fe80::d2d0:fdff:fe91:e260/64

DHCP Information

  Primary DHCP Server      10.10.100.100

  Secondary DHCP Server

  DHCP Proxy Mode          Global    ▼

  Enable DHCP Option 82
```

Figure 2-80 *Example Employee Interface*

Create the Guest Dynamic Interface

The guest dynamic interface will be used for all devices connecting to the Guest WLAN, as well as unsuccessful or unauthorized authentications to the Corporate Wireless LAN. This interface will have Internet access only.

From the WLC GUI:

Step 1.   Navigate to **Controller > Interfaces**.

Step 2.   Click **New**.

Step 3.   In the Interface Name field, name your interface. We will use the name **guest** in our example.

Step 4.   Provide the VLAN ID to be used in the 802.1Q tag (**42** in the example).

Step 5.   Click **Apply**.

Step 6.   Click on the new interface named **guest**.

Note   You will most likely leave the settings at their defaults until you reach the Physical Information section. Do not check the Guest Lan check box. This is not for Guest WLANs; it is for providing guest access to directly connected wired LANs.

Step 7.   In the Interface Address section, provide an IP address, netmask, and gateway for the VLAN in the corresponding fields.

Step 8.   In the DHCP Information section, provide the primary DHCP server address.

Step 9.   Click **Apply.**

Figure 2-81 shows an example guest dynamic interface configuration.

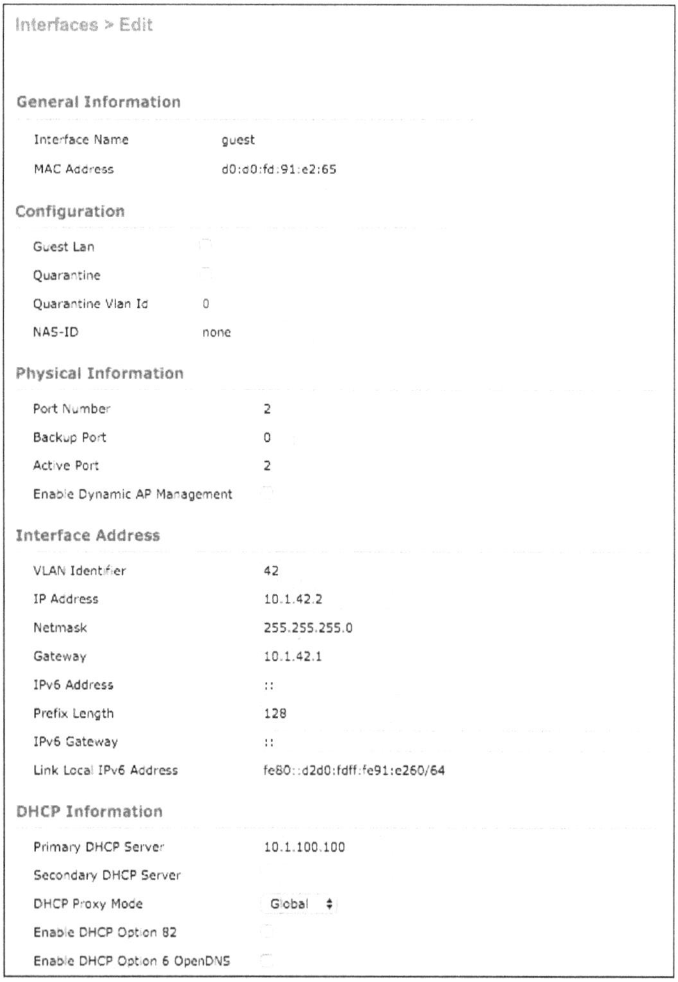

Interfaces > Edit

General Information

Interface Name	guest
MAC Address	d0:d0:fd:91:e2:65

Configuration

Guest Lan	
Quarantine	
Quarantine Vlan Id	0
NAS-ID	none

Physical Information

Port Number	2
Backup Port	0
Active Port	2
Enable Dynamic AP Management	

Interface Address

VLAN Identifier	42
IP Address	10.1.42.2
Netmask	255.255.255.0
Gateway	10.1.42.1
IPv6 Address	::
Prefix Length	128
IPv6 Gateway	::
Link Local IPv6 Address	fe80::d2d0:fdff:fe91:e260/64

DHCP Information

Primary DHCP Server	10.1.100.100
Secondary DHCP Server	
DHCP Proxy Mode	Global ⬍
Enable DHCP Option 82	
Enable DHCP Option 6 OpenDNS	

Figure 2-81   *Example Guest Interface*

Note   Checking the Guest Lan check box shown in Figure 2-81 enables the WLC to capture wired traffic and combine it with the wireless traffic in the CAPWAP tunnels. Do not check that check box unless you won't be using ISE for wired guest access and you specifically plan to use anchor controllers and need your wired and wireless traffic to both exit from the same anchor controller.

Create the PCI Dynamic Interface

The PCI dynamic interface will be used for all successful authentications to the Corporate Wireless LAN, providing full access to the entire network.

From the WLC GUI:

Step 1.   Navigate to **Controller > Interfaces.**

Step 2.   Click **New.**

Step 3.   In the Interface Name field, name your Interface. We will use the name **pci** in the example.

Step 4.   Provide the VLAN ID to be used in the 802.1Q tag (**22** in the example).

Step 5.   Click **Apply.**

Step 6.   Click on the new interface named **pci.**

Note   You will most likely leave the settings at their defaults until you reach the Physical Information section.

Step 7.   In the Interface Address section, provide an IP address, netmask, and gateway for the VLAN in the corresponding fields.

Step 8.   In the DHCP Information section, provide the dynamic DHCP server address.

Step 9.   Click **Apply.**

Create the Wireless LANs

Now that the RADIUS servers, ACLs, and dynamic interfaces are all created and configured, we will move into creating two WLANs: one for guests and one for corporate users. The Guest WLAN will be an "open" WLAN, while the corporate WLAN will be configured to use 802.1X to authenticate devices. With WLC version 8.3 and higher, the guest network could also use WPA/WPA2 with a pre-shared key.

Create the Guest WLAN

The Guest WLAN will be created as an open SSID but will send the endpoint MAC addresses to ISE over RADIUS for MAB, just like the wired networks.

From the WLC GUI:

Step 1.   Navigate to **WLANs.**

Step 2.   From the drop-down list, select **Create New** and then click **Go.**

Step 3.   In the Type drop-down list, select **WLAN.**

Step 4.   In the Profile Name field, give the WLAN profile a name (we will use **ISE-Guest** in this example).

Step 5.   In the SSID field, provide an SSID name (**ISE-Guest** in this example).

Step 6.   Click **Apply.**

Figure 2-82 shows an example Guest WLAN being added.

Figure 2-82   *Example Guest WLAN Creation*

General Tab

Configure the General tab to enable the SSID and configure it to use the guest interface.

Step 1.   If you are ready to work with this SSID, ensure the **Enabled** check box is checked.

Step 2.   In the Interface/Interface Group(G) spin box, choose the **guest** interface that we created previously.

Step 3.   The general practice for open guest networks is to enable broadcast SSID, so check the Broadcast SSID **Enabled** check box.

Figure 2-83 shows the example Guest WLAN's General tab.

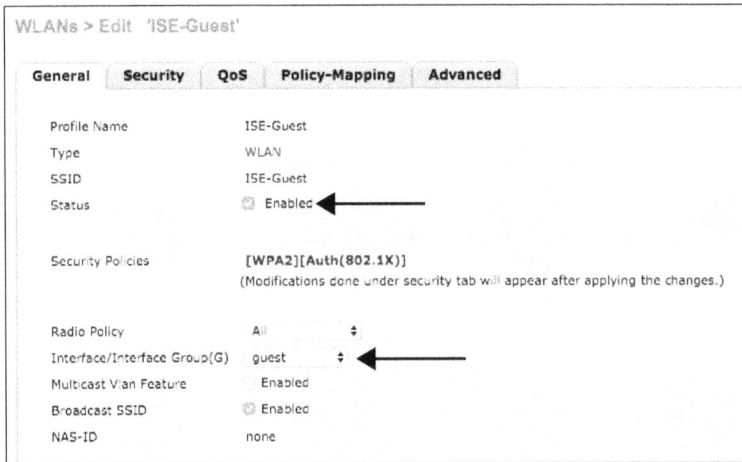

Figure 2-83 *Example Guest WLAN: General Tab*

Note The default security for policy is for WPA2 and 802.1X. We will change that in the Security Tab.

Layer 2 Security Tab

Click the **Security** tab, which displays the Layer 2 tab first, and configure the Layer 2 security for wireless MAC Authentication Bypass as follows:

Step 1. Change the Layer 2 Security spin box from the default (WPA+WPA2) to **None.**

Step 2. Check the **MAC Filtering** check box (which is wireless MAB).

Figure 2-84 shows the example Guest WLAN's Layer 2 Security tab.

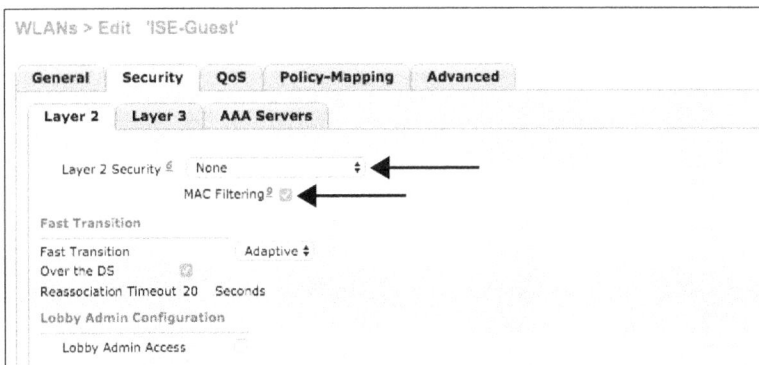

Figure 2-84 *Example Guest WLAN: Layer 2 Security Tab*

Layer 3 Security Tab

Click the **Layer 3 Security** tab and configure it as follows:

Step 1.   Ensure the Layer 3 Security spin box is set to **None**.

Step 2.   Set the Captive Network Assistant Bypass spin box to **Enable**.

The Captive Network Assistant Bypass option configures the WLC to lie to the endpoint about being connected to the Internet. Most OS vendors test their connectivity to the Internet to look for a captive portal, and to assist the end user in gaining network access, the OS will automatically pop up a web browser or a pseudo-browser like Apple's "web sheet."

Apple iOS uses the web sheet instead of the full-blown Safari browser as a way to isolate saved passwords and other private data from accidently being entered into an untrusted network connection. However, this pseudo-browser is missing a lot of functionality needed for advanced guest networking and BYOD functions, and therefore it is best to enable the Captive Network Assistant Bypass on the WLC to trick iOS into believing there is no captive portal, and thereby preventing the web sheet from ever popping up.

Captive Network Assistant Bypass was added to the WLC GUI in version 8.4. If you are using a version lower than 8.4, the configuration is still there, but is only available in the CLI.

Figure 2-85 shows the example Guest WLAN's Layer 3 Security tab.

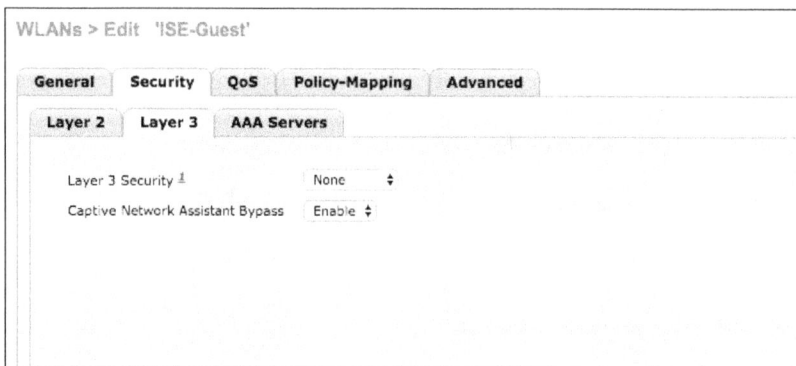

Figure 2-85   *Example Guest WLAN: Layer 3 Security Tab*

AAA Servers Tab

The Cisco WLC allows for the administrator to specify different authentication and accounting servers; however, this is a configuration that is incompatible with an ISE RADIUS server. ISE provides session services that are tied together from the session ID in the authentication packet and the session ID in the accounting packet.

Step 1.   Click the **AAA Servers** tab and check the Apply Cisco ISE Default Settings **Enabled** check box.

This automatically ensures that your authentication and accounting servers are the same per line, and configures the values called out in Steps 3 and 4. If you are using a WLC version lower than 8.4, then this setting is not available and you must proceed with Steps 3 and 4 manually.

Step 2.   Select your ISE Policy Service Node(s) for both **Authentication** and **Accounting**.

Step 3.   In the RADIUS Server Accounting section, check the **Interim Update** check box.

Step 4.   Set the Interim Interval to **0** seconds.

Note   For WLC versions 7.6 and lower, the recommendation to is to clear the Interim Updates check box. For version 8.0 and later, it should be checked, with an Interim Interval setting of 0 seconds. The setting will ensure that an accounting update is sent only when the client IP address changes. Device Sensor updates will not be impacted.

Step 5.   Click **Apply**.

Figure 2-86 shows the example Guest WLAN's AAA Servers Security tab.

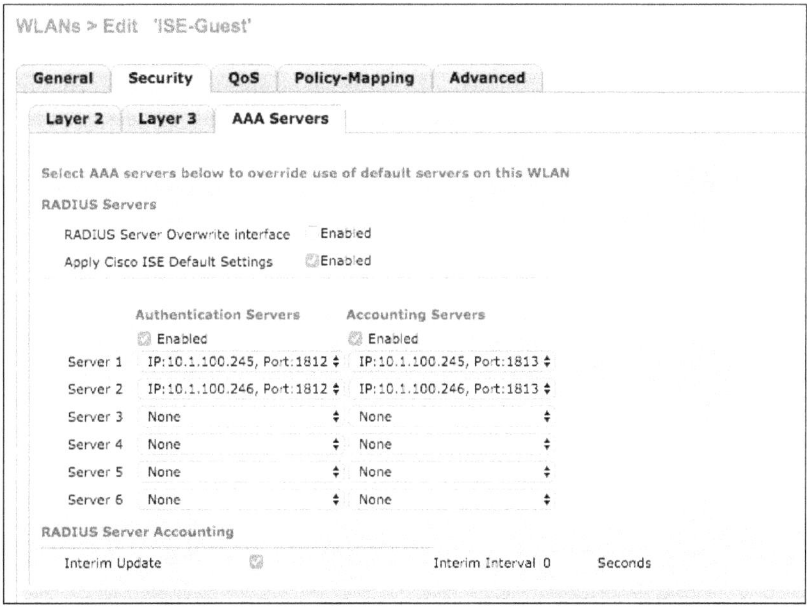

Figure 2-86   *Example Guest WLAN: AAA Servers Security Tab*

Advanced Tab

There are several settings on the Advanced tab that are required for the seamless operation with ISE for all applicable use cases. When you have selected ISE as the RADIUS server, all of these settings are configured for you.

Step 1. Check the Allow AAA Override **Enabled** check box.

This will enable ISE to assign a different VLAN and ACL than what is configured on the WLAN and interface by default. This may be checked and grayed out depending on your WLC version and if you used the "easy check boxes for ISE."

Step 2. Leave the **Enable Session Timeout** check box checked.

Step 3. Ensure that the Client Exclusion **Enabled** check box is checked.

Step 4. Change the NAC State spin box to **ISE NAC**.

In WLC versions lower than 8.3, this setting is named "Radius NAC"—yes, it should be all caps, RADIUS, because it is an acronym. The name and spelling of the setting is unimportant. The setting itself, however, is critical to allow for URL redirection, CWA, posture assessment, native supplicant provisioning, MDM redirections, and more.

Step 5. Scroll down to the Radius [*sic*] Client Profiling section and check both **DHCP Profiling** and **HTTP Profiling** check boxes.

The Cisco WLC has two different client profiling options: Radius Client Profiling, which sends the attributes to ISE within RADIUS accounting packets, and Local Client Profiling, where the WLC keeps the information and uses it locally. Although the interface appears to be able to use both types of profiling, they are mutually exclusive and cannot be enabled at the same time.

Step 6. Click **Apply**.

Step 7. Click **Save Configuration**.

The Advanced tab is quite long, and the UI requires you to scroll. Therefore, the tab has been broken into three different images. Figures 2-87, 2-88, and 2-89 show the example Guest WLAN's Advanced tab.

WLANs > Edit 'ISE-Guest'

General   **Security**   **QoS**   **Policy-Mapping**   **Advanced**

Allow AAA Override	✓ Enabled	
Coverage Hole Detection	✓ Enabled	
Enable Session Timeout	✓ 1800	
	Session Timeout (secs)	
Aironet IE	✓ Enabled	
Diagnostic Channel ¹⁸	Enabled	
Override Interface ACL	IPv4	IPv6
	None ÷	None ÷
Layer2 Acl	None ÷	
URL ACL	None ÷	
P2P Blocking Action	Disabled ÷	
Client Exclusion ²	✓ Enabled 180	
	Timeout Value (secs)	
Maximum Allowed Clients ⁸	0	
Static IP Tunneling ¹¹	Enabled	
Wi-Fi Direct Clients Policy	Disabled ÷	
Maximum Allowed Clients Per AP Radio	200	
Clear HotSpot Configuration	Enabled	

DHCP

DHCP Server	Override
DHCP Addr. Assignment	Required

OEAP

Split Tunnel	Enabled

Management Frame Protection (MFP)

MFP Client Protection ⁴	Optional ÷

DTIM Period (in beacon intervals)

802.11a/n (1 - 255)	1
802.11b/g/n (1 - 255)	1

NAC

NAC State	ISE NAC ÷

Load Balancing and Band Select

Client Load Balancing

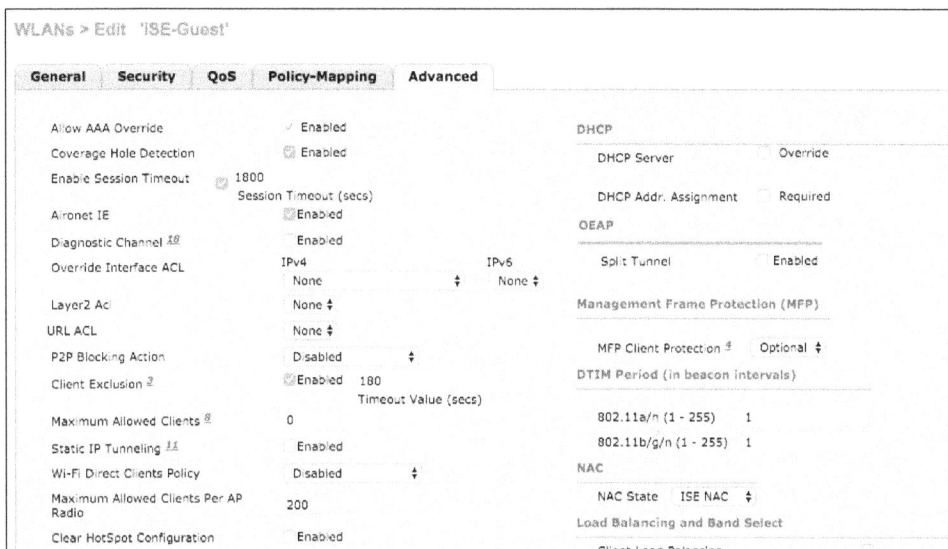

Figure 2-87   *Example Guest WLAN: Advanced Tab, Part 1*

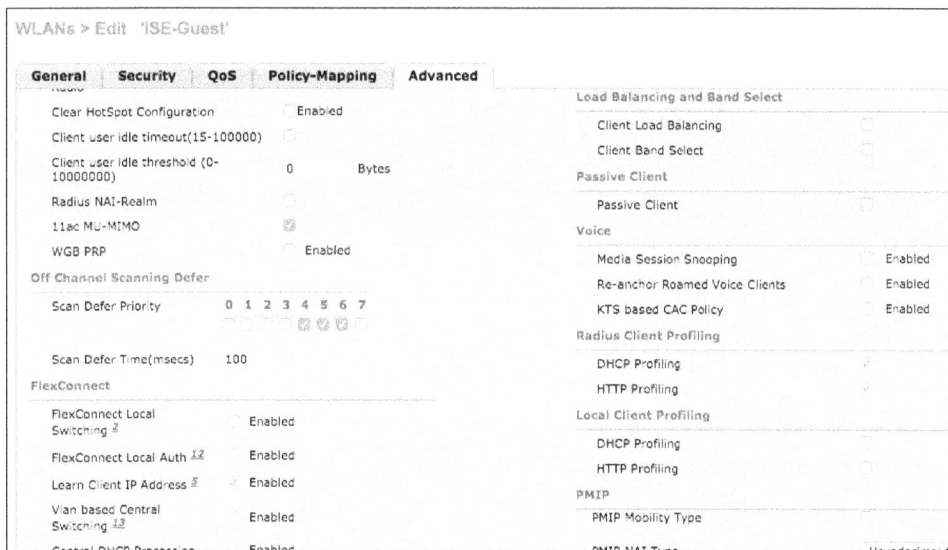

WLANs > Edit 'ISE-Guest'

General   **Security**   **QoS**   **Policy-Mapping**   **Advanced**

Clear HotSpot Configuration	Enabled	
Client user idle timeout(15-100000)		
Client user idle threshold (0-10000000)	0	Bytes
Radius NAI-Realm		
11ac MU-MIMO	✓	
WGB PRP	Enabled	
Off Channel Scanning Defer		
Scan Defer Priority	0 1 2 3 4 5 6 7	
Scan Defer Time(msecs)	100	
FlexConnect		
FlexConnect Local Switching ²	Enabled	
FlexConnect Local Auth ¹²	Enabled	
Learn Client IP Address ⁵	Enabled	
Vlan based Central Switching ¹³	Enabled	
Central DHCP Processing	Enabled	

Load Balancing and Band Select

Client Load Balancing	
Client Band Select	

Passive Client

Passive Client	

Voice

Media Session Snooping	Enabled
Re-anchor Roamed Voice Clients	Enabled
KTS based CAC Policy	Enabled

Radius Client Profiling

DHCP Profiling	
HTTP Profiling	

Local Client Profiling

DHCP Profiling	
HTTP Profiling	

PMIP

PMIP Mobility Type	
PMIP NAI Type	Hexadecimal ÷

Figure 2-88   *Example Guest WLAN: Advanced Tab, Part 2*

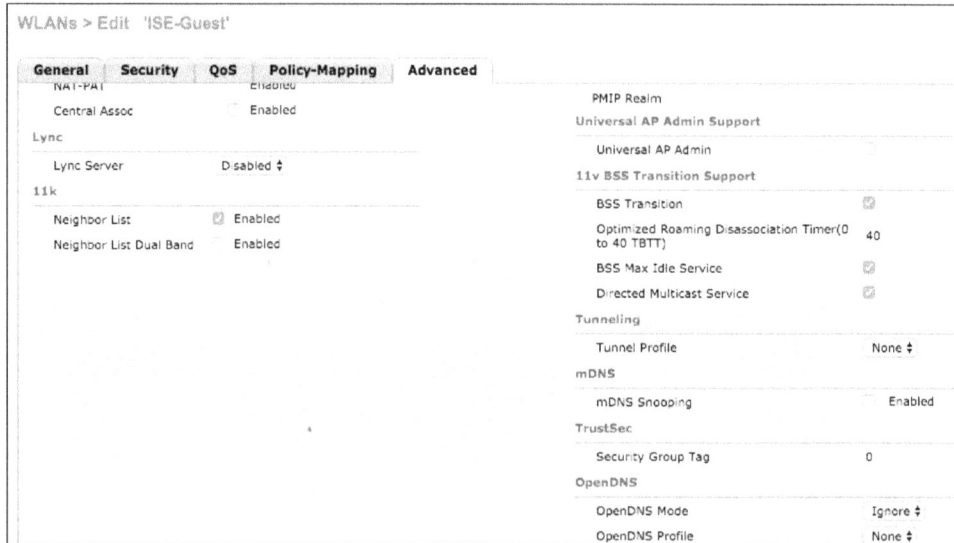

Figure 2-89   *Example Guest WLAN: Advanced Tab, Part 3*

Create the Corporate WLAN

The Corporate WLAN will be created as a *closed* SSID and will require 802.1X authentication in order for an endpoint to associate to the WLAN. Unlike wired networks, wireless networks have the added benefit of truly rejecting all access without a successful authentication. Users are attuned to the requirement of configuring software in order to connect to a wired network. The same is very much untrue when it comes to wired networks.

From the WLC GUI:

Step 1.   Navigate to **WLAN**.

Step 2.   From the drop-down list, select **Create New** and then click **Go**.

Step 3.   In the Type drop-down list, select **WLAN**.

Step 4.   In the Profile Name field, give the WLAN profile a name (we will use **ISE** in this example).

Step 5.   In the SSID field, provide an SSID name (**ISE** in this example).

Step 6.   Click **Apply**.

In this example, the SSID name of ISE is used because it is the SSID name that is preconfigured in the smart-default prebuilt native supplicant profile for ISE 2.0 and higher. Using this SSID name will help speed up your installation and demo ability, just like using the ACL_WEBAUTH_REDIRECT name for the Airespace ACL.

Figure 2-90 shows an example corporate WLAN named ISE being added.

Figure 2-90   *Example Corporate WLAN Creation*

General Tab

Configure the General tab to enable the SSID and configure it to use the employee interface.

Step 1.   If you are ready to work with this SSID, ensure the **Enabled** check box is checked.

Step 2.   In the Interface/Interface Group(G) spin box, choose the **employee** interface that we created previously.

Figure 2-91 shows the example corporate WLAN's General tab.

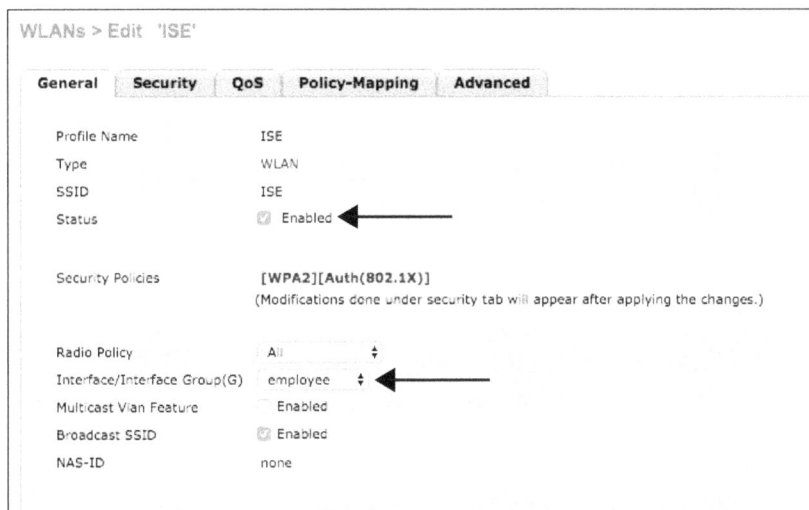

Figure 2-91   *Example Corporate WLAN: General Tab*

Note   The authorization results you created in the "Creating a Policy for Differentiated Access" section will assign the VLAN 44 for employees, and 22 for PCI users. The VLAN assigned from ISE will overwrite the assigned interface on this tab.

Layer 2 Security Tab

Click the **Security** tab and configure the Layer 2 security to use secure key management with 802.1X as follows:

Step 1.   Leave the Layer 2 Security spin box at its default setting of **WPA+WPA2**.

Step 2.   We will not be enabling MAC filtering, so leave the MAC Filtering check box clear.

Step 3.   In the Authentication Key Management section, ensure that 802.1X **Enable** check box is checked.

Figure 2-92 shows the example corporate WLAN's Layer 2 Security Tab.

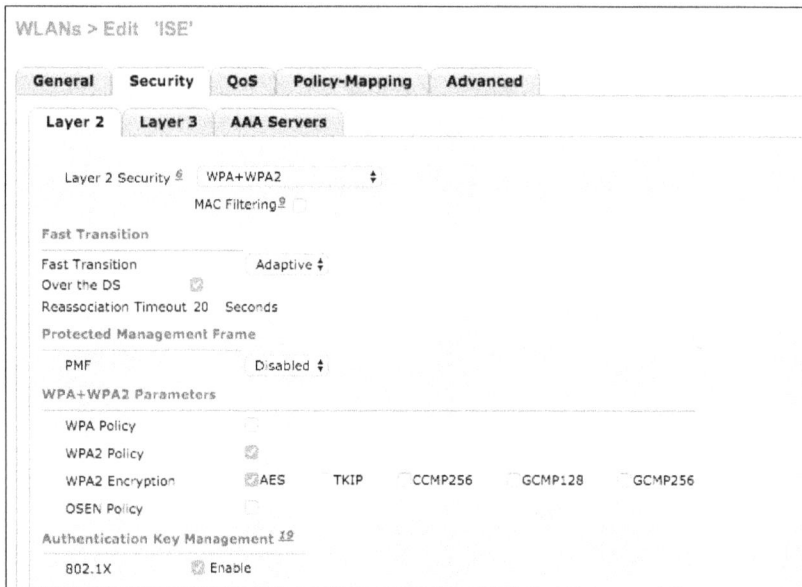

Figure 2-92   *Example Corporate WLAN: Layer 2 Security Tab*

Layer 3 Security Tab

Click the **Layer 3 Security** tab and configure it as follows:

Step 1.   Ensure the Layer 3 Security spin box is set to **None**.

Step 2.   Set the Captive Network Assistant Bypass spin box to **Enable**.

Just like with the Guest WLAN, you are configuring this network to lie to Apple iOS devices. You need it on the corporate SSID for the single-SSID onboarding scenarios.

Figure 2-93 shows the example corporate WLAN's Layer 3 Security tab.

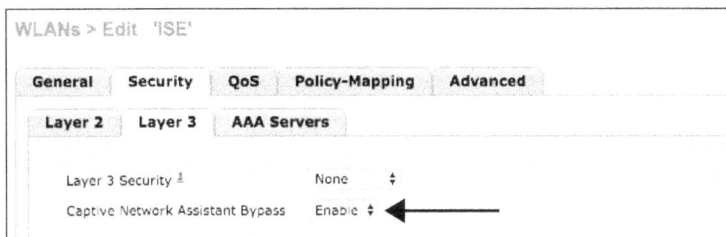

Figure 2-93   *Example Corporate WLAN: Layer 3 Security Tab*

AAA Servers Tab

The Cisco WLC allows for the administrator to specify different authentication and accounting servers; however, this is a configuration that is incompatible with an ISE RADIUS server. ISE provides session services that are tied together from the session ID in the authentication packet and the session ID in the accounting packet.

Step 1.   Click the **AAA Servers** tab and check the Apply Cisco ISE Default Settings **Enabled** check box.

This automatically ensures that your authentication and accounting servers are the same per line, and configures the values called out in Steps 3 and 4. If you are using a WLC version earlier than 8.4, then this setting is not available, and you must proceed with Steps 3 and 4 manually.

Step 2.   Select your ISE Policy Service Node(s) for both **Authentication** and **Accounting**.

Step 3.   In the RADIUS Server Accounting section, check the **Interim Update** check box.

Step 4.   Set the Interim Interval to **0** seconds.

Note   For WLC versions 7.6 and lower, the recommendation to is to clear the Interim Updates check box. For version 8.0 and later, it should be checked, with an Interim Interval setting of 0 seconds. The setting will ensure that an accounting update is sent only when the client IP address changes. Device Sensor updates will not be impacted.

Step 5.   Click **Apply**.

Advanced Tab

There are a number of settings on the Advanced tab that are required for the seamless operation with ISE for all applicable use cases. This is set up exactly the same way as the Guest WLAN, so you can refer to Figures 2-87, 2-88, and 2-89 for a visual of the

Advanced tab settings. Remember, with WLC version 8.4 and higher, when you have selected ISE as the RADIUS server, all of these settings are configured for you.

Step 1.   Check the Allow AAA Override **Enabled** check box.

This will enable ISE to assign a different VLAN and ACL than what is configured on the WLAN and interface by default. This may be checked and grayed out depending on your WLC version and if you used the "easy check boxes for ISE."

Step 2.   Leave the **Enable Session Timeout** check box checked.

Step 3.   Ensure that Client Exclusion **Enabled** check box is checked.

Step 4.   Change the NAC State spin box to **ISE NAC**.

In WLC versions earlier than 8.3, this setting is named "Radius NAC" (yes, it should be all caps, RADIUS). The name and spelling of the setting is unimportant. The setting itself, however, is critical to allow for URL redirection, CWA, posture assessment, native supplicant provisioning, MDM redirections, and more.

Step 5.   Scroll down to the Radius [sic] Client Profiling section and check both the **DHCP Profiling** and **HTTP Profiling** check boxes.

The Cisco WLC has two different client profiling options: Radius Client Profiling, which sends the attributes to ISE within RADIUS accounting packets, and Local Client Profiling, where the WLC keeps the information and uses it locally. Although the interface appears to be able to use both types of profiling, they are mutually exclusive and cannot be enabled at the same time.

Step 6.   Click **Apply**.

Step 7.   Click **Save Configuration**.

Configuring ISE for Wireless Network Access Control

Most of the ISE configuration was completed in the "Configuring ISE for Basic Wired Network Access Control" section; however, we used the "device-type = switches" condition for the policy set, and now we have to update that to include wireless controllers.

From the ISE UI:

Step 1.   Navigate to **Work Centers > Network Access > Policy Sets**.

Step 2.   Hover over the Conditions cell for the policy set and click it to edit, as shown in Figure 2-94.

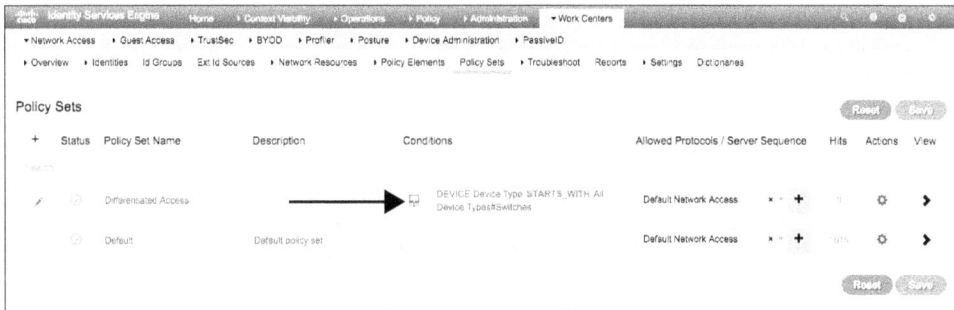

Figure 2-94   *Editing the Policy Set Condition*

Step 3.   Click **New**.

Step 4.   Set the attribute to **Device: Device Type**, the operator to **StartsWith**, and the value to the **WiFi NDG**.

Step 5.   Ensure the operator is **OR**, not AND, as shown in Figure 2-95.

Step 6.   Click **Save**.

Figure 2-95 shows the top-level policy set rule with Wi-Fi devices added.

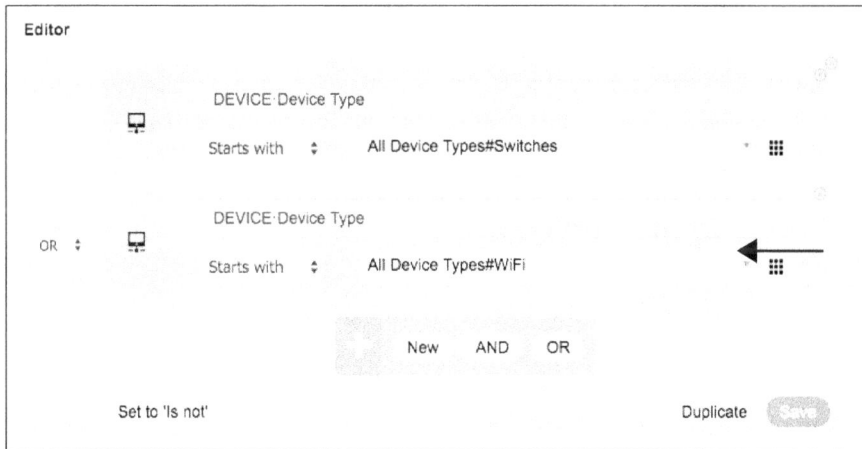

Figure 2-95   *Adding Wi-Fi to the Device Types for Policy Set*

In the section "Configuring a Policy for Differentiated Access," you built a policy set that would work perfectly for authorizing these wireless authentications right along with the wired authentications. The SGTs will be assigned just as they were for the switches, and the dACLs will be ignored because the WLC does not understand dACLs. If an ACL to limit traffic is desired, you would simply add the Airespace ACL name to the authorization profile.

That's it! You've finished configuring your network access devices and creating your policies in ISE, for now. In the next section, you will test your work and learn a bit about troubleshooting.

Verifying Dot1X and MAB

There are numerous ways to verify the authentication operations of switches and wireless controllers. There are always three locations that must be examined to validate a complete end-to-end transaction. Two of those three locations are much more common and easy to use. The three locations are:

- **Endpoint Supplicant:** For 802.1X authentications

- **Network Access Device (NAD):** For all authentications

- **Cisco ISE:** For all authentications

Endpoint Supplicant Verification

Verifying the authentications from the supplicant is a bit outside of the exam blueprint, so this book will not focus on it much. With Cisco AnyConnect NAM as your supplicant, you can use the DART tool to get a detailed communication, even perform packet captures at the endpoint. If the supplicant is an Apple supplicant (macOS or iOS), you must use the Apple Configurator app to extract and examine the supplicant logs.

With Windows, no supplicant logging is on by default. You must use the command line **netsh ras set tracing * enable** in order to enable the supplicant's logging capabilities. Once enabled, the logs will be added to the *%systemroot%\tracing* folder.

Network Access Device Verification

There are two NADs that we will focus on: Cisco switches and Cisco Wireless LAN Controllers. Each is quite different in how authentications are verified and will therefore be discussed in two separate sections.

Verifying Authentications with Cisco Switches

There are many items to test with a Cisco switch, with many tools being provided in Cisco IOS. The ones used most often are described in this section.

show aaa servers Command

One of the first things to check with a Cisco switch is the status of the RADIUS server (ISE). The **show aaa servers** command is a quick and simple way to see the current status of the ISE server from the switch's perspective. Example 2-1 shows the use of this command and its output. The main item of interest with this commands output is the State field. In Example 2-1, the current state is UP. Use this command to validate the server is up. If it is down, then communication to the RADIUS server will not occur.

Example 2-1 *show aaa servers Command*

```
3750-X#sho aaa servers

RADIUS: id 1, priority 1, host 10.1.100.232, auth-port 1812, acct-port 1813
     State: current UP, duration 93974s, previous duration 0s
     Dead: total time 0s, count 0
     Quarantined: No
     Authen: request 29, timeouts 0, failover 0, retransmission 0
             Response: accept 28, reject 0, challenge 0
             Response: unexpected 0, server error 0, incorrect 0, time 247795ms
             Transaction: success 29, failure 0
             Throttled: transaction 0, timeout 0, failure 0
     Author: request 0, timeouts 0, failover 0, retransmission 0
             Response: accept 0, reject 0, challenge 0
             Response: unexpected 0, server error 0, incorrect 0, time 0ms
             Transaction: success 0, failure 0
             Throttled: transaction 0, timeout 0, failure 0
     Account: request 35, timeouts 0, failover 0, retransmission 0
             Request: start 4, interim 4, stop 1
             Response: start 4, interim 4, stop 1
             Response: unexpected 0, server error 0, incorrect 0, time 16ms
             Transaction: success 35, failure 0
             Throttled: transaction 0, timeout 0, failure 0
     Elapsed time since counters last cleared: 1d2h6m
     Estimated Outstanding Access Transactions: 0
     Estimated Outstanding Accounting Transactions: 0
     Estimated Throttled Access Transactions: 0
     Estimated Throttled Accounting Transactions: 0
     Maximum Throttled Transactions: access 0, accounting 0
     Requests per minute past 24 hours:
             high - 2 hours, 15 minutes ago: 3
             low  - 2 hours, 6 minutes ago: 0
             average: 0
3750-X#
```

test aaa Command

Cisco switches have a built-in mechanism to send test authentications to the AAA servers they are configured to use. Using the **test aaa** command, you can verify that an authentication is successfully sent to and received by the RADIUS server. Example 2-2 shows the use of the **test aaa** command, and the successful response. The **test aaa** command will send an authentication request using PAP_ASCII, and return a RADIUS Access-Accept if successful or an Access-Reject if the password was incorrect. If no response is received, then the communication between the switch and the RADIUS server is not occurring. It is also possible that the authentication Allowed Protocols may not permit PAP_ASCII. So ensure the authentication is not being rejected for that reason.

Example 2-2   *test aaa command*

```
3750-X#test aaa group radius employee1 Cisco123 legacy
Attempting authentication test to server-group radius using radius
User was successfully authenticated.

3750-X#
```

show authentication session interface Command

One of the go-to commands that is in every implementer's "bag of tools" is the **show authentication session interface** command. Yes, the **interface** option is added to the base command of **show authentication session**, but that is to provide more detail. Example 2-3 shows the use of this command, and the output, which displays a successful MAB authentication. Use this command to validate that the authentications are being attempted, which are successful, what authorization results have been assigned, and much more.

Example 2-3   *show authentication session interface Command*

```
3750-X#show authentication session int g1/0/2
            Interface: GigabitEthernet1/0/2
          MAC Address: 0050.5687.0004
           IP Address: 10.1.10.50
            User-Name: 00-50-56-87-00-04
               Status: Authz Success
               Domain: DATA
      Security Policy: Should Secure
      Security Status: Unsecure
        Oper host mode: multi-auth
      Oper control dir: both
         Authorized By: Authentication Server
           Vlan Policy: N/A
       Session timeout: N/A
          Idle timeout: N/A
     Common Session ID: 0A013002000000110073D1F6
       Acct Session ID: 0x00000002
                Handle: 0xA9000012

Runnable methods list:
        Method   State
        mab      Authc Success
        dot1x    Not run
```

There are many facets of the authentication session that are displayed in this command's output. As this is one of the most important commands, the most important fields of the output are described in this list:

- **Interface:** This is the switch interface controlling the authentication session.

- **MAC Address:** This is the MAC address of the endpoint being authenticated.

- **IP Address:** The **ip device tracking** command enables the switch to keep track of which IP addresses are associated to the endpoints connected to the switch interface. This applies to both static IP addresses and DHCP assigned addresses. Once the switch has learned the endpoint's IP address, it will be listed here.

- **User-Name:** The RADIUS username is displayed here, when using 802.1X. When the authentication method is MAB, the username will be the same as the MAC address.

- **Status:** This lists the status of the authentication session, which may be Idle, Running, No Methods, Authc Success, Authc Failed, Authz Success, or Authz Failed.

- **Domain:** This lists the domain related to the host mode of the switch interface. With Multi-Auth, MDA, and Multi-Host modes, there are two domains: DATA and VOICE. Each authentication session may be assigned to one and only one of the domains.

- **Security Policy:** A better name for this would be MACSec Policy, as that is exactly what the field is referring to. MACSec is the friendly name for IEEE 802.1AE, a Layer 2 encryption standard. The three options are Should Secure, Must Secure, and Must Not Secure.

- **Security Status:** This displays the current MACSec encryption applied. When secure, there is encryption. When unsecure, there is no encryption.

- **Oper host mode:** This lists the host mode of the switch interface. Single-mode, multi-domain, multi-auth, and multi-host are the available modes of operation.

- **Common Session ID:** The session ID is used to correlate authentication session information between the NAD and the Cisco RADIUS server. When troubleshooting, it is often necessary to compare this value with the one shown within Cisco ISE.

- **Runnable methods list:** The available methods are mab, dot1x, or webauth. Possible states of the methods are Not Run, Running, Failed over, Authc Succeeded, and Authc Failed.

Sending Syslog to ISE

Syslog may be generated on Cisco IOS Software in many events. Some of the syslog messages can be sent to the ISE Monitoring Node (MNT) to be used in troubleshooting purposes. The ISE MNT node will correlate the syslog data with the RADIUS data, and display both together in a report. This can be very useful when checking to see if dACLs have been applied correctly, as well as other important validations.

It is not recommended to enable the sending of syslog messages to ISE from all NADs at all times, but to enable it only when troubleshooting.

To ensure Cisco ISE is able to compile appropriate syslog messages from the switch, use the following commands.

Step 1.   Enable syslog on the switch.

```
C3560X(config)#logging monitor informational
C3560X(config)#logging origin-id ip
C3560X(config)#logging source-interface <interface_id>
C3560X(config)#logging host <ISE_MNT_PERSONA_IP_Address_x>
transport udp port 20514
```

EPM is a part of the Cisco IOS Software module responsible for features such as Web Authentication and dACLs. Enabling EPM logging generates a syslog related to Downloadable ACL authorization, and part of the log can be correlated inside Cisco ISE when such logs are sent to Cisco ISE.

Step 2.   Set up standard logging functions on the switch to support possible troubleshooting/recording for Cisco ISE functions.

```
C3560X(config)#epm logging
```

Only the following NAD syslog messages are actually collected and used by Cisco ISE:

- AP-6-AUTH_PROXY_AUDIT_START
- AP-6-AUTH_PROXY_AUDIT_STOP
- AP-1-AUTH_PROXY_DOS_ATTACK
- AP-1-AUTH_PROXY_RETRIES_EXCEEDED
- AP-1-AUTH_PROXY_FALLBACK_REQ
- AP-1-AUTH_PROXY_AAA_DOWN
- AUTHMGR-5-MACMOVE
- AUTHMGR-5-MACREPLACE
- MKA-5-SESSION_START
- MKA-5-SESSION_STOP
- MKA-5-SESSION_REAUTH
- MKA-5-SESSION_UNSECURED
- MKA-5-SESSION_SECURED
- MKA-5-KEEPALIVE_TIMEOUT
- DOT1X-5-SUCCESS/FAIL

- MAB-5-SUCCESS/FAIL

- AUTHMGR-5-START/SUCCESS/FAIL

- AUTHMGR-SP-5-VLANASSIGN/VLANASSIGNERR

- EPM-6-POLICY_REQ

- EPM-6-POLICY_APP_SUCCESS/FAILURE

- EPM-6-IPEVENT:

- DOT1X_SWITCH-5-ERR_VLAN_NOT_FOUND

- RADIUS-4-RADIUS_DEAD

Verifying Authentications with Cisco WLCs

Cisco WLCs have a number of built-in mechanisms that may be used to verify authentications.

Current Clients

From the Cisco WLC GUI, navigate to **Monitor > Clients**, as shown in Figure 2-96. Figure 2-96 is a modified screen capture of the Clients UI, in an attempt to squeeze the important information onto the page of this book while retaining legibility of the text on the screen. If you are following along on your own WLC, you will see more fields displayed in the table.

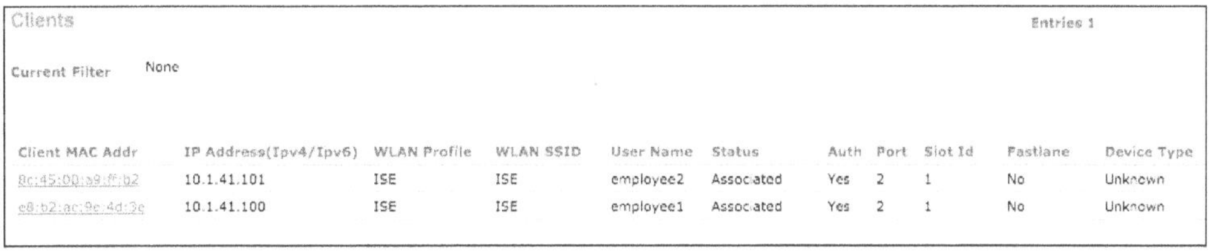

Clients											Entries 1
Current Filter	None										
Client MAC Addr	IP Address(Ipv4/Ipv6)	WLAN Profile	WLAN SSID	User Name	Status	Auth	Port	Slot Id	Fastlane	Device Type	
8c:45:00:a9:ff:b2	10.1.41.101	ISE	ISE	employee2	Associated	Yes	2	1	No	Unknown	
c8:b2:ac:9c:4d:3c	10.1.41.100	ISE	ISE	employee1	Associated	Yes	2	1	No	Unknown	

Figure 2-96 *Monitor Clients*

As shown in Figure 2-96, the Clients screen shows all current clients associated to the WLC, along with very valuable information, such as:

- **IP Address:** The IP address of the endpoint, when known.

- **AP Name:** The name of the Access Point to which the endpoint is associated.

- **WLAN Profile:** The name of the WLAN profile created in the WLC.

- **WLAN SSID:** The name of the SSID for the WLAN profile, of which the endpoint has associated.

- **User Name:** With 802.1X, the username is displayed. When the endpoint is authenticated via wireless MAB, the MAC address will be displayed.

■ **Auth:** If the endpoint/supplicant has authenticated successfully, it will be listed here.

■ **Device Type:** When the endpoint profile of the device is known, it will be displayed in this field.

For much more detail, click on the endpoint's MAC address. This brings up the details related to the individual endpoint's wireless session. As shown in Figure 2-97, a key value to verify for authentication is that the Policy Manager is in the "RUN" state. This means that "all systems are go" and the endpoint's traffic will flow through the wireless controller normally.

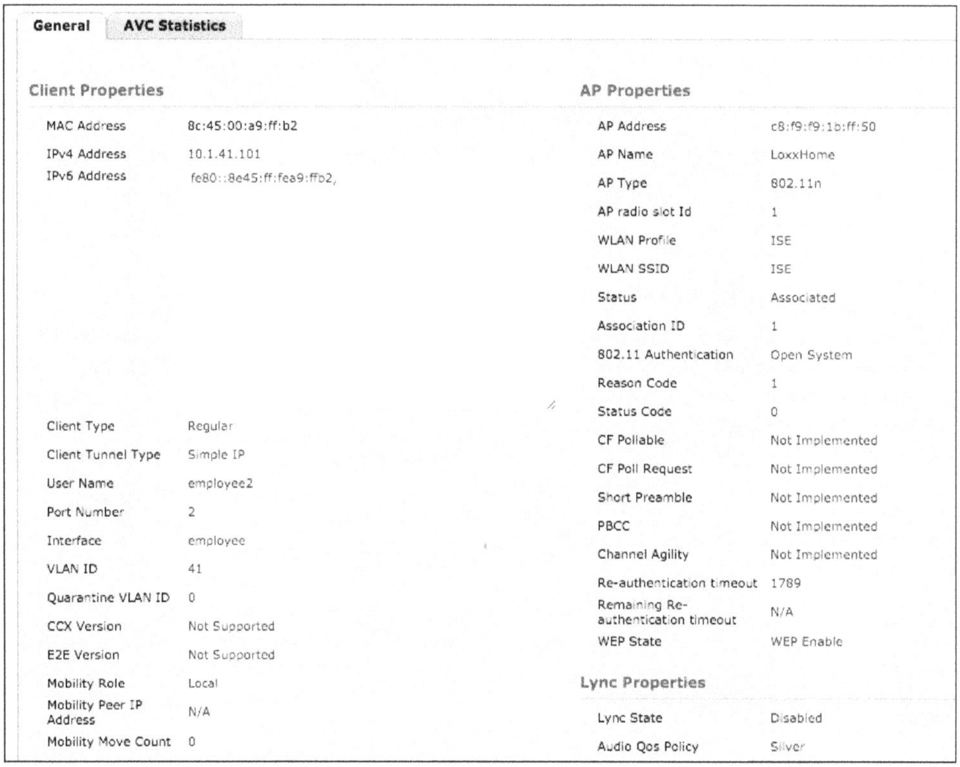

General	AVC Statistics		
Client Properties		**AP Properties**	
MAC Address	8c:45:00:a9:ff:b2	AP Address	c8:f9:f9:1b:ff:50
IPv4 Address	10.1.41.101	AP Name	LoxxHome
IPv6 Address	fe80::8e45:ff:fea9:ffb2,	AP Type	802.11n
		AP radio slot Id	1
		WLAN Profile	ISE
		WLAN SSID	ISE
		Status	Associated
		Association ID	1
		802.11 Authentication	Open System
		Reason Code	1
		Status Code	0
Client Type	Regular	CF Pollable	Not Implemented
Client Tunnel Type	Simple IP	CF Poll Request	Not Implemented
User Name	employee2	Short Preamble	Not Implemented
Port Number	2	PBCC	Not Implemented
Interface	employee	Channel Agility	Not Implemented
VLAN ID	41	Re-authentication timeout	1789
Quarantine VLAN ID	0	Remaining Re-authentication timeout	N/A
CCX Version	Not Supported	WEP State	WEP Enable
E2E Version	Not Supported		
Mobility Role	Local	**Lync Properties**	
Mobility Peer IP Address	N/A	Lync State	Disabled
Mobility Move Count	0	Audio Qos Policy	Silver

Figure 2-97   *Client Details*

Debug Client

The WLC provides a few very useful debug commands: **debug dot1x** and **debug client** *<mac-address>*. **debug dot1x** can be a bit overwhelming on a live network, but the **debug client** command will show only events related to that specific endpoint. Example 2-4 shows an example of the **debug client** command.

Example 2-4 *debug client <mac-address>*

```
(Cisco Controller) >debug client 10:bf:48:d0:05:67


*Dot1x_NW_MsgTask_7: Jul 12 18:40:28.059: 10:bf:48:d0:05:67 Received EAPOL EAPPKT
  from mobile 10:bf:48:d0:05:67
*Dot1x_NW_MsgTask_7: Jul 12 18:40:28.059: 10:bf:48:d0:05:67 Received Identity
  Response (count=1) from mobile 10:bf:48:d0:05:67
*Dot1x_NW_MsgTask_7: Jul 12 18:40:28.059: 10:bf:48:d0:05:67 Resetting reauth count 1
  to 0 for mobile 10:bf:48:d0:05:67
*Dot1x_NW_MsgTask_7: Jul 12 18:40:28.059: 10:bf:48:d0:05:67 EAP State update from
  Connecting to Authenticating for mobile 10:bf:48:d0:05:67
*Dot1x_NW_MsgTask_7: Jul 12 18:40:28.059: 10:bf:48:d0:05:67 dot1x - moving mobile
  10:bf:48:d0:05:67 into Authenticating state
*Dot1x_NW_MsgTask_7: Jul 12 18:40:28.059: 10:bf:48:d0:05:67 Entering Backend Auth
  Response state for mobile 10:bf:48:d0:05:67
*Dot1x_NW_MsgTask_7: Jul 12 18:40:28.067: 10:bf:48:d0:05:67 Processing
  Access-Challenge for mobile 10:bf:48:d0:05:67
```

Cisco ISE Verification

Validating the authentication from the NAD has a lot of value, but many times it is preferable to see the authentications from a central console. Cisco ISE is that central console. ISE has the Live Authentications Log (commonly known as Live Log).

Live Authentications Log

To view the Live Log, navigate to **Work Centers > Network Access > Overview > RADIUS Livelog**, as shown in Figure 2-98.

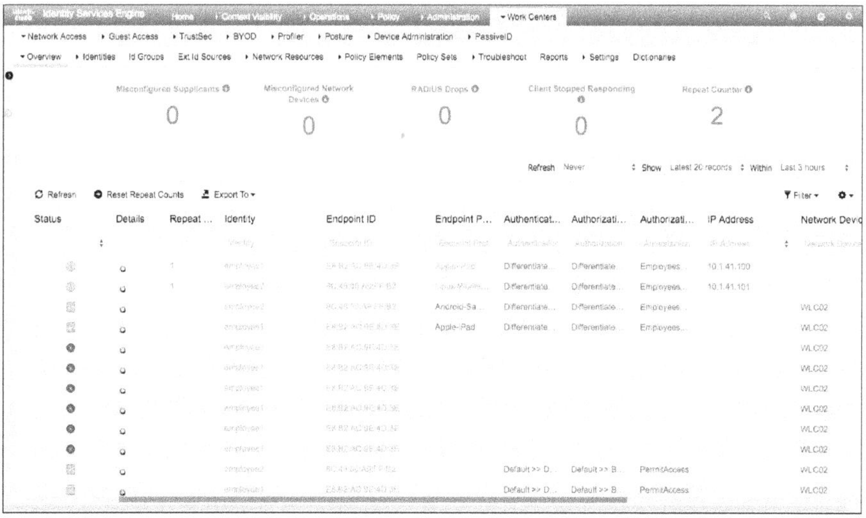

Figure 2-98 *RADIUS Live Log*

As shown in Figure 2-98, Live Log displays a near real-time display of authentication activity for the ISE Cube (a.k.a. ISE deployment). You can see successful wireless authentications from employee1 and employee2 on different devices. You will become very familiar with the Live Log as you practice with ISE.

Note For more on Live Log and the other troubleshooting tools in ISE, *Cisco ISE for BYOD and Secure Network Access, Second Edition*, which has a very detailed chapter on troubleshooting with ISE.

Summary

In this chapter, you learned all about basic network access controls with Cisco ISE and configuring the wired and wireless network access devices themselves. The next chapter will extend your knowledge with some not-so-basic network access control concepts such as profiling and web authentication, and more advanced concepts like passive authentications and EZ Connect.

Even with all the ISE topics covered in Chapters 2, 3, and 4 of this book, there is a lot more ground to cover, and there are entire books dedicated to ISE, such as the previously referenced *Cisco ISE for BYOD and Secure Unified Access, Second Edition*. If you are attempting the CCIE Security exam, it's highly recommended to also read that book in addition to this one.

Chapter 3

Beyond Basic Network Access Control

The previous chapter, "Basic Network Access Control," focused on network access authentication, authorization, and accounting (AAA), the process of validating who and what is allowed to access the network before providing that access. Within that scope, Chapter 2 focused on access controls for strong identities with 802.1X, as well as how to use MAC Authentication Bypass (MAB) to deal with the devices that do not have a (configured) supplicant.

For all authentication mechanisms, the authorization decision can include many different attributes, including the attributes of the endpoint type that is connecting to the network.

Besides the active authentication with 802.1X that ISE is well known for, it also provides additional authentication capabilities for sharing identities from other sources, it includes the ability to collect and leverage attributes to use within the authorization policy through profiling and posture services.

In this chapter, we will examine the topics of endpoint profiling with ISE and the many collaborative tools to aid with profiling. This chapter will also examine how to effectively integrate security solutions together with ISE as the center of a security ecosystem leveraging the platform exchange Grid (pxGrid).

Profiling with ISE

The Cisco Identity Services Engine Profiler is the component of the Cisco Identity Services Engine platform that is responsible for endpoint detection and classification. It does so by using a probe or series of probes that collects attributes about an endpoint. The Profiler then compares the collected attributes to predefined device profiles (basically, a set of signatures) to locate a match.

Why would profiling be an important technology for a company rolling out an identity solution? I'm glad you asked.

In the early days of identity-based networks and 802.1X, countless man-hours were spent identifying all the devices that did not have supplicants—in other words, the devices that could not authenticate to the network using 802.1X, such as printers and fax machines. You needed to identify all the switch ports that were connected to the printer and configure those ports to either:

- Not use 802.1X

- Use MAC Authentication Bypass (MAB)

MAB is an extension to 802.1X that allows the switch to send the device's MAC address to the authentication server. If that MAC address is in the "approved list" of devices, then the authentication server sends back an "accept" result, thereby allowing specific MAC addresses to skip authentication.

I'm sure you can imagine just how many man-hours were spent collecting and maintaining this list of MAC addresses. A company would need to institute a new onboarding process, so that when a new printer was added to the network, its MAC address was added to the list, and so forth.

Obviously, some enhancements to this onboarding process were required. There had to be some way to build this list more dynamically and save all those man-hours of prep and maintenance.

This is where profiling technology enters the picture. It allows you to collect attributes about devices from a multitude of sources such as DHCP, NetFlow, HTTP User-Agent strings, NMAP scans, and more. Those collected attributes are then compared to a set of signatures—similar to the way an intrusion prevention system (IPS) works. These signatures are more commonly referred to as *profiles*, or *profile policies*.

An example of building a profile would be:

1. Collecting a MAC address that belongs to Epson, inc.

2. Doing an NMAP scan on the IP address, and seeing common printer ports being open.

3. Based on those two attributes, assigning that device to the profile of "Epson Printer."

Profiling technology has evolved, as technology often does. Nowadays, your authentication server has the capability to use that profiling data for much more than just building the list of MAC addresses permitted to use MAB.

Cisco ISE uses the resulting collection and classification data from the profiler as conditions in the authorization policy. Now you can build an authorization policy that looks at much more than your identity credentials. You can combine a user's identity with the classification result and invoke specific authorization results.

Figures 3-1 and 3-2 show an example of a differentiated authorization policy based on profiling.

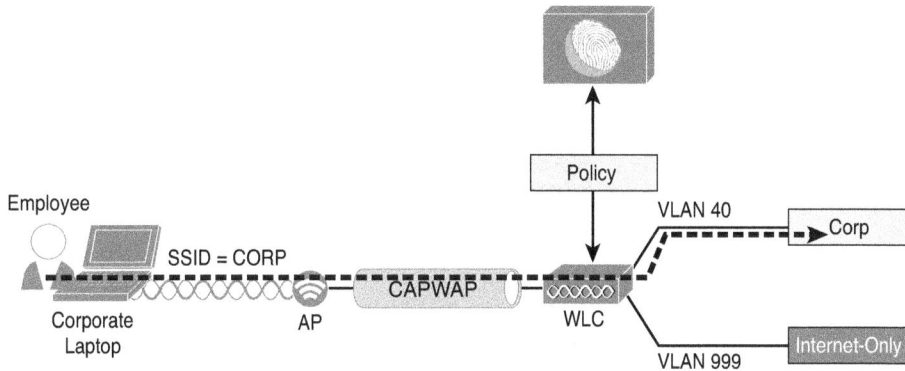

Figure 3-1   *Employee Using Corporate Laptop to Gain Full Access*

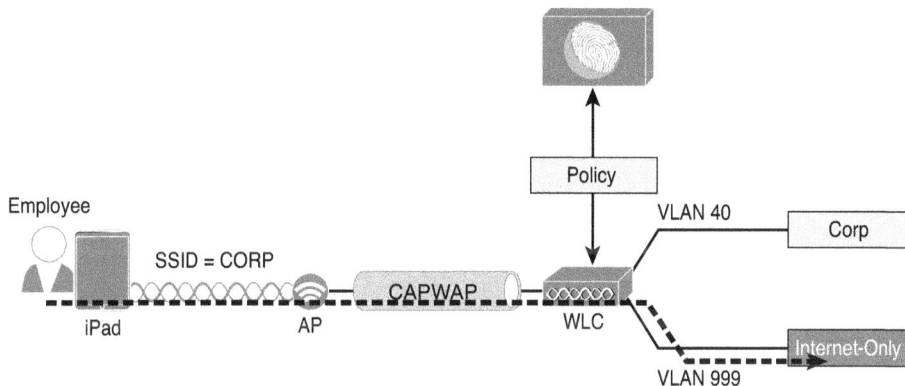

Figure 3-2   *Same Employee Credentials on an iPad Gets Limited Access*

Users who are using the same wireless SSID and the same credentials can be associated to different wired VLAN interfaces based on the device profile:

- Employees using a corporate laptop with their Active Directory user ID are assigned to the corporate VLAN and given full access to the network.

- Employees using mobile devices with their same Active Directory user ID are assigned to a Guest VLAN and provided Internet access only.

Although it might be quite intuitive to visualize the types of network access policies you will be able to create based on the device's profile, the design of where and how the Profiler collects the data about the endpoints requires thought and planning.

One of the first questions a security team may ask when discovering profiling with any network access control solutions is, "Can we use this as an anti-spoofing solution?" Remember that MAC Authentication Bypass is really a very limited replacement for a strong authentication. It would be fairly easy for a malicious user to unplug a printer from the wall, configure their laptop to use the same MAC address as the printer (spoofing), and gain access to the network.

You should always keep in mind that profiling is a technology that compares collected attributes about an endpoint to a set of signatures called *profiling policies* to make the best guess of what a device is. Can this type of technology be used to prevent spoofing? Sure. However, it is very difficult to accomplish anti-spoofing with this type of technology. It would require a lot of tuning, trial and error, and constant adjustment, which makes it too operationally expensive and untenable.

A best-practice approach is to use a least-privilege strategy instead. If the previously mentioned malicious user is successful in spoofing the MAC address of the printer and gains network access, what level of network access should that device have? In other words, the authorization policy for printers should not provide full network access but should provide a very limited subset of access instead; that is, a printer should be permitted to communicate using only network ports critical to printer operations (such as TCP port 9100 or 9600).

Profiling technology and the value it provides continue to evolve beyond MAB lists, beyond attributes in an authorization policy, and toward inventory of network-attached assets. Figure 3-3 illustrates this evolution of profiling, which will be evident in many aspects of ISE version 2.1 and beyond.

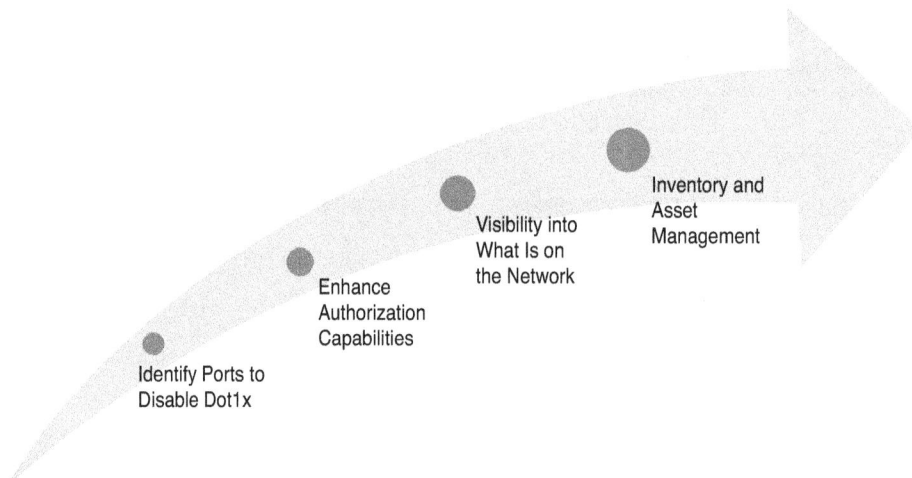

Inventory and Asset Management

Visibility into What Is on the Network

Enhance Authorization Capabilities

Identify Ports to Disable Dot1x

Figure 3-3 *Profiling Technology Evolution*

ISE Profiler Work Center

The ISE Profiler work center (**Work Centers > Profiler**) is designed to provide you, the ISE admin, with a single section of the GUI to accomplish all the tasks related to profiling. As with all work centers in the ISE GUI, you can pretty much get everything configured if you just follow the Profiler work center from top to bottom and left to right.

ISE Profiling Probes

The Cisco ISE solution is capable of providing access policies where the decisions may be made based on: Who, What, Where, When, How, and Other. Profiling is focused on the "what" elements of the policy; however, before the policy engine can know what the device is, you must first collect that data.

The Cisco ISE solution uses a number of collection mechanisms known as *probes*, software designed to collect data to be used in a profiling decision. An example of this would be the HTTP probe, which captures HTTP traffic to allow the Profiler to examine attributes from the traffic, such as HTTP User-Agent strings.

Without the probe being enabled on the policy server, the data would never be collected. The good news is that starting in ISE version 1.3, profiling and a default set of probes are enabled by default.

Probe Configuration

You enable the probes on each Policy Service Node (PSN) where appropriate. In the Administration GUI of the Policy Admin Node (PAN), navigate to **Work Centers > Profiler > Node Config**. The same screen may also be found under **Administration > System > Deployment**. From here, select the PSN that you are configuring the probes for. You will repeat these steps for each PSN in your deployment:

Step 1.   Select one of the Policy Service Nodes, as shown in Figure 3-4.

Step 2.   On the General Settings tab (not shown in Figure 3-4), the **Enable Profiling Service** check box is checked by default. This service is enabled by default on all PSNs, and is not configurable when in standalone mode.

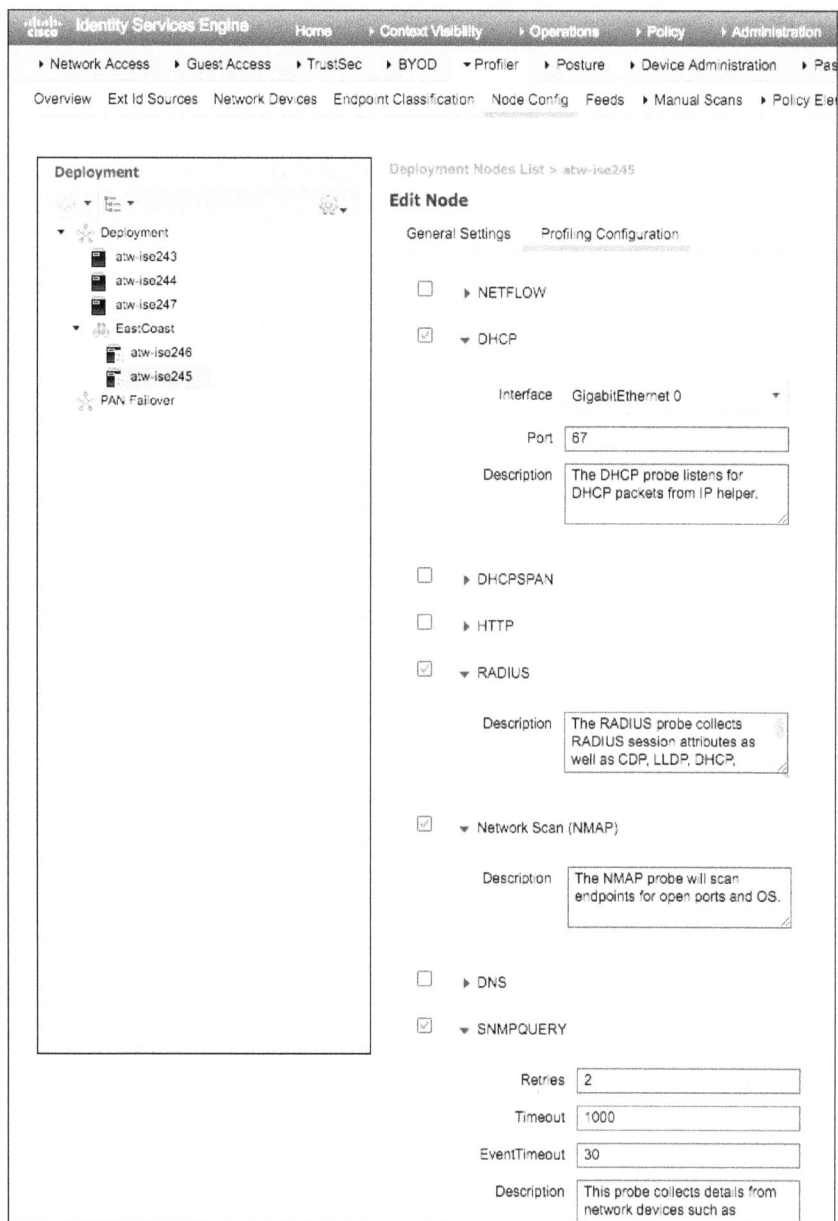

Figure 3-4 *ISE Deployment Screen*

Step 3.   Select the **Profiling Configuration** tab, as shown in Figure 3-4

There are 11 different probes on each Policy Services Node:

- NETFLOW

- DHCP

- DHCPSPAN

- HTTP

- RADIUS

- Network Scan (NMAP)

- DNS

- SNMPQUERY

- SNMPTRAP

- Active Directory

- PxGrid (added in ISE 2.4)

Each probe will be examined in detail, but not in order.

DHCP and DHCPSPAN Probes

DHCP can be one of the most useful data sources for an endpoint device. A primary use of DHCP in profiling is to capture the device MAC address; however, there are many other uses for the data. Much like HTTP, DHCP requests will also carry a User-Agent field that helps to identify the operating system of the device. Some organizations have been known to use a custom DHCP User-Agent string, which helps to identify the device as a corporate asset.

Very useful in classifying the device are not only the populated fields from the DHCP client, but other attributes, such as requested DHCP Options, DHCP Host-Name, and more.

There are two DHCP probes, each working in a slightly different way: DHCP an DHCPSPAN.

DHCP Probe

The DHCP probe requires the DHCP requests to be sent directly to the ISE PSN(s). This is often done by using the **ip helper-address** interface configuration command and is illustrated in Figure 3-5. Recall that you configured the **ip helper-address** command on the Catalyst switches in the "Configuring Cisco Catalyst Switches" section of Chapter 2.

The **ip helper-address** command on a Layer 3 interface will convert a DHCP broadcast (which is a Layer 2 broadcast) to a unicast or directed broadcast (which is sending the broadcast to all hosts on a specific subnet). Simply add the IP address of your PSN(s) to the list of "helper addresses" and it will be copied on all DHCP requests.

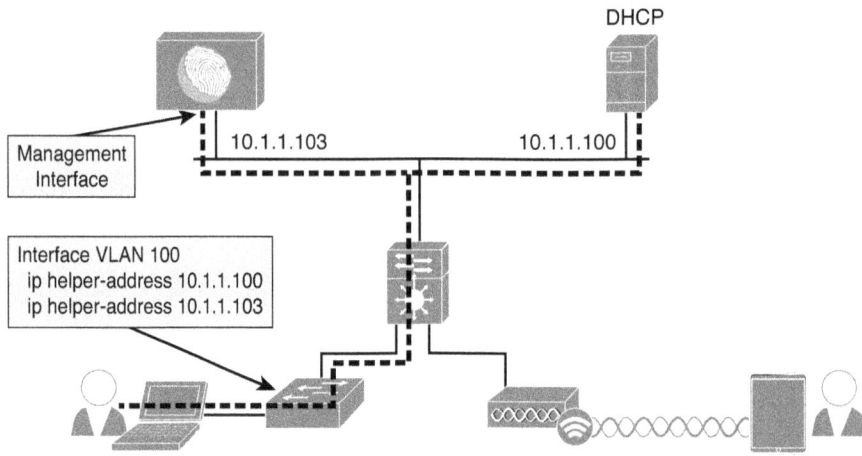

Figure 3-5 *DHCP with ip helper-address Logical Design*

DHCPSPAN Probe

Another way for ISE to glean the DHCP requests and even the DHCP responses is the use of a Switched Port Analyzer (SPAN) session in true promiscuous mode. A SPAN session copies all traffic to and from a source interface on a switch to the destination interface, which would be one of ISE's interfaces assigned to the DHCPSPAN probe. Figure 3-6 illustrates the logical design of using SPAN.

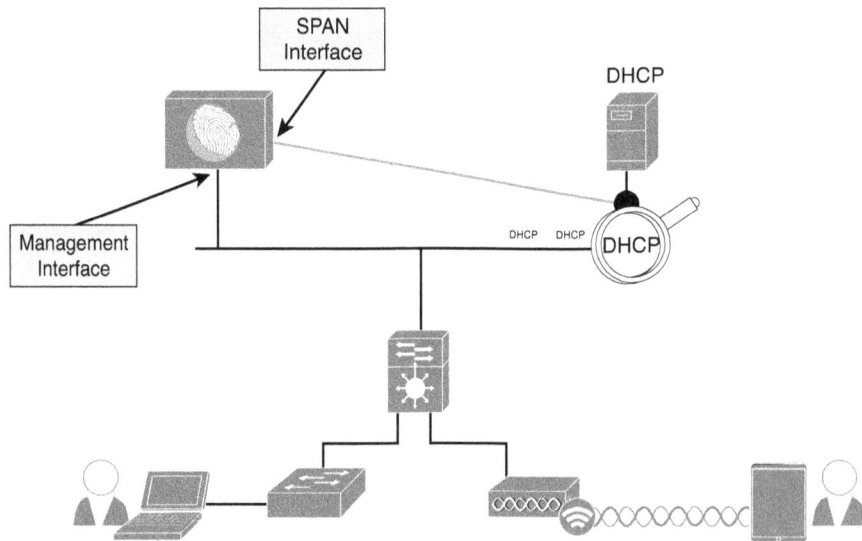

Figure 3-6 *DHCP SPAN Logical Design*

When using the SPAN method, you will need to consider where the best location is to create the SPAN session and gather the data. One recommended location is the DHCP server, where the DHCP probe will see both ends of the conversation (request and response). However, there are caveats to this method, such as, "What if the organization uses distributed DHCP servers?" This is why the non-SPAN method tends to be the most commonly deployed.

Note   The DHCPSPAN probe is actually more efficient under the covers with ISE. When doing performance tuning, we will often turn off DHCP and turn on DHCP SPAN. Keep in mind, we're still using the **ip helper-address** method of sending the data, but ISE will actually perform better when processing the DHCP data if it's parsed using the SPAN probe.

Considerations with the Cisco WLC

It is important to note that regardless of the SPAN or "helper-address" methods of using the DHCP probe(s), when using a Wireless LAN Controller (WLC), the WLC has a default configuration of acting as a DHCP proxy, which is its own form of a "helper address" where the WLC acts as a middleman for all DHCP transactions. Unfortunately, this behavior will have a negative effect on the DHCP probe, and must be disabled on the WLC. Upon doing so, the DHCP requests from wireless endpoints will appear as broadcast messages on the VLAN, and an **ip helper-address** statement should be configured on the Layer 3 interface of that VLAN (the switch or router).

Probe Configuration

There is minimal configuration required on the ISE side to enable the DHCP probe(s). On the Profiling Configuration tab, partially displayed in Figure 3-7, note the following:

- The DHCP Probe is enabled by default. This default setting has existed since ISE 1.3.

- GigabitEthernet 0 is the default interface. You can choose another interface or all interfaces. Multiple interfaces might not be individually selected. The choices are a single interface or all interfaces.

Figure 3-7 shows the DHCP probes. There should never be a need to enable both probes for the same interface. That would cause double processing of DHCP packets and be wasteful of system resources.

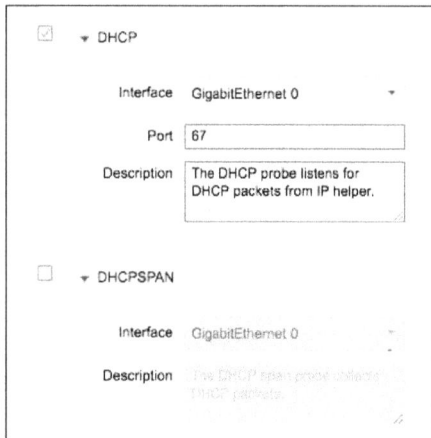

Figure 3-7   *DHCP Probes*

Note   If you are using only Device Sensor-capable infrastructure, neither DHCP probe needs to be enabled.

RADIUS Probe

RADIUS is the primary communication mechanism from a network access device (NAD) to the authentication server (ISE). There is very useful data to help classify a device that exists within RADIUS communication.

Originally, the RADIUS probe was focused on the MAC address and IP address of the device. By having this data conveyed in the RADIUS packet, ISE is able to build the all-important MAC-to-IP address bindings. Because the endpoint database uses MAC addresses as the unique identifier for all endpoints, these bindings are absolutely critical. Without them, the Layer 3 probes such as HTTP and NMAP would never work correctly.

The Calling-Station-ID field in the RADIUS packet provides the endpoint's MAC address, and the Framed-IP-Address field provides its IP address in the RADIUS accounting packet.

Additionally, the RADIUS probe will trigger the SNMPQUERY probe to poll the NAD (as described in the upcoming "SNMPQUERY and SNMPTRAP Probes" section).

Most importantly, with the proliferation of Device Sensor-capable switches and wireless controllers, the RADIUS probe becomes even more critical. Device Sensor is a feature in the switch or controller that collects endpoint attributes locally and then sends those attributes to ISE within RADIUS accounting packets.

By allowing the network device to proactively send the profiling data to ISE, the architecture has placed the collection agents as close to the endpoint as possible, at the point of access to the network. Additionally, the Device Sensor technology can eliminate the need to send the **ip helper-address** information to ISE as well as the need to reactively query the switches for CDP/LLDP information (again, see the "SNMPQUERY and SNMPTRAP Probes" section).

Considerations with RADIUS Probe

All NADs used with ISE should be configured to send RADIUS accounting packets. It is also important to note that the Cisco switch must learn the endpoint's IP address via DHCP snooping or through the ip-device-tracking function in order to fill in the Framed-IP-Address field.

It is possible for a network device to send too much information, or to send accounting packets too often. Cisco has gone to great lengths to ship switches and WLCs with default settings that are tuned for the best blend of performance and stability. It is not recommended to change the settings unless directed by Cisco TAC.

Probe Configuration

The RADIUS probe has been enabled by default since ISE version 1.3. There is minimal configuration available on the ISE side to enable or configure the RADIUS probe. From the Profiling Configuration tab (displayed earlier in Figure 3-4), just check the check box next to RADIUS to enable the RADIUS probe, as shown in Figure 3-8.

Notice there is not really any configuration possible with this probe; however, it is one of the most useful probes, especially when combined with Device Sensor.

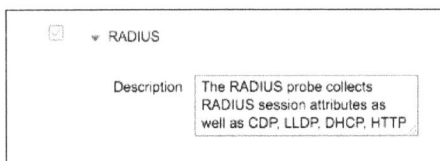

Figure 3-8 *RADIUS Probe*

Network Scan (NMAP) Probe

A very welcome improvement to ISE version 1.1 was the addition of the Endpoint Scanning (NMAP) probe (renamed to Network Scan). NMAP is a tool that uses port scans, SNMP, and other mechanisms to identity a device's operating system, or other attributes of the device. The NMAP probe may be manually run against a single IP address or subnet. More importantly, the profiling engine can be configured to react to a profiling event with a reactive NMAP probe.

For example, when an endpoint is discovered to be an "Apple-Device," ISE will automatically launch an NMAP OS scan against that endpoint to determine if the device is running macOS, or iOS. From the results of that scan, ISE will further classify the device as a MAC device or an iOS device, the latter of which can be further classified as an iPhone or iPad.

ISE version 2.1 enhances that NMAP probe even further by leveraging the Server Message Block (SMB) protocol for probing Windows devices, leveraging McAfee ePolicy Orchestrator (ePO) ports to recognize corporate assets, and allowing custom ports to be configured to help identify custom devices.

Considerations with the NMAP Probe

The NMAP probe is executed against an IP address or range of IP addresses; however, it is absolutely crucial to keep in mind that the endpoint database uses a MAC address as the unique identifier of any endpoint. As such, the Policy Services Node will rely on the MAC address-to-IP address binding to update an endpoint's attributes with the results of the NMAP scan; therefore, it is absolutely critical that the PSN has received valid information from the other probes.

The NMAP probe may be manually run against a single IP address or subnet, or (more commonly) an NMAP scan may be triggered as an action of a profile.

Probe Configuration

As with all the other probes, only minimal configuration is needed in this portion of the ISE GUI. From the Profiling Configuration tab (previously displayed in Figure 3-4), just check the check box next to the Network Scan (NMAP) probe to enable it, as shown in Figure 3-9.

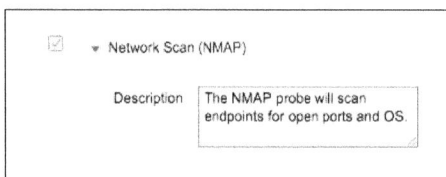

Figure 3-9 *Network Scan (NMAP) Probe*

In ISE version 2.0 and earlier, there was a manual scan option in the probe configuration; however, beginning with ISE 2.1, NMAP configuration can be found in **Work Centers > Profiler > Manual Scans**, as shown in Figure 3-10. This is a brilliant enhancement and provides a lot of control and visibility from a single place. To configure the NMAP probe:

Step 1.   From the Node drop-down list, select which node in the deployment to run the scan from. This is important, because certain nodes may be closer to the target network, or certain nodes may not be able to reach some networks.

Step 2.   In the Manual Scan Subnet field, provide a subnet or host address (/32) to scan from that host.

Step 3.   Under Scan Options, choose either the **Specify scan options** radio button, as shown in Figure 3-10, or the **Select an existing NMAP scan action** radio button, for saved scans.

If you choose Specify scan options, you can click **Save As Scan Action** to store it and add it to the library of available scan actions. Those available scan actions are listed in the drop-down list when you choose Select an existing NMAP scan action.

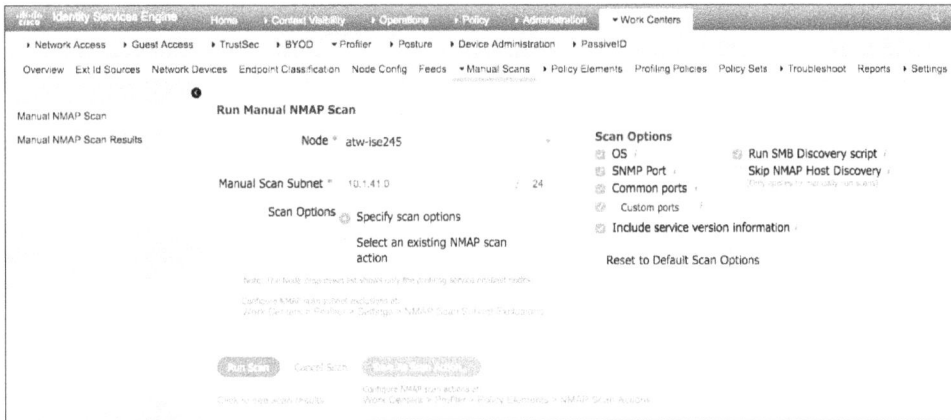

Figure 3-10   *Specifying Scan Options*

Let's examine the options that are available in the Scan Options section on the right side of Figure 3-10:

- **OS:** This option leverages the NMAP capability to attempt operating system detection by examining TCP/IP fingerprints. In other words, it tries to detect what the operating system is by the window size and other default settings in the TCP/IP stack.

- **SNMP Port:** Selecting this option will check to see if SNMP is listening on the discovered host. If it is, the SNMP probe can be used to perform an SNMP walk of the device.

- **Common ports:** This option will have NMAP scan a predefined set of TCP and UDP ports.

- **Custom ports:** Many times an organization will have devices that are rather unique to the environment, especially when Internet of Things (IoT) devices are in use. This option is used to define specific ports that would help identify those machines.

- **Include service version information:** When using this option, the NMAP scan will capture any detailed information that the vendor may display in banners associated to different services. This setting requires Common or Custom ports to be enabled as a prerequisite.

- **Run SMB Discovery script:** As previously mentioned, SMB is a protocol used mainly by Microsoft operating systems. SMB can be used to try to determine the OS, computer name, domain name, NetBIOS computer name, NetBIOS domain name, workgroup, time zone, and more.

- **Skip NMAP Host Discovery:** NMAP host discovery is used to probe to ensure an endpoint exists before performing deeper scans. The host discovery mechanism will provide better performance, by not wasting cycles trying to scan endpoints that are not there. Enabling this bypass option will ensure the deeper scans are always attempted on each IP address in the scan range. This setting only applies to manual scans. When an NMAP scan action is triggered, the host discovery will always be skipped and the endpoint will be deep scanned.

Note   Many environments will have pockets of devices that are fragile, and network scans can possibly cause them to reboot or fail in some way. Be sure that you filter those subnets when possible, and if you are a consultant—ensure that you have permission before manually scanning the network.

DNS Probe

The DNS probe is used to collect the fully qualified domain name (FQDN) of an endpoint using a DNS reverse lookup for the static or dynamic DNS registration of that endpoint. It is quite useful when looking for a specific DNS name format of corporate assets (Active Directory members).

Note   A reverse DNS lookup will be completed only when an endpoint is detected by one of the DHCP, RADIUS, HTTP, or SNMP probes.

To enable the DNS probe, simply check the check box next to DNS to enable it, as shown in Figure 3-11. This probe will use the name-server configuration from the Identity Services Engine node itself.

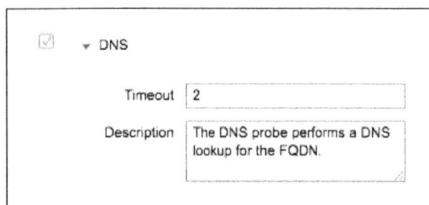

Figure 3-11   *DNS Probe*

SNMPQUERY and SNMPTRAP Probes

SNMP is used to query network access devices that do not yet support Device Sensor. After enabling the SNMPQUERY probe, ISE will poll all the SNMP-enabled NADs at the configured polling interval.

Note It is recommended to remove SNMP settings from NADs that support IOS Device Sensor, to avoid double work and wasted processing.

There are two SNMP probes: SNMPTRAP and SNMPQUERY.

SNMPTRAP Probe

The SNMP trap probe receives information from the configured NAD(s) that support MAC notification, linkup, linkdown, and informs. The purpose of this probe is twofold: it is used to trigger the SNMPQUERY probe and it is used as a toggle switch to allow the SNMPQUERY probe to reactively query a NAD instead of waiting for the periodic polling interval. Therefore, in order for SNMPTRAP to be functional, you must also enable the SNMPQUERY probe.

The SNMPTRAP probe receives information from the specific NAD(s) when the MAC address table changes or when link state changes on a switch port. To make this feature functional, you must configure the NAD to send SNMP traps or informs.

SNMPQUERY Probe

SNMPQUERY does the bulk of the work. There are actually three different kinds of SNMPQUERY probes:

- The System probe will poll all NAD that are configured for SNMP at the configured interval.

- The Interface probe occurs in response to an SNMPTRAP or RADIUS Accounting "Start" packet (only if the SNMPTRAP probe is enabled).

- The NMAP probe will trigger the SNMP walk of an endpoint.

When querying a NAD, ISE looks for interface data (which interface, which VLAN), session data (if the interface is Ethernet), and Cisco Discovery Protocol (CDP) and Link Layer Discovery Protocol (LLDP) data. The CDP and LLDP data can be very useful in identifying a device type by its registered capabilities and similar attributes.

Note For distributed deployments, NAD polling is distributed among all PSNs enabled for SNMPQUERY probes.

Probe Configuration

Although these probes have configuration options, such as the trap types to examine and the SNMP port, it is recommended to leave these at their default settings unless directed otherwise by Cisco TAC.

Step 1.   Check the check boxes next to the SNMPQUERY and SNMPTRAP probes to enable them.

Step 2.   For the SNMPTRAP probe, select either the GigabitEthernet 0 interface or all interfaces. You can't select multiple interfaces individually. The choice is a single interface or all interfaces.

Figure 3-12 shows the enabling of the SNMP probes and their default settings.

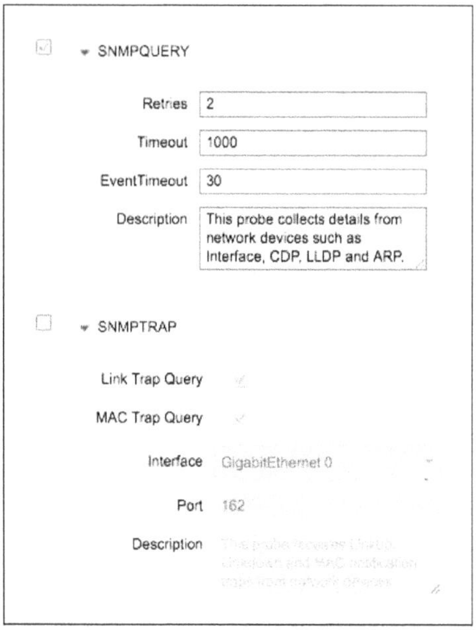

Figure 3-12   *SNMP Probes*

Active Directory Probe

Added to ISE in version 2.1, the Active Directory (AD) probe is designed to help answer the question, "Is this endpoint a corporate asset?" This probe leverages what is known as the Active Directory Run Time (ADRT), which is the powerful Active Directory connector introduced back in ISE 1.3. Once a computer hostname is learned from either the DHCP or DNS probe, the AD probe will search in AD for attributes and allow the following attributes to be used in profiler policy creation:

■ **AD-Host-Exists:** If the endpoint exists in AD, then it helps identify that it could be a corporate system.

- **AD-Join-Point:** Defines the AD domain where the host is located.

- **AD-Operating-System:** The OS type version of the endpoint.

- **AD-OS-Version:** The version of that endpoint's OS.

- **AD-Service-Pack:** The service pack version of the endpoint.

As you can see in the list of attributes above, this probe provides ISE admins some decent flexibility when identifying systems and gleaning some inventory of those systems. Figure 3-13 shows the Active Directory probe configuration, where you can that the configuration is to enable or disable the probe, and to configure the number of days before rescanning for attributes.

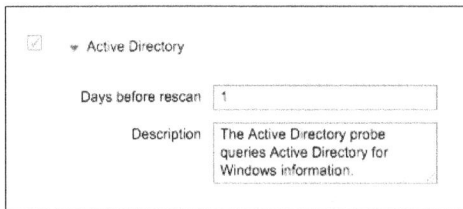

Figure 3-13 *Active Directory Probe Configuration*

HTTP Probe

When an application uses HTTP, such as a web browser or even software like Microsoft Outlook and Windows Update, it typically identifies itself, its application type, operating system, software vendor, and software revision by submitting an identification string to its operating peer. This information is transmitted in an HTTP request-header field called the User-Agent field.

Cisco Identity Services Engine will utilize the information in HTTP packets, especially the User-Agent field, to help match signatures of what "profile" a device belongs in.

The User-Agent field can tell ISE the difference between the various Windows versions, Android, Linux, macOS/Mac OS X, and iOS device types, sometimes delivering OS and version details not available from other profile attributes. Example 3-1 shows the User-Agent string for Mac OS X 10.11.

Example 3-1 *User-Agent String for Mac OS X 10.11 (El Capitan)*

```
Mozilla/5.0 (Macintosh; Intel Mac OS X 10_11) AppleWebKit/601.1.27 (KHTML, like
  Gecko) Version/8.1 Safari/601.1.27
```

Example 3-2 shows the User-Agent string for Windows 8.1.

Example 3-2   *User-Agent String for Windows 8.1*

```
Mozilla/5.0Mozilla/5.0 (Windows NT 6.3; WOW64; Trident/7.0; Touch; rv:11.0)
  like Gecko
```

You can see that the HTTP packet inspection is a key element to profiling effectively, and Figure 3-14 illustrates the logical design of ISE examining the HTTP packets.

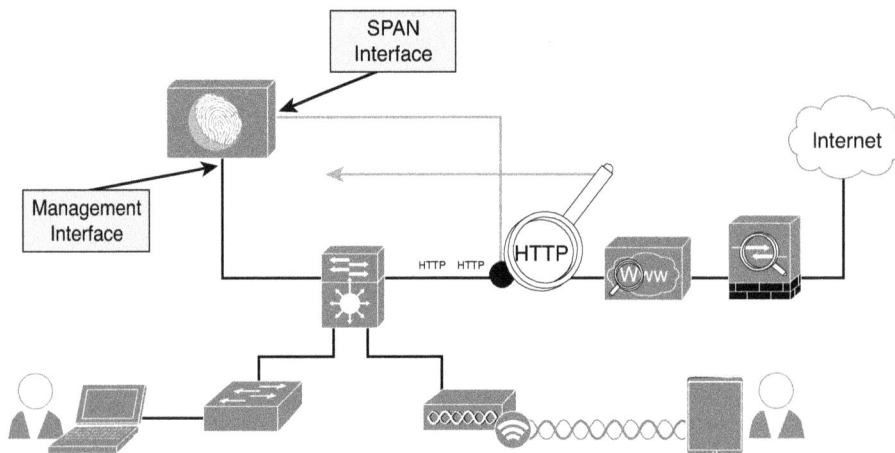

Figure 3-14   *HTTP SPAN Logical Design*

There are two primary mechanisms for the HTTP probe to collect the HTTP traffic:

■ **Use a SPAN session in true promiscuous mode:** When using the SPAN method, you will need to consider where the best place is to create the SPAN session and gather the data. One recommended location is the Internet edge, where a network organization would typically deploy a web security appliance such as the Cisco IronPort WSA.

■ **Use a SPAN session in conjunction with a filter to limit the traffic visible to ISE:** Another option with the SPAN design is the use of VLAN ACLs (VACLs) on a Catalyst 6500 Series switch, or ACL-based SPAN sessions on a Nexus 7000 Series switch. These options allow you to build an ACL that defines exactly what traffic you wish to capture and send along to ISE—instead of a pure promiscuous SPAN, where the ISE interface will see all traffic. This is a better way to manage the resource utilization on your ISE server, when available.

As you can see, there are multiple ways to use the HTTP probe, and you should consider what works best for your environment and then deploy with that approach. In many environments, it is best to not use SPAN at all, but to leverage ISE's own portals to capture the User-Agent strings.

To configure the HTTP probe, check the check box next to the HTTP probe, as shown in Figure 3-15. Select either the GigabitEthernet 0 interface or all interfaces.

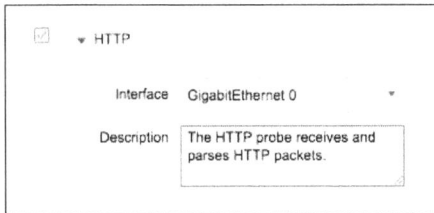

Figure 3-15 *HTTP Probe*

HTTP Profiling Without Probes

ISE deployments do not require the use of SPAN sessions or VACLs to receive the HTTP User-Agent strings. The Web Portal system within ISE itself has been outfitted to collect the User-Agent details from the web browser that is communicating with an ISE portal. This occurs regardless of profiling being enabled or not. The User-Agent is used to know which operating system is connecting and therefore which agent or client to send to the endpoint (in the cases of client provisioning and native supplicant provisioning).

When any portal collects that User-Agent, it is automatically passed over to the profiling engine within ISE, without requiring the HTTP probe to be enabled. It is a simple and efficient way to get the extremely valuable User-Agent string without having to rely on the computationally expensive SPAN methods.

NetFlow Probe

NetFlow is an incredibly useful and undervalued security tool. Essentially, it is similar to a phone bill. A phone bill does not include recordings of all the conversations you have had in their entirety; instead, it is a summary record of all calls sent and received.

Cisco routers and switches support NetFlow, sending a "record" of each packet that has been routed, including the ports and other very usable information.

Just enabling NetFlow in your infrastructure and forwarding it all to ISE can quickly oversubscribe your PSN. If you are planning to use the NetFlow probe, it is highly recommended that you have a robust solution, such as Cisco Stealthwatch (from Cisco's acquisition of Lancope), to filter out any unnecessary data and only send what you truly need to ISE. For that reason, this probe is not focused on heavily in this book, and it is recommended to perform extensive planning prior to its use.

Configuring the NetFlow probe is limited to checking the check box next to the NetFlow probe and selecting either the GigabitEthernet 0 interface or all interfaces. Figure 3-16 shows the enabled NetFlow probe.

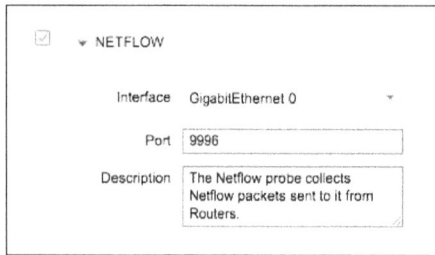

Figure 3-16 *NetFlow Probe*

Aaron Woland and Vivek Santuka developed a methodology for enabling NetFlow to ISE as needed, with a goal of using the NetFlow probe in environments where it is required for profiling of IoT-style devices, such as medical endpoints. You can read about the solution, titled "Triggered NetFlow," on Aaron's blog: https://www.networkworld.com/blog/secure-network-access/.

pxGrid Probe

Added in ISE version 2.4, the pxGrid probe allows external systems to publish profiling data that ISE can ingest. At the time of writing, only a few ecosystem partners were publishing to this probe, such as CloudPost (an IoT profiling solution).

Profiling Policies

Collecting the data for profiling is only part of the solution. You also need to have endpoint signatures and a policy engine to compare the collected attributes to those signatures, which will lead to the assignment of the endpoint profile.

The profiling engine works a lot like an intrusion detection system (IDS), comparing traffic to a set of signatures to identify suspicious activity. The profiling engine has hundreds of built-in signatures, called *profiles (aka: profiling policies)*, that are designed to match when certain attributes exist. Additionally, much like an IDS, there is an update service to allow the engine to download new signatures.

Profiling Feed Service

Although ISE comes with a very large and comprehensive list of signatures to classify endpoints (profiles), many more devices are produced almost daily (think of the next smartphone, or version of the phone's OS), and there is a constant stream of new profiles created by Cisco that should be shared to the ISE deployments of the world.

That's why Cisco created a profiler feed service. As new devices are released to market: Cisco, Cisco partners and device manufacturers create profiles for them. Cisco also has a team that focuses on profile creation. The ISE profiler feed service is used to distribute these new profiles after the Quality Assurance (QA) team has approved them.

Configuring the Profiler Feed Service

Configuring the feed service is straightforward. Once enabled, it will reach out to Cisco.com at the set time interval and download any published profiles. There is an option to send an email alert to the administrator when an update occurs, an undo button for reversing the latest update, a test button to ensure the feed service is reachable and working, a link to view a report on the latest updates, and lastly a section to send your information to Cisco, to help with understanding how many customers are utilizing the feed service.

Figure 3-17 shows an enabled and configured Profiler Feed Service screen, which is located under **Work Centers > Profiler > Feeds.**

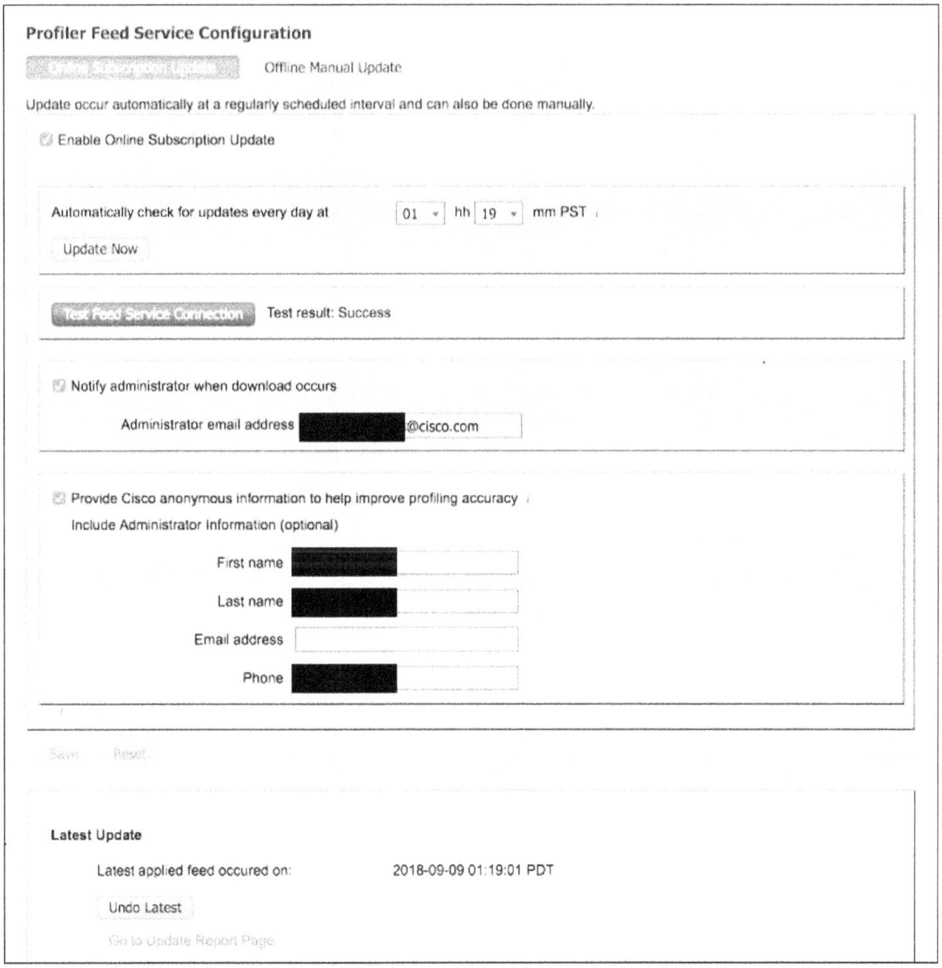

Figure 3-17 *Configured Profiler Feed Service*

When you don't want to wait for a configured interval for the feed service to run, click the **Update Now** button. Be cautious with manually updating the profiles during a production workday. When the profiles are updated, it will cause all endpoints in the endpoint database to be compared against the new list of profiles. In other words, a complete re-profiling of endpoints occurs, and that can be very processor intensive.

Endpoint Profile Policies

The profiler probes are collecting attributes of endpoints, while the profiler policies are similar to "signatures," which are defining the endpoint profiles themselves. For example, in order to match an Apple-Device profile, the endpoint must have a MAC address beginning with one of Apple's OUIs.

Each endpoint profile policy defines a set of attributes that must be matched for a device to be classified as that endpoint type. ISE has a very large number of predefined profile policies, and you have just read about the feed service that's used to update those policies and provide new ones.

You can view the endpoint profile policies by navigating to **Work Centers > Profiler > Profiling Policies**, as shown in Figure 3-18.

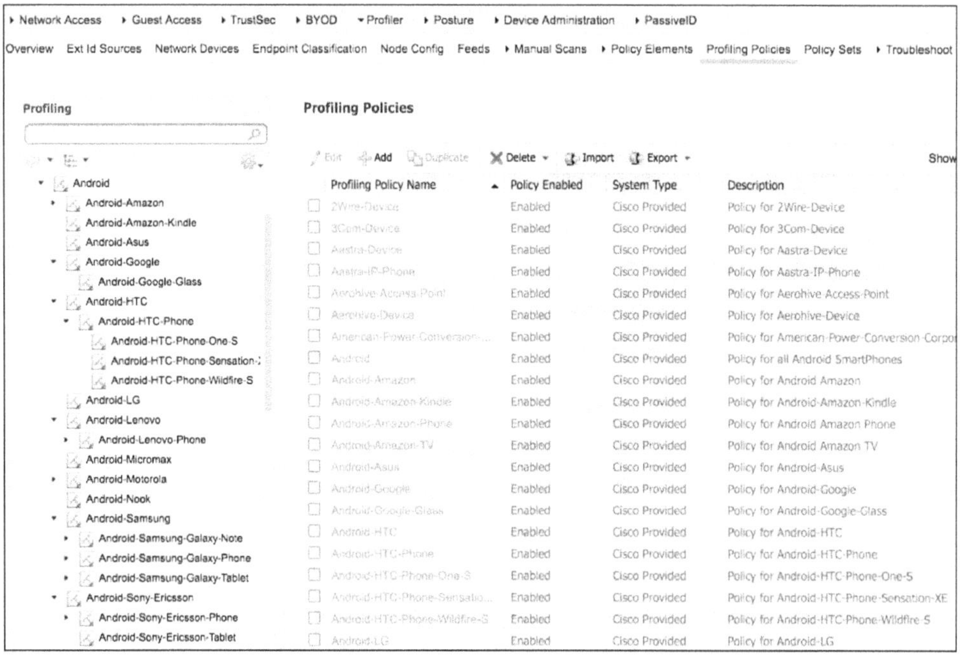

Figure 3-18 *Viewing Profiling Policies*

Each profile is listed as either Cisco Provided or Administrator Modified. This classification ensures that the feed service will not override a profile that has been changed by the administrator.

Profiles are hierarchical and inclusive in nature, and you may pick any level to use within your authorization policies, enabling you to be very specific or broad in your rules. As an example, examining Figure 3-19, you see the existence of a parent policy named Android with a child policy named Android HTC, which has another child policy named Android HTC-Phone (**Android > Android-HTC > Android-HTC-Phone**).

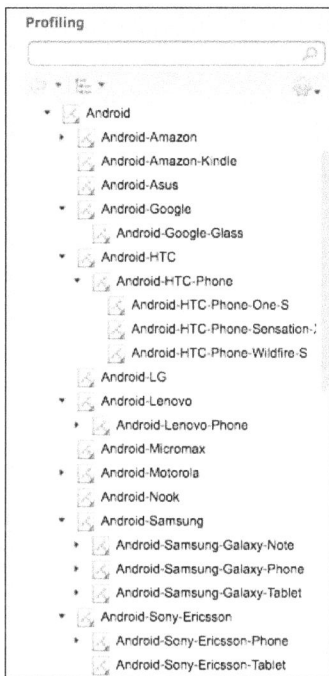

Figure 3-19 *Android Profile Hierarchy Example*

When building an authorization policy, you can choose to use the profile at any point in that chain. If you were to select Android, it would apply to all devices classified as Android as well as anything classified as a child profile of Android. For example, it would include Android-Sony-Ericsson-Tablet.

Context Visibility

In ISE 2.0 and earlier, the endpoints were kind of hidden under Administration > Identity Management > Identities > Endpoints. Beginning with ISE 2.1, the endpoints have been brought front and center with a major presence on the main dashboard, a full Profiler work center, and a new GUI area known as Context Visibility.

Start by examining the endpoint attributes and comparing them to the profiling policies:

Step 1.   Navigate to **Context Visibility > Endpoints**.

Context Visibility is meant to be a centralized location to work with your entire asset inventory. It maintains the users, applications, network devices, and endpoints that have been seen along with their attributes and information about the authentications they have been involved with; as well as the threats and vulnerabilities associated with the endpoints when ISE is configured for Threat Centric NAC (TC-NAC).

Step 2.   Click the **Endpoint Classification** tab, as shown in Figure 3-20.

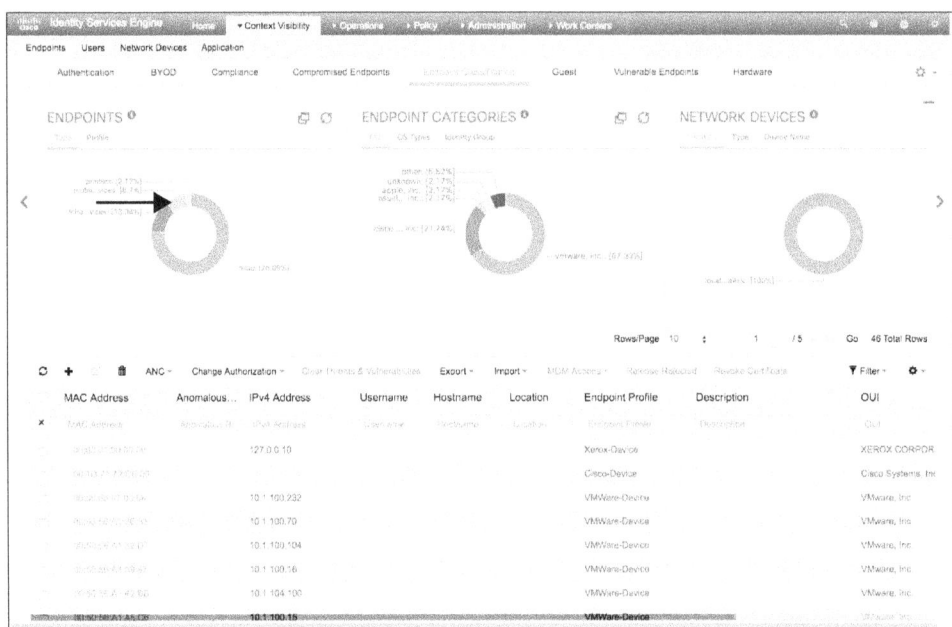

Figure 3-20   *Endpoint Classification*

Step 3.   In the Endpoints dashlet in the upper-left, click on **mobile devices**. This begins to filter the list, as pointed out in Figure 3-21.

Step 4.   Click the MAC address **E8:B2:AC:9E:4D:3E** (in this example) to bring up the endpoint details, shown in Figure 3-22. Notice that the Endpoint Policy (the profile of the device) is Apple-iPad. However, the Identity Group Assignment is Profiled.

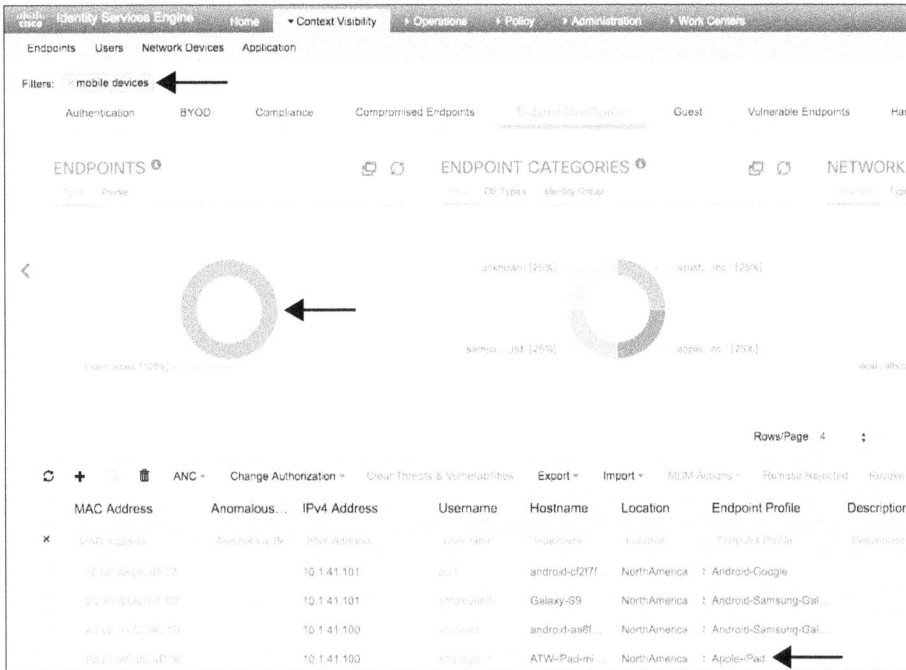

Figure 3-21 *Endpoint Classification: Filtered for Mobile Devices*

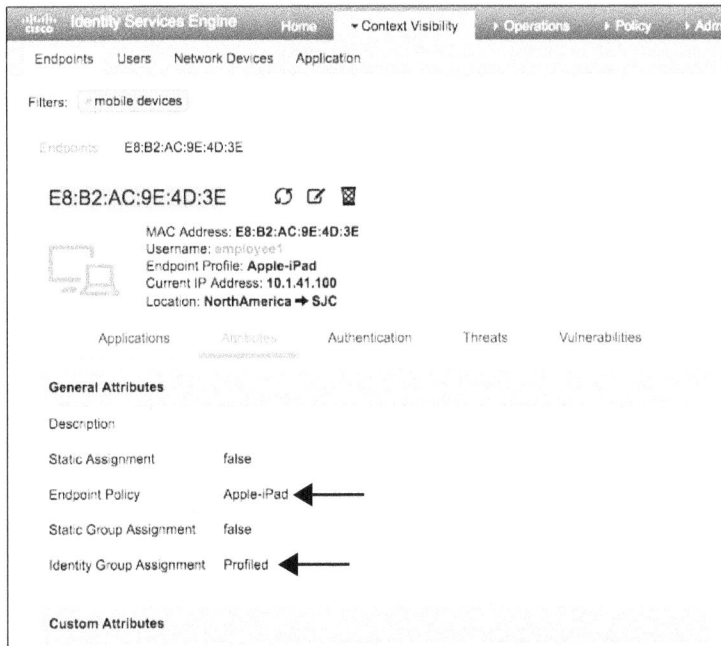

Figure 3-22 *Endpoint Details: E8:B2:AC:9E:4D:3E*

Step 5.   Scroll down in the endpoint details and you see that the EndPointSource is the SNMPQuery Probe, as shown in Figure 3-23. This is actually a misnomer. It was actually learned through multiple probes, including DHCP, HTTP, and then finally with the NMAP probe's SNMP walk of the endpoint.

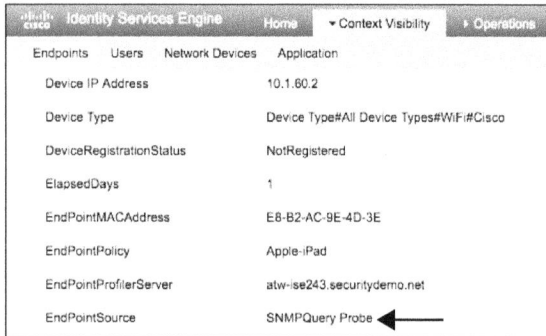

Figure 3-23   *Endpoint Details: EndPointSource*

Logical Profiles

When ISE 1.0 was first released it was quickly requested by many customers to have a grouping of profiles that is not hierarchical; for example, to create a profile group named "IP-Phones" that contains all the individual profiles of IP phones, Cisco and non-Cisco alike.

ISE 1.2 answered that request. With that release, Cisco introduced the new concept of *logical profiles*. These logical profiles are exactly what customers requested: a grouping of profiles. ISE version 2.1 adds more logical profiles such as Cameras, Gaming Devices, Home Network Devices, Medical Devices, and more.

To examine the logical profiles in ISE, navigate to **Work Centers > Profiler > Profiling Policies > Logical Profiles**, as shown in Figure 3-24.

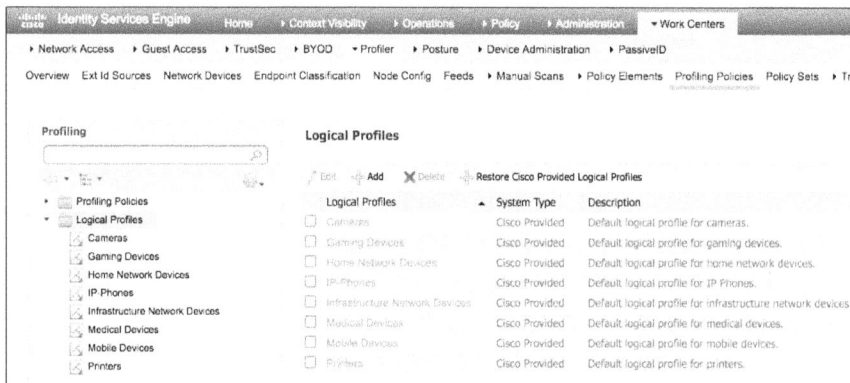

Figure 3-24   *Logical Profiles*

Click the **Mobile Devices** logical profile to examine its contents, as shown in Figure 3-25. Notice that the logical profile contains Android, Apple-iPad, and other mobile endpoint profiles.

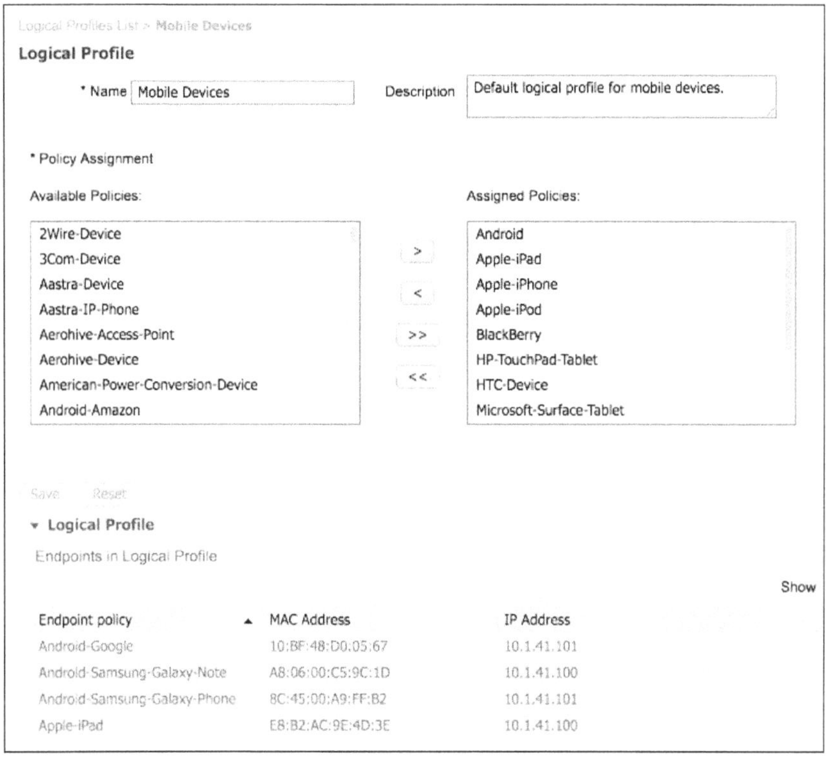

Figure 3-25 *Mobile Devices Logical Profile*

Logical profiles are not limited to being defined by Cisco only. You can also create your own.

ISE Profiler and CoA

When using an endpoint profile as an attribute within your authorization policy, you will be providing differentiated results for specific profiles. However, there is often a "chicken and egg" phenomenon happening simultaneously. You cannot provide the right access to a device without knowing what that device is, yet you cannot find out what the device is without providing some level of access so the endpoint will be active on the network and ISE can identify the endpoint profile.

Welcome to the concept of Change of Authorization (CoA). Without CoA, the only time a policy server such as ISE is permitted to send a command to the NAD is during a response to an authentication request. This creates numerous issues because there is not a way to disconnect a bad actor from the network or change the level of access an endpoint is permitted to have based on a newer data element that has been learned at the policy engine. The current authorization to the network would have to be sustained until the next time the endpoint has to authenticate.

Because the authorization policy can be configured to send different results for an endpoint before it is profiled, and then send another level of authorization after the endpoint profile becomes more solidified, and the final result after the endpoint profile is definitely known, you cannot wait for the next authentication request each time. Instead, the profiling engine can use CoA to change the level for each state the endpoint goes through.

To describe that a little bit more succinctly, because ISE will learn more about endpoints at any time, ISE may send a Change of Authorization (CoA) to the network access device, in order to have a different level of access applied to the session.

Two main areas for configuring CoA with profiling exist:

- A global setting that enables CoA for profiling in the ISE deployment

- The capability to configure a CoA on a per-profile basis

Global CoA

To enable CoA for profiling in the ISE cube, and to configure the CoA type used by profiling globally, navigate to **Work Centers > Profiler > Settings**, as shown in Figure 3-26.

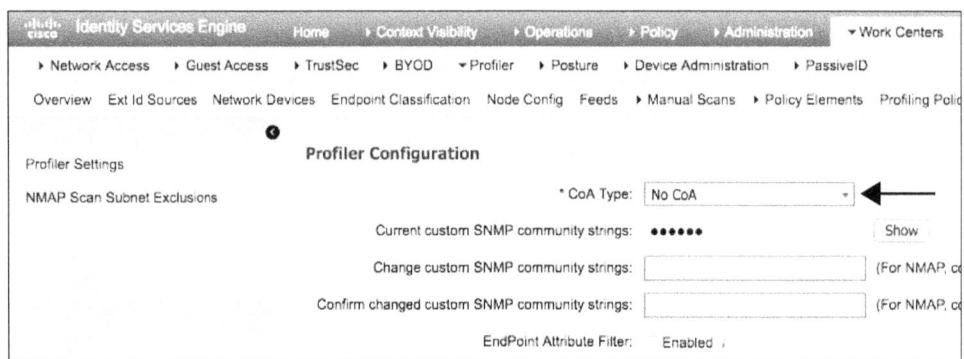

Figure 3-26 *Profiler Global Settings*

As shown in Figure 3-26, the default CoA Type setting is **No CoA**. Click the drop-down arrow to see the other two choices: Port Bounce and Reauth.

The Port Bounce CoA option will perform a **shutdown** on the switch port and then perform a **no shutdown** to re-enable it. This causes the link state to change, simulating the unplugging and plugging of network cable. The benefit to this type of CoA is that many devices will try to renew their DHCP-assigned IP addresses when the link state changes.

Additionally, there is a built-in failsafe to never send a Port Bounce when there is more than one MAC address seen on the switch port. That failsafe is in place to ensure there is no negative impact on IP telephony. When more than one MAC address exists on the switch port, a Reauth will be sent instead.

The Reauth CoA will instruct the NAD to initiate a new authentication to the endpoint, sending another EAPoL Start message to trigger the supplicant to send the credentials again, or (in the case of MAB) the NAD will resend a RADIUS authentication with the endpoint MAC address as the identity credential. Either way, there will be a new authentication, but that authentication will maintain the same authentication session ID. By maintaining the session ID, ISE is able to stitch together the multiple states of the endpoint.

Regardless of the CoA type used, ISE has now forced a new authentication attempt so that a different authorization result may be sent to the NAD, providing the correct level of network access with the latest profiling information being used. Setting a global CoA type to Port Bounce is not recommended, however. The safer bet is to use the Reauth option.

Once the profiler CoA is enabled globally, a CoA will automatically be sent for any endpoint that transitions from unknown to any known profile.

Global Profiler Settings

There are additional settings related to profiling that are set at the global (system-wide) level, not just the global CoA type. There are the SNMP community strings for NMAP SNMP walks, and the Enabled setting for endpoint attribute filtering.

Configure SNMP Settings for Probes

The SNMPQUERY probe will use the SNMP community strings that are defined as part of the NAD entry under **Administration > Network Resources > Network Devices.** Each NAD could theoretically have a different community string.

As described in the "Network Scan (NMAP)" section, NMAP will use SNMP to examine endpoints. In order for this to function, ISE profiler must know what SNMP community strings to use. The community strings to use are configured within **Work Centers > Profiler > Settings** by listing each community string one by one with a comma separating each value. Once they are saved, the two text boxes are erased, and you click the **Show** button to see the configured strings.

Endpoint Attribute Filtering

Profiler can and does collect a lot of data about endpoints. It will store all that data and replicate that data to the other ISE nodes in the deployment. In order to help keep the replication traffic down, ISE has Endpoint Attribute Filters, which are enabled by navigating to **Work Centers > Profiler > Settings** (previously shown in Figure 3-26) and clicking the **Enabled** check box.

When endpoint attribute filtering is enabled, profiler will build a white list of attributes that are used in the existing profiler policies. In other words, profiler will examine every policy that is enabled and create a list of attributes that are needed for all those policies. Only those attributes will now be collected and stored in the endpoint database.

Use of the Endpoint Attribute Filter is highly recommended but only after a deployment has been up and running properly for an extended period of time, in order to filter out unnecessary attributes, but do not enable it too quickly, or you could accidently filter out critical attributes.

NMAP Scan Subnet Exclusions

Another global setting for the Profiler service is NMAP Scan Subnet Exclusions, shown in Figure 3-27. Many organizations have special devices that can be negatively impacted by being scanned, and therefore the organizations prohibit it. That is where this setting comes into play. It provides the ability to prevent the NMAP engine from scanning those networks.

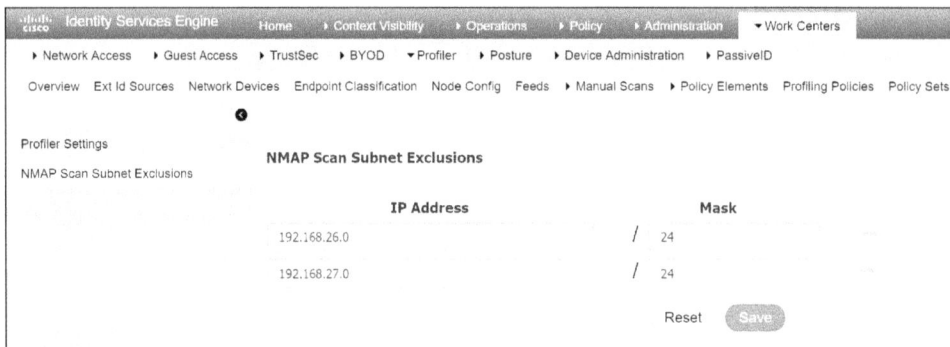

Figure 3-27   *NMAP Scan Subnet Exclusions*

Profiles in Authorization Policies

As you saw earlier in this chapter, the profile may be used as a condition of an authorization policy rule in the form of an Identity Group. Originally, ISE required an Identity Group in order to use any of the profiling policies in the rule, but it has evolved to be able to use the profile directly (called the EndPointPolicy).

Endpoint Identity Groups

Local Identities within the ISE database may be in the form of User Identities or Endpoint Identities. There are also Identity Groups that may contain multiple identities, although an identity (user or endpoint) may be a member of only one Identity Group at a time.

To create an Identity Group based on the profile, you simply select the option named **Yes, create matching Identity Group**, as displayed in Figure 3-28.

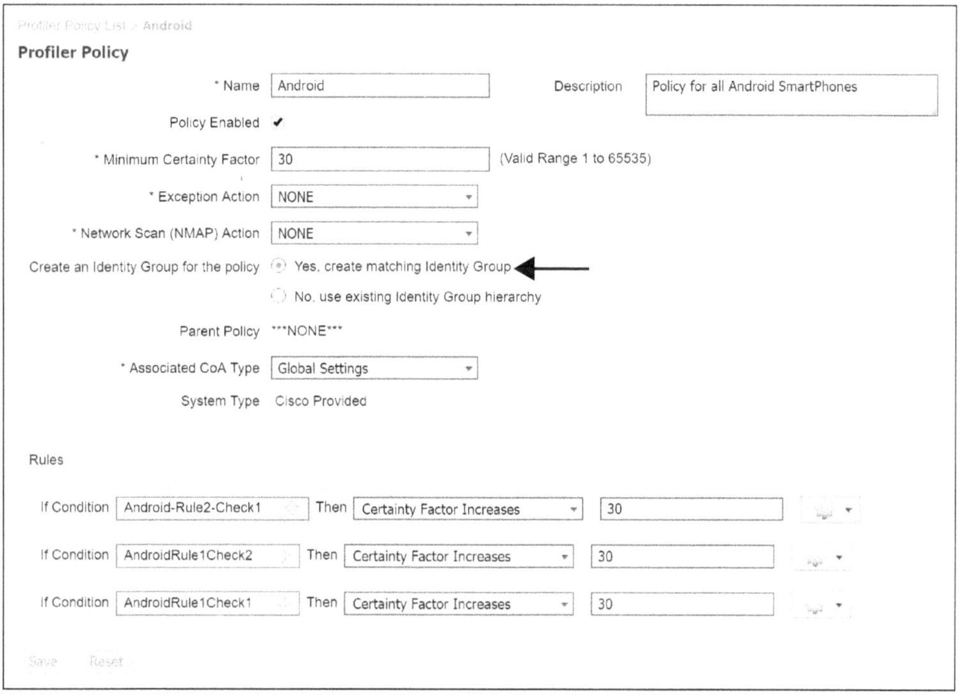

Figure 3-28   *Create Matching Identity Group*

If that option is selected, you can find the matching Identity Group under **Work Centers > Network Access > Id Groups > Endpoint Identity Groups** (as shown in Figure 3-29).

Back in ISE 1.0, the use of Endpoint Identity Groups was the only way to include profiles in authorization policies. The use of these Identity Groups for profiling has been deprecated in favor of using the actual endpoint profile or logical profiles directly in the authorization policy. It is a lot more flexible and less operationally expensive.

Therefore, starting with ISE 1.2, Endpoint Identity Groups are used for a different purpose. They are used for more of a MAC address management (MAM) model—where you can create a static list of MAC addresses to be authorized specifically. For example, you can create a list of all Apple iPads that are owned by the company, so they can be differentiated from personally owned iPads.

The Blacklist Identity Group is a perfect example of Identity Group usage in this manner. If a user were to lose their personal device, they could log in to the My Devices Portal and mark the device as Stolen, which immediately adds the endpoint to the Blacklist Identity Group—which will be denied network access by default.

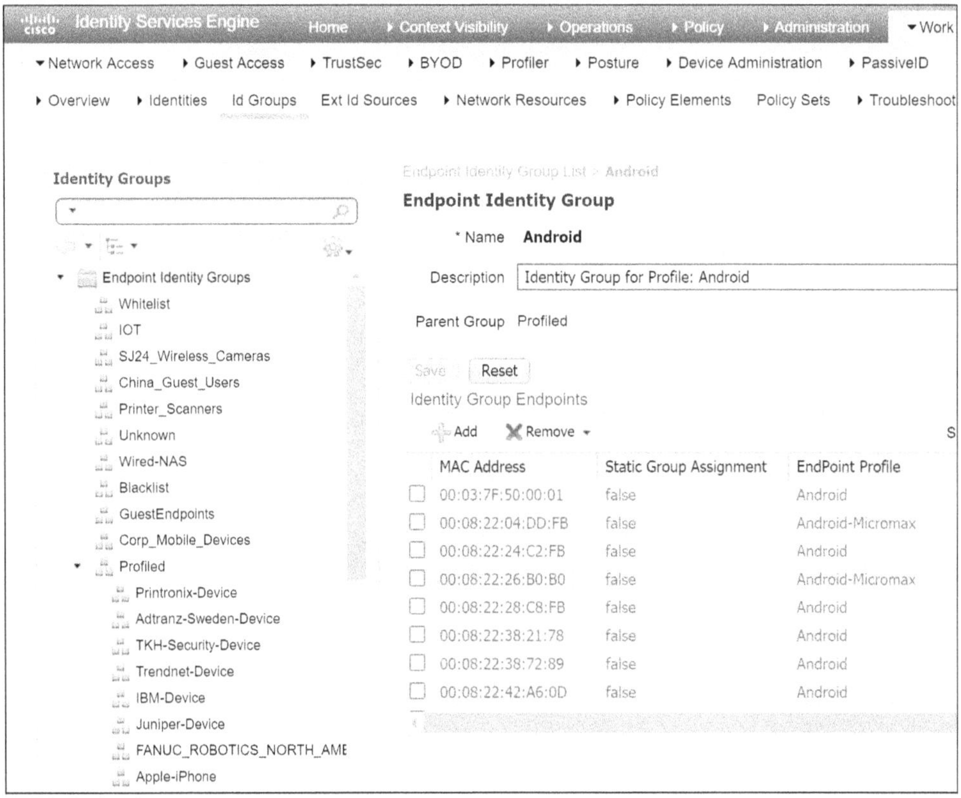

Figure 3-29 *Endpoint Identity Groups*

Passive Identities and EasyConnect

One of the most common functions of secure network access is to identify who is attempting to access the network before granting them access. Throughout this chapter and Chapter 2, you have learned about technologies such as supplicants, authenticators, authentication servers, 802.1X, WebAuth, MAB, and even Active Directory integration.

Up until this point, the identities have been presented directly to ISE, meaning either the endpoint's supplicant is configured to pass the user credentials inside of an EAP packet to ISE itself (802.1X) or the user credentials are entered directly into a web page hosted on ISE (WebAuth). ISE isn't the only server or service on the network performing authentications day in and day out, however. The vast majority of organizations are using Microsoft Active Directory, so wouldn't it be neat if we could piggyback off that for network access, even if only temporarily as 802.1X is being deployed across the organization?

The function of learning about identities that have been authenticated by another server or service is known as *passive authentication*, and the identities that have been learned are referred to as *passive identities*.

Passive Authentication

Many security products on the market today use passive authentication to learn user identities and which IP addresses are assigned to those users. For example, most modern firewall and next-generation firewall (NGFW) solutions use user identities within their firewall policies instead of constructing the policies with source IP addresses.

The Cisco Adaptive Security Appliance (ASA) has used a solution known as Cisco Context Directory Agent (CDA) for years. The Cisco Sourcefire Firepower solution leveraged an Active Directory agent named Source Fire User Agent (SFUA). Both solutions would integrate with Active Directory using Windows Management Instrumentation (WMI) to learn about user authentications and their corresponding IP addresses, and then leverage that information within the firewall policies.

An active authentication, by contrast, learns the identity directly from the user, and a firewall usually only does active authentication by sending the user through a web authentication process. By leveraging passive authentications, the firewall is able to transparently authenticate the user's IP address and apply the correct firewall rule to the traffic traversing the firewall.

To visualize the distinction, Figure 3-30 illustrates an active authentication and Figure 3-31 illustrates a passive authentication.

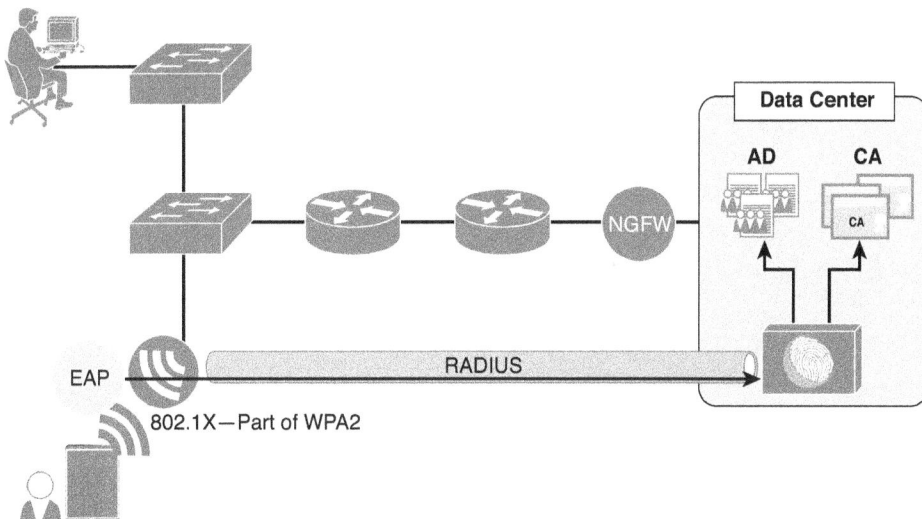

Figure 3-30 *Example Active Authentication*

Figure 3-30 shows an EAP packet from the endpoint traversing the RADIUS connection to ISE.

The following list describes the process that is occurring within an active authentication, such as what is depicted in Figure 3-30:

1. The identity is contained within the EAP packet and is sent from the supplicant to the network, which passes the packet to ISE within the RADIUS connection.

2. ISE validates the credentials against the correct ID store, ensuring the identity is valid. The identity may be in the form of a username and password, or it could be a certificate, etc.

3. As part of the authorization process, ISE learns the group membership and other attributes of the user's identity and adds this to ISE's session directory.

4. ISE provides the end result back to the network, authorizing the user to have the assigned level of access.

5. The session directory information can be shared with ecosystem partners, such as firewalls and web security appliances.

Figure 3-31 illustrates ISE learning about a user with a Windows workstation authenticating to Active Directory, which leverages Kerberos.

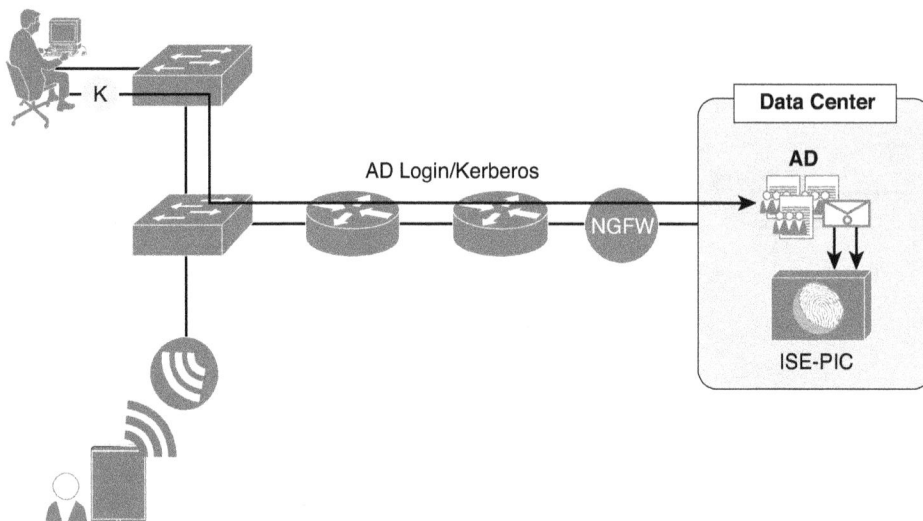

Figure 3-31 *Passive Authentication Using WMI*

The following list describes the process that is occurring within a passive authentication flow, such as what is depicted in Figure 3-31:

1. The identity is part of the Kerberos authentication that occurs as part of the normal Active Directory processes.

2. The AD authentication triggers a notification through WMI.

3. ISE is subscribed to those WMI messages and learns about the authentication event, the user ID, and the source IP address of that authentication.

4. ISE performs an AD lookup and learns the user's group membership, adding the information to the session directory.

5. The session directory information can be shared with ecosystem partners, such as firewalls and web security appliances.

EasyConnect

EasyConnect extends the concepts of passive identity by providing network authorization without requiring 802.1X on the endpoints. Active Directory logins are used to map user information to network connections, which is then used for authorizing users on the network even when ISE is not involved in the user authentication process. EasyConnect can be used as a backup authentication method or way to add a second level of identity.

Some customers use it as a stepping-stone toward a full 802.1X environment. They use EasyConnect in some locations to provide network access control before the supplicant is fully deployed on all endpoints. The deployment is capable of mixed authorizations, so as the desktop team rolls out the supplicant configuration to the managed endpoints, both Dot1x-capable systems and non-capable systems can coexist.

Note   It's important that you understand that EasyConnect is not a client and it is not an agent—it is a solution that combines multiple features to meet a need of certain environments. It combines technologies such as MAB with passive identity technologies to provide a solution for identity without 802.1X.

The following are some basic concepts about EasyConnect (EZC):

- EZC requires a network authentication, usually MAB.

- EZC is for Microsoft AD-joined computers—Windows only.

- EZC identity is based on AD User login, *not* AD machine login.

- It is possible to combine authentications:

    - Combine MAB identity (endpoint MAC address) with EZC; this is the most common use of EZC.

    - Combine 802.1X machine authentication with EZC user information for a dual-factor authentication.

- EZC requires an AD login event to be processed from the endpoint to AD. If access to the domain controllers is not permitted at time of user login, EZC will fail.

- The NADs are not configured any differently:

    - They must still process network authentications (MAB and 802.1X).

    - ISE must still be configured as the RADIUS server.

When a machine joins the network, a MAB is processed. The authorization result must include the Passive Identity Tracking option checked, such as shown in Figure 3-32.

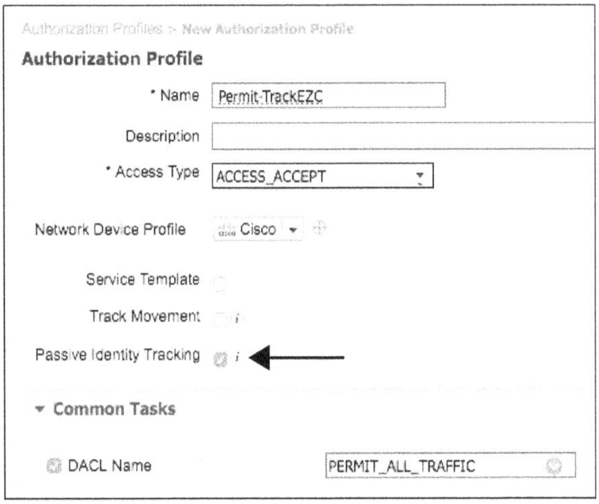

Figure 3-32   *Authorization Profile with Passive Identity Tracking Enabled*

When a network session is authorized with this flag, ISE will monitor the session and look for WMI events that leverage the same endpoint ID (MAC address), to stitch the passive identity together with the network session.

After the WMI event for that endpoint is stitched together, a CoA-Reauth is sent to the NAD and a new authorization result may be applied to that based on the combined authentication (MAB + EZC).

Figures 3-33 and 3-34 show the EasyConnect flow leveraging MAB for the network session.

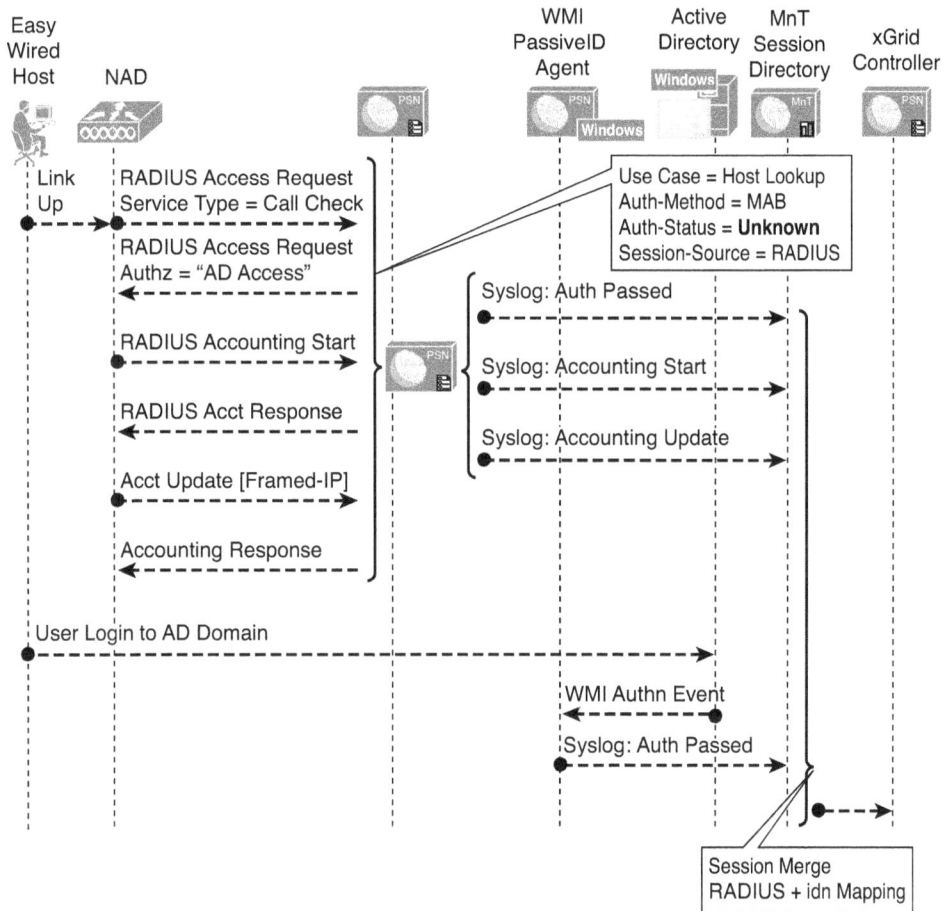

Figure 3-33 *EasyConnect Flow with MAB*

Windows Management Instrumentation

Windows Management Instrumentation (WMI) is a core Windows management technology that enables you to manage Windows servers or workstations locally or remotely. WMI acts as a publish/subscribe (pub/sub) messaging system within Microsoft Active Directory.

ISE may remotely communicate with AD using WMI and subscribe to certain security events, such as logins. When those events occur, ISE is notified by AD.

The main benefits to using this WMI method to learn about the passive authentication is that it does not require installation of an agent on a domain controller or a member server. Before WMI can be used, connectivity requirements for successful WMI connections must be met. The good news is that the *Config WMI* function from ISE's UI will perform that configuration for you.

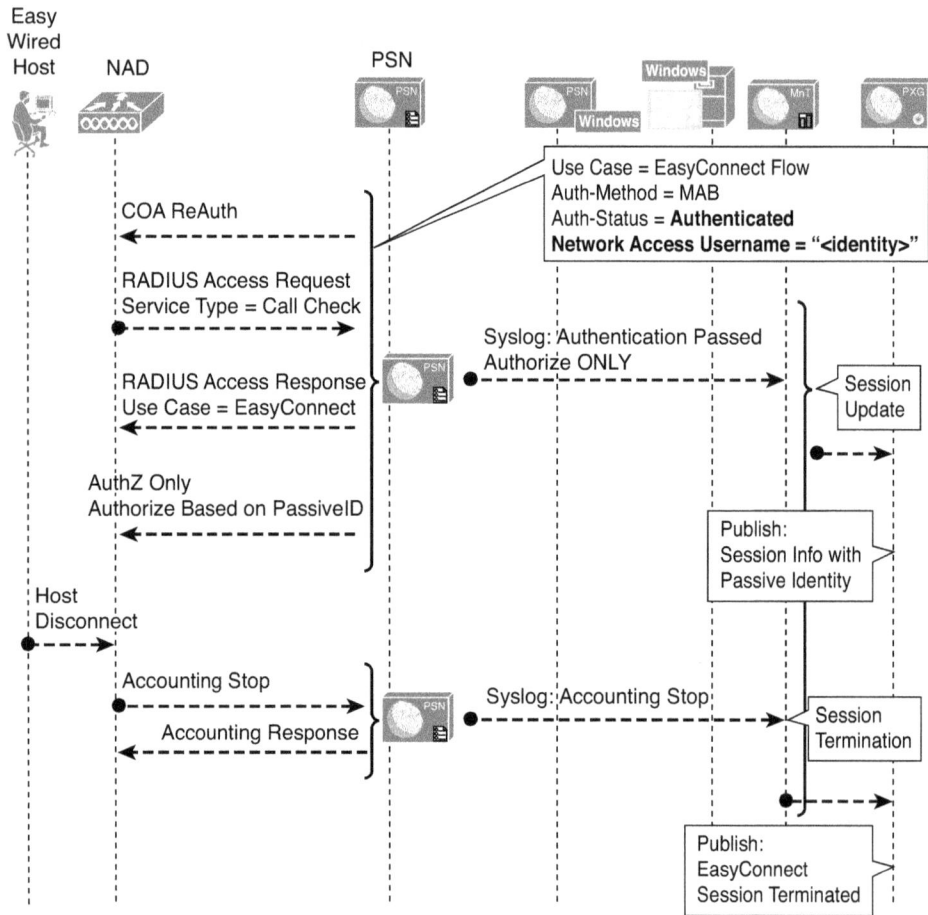

Figure 3-34   *EasyConnect Flow with MAB (continued)*

This type of connection to AD has been around for a very long time. The Cisco Context Directory Agent (CDA) used it, and it's been a part of ISE since version 1.3. In ISE, it was previously referred to as "pxGrid Identity Mapping" and was designed to bring the passive identity functionality of CDA into ISE for sharing with pxGrid subscribers.

This functionality was extended to create the EasyConnect deployment method in ISE version 2.1 and then given a tremendous boost in capability and ease of use in ISE version 2.2.

The WMI connection allows ISE to remotely communicate to an AD domain controller as a subscriber of WMI security events. Specifically, ISE looks for new Kerberos tickets that are granted and when those tickets are renewed. The granting of a ticket shows that a new Windows authentication session has occurred; it could be a user authentication or a machine authentication, but that is for ISE to sort through after it is notified. The renewing of Kerberos tickets shows that the session is still active and should not be timed out or purged.

Note   At the time of writing, with ISE version 2.4, WMI is the only passive identity source that can be used with EasyConnect.

Configuring WMI

To integrate ISE with Active Directory via WMI:

Step 1.   Navigate to **Administration > System > Deployment.** Ensure that at least one PSN has the Passive Identity service enabled, as shown in Figure 3-35.

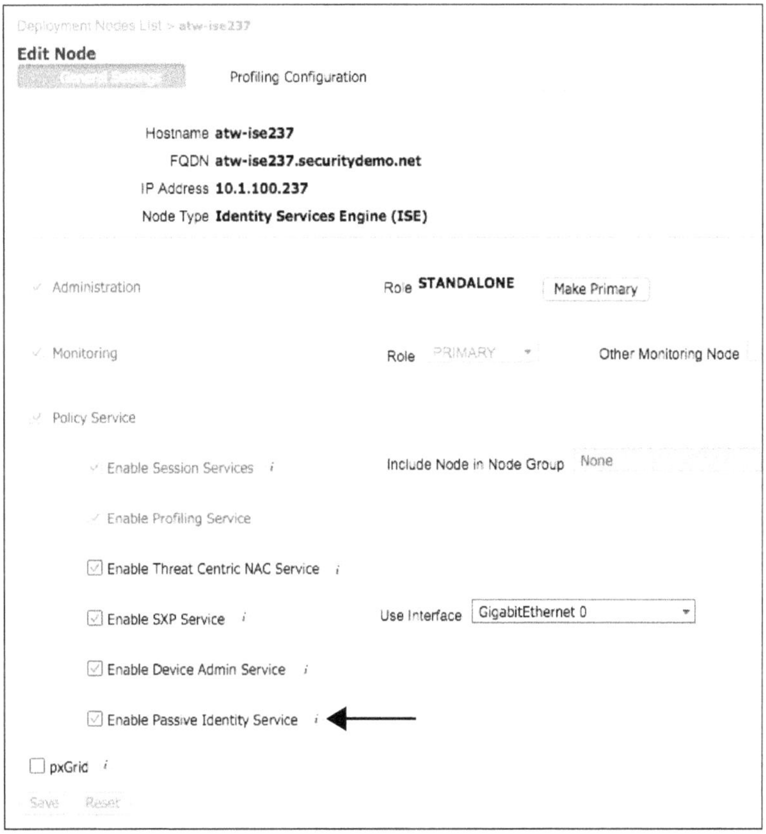

Figure 3-35   *Passive Identity Service Enabled for PSN*

Step 2.   Navigate to **Work Centers > PassiveID > Providers > Active Directory.**

Step 3.   Select your Active Directory join point that you previously created. In the example used in this book, it is named AD-SecurityDemo.

Step 4.   Click the **PassiveID** tab, shown in Figure 3-36.

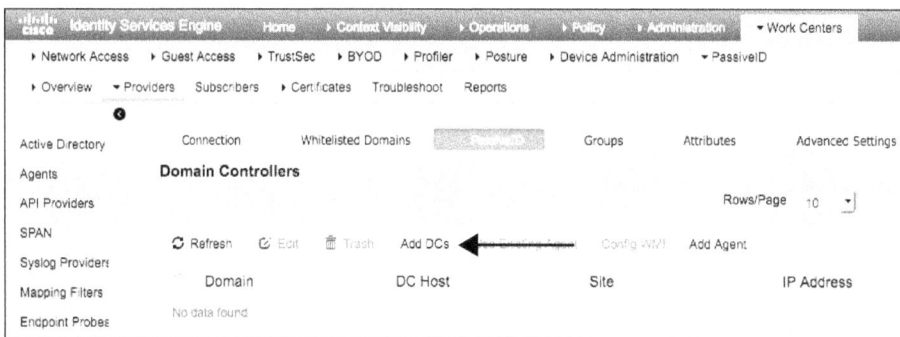

Figure 3-36   *PassiveID Tab*

Step 5.   Click **Add DCs.** The list of domain controllers is displayed, as shown in Figure 3-37.

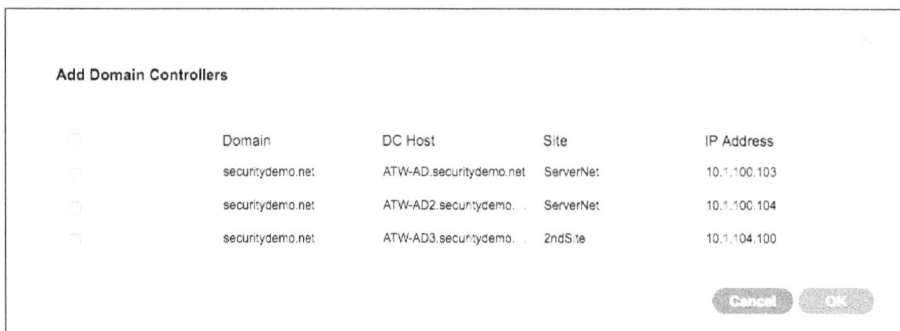

Figure 3-37   *Adding Domain Controllers*

Step 6.   Check the check boxes for the domain controller(s) that you wish to monitor and click **OK.**

Step 7.   The domain controllers are added to the list of PassiveID Domain Controllers. Check the check boxes for the DCs and click **Config WMI**, as highlighted in Figure 3-38.

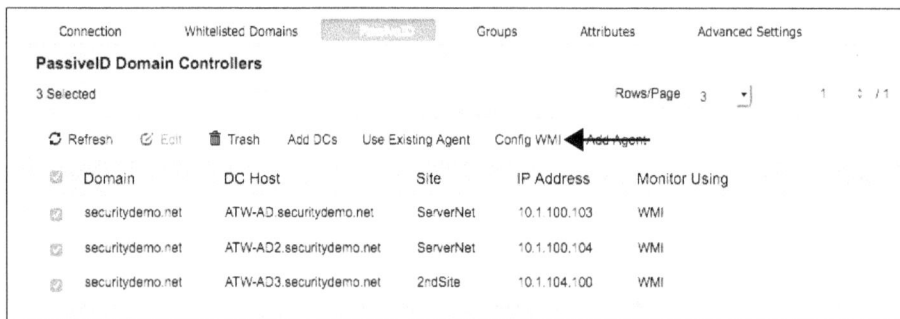

Figure 3-38   *Configuring WMI on Selected DCs*

The "Config WMI in process" message is displayed, as shown in Figure 3-39.

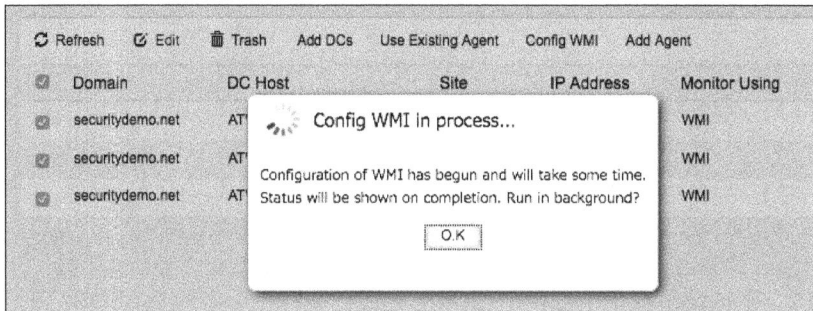

Figure 3-39 *Configuration of WMI in Process*

When the configuration process is complete, a success message is displayed. The process performed by the Config WMI function is quite extensive and detailed after these configuration steps.

ISE is now configured to subscribe to the WMI security events, and the AD controllers are configured to send those events to ISE. When AD authentications occur, those sessions will be displayed in the Live Sessions screen, as shown in Figure 3-40.

Figure 3-40 *Live Sessions*

What Does That Config WMI Button Do?

The Config WMI process performs an awful lot in the background. Prior to ISE version 2.2, everything detailed in this section needed to be performed manually. To see more of the painful process of the past, check out the *Cisco Identity Services Engine Administrator Guide* for ISE version 1.3 or 1.4 and the process for setting up the pxGrid Identity Mapping function.

There are five main things that Config WMI must complete for you:

- **Registry changes:** ISE must create two registry keys that add the ID of the WMI client used by ISE. The key name is 76A64158-CB41-11D1-8B02-00600806D9B6, and it must be added in two locations:

  - HKEY_CLASSES_ROOT\CLSID\{76A64158-CB41-11D1-8B02-00600806D9B6}

  - HKLM\Software\Classes\Wow6432Node\CLSID\{76A64158-CB41-11D1-8B02-00600806D9B6}

  - These keys are being used to list the ID as a valid App for DCOM.

- **Permissions to use DCOM:** ISE will communicate to the domain controllers using a Windows account, which needs to have local and remote access to DCOM. The **dcomcnfg** command could be used to configure DCOM permissions manually.

- **Permissions to use WMI remotely:** By default, Active Directory users do not have the Execute Methods and Remote Enable permissions. These can be granted manually by using the wmimgmt.msc tool.

- **Access to read the security event log of the AD DC:** To allow the AD user to read the security event log of the DC, the user must be added to two different security groups:

  - Event Log Readers group

  - Distributed COM Users group

- **Configure Windows Firewall to allow traffic to and from ISE:** By default, Windows Firewall on the domain controller would block the communication, so a rule must be added to allow ISE to remotely access the server for DCOM/WMI.

Logoff Detection with the Endpoint Probe

Users do not always log off from their computers before leaving the network. Often, they just close the lid on their laptop and pack up for the day. ISE 2.2 introduced an endpoint probe to aid with logoff detection. The probe is designed to answer the burning questions: Is the endpoint still there? If so, is the same user logged in?

The endpoint probe uses WMI to remotely communicate with the endpoint and check if the user is still active. If the endpoint is on the network but WMI is not responding, ISE will try to remotely log in to the endpoint using the saved Domain Admin credentials and enable WMI. If you chose to not save the credential when joining AD, then the endpoint probe will not function.

If the endpoint is not there or if a different user is logged in, the session will be cleared.

Keep in mind that the endpoint probe relies on reverse DNS to map IP addresses to hostnames, and the probe will run every four hours. If the endpoint is online but is not responding to WMI, then ISE will remotely log in with the saved domain admin credentials and enable WMI. This behavior is not configurable; if it is not desirable for your organization, the only option is to disable the endpoint probe.

ISE also allows you to map subnets to PSNs for the endpoint probe. This way you can design and plan which PSN is responsible for specific areas of your network. If a subnet does not exist in the list, then the endpoint probe will not operate in that subnet.

Summary

In this chapter, you learned all about extending basic network access control with profiling, web authentication, and advanced concepts like passive authentications and EasyConnect. You learned about the different profiling probes, including where each is useful and how to configure them. You learned the difference between active and passive authentications, why ISE would care about passive IDs, and how to combine multiple technologies together to provide an identity solution for access control without 802.1X.

This chapter covered a lot of information about extending basic NAC, but it merely scratched the surface of what you can do with Cisco Identity Services Engine. Entire books are dedicated to the topic, such as *Cisco ISE for BYOD and Secure Unified Access, Second Edition* (Cisco Press, 2017). If you are attempting the CCIE Security exam, it's highly recommended to also read that book in addition to this one.

Chapter 4

Extending Network Access with ISE

In Chapter 2, "Basic Network Access Control," we discussed 802.1X and MAC Authentication Bypass (MAB) and how to configure ISE and the network devices for it. As you probably realized, choice of authentication method depends on the endpoints being authenticated. On one side, classic enterprise-owned devices such as laptops and desktops support and can be easily configured for 802.1X. For a large enterprise, configuring thousands of devices using Active Directory Group Policy Objects (GPOs) is very easy. On the other side, common unmanaged devices such as printers and IP Phones can be granted access with MAB based on profiling results.

Unfortunately for network administrators, modern networks are no longer limited to these kinds of devices only. With the increase in mobile device usage, employees, partners, vendors, and guests expect access to the Internet, at least. Sometimes, organizations even allow employees to bring their own devices for work purposes. Because these devices are not owned by the organization, it has no control over them nor does it have the ability to configure these devices for authentication. This introduces the need to implement different kinds of access control mechanisms for these devices. The Bring Your Own Device (BYOD) provisioning and Guest access features of ISE are used to provide access in such cases. This chapter will discuss both of these features in detail.

While network access control has traditionally meant authenticating the user and/or device before granting access, it does not need to stop there. In addition to confirming the identity of the user and device, the posture of the device should also be considered before granting access. The posture of a device refers to the security applications running on the device and their state. If the posture does not comply with the organization's security policies, the device should not be allowed on the network. For example, if a laptop does not have the correct and updated anti-malware application running, then it is more likely to have been infected. Allowing such a device on the network increases the risk to other devices in the network. The posture validation features of ISE are used to verify and remediate the posture of a device before granting it access. This chapter will also discuss how to configure the posture features of ISE.

Finally, though access control is a must-have for network security, its real advantage can only be derived by applying granular permissions and micro-segmentation. This chapter will also discuss micro-segmentation with Cisco TrustSec and how to configure ISE and the network for it.

Get Ready, Get Set, Prerequisites

Most of the advanced ISE features discussed in this chapter use some common foundational features on network devices such as switches and Wireless LAN Controllers (WLCs). This section discusses those features and how to configure them. This section also shows examples of the typical device configuration that will be used for the rest of the chapter.

URL Redirection

Almost all features discussed in this chapter rely on the URL Redirection capability of the network device. As the name suggests, this feature is used to intercept traffic coming from the endpoint and redirect it. In particular, the redirect is applied to HTTP and HTTPS traffic.

This is especially useful when you require the endpoint to interact with ISE before it can interact with anything else on the network. For instance, when a guest device connects to the wireless network, URL Redirection forces it to go to the ISE guest portal and authenticate before it can go out to the Internet.

To understand how URL Redirection works, consider the flow shown in Figure 4-1.

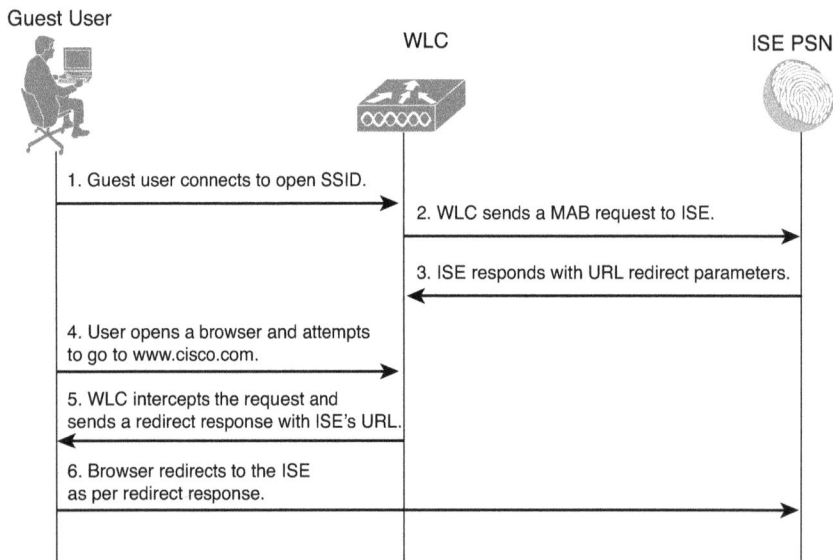

Guest User   WLC   ISE PSN

1. Guest user connects to open SSID.

                     2. WLC sends a MAB request to ISE.

                     3. ISE responds with URL redirect parameters.

4. User opens a browser and attempts to go to www.cisco.com.

5. WLC intercepts the request and sends a redirect response with ISE's URL.

6. Browser redirects to the ISE as per redirect response.

Figure 4-1   *URL Redirection Flow*

A session begins with the user connecting to an SSID or a switch port and results in the network device, a WLC in this case, sending an authentication request to ISE. Upon receiving the authentication request, ISE sends a URL Redirection authorization response with its own URL. This URL is unique to every session.

Note   Figure 4-1 shows a MAB authentication, but this authentication can be 802.1X for different use cases such as posture validation.

Note   Configuring ISE to send a URL Redirection is covered in relevant sections later in the chapter. This section introduces the URL Redirection function and the configuration required on the network devices.

On receiving the response, the network device applies a URL Redirection enforcement on the session. After this point, all traffic from the endpoint is dropped until HTTP or HTTPS traffic is received. When the user opens a browser and attempts to access a website, this request is intercepted by the WLC and a redirect response, with the appropriate session-specific URL, is sent back to the browser. This results in the user's browser connecting to the URL specified by ISE.

Note   Use of URL Redirection is so common that most current operating systems check for it when they connect to a network. If they detect a URL Redirection, they will open a browser or browser-like app and send a simple HTTP request to get redirected, so that the user can authenticate. So, in most cases, users will not have to open a browser manually to authenticate.

Note   What happens after the redirect depends on the configuration of ISE and differs based on the feature being used and will be covered in relevant sections later in this chapter.

For URL Redirection to work on the network device, a few things must be configured on it:

- **Redirect ACL:** When URL Redirection is applied, some traffic, such as that to ISE, DNS, and DHCP and other flow-specific traffic, will need to be allowed through without redirection while all other traffic will need to be blocked and redirected. A redirect ACL is used by the network device to determine what traffic gets redirected or allowed. This ACL is a standard or extended IP ACL defined on the device itself. The **permit** and **deny** statements are used to specify what traffic gets redirected or is allowed. This ACL needs to be configured on all network devices that will be used in a flow that requires URL Redirection. ISE will specify the name of the redirect ACL along with the URL Redirection response it sends (Step 3 in Figure 4-1).

At the minimum, the redirect ACL needs to allow communication between the endpoint, ISE, DNS server, and DHCP server to go through without redirection. Each network device type treats redirect ACLs differently. Care should be taken when creating redirect ACLs on different devices.

For example, on Cisco switches, a **deny** statement in an ACL specifies the traffic that should not be redirected, while a **permit** statement specifies the traffic that should be redirected. On a Cisco WLC this is reversed—a **deny** statement defines traffic that needs to be redirected while a **permit** statement defines traffic that should be allowed without redirection.

Example 4-1 shows a redirect ACL on a Cisco switch, and Figure 4-2 shows a similar redirect ACL created on a Cisco WLC. The IP address shown in both examples—192.168.1.11—is the ISE PSN.

Example 4-1   *Redirect ACL on a Cisco Switch*

```
ip access-list extended redirect
 deny    ip any host 192.168.1.11
 deny    udp any any eq domain
 permit ip any any
```

redirect

0

Source IP/Mask		Destination IP/Mask		Protocol	Source Port	Dest Port	DSCP	Direction	Number of Hits	
0.0.0.0 0.0.0.0	/	192.168.1.11 255.255.255.255	/	Any	Any	Any	Any	Any	0	🔽
192.168.1.11 255.255.255.255	/	0.0.0.0 0.0.0.0	/	Any	Any	Any	Any	Any	0	🔽
0.0.0.0 0.0.0.0	/	0.0.0.0 0.0.0.0	/	UDP	DHCP Client	Any	Any	Any	0	🔽
0.0.0.0 0.0.0.0	/	0.0.0.0 0.0.0.0	/	UDP	DHCP Server	Any	Any	Any	0	🔽
0.0.0.0 0.0.0.0	/	0.0.0.0 0.0.0.0	/	UDP	DNS	Any	Any	Any	0	🔽
0.0.0.0 0.0.0.0	/	0.0.0.0 0.0.0.0	/	UDP	Any	DNS	Any	Any	0	🔽
0.0.0.0 0.0.0.0	/	0.0.0.0 0.0.0.0	/	Any	Any	Any	Any	Any	0	🔽

Figure 4-2   *Redirect ACL on Cisco WLC*

- **HTTP/HTTPS server:** Cisco switches require their HTTP and HTTPS servers to be enabled before they can intercept or redirect traffic. These can be enabled with the **ip http server** and **ip http secure-server** commands.

- **Routing and switch virtual interface (SVI):** Cisco switches use their management VLAN IP address to respond to the intercepted HTTP request. To allow redirect to work properly, the switch must have a route from the management VLAN to the endpoint's VLAN. One way to get around this is to assign an IP address to the endpoint's VLAN SVI.

■ **IP Device Tracking (IPDT):** The switch needs to learn the IP address of the endpoint for URL Redirection to work correctly. IPDT can be enabled on the switch using the **ip device tracking** command.

When designing a solution based on URL Redirection, two important things must be considered in the design:

■ **HTTPS redirection:** HTTPS redirection is a dual-edged sword—on one hand, most common websites now use HTTPS, so when a browser opens and the user attempts to go to a website, it will most likely be an HTTPS session. If HTTPS is not redirected, the user will never reach the ISE portal. On the other hand, HTTPS redirection has a big impact on the network device, specially the WLC. On a busy network, redirecting HTTPS can be prohibitively resource extensive. To add to that, HTTPS redirection will result in certificate warnings because the certificate presented on redirection is not going to match the hostname of the original HTTPS request. In some cases, the browser will not even allow the user to add an exception and continue to the ISE portal. Hence, before designing a URL Redirection-based solution, consider whether you want to redirect HTTPS traffic. Given that most current operating systems can consistently detect URL Redirection and eliminate the need for the user interaction in the redirection process, HTTPS redirection is not worth the effort in most cases.

■ **DNS:** The URL sent from ISE for redirection will mostly use the FQDN of the node. In some cases, the endpoint will even need to resolve some public addresses such as that of the Google Play store. Hence, it is important that the end-user VLAN have access to a DNS server that can resolve the ISE hostnames as well as external addresses.

Note The CCIE lab may not have proper DNS setup. It is possible to configure ISE to use its IP address in the redirect URL. The relevant sections will point that out.

AAA Configuration

Every feature discussed in this chapter will depend on the AAA configuration on the network device, including RADIUS, 802.1X, and MAB configuration. These were discussed in Chapter 2, so if you have skipped that chapter, it is strongly recommended that you read it before continuing. Particular attention should be paid to the RADIUS Change of Authorization (CoA) configuration on the network devices. None of the flows discussed in this chapter will work without RADIUS CoA.

BYOD Onboarding with ISE

Even a decade ago, employees connecting their personal devices to the corporate network was very uncommon. IT departments had strict policies defining what devices could connect to the network. The enterprise-owned devices used a specific operating system image and had the same applications and security policies. Fast-forward a few years and personal mobile devices have become omnipresent. Employees expect some degree of access to apps, data, and the network on their personal devices. Allowing such access even increases productivity and benefits the organization.

Unfortunately, BYOD brings a whole new shift in network access policies and a risk that needs to be mitigated. Because the IT departments no longer have control over a substantial share of devices that connect to the network, it becomes difficult to ensure malicious or infected devices do not connect. Because personal devices often lack the preventive protection that enterprise-owned devices have, there is inherent risk of unauthorized access and data loss.

To mitigate such risk, varying degrees of access policies are put into place. In some organizations, all personal devices are segmented into networks separate from the corporate network and access is limited to the Internet or a few servers in the DMZ and cloud. In other organizations, full corporate access is granted after a device is registered. There are forms of policies that fall in the spectrum between these two ends.

Building Blocks of a BYOD Solution

Although risks of BYOD can be mitigated with a well-designed access policy, any policy decision will need to be based on the identification and authentication of the user and the device trying to connect to the network.

Identification and authentication of personal devices is not as easy as that of enterprise-owned devices. With enterprise-owned devices, most of the required configuration, including certificates, can be pushed via centralized management systems such as Active Directory or a mobile device management (MDM) solution. That is not the case with personal devices. There are three primary questions that need to be addressed for a BYOD solution:

- **What identification method will be used?** Access is granted based on the identity of the user or device trying to connect to the network. So what form of identity will be used for personal devices? There are three common answers to this question:

  - **Existing corporate identity:** The most common answer is to use the same identity, credentials, and database as that used on corporate assets. This is often the username and password in Active Directory. This option is very simple because a functional method to identify users and maintain password hygiene already exists. It is also easy for users to remember just a single set of credentials. So why consider any other identity methods? Because convenience often comes at the cost of security. Because personal devices are often less secure, there is a high risk of the credentials being stolen. There is also a risk of the device itself being stolen. Imagine what an attacker can do with a perfectly valid set of credentials that is used for application, data, and network access.

■ **Separate set of credentials:** With this method, users are provided with a single-purpose set of credentials that is different from the corporate set. This increases security because even if the credentials are stolen, they cannot be used anywhere else. Of course, because security is increased, convenience will decrease. In this case, the end users will need to remember a new set of credentials, and that can become inconvenient. Most end users will try to increase the convenience by using a single password across all accounts and hence decrease the security back again. With this option you will also need to consider the cost of creating and maintaining the infrastructure required for the special credentials. In the end this is probably the worst option in terms of security and cost.

■ **Certificates:** With this method, a certificate is used as identity. A certificate is specific to a user and device and cannot be easily stolen, making it the most secure method of identification. Following the "Inverse Proportionality of Convenience and Security" rule (not an actual rule, but this has a nice sound to it!), because this is the most secure method, it has to be the most inconvenient method! It actually is. Installing certificates on personal devices without using a centralized management system is difficult. The end users will need to be significantly technical (some of you laughed out loud here!) or have to be provided with complicated instructions (you laughed again!).

■ **What authentication method will be used?** The second key consideration when designing a BYOD solution is the choice of authentication method. There are two common option available for this:

   ■ **802.1X:** This method is self-explanatory. Using some kind of EAP authentication with 802.1X is the best way to provide secure access, especially with wireless networks because the connection can be encrypted with dynamic keys. The problem with 802.1X is being able to configure the supplicant and has the same challenges as using certificates for authentication.

   ■ **Web portals:** Using web portals for authentication is almost the same as providing guest access, which will be discussed later in the chapter. One key problem with using portals-based authentication, especially on wireless networks, is that an open SSID may need to be used, and that leaves the connections unencrypted.

■ **How will the devices be configured?** Irrespective of the identification and authentication methods selected, the device will need to be configured to access the network. This process is commonly referred to as *onboarding*. A few common methods used are:

   ■ **User education:** The simplest way is to create guides that users can follow to configure their devices. The problem with this method is that most users are not technical enough to correctly follow the guides, and that can result in increased help desk cost. This method often results in user dissatisfaction and a feeling of the solution being complicated.

■ **Mobile device management solution:** An MDM solution can make the provisioning process trivial for end users. The problem with such a system, though, is twofold. First, there is an inherent privacy concern among end users when their employer puts an application on their personal devices. Secondly, the cost of MDM solutions is tied to the number of endpoints. Procuring enough licenses to cover an uncertain or large number of endpoints is not often feasible.

■ **Web-based provisioning:** With this option a product such as Cisco ISE is used to provision an endpoint with SSID details and credentials, including certificates. The process is end-user driven and does not require any applications to be installed. This provides a good way to operate a solution with good security, fair convenience, and manageable cost.

That was a long introduction to BYOD solutions, but it was important to discuss the need for BYOD and various options available to understand the configuration options available in ISE. With the BYOD features of ISE, it is possible to provision a device with the required identity and authentication information thorough a convenient user-driven web portal.

The BYOD provisioning process and configuration can be divided into three parts:

■ **Initial authentication:** To be able to reach the ISE portal for onboarding, the device will need a way to access the network in the first place. This creates a catch-22 situation and can be resolved in two ways—Single SSID flow and Dual SSID flow (and wired access, of course). These flows are discussed in the next section.

■ **Provisioning:** After the initial authentication completes, the user is redirected to a provisioning web portal on ISE. Provisioning, in case of BYOD, refers to the process of configuring the device to connect to a specific network using a specific method and set of credentials. It can, optionally, also push identity certificates to the device. For example, ISE can install certificates on an endpoint and then configure it to connect to a specific SSID using EAP-TLS.

■ **End state:** Once the device is able to connect to the desired SSID using the correct method, onboarding is deemed to be successful.

Single SSID and Dual SSID Provisioning

ISE provides two methods for initial authentication on a wireless network for onboarding purpose—Single SSID and Dual SSID. There is a big difference between these two methods but both result in the user being redirected to a provisioning portal on ISE after successful authentication.

Figure 4-3 illustrates the Dual SSID flow for initial authentication, described further in the list that follows.

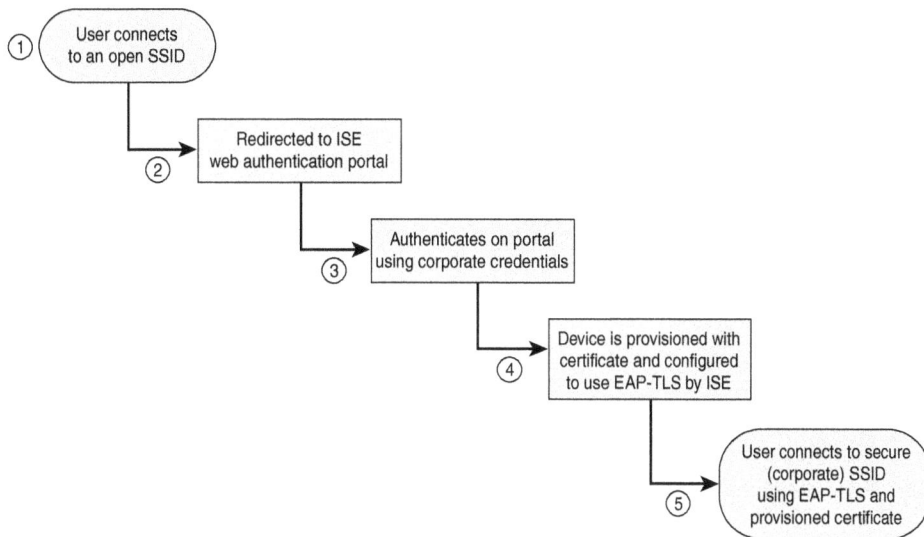

Figure 4-3   *Dual SSID Flow*

   1. In a Dual SSID flow, a dedicated onboarding SSID is used for onboarding. Once provisioned, the device can connect to the target corporate or secure SSID.

   2. The dedicated SSID is usually an open SSID that uses MAB initially and then redirects the user to a web portal on ISE for authentication. If an open SSID is used, the end user will not need to configure the supplicant on their endpoint manually.

Note   The dedicated SSID is required because, unlike wired networks, wireless networks cannot fail over to different authentication methods (802.1 to MAB). Although open SSID is most commonly used, starting in Cisco WLC version 8.4, a WPA2-PSK–based SSID can also be used with MAB for this purpose. The additional benefit is mostly not worth having the extra burden of educating users. The authentication and provisioning process happens securely over HTTPS even though the SSID is open.

   3. After the user authenticates on the web portal, usually with their corporate credentials, they are redirected to the provisioning portal and onboarding begins.

   4. During onboarding, ISE uses OS-specific methods to push a wireless network profile onto the device. It can also provision a certificate during this process, if required.

   5. After provisioning, the user disconnects from the onboarding SSID and connects to the corporate SSID using the provisioned profile.

   Figure 4-4 shows the Single SSID flow for initial authentication, where onboarding is done on the corporate or secure SSID itself. The list that follows describes this flow.

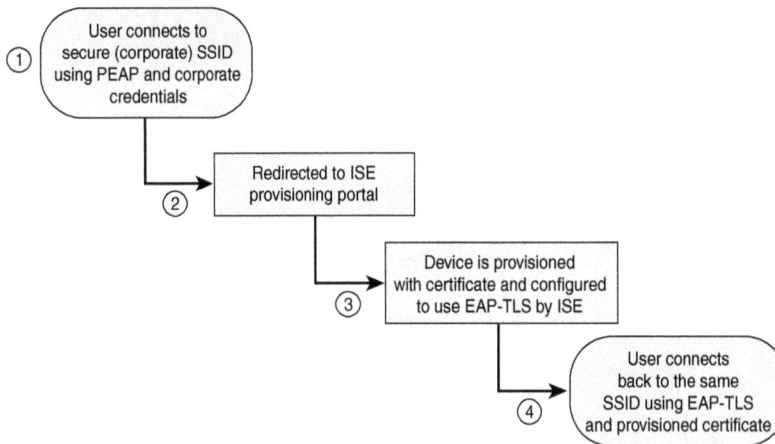

Figure 4-4   *Single SSID Flow*

1. The initial authentication is done using a username/password-based EAP protocol such as PEAP.

   The user will need to configure the device supplicant to use the required protocol and credentials.

2. After the initial authentication, the user is redirected to the provisioning portal for certificate and SSID configuration provisioning.

3. During onboarding, ISE uses OS-specific methods to push a wireless network profile and certificate onto the device.

4. After provisioning, the device connects back to the same SSID using EAP-TLS and the provisioned certificate.

Note   BYOD onboarding is supported on wired networks also but this chapter focuses on wireless network onboarding because wired onboarding is rarely used. The configuration required for wired onboarding is the same as those for wireless. Because switches can fail over to different authentication methods, a web portal-based authentication followed by provisioning works well.

Configuring ISE for BYOD Onboarding

Configuring ISE for BYOD onboarding requires configuring the following three components. As with everything else on ISE, each component will require configuring smaller elements first.

■ **Client Provisioning Policy (CPP):** The rules for this policy are used to determine the action that ISE will take when a user reaches the provisioning portal. The rules are OS-specific and define the provisioning method to use and what to provision.

- **Web portals:** Actual onboarding and provisioning of the end-user device begins on a web portal on ISE. In case of Dual SSID flow, even the user authentication is done on the portal. This requires configuration of the portal and optional customization to meet branding needs.

- **Policy sets:** Every flow in ISE starts with an authentication. BYOD starts with an initial authentication using MAB or 802.1X also, so it requires policy sets, which are authentication rules and authorization rules to enforce redirection for provisioning and then to allow access after onboarding.

Note   All features discussed in this chapter require multiple components to be configured on ISE. Each component then has multiple elements to be configured. For the CCIE Security exam, it is easier to break down the required configuration into such components and elements to avoid missing anything. An easy way to remember the required components is to visualize the flow. For example, BYOD flow starts with MAB or 802.1X, so that requires policy sets. Then it redirects to a portal, so that requires a portal configuration. Finally, it provisions, so it requires a Client Provisioning Policy.

Understanding Client Provisioning Policy for BYOD Onboarding

While provisioning begins on the ISE portal, the actual job of configuring the endpoint supplicant and installing certificates is done by a provisioning agent called *Config Wizard* or *Supplicant Provisioning Wizards (SPWizards)*. The primary function of the portal is to provision the agent, except in case of devices running the Apple iOS operating system.

The type of agent, as well as the method to install and execute it, depends on the operating system of the endpoint, as discussed in the list that follows:

- **Windows and Apple OS X:** For these operating systems, Cisco provides agents known as SPWizards that are pushed to the endpoint directly from the provisioning portal. These agents are sent as executable files and users have to manually execute them after the download is complete.

- **Apple iOS:** Apple iOS provides an over-the-air (OTA) provisioning method and does not require any agent to be installed. The portal directly pushes the profiles and certificates to the endpoint using the OTA process.

- **Android:** Android devices also require an agent for the provisioning process but the agent can only be installed from the Google Play store. The provisioning portal redirects the user to the Google Play store to download the agent, which is an application in the Play store called *Cisco Network Setup Assistant*. Once the application is installed, users have to open it to start the onboarding process.

Table 4-1 provides a handy visual reference of the agents and installation methods for each operating system.

Table 4-1   *Provisioning Agents and Their Installation Methods by Operating Systems*

Operating Systems	Agent Required	Installed by ISE
Windows and Apple OS X	Y	Y
Android	Y	N
Apple iOS	N	—

Once the agent is executed on the endpoint, it communicates back to ISE to receive instructions. Using the agent or the OTA process on iOS, ISE executes the following tasks to onboard the endpoint:

1. Configure the supplicant on the endpoint such that it can connect to the network using the required authentication protocols and credentials.

2. Add the ISE server certificate chain to the trust store on the endpoint.

3. Install an identity certificate on the endpoint, if EAP-TLS is to be used for authentication.

The supplicant configuration and certificate generation instructions are defined on ISE in what is called a *Native Supplicant Profile (NSP)*. (In some places on ISE, NSP is called *Wizard Profile*.)

The NSP and the agent details combined create the *client provisioning rules*. These rules are used to provision the correct agent and to send the configuration and certificates to the provisioning agents. Figure 4-5 shows the various elements that combine together to create the client provisioning rule.

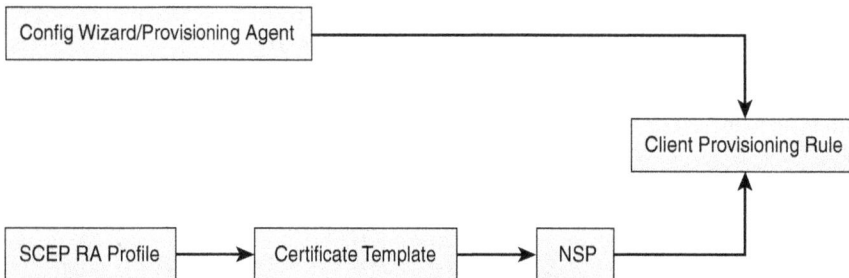

Figure 4-5   *Components of a Client Provisioning Rule*

Although Figure 4-5 appears to make the configuration of the client provisioning rules look complicated, most of the elements shown are prebuilt in ISE and can be used with little or no modification. Also remember that Simple Certificate Enrollment Protocol (SCEP) Registration Authority (RA) Profile and certificate templates are required only when creating an NSP for EAP-TLS provisioning.

Configuring SCEP RA Profile and Certificate Templates

If an endpoint is being onboarded to authenticate using EAP-TLS, then the endpoint will need to be provisioned with a certificate. The *SCEP RA profile* tells ISE which certificate authority (CA) to use to generate the certificate for the endpoint.

There is a CA server built into ISE that can be used to generate a certificate for the endpoint. The SCEP RA profile for the internal CA server is prebuilt and can be used in the certificate template directly.

If you plan to use an external CA, you will need to create a SCEP RA profile for it, as shown in Figure 4-6, by navigating to **Work Centers > BYOD > Portals & Components > Certificates > External CA Templates**.

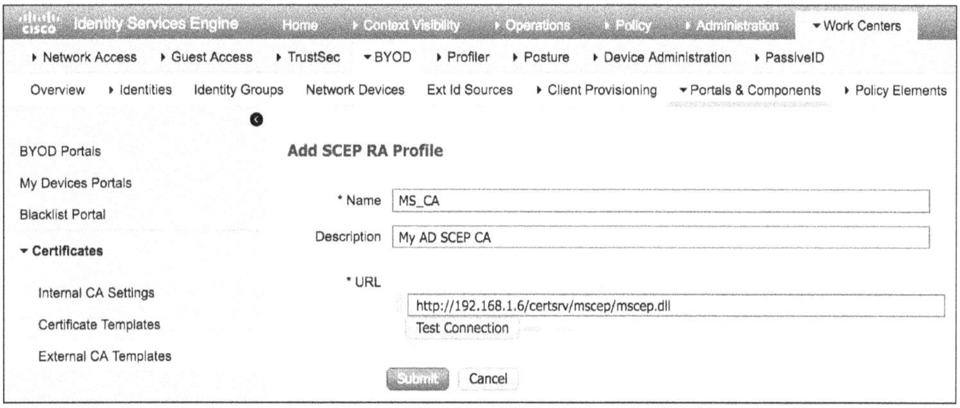

Figure 4-6 *Creating a SCEP RA Profile*

Note Using an external CA is not recommended because most CAs that support SCEP will require their security configuration to be reduced significantly to allow them to respond to requests from ISE. Instead of using SCEP to request a certificate from an external CA, consider making ISE a subordinate CA (sub CA) in the existing public key infrastructure (PKI). By doing so, you can use the internal ISE CA to issue certificates while still maintaining a single chain of trust.

For the purpose of the CCIE exam and this book, we will not discuss using an external CA or the mechanics of the internal CA. It is sufficient to know that the internal CA in ISE is enabled by default and creates the required PKI on first boot. Each PSN acts as a sub CA and can issue certificates to clients. The provided *Internal CA SCEP RA Profile* can be used in certificate templates directly without any additional configuration.

The *certificate template* defines the attributes of the certificate that will be generated for the endpoint during onboarding. ISE provides a default template that can be used in NSP, called *EAP_Authentication_Certificate_Template*. The certificate template, shown in Figure 4-7, can be viewed or edited by navigating to **Work Centers > BYOD > Portals & Components > Certificates > Certificate Templates**.

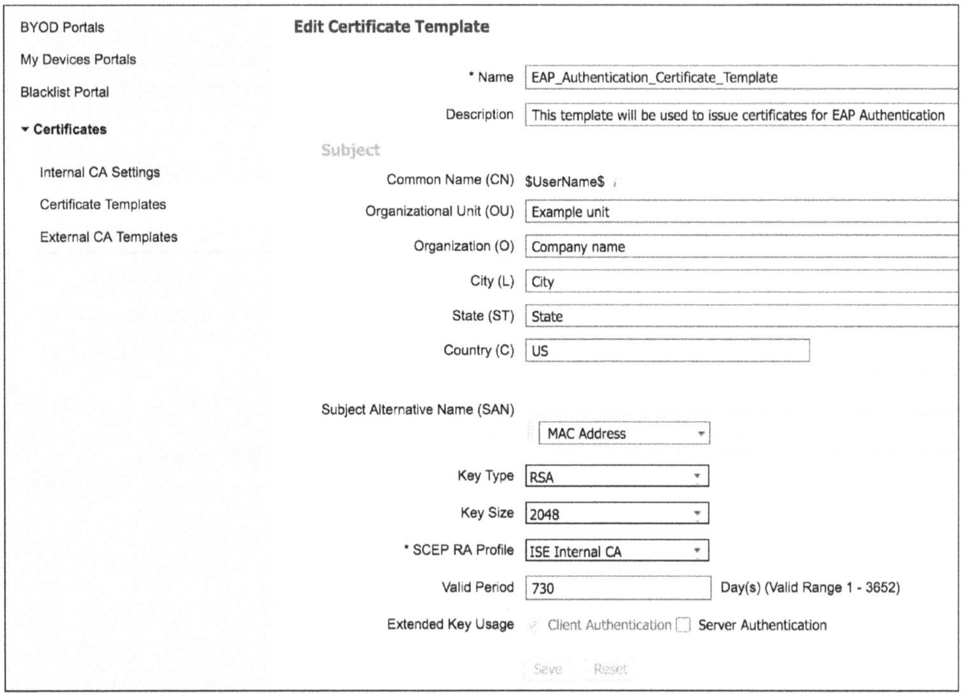

Figure 4-7 *Certificate Template*

The key components of the certificate template, show in Figure 4-7, are as follows:

- The Common Name (CN) field has a fixed value of $UserName$ and is replaced with the actual username from initial authentication.

- The Organizational Unit (OU), Organization (O), City (L), State (ST) and Country © fields have placeholder values and can be edited as needed.

- The Subject Alternative Name (SAN) field has a single option in the drop-down field for now—MAC Address. This is substituted with the actual MAC address of the endpoint received in the RADIUS request during initial authentication.

- The Key Type field allows the selection of RSA or ECC. ECC support is limited in operating systems and should be used carefully.

- Depending on the key type used, you can select the appropriate Key Size (RSA) or Curve Type (ECC).

- The SCEP RA Profile drop-down list shows the available SCEP profiles. This field defines the CA server that will be used to generate the certificate. Notice in Figure 4-7 that the prebuilt ISE Internal CA profile is available as an option

- The Valid Period field defines the length of time for which the certificate will be considered valid. Once this period expires, the endpoint will need to go through the onboarding process again.

■ The Extended Key Usage field defines the EKUs that will be added to the certificate. Most often, only the Client Authentication EKU is required for endpoints.

We will use the prebuilt EAP Authentication Certificate Template for the purpose of this chapter.

Note   You will notice a similar theme of using prebuilt elements throughout this chapter. Using prebuilt elements in your CCIE lab, where possible, will save a lot of time.

Configuring the Native Supplicant Profile

Referring back to Figure 4-5, the Native Supplicant Profile (NSP) is a key component required to create the client provisioning rule. We have now configured the two elements required to configure the NSP itself. ISE comes with a prebuilt NSP profile that can be modified as required. To edit the prebuilt profile, Cisco-ISE-NSP, navigate to **Work Centers > BYOD > Client Provisioning > Resources**, select **Cisco-ISE-NSP**, and click **Edit**. Figure 4-8 shows the profile that opens.

Figure 4-8 *Native Supplicant Profile*

Notice in Figure 4-8 that this NSP is divided into two sections—Wireless Profile(s) and Wired Profile—and applies to all operating systems. The Wireless Profile(s) section shows the configuration for the secure SSID, *CCIE-Secure*, that has already been configured for this example. To see the details of a profile in that section, check the check box to the left of the profile and click **Edit**. Figure 4-9 shows the details of the CCIE-Secure profile from our example.

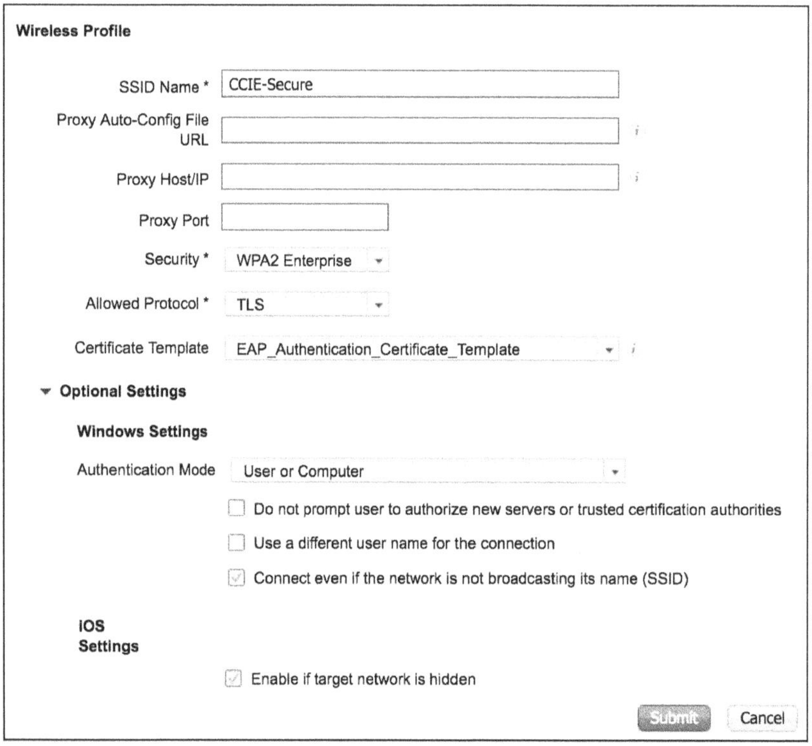

Figure 4-9 *Details of an SSID Profile in NSP*

As shown in Figure 4-9, the profile is configured to connect to an SSID named CCIE-Secure using EAP-TLS, and the prebuilt certificate template, discussed earlier, will be used to generate the certificate. In the Optional Settings section, Windows- and iOS-specific settings have been enabled to allow the endpoint to connect to the SSID even if it is not being broadcasted.

The NSP can be similarly configured to provision the endpoint for multiple SSIDs or wired network. You can also create OS-specific NSPs if you need different device types to connect to different SSIDs.

Downloading Supplicant Wizards

Referring back to Figure 4-5 again, we now have configured one of the two key components required to configure the client provisioning rules. The second key component required is the provisioning agent. Particular, the *SPWizard* for Windows and Apple OS X. The agents will need to be downloaded directly to ISE from a Cisco site. To download the agents:

Note   Downloading the SPWizards requires Internet connection from the ISE PAN. If a direct Internet connection is not available, then configure a proxy by navigating to **Administration > System > Settings > Proxy.**

Step 1.   Navigate to **Work Centers > BYOD > Client Provisioning > Resources.**

Step 2.   Click **Add.**

Step 3.   Choose **Agent resources from Cisco site.** This open the a pop-up window shown in Figure 4-10 and populates it with options from the Cisco site.

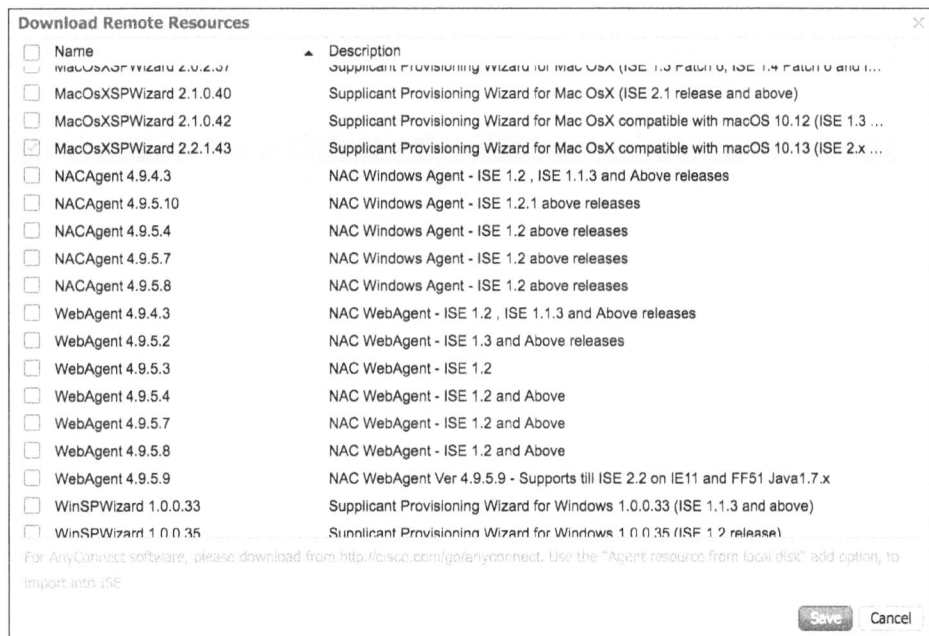

Download Remote Resources   ✕

	Name	▲	Description
	MacOsXSPWizard 2.0.2.37		Supplicant Provisioning Wizard for Mac OsX (ISE 1.3 Patch 6, ISE 1.4 Patch 6 and I...
	MacOsXSPWizard 2.1.0.40		Supplicant Provisioning Wizard for Mac OsX (ISE 2.1 release and above)
	MacOsXSPWizard 2.1.0.42		Supplicant Provisioning Wizard for Mac OsX compatible with macOS 10.12 (ISE 1.3 ...
☑	MacOsXSPWizard 2.2.1.43		Supplicant Provisioning Wizard for Mac OsX compatible with macOS 10.13 (ISE 2.x ...
	NACAgent 4.9.4.3		NAC Windows Agent - ISE 1.2 , ISE 1.1.3 and Above releases
	NACAgent 4.9.5.10		NAC Windows Agent - ISE 1.2.1 above releases
	NACAgent 4.9.5.4		NAC Windows Agent - ISE 1.2 above releases
	NACAgent 4.9.5.7		NAC Windows Agent - ISE 1.2 above releases
	NACAgent 4.9.5.8		NAC Windows Agent - ISE 1.2 above releases
	WebAgent 4.9.4.3		NAC WebAgent - ISE 1.2 , ISE 1.1.3 and Above releases
	WebAgent 4.9.5.2		NAC WebAgent - ISE 1.3 and Above releases
	WebAgent 4.9.5.3		NAC WebAgent - ISE 1.2
	WebAgent 4.9.5.4		NAC WebAgent - ISE 1.2 and Above
	WebAgent 4.9.5.7		NAC WebAgent - ISE 1.2 and Above
	WebAgent 4.9.5.8		NAC WebAgent - ISE 1.2 and Above
	WebAgent 4.9.5.9		NAC WebAgent Ver 4.9.5.9 - Supports till ISE 2.2 on IE11 and FF51 Java1.7.x
	WinSPWizard 1.0.0.33		Supplicant Provisioning Wizard for Windows 1.0.0.33 (ISE 1.1.3 and above)
	WinSPWizard 1.0.0.35		Supplicant Provisioning Wizard for Windows 1.0.0.35 (ISE 1.2 release)

For AnyConnect software, please download from http://cisco.com/go/anyconnect. Use the "Agent resource from local disk" add option to import into ISE

Save   Cancel

Figure 4-10   *Downloading SPWizards*

Note   The pop-up window consists of files required for other flows such as posture. For the purpose of BYOD onboarding, we only need the MacOsXSPWizard and WinSPWizard files.

Step 4.   Check the check boxes to the left of the latest MacOsXSPWizard and WinSPWizard files.

Note   Select the latest file in a major version series such as 1.x or 2.x depending on the ISE version being used. In case of Windows SPWizard, also pay attention to the minor version because some of the versions, such as 2.4.0.1, are specific to the switch code also. The description text next to the filename in the pop-up window is self-explanatory.

Step 5.   Click **Save.**

Once downloaded, the files will be available in the Resources section, as shown in Figure 4-11.

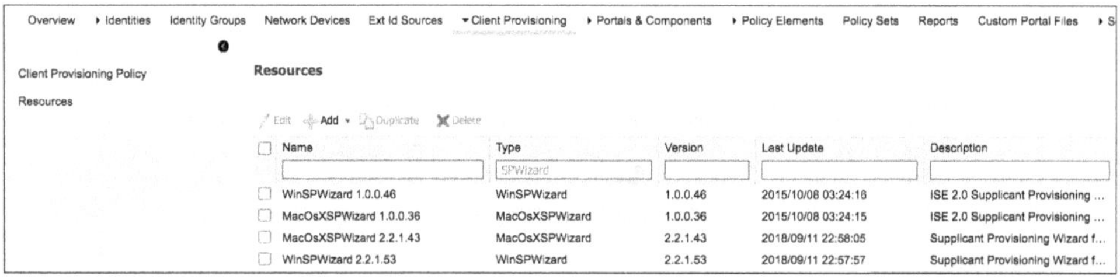

Figure 4-11   *Downloaded SPWizards*

Configuring Client Provisioning Policy

Once all the required components have been downloaded or configured, you can create the Client Provisioning Policy (CPP) finally. Remember that client provisioning rules in the CPP are used to provision the agents as well as to push the required certificates and supplicant configuration.

The CPP can be configured by navigating to **Policy > Client Provisioning.** By default, ISE provides one preconfigured rule for each supported operating system using the prebuilt elements previously discussed. Figure 4-12 shows an example of this page.

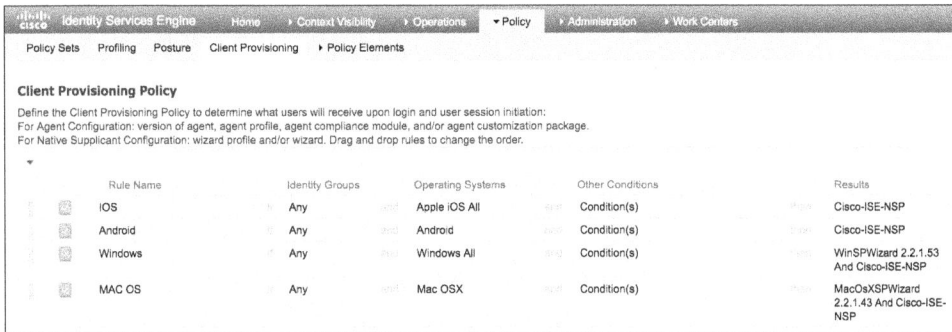

Figure 4-12   *Client Provisioning Policy*

Notice that the IOS and Android rules only have the NSP defined as a result in the Results column, whereas the Windows and MAC OS rules have the SPWizard and NSP defined. This is because ISE does not push any agent for Apple iOS and Android. While OTA is used to provision devices running Apple iOS, the users are redirected to the Google Play store to download the required agent on Android.

You can choose to use the existing rules as they are, edit them, or delete them and add new custom rules. To edit these rules, follow these steps:

Step 1.   Click **Edit** at the end of the row containing the rule.

Step 2.   Click the **+** symbol in the Results column. The configuration options displayed in the drop-down window will differ based on the operating system. Windows and MAC OS rules have more options, as shown in Figure 4-13, while Android and iOS rules have a single option, as shown in Figure 4-14.

Figure 4-13   *Windows Client Provisioning Rule*

Figure 4-14   *Apple iOS Client Provisioning Rule*

Note Ignore the Agent Configuration section shown in the results section of the Windows and MAC OS rules. These are used for posture agent provisioning and will be discussed later in the chapter.

Step 3. Select the desired NSP and/or SPWizard in the respective drop-down list in the Results column.

Step 4. Click the minus (–) sign in the Results column.

Step 5. Click **Done** at the end of the row.

Step 6. Repeat Steps 1 to 5 for each rule that you need to edit.

Step 7. Click **Save** at the end of the page.

Note While we only discussed the Results column of the rule for the purpose of the exam, note the Other Conditions column of the rule also. This can be used to create multiple provisioning policies for an operating system depending on the use case. For example, you might need to create two policies for Apple iOS based on the provisioning SSID to which the device is connected.

Configuring Portals for BYOD Onboarding

Now that you have configured the first of the three main components of a BYOD flow, it is time to look at the second component—portals. These are the provisioning portals that will help the end user navigate the onboarding process.

There are multiple types of portals that can be created on ISE. Each portal type serves a particular function. Out of those, two types of portals can be configured for BYOD depending on the initial authentication method. For a MAB-based flow, such as the Dual SSID flow (or a wired MAB authentication), a guest portal needs to be configured with onboarding enabled to allow user to authenticate before provisioning begins. For an 802.1X-based flow, such as the Single SSID flow, because the authentication is already completed using 802.1X, a BYOD portal will need to be configured.

First, let's look at the steps to create the guest portal required for a Dual SSID flow:

Step 1. Navigate to **Work Centers > Guest Access > Portals & Components > Guest Portals.**

Step 2. Click **Create.**

Step 3. Select **Sponsored-Guest Portal** and click **Continue.**

Step 4. Provide a name for the portal. For this example, we will use **Dual SSID Onboard** as the name of the portal.

Step 5. Expand the **Portal Settings** section as shown in Figure 4-15.

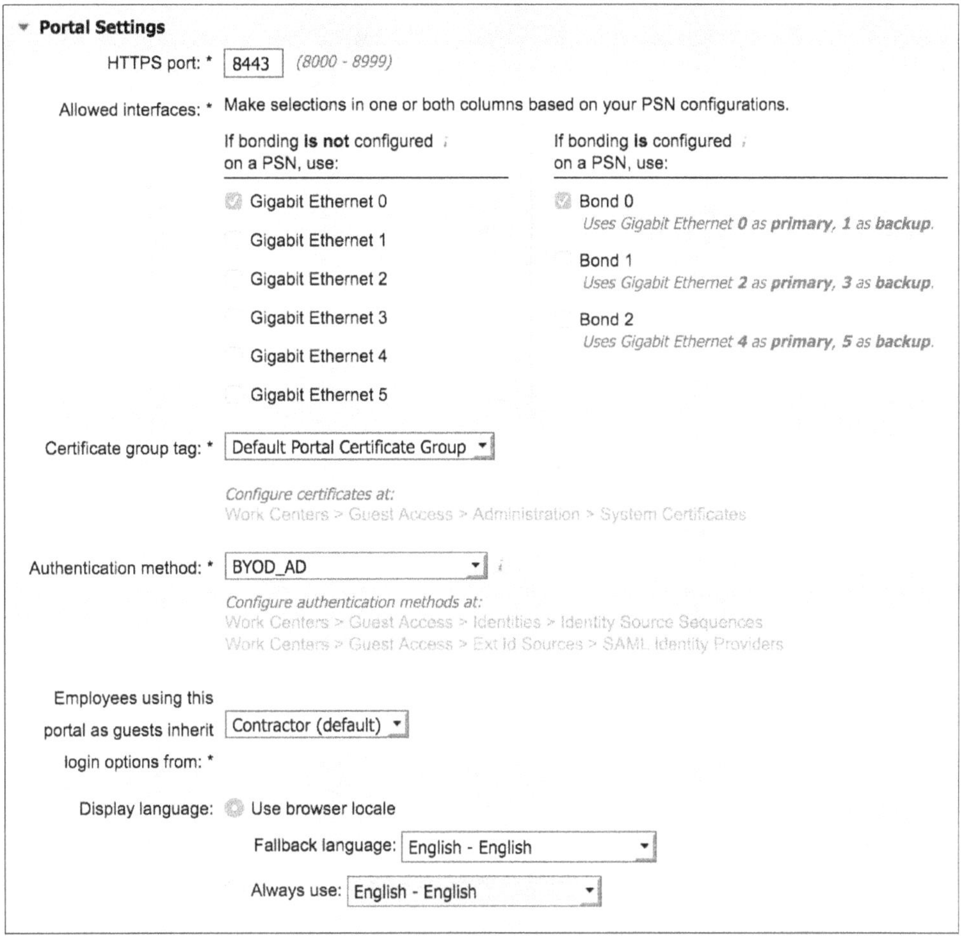

Portal Settings

HTTPS port: * `8443` *(8000 - 8999)*

Allowed interfaces: * Make selections in one or both columns based on your PSN configurations.

If bonding **is not** configured ⓘ
on a PSN, use:

If bonding **is** configured ⓘ
on a PSN, use:

☑ Gigabit Ethernet 0
☐ Gigabit Ethernet 1
☐ Gigabit Ethernet 2
☐ Gigabit Ethernet 3
☐ Gigabit Ethernet 4
☐ Gigabit Ethernet 5

☑ Bond 0
*Uses Gigabit Ethernet **0** as **primary**, **1** as **backup**.*

Bond 1
*Uses Gigabit Ethernet **2** as **primary**, **3** as **backup**.*

Bond 2
*Uses Gigabit Ethernet **4** as **primary**, **5** as **backup**.*

Certificate group tag: * `Default Portal Certificate Group ▾`

Configure certificates at:
Work Centers > Guest Access > Administration > System Certificates

Authentication method: * `BYOD_AD ▾` ⓘ

Configure authentication methods at:
Work Centers > Guest Access > Identities > Identity Source Sequences
Work Centers > Guest Access > Ext Id Sources > SAML Identity Providers

Employees using this
portal as guests inherit `Contractor (default) ▾`
login options from: *

Display language: ◉ Use browser locale
Fallback language: `English - English ▾`
Always use: `English - English ▾`

Figure 4-15 *Portal Settings on Guest Portal for BYOD*

The key fields that you need to configure for BYOD are as follows:

- **Ports and interfaces:** The default is for ISE to listen on interfaces Gigabit Ethernet 0 and Bond 0 and port 8443. Change these only if your network design calls for different interfaces and ports.

- **Certificate group tag:** Defines the tag that maps to the certificate that will be used for this portal.

- **Authentication method:** Defines the ID source sequence that will be used to authenticate this portal. For BYOD, this will usually point to a corporate directory such as AD.

Note For this example, an ID source sequence named BYOD_AD, which points to AD for authentication, was pre-created.

Step 6. Expand the BYOD Settings section as shown in Figure 4-16.

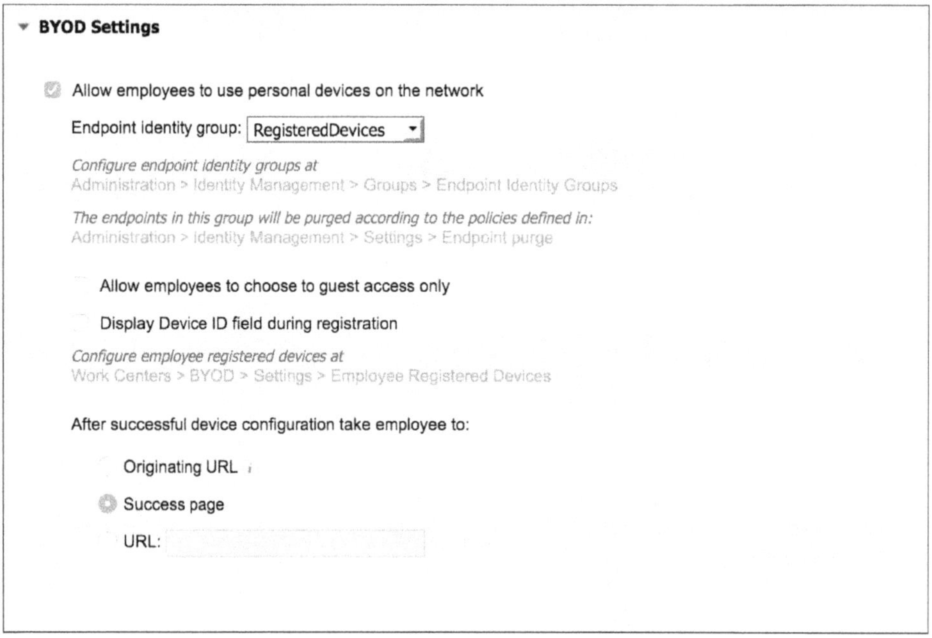

▾ **BYOD Settings**

☑ Allow employees to use personal devices on the network

Endpoint Identity group: | RegisteredDevices ▾ |

Configure endpoint identity groups at
Administration > Identity Management > Groups > Endpoint Identity Groups

The endpoints in this group will be purged according to the policies defined in:
Administration > Identity Management > Settings > Endpoint purge

Allow employees to choose to guest access only

Display Device ID field during registration

Configure employee registered devices at
Work Centers > BYOD > Settings > Employee Registered Devices

After successful device configuration take employee to:

Originating URL

⦿ Success page

URL:

Figure 4-16 *BYOD Settings on Guest Portal*

Step 7. Check the **Allow employees to use personal devices on the network** check box, as shown in Figure 4-16. This is the option that will result in the BYOD flow starting after authentication.

Note These steps configure the minimum required options on the portal. There are various other options for configuration such as Acceptable User Policy (AUP) that can be configured to meet other requirements. In addition to that, the Portal Page Customization tab contains various options to customize the look of the portal to meet any branding requirements. These are not covered in this book to keep it more relevant to the CCIE exam.

Step 8. Click **Save** at the top of the page.

For a Single SSID or similar 802.1X-based flow (wired 802.1X, for example), because the initial authentication is taken care of during the 802.1X exchange, the user does not need to authenticate again on the portal. Hence, for such flows, ISE provides a separate BYOD portal and has a default one prebuilt. While you can create a custom BYOD portal, the default one can be edited to suit most needs. The default BYOD portal can be edited as follows:

Step 1.   Navigate to **Work Centers > BYOD > Portals & Components > BYOD Portals.**

Step 2.   Click **BYOD Portal (default).** You will notice that this portal has far fewer options than the guest portal. This is because this portal can only be used for BYOD onboarding.

Step 3.   Expand the **Portal Settings** section as shown in Figure 4-17. The options available in this section are very similar to those available in the guest portal. The key difference is that there is no option for ID Store. Instead, there is an option to select the group to which the device will be registered.

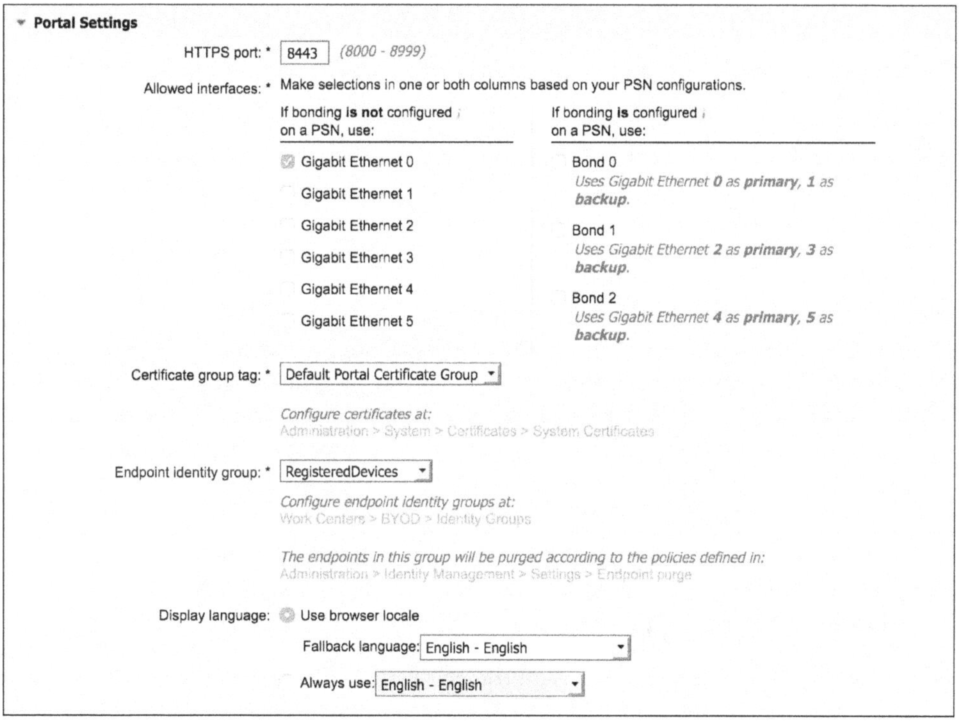

Figure 4-17   *Portal Settings on BYOD Portal*

Step 4.   Expand the **BYOD Settings** section as shown in Figure 4-18. All the options in this section are optional and what you select here will depend on your policy requirements.

```
▼ BYOD Settings

    ☑ Include an AUP on page ▾
            Require acceptance

                Require scrolling to end of AUP

    ☑ Display Device ID field during registration
    Configure employee registered devices at
    Work Centers > BYOD > Settings > Employee Registered Devices

    After successful device configuration take employee to:

        Originating URL

    ⚙ Success page
        URL:
```

Figure 4-18   *BYOD Settings on the BYOD Portal*

> **Step 5.**   Click **Save** at the top of the page.

Note   As with the guest portal, we configured the minimum required settings. Other settings, including those under the Portal Page Customization tab, can be used as required for policy and branding needs.

Configuring Policy Set for BYOD Onboarding

Two down, one to go! Out of the three required components, we have configured two. You should already be very familiar with the third component—Policy Sets. As you saw in Chapter 2, policy sets and the authentication and authorization rules contained in them are the foundation of ISE. They tie up the various components and make the magic happen. Even with BYOD onboarding, the policy sets play the key role and redirect the users to the correct portals and grant access after onboarding.

As usual, before configuring the authentication and authorization rules, you need to configure authentication and authorization profiles. For the two BYOD flows, the following four profiles are needed:

- **Authentication profile (Allowed Protocols list):** For the purpose of BYOD onboarding, host lookup (MAB), PEAP, and EAP-TLS need to be allowed for the different flows. The Default Network Access profile allows all of these protocols, so we will use that for our examples.

- **Authorization profile for Dual SSID flow:** During a Dual SSID flow, the network device will send an initial MAB request and the user will need to be redirected to the Guest Authentication portal that has BYOD onboarding enabled. For this, we need to create an authorization profile as shown in Figure 4-19. The profile is named Dual_SSID_Onboard and has Web Redirection enabled, with Centralized Web Auth selected. The ACL for URL Redirection is set to **redirect**. This is the URL

Redirection ACL created on the network device as shown previously in Figure 4-1 and Figure 4-2. Lastly, the Value field is set to the Dual SSID Onboard portal that we created previously (see Figure 4-15).

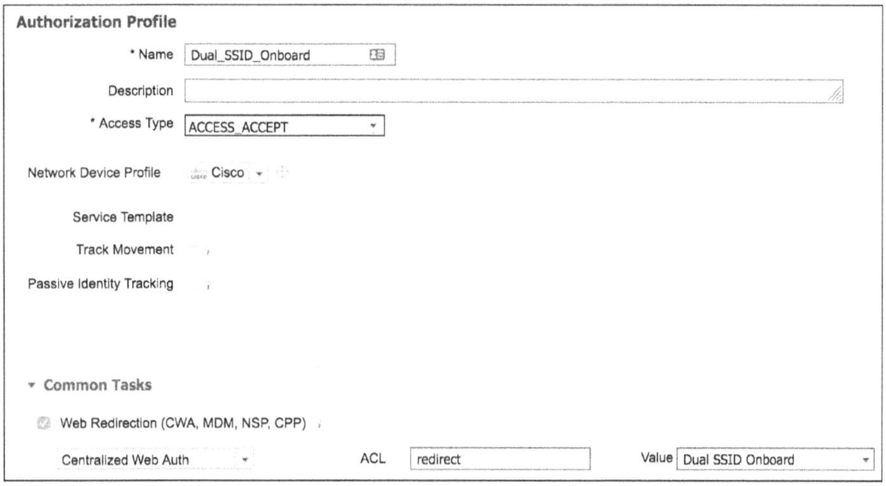

Figure 4-19 *Authorization Profile for Dual SSID Flow*

■ **Authorization profile for Single SSID flow:** During a Single SSID flow, the user authenticates using a less secure EAP method and is redirected to the BYOD portal for onboarding. For this, we need to create an authorization profile as shown in Figure 4-20. The profile is named Single_SSID_Onboard and has Web Redirection enabled, with Native Supplicant Provisioning selected. The ACL value is again set to **redirect** but the Value field is set to BYOD Portal (default) to redirect users to the BYOD portal we edited earlier (see Figure 4-17).

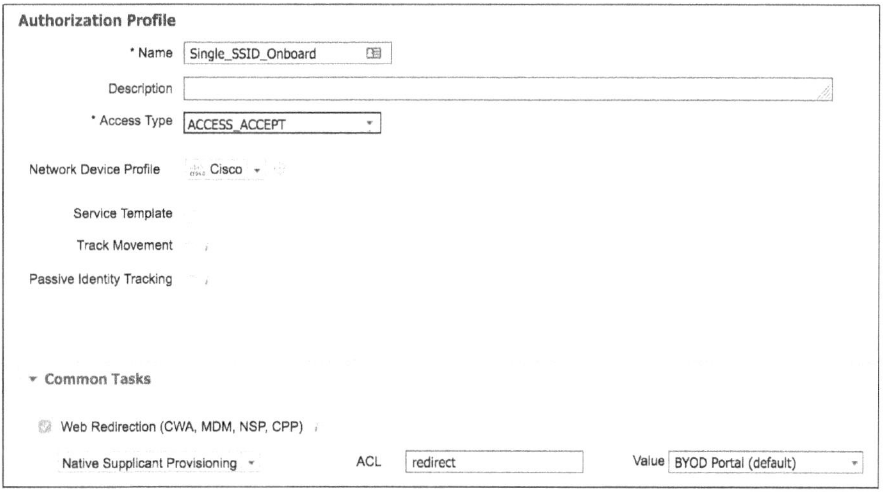

Figure 4-20 *Authorization Profile for Single SSID Flow*

■ **Authorization profile for onboarded devices:** The last profile that we need is to grant access to devices after onboarding. For the purpose of our example, we will use the pre-built PermitAccess profile.

Now that we have created the required profiles, we have everything we need to create the policy set. For the purpose of example, we will use two SSIDs: CCIE-Secure and CCIE-Onboard. As the names suggest, CCIE-Secure is used as the secure or corporate SSID that the device should connect to after onboarding. It is also the SSID that the device connects to for onboarding in Single SSID flow. CCIE-Onboard is the open SSID that the device connects to for onboarding in Dual SSID flow. Configuration of these SSIDs on the WLC will be discussed in the next section.

Note   For purpose of example, this section uses simplistic conditions to create a policy set and its authentication and authorization rules. As you know by now, various types of conditions can be used in ISE to accomplish the same result. While such simplistic conditions are recommended for the CCIE lab, an actual production setup will most likely require more refined conditions and rules.

Given that we know the SSID names, we can create a policy set that matches any session connected to these SSIDs. To match such sessions, we will use the RADIUS:Called-Station-ID AV pair in the condition.

Note   When defining a RADIUS server on the Cisco WLC, one of the configuration options allows the value of the Called-Station-ID attribute to be set to AP MAC Address:SSID. We are using this AV pair to match sessions connecting to any SSID that contains CCIE in its name.

The policy set can be created using the following steps:

Step 1.   Navigate to **Policy > Policy Sets** (or **Work Centers > BYOD > Policy Sets**).

Step 2.   Click the **+** sign in the top left corner of the table.

Step 3.   Enter a name for the policy set. For this example, we will use **CCIE-BYOD**.

Step 4.   Click the **+** sign in the Conditions column.

Step 5.   In the Editor section, click the field that reads **Click to add an attribute**.

Step 6.   Type **Called** in the search box under the Attribute column.

Step 7.   Select the **Called-Station-ID** attribute.

Step 8.   Select **Contains** from the drop-down list.

Step 9.   Type **CCIE** in the Attribute value text box, as shown in Figure 4-21.

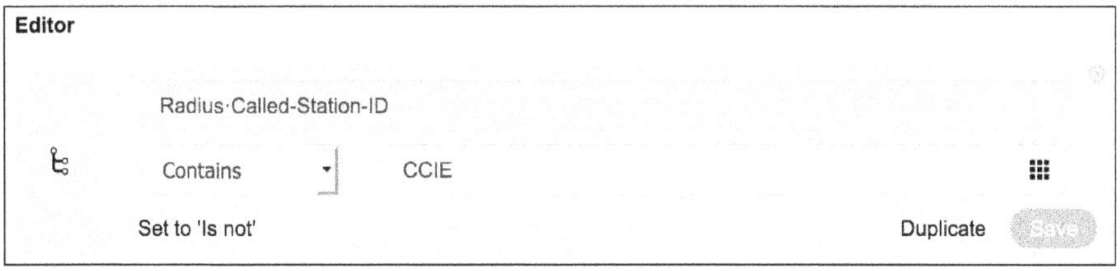

Figure 4-21   *Policy Set Condition*

Step 10.   Click **Use**.

Step 11.   Select **Default Network Access** from the Allowed Protocols/Server Sequence drop-down list, as shown in Figure 4-22.

Step 12.   Click **Save**.

Figure 4-22   *Creating the Policy Set*

Because we are creating a single policy set for both the flows, we will require three authentication rules in the policy set. The first authentication is required for MAB authentication received at the start of the Dual SSID flow. The second rule is required to authenticate PEAP authentication received during the initial authentication of the Single SSID flow. The final rule is required to allow certificate-based authentication after onboarding. The three authentication rules can be created using the following steps:

Step 1.   Click the **>** symbol in the View column next to the new policy set (CCIE-BYOD in our example).

Step 2.   Expand the **Authentication Policy** section.

Step 3.   Select **Preloaded_Certificate_Profile** in the Use column of the Default rule, as shown in Figure 4-23. This allows EAP-TLS authentication after onboarding.

Figure 4-23   *Authentication Rule to Allow Certificate-Based Authentication*

Step 4.   Click the gear icon in the Actions column for the Default rule and click **Insert new row above**.

Step 5.   Enter **Single_SSID_Onboard** as the name of the new rule.

Step 6.   Click the **Conditions** column in the new rule.

Step 7.   Select **EAP-MSCHAPv2** from the Library section on the left and drag it to the Editor section on the right, as shown in Figure 4-24. This condition checks for PEAP authentication from the Single SSID flow.

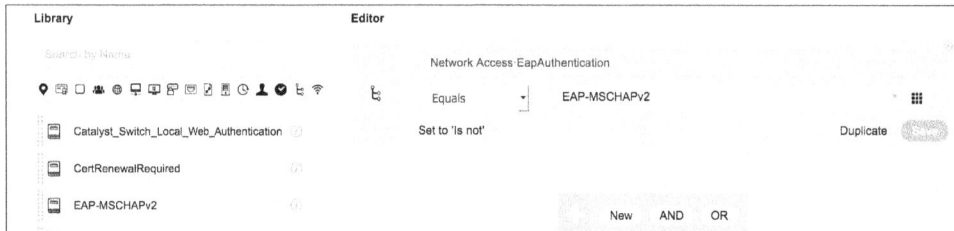

Figure 4-24   *Condition for Single SSID Authentication Rule*

Step 8.   Click **Use**.

Step 9.   Select an ID store from the drop-down list in the Use column. In this example, **AD** is selected.

Step 10.   Click the gear icon in the Actions column for the new rule just created and select **Insert new row above**.

Step 11.   Enter **Dual_SSID_Onboard** as the name of the rule.

Step 12.   Click the **Conditions** column in the new rule.

Step 13.   Select **Wireless_MAB** from the Library section on the left and drag it to the Editor section on the right, as shown in Figure 4-25. This condition checks for MAB authentication from the Dual SSID flow.

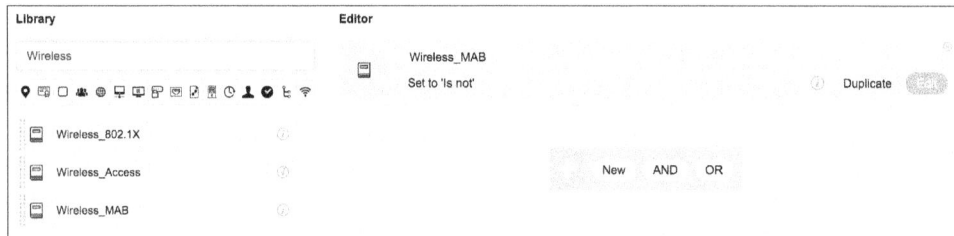

Figure 4-25   *Condition for Dual SSID Authentication Rule*

Step 14.   Select **Internal Endpoints** from the drop-down list in the Use column.

Step 15.   Expand the **Options** section in the same column.

Step 16.   Set the If Auth Fail and If User not found drop-down list boxes to **CONTINUE**, as shown in Figure 4-26. This is required to allow MAB sessions to continue to authorization even if the MAC address is not present in the database.

Figure 4-26 shows the completed Authentication Policy section.

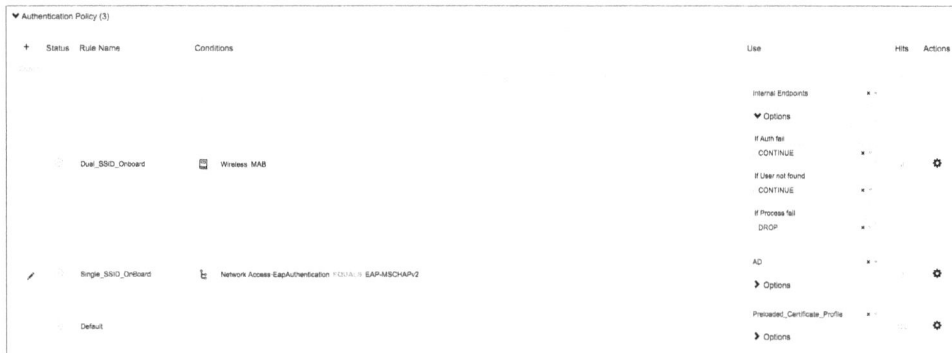

Figure 4-26   *Completed Authentication Policy for BYOD Onboarding*

The last thing we need to complete the configuration for BYOD onboarding on ISE is the authorization policy in the policy set. As with the authentication policy, we need three rules in the authorization policy. The first rule is to allow access after onboarding, the second is to redirect MAB requests to the web authentication portal, and the last is to redirect PEAP authentication to the BYOD portal. The rules can be created using the following steps:

Step 1.   Expand the **Authorization Policy** section.

Step 2.   Replace the Profile for the Default rule with **DenyAccess**.

Step 3.   Click the gear icon in the Actions column for the Default rule and select **Insert new row above.**

Step 4.   Name the new rule **CCIE-Secure-EAP_TLS.**

Step 5.   Click the **Conditions** column in the new rule.

Step 6.   Select **EAP-TLS** from the Library section on the left and drag it to the Editor section on the right, as shown in Figure 4-27. This condition checks for EAP-TLS authentication that is expected after onboarding.

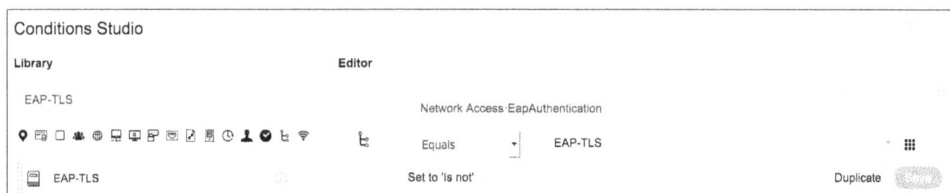

Figure 4-27   *Condition for EAP-TLS Authorization*

Step 7.   Click **Use.**

Step 8.   Select **PermitAccess** from the drop-down list in the Profiles column of the new rule.

Step 9.   Click the gear icon in the Actions column for the rule and select **Insert new row above.**

Step 10.   Name the new rule **Dual_SSID_Initial_Auth.**

Step 11.   Click the **Conditions** column in the new rule.

Step 12.   Select **Wireless_MAB** from the Library section on the left and drag it to the Editor section on the right, as shown in Figure 4-28. This condition checks for the MAB authentication expected during Dual SSID flow.

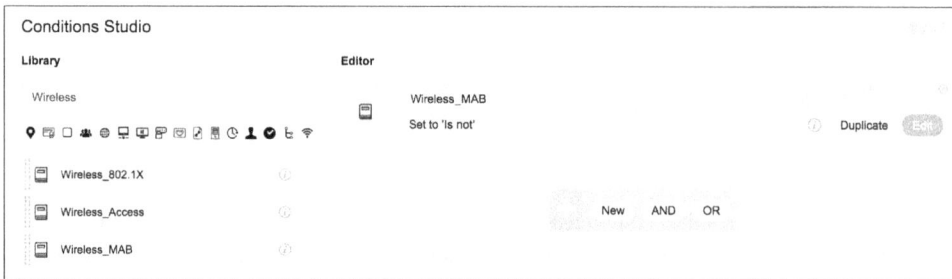

Figure 4-28   *Condition for Dual SSID Authorization*

Step 13.   Click **Use.**

Step 14.   Select **Dual_SSID_Onboard** from the drop-down list in the Profiles column of the new rule. This authorization profile was created earlier to redirect Dual SSID flow to the web authentication portal.

Step 15.   Click the gear icon in the Actions column for the rule and select **Insert new row above.**

Step 16.   Name the new rule **Single_SSID_Initial_Auth.**

Step 17.   Click the **Conditions** column in the new rule.

Step 18.   Select **EAP-MSCHAPv2** from the Library section on the left and drag it to the Editor section on the right, as shown in Figure 4-29. This condition checks for PEAP authentication expected during Single SSID flow.

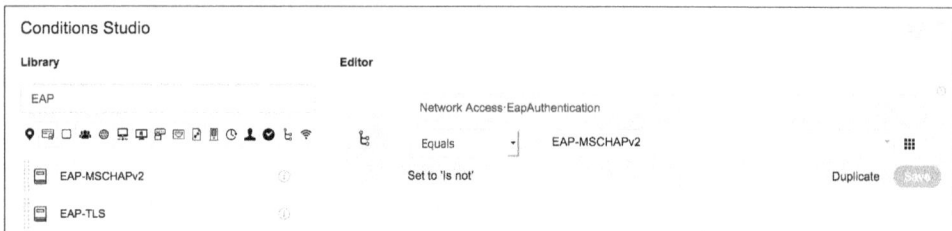

Figure 4-29   *Condition for Single SSID Authorization*

Step 19. Click **Use**.

Step 20. Select **Single_SSID_Onboard** from the drop-down list in the Profiles column of the new rule. This authorization profile was created earlier to redirect Single SSID flow to the web authentication portal.

Step 21. Click **Save**.

Figure 4-30 shows the completed authorization policy.

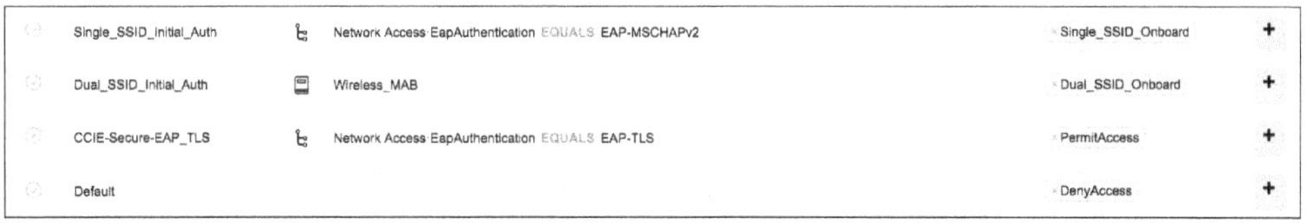

Single_SSID_Initial_Auth	Network Access:EapAuthentication EQUALS EAP-MSCHAPv2	Single_SSID_Onboard	+
Dual_SSID_Initial_Auth	Wireless_MAB	Dual_SSID_Onboard	+
CCIE-Secure-EAP_TLS	Network Access:EapAuthentication EQUALS EAP-TLS	PermitAccess	+
Default		DenyAccess	+

Figure 4-30 *Authorization Policy for BYOD Onboarding*

Network Device Configuration for BYOD Onboarding

After configuring ISE, the network device (WLC in this case) needs to be configured for BYOD onboarding. The configuration of the WLC was covered in Chapter 2, so we will only focus on creating the two example SSIDs and the redirect ACLs in this section. The first SSID will be the CCIE-Onboard SSID used for the Dual SSID flow and the second will be the CCIE-Secure SSID used for the Single SSID flow and post-onboarding access.

Note Add ISE as a RADIUS server on the WLC before creating the SSIDs.

The steps to create the SSIDs are as follows:

Step 1. Navigate to the **WLAN** menu on the WLC UI.

Step 2. Click **Go** at the top of the page.

Step 3. In the Profile Name and SSID fields, enter **CCIE-Onboard**.

Step 4. Click **Apply**.

Step 5. Check the Status **Enabled** check box, as shown in Figure 4-31.

Step 6. Click the **Security** tab.

Step 7. Set the Layer 2 Security spin box to **None**.

Step 8. Check the **MAC Filtering** check box, as shown in Figure 4-32.

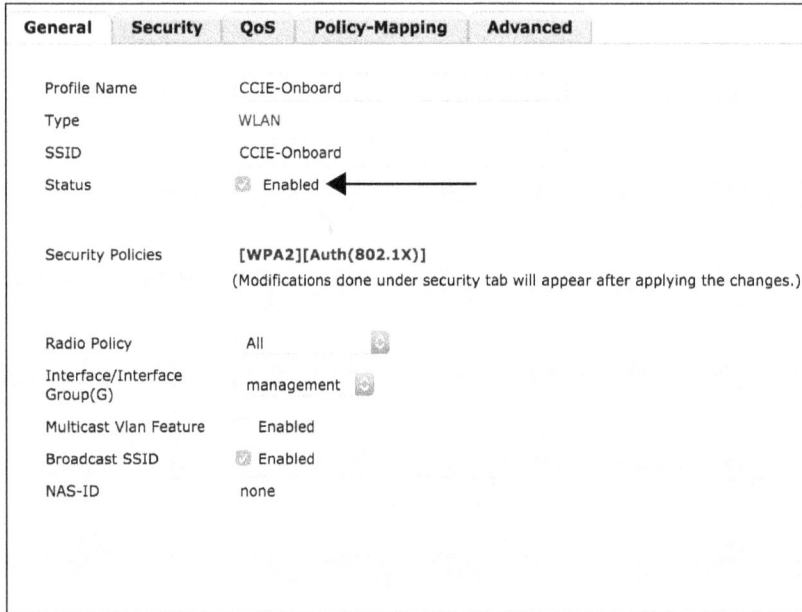

Figure 4-31   *Enabling Onboarding SSID*

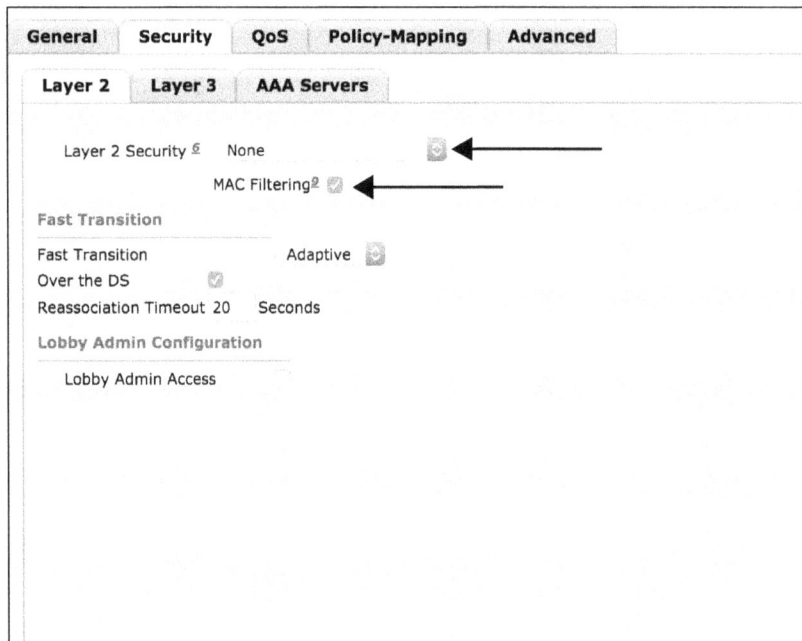

Figure 4-32   *Security Configuration for Onboarding SSID*

Step 9.   Click the **AAA Servers** tab.

Step 10.   Select the IP address or name of ISE as the Authentication and Authorization Server. Figure 4-33 shows 192.168.1.11, the ISE PSN, selected as Authentication and Authorization Server.

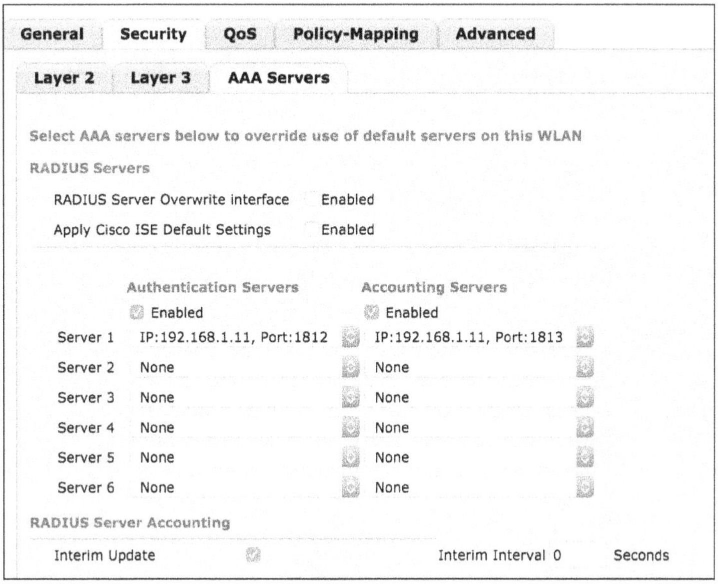

Figure 4-33   *AAA Server Configuration for Onboarding SSID*

Step 11.   Click the **Advanced** tab.

Step 12.   Check the DHCP Addr. Assignment **Required** check box.

Step 13.   Set the NAC State spin box to **ISE NAC**, as shown in Figure 4-34.

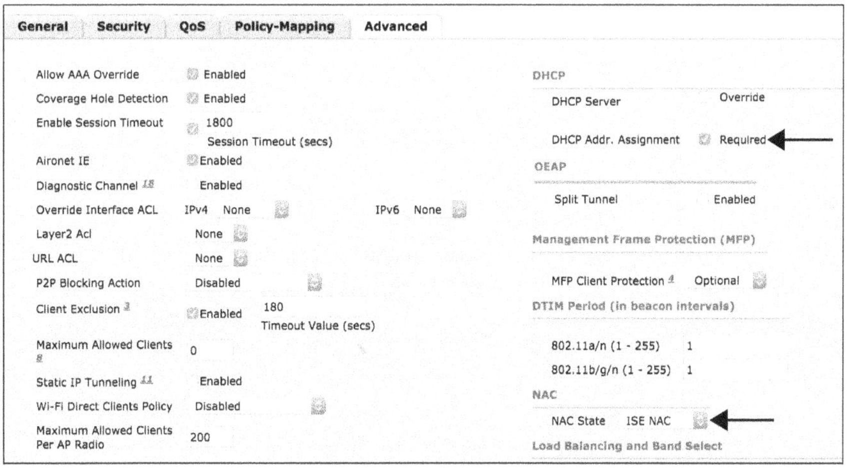

Figure 4-34   *Configuring Advanced SSID Options*

Step 14. Click **Apply** and then click **Back**.

Step 15. To start creating the second SSID, repeat Steps 1 and 2.

Step 16. Enter **CCIE-Secure** in the Profile Name and SSID fields.

Step 17. Repeat Steps 4 to 6 to apply the change and enable the SSID.

Step 18. Ensure that the Layer 2 Security field is set to **WPA+WPA2** and, in the Authentication Key Management section, that the 802.1X **Enable** check box is checked, as shown in Figure 4-35.

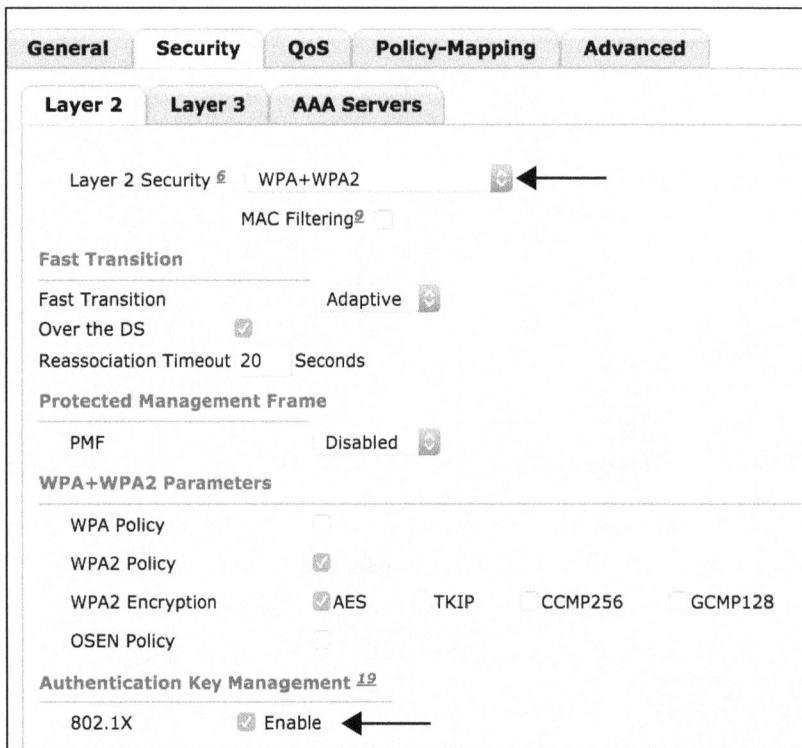

Figure 4-35 *Security Configuration for Secure SSID*

Step 19. Repeat Steps 9 to 14 to complete the configuration of the second SSID.

After creating the SSIDs, you need to create the redirect ACL. Apart from creating the normal IP-based redirect ACL as discussed in the beginning of the chapter, you will also need to create DNS-based ACLs. The DNS-based ACLs are required for two reasons:

■ Android users will need to connect to the Google Play store to download the provisioning agent. To connect to the Play store and download a file, Android has to connect to multiple hosts that reside behind load balancers. It is not practical to list every IP address or subnet that Android can connect to in the redirect ACL. To add to the problem, these IP addresses and subnets can change often. With DNS ACLs, traffic to DNS domains can be permitted without worrying about IP addresses and subnets.

■ When an Apple iOS–based device connects to a network, it sends an HTTP request to captive.apple.com. If this connection succeeds, the OS assumes it has full Internet access. If the connection is redirected, then it opens a utility called Captive Network Assistant (CNA) and displays the redirected page to allow users to authenticate. CNA is limited in functionality and cannot support a full BYOD onboarding flow. Hence, the flow requires the OS to not open CNA and allow the user to open a browser. This can be done by allowing the initial HTTP request from the device to go through by allowing the URL in a DNS ACL.

DNS ACLs in the WLC are added as part of the redirect IP ACL. Here are a few things to remember regarding DNS ACL:

■ DNS ACLs in the WLC are also known as URL lists.

■ When you add a URL, the WLC adds a preceding implicit wildcard. For example, if you add cisco.com, the WLC will assume *.cisco.com.

■ The implicit wildcard does not extend beyond one level. That means when you add cisco.com, it equates only to *.cisco.com and not to *.*.cisco.com.

■ The URLs that devices use for any function can change—especially at the sub-domain level. For example, Google may decide to change the subdomain where the Play store files reside. You can choose to create a broad URL list to protect against such changes but that will result in the users having more access than planned before onboarding. On the other hand, a restrictive URL list will mean the flow can break sometimes.

■ Google does change the domains often. It is difficult to pin down an accurate and specific list of URLs that Android requires to download a file from the Play store. This is even more so when the users are outside the United States. The following list is known to work the best:

google.com	googleusercontent.com
gstatic.com	googleapis.com
google-analytics.com	play.google.com
ggpht.com	gvt1.com
goo.gl	clients.google.com
android.clients.google.com	android.com

To configure DNS ACLs, first create a normal IP-based redirect ACL, as shown in Figure 4-2 at the start of the chapter, and then use the following steps:

Step 1.   Navigate to **Security > Access Control Lists > Access Control Lists** on the WLC UI.

Step 2.   Find the IP ACL that you created and then hover your mouse over the blue down-arrow icon at the end of that row.

Step 3.   Click **Add-Remove URL** as shown in Figure 4-36.

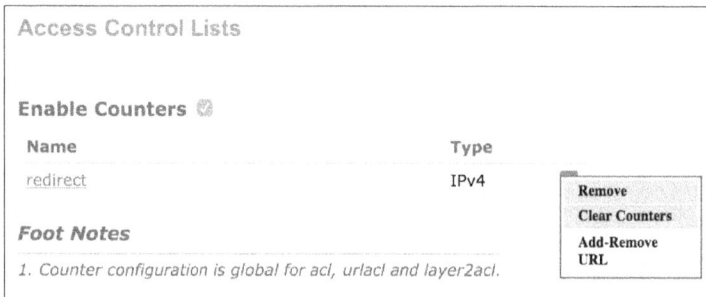

Figure 4-36   *Creating a URL List in WLC*

Step 4.   Type **captive.apple.com** in the URL String Name text field.

Step 5.   Click **Add**.

Step 6.   Repeat Steps 4 and 5 for all the URLs required, which are shown in Figure 4-37.

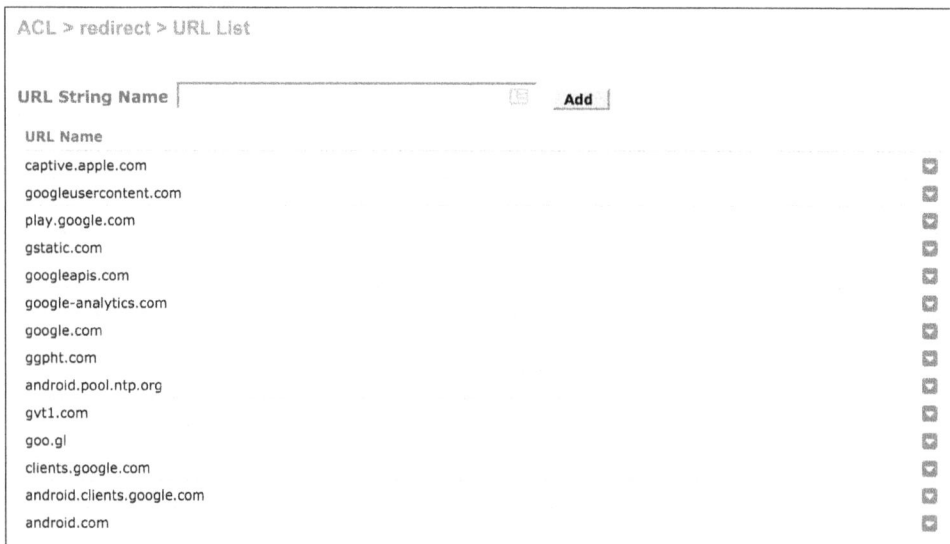

Figure 4-37   *URL List for BYOD Onboarding*

Step 7.   Click **Back**.

BYOD Onboarding Verification and End-User Experience

After configuring ISE and the network device, it is time to verify the configuration. This section will also show you what the end-user experience should look like when BYOD onboarding is configured correctly. Two examples will be discussed here: the onboarding experience on an Apple iPad and on an Android device.

To verify the configuration on an Apple iPad, use the following steps:

Step 1.   On the iPad, navigate to **Settings > Wi-Fi** and connect to the CCIE-Onboard SSID, as shown in Figure 4-38.

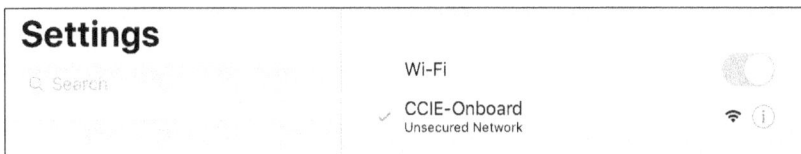

Figure 4-38   *Connecting to Onboarding SSID*

Step 2.   Open the web browser and attempt to connect to **www.ciscopress.com**. You will be redirected to the ISE web authentication portal, as shown in Figure 4-39.

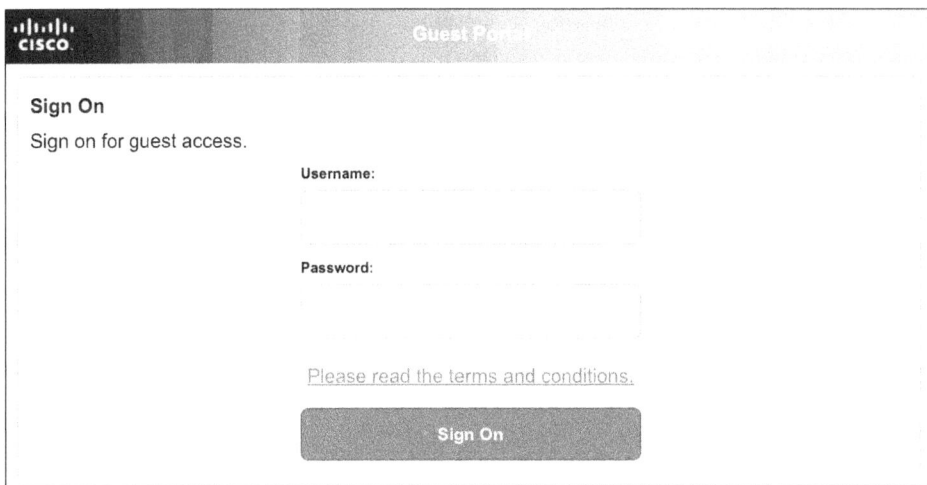

Figure 4-39   *Redirect to Authentication Portal*

Step 3.   Type in a valid username and password and click **Sign On**.

Step 4.   After successful authentication, the BYOD onboarding process will start and you will see a BYOD Welcome page, as shown in Figure 4-40. Click **Start**.

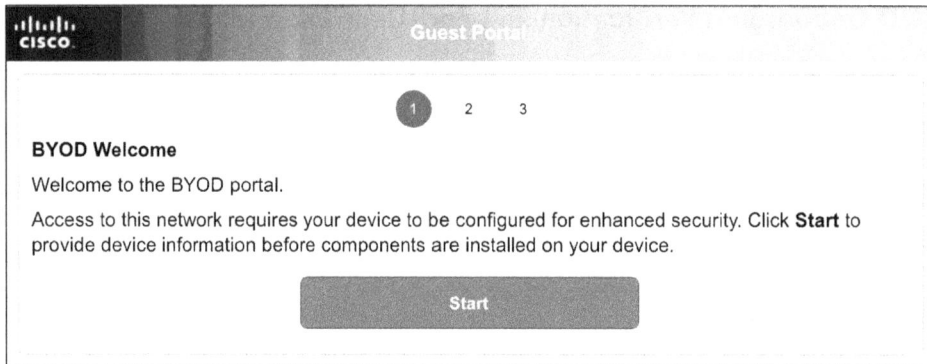

Figure 4-40   *BYOD Start Page*

Step 5.   On the Device Information page, enter a name for the device and an optional description to register the device, as shown in Figure 4-41. Click **Continue**.

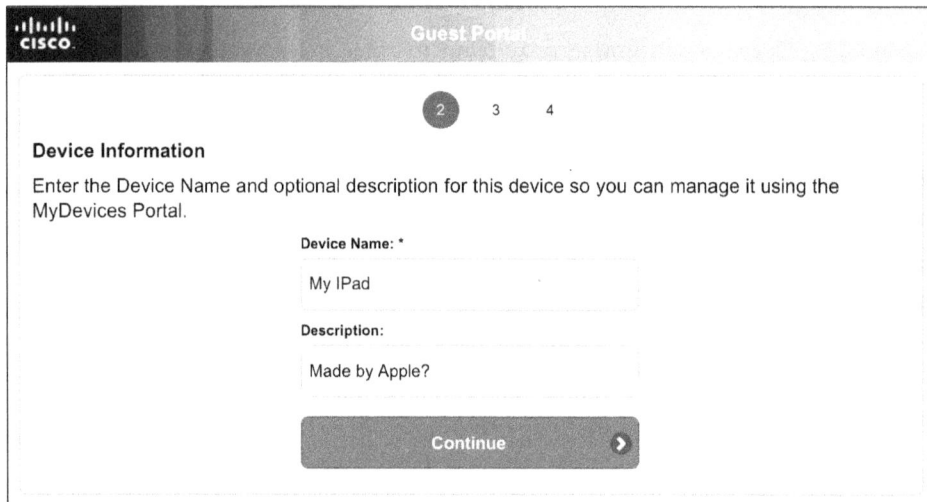

Figure 4-41   *Registering the Device*

Step 6.   The Install page starts the actual onboarding process. Click the **Launch Apple Profile and Certificate Installers Now** button, shown in Figure 4-42.

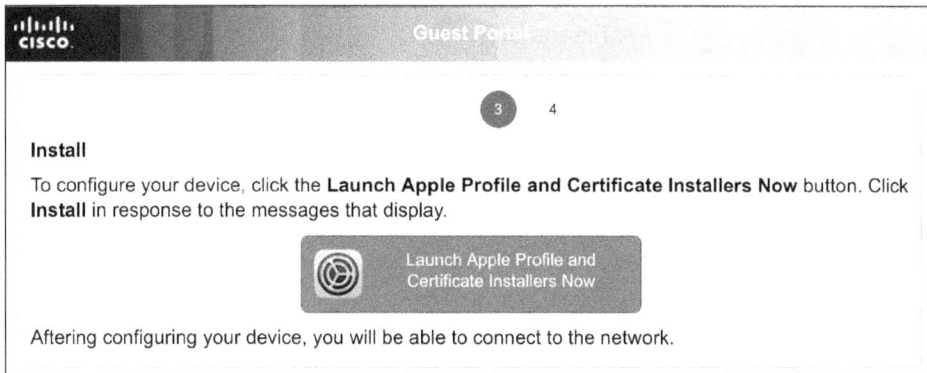

Figure 4-42 *Starting the Onboarding Process*

Step 7.   After this, the iPad will show a series of prompts to install certificates and profiles, starting with the prompt to install the profile shown in Figure 4-43 and ending with the installation complete prompt shown in Figure 4-44. Follow the onscreen prompts to complete onboarding.

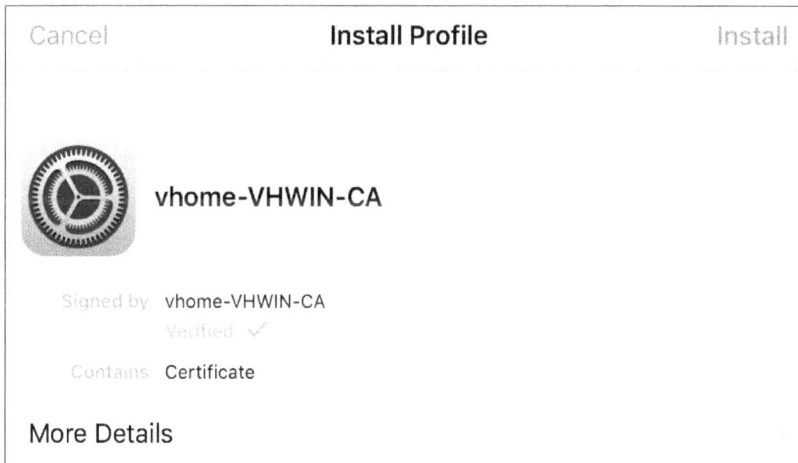

Figure 4-43 *Installing Profiles and Certificates*

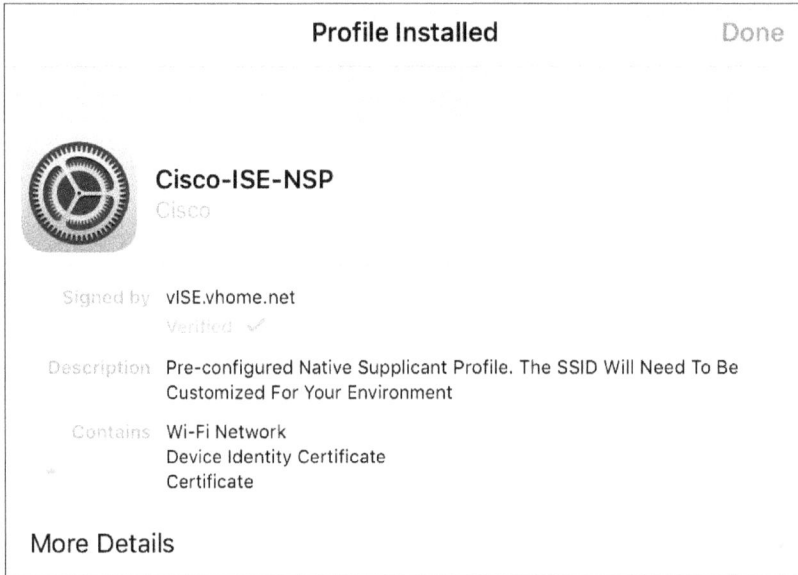

Profile Installed   Done

Cisco-ISE-NSP
Cisco

Signed by   vISE.vhome.net
            Verified ✓

Description Pre-configured Native Supplicant Profile. The SSID Will Need To Be
             Customized For Your Environment

Contains   Wi-Fi Network
            Device Identity Certificate
            Certificate

More Details

Figure 4-44   *Profiles and Certificates Installed*

Step 8.   The browser will show a Success message, as shown in Figure 4-45, after the
process is completed. Close your browser.

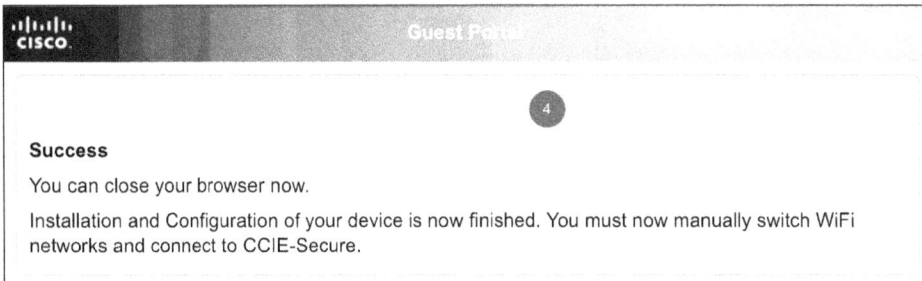

cisco   Guest Portal

                                  4

Success

You can close your browser now.

Installation and Configuration of your device is now finished. You must now manually switch WiFi
networks and connect to CCIE-Secure.

Figure 4-45   *Onboarding Success*

Step 9.   Navigate to **Settings > Wi-Fi** and connect to the CCIE-Secure SSID, as shown
in Figure 4-46.

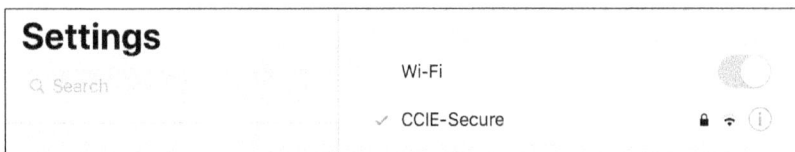

Settings

Q Search

                    Wi-Fi

                 ✓ CCIE-Secure   🔒 ᯤ ⓘ

Figure 4-46   *Connecting to Secure SSID*

Step 10. Navigate to **Operations > RADIUS > Live Logs** on the ISE UI. You will notice that the last authentication from the iPad used EAP-TLS, as shown in Figure 4-47. This shows that the device was successfully provisioned.

Figure 4-47 *Verifying Authentication on ISE Live Logs*

In the previous example you saw the OTA onboarding process on an Apple iOS device. The experience on other operating systems is a little different because they all use an agent for onboarding. The next example uses an Android device for verification. The first five steps are similar to that on an iOS device wherein you connect to the onboarding SSID, get redirected, authenticate using valid credentials, and then register the device. To continue verification beyond that, follow these steps:

Step 1. After authentication and registration, the portal will show the Install page, as shown in Figure 4-48. Click the **Get Cisco Network Setup Assistant Now** button.

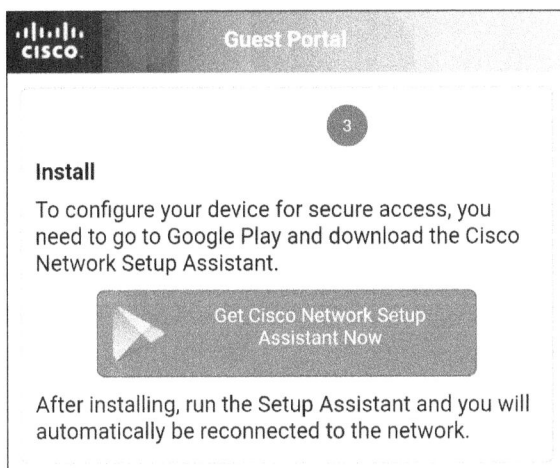

Figure 4-48 *Starting Onboarding on Android*

Step 2. The Google Play store app opens and shows the Cisco Network Setup Assistant application, as shown in Figure 4-49. Click **Install**.

Step 3. After installation completes, click **Open**.

Step 4. The Network Setup Assistance app opens, as shown in Figure 4-50. Click **Start**.

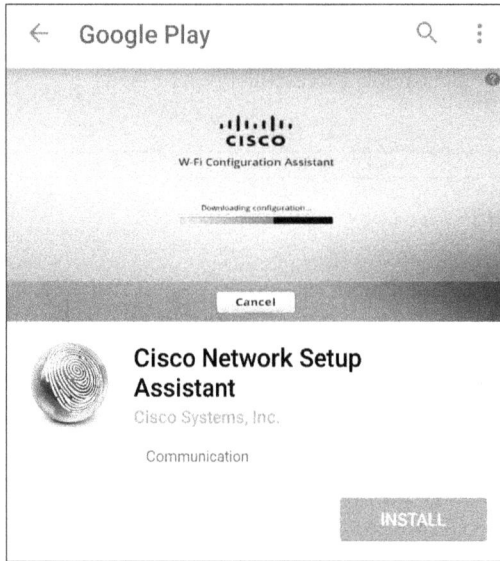

Figure 4-49   *Downloading the Network Setup Assistant Application*

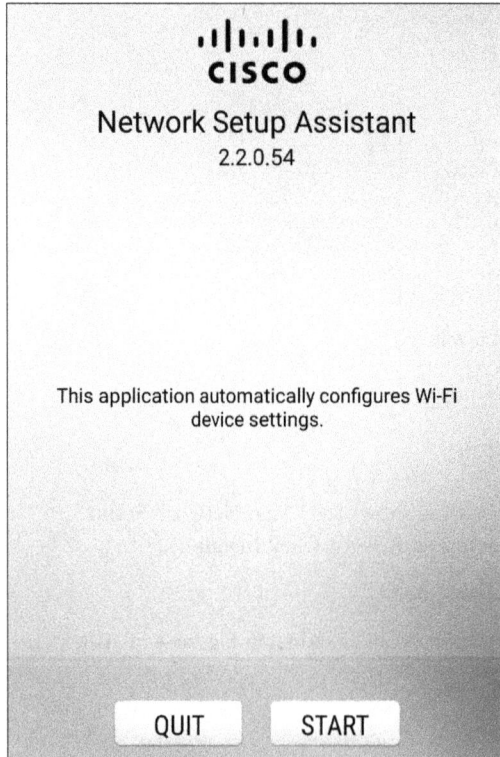

Figure 4-50   *Starting the Cisco Network Setup Assistant Application*

Step 5.   The app contacts ISE and goes through the process of installing certificates and profiles, as shown in Figure 4-51.

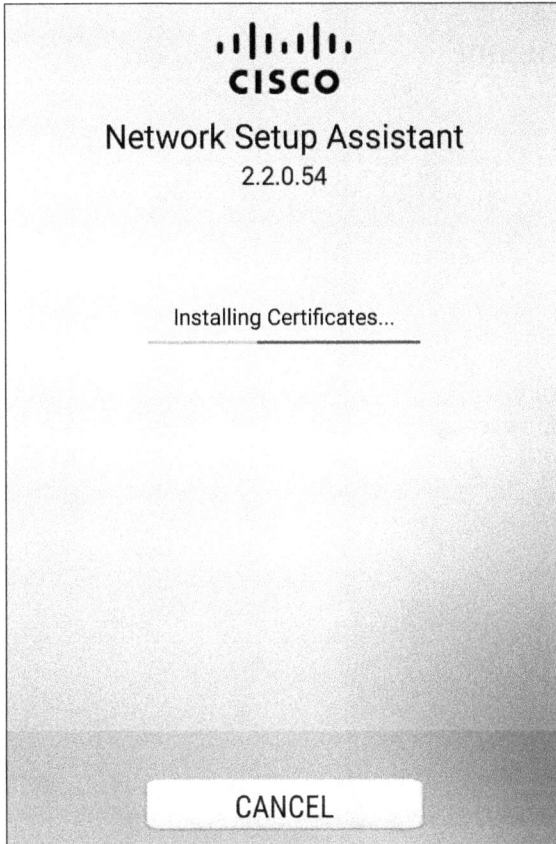

Figure 4-51   *Onboarding Android Using the Network Setup Assistant Application*

Step 6.   When the process finishes, the app will automatically connect to the provisioned SSID, CCIE-Secure in this case, as shown in Figure 4-52.

Note   Phew! That was a really long section. It is strongly suggested that you take a break here and get some hands-on time in the lab practicing everything covered in this section. A practical understanding of BYOD onboarding will help with the rest of the chapter. Some configurations will be repeated for other features and we will not discuss those step by step again.

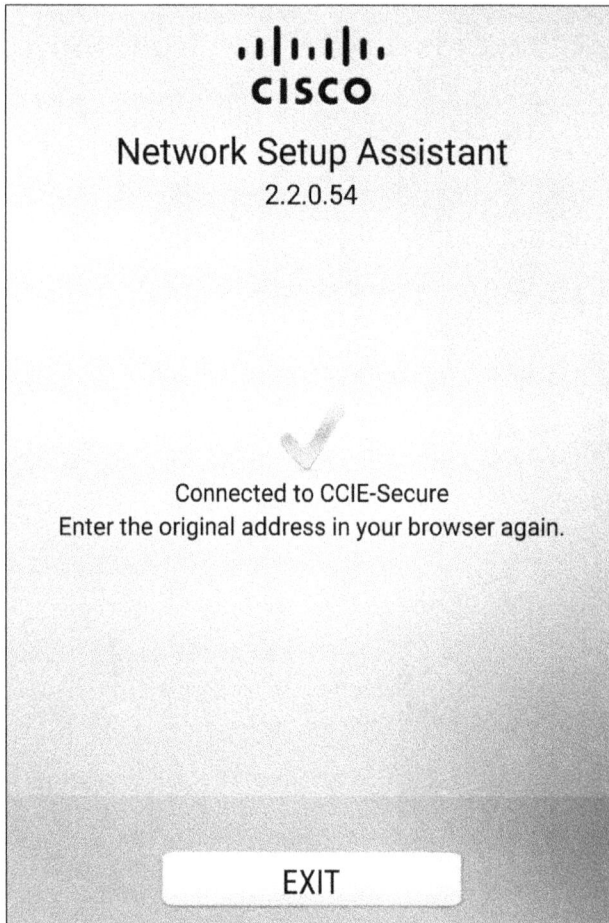

Figure 4-52   *Onboarding Completes on Android*

MDM Onboarding and Enforcement with ISE

Earlier in the chapter we discussed the need and benefits of allowing mobile devices onto the network. Mobile devices, especially personal devices, carry an inherent risk due to lack of preventative measures on them. On top of that, there has been a big increase in the availability of malicious applications in official application stores for common mobile operating systems.

To mitigate that risk, organizations turn to mobile device management (MDM) solutions, which can help in two ways:

■ **Provisioning:** MDM solutions can provision applications and settings on a device. This helps ensure that the devices have appropriate security applications and settings. Some MDM solutions can even provision certificates and supplicant profiles just like ISE.

■ **Enforcement:** MDM solutions help enforce good security practices such as screen lock and minimum pin size. In addition to that, they help monitor the device for potentially hazardous conditions such as jail-break. If a device is found in violation of security policies, corporate applications and data can be removed from the device and further access can be restricted.

Although they are very useful, MDM solutions have a few inherent downsides in their usability and enforcement capabilities:

■ The device needs to be onboarded to the MDM solution before it can begin monitoring and enforcement. Typically, users are provided written instructions to follow and start the onboarding process. This results in a high volume of help desk calls and a bad end-user experience.

■ MDM devices can enforce at an operating system level or even an application level. They usually do not have the ability to enforce network access restriction for a noncompliant device. So, if a device becomes non-compliant after onboarding, it cannot generally be kept out of the network but can be denied access to applications and data.

Given that ISE has onboarding and network enforcement capabilities that MDMs lack, MDM vendors and Cisco announced a partnership during the early days of ISE and worked on an integration strategy. Today ISE can integrate with all major MDM vendors to provide two functions:

■ **Onboarding:** Just like BYOD onboarding, ISE can help onboard a device to an MDM solution. MDM onboarding either can be a sequential step after BYOD onboarding or can be done without BYOD onboarding.

■ **Enforcement:** ISE can be configured to grant or deny network access based on the compliance status of the device in the MDM solution. This helps ensure that network access is only granted if the device conforms to the security policy of the organization. If the compliance status changes while the device is connected to the network, ISE can send a CoA and quarantine the device. Figure 4-53 shows a list of attributes that can be used in an authorization policy to check for various compliance statues of a device from the MDM server.

Name	Internal Name	Description
DaysSinceLastCheckin	days_since_lastcheckin	Number of days since last checkin
DeviceCompliantStatus	compliant_status	Compliant Status of device on M...
DeviceRegisterStatus	register_status	Status of device registration on M...
DiskEncryptionStatus	disk_encryption_on	Device disk encryption on MDM
IMEI	imei	IMEI
JailBrokenStatus	jail_broken	Is device jail broken
Manufacturer	manufacturer	Manufacturer name
MDMFailureReason	mdm_failure_reason	Reason for MDM Server connecti...
MDMServerName	mdmServerName	MDM server name
MDMServerReachable	MDMserverReachable	MDM server reachability
MEID	meid	MEID
Model	model	Device model
OsVersion	os_version	Device Operating System
PhoneNumber	phone_number	Phone number
PinLockStatus	pin_lock_on	Device Pin lock status
SerialNumber	serial_number	Device serial number
ServerType	server_type	Type of device management server
UDID	udid	UDID
UserNotified	user_notified	Has the user been notified

Figure 4-53   *List of MDM Attributes on ISE*

The configuration required for MDM integration on ISE can be divided into three parts:

1. **Add the MDM server in ISE:** Before you can configure MDM policies in ISE, you need to add the MDM server. The MDM dictionaries will not be available for creating authorization rules until this is completed.

2. **Configure the MDM portal (optional):** The MDM portal is used to redirect the user for MDM onboarding, just like the BYOD portal. The default portal is usually sufficient and has the exact same configuration options as the BYOD portal. Because the BYOD portal was covered earlier, we will not discuss the MDM portal. The default portal can be found at **Administration > Device Portal Management > Mobile Device Management.**

3. **Create MDM Policies:** As with any other feature on ISE, MDM integration requires authentication and authorization policies in a policy set. Refer back to Figure 4-53 to see the list of attributes that are available to create MDM authorization rules.

Adding MDM Server in ISE

Because ISE will use HTTPS to communicate with the MDM server, it will need to trust the server's certificate. To establish this trust, you need to add the CA certificate of the MDM server in ISE's trust store using the following steps:

Step 1.   Navigate to **Administration > Certificates > Certificate Management > Trusted Certificates.**

Step 2.   Click **Import.**

Step 3.   Click the **Browse** button and select the certificate file, as shown in Figure 4-54.

Import a new Certificate into the Certificate Store

* Certificate File	Browse... GoDaddyRootCertificateAuthority-G2.crt
Friendly Name	

Trusted For: ⓘ

☑ Trust for authentication within ISE

☐ Trust for client authentication and Syslog

☐ Trust for authentication of Cisco Services

☐ Validate Certificate Extensions

Description

[Submit]   [Cancel]

Figure 4-54   *Importing an MDM CA Certificate*

Step 4.   Click **Submit.**

Now that ISE trusts the certificate, you can add the MDM server using the following steps:

Step 1.   Navigate to **Administration > Network Resources > External MDM.**

Step 2.   Click **Add.**

Step 3.   In the Name field, enter a name for the MDM instance.

Step 4.   In the Host Name / IP Address field, enter the IP address or hostname of the server.

Step 5.   In the Port field, enter a port number. This usually is 443.

Step 6.   In the Username and Password fields, enter a username and password.

Step 7.   Select **Enabled** from the Status drop-down list.

Step 8.   Select **Submit**.

Note   These steps describe a typical MDM configuration. Some MDM providers may use a different port, have a different authentication type, or even be multitenant aware and require you to use an instance name. Confirm the settings required with your MDM administrator or vendor.

Figure 4-55 shows an MDM server added to ISE.

Name *	Meraki-MDM
Server Type	Mobile Device Manager
Authentication Type	Basic
Host Name / IP Address *	n180.meraki.com
Port *	443 (max length: 5)
Instance Name	
Username *	0b49e939531a040eeedc93b8543736fb342230de
Password *	••••••••••••••••••••••••••••••••••••
Description	
Polling Interval *	240 (minutes)
Time Interval For Compliance Device ReAuth Query *	1 (minutes)
Status	Enabled

Figure 4-55   *Adding an MDM Server in ISE*

Configuring MDM Policies

Before creating MDM policies, you need to create the required authorization profile. Apart from the in-built profiles, an authorization profile to redirect users to MDM is required, as shown in Figure 4-56. The figure shows an authorization profile named

MDM_Onboard that has Web Redirection enabled, with MDM Redirect selected. The ACL value is again set to **redirect** but the Value field is set to MDM Portal (default) to redirect users to the in-built MDM portal we discussed earlier. Because ISE can integrate with multiple MDM servers, the MDM server will need to be identified in the authorization profile. In Figure 4-56, the Meraki MDM we created earlier is selected.

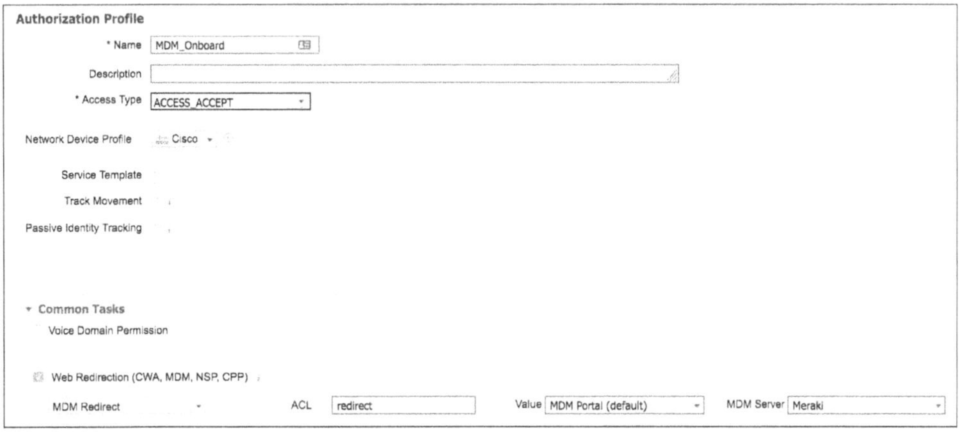

Figure 4-56 *Authorization Profile for MDM Redirection*

As you know, policy sets, authentication polices, and authorization policies can be created using different combination of conditions to achieve the same result. For the purpose of example, we will create a policy set using the exact same condition we used for the BYOD policy set. The authentication policy will be configured to allow EAP-TLS authentication only. Figure 4-57 shows the policy set and authentication policy configuration.

Figure 4-57 *Policy Set and Authentication Policy Configuration for MDM Integration*

The authorization policy for this policy set will be configured to redirect devices that are not registered in MDM and allow access for devices that are registered and compliant in the MDM server. All other devices will be denied access.

Note   Organizations usually have more complicated rules to limit the number of devices that get onboarded to MDM. Onboarding and enforcement rules are usually created based on user group membership, device type, SSID name, or authentication methods. This example was designed to show specific conditions required for MDM integration, but other conditions can be added in the rules to meet requirements.

To configure the authorization policy, follow these steps:

Step 1.   Expand the **Authorization Policy** section.

Step 2.   Replace the Profile for the Default rule with **DenyAccess**.

Step 3.   Click the gear icon in the Actions column for the Default rule and select **Insert new row above.**

Step 4.   Name the new rule **MDM_Compliant.**

Step 5.   Click the **Conditions** column in the new rule.

Step 6.   In the Editor section on the right, click the field that reads **Click to add an attribute.**

Step 7.   Select **MDM** from the Dictionaries drop-down list.

Step 8.   Select **DeviceRegisterStatus** from the Attribute column.

Step 9.   Click the drop-down arrow for the field that reads Choose from list of type and select **Registered.**

Step 10.   Click **New.**

Step 11.   Click the field that reads **Click to add an attribute.**

Step 12.   Select **MDM** from the Dictionaries drop-down list.

Step 13.   Select **DeviceCompliantStatus** from the Attribute column.

Step 14.   Click the drop-down arrow for the field that reads Choose from list of type and select **Compliant.** After this, the Editor section should look as shown in Figure 4-58.

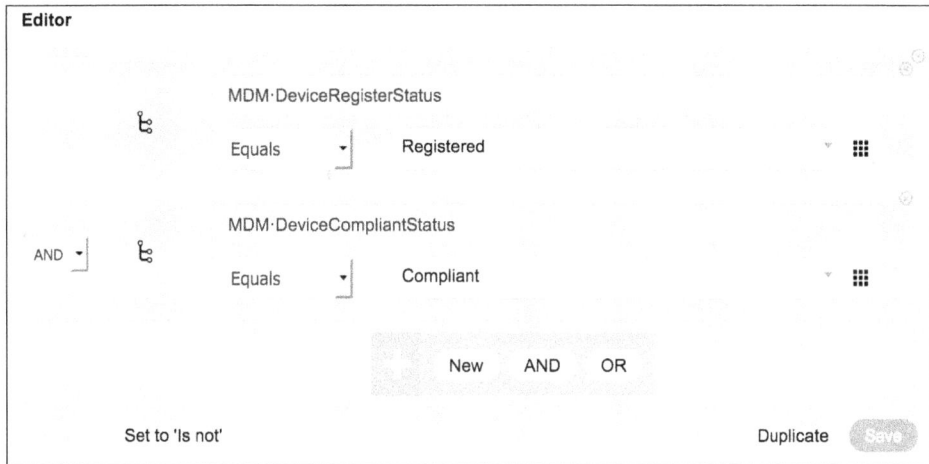

Figure 4-58 *Conditions for MDM Compliance Check*

Step 15. Click **Use**.

Step 16. Select **PermitAccess** from the drop-down list in the Profiles column of the new rule. This authorization rule will permit access if the device is registered and compliant in MDM.

Step 17. Click the gear icon in the Actions column for the rule and select **Insert new row above.**

Step 18. Name the new rule **MDM_Onboard.**

Step 19. Click the **Conditions** column in the new rule.

Step 20. In the Editor section on the right, click the field that reads **Click to add an attribute.**

Step 21. Select **MDM** from the Dictionaries drop-down list.

Step 22. Select **DeviceRegisterStatus** from the Attribute column.

Step 23. Click the drop-down arrow in the field that reads Choose from list of type and select **UnRegistered**, as shown in Figure 4-59.

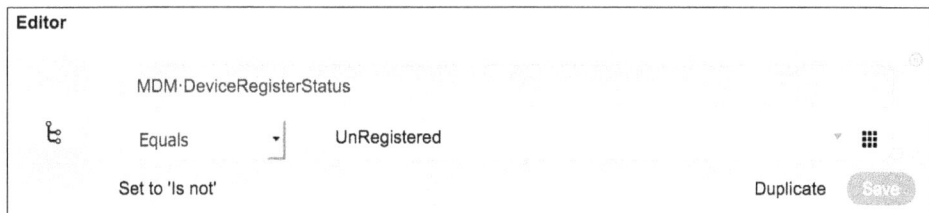

Figure 4-59 *Condition for MDM Onboarding*

Step 24.   Click **Use.**

Step 25.   Select **MDM_Onboard** from the drop-down list in the Profiles column of the new rule. This authorization profile was created earlier to redirect to the MDM portal. This rule will redirect any device to the MDM portal if it is not registered in MDM.

Step 26.   Click **Save.**

Figure 4-60 shows the completed authorization policy.

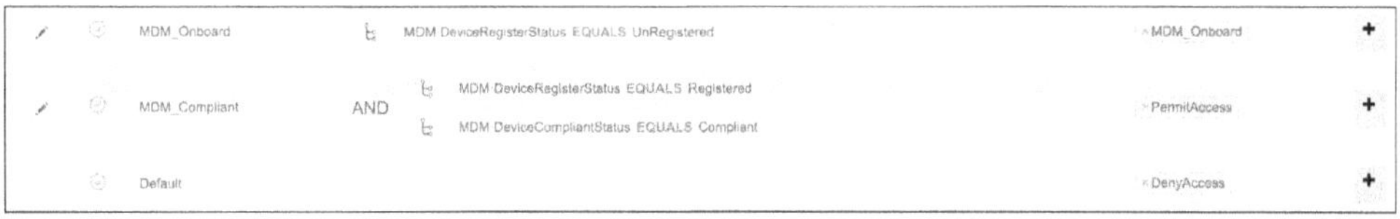

		MDM_Onboard		MDM:DeviceRegisterStatus EQUALS UnRegistered		MDM_Onboard	+
		MDM_Compliant	AND	MDM:DeviceRegisterStatus EQUALS Registered		PermitAccess	+
				MDM:DeviceCompliantStatus EQUALS Compliant			
		Default				DenyAccess	+

Figure 4-60   *Authorization Profile for MDM Onboarding and Enforcement*

Posture Assessment and Remediation with ISE

The key advantage of implementing a network access control solution is the ability to control which devices and users can connect. This is not limited to just checking if the devices and users are authorized. It can be extended to check the posture or compliance status of a device. Generally, this means checking if the device has the required anti-malware software, firewall, and latest operating system patches and such installed and running. Sometimes compliance requirements can also include checking for disk encryption, registry settings, and certain applications or processes or files. We discussed an example of this in the previous section with MDM enforcement for mobile devices. With an MDM integration we can check for the compliance status of a mobile device before allowing it on to the network.

For devices running Windows or Apple OS X, ISE provides a separate posture assessment feature that does not require integration with a third-party software. ISE, working with Cisco AnyConnect, can check the compliance status of a Windows or Apple OS X device before allowing it access. If the device is found to be non-compliant, it can be remediated before being allowed access.

It is important to understand how posture assessment features work with the AAA features. Figure 4-61 shows the interaction between the endpoint, network device, and ISE starting from a typical 802.1X authentication and ending with successful posture assessment.

Windows/Apple OS X

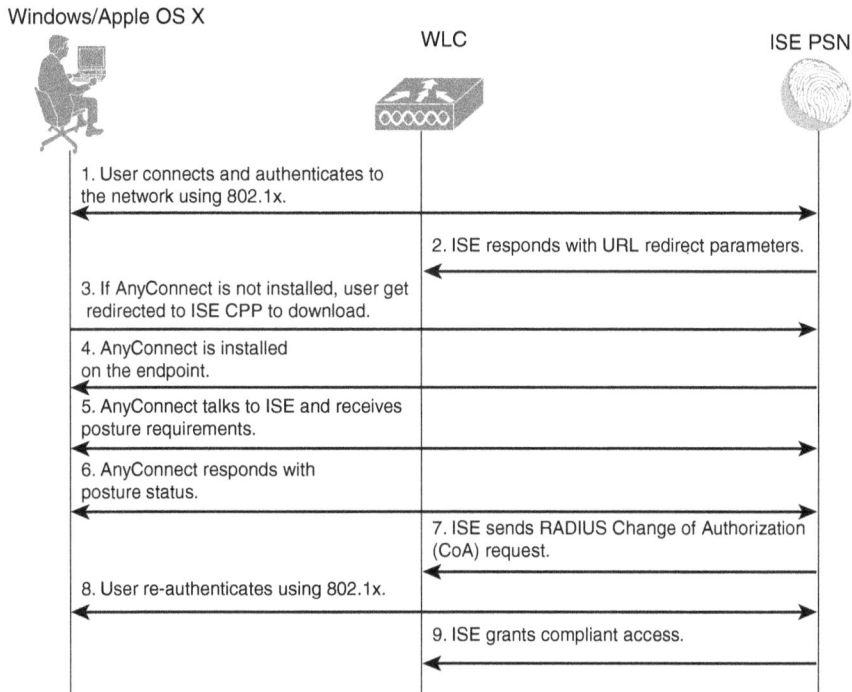

Figure 4-61 *Posture Assessment with ISE*

The steps shown in the posture assessment flow in Figure 4-61 are as follows:

1. The flow starts with a normal 802.1X authentication to ISE after the user connects to the network through a WLC or a switch.

2. Because the posture status is unknown at this time, ISE responds with a URL Redirection. Only traffic that is required to complete posture assessment and potential remediation is allowed through.

3. If the device has the AnyConnect posture module installed, it skips to Step 5. Otherwise, the user opens a browser and gets redirected to the ISE Client Provisioning Portal (CPP).

4. The user downloads the AnyConnect installation file from the CPP and installs it on the device.

5. Once AnyConnect is installed, it discovers the IP address of the ISE PSN and, upon connecting to it, receives the posture requirement for the device.

6. AnyConnect checks the applications and updates installed on the device based on the posture requirements received from ISE and sends a posture status report back to ISE.

7. On receiving a compliant status, ISE sends a CoA to the network device requesting a re-authentication.

8. The device/user re-authenticates to ISE.

9. Because the posture is now known to be compliant, ISE responds with a permit access authorization.

The configuration required to implement this posture flow on ISE can be broken down into the following three buckets. Each of these will be discussed in detail in the sections ahead.

- **AnyConnect provisioning:** ISE requires an agent to check the compliance status on the endpoint. Although there are web-based agents that can be used, their functionality is very limited. Hence, the AnyConnect agent is almost always used. The agent can be provisioned either out-of-band using software management systems or during the installation of the operating system. It can also be installed in-band from ISE directly when the device connects to the network for the first time. This works very similarly to BYOD provisioning of Windows and Apple OS X devices and is done by redirecting the user to the Client Provisioning Portal on ISE. In this chapter we will discuss the configuration required for in-band provisioning.

Note Older versions of ISE used a standalone NAC agent. ISE 2.x and later require the AnyConnect application and its posture module to be used. AnyConnect is a separately licensed product.

- **Posture policies:** Posture policies define what compliance means for a particular deployment. These policies define the posture requirements that AnyConnect checks on the endpoint to ensure the device is compliant. The policies can range from a simple check to ensure that an updated anti-malware is running on the device to a list of multiple requirements checking for various applications, services, and registry entries. Posture policies are operating system specific.

- **Policy sets:** As usual, everything needs to be tied back to policy sets, authentication policies, and authorization policies. Posture assessment is no exception. ISE will need policies that define what action to take when a device with unknown, noncompliant, or compliant posture status authenticates.

Preparing to Configure Posture

Before starting to configure any of the three sets of requirements discussed in the preceding list, there are a few prerequisite configuration tasks that you need to complete, which consist of the following:

Step 1.   **Update posture data:** When ISE is installed, it does not have a comprehensive list of vendors and applications that can be used to create posture checks. You have to run the posture update process on ISE before it receives the most current list from Cisco. Either ISE can directly download that list from a Cisco site or you can upload the update file manually after downloading it yourself. It is strongly recommended that you allow ISE to download this list directly and also allow it to automatically download updates periodically. To run the update process, navigate to **Administration > System > Settings > Posture > Updates** and click **Update Now**. The process can take up to 15 minutes or more to complete depending on available bandwidth.

Note   If ISE does not have direct Internet connectivity, you may need to configure it to use a proxy. You can configure the details of the proxy by navigating to **Administration > System > Settings > Proxy**.

Step 2.   **Upload AnyConnect installation package to ISE:** Because AnyConnect is separately licensed software, ISE cannot directly download it from the Cisco software repository (as it can download posture updates or SPWizards). You need to download it manually from Cisco and upload it to ISE before it can be provisioned in-band. To download the files, search for **AnyConnect Secure Mobility Client v4.x** on Cisco.com and download the appropriate version of the **Headend Deployment Package**. You need individual packages for Windows and Apple OS X if you want to enforce posture assessment on both operating systems. Once downloaded, follow these steps to upload the package(s) to ISE:

   a. Navigate to **Work Centers > Posture > Client Provisioning > Resources**.

   b. Click **Add** and select **Agent resources from local disk**.

   c. Select **Cisco Provided Packages** from the Category drop-down list, as shown in Figure 4-62.

   d. Click **Browse** and select the file you downloaded.

   e. Click **Submit**.

   f. Repeat the steps if you need to upload another OS package.

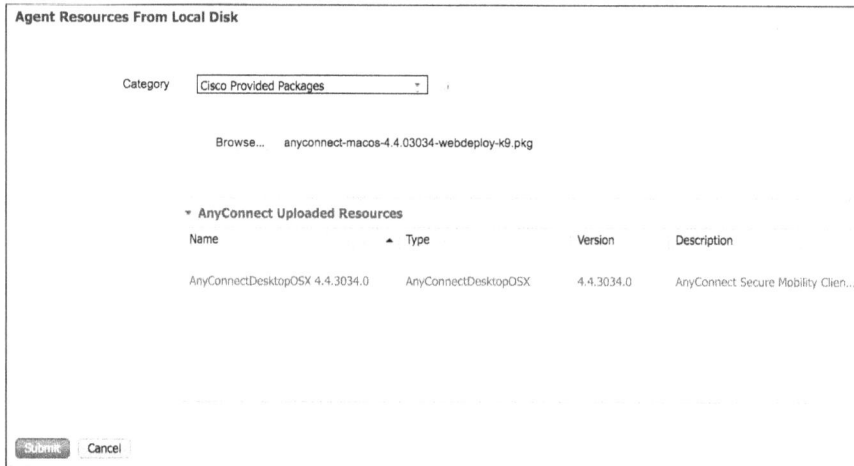

Figure 4-62   *Uploading AnyConnect Installation Package on ISE*

Step 3.   **Download the compliance module:** Similar to posture updates on ISE, AnyConnect needs information regarding various applications and how to check for their status. This is provided by the compliance module. The compliance module is provided by Cisco and can be downloaded on ISE directly. If a device does not have a compliance module or has an outdated compliance module, ISE will push the required module at the start of the posture assessment session. To download the latest compliance module on ISE, follow these steps:

   a. Navigate to **Work Centers > Posture > Client Provisioning > Resources.**

   b. Click **Add** and select **Agent resources from Cisco site.** This opens the Download Remote Resources window (which should be familiar from the "Configuring ISE for BYOD Onboarding" section).

   c. Check the check boxes for the latest: AnyConnectComplianceModuleWindows and AnyConnectComplianceModuleOSX files, as shown in Figure 4-63.

   d. Click **Save.**

Note   Compliance modules are specific to the version of AnyConnect you are using. The major version of the compliance module and AnyConnect should match. Cisco releases one compliance module almost every month. It is not necessary to always use the latest module though. As long as the module can recognize the applications you want to check for, you don't need to update it. In any case, the compliance module can be updated on the endpoint inline when AnyConnect reaches out to ISE to get posture requirements.

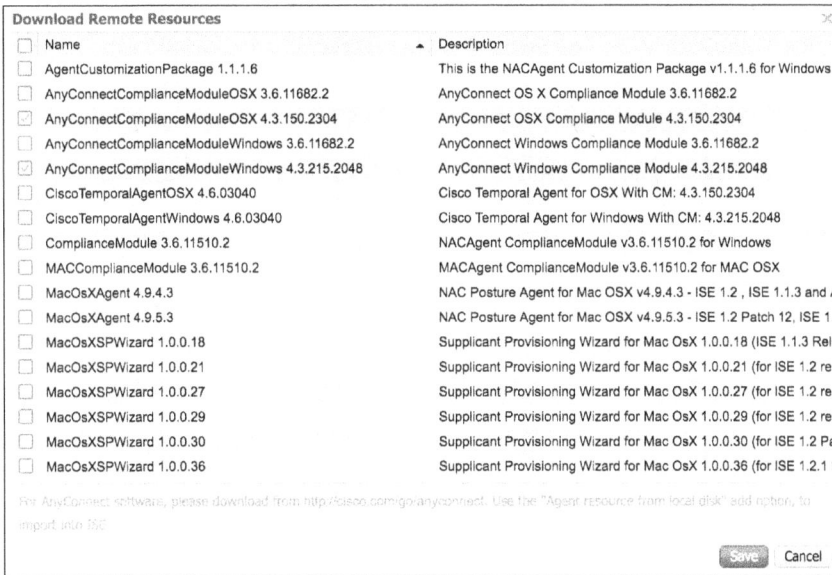

Figure 4-63   *Downloading Compliance Modules on ISE*

Step 4.   **Network device configuration:** Provisioning works in conjunction with 802.1X authentication. So, the network devices will need to be configured for 802.1X, URL Redirection, and CoA, as discussed earlier in this chapter and in Chapter 2. For purposes of the example, we will continue to use the CCIE-Secure SSID and redirect ACL discussed in the BYOD section. The configuration of the SSID will remain unchanged.

Configuring AnyConnect Provisioning

In-band provisioning of AnyConnect requires a Client Provisioning Policy (CPP) similar to the CPP required for BYOD provisioning. Though both CPPs are configured in the exact same place, the components required for AnyConnect provisioning are different. Figure 4-64 shows the components that are required to create the CPP for AnyConnect.

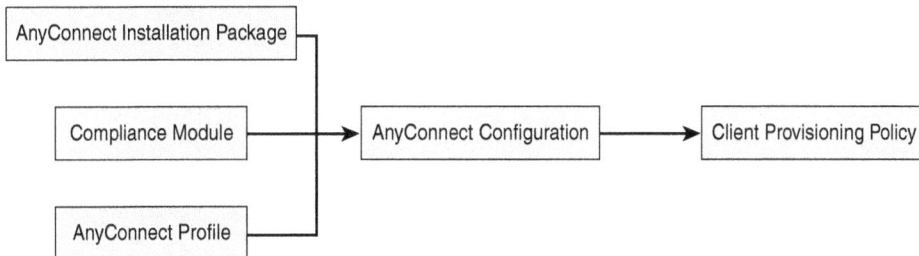

Figure 4-64   *Components Required to Create Client Provisioning Policy for AnyConnect*

As shown in Figure 4-64, creating the CPP for AnyConnect requires something called AnyConnect Configuration (AnyConnect provisioning configuration would have been a better name). To create the AnyConnect configuration, you need three components:

■ The AnyConnect installation package

■ The compliance module

■ An AnyConnect profile

All of these three components get pushed to the endpoint from ISE. Out of the three, we already discussed the first two components. The third, an AnyConnect profile, defines various characteristics of the AnyConnect agent on the endpoint and can be created within the ISE GUI. To create an AnyConnect profile, follow these steps:

Step 1.   Navigate to **Work Centers > Posture > Client Provisioning > Resources.**

Step 2.   Click **Add** and select **NAC Agent or AnyConnect Posture Profile.**

Step 3.   Select **AnyConnect** from the Category drop-down list.

Step 4.   Enter a name for the profile. For this example, we will use **CCIE-AC-Profile.**

Step 5.   Examine the Agent Behavior section, shown in Figure 4-65. Most of the settings in the section can be left at default, but two options need to be carefully considered:

■ **Stealth Mode:** AnyConnect can be configured to run in an agent-less mode as a service only. This mode can be enabled to prevent AnyConnect from being visible to the end user.

■ **Periodic probing:** This setting defines how often AnyConnect will send probes when trying to reach an ISE node. When AnyConnect is not able to reach an ISE node after the defined number of tries, it enters a back-off period during which it will not send out probes. This setting defines the number of times the probes will be sent out during that window.

Step 6.   Examine the IP Address Change section, shown in Figure 4-66. This section defines how AnyConnect will detect a VLAN change on the network, if one occurs after posture assessment. If a VLAN change is detected, AnyConnect can force the device to request a new IP address. The default values in this section should be changed only if AnyConnect is not able to detect VLAN change properly in your setup.

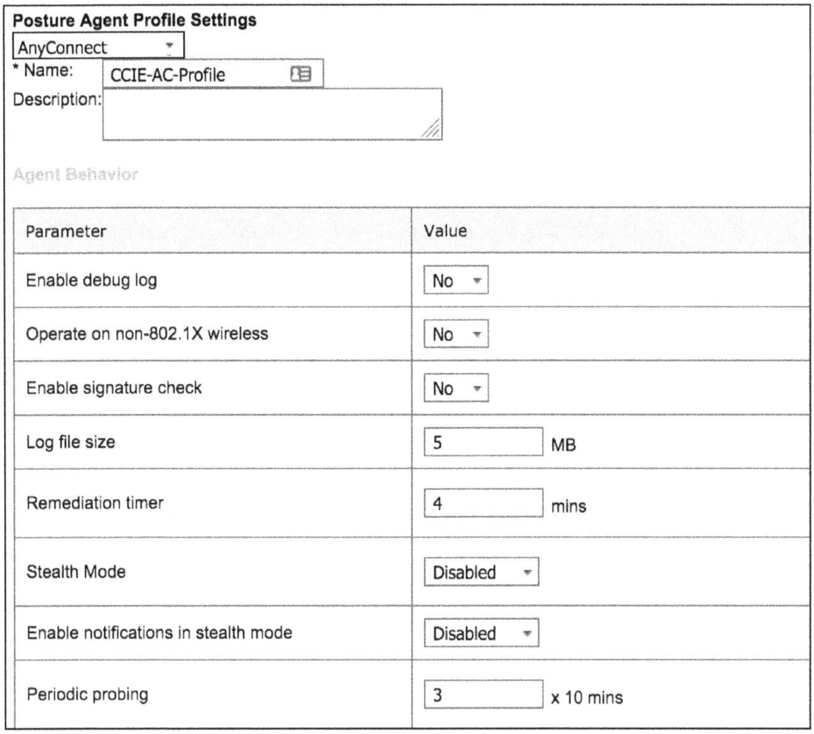

Posture Agent Profile Settings

AnyConnect ▾

* Name: CCIE-AC-Profile   ⬚

Description:

Agent Behavior

Parameter	Value
Enable debug log	No ▾
Operate on non-802.1X wireless	No ▾
Enable signature check	No ▾
Log file size	5 MB
Remediation timer	4 mins
Stealth Mode	Disabled ▾
Enable notifications in stealth mode	Disabled ▾
Periodic probing	3 x 10 mins

Figure 4-65 *Agent Behavior Section of AnyConnect Profile*

IP Address Change

Parameter	Value
Enable agent IP refresh	Yes ▾
VLAN detection interval	0 secs
Ping or ARP	Ping ▾
Maximum timeout for ping	1 secs
DHCP renew delay	1 secs
DHCP release delay	4 secs
Network transition delay	3 secs

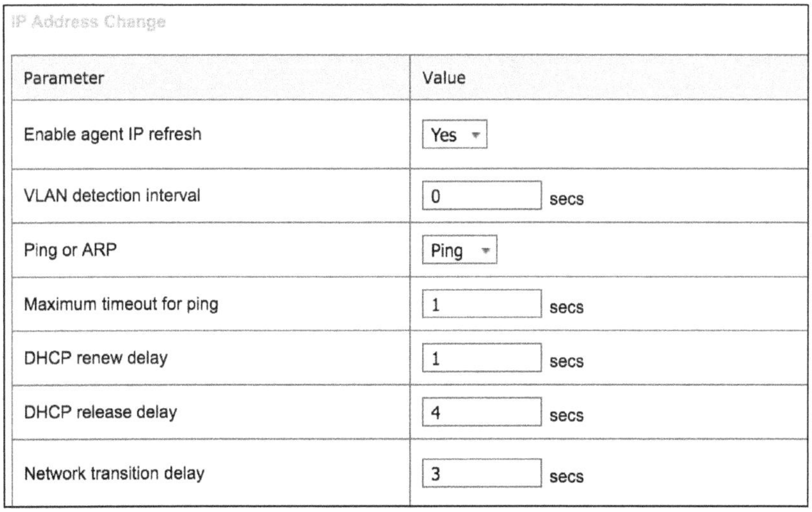

Figure 4-66 *IP Address Change Section of AnyConnect Profile*

Step 7.   Edit the settings in the Posture Protocol section, as shown in Figure 4-67:

■ **Discovery host:** AnyConnect relies on URL Redirection on the network device to reach the correct ISE node. To do so, it sends out probes to different IP addresses in sequence. The configured discovery host is one of the addresses that it sends a probe to. Because we need this probe to be redirected, the Discovery host setting should be set to an IP address on the network that we know will be redirected. Usually this will be an IP address in the endpoint's subnet but not the default gateway or the endpoint's own address.

■ **Server name rules:** Defines the names of ISE PSNs that AnyConnect can connect to. This is a security feature that prevents AnyConnect from communicating with a rogue ISE server. You can either define the name of each ISE PSN in your network as a comma-separated value, or specify a wildcard-based value such as *.domain. To allow communication with any ISE node, set the value as *.

■ **Call Home List:** This is a list of ISE PSNs that the AnyConnect will reach out to if discovery fails. Normally, this should not be configured, but in the CCIE lab, there is a benefit to setting this value to the IP address of the ISE PSN, especially if the lab consists of a single ISE node only. This will allow posture to work even if redirect is not working correctly and can save some time in the lab.

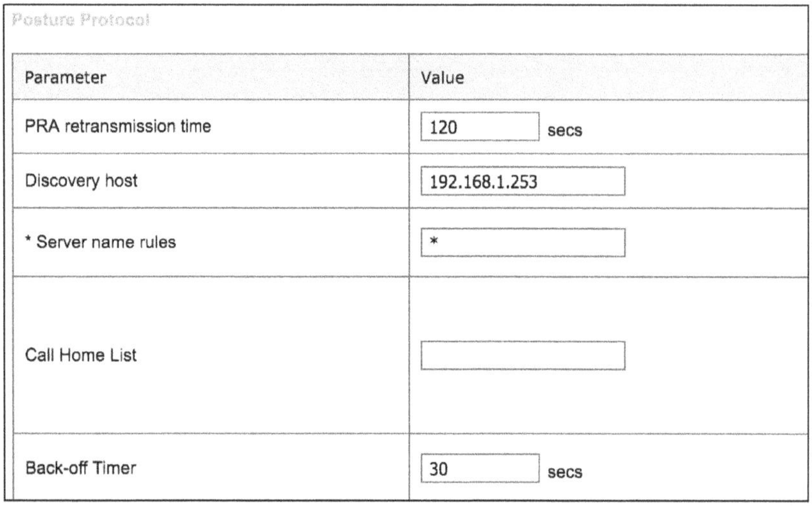

Posture Protocol	
Parameter	Value
PRA retransmission time	120 secs
Discovery host	192.168.1.253
* Server name rules	*
Call Home List	
Back-off Timer	30 secs

Figure 4-67 *Posture Protocol Setting in AnyConnect Profile*

Step 8.   Click **Submit.**

After creating the AnyConnect profile, we have all three components required to create the AnyConnect configuration. To create it, follow these steps:

Step 1.   Navigate to **Work Centers > Posture > Client Provisioning > Resources.**

Step 2.   Click **Add** and select **AnyConnect Configuration.**

Step 3.   From the Select AnyConnect Package drop-down list, select the **AnyConnect** installation package that you uploaded to ISE earlier.

Step 4.   In the Configuration Name field, edit the name of the configuration. For this example, we will use **CCIE-AC-Config.**

Step 5.   From the Compliance Module drop-down list, select the compliance module you downloaded earlier, as shown in Figure 4-68.

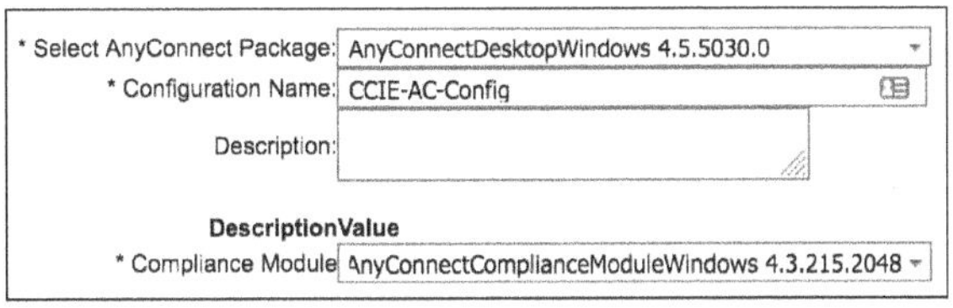

Figure 4-68   *Selecting a Compliance Module in AnyConnect Configuration*

Step 6.   In the Profile Selection section, select the AnyConnect profile in the ISE Posture drop-down list. For this example, select the **CCIE-AC-Profile** profile we created earlier, as shown in Figure 4-69.

Figure 4-69   *Selecting a Profile in AnyConnect Configuration*

Step 7.   Examine the rest of the configuration options. A few of the key options to consider are as follows:

■ **Customization Bundle:** This is a bundle that can be uploaded in ISE and used in the configuration to change the look of the AnyConnect UI to meet any branding requirements.

■ **Localization Bundle:** This is also a bundle that can be uploaded on ISE and used in the configuration. This bundle allows the language on the AnyConnect UI to be changed to the preferred one.

■ **Deferred Update:** This section controls the inline update function. If you need to update the AnyConnect software or the compliance module inline, you can use the settings in this section to do so.

Step 8.   Click **Submit**.

Now that all the required components are available, we can finally create a CPP. You should already be familiar with CPP creation from the BYOD onboarding discussion earlier in the chapter. As a refresher, CPP can be configured by navigating to **Policy > Client Provisioning**. Remember that ISE provides one preconfigured rule for each supported operating system. To edit these rules, follow these steps:

Step 1.   Click **Edit** at the end of the row containing the Windows rule.

Step 2.   Click the **+** symbol in the Results column.

Step 3.   Select the AnyConnect configuration created earlier from the Agent drop-down list, as shown in Figure 4-70. For this example, we will select **CCIE-AC-Config**.

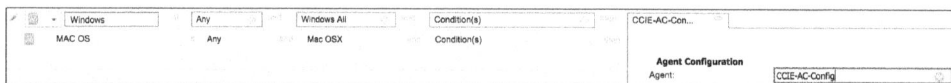

Figure 4-70   *Edit Client Provisioning Rules for AnyConnect Provisioning*

Step 4.   Click the minus (–) sign in the Results column.

Step 5.   Click **Done** at the end of the row.

Step 6.   Repeat the steps for the APPLE OS X rule, if required.

Step 7.   Click **Save** at the end of the page.

Note   You will need to create separate AnyConnect configurations for Windows and Apple OS X. You can leave the Config Wizard and Wizard Profile drop-down list boxes blank if BYOD onboarding is not required.

As mentioned previously, the portal that AnyConnect is provisioned from is called the Client Provisioning Portal. Like other portals on ISE, you can either use the provided default or create a custom one. The portal can be found at **Work Centers > Posture > Client Provisioning > Client Provisioning Portal**. As shown in Figure 4-71, this portal is very similar to the BYOD portal, with the same configuration sections. We will not discuss configuring the portal again because it was covered in the BYOD onboarding section. For the purpose of example, we will use the default portal in our authorization profile.

Portals Settings and Customization

Save

Portal Name: *   Description:

Client Provisioning Portal (default)   Default portal and user experience used to install the posture agents and   Portal test URL   Language File ▾

Portal Behavior and Flow Settings
Use these settings to specify the guest experience for this portal.

Portal Page Customization
Use these settings to specify the guest experience for this portal.

Portal & Page Settings

▸ **Portal Settings**

▸ **Login Page Settings**

▸ **Acceptable Use Policy (AUP) Page Settings**

▸ **Post-Login Banner Page Settings**

▸ **Change Password Settings**

▸ **Support Information Page Settings**

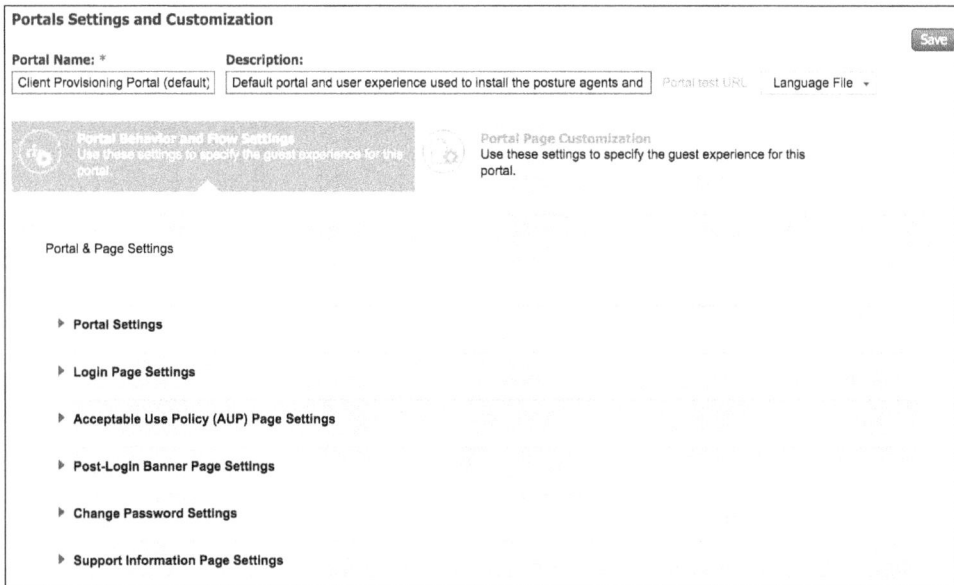

Figure 4-71 *Default Client Provisioning Portal*

Configuring Posture Policy

When AnyConnect communicates with ISE, it receives a list of posture requirements. This list of requirements is defined in the rules in the posture policy on ISE. The device must pass all requirements in the posture policy that apply to its operating system before the device will be considered compliant. Like any other policy rule on ISE, posture rules also require multiple elements to be configured. Figure 4-72 shows the elements required to create a posture policy rule and the relationship between them.

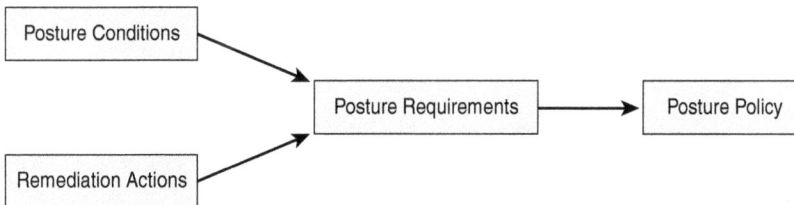

Figure 4-72 *Elements Required to Create a Posture Policy*

As shown in Figure 4-72, the three elements required to create a posture policy rule are posture condition, remediation action, and posture requirement.

Posture Condition

The main element required for a posture rule is the condition. The condition defines what is being checked on the endpoint, and the endpoint is deemed compliant only if the condition is met. ISE allows many types of conditions, as shown in Figure 4-73.

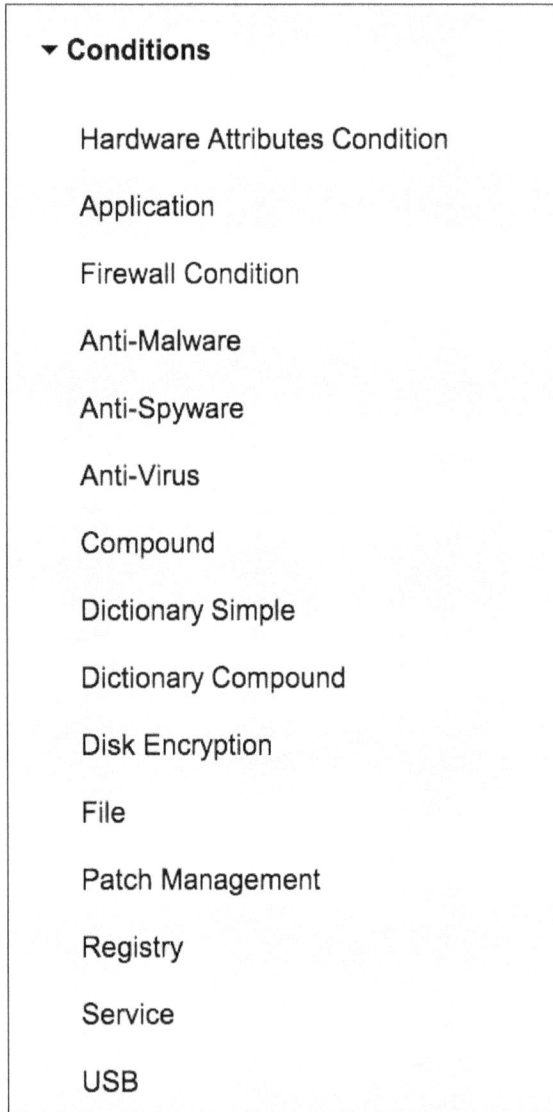

▼ **Conditions**

Hardware Attributes Condition

Application

Firewall Condition

Anti-Malware

Anti-Spyware

Anti-Virus

Compound

Dictionary Simple

Dictionary Compound

Disk Encryption

File

Patch Management

Registry

Service

USB

Figure 4-73   *List of Types of Conditions Supported by ISE*

Note Not every condition shown in Figure 4-73 is supported on Apple OS X at this time; however, each new release of ISE adds support for more conditions on Apple OS X. Release notes for each ISE version will clearly state whether there is a change in support for Apple OS X in any check. Similarly, Cisco adds new types of conditions every few releases of ISE.

Although the list may seem long, as with other elements, ISE has prebuilt conditions for most of the condition types. These prebuilt conditions can often be modified, but it is highly recommended that you duplicate them and edit the copies.

Note Prebuilt conditions of some types cannot be modified. This is often the case with prebuilt *compound* conditions.

Each condition is specific to an operating system and can be applied to all or specific versions of the operating system. While the details required to configure the conditions differ by the condition types, the general process to create them is similar. For the purposes of this section, we will discuss the steps required to create an Anti-Malware condition that checks from the presence of Cisco AMP on a Windows endpoint. The steps to create an Anti-Malware condition are as follows:

Step 1. Navigate to **Work Centers > Posture > Policy Elements > Conditions > Anti-Malware** and click **Add**.

Step 2. In the Name field, enter a name for the condition. For this example, we will use **CCIE-AMP-Condition**.

Step 3. Click the **+** sign in the field labeled Operating System.

Step 4. Select **Windows All** from the drop-down list. If we were creating a condition for Apple OS X, we would have selected **Mac OSX**. Also note that there is an arrow next to the name of the operating system. If you click it, a list of specific Windows or Apple OS X versions will be displayed for selection. That can be used to create conditions for specific operating system versions.

Step 5. Select **Cisco Systems, Inc.** from the Vendor drop-down list. Notice the list of vendors available. This list of vendors comes from the posture update process we discussed earlier. As soon as you make a selection, all anti-malware products from that vendor will be displayed in the Products for Selected Vendor list, as shown in Figure 4-74 for Cisco anti-malware products.

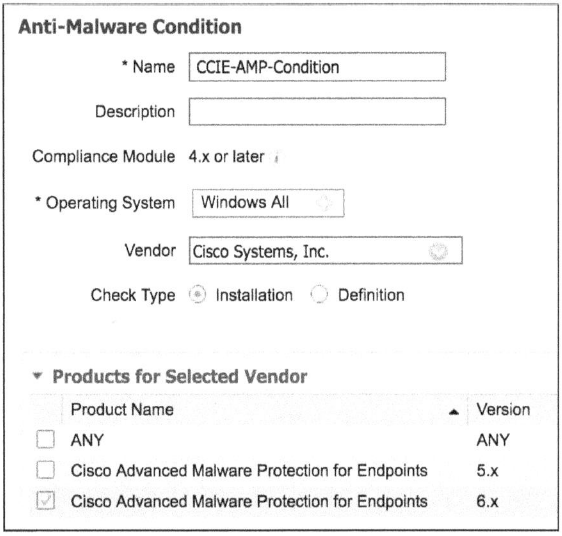

Anti-Malware Condition

* Name	CCIE-AMP-Condition
Description	
Compliance Module	4.x or later ⓘ
* Operating System	Windows All
Vendor	Cisco Systems, Inc.
Check Type	⦿ Installation ◯ Definition

▾ **Products for Selected Vendor**

Product Name	▲	Version
☐ ANY		ANY
☐ Cisco Advanced Malware Protection for Endpoints		5.x
☑ Cisco Advanced Malware Protection for Endpoints		6.x

Figure 4-74 *Creating an Anti-Malware Condition*

Step 6. For Check Type, click the **Installation** radio button. Anti-Malware conditions can be created to check if a product is installed or if its definition is updated. In this case, because we want to check if AMP is installed, we select Installation.

Step 7. Check the **Cisco Advanced Malware Protection for Endpoints v 6.x** check box in the list of products displayed, as shown in Figure 4-74. You can select a specific product and version or ANY product from the selected vendor.

Step 8. Click **Submit**.

Remediation Action

Remediation actions are actions that can be taken when a posture condition check fails on an endpoint. The actions can be as simple as displaying a message or as advanced as automatically attempting to remediate the problem through AnyConnect. Creating a remediation action is optional for a posture rule. ISE provides an in-built Message Text Only action that can be used as remediation and will result in the end user seeing a message on failure.

Like conditions, ISE supports multiple remediation types, as shown in Figure 4-75, and most of the prebuilt actions available for use.

> **▸ Remediations**

  Application

  Anti-Malware

  Anti-Spyware

  Anti-Virus

  File

  Firewall

  Launch Program

  Link

  Patch Management

  Windows Server Update Services

  Windows Update

  USB

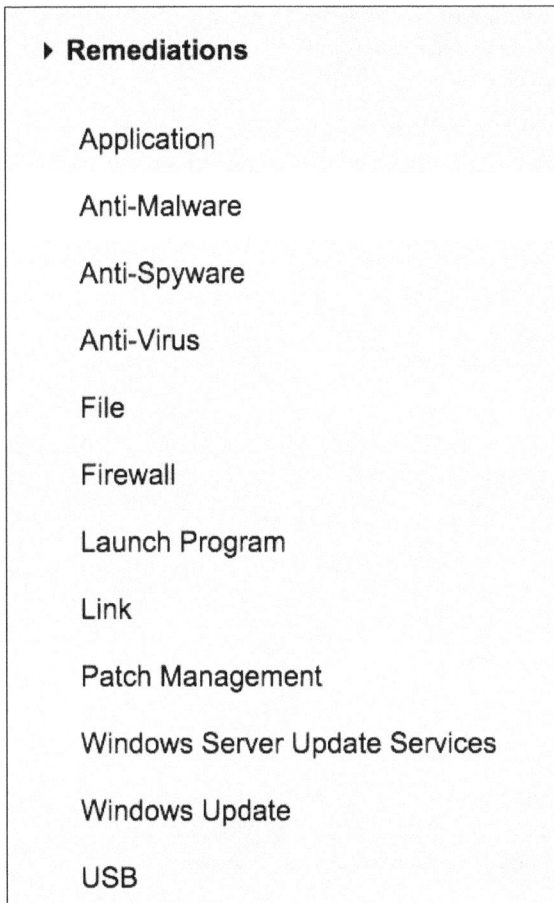

Figure 4-75 *Supported Remediation Actions in ISE*

Most prebuilt actions can be edited, but it is recommended to duplicate them and edit the copy. For the purpose of this section, let's examine a prebuilt Anti-Malware remediation action using the following steps:

Step 1. Navigate to **Work Centers > Posture > Policy Elements > Remediation > Anti-Malware.**

Step 2. Select **AnyAMDefRemediationWin** from the list. This action was created to automatically remediate the malware definition database of any installed anti-malware on the endpoint.

Step 3. Examine the various fields of the action as discussed in the following list and shown in Figure 4-76:

■ Notice that Windows is selected as the operating system and the Remediation Type field is set to Automatic.

■ The Interval and Retry Count fields define how many times and within what time period AnyConnect will attempt to execute the update program of the anti-malware application.

■ The Anti-Malware Vendor Name field is set to **ANY**. This means AnyConnect will attempt to update the definition files of any supported anti-malware product it finds. A specific vendor can be selected to limit the actions of AnyConnect to specific products.

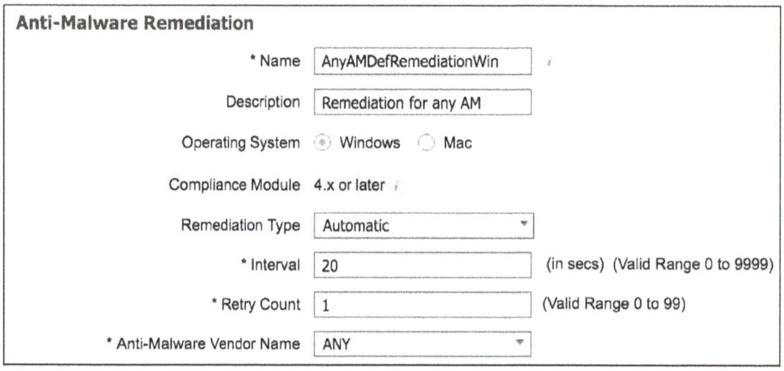

Anti-Malware Remediation

* Name	AnyAMDefRemediationWin
Description	Remediation for any AM
Operating System	⦿ Windows ○ Mac
Compliance Module	4.x or later
Remediation Type	Automatic ▾
* Interval	20 (in secs) (Valid Range 0 to 9999)
* Retry Count	1 (Valid Range 0 to 99)
* Anti-Malware Vendor Name	ANY ▾

Figure 4-76 *Examining a Remediation Action*

Posture Requirement

The final element required for a posture policy rule is the posture requirement. A posture requirement ties a remediation action to a condition. It essentially tells ISE what action needs to be taken when a particular condition check fails on an endpoint.

As with other elements, ISE contains prebuilt requirements created with prebuilt conditions and actions. These requirements can be edited or used as they are in a posture policy rule. Figure 4-77 shows examples of the prebuilt requirements from ISE.

Name	Operating Systems	Compliance Module	Posture Type	Conditions	Remediation Actions
Any_AM_Definition_Win	Windows All	4.x or later	AnyConnect	ANY_am_win_def	AnyAMDefRemediationWin
Any_AV_Installation_Mac	Mac OSX	3.x or earlier	AnyConnect	ANY_av_mac_Inst	Message Text Only

Figure 4-77 *Prebuilt Posture Requirements in ISE*

As shown in Figure 4-77, requirements are simple rules that define what actions apply to what conditions. Let's look at the steps required to create a requirement using the AMP Anti-Malware condition we created earlier:

Step 1.   Navigate to **Work Centers > Posture > Policy Elements > Requirements**.

Step 2.   Click the down arrow at the right end of the last requirement and select **Insert new requirement**.

Step 3. Enter a name for the requirement. We will use **CCIE-AMP** for this example.

Step 4. Click the **+** sign and then select **Windows** from the drop-down list in the Operating Systems column.

Step 5. Select **4.x or later** from the drop-down list in the Compliance Module column.

Step 6. Select **AnyConnect** from the Posture Type column.

Step 7. Click the **+** sign in the Conditions column.

Step 8. Select **User Defined > Anti-Malware Condition > CCIE-AMP-Condition** from the drop-down list.

Step 9. Click the **+** sign in the Remediation Actions column.

Step 10. Select **Message Text Only** from the Action drop-down list and type any text in the Message box.

Step 11. Click **Done.**

Step 12. Click **Save.**

Figure 4-78 shows the requirement created by the preceding steps. This requirement will check if AMP is installed on a Windows operating system. If the check fails, the device will be marked noncompliant and the user will be shown a message.

| CCIE-AMP | Windows All | 4.x or later | AnyConnect | CCIE-AMP-Condition | Message Text Only |

Figure 4-78 *Creating a Posture Requirement*

Note   The Compliance Module column no longer has any relevance because current ISE versions only support AnyConnect 4.x and compliance module 4.x. Similarly, the Posture Type column will always be AnyConnect unless you are using AnyConnect in stealth mode or the Web Agent.

Configuring Posture Policy Rule

Now that all the elements have been created, we can create a posture policy rule. These rules can be created based on operating system, identity group, or conditions such as SSID name and authentication protocol. These conditions are very similar to those used to create policy sets and authorization rules, but only a subset of dictionaries is available for posture rules.

One key aspect of a posture rule is that it can contain multiple requirements and the requirements are cumulative. Each requirement in a posture policy rule has its own status setting of Mandatory, Optional, or Audit (as shown in Figure 4-79). Mandatory means that the requirement must be met in order for the endpoint to be marked compliant. Optional means the endpoint will be considered compliant even if the requirement is not met but the remediation action will be attempted. Audit only logs the requirement result and does not affect the client's compliance status.

Let's look at the steps required to create a posture rule for the AMP requirement created earlier:

Step 1.   Navigate to **Work Centers > Posture > Posture Policy.**

Step 2.   Select the down arrow at the right end of the last rule and select **Insert new policy.**

Step 3.   Enter a name. For this example, we will use **CCIE-Check-AMP.**

Step 4.   Click the **+** sign and then select **Windows** from the drop-down list in the Operating Systems column.

Step 5.   Select **4.x or later** from the drop-down list in the Compliance Module column.

Step 6.   Select **AnyConnect** from the Posture Type column.

Step 7.   Click the **+** sign and then select **CCIE-AMP** from the drop-down list, as shown in Figure 4-79.

Step 8.   Click **Done.**

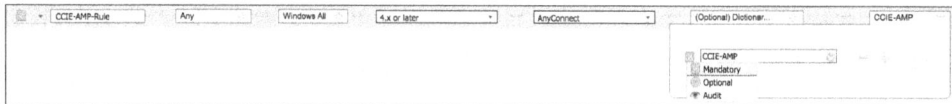

Figure 4-79   *Creating a Posture Policy Rule*

The preceding steps can be repeated to create multiple rules. One unique thing about posture rules is that they are not first-match only like other rules in ISE. If a device or session matches multiple rules in the posture policy, then all the requirements of each matched rule are applied to the endpoint. It must pass every mandatory requirement of these rules to be marked compliant.

Configure Policy Set for Posture

Before creating a policy set based on posture status, the required authorization profile will need to be created. Apart from the built-in profiles, an authorization profile to redirect users to the provisioning portal is required, as shown in Figure 4-80. The figure shows an authorization profile named Posture_Redirect that has Web Redirection enabled and Client Provisioning (Posture) selected. The ACL value is again set to **redirect** but the Value field is set to Client Provisioning Portal (default) to redirect users to the in-built provisioning portal we discussed earlier.

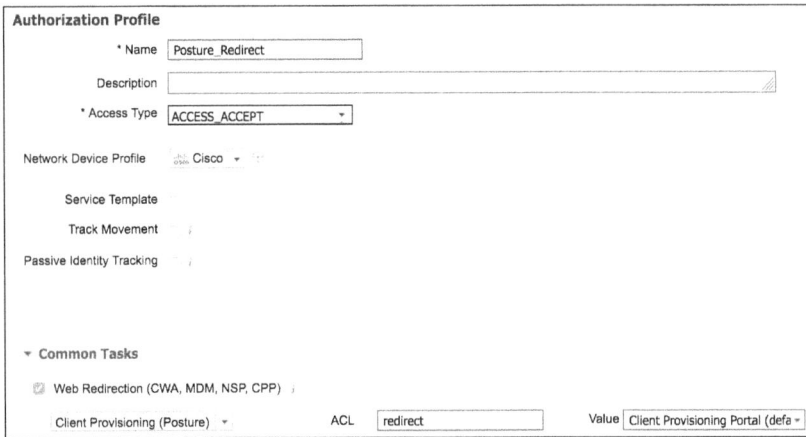

Figure 4-80 *Authorization Profile for Posture Redirection*

As you know, policy sets, authentication polices, and authorization policies can be created using different combinations of conditions to achieve the same result. For the purpose of example, we will create a policy set using the exact same condition we used for the BYOD and MDM policy sets. The authentication policy will be configured to allow EAP-TLS authentication only. Figure 4-81 shows the policy set and authentication policy configuration.

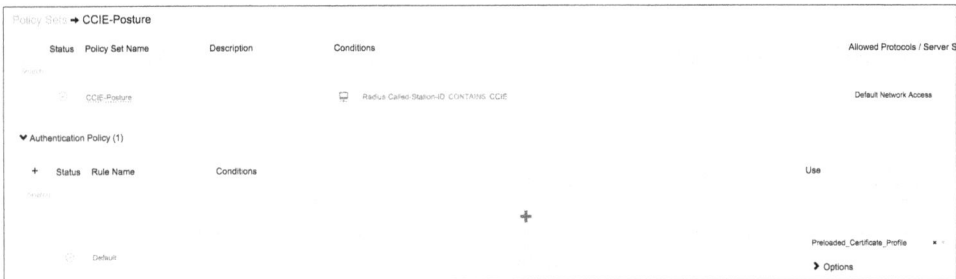

Figure 4-81 *Policy Set and Authentication Policy Configuration for Posture*

The authorization policy for this policy set will be configured to redirect devices that are not compliant or those with an unknown posture status. Devices with compliant posture status will be allowed access.

To configure the authorization policy, follow these steps:

Step 1. Expand the **Authorization Policy** section.

Step 2. Replace the Profile for the Default rule with **DenyAccess.**

Step 3. Click the gear icon in the Actions column for the Default rule and select **Insert new row above.**

Step 4.   Name the new rule **Posture_Compliant**.

Step 5.   Click the **Conditions** column in the new rule.

Step 6.   Drag the **Compliant_Devices** rule from the Library section on the left to the Editor section on the right, as shown in Figure 4-82.

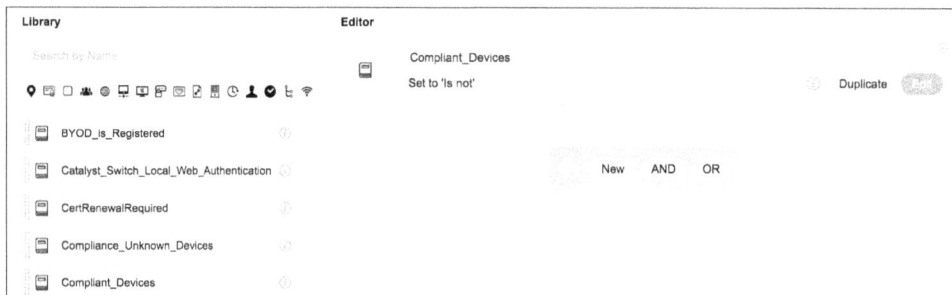

Figure 4-82   *Conditions for Posture Compliance Check*

Step 7.   Click **Use**.

Step 8.   Select **PermitAccess** from the drop-down list in the Profiles column of the new rule.

This authorization rule will permit access if the posture status of the device is compliant.

Step 9.   Click the gear icon in the Actions column for the rule and select **Insert new row above**.

Step 10.   Name the new rule **Posture_Other**.

Step 11.   Click the **Conditions** column in the new rule.

Step 12.   Drag the **Compliant_Unknown** rule from the Library section on the left to the Editor section on the right, as shown in Figure 4-83.

Step 13.   Drag the **Non_Compliant_Devices** rule from the Library section on the left to the Editor section on the right, as shown in Figure 4-83.

Step 14.   Select **OR** from the drop-down list in the first column of the Editor section, as shown in Figure 4-83.

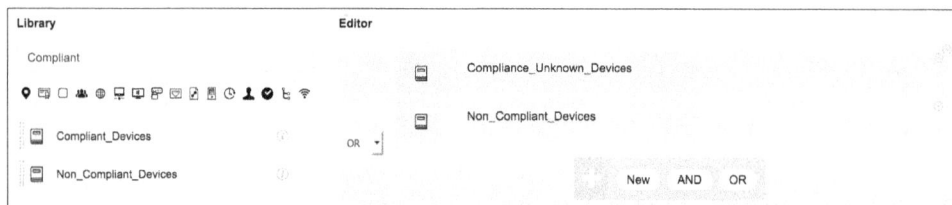

Figure 4-83   *Condition for Posture Noncompliance and Unknown Posture Status*

Step 15. Click **Use**.

Step 16. Select **Posture_Redirect** from the drop-down list in the Profiles column of
the new rule.

This authorization profile was created earlier to redirect to the Client
Provisioning Portal. This rule will redirect non-compliant devices or those
with an unknown posture status to the portal.

Step 17. Click **Save**.

Figure 4-84 shows the completed authorization policy.

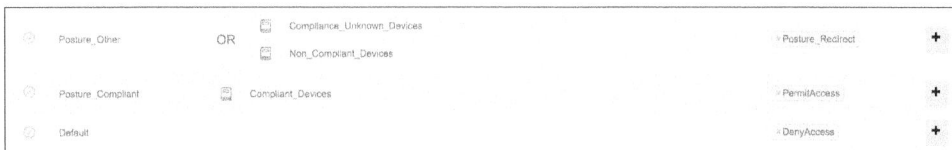

Figure 4-84   *Authorization Profile for Posture Enforcement*

Guest Access with ISE

As discussed earlier in this chapter, with use of mobile devices becoming common,
employees, vendors, and guests visiting an organization expect Internet access. This is
even more so in the retail and hospitality industries, where customers demand this access.
Although traditional methods such as 802.1X, with or without onboarding, can help with
employee and vendor access, customer and guest access presents two unique challenges:

■ Customers and guests will not allow an organization to install a profile or app on
their devices. Neither will they appreciate being asked to follow complicated
procedures to get access.

■ If open access to the network is provided, then unauthorized users may take
advantage of it and at the very least consume resources meant for authorized
users. Users may also use the access for illegal purposes such as pirating copyright
material. With open access and no user identification, the accountability of such
actions cannot be attributed to individuals, and the organization providing the
access may become liable.

To solve these challenges, a guest access solution needs to provide a simple method of
access that does not require any configuration on the endpoint. The industry as a whole
has adopted URL-redirect and web-portal-based solutions as the standard for guest
access. You may have seen examples of that in hotels, restaurants, stores, and airplanes
where upon connecting to an open SSID, you are redirected to a web portal. Once you
provide the required information, such as payment details or identification of some sort,
or you accept use policies, you are granted access.

While portal-based authentication does solve the problem of complexity, the problem of identification remains. Any sort of authentication will require credentials of some kind. The problem is, how does a guest user get valid credentials? ISE provides a full suite of guest access features that solve this problem with three types of guest access:

- **Hotspot guest access:** With this method, the web portal simply contains an Acceptable User Policy (AUP) and does not require authentication of any kind. By accepting the AUP, the users agree to use the provided access within the limits of the policy. Their MAC address and acceptance of AUP is stored in the database. Such access is usually limited to a time period. An example of this can be seen when visiting coffee shops or airports.

- **Sponsored guest access:** With this method, the guest user accounts are created by employees with corporate credentials. The employees that create the accounts are generally the hosts of the guest or lobby administrators. The created credentials can be sent to the guest through email or SMS. They can also be printed and provided to the guest.

- **Self-registered guest access:** With this method, the guest users can create their own account on the portal by providing some identifying information such as email or phone number. The account can either be created immediately or require an employee of the organization to approve the request. Once the account is created, the credentials are sent to the guest through email or SMS.

The type of guest access depends on the portal configuration in ISE. Irrespective of the type, the basic flow of guest access with ISE remains the same. Figure 4-85 shows the interaction between the endpoint, the network device, and ISE that allows guest access.

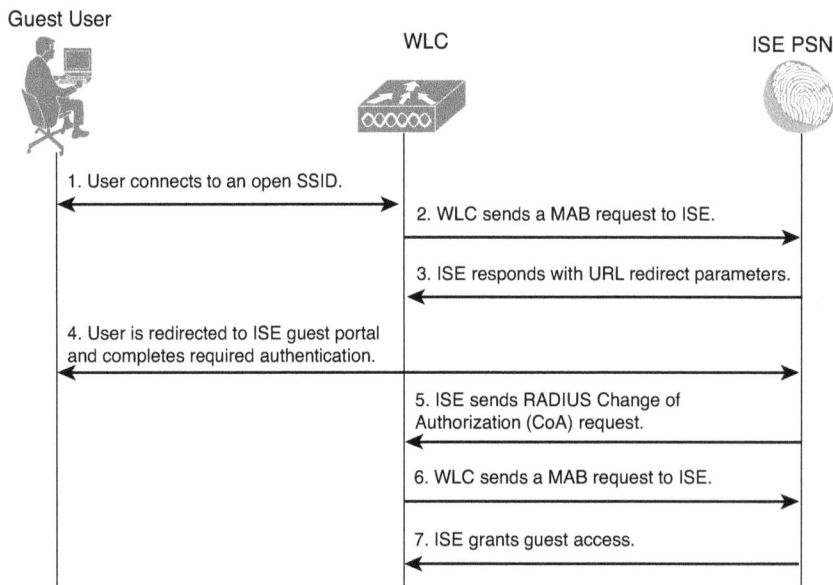

Figure 4-85   *Guest Access with ISE*

The steps shown in the guest flow in Figure 4-85 are as follows:

1. The flow starts with the user connecting to an open SSID.

Note   Starting with Cisco WLC version 8.4, MAB authentication is allowed on an SSID that is protected by a preshared key. So, connecting to an open SSID is no longer the only option, but distributing the preshared key to guests is a problem, so an open SSID is used in most cases. Also, remember that while this section uses a wireless network as an example, guest access can be provided on wired networks also through a MAB authentication.

2. The network device, the WLC in this case, sends a MAB request to ISE.

3. Because this is a new session, ISE responds with a URL Redirection response.

4. The user is redirected to the ISE guest portal where they authenticate. The type of authentication depends on the portal configuration.

Note   Remember that redirect can be triggered either by the operating system testing for the presence of redirect or by the user opening a browser and attempting to connect to a URL.

5. After successful authentication (or AUP acceptance in case of hotspot access), ISE sends a RADIUS CoA request to the network device.

6. The network device sends a MAB request again to ISE with the same session ID.

7. ISE recognizes this as a re-authentication request after CoA and grants guest access based on the authentication completed in Step 4.

Note   With the redirect and CoA based solution, the session ID is very important. The ISE PSN maintains a state table of session IDs and records all associated attributes in it. The MAB session is tied to the portal authentication in this table. The network device needs to preserve the session ID across requests for the solution to work properly.

Because we already discussed the configuration of BYOD onboarding and posture provisioning features, the configuration required for guest access will feel very familiar. It can be broken into two parts:

1. **Portal configuration:** Guest access features primarily depend on the configuration of the guest portal. The guest access type—hotspot, sponsored, or self-registered— is defined by the portal configuration. There are various settings in a guest portal that define the guest experience and will be discussed in depth in later sections.

2. **Policy set configuration:** The policy set, authentication policies, and authorization policies are required to redirect users to the guest portal and grant access after authentication.

Preparing to Configure Guest Access

Before configuring the guest portals or the policy set for guest access, there are a few prerequisite configuration tasks that you need to complete, as described in the sections that follow.

Configure Network Devices

Guest access works in conjunction with MAB authentication. So, the network devices need to be configured for MAB, URL Redirection, and CoA, as discussed earlier in this chapter and in Chapter 2. For example purposes, create an open SSID named **CCIE-Guest** and configure it in the same way we configured the CCIE-Onboard SSID for the Single SSID flow BYOD onboarding earlier in the "Network Device Configuration for BYOD Onboarding" section (see Figures 4-31 to 4-34).

Define an SMTP Server on ISE

When a sponsor or self-registered guest account is created, ISE can send credentials to the guest directly. For this, an SMTP server needs to be defined on ISE. The SMTP server address can be configured by navigating to **Administration > Settings > SMTP Server.** You can enter the SMTP server hostname or IP address, as shown in Figure 4-86.

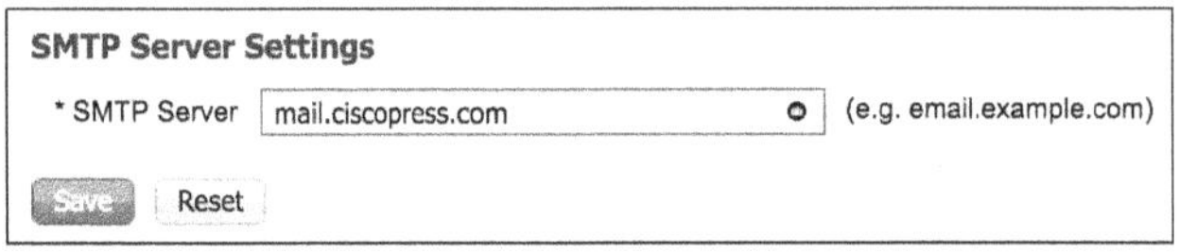

SMTP Server Settings

* SMTP Server   `mail.ciscopress.com`   (e.g. email.example.com)

Save   Reset

Figure 4-86 *Configuring SMTP Server Address on ISE*

Create Guest Types

All guest accounts in ISE have to belong to a guest type. A guest type is a collection of settings that apply to guest accounts. These settings include access duration and time restrictions, limit on simultaneous logins, and account expiration notice, among others. ISE contains a few prebuilt guest types such as Contractors, Daily, and Weekly, but you can create custom guest types. To create a guest type, follow these steps:

Step 1. Navigate to **Work Centers > Guest Access > Portals & Components > Guest Types** and click **Create.**

Step 2.   Enter a name for the guest type. We will use **CCIE-Guest** as an example here.

Step 3.   Configure the following settings in the Maximum Access Time section (shown in Figure 4-87):

- **Account duration starts:** This setting specifies the date from which a guest account will be active. It can be either from the first time the account is used or from a date specified while creating the account. Because guest accounts have a validity period, this setting is important to ensure the guest has access during the time they are visiting and not before or after that. It is generally recommended to select the first option—From first login—to avoid time zone problems.

- **Maximum account duration:** This specifies the maximum validity for a guest account.

- **Allow access only on these days and times:** This applies day and time limits to guest accounts. This is particularly useful if you want to prevent access outside of office hours.

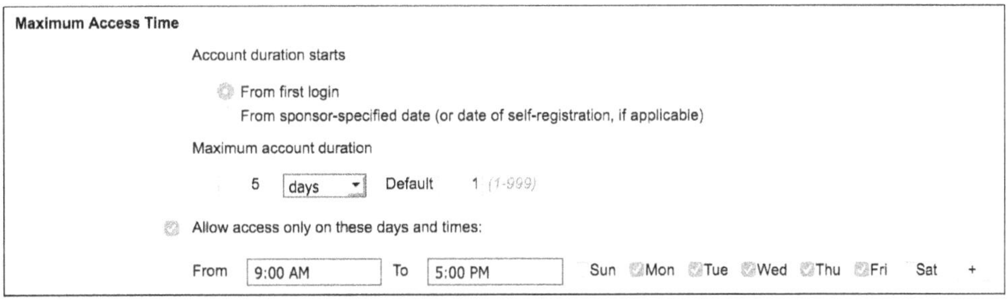

Maximum Access Time

Account duration starts

  ○ From first login
  From sponsor-specified date (or date of self-registration, if applicable)

Maximum account duration

  5 [days ▾] Default   1 *(1-999)*

  ☑ Allow access only on these days and times:

  From [9:00 AM]   To [5:00 PM]   Sun ☑Mon ☑Tue ☑Wed ☑Thu ☑Fri   Sat   +

Figure 4-87   *Maximum Access Time Settings for Guest Type*

Step 4.   Configure the following settings in the Login Options section (shown in Figure 4-88):

- **Maximum simultaneous logins:** Defines the maximum simultaneous devices that can log in using the same guest account and the action to take when the configured number is exceeded.

- **Maximum devices guests can register:** Defines the maximum number of devices that can be registered under the same guest name and the group to register devices under.

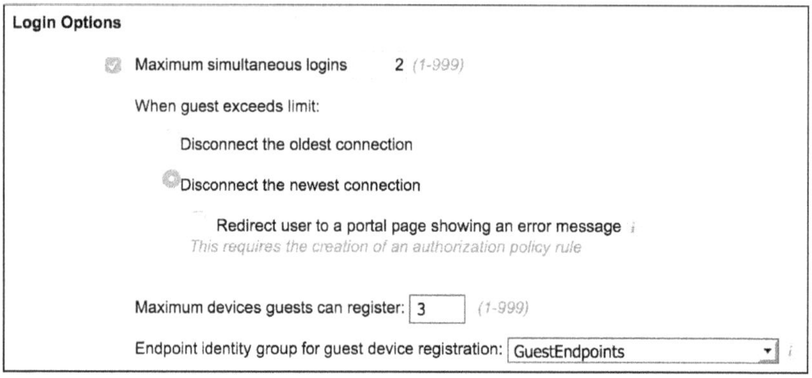

Figure 4-88   *Login Options Settings for Guest Type*

Step 5.   Configure the Account Expiration Notification section as shown in Figure 4-89. This section specifies if an account expiration notification will be sent to the guest and how it will be sent.

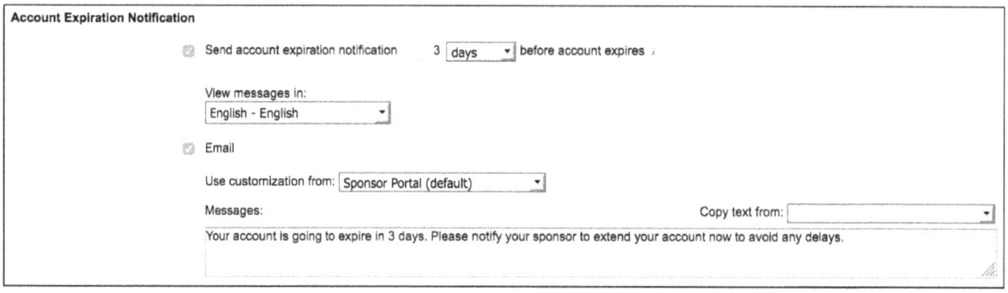

Figure 4-89   *Account Expiration Notification Settings for Guest Type*

Step 6.   Click Save.

Sponsor Groups and Portal

Earlier, we discussed that sponsored guest access requires a sponsor, most often an employee of the organization, to create a guest account. Similarly, a self-registered guest access requires the guest to create a guest account. These *guest accounts* are different from the *internal user accounts* in ISE. All guest accounts are saved in a separate database called Guest Users. This database is different from the Internal Users database where all user accounts created from the ISE GUI are stored.

Guest accounts can only be created from the self-registered guest portal or the *sponsor portal* (or using APIs). The sponsor portal is a dedicated UI that employees can log in to and create a guest account. The sponsor portal provides a convenient method to create guest accounts without requiring administrative access to the ISE GUI.

ISE provides a prebuilt sponsor portal that can be customized. You can also choose to create a custom portal, but that is often not required. You can use any supported mechanism for authentication to the sponsor portal, such as Active Directory and an internal ISE database. ISE also provides a role-based authorization method called *sponsor groups* to control access to the portal. Before using the sponsor or self-registered guest portals, it is necessary to configure sponsor groups and the sponsor portal.

Note   If a self-registered guest portal requires the guest-created accounts to be approved by a sponsor, then the sponsor will need to use the sponsor portal to grant that approval also.

Configuring Sponsor Groups

Sponsor groups define the access control policy for the sponsor portal. They define the level of access a sponsor gets on the portal based on their group membership.

ISE provides three default sponsor groups, as shown in Figure 4-90:

- **ALL_ACCOUNTS:** Members of this group can manage all guest accounts created on that ISE deployment, irrespective of who created those accounts.

- **GROUP_ACCOUNTS:** Members of this group can manage guest accounts from other sponsors in this group.

- **OWN_ACCOUNTS:** Members of this group can only manage guest accounts created by them.

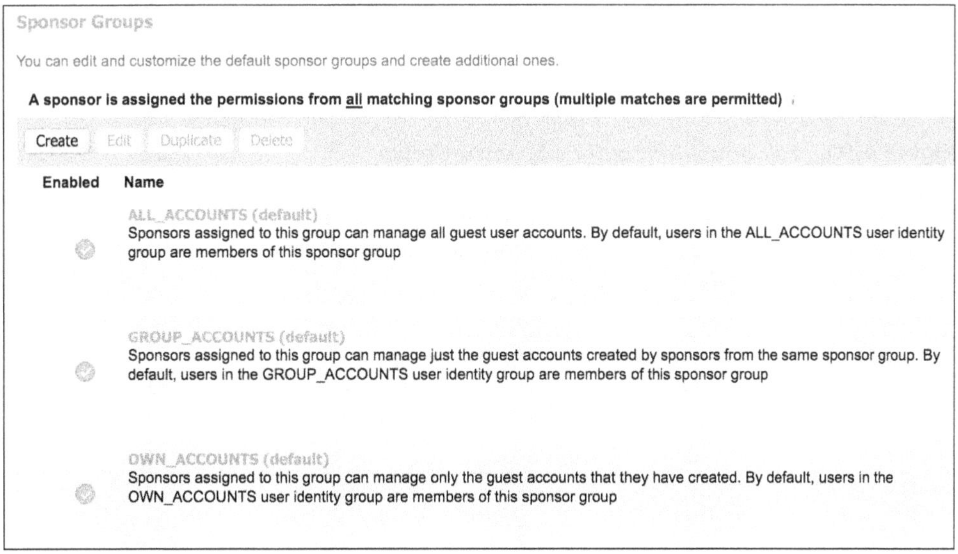

Figure 4-90 *Default Sponsor Groups*

To examine and edit a sponsor group, follow these steps:

Step 1.   Navigate to **Work Centers > Guest Access > Portals & Components > Sponsor Groups.**

Step 2.   Select the **ALL_ACCOUNTS (default)** group.

Step 3.   The Match Criteria section defines the groups of users that will be mapped to this sponsor group. This is commonly an Active Directory group or an internal ISE user group. Click the **Members** button to open a list of available groups and select the desired groups. Figure 4-91 shows the ALL_ ACCOUNTS and Employee internal ISE groups selected.

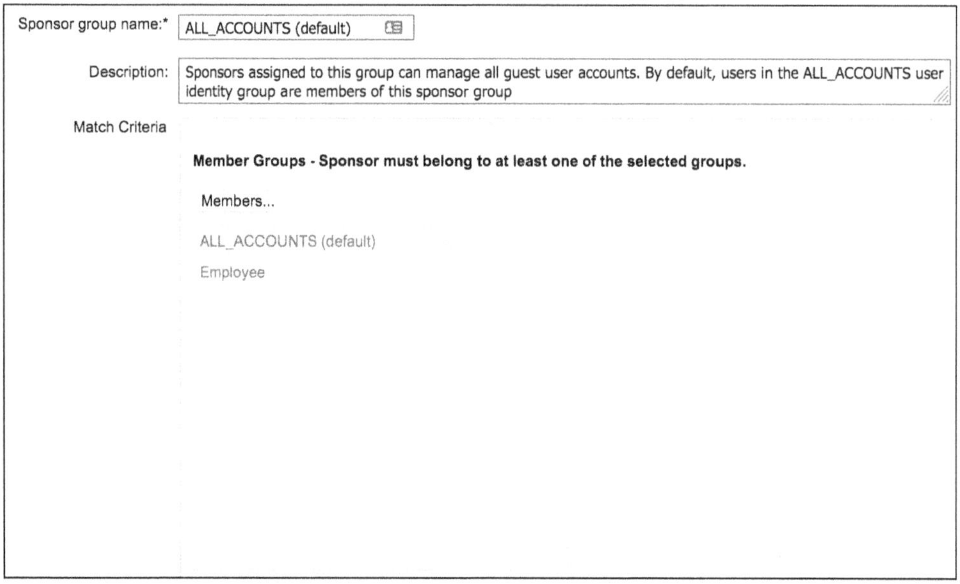

Sponsor group name:*	ALL_ACCOUNTS (default)
Description:	Sponsors assigned to this group can manage all guest user accounts. By default, users in the ALL_ACCOUNTS user identity group are members of this sponsor group
Match Criteria	

Member Groups - Sponsor must belong to at least one of the selected groups.

Members...

ALL_ACCOUNTS (default)

Employee

Figure 4-91   *Selecting Members of a Sponsor Group*

Step 4.   Assign the guest types that the members of this group can create guest accounts for. Figure 4-92 shows the previously created CCIE-Guest type selected.

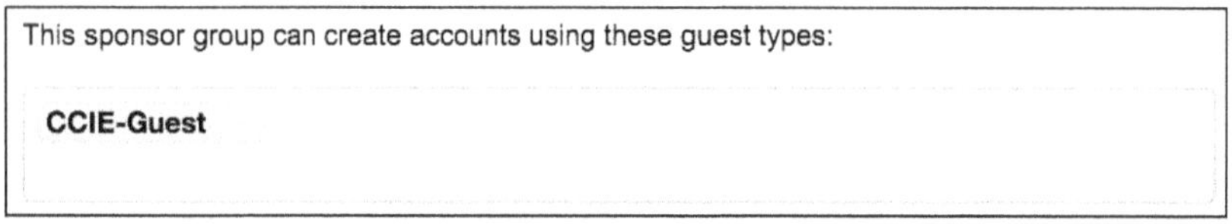

This sponsor group can create accounts using these guest types:

CCIE-Guest

Figure 4-92   *Adding Guest Types to a Sponsor Group*

Step 5. In the Sponsor Permissions section, shown in Figure 4-93, select the various permissions that the members of this group will get on the sponsor portal. Some key permissions that can be selected are:

- Ability to bulk create guest accounts

- Ability to manage all accounts, group accounts, or own accounts

- View or rest guest passwords

- Update, extended, delete, or suspend guest accounts

- Approve self-registered guest accounts

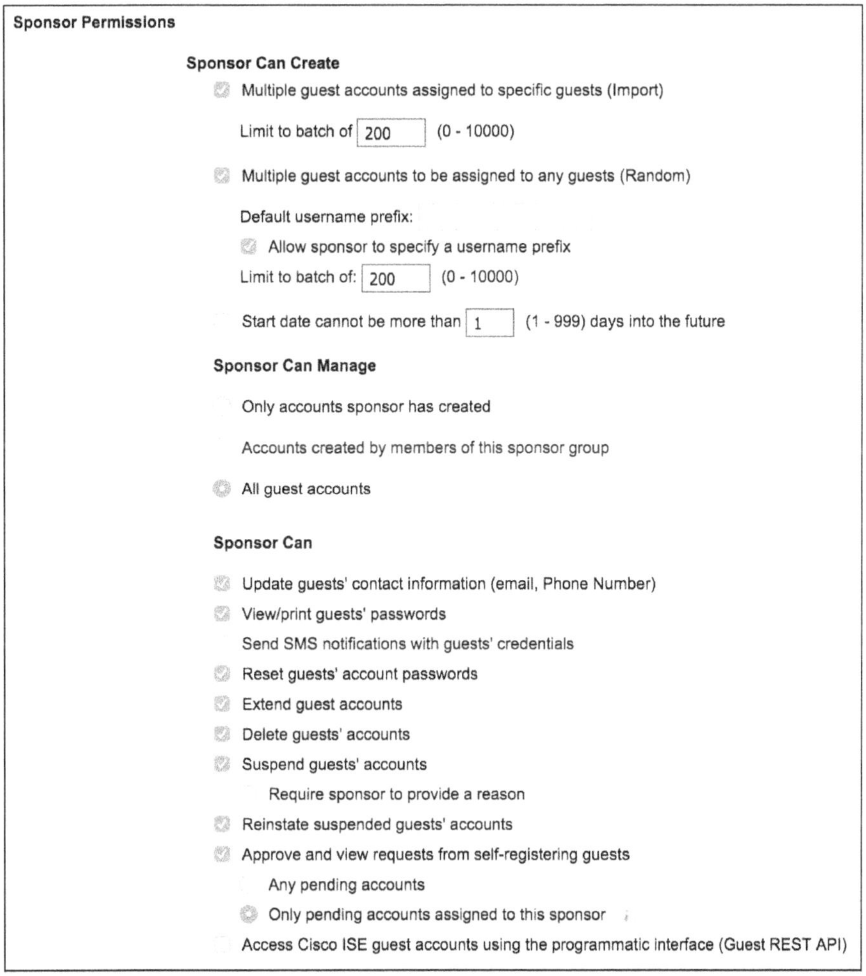

Sponsor Permissions

Sponsor Can Create

☑ Multiple guest accounts assigned to specific guests (Import)

Limit to batch of [200] (0 - 10000)

☑ Multiple guest accounts to be assigned to any guests (Random)

Default username prefix:

☑ Allow sponsor to specify a username prefix

Limit to batch of: [200] (0 - 10000)

Start date cannot be more than [1] (1 - 999) days into the future

Sponsor Can Manage

Only accounts sponsor has created

Accounts created by members of this sponsor group

⦿ All guest accounts

Sponsor Can

☑ Update guests' contact information (email, Phone Number)
☑ View/print guests' passwords
Send SMS notifications with guests' credentials
☑ Reset guests' account passwords
☑ Extend guest accounts
☑ Delete guests' accounts
☑ Suspend guests' accounts
Require sponsor to provide a reason
☑ Reinstate suspended guests' accounts
☑ Approve and view requests from self-registering guests
Any pending accounts
⦿ Only pending accounts assigned to this sponsor
Access Cisco ISE guest accounts using the programmatic interface (Guest REST API)

Figure 4-93 *Selecting Sponsor Permissions*

Step 6. Click Save.

Configuring the Sponsor Portal

ISE provides a prebuilt default sponsor portal that is usually sufficient for most deployments but can be edited to meet requirements. Editing the sponsor portal is similar to editing any other portal discussed earlier in the chapter. Perform the following steps to edit the default sponsor portal:

Step 1.   Navigate to **Work Centers > Guest Access > Portals & Components > Sponsor Portals.**

Step 2.   Select **Sponsor Portal (default)** to open the familiar layout of a portal configuration page, as shown in Figure 4-94.

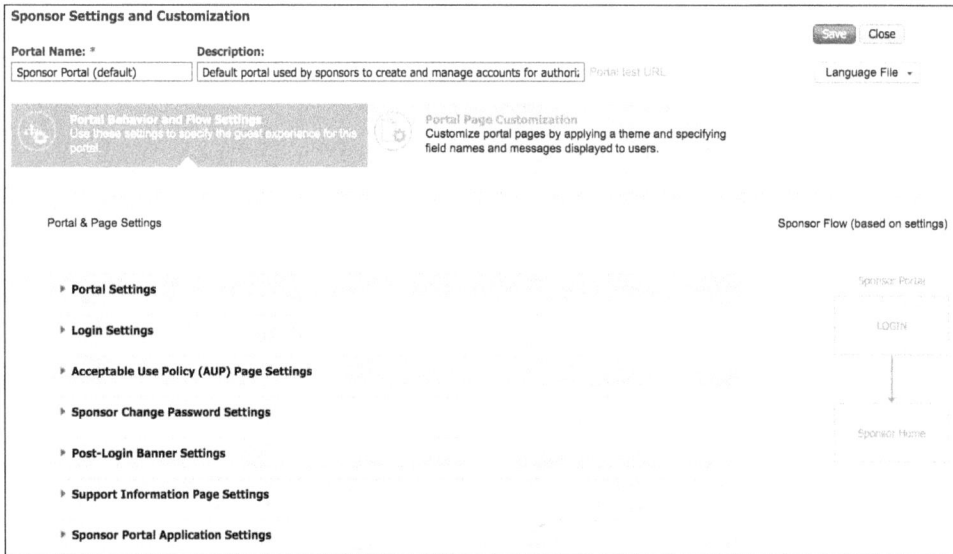

Figure 4-94   *Default Sponsor Portal*

Step 3.   Expand the **Portal Settings** section as shown in Figure 4-95. Just like other portals, this section allows you to select the interface, port, and identity source sequence. One setting to note is the FQDN of the portal. Recommended practice dictates that you enter an easy-to-remember FQDN for employees to access the portal. Make sure the FQDN can resolve to the IP address of the interface on which the sponsor portal is listening.

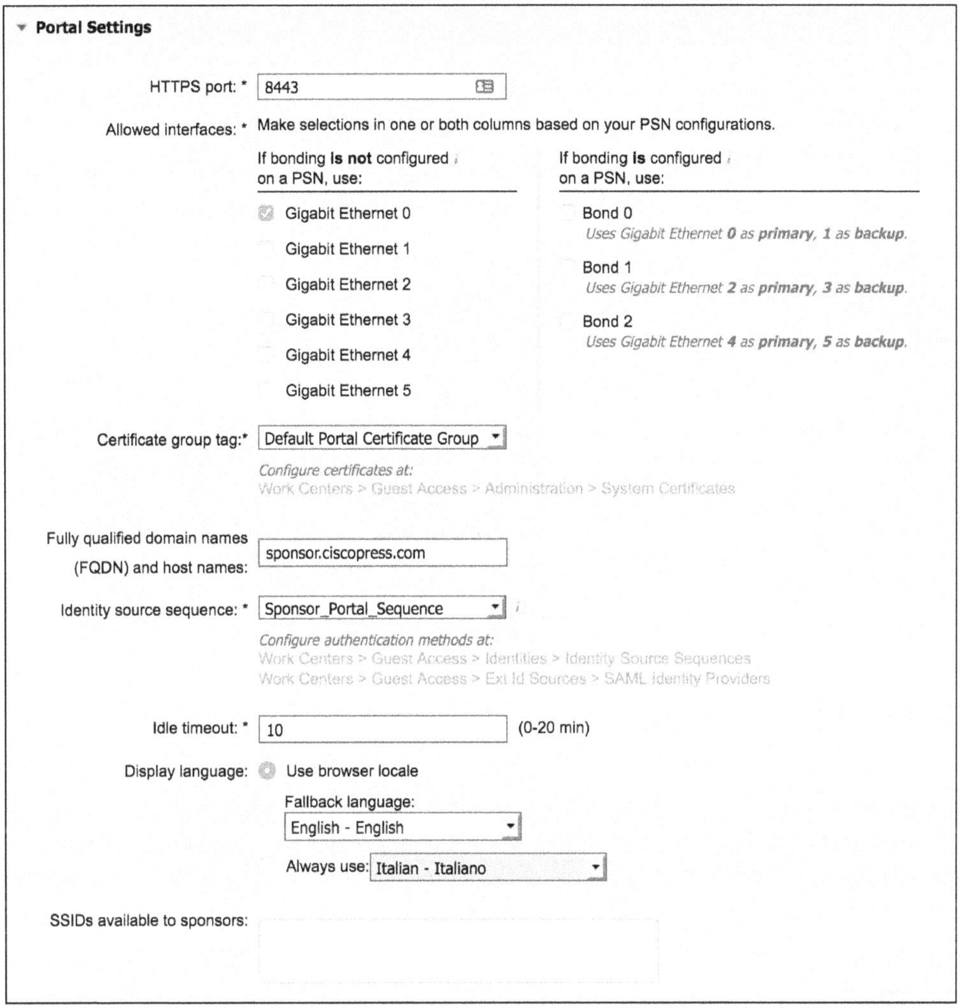

Figure 4-95 *Sponsor Portal Login Settings*

Note The Sponsor_Portal_Sequence ID sequence group, shown in Figure 4-95, is a prebuilt element. Edit it to authenticate to the desired database. For this example, only Internal User is selected in the ID sequence group.

Step 4.   Expand the rest of the sections to configure options such as the AUP and banners.

Step 5.   Click Save.

Using the Sponsor Portal

Once the sponsor groups and sponsor portal have been configured, you can navigate to the portal and start creating guest accounts. To use the sponsor portal, perform the following steps:

Step 1.   Open a browser and enter the FQDN you entered in the portal configuration to open the sponsor portal, as shown in Figure 4-96.

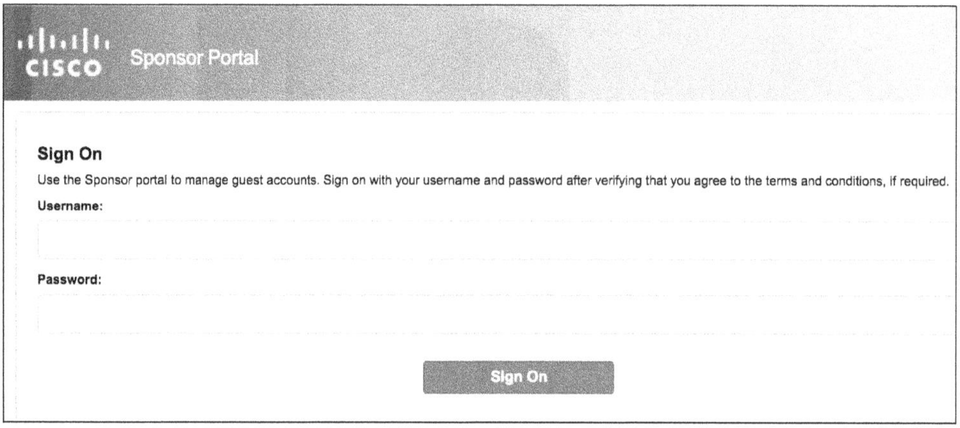

Figure 4-96   *Sponsor Portal*

Note   You can also log in to the sponsor portal by navigating to **Work Centers > Guest Access > Manage Accounts** and clicking the **Manage Accounts** button, but this is not a true verification of the sponsor portal configuration because this uses the ISE UI admin account to log in to the portal.

Step 2.   Log in using a user account from the database selected in the portal settings. For this example, we will use an account from the Internal Users database that belongs to the Employee group. After login, the sponsor portal is displayed as shown in Figure 4-97.

Note   User should belong to the ALL_ACCOUNTS or Employee group because we mapped these groups to the ALL_ACCOUNTS sponsor group earlier.

Step 3.   Fill out the guest details as shown in Figure 4-97.

Step 4.   Click **Create**.

Step 5.   The guest account will be created and the details will be displayed, as shown in Figure 4-98.

Step 6.   Click **Notify** to send the credentials to the guest by email.

Figure 4-97 *Creating a Guest Account on Sponsor Portal*

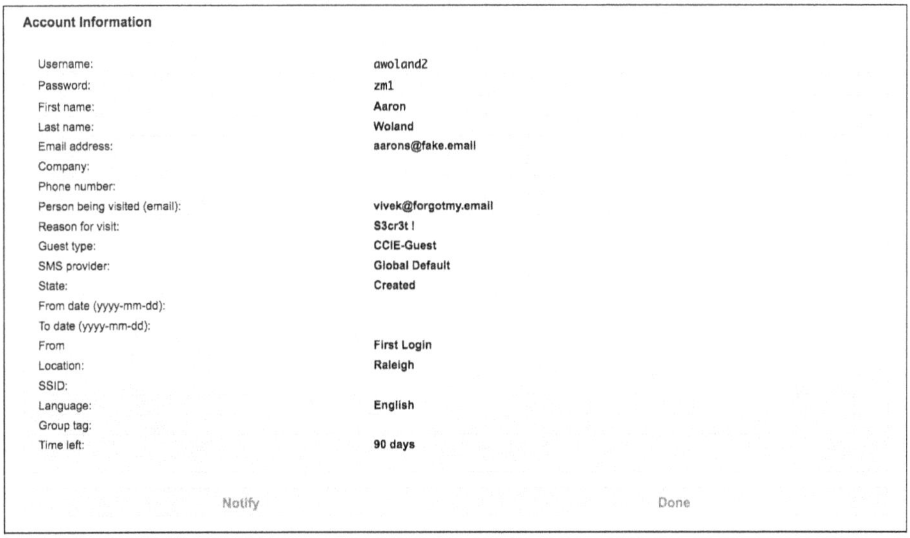

Figure 4-98 *Guest Account Confirmation*

Hotspot Portal

With all the required elements already configured, it is time to configure the guest portals. We will start with the hotspot portal. Because hotspot guest access requires only an AUP to be accepted, this portal is the simplest to configure. Perform the following steps to configure the portal:

Step 1.   Navigate to **Work Centers > Guest Access > Portals & Components > Guest Portals.**

Step 2.   Select **Hotspot Guest Portal (default)** to open the familiar layout of a portal configuration page, as shown in Figure 4-99.

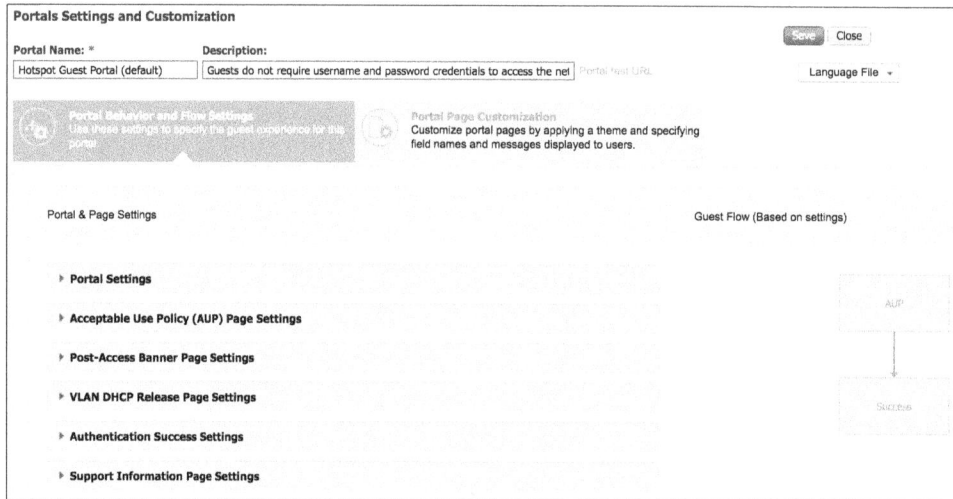

Figure 4-99   *Hotspot Guest Portal*

Step 3.   Expand the **Portal Settings** section as shown in Figure 4-100. Just like other portals, this section allows you to select the interface and port. There are two other options in this section that you should carefully consider:

■ **Endpoint identity group:** This is the group to which the endpoint will be added. This group can be used in the authorization rule to grant access.

■ **CoA Type:** Depending on how the authorization rule will be configured, you need to select the CoA type that will be sent after the AUP is accepted on the hotspot portal. Most often, this will be set to **CoA Reauthenticate.**

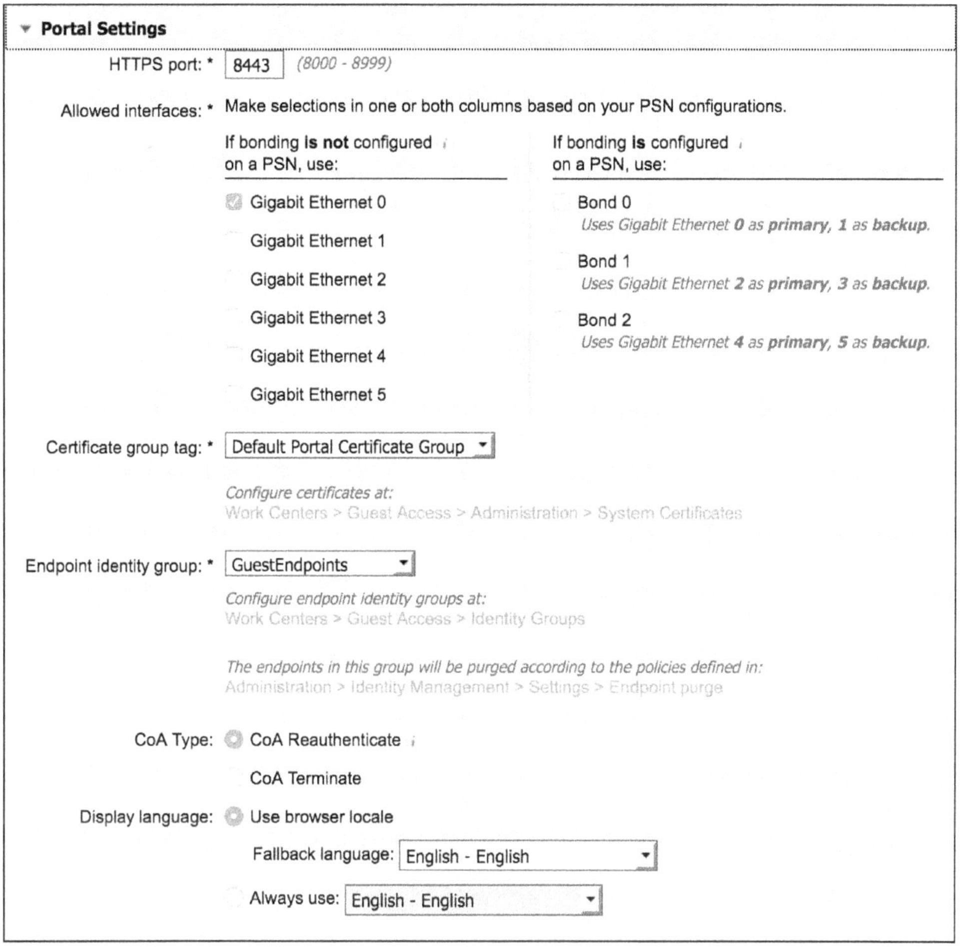

Portal Settings

HTTPS port: * `8443`   *(8000 - 8999)*

Allowed interfaces: *   Make selections in one or both columns based on your PSN configurations.

If bonding **is not** configured *i*
on a PSN, use:

If bonding **is** configured *i*
on a PSN, use:

☑ Gigabit Ethernet 0

Gigabit Ethernet 1

Gigabit Ethernet 2

Gigabit Ethernet 3

Gigabit Ethernet 4

Gigabit Ethernet 5

Bond 0
  *Uses Gigabit Ethernet **0** as **primary**, **1** as **backup**.*

Bond 1
  *Uses Gigabit Ethernet **2** as **primary**, **3** as **backup**.*

Bond 2
  *Uses Gigabit Ethernet **4** as **primary**, **5** as **backup**.*

Certificate group tag: * `Default Portal Certificate Group ▼`

Configure certificates at:
Work Centers > Guest Access > Administration > System Certificates

Endpoint identity group: * `GuestEndpoints ▼`

Configure endpoint identity groups at:
Work Centers > Guest Access > Identity Groups

The endpoints in this group will be purged according to the policies defined in:
Administration > Identity Management > Settings > Endpoint purge

CoA Type: ⦿ CoA Reauthenticate *i*

CoA Terminate

Display language: ⦿ Use browser locale

Fallback language: `English - English ▼`

Always use: `English - English ▼`

Figure 4-100   *Hotspot Portal Settings*

Step 4.   Expand rest of the sections to configure options such as the AUP and banners.

Step 5.   Click Save.

Sponsored and Self-Registered Guest Portals

The sponsored guest portal is the Swiss-army knife of portals. While its primary use is allowing access to users with a guest account, it can easily be used to provide portal-based authentication for employees, BYOD onboarding, client provisioning, and self-registration for guests. In fact, in the BYOD onboarding section, we used a sponsored guest portal for Single SSID flow. You can configure the default sponsor portal to be sponsored or self-registered guest access using the following steps:

Step 1.   Navigate to **Work Centers > Guest Access > Portals & Components > Guest Portals.**

Step 2.   Select **Sponsored Guest Portal (default)** to open the familiar layout of a portal configuration page, as shown in Figure 4-101.

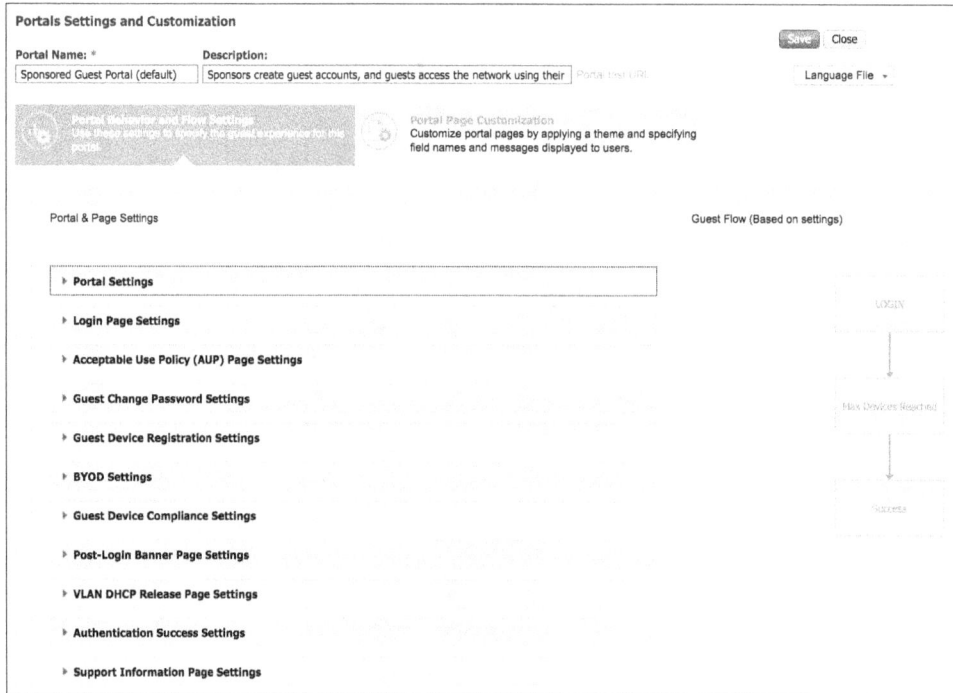

Portals Settings and Customization

			Save Close
Portal Name: *	**Description:**		
Sponsored Guest Portal (default)	Sponsors create guest accounts, and guests access the network using their	Portal test URL	Language File ▾

Portal Behavior and Flow Settings
Use these settings to specify the guest experience for this portal.

Portal Page Customization
Customize portal pages by applying a theme and specifying field names and messages displayed to users.

Portal & Page Settings   Guest Flow (Based on settings)

▸ **Portal Settings**

▸ **Login Page Settings**   LOGIN

▸ **Acceptable Use Policy (AUP) Page Settings**   │

▸ **Guest Change Password Settings**

▸ **Guest Device Registration Settings**   Max Devices Reached

▸ **BYOD Settings**   │

▸ **Guest Device Compliance Settings**

▸ **Post-Login Banner Page Settings**   Success

▸ **VLAN DHCP Release Page Settings**

▸ **Authentication Success Settings**

▸ **Support Information Page Settings**

Figure 4-101   *Sponsored Guest Portal*

Step 3.   Expand the **Portal Settings** section as shown in Figure 4-102. Just like other portals, this section allows you to select the interface and port. There are two other options in this section that you should carefully consider:

■ **Authentication method:** This is the ID store sequence that will be used for authentication. The prebuilt Guest_Portal_Sequence maps to the Guest User database and is used for sponsored or self-registered users. You can change this to a sequence that points to Active Directory or other databases to allow this portal to authenticate employees instead, as we did for BYOD onboarding earlier.

■ **Employees using this portal as guests inherit login options from:** If a database other than Guest User is used, the users are considered employees and the guest type selected here will apply to those users.

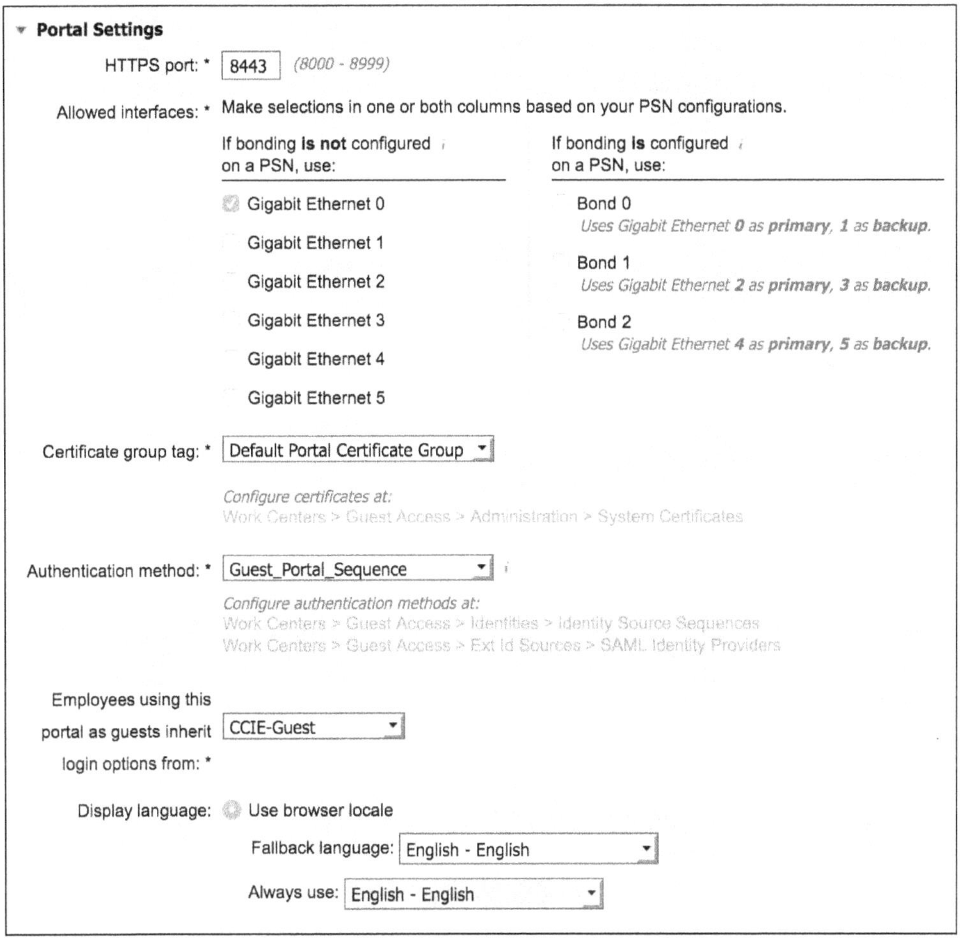

▼ **Portal Settings**

HTTPS port: * [8443]   *(8000 - 8999)*

Allowed interfaces: * Make selections in one or both columns based on your PSN configurations.

If bonding **is not** configured on a PSN, use:	If bonding **is** configured on a PSN, use:
☑ Gigabit Ethernet 0	Bond 0 *Uses Gigabit Ethernet **0** as **primary**, **1** as **backup**.*
☐ Gigabit Ethernet 1	
☐ Gigabit Ethernet 2	Bond 1 *Uses Gigabit Ethernet **2** as **primary**, **3** as **backup**.*
☐ Gigabit Ethernet 3	Bond 2 *Uses Gigabit Ethernet **4** as **primary**, **5** as **backup**.*
☐ Gigabit Ethernet 4	
☐ Gigabit Ethernet 5	

Certificate group tag: * [Default Portal Certificate Group ▼]

Configure certificates at:
Work Centers > Guest Access > Administration > System Certificates

Authentication method: * [Guest_Portal_Sequence ▼]

Configure authentication methods at:
Work Centers > Guest Access > Identities > Identity Source Sequences
Work Centers > Guest Access > Ext Id Sources > SAML Identity Providers

Employees using this
portal as guests inherit   [CCIE-Guest ▼]
login options from: *

Display language: ◉ Use browser locale

Fallback language: [English - English ▼]

Always use: [English - English ▼]

Figure 4-102 *Sponsored and Self-Registered Portal Settings*

Step 4.   Expand the Login Page Settings section as shown in Figure 4-103. Some important options to consider in this section are as follows:

■ **Include an AUP:** Check this check box to display the AUP and choose whether to display it on the page or display a link to the AUP. You can check the **Require acceptance** check box to make acceptance of the AUP mandatory.

■ **Allow guests to create their own accounts:** Check this check box to enable self-registration on the portal and convert this to a self-registered portal. This will also add two new sections to the portal configuration page specific to self-registration.

■ **Allow social login:** Check this check box to enable users to authenticate using social media accounts such as Facebook. This is particularly useful in the hospitality industry.

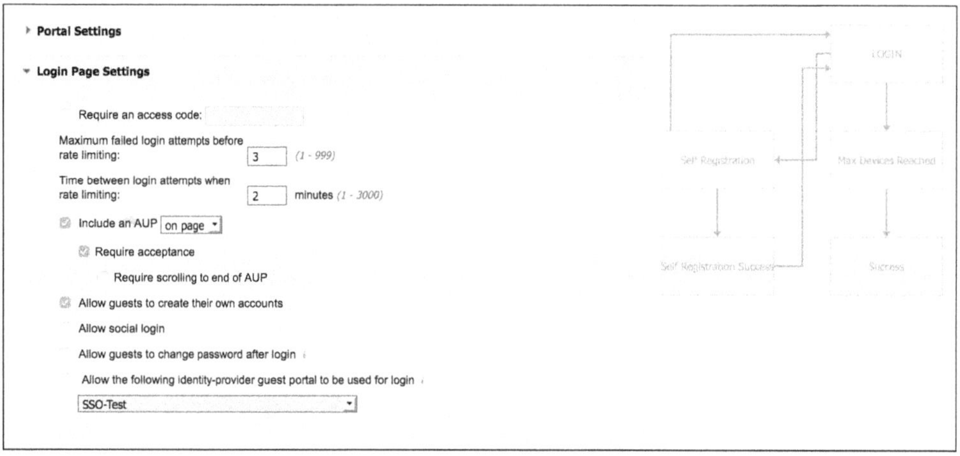

Figure 4-103   *Sponsored and Self-Registered Portal Login Page Settings*

Step 5.   If self-registration is enabled, expand the Registration Form Settings page as shown in Figures 4-104 and 4-105. Key options to consider in this section are as follows:

■ **Assign to guest type:** Choose the guest type that self-registered accounts will be assigned to.

■ **Fields to include:** Choose mandatory and optional information you want the guest to enter in the registration form.

■ **Only allow guests with an email address from:** Check this check box and enter email domains that are accepted for registration. This is particularly useful if you want users to use a corporate email address instead of personal ones.

■ **Do not allow guests with an email address from:** Check this check box and enter email domains that are not accepted for registration.

■ **Require guests to be approved:** Check this check box to enforce sponsor approval for self-registered guest accounts.

■ **Send credential notification:** Choose this method to use to send credentials to the guest.

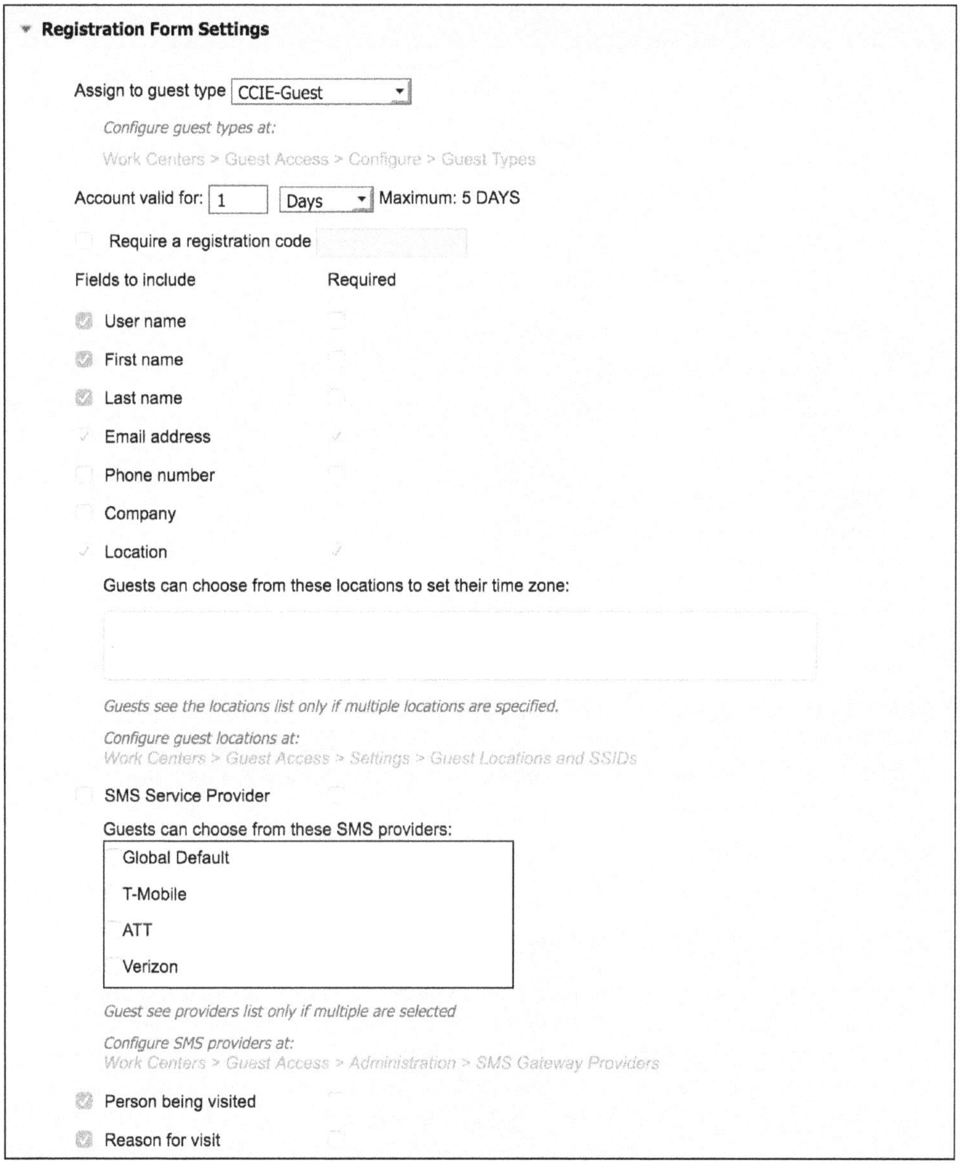

Figure 4-104 *Self-Registration Form Settings*

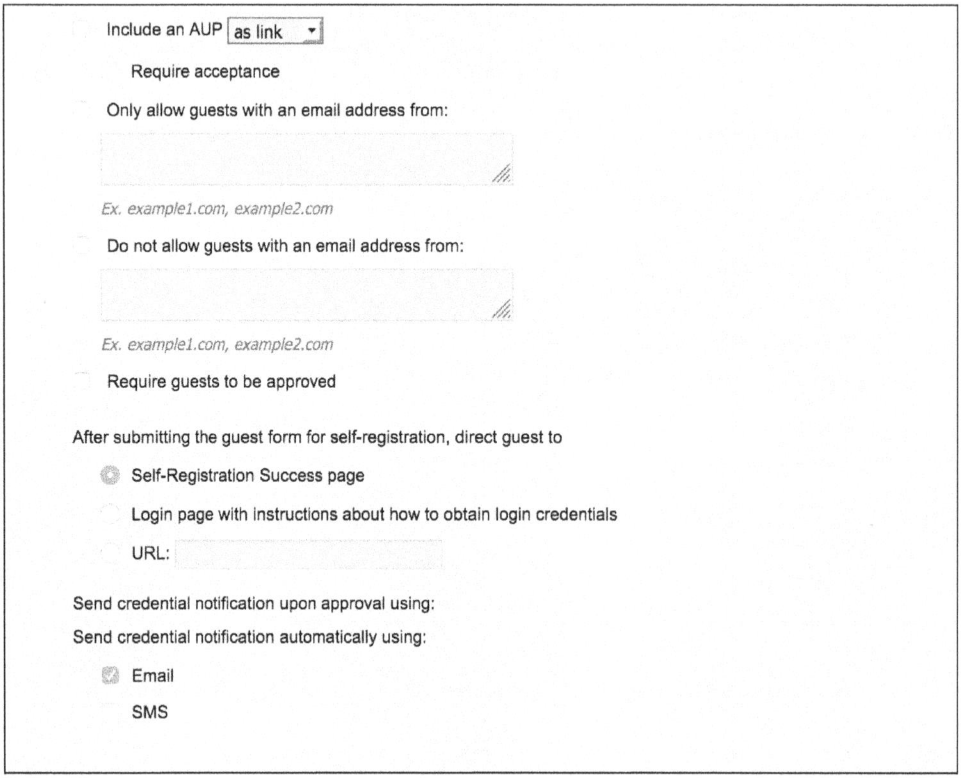

Include an AUP [as link ▾]

Require acceptance

Only allow guests with an email address from:

Ex. example1.com, example2.com

Do not allow guests with an email address from:

Ex. example1.com, example2.com

Require guests to be approved

After submitting the guest form for self-registration, direct guest to

◉ Self-Registration Success page

Login page with instructions about how to obtain login credentials

URL:

Send credential notification upon approval using:

Send credential notification automatically using:

☑ Email

SMS

Figure 4-105 *Self-Registration Form Settings (continued)*

Step 6. Examine the rest of the settings to configure AUP, post-login banner, and success page options.

Step 7. Click **Save**.

Configuring Policy Sets for Guest Access

Before creating a policy set for guest access, you need to create the required authorization profile. Apart from the in-built profiles, an authorization profile to redirect users to the guest portal is required, as shown in Figure 4-106. The figure shows an authorization profile named Guest_Redirect that has Web Redirection enabled, with Centralized Web Auth selected. The ACL value is again set to **redirect** but the Value field is set to Sponsored Guest Portal (default) to redirect users to the in-built sponsored guest portal we edited in the previous section.

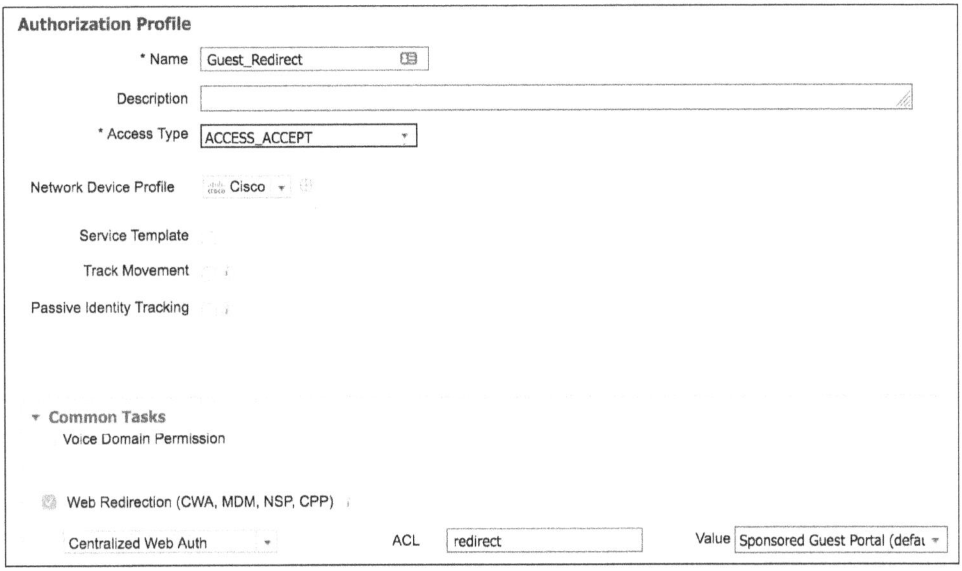

Authorization Profile

* Name	Guest_Redirect
Description	
* Access Type	ACCESS_ACCEPT
Network Device Profile	Cisco ▾
Service Template	
Track Movement	
Passive Identity Tracking	

▼ **Common Tasks**
   Voice Domain Permission

☑ Web Redirection (CWA, MDM, NSP, CPP)

Centralized Web Auth ▾	ACL	redirect	Value	Sponsored Guest Portal (defau ▾

Figure 4-106   *Authorization Profile for Guest Redirection*

As you know, policy sets, authentication polices, and authorization policies can be created using different combinations of conditions to achieve the same result. For the purpose of example, we will create a policy set using the exact same condition we used for the BYOD and MDM policy sets. The authentication policy will be configured to allow MAB authentication. Figure 4-107 shows the policy set and authentication policy configuration.

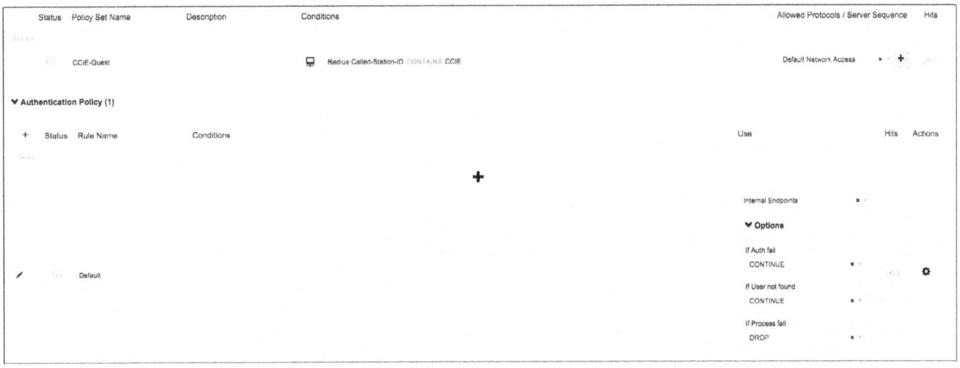

Figure 4-107   *Policy Set and Authentication Policy Configuration for Guest Access*

The authorization policy for this policy set will be configured to allow access after guest authentication and to redirect everything else to the guest portal.

To configure the authorization policy, perform the following steps:

Step 1.   Expand the **Authorization Policy** section.

Step 2.   Replace the Profile for the Default rule with the **Guest_Redirect** profile created earlier.

This will apply redirection on all MAB sessions that have not authenticated on the guest portal.

Step 3.   Click the gear icon in the Actions column for the Default rule and select **Insert new row above**.

Step 4.   Name the new rule **Authenticated_Guest**.

Step 5.   Click the **Conditions** column in the new rule.

Step 6.   Drag the **Guest_Flow** rule from the Library on the left to the Editor section on the right, as shown in Figure 4-108.

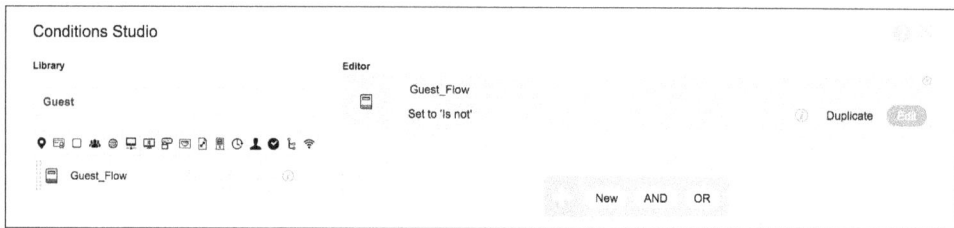

Figure 4-108   *Condition for Guest Access*

Step 7.   Click **Use**.

Step 8.   Select **PermitAccess** from the drop-down list in the Profiles column of the new rule.

This authorization rule will permit access if the authentication on the guest portal was successful.

Step 9.   Click **Save**.

Figure 4-109 shows the completed authorization policy.

Figure 4-109   *Authorization Profile for Guest Access*

Note   In Step 6, we selected the in-built Guest_Flow condition to allow access after successful authentication on the portal. For hotspot access, you will need to use the endpoint ID group as a condition instead.

TrustSec with ISE

In the previous two and the current chapter, you learned about various methods to control access to the network. The purpose of access control is not limited to just allowing authorized users or devices to connect to the network. Defining what the authorized devices or users can do on the network is the larger goal of implementing an access control solution. In Chapter 2, you discovered that using dynamic VLAN assignments and downloadable ACLS (dACLs) are the common methods of defining what a device or user can do on the network.

VLANs and ingress ACLs, whether configured manually on the network device or assigned dynamically during authentication, have been the two primary ways of access control enforcement for decades. With ever-growing network infrastructure, device types, and business needs, these two methods are no longer sufficient.

In case of VLANs, users and devices are assigned based on some context such as the department the user works in or the device type or such. Filtering on inter-VLAN traffic and traffic to other destination such as data centers is applied on an upstream device such as a router or firewall based on source address, destination address, source port, and destination port. As the number of VLANs and destinations grows, so do the number of access control entries (ACEs) in an ACL. To calculate the number of ACEs required, a simple formula can be used:

Number of sources × Number of destinations × Permissions

In the formula, permissions refer to the source and destination combinations. As a rough example, if there are 100 source VLANs, 100 destinations, and 4 permissions per destination, the number of ACEs required would be 40,000. That is a lot of ACEs just from a small example. Now imagine a large enterprise where sources, destinations, and permissions are far more than that. We have seen organizations with over 11 million ACEs on their firewalls. Let's call this phenomenon *ACE explosion*. Managing large ACLs becomes impossible and requires a large team, thereby increasing the cost. On top of that, how often do you think such large ACLs are audited? Over the years, nobody remembers why an ACE was added and everyone is very reluctant to remove it. Eventually the firewall just becomes a big hole in the network and provides less than desirable security.

Another common method of access control and filtering is the use of ingress ACLs on the switch port. When combined with AAA, this can be done with dACLs for centralized management. Because each dACL will have a single source—the host connected to the switch port—even with 100 destinations and 4 permissions each, the ACL will be 400 lines long only. However, there is a major drawback to using dACLs. The access layer switches are made for the specific purpose of switching frames fast. Adding any other function such a filtering will increase the burden on the switch. On Cisco switches, ACLs are loaded into and used from the Ternary Content-Addressable Memory (TCAM). TCAM space on every switch is limited. So, depending on the type of switch, the number of ACEs per ACL cannot exceed a certain number. For most access layer switches, the recommended number of maximum ACEs would fall between 25 and 64. This severely limits the use of ingress ACLs.

A combination of dACLs and VLANs is also often used for access control enforcement. dACLs can be used for macro-level filtering while upstream filtering based on VLANs can be used for micro-level filtering. Unfortunately, this approach creates a bigger operational challenge because now the ACLs are defined in two places and are more difficult to audit and correlate. On top of that, this approach may still not help with ACE explosion.

Given the problems with the existing options, a new way of access control enforcement was needed. This came in form of TrustSec.

Introducing TrustSec

TrustSec is the next-generation access control enforcement solution that was created by Cisco to address the growing operational challenges with maintaining firewall rules and ACLs. TrustSec is a complementary enforcement technology that removes the concerns of TCAM space and ACE explosion.

TrustSec works by assigning a tag, known as a Security Group Tag (SGT), to the user/device's traffic as it enters the network (ingress), and then filtering based on the SGT at an upstream device such as a firewall in the data center.

Note   In some places SGTs are called Scalable Group Tags instead of Security Group Tags. Both are correct, but calling them Scalable Group Tags is a new rebranding effort and may not be reflected in most documents, books, or CCIE exam questions.

Think of TrustSec as QoS for security. You "color" a packet in some way and then act based on that. In this case, the color is SGT. SGT is a 16-bit value that ISE assigns to the user's or endpoint's session upon login. The network device views the SGT as another attribute to assign to the session, and inserts the Layer 2 tag into all traffic from that session. In some cases where the device is not capable of inserting the tag in the frame, it will maintain a list of SGT mappings and act based on that. More on that in later sections.

SGT represents the context of the user, device, and session. What that means is that SGTs are often named after a particular business use case. For example, a session from a user belonging to the HR department and using a Windows 7 laptop can be assigned an SGT named HR_Windows7. If the device is not compliant to posture requirements, then it can be assigned an SGT named HR_Windows7_NonCompliant. When the context of the user, device, and session is reflected in the SGT, it allows the administrator to make business-relevant enforcement policies. When policies are made based on the context and business relevance, instead of IP addresses, auditing and maintaining them becomes much easier. Figure 4-110 shows an example of this.

Security Groups
For Policy Export go to Administration > System > Backup & Restore > Policy Export Page

	Icon	Name ↓↑	SGT (Dec / Hex)	Description
		Auditors	9/0009	Auditor Security Group
		AV_Devices	17/0011	
		BYOD	15/000F	BYOD Security Group
		Contractors	5/0005	Contractor Security Group
		Developers	8/0008	Developer Security Group
		Development_Servers	12/000C	Development Servers Security Group
		Employees	4/0004	Employee Security Group

Figure 4-110   *SGTs on ISE*

Figure 4-110 shows a list of SGTs on ISE. Notice that the SGTs all have a business-relevant name and description. ISE acts as sort of a controller for TrustSec and maintains a list of SGTs. SGTs can be viewed, edited, and added by navigating to **Work Centers > TrustSec > Components > SGTs**. ISE considers an SGT a policy result. Therefore, create one SGT result for each SGT you want to define in the environment. To help customers, ISE also comes with a large number of preexisting SGTs with assigned icons, as shown in Figure 4-110.

Note   SGTs themselves are numerical when applied to a session or inserted in a frame, but the associated name is available on ISE and network devices to create policies.

TrustSec and its configuration can be divided into three different phases to make it simple to understand and implement:

- **Classification:** Assignment of an SGT to a session is called *Classification*. ISE and network devices need to be configured to assign SGTs to sessions. This can be done dynamically based on authorization policies or statically, where required.

- **Propagation:** Propagation is the process of communicating session-to-SGT mappings and policies to network devices for enforcement. The supported distribution methods vary by network devices and not all methods are supported by all devices.

■ **Enforcement:** The final phase of TrustSec is the actual enforcement. Network devices need to apply policies based on SGT assignment received during the distribution phase. As with distribution, different devices support different methods of enforcement.

Classification

To use the Security Group Tag, the tag needs to be assigned to a session, which can happen in one of two ways:

■ **Dynamic assignment:** The SGT can be assigned dynamically and be downloaded as the result of an ISE authorization. This is commonly used with 802.1X and MAB authentication to assign SGTs based on context.

■ **Manual assignment:** In data centers and other environments that do not support 802.1X or MAB authentication, dynamic SGT assignment is not possible. In such cases, SGTs can be mapped manually and statically either on ISE or on a network device. Manual assignment on a device depends on the platform and code level of the device but can generally be one of the following:

   ■ **IP to SGT:** Manual IP-to-SGT mappings can be created on ISE or the network device to be distributed and used for enforcement.

   ■ **Subnet to SGT:** Similar to IP-to-SGT mappings, subnet-to-SGT mappings can be created on ISE or a network device for distribution and enforcement.

   ■ **VLAN to SGT:** Where it is not feasible to use authentication or create IP or subnet mappings, VLAN-to-SGT mappings can be created on a device. All endpoints in that VLAN will be assigned to the specified SGT.

   ■ **Port to SGT:** In some cases, where an endpoint such as a server is connected to a particular switch port, a port-to-SGT mapping can be created. Endpoints connected to the specific port will be assigned that SGT.

Note   Higher-end routers and switches such as the Nexus 9000 support other forms of static SGT assignment. In this chapter, we focus only on the devices that are available in the CCIE lab.

Dynamically Assigning an SGT with ISE

Assigning an SGT is as simple as adding it as another result of in an authorization rule. This chapter discussed various examples of authorization rules. In all those rules, we selected an authorization profile as the result. In addition to an authorization profile, each authorization rule can also have an SGT assignment as a result. Figure 4-111 shows two examples of this. In the figure, notice that the Posture_Compliant rule applies the PermitAccess profile and the Workstations SGT to devices that authenticate using

EAP-TLS and are posture compliant. Similarly, the Authenticated_Guest rule applies the PermitAccess profile and the Guests SGT to guest sessions.

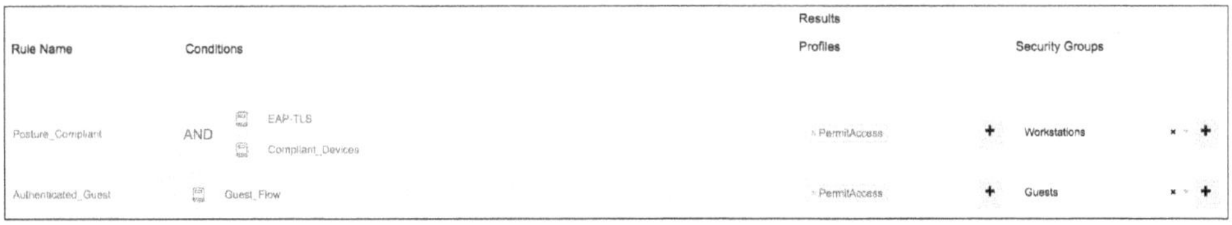

Rule Name	Conditions		Results		
			Profiles		Security Groups
Posture_Compliant	AND	EAP-TLS / Compliant_Devices	PermitAccess	+	Workstations
Authenticated_Guest		Guest_Flow	PermitAccess	+	Guests

Figure 4-111 *SGT as a Result of an Authorization Rule*

Using an SGT as a result of an authorization rule is as simple as selecting the SGT in the Security Groups column of the rule.

Manually Assigning an SGT with ISE

To manually assign an IP-to-SGT mapping on ISE, perform the following steps:

Step 1.   Navigate to **Work Centers > TrustSec > Components > IP SGT Static Mapping.**

Step 2.   Click **Add.**

Step 3.   Enter an IP address as shown in Figure 4-112.

Step 4.   Select an SGT from the **SGT** drop-down list.

Step 5.   Select the default domain from the Send to SXP Domain drop-down list.

Step 6.   Click **Save.**

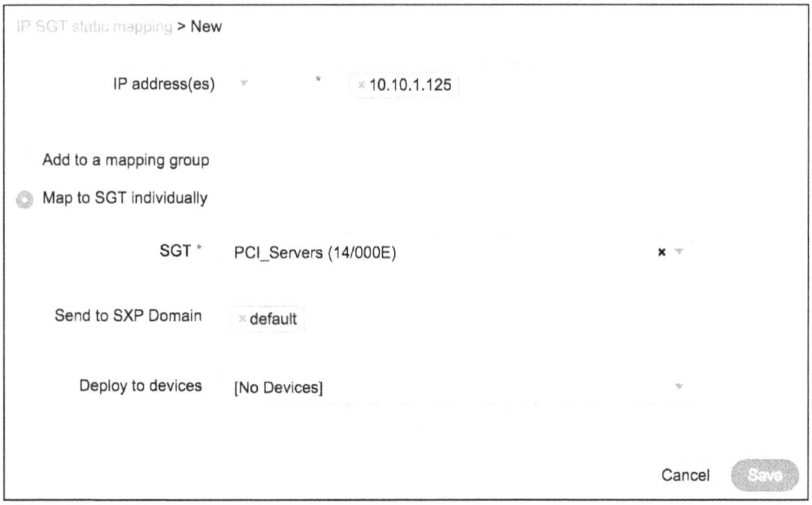

Figure 4-112 *Adding a Static IP-to-SGT Mapping in ISE*

Once the IP-to-SGT mapping is created, it will be downloaded to network devices such as Cisco switches and NGFWs using the methods discussed in the next section.

In cases where an endpoint cannot authenticate to ISE, static mapping can be defined on the network device itself. Static mappings on Cisco IOS can be defined using the **cts role-based sgt-map** command. This command allows mapping an individual IP address, subnet, or VLAN to an SGT.

To map an IP address to an SGT, use the **cts role-base sgt-map** {*ipv4 address* | *ipv6 address*} **sgt** *tag-value* command as demonstrated in the following example:

```
C3k(config)#cts role-based sgt-map 10.1.1.50 sgt 10
```

To map a subnet to an SGT, use the **cts role-based sgt-map** {*ipv4 prefix /length* | *ipv6 prefix /length*] **sgt** *tag-value* command as demonstrated in the following example:

```
C3k(config)#cts role-based sgt-map 10.1.1.0/8 sgt 10
```

To map a VLAN to an SGT, use the **cts role-based sgt-map vlan-list** *vlans* **sgt** *tag-value* command as demonstrated in the three examples that follow. Note the use of a comma or a hyphen to map multiple VLANs in a single command.

```
C3k(config)#cts role-based sgt-map vlan-list 4 sgt 10
C3k(config)#cts role-based sgt-map vlan-list 4-10 sgt 10
C3k(config)#cts role-based sgt-map vlan-list 4,6 sgt 10
```

Apart from mapping an IP address, subnet, or VLAN manually, you can map a switch port to an SGT also, as shown in the following example:

```
C3k(config)#interface gi0/5
C3k(config-if)#cts manual
C3k(config-if-cts-manual)#policy static sgt 4
```

Propagation

Now that classification is configured and an SGT will be assigned to the sessions, the next step is to communicate the mapping to network devices that will enforce policy based on SGTs. This communication process is called *propagation*. There are two methods to propagate an SGT: by inline or native tagging and by SXP.

With inline or native tagging, the switch can insert the tag inside the frame to allow upstream devices to read and apply policy. The frame continues to retain a tag throughout the network infrastructure until the destination. Native tagging allows the technology to scale almost endlessly, and it remains completely independent of any Layer 3 protocol. The tag is completely independent and consumes much less resources on the network device. The downside to native tagging is that the network device needs to support it. If the tagged frame is received by a device that does not support native tagging, it will drop the frame.

For devices that do not support native tagging, Cisco developed a peering protocol called SGT Exchange Protocol (SXP). Using this protocol, ISE and other network devices can communicate their SGT mapping database. With SXP, devices that do not support native tagging will still have an SGT mapping database to check packets against and enforce policy.

Figure 4-113 shows an example of one access switch that has native tagging. The packets get tagged on the uplink port and through the infrastructure. It also shows a switch that is not inline-tagging capable, which uses SXP to update the upstream switch. In both cases, the upstream switch continues to tag the traffic throughout the infrastructure.

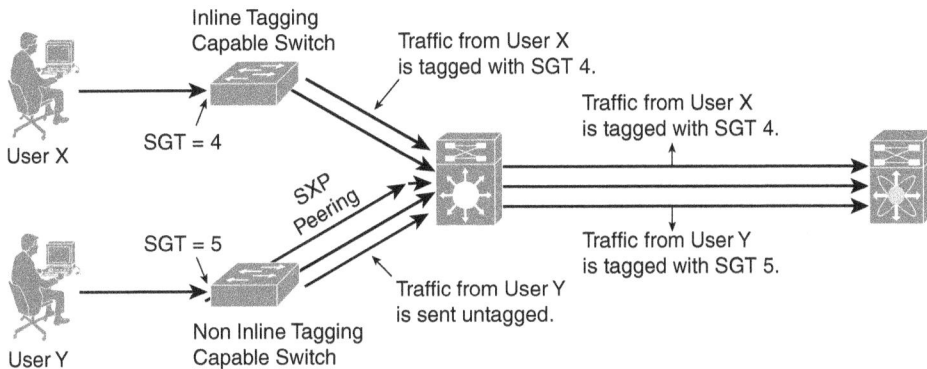

Figure 4-113   *Mixed Propagation Environment with Inline Tagging and SXP*

Figure 4-114 shows another example where the switching infrastructure does not support inline tagging or SXP but authenticates users to ISE. ISE assigns an SGT and sends the mapping through SXP to an upstream Cisco Adaptive Security Appliance (ASA). The ASA will use this mapping to enforce policy on the untagged traffic coming from the network.

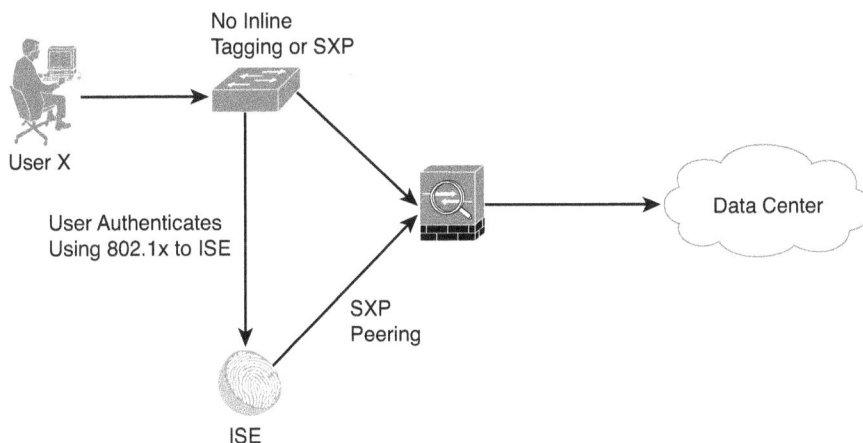

Figure 4-114   *Using SXP Peering between ISE and Network Device*

Note   There is a third method of SGT propagation that uses pxGrid from ISE. Cisco NGFW, for example, supports receiving mappings through pxGrid instead of SXP. pxGrid is covered in Chapter 6, "Sharing the Context."

Configuring Inline Tagging

Although the principle behind configuring inline tagging is similar across all Cisco switches, the exact steps and commands differ. This section discusses the configuration of SGT propagation on access layer switches, such as the Cisco Catalyst 3560-X and Cisco Catalyst 3750-X, that have the ability to use native tags. The rest of the switches will not be covered in this book to keep the focus on devices available in the CCIE lab.

When it comes to inline tagging, the communication between two switches can be secured using Cisco TrustSec Network Device Admission Control (NDAC). For the sake of simplicity, this section will use unsecured inline tagging.

To enable inline tagging and enforcement globally, enter the **cts role-based enforcement** command in the global configuration mode. To configure inline tagging between two switches, follow these steps:

Step 1.   Enter the interface configuration mode of the port connected to another switch by typing **interface** *interface-name*.

Step 2.   Enter the **cts manual** command.

Note   We are using **cts manual** because we do not require encryption. Without the **cts** mode set to **manual**, we will need to configure NDAC between the switches.

Step 3.   Enter the **policy static sgt** *sgt-value* **trusted** command. Replace *sgt-value* with a valid SGT.

Note   ISE has predefined SGTs. One of those SGTs is a special group for network access devices named TrustSec_Devices with a value of 2 (0x02). That SGT should be used in the command in Step 3. The **trusted** keyword in this command ensures that no changes are made to the incoming tags, as they are from a trusted source.

Example 4-2 shows the inline tagging configuration applied to an interface.

Example 4-2   *Enabling Inline Tagging on a Switch Interface*

```
C3k(config)#cts role-based enforcement
C3k(config)#interface Gi0/1
C3k(config-if)#cts manual
C3k(config-if-cts-manual)#policy static sgt 2 trusted
```

Inline tagging configuration can be verified with the **show cts interface** command, as shown in Example 4-3.

Example 4-3 *Verifying Inline Tagging Configuration*

```
C3k#show cts interface Gi0/1
Interface GigabitEthernet0/1:
    CTS is enabled, mode:     MANUAL
    IFC state:                OPEN
    Interface Active for 00:01:00.202
    Authentication Status:    NOT APPLICABLE
        Peer identity:        "unknown"
        Peer's advertised capabilities: ""
    Authorization Status:     SUCCEEDED
        Peer SGT:             2:TrustSec_Devices
        Peer SGT assignment:  Trusted
    SAP Status:               NOT APPLICABLE
    Propagate SGT:            Enabled
<truncated for brevity>
```

Configuring SXP

SXP support is available in most Cisco switches, Cisco WLC, and ASA, to name a few devices. This section discusses enabling SXP on these devices and ISE.

To configure SXP on a Cisco IOS device, use the following steps:

Step 1.   Enter the **cts sxp enable** command in the global configuration mode. This command enables SXP globally on the device.

Step 2.   Enter the cts **sxp default password** *password* command.

Step 3.   Enter the **cts sxp connection peer** *peer-ip-address* **password** [default | none] **mode** [local | peer] [listener | speaker | both] command to define SXP peers. The command parameters are explained as follows:

   ■ **password:** The SXP connection can be optionally password protected. At present only a globally defined default password can be used. The **default** keyword refers to the default password defined in Step 2.

   ■ **mode:** The mode command allows defining either the local role or the role of the peer.

■ **listener and speaker:** SXP peers can have a listener, speaker, or both roles. A listener receives SXP mappings, while a speaker sends SXP mappings. Some devices can have both roles also.

Example 4-4 shows an example of SXP configuration on Cisco IOS.

Example 4-4   *Configuring SXP on Cisco IOS*

```
C3k(config)#cts sxp enable
C3k(config)#cts sxp default password s3cr3t!
C3k(config)#cts sxp connection peer 192.168.1.11 password default mode
  local both
```

SXP configuration can be verified using the **show cts sxp connections** command, as shown in Example 4-5.

Example 4-5   *Verifying SXP Configuration on Cisco IOS*

```
C3k#show cts sxp connections
 SXP               : Enabled
 Highest Version Supported: 4
 Default Password : Set
 Default Source IP: Not Set
Connection retry open period: 120 secs
Reconcile period: 120 secs
Retry open timer is running
---------------------------------------------
Peer IP          : 192.168.1.11
Source IP        : 192.168.1.3
Conn status      : On (Speaker) :: On (Listener)
Conn version     : 4
Conn capability  : IPv4-IPv6-Subnet
Speaker Conn hold time   : 120 seconds
Listener Conn hold time  : 120 seconds
Local mode       : Both
Connection inst# : 1
TCP conn fd      : 1(Speaker) 2(Listener)
TCP conn password: default SXP password
Keepalive timer is running
```

You can enable SXP on the ASA also using the exact same commands used on Cisco IOS. The only difference between SXP support on the ASA and IOS is that the ASA can only support a listener or speaker mode. Example 4-6 shows how to enable SXP on the ASA.

Example 4-6   *Enabling SXP on ASA*

```
ASA(config)#cts sxp enable
ASA(config)#cts sxp default password s3cr3t!
ASA(config)#cts sxp connection peer 192.168.1.11 password default mode
  local listener
```

You can use the **show cts sxp connections** command on the ASA also to verify the SXP configuration, as shown in Example 4-7.

Example 4-7   *Verifying SXP Configuration on ASA*

```
ASA#show cts sxp connections
SXP                  : Enabled
Highest version   : 3
Default password   : Set
Default local  IP : Not Set
Reconcile period   : 120 secs
Retry open period : 120 secs
Retry open timer   : Not Running
Total number of SXP connections: 1
Total number of SXP connections shown: 1
-----------------------------------------------------------
Peer IP            : 192.168.1.11
Source IP          : 192.168.1.22
Conn status        : On
Conn version       : 3
Local mode         : Listener
Ins number         : 2
TCP conn password : Default
Reconciliation timer   : Not Running
Delete hold down timer : Not Running
```

To enable SXP on Cisco WLC (version 7.2 and later only), perform the following steps:

Step 1.   Navigate to **Security > TrustSec > SXP Config on the WLC UI.**

Step 2.   Select **Enabled** in the SXP State spin box.

Step 3.   In the Default Password field, enter a default password.

Step 4.   Click **Apply.**

Step 5.   In the Peer IP Address field, enter the peer IP address and then click **ADD**, as shown in Figure 4-115.

Step 6.   Click **Apply.**

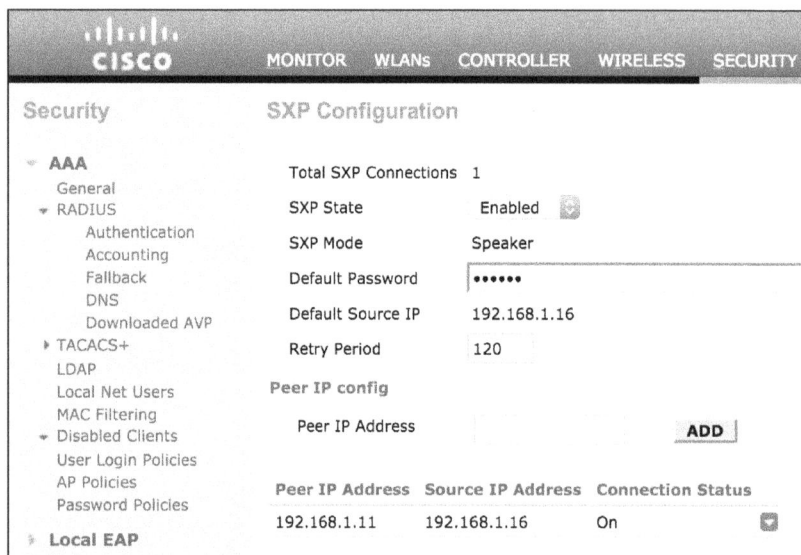

Figure 4-115   *Configuring SXP on Cisco WLC*

ISE can act as an SXP speaker and listener to collect and propagate SGT mappings from a central location. This helps in keeping SXP connections simple and avoiding any redundant peering. In an environment where 802.1X authentication is done on a network infrastructure that does not support inline tagging or SXP, peering with ISE is the only option to implement TrustSec on an upstream device. To configure SXP on ISE, perform the following steps:

Step 1.   Navigate to **Administration > System > Deployment** and select a node on which to enable SXP.

Step 2.   Check the **Enable SXP Service** check box, as shown in Figure 4-116.

Step 3.   Navigate to **Work Centers > TrustSec > Settings > SXP Settings**.

Step 4.   Enter a default password in the Global Password textbox, as shown in Figure 4-117.

Step 5.   Click **Save**.

Step 6.   Navigate to **Work Centers > TrustSec > SXP > SXP Devices** and click **Add**.

Step 7.   Enter the name and IP address of the peer.

Step 8.   In the Peer Role drop-down list, select the role of the peer.

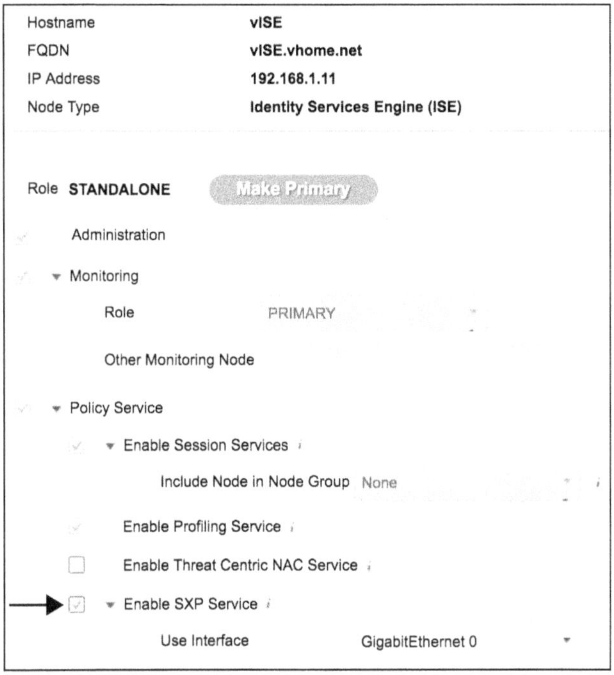

Figure 4-116 *Enabling SXP Service on an ISE Node*

Figure 4-117 *Configuring SXP Global Settings on ISE*

Step 9.   In the Connected PSNs field, select the PSN that the peer will talk to, as shown in Figure 4-118.

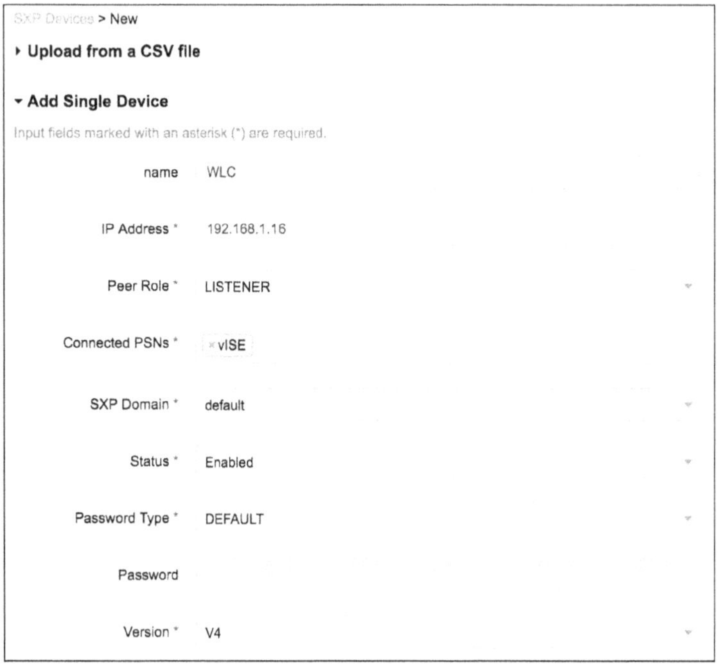

SXP Devices > New

▸ **Upload from a CSV file**

▾ **Add Single Device**

Input fields marked with an asterisk (*) are required.

name	WLC
IP Address *	192.168.1.16
Peer Role *	LISTENER
Connected PSNs *	×vISE
SXP Domain *	default
Status *	Enabled
Password Type *	DEFAULT
Password	
Version *	V4

Figure 4-118   *Adding SXP Peers on ISE*

Step 10.   Click **Save**.

Step 11.   Repeat Steps 6 to 10 to add other peers.

Enforcement

Now that classification and propagation have been configured on ISE and the network devices, it is time to configure the third and most important phase of TrustSec: enforcement.

Enforcement with tags is done using Security Group ACLs (SGACLs). Most devices, such as Cisco switches and routers, that support TrustSec can download SGACLs and related TrustSec policy from ISE directly and enforce them. Firewalls such as Cisco ASA and NGFW, though, require the tag-based rules to be defined locally on the device.

Configuring TrustSec Policy in ISE

TrustSec policy for enforcement is configured in a visual matrix. The rows and columns of the matrix represent source and destination tags. The portion of the matrix shown in

Figure 4-119 displays various policies configured. Some of these policies are explained in the list that follows:

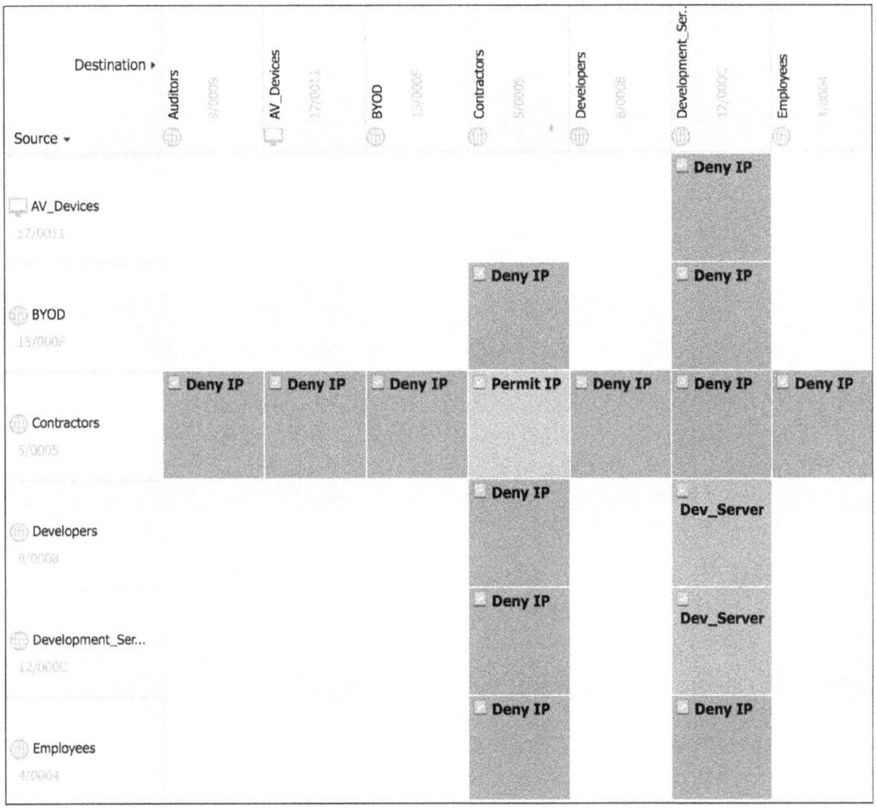

Figure 4-119 *TrustSec Policy Matrix in ISE*

■ Devices that get the Contractors SGT are not allowed to talk to anything other than devices belonging to the same SGT. Deny rules are indicated by red boxes while permits are represented by green boxes.

■ Devices that get the Development_Servers tag are not allowed to talk to devices with any tags other than Developers and Development_Servers. Even for those two tags, the traffic is limited by an SGACL named Dev_Server. Blue boxes represent rules that have an SGACL applied. If you hover the mouse over the *target* icon in the blue box, the contents of the SGACL will be displayed, as shown in Figure 4-120.

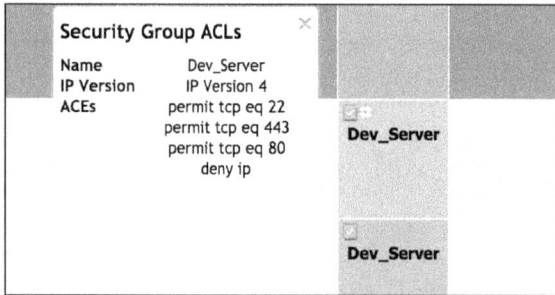

Figure 4-120   *Viewing the Contents of SGACL*

To create or edit an SGACL, perform the following steps:

Step 1.   Navigate to **Work Centers > TrustSec > Components > Security Group ACLs**.

Step 2.   Click **Add** to create a new ACL or select an existing ACL.

Step 3.   Enter a name.

Step 4.   Click the **IPv4**, **IPv6**, or **Agnostic** radio button depending on the protocol the ACL will apply to.

Step 5.   Add the required ACEs in the Security Group ACL content box, as shown in Figure 4-121. The example shown will permit traffic to ports 22, 443, and 80 and deny everything else.

Step 6.   Click **Save**.

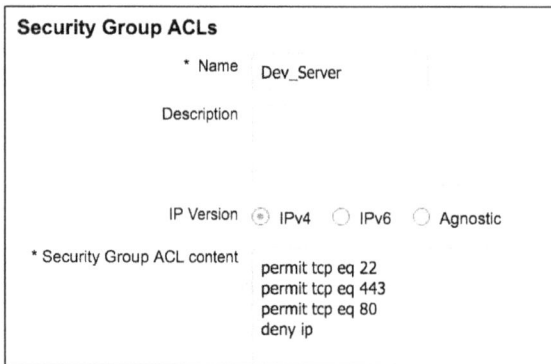

Figure 4-121   *Creating SGACL in ISE*

Configuring ISE to Allow Download of Policies

After creating the TrustSec policy and SGACLs, ISE will need to be configured to allow the network devices to download them. This configuration is applied inside the network device configuration in ISE. You are already familiar with adding network devices to ISE, so add the TrustSec-capable device and configure the RADIUS shared key. After that, perform the following steps:

Step 1. Navigate to **Administration > Network Resources > Network Devices** and select the device you added.

Step 2. Scroll down and expand the **Advanced TrustSec Settings** section.

Step 3. Under Device Authentication Settings, check the **Use Device ID for TrustSec** check box, as shown in Figure 4-122.

Remember this device ID and password for configuration on the network device. They should match on ISE and the device for the communication to work.

Step 4. Enter a password.

Step 5. Under Device Configuration Deployment, check the check box and enter the exec mode username, password, and enable password.

Step 6. Repeat these steps for all devices that need to download the TrustSec policy.

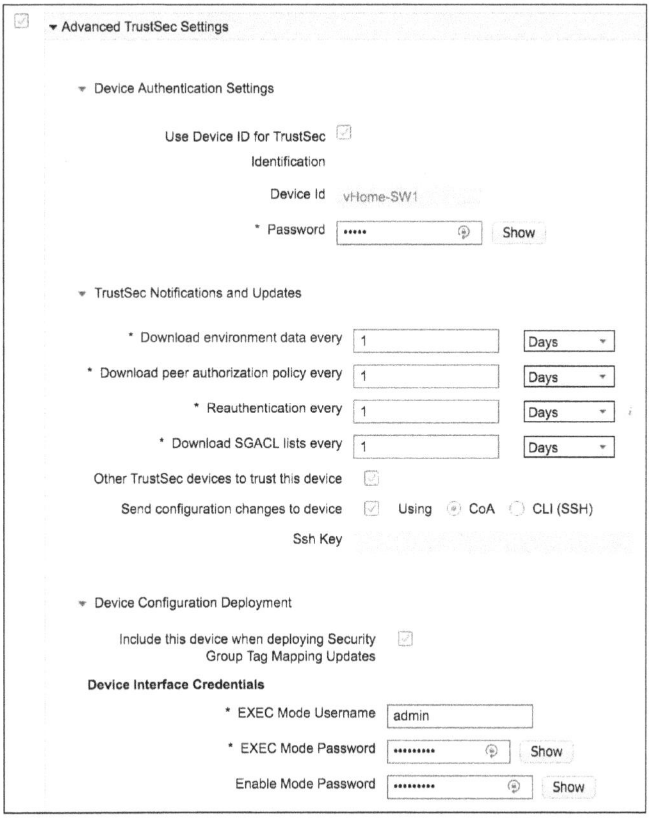

Figure 4-122 *Configuring ISE to Allow TrustSec Policy Download*

Configuring Network Devices to Download Policies

To download the TrustSec policy from ISE, the device will need to download a PAC file and authenticate to ISE. To configure the device for authentication, use the following steps:

Step 1.   Add ISE as a RADIUS server and configure the AAA commands as you would for 802.1X or MAB.

Step 2.   Create a named authorization list using the **aaa authorization network** *list-name group-name* command.

Step 3.   Enter the **cts authorization list** *list-name* command.

Step 4.   Configure the device ID and password using the **cts credentials id** *device-id* password *password* command in the exec mode. Make sure the ID and password match those configured on ISE for this device. This command will also kick-start the download process.

Note   The exact configuration commands will vary by device and OS type and sometimes by version. Ensure that you are testing on the device and OS versions published for CCIE Security v5.

Example 4-8 shows an example of the configuration outlined in the preceding list.

Example 4-8   *Configuring Network Device to Download TrustSec Policy*

```
C3k(config)#radius server ise
C3k(config-radius-server)#address ipv4 192.168.1.11
C3k(config-radius-server)#pac key s3cr3t!
C3k(config-radius-server)#exit
C3k(config)#aaa group server radius ise-group
C3k(config-sg-radius)#server name ise
C3k(config-sg-radius)#exit
C3k(config)#aaa authorization network mlist group ise-group
C3k(config)#cts authorization list mlist
C3k(config)#exit
C3k#cts credentials id C3k password s3cr3t!
```

To verify the configuration, use the **show cts environment-data** command, as shown in Example 4-9.

Example 4-9 *Verify TrustSec Configuration on Cisco IOS*

```
C3k#show cts environment-data
CTS Environment Data
====================
Current state = COMPLETE
Last status = Successful
Local Device SGT:
  SGT tag = 0-00:Unknown
Server List Info:
Installed list: CTSServerList1-0001, 1 server(s):
 *Server: 192.168.1.11, port 1812, A-ID 1B073DFDE298D9661C3887962B53DC55
          Status = ALIVE
          auto-test = TRUE, keywrap-enable = FALSE, idle-time = 60 mins, deadtime =
  20 secs
Multicast Group SGT Table:
Security Group Name Table:
    0-ec:Unknown
    2-ec:TrustSec_Devices
<truncated for brevity>
```

Configuring Tag-Based ACL on ASA

The Cisco ASA cannot download policies and SGACLs from ISE, but SGT-based ACLs can be defined locally on the ASA. SGT-based ACLs are created and applied in the same way as normal IP ACLs but the SGT name or ID is used as the source and destination. Example 4-10 shows the Dev_Server SGACL from earlier example re-created on the ASA.

Example 4-10 *SGT-Based ACL on ASA*

```
ASA(config)#access-list dev_server permit tcp security-group name
  Developers any security-group name Development_Servers any eq 22
ASA(config)#access-list dev_server permit tcp security-group name
  Developers any security-group name Development_Servers any eq 443
ASA(config)#access-list dev_server permit tcp security-group name
  Developers any security-group name Development_Servers any eq 80
```

Configuring Tag-Based Policies on Cisco NGFW

Like the ASA, the Cisco NGFW cannot download TrustSec policies and SGACLs from ISE but it can receive SGT-to-IP mappings using pxGrid (discussed in Chapter 6). Once the Firepower Management Console (FMC) can download SGTs, access policy rules can be created using them. The process to create an SGT-based rule is the same as the process to create a normal IP-based rule. To use SGTs, create or edit a rule in an access policy and select the required SGTs in the SGT/ISE Attributes tab, as shown in Figure 4-123. Notice that FMC downloads SGTs from ISE to allow you to use them in the rule.

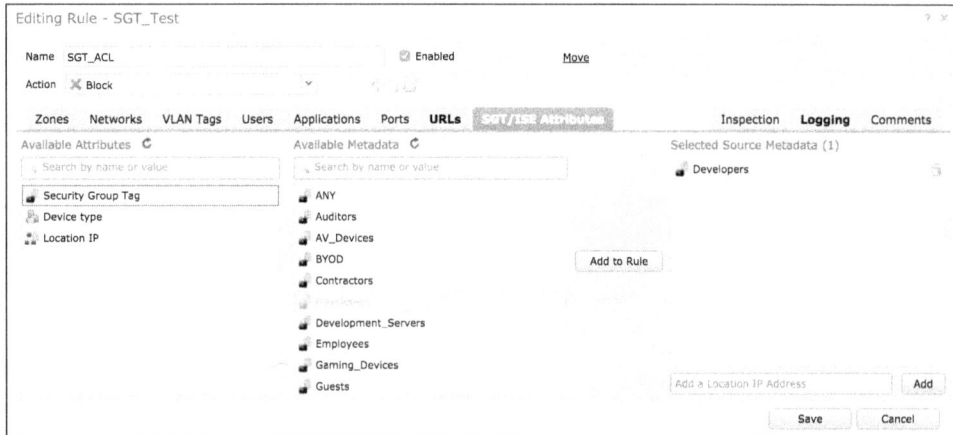

Figure 4-123   *Creating SGT-Based Rules in FMC*

Note   At the time of writing, the Cisco NGFW can only use SGTs as the source. Support for SGTs as the destination is planned for a release in the near future.

Summary

Wow, this was a really long chapter! ISE is 25 percent of the CCIE exam blueprint, and topics covered in this chapter make up a large chunk of that. We covered BYOD onboarding, MDM onboarding and enforcement, posture assessment and enforcement, guest services, and TrustSec. While that might sound like a lot, you would have noticed that there is a similarity in configuration of most of the portal-based features. Breaking down each feature into required components and elements helps in simplifying the configuration.

In the end, ISE can be the easiest portion of the CCIE exam and, if practiced properly, can save a lot of time in the lab for the rest of the sections.

Chapter 5

Device Administration Control with ISE

The previous chapters in this book discussed the various methods to control user access to the network with Cisco ISE. Another key function of ISE is the ability to control access to the network device itself for administrative purposes.

This chapter discusses the benefits of using a centralized access control for device administration and the use of Remote Authentication Dial-In User Service (RADIUS) and Terminal Access Controller Access-Control System Plus (TACACS+) protocols to do that. It also discusses how to configure ISE and different Cisco network devices to enforce granular device administration control.

The Case for Centralized AAA

One of the first steps for securing a network should be securing the network devices themselves. Chapter 2, "Infrastructure Security and Segmentation," of Volume I of this series discusses the three planes of a network device (management, control, and data) and the various measures available to secure them. Of the three planes of a network device, breach of the management plane most drastically affects the security of the device because the management plane can be used to change the functions of the other planes as well.

Securing the management plane of a device requires ensuring strict access control on all of the access points into the management plane. Commonly, the command-line interface (CLI), graphical user interface (GUI), Simple Network Management Protocol (SNMP), and application programming interfaces (APIs) provide access to the management plane.

Every network device has local methods to control access to the management plane—most often locally stored and managed credentials. Some of these methods were discussed, with examples, in Chapter 2 of Volume I. While such local methods are usually sufficient to secure the management plane, managing them across hundreds or thousands of individual devices can allow inconsistencies to creep in. In addition to that, it becomes difficult to manage changes across a large number of devices.

This is where centralized methods for controlling management plane access come to the rescue. Most network devices provide options to use protocols such as RADIUS, TACACS+, Lightweight Directory Access Protocol (LDAP), and Kerberos to control management plane access from a centralized server.

While most of the benefits of a centralized access control are operational in nature, there are some security benefits also. Some of the key benefits of a centralized access control are as follows:

- It allows enforcement of a consistent policy across all network devices.

- It allows role-based access control to be implemented uniformly.

- It helps organizations prevent access creep or stale access when user roles change or users leave an organization.

- It makes it easy to implement very granular access control—even down to every command that a user can execute.

- It allows easy enforcement of good credential hygiene such as frequent password changes.

- It allows for centralized accounting and audit of administrative actions taken across all network devices in a network.

- Because access credentials are maintained on a central server, network device configuration does not risk exposure of credentials.

Cisco ISE supports both RADIUS and TACACS+ protocols for enforcing granular access control of the management plane. The choice of protocol is dictated by various factors such as the support on the network device and the kind of access control required.

RADIUS Versus TACACS+ for Device Administration

While ISE supports both RADIUS and TACACS+ and they basically do the same thing, the difference in how they function dictates the choice of protocol for device administration.

As you read in Chapter 1, "Who and What: AAA Basics," there is one big difference in how RADIUS and TACACS+ operate. Whereas RADIUS combines authentication and authorization in a single request, TACACS+ sends separate requests for authentication and authorization. What this means is that RADIUS needs to return all authorization parameters in a single reply, while TACACS+ can request authorization parameters separately and multiple times throughout the session.

In practical terms, when using RADIUS, whatever a user can do after logging into the device needs to be sent to the device right at the beginning of the session. On the other hand, when using TACACS+, the device can request authorization at every step of the session. For example, an IOS device, such as a Cisco switch or router, can request a TACACS+ server to authorize every command that a user tries to execute after logging into the device.

Given these differences, TACACS+ is preferred for device administration, although RADIUS and TACACS+ both have their uses. For example, most devices that have a GUI-based management interface might prefer RADIUS because all authorization information is available before the GUI is rendered. Because a GUI consists of many elements, such as links and images, authorizing every object or action using TACACS+ will become prohibitively overwhelming for the device and the TACACS+ server—as was seen in legacy Cisco Access Points.

With a CLI-based management interface, however, authorizing every command that a user can execute with RADIUS will require those commands to be sent in the initial authentication response. Given that most CLI-based management systems can have thousands of command combinations, a large authorization result list can cause memory exhaustion on the network device. With CLI-based devices, using TACACS+ is more practical because the device can generate an authorization request for every command that the user is attempting to execute.

Of course, this assumes that command authorization is required. If only a simple user authentication is required, there is no practical difference between using RADIUS or TACACS+. Hence, the choice between RADIUS and TACACS+ depends primarily on what is supported by the network device and the security requirements.

The rest of this chapter is divided into two main sections—TACACS+ and RADIUS. The first section will discuss configuring ISE, Cisco IOS devices, Cisco Adaptive Security Appliance (ASA), and Wireless LAN Controller (WLC) for TACACS+-based AAA for device administration. The second section will discuss configuring ISE, Cisco Firepower Management Center (FMC), Web Security Appliance (WSA), and Email Security Appliance (ESA) for RADIUS-based AAA for device administration. The chapter will discuss these devices in particular because they are the ones available in the CCIE lab.

Using TACACS+ for Device Administration

Because TACACS+ can request authentication and authorization multiple times during a session and for different reasons, before configuring the network device or ISE, it is important to know what can be authenticated and authorized on a device. You will need to configure the network device for each type of authentication and authorization required, as well as configure the appropriate authentication and authorization policies on ISE. Generally, on Cisco devices that support TACACS+, you can authenticate or authorize the following:

- Login to the device. For example, when a user tries to log in to the CLI of a Cisco router using SSH or console, the session can be authenticated using TACACS+.

- Login to privileged EXEC mode. For example, switching to privilege level 15 on a Cisco router using the **enable** command.

- Commands executed at various privilege levels.

Figure 5-1 shows a visual representation of how the communication works between the end user, the network device, and ISE when TACACS+ is used to authenticate and authorize.

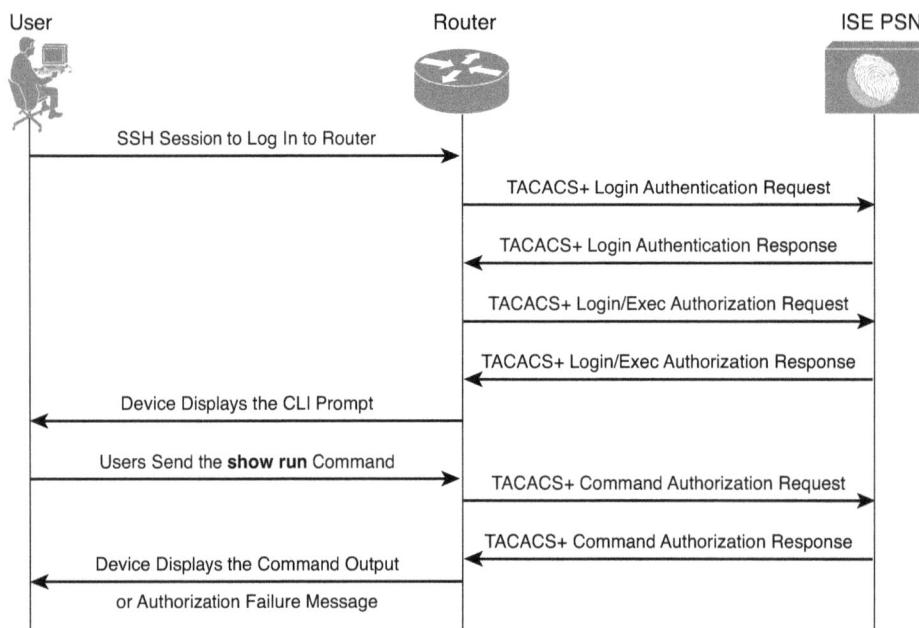

Figure 5-1 *Authentication and Authorization Flows with TACACS+*

Once you decide on the type of authentication and authorization you require on a device, you can begin configuring the network device and ISE with the appropriate policies.

Configuring ISE for TACACS+

Configuring ISE for TACACS+ is very similar to configuring it for any of the RADIUS use cases covered in the previous chapters, such as 802.1X. The difference primarily lies in specific elements needed and the location where they are configured. The steps required to configure TACACS+ are as follows:

Step 1. Enable TACACS+ service.

Step 2. Add TACACS+ network devices.

Step 3. Create TACACS+ policy elements.

Step 4. Create TACACS+ policy sets and rules.

The sections that follow cover these steps in depth.

Enabling TACACS+ Service on ISE

Before ISE can start accepting TACACS+ requests, you need to enable the *Device Admin Service* on a node. Chapter 2 discussed the various ways to deploy ISE by selecting different personas of a node. In that chapter, you learned that to enable RADIUS authentication on a node, you need to enable *Policy Service* and *Session Service* on a node. Similarly, to enable TACACS+ service on ISE, the *Policy Service* and *Device Admin Service* need to be enabled on a node.

Note   To enable and use TACACS+ service, the deployment requires at least 100 Base licenses. In addition to that, starting with ISE 2.4, one device administration license is required for each node that will have *Device Admin Service* enabled. In versions earlier than 2.4, a single device administration license is required for the whole deployment.

Device Admin Service can be enabled in two ways. The first method is to enable the service in the node configuration page using the following steps and as shown in Figure 5-2:

Step 1.   Navigate to **Administration > System > Deployment**.

Step 2.   Select the name of the ISE node.

Step 3.   Check the **Policy Service** check box, if not already selected.

Step 4.   Check the **Enable Device Admin Service** check box.

Step 5.   Click **Save**.

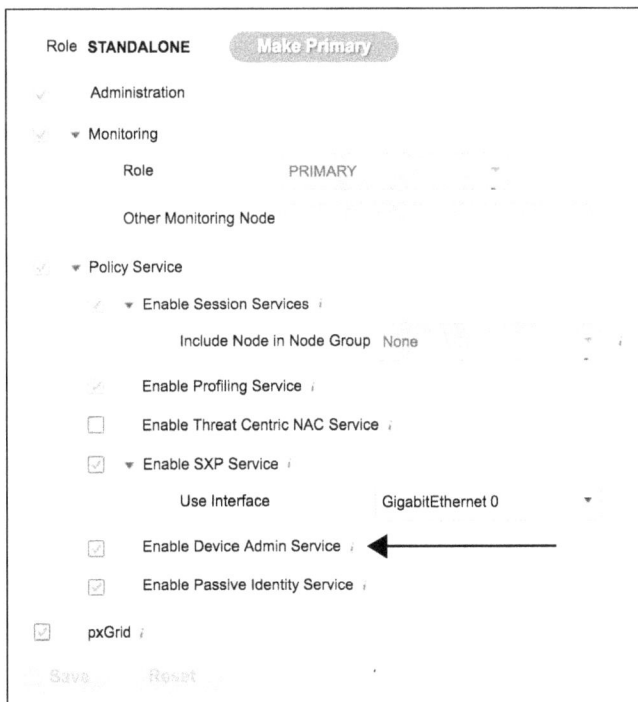

Figure 5-2   *Enabling TACACS+ Service on an ISE Node*

Repeat Steps 2 to 5 for each node that you need to enable the service on.

The Device Admin Service can also be enabled on multiple nodes at one go, by using the method described in the steps that follow and shown in Figure 5-3:

Step 1.   Navigate to **Work Centers > Device Administration > Overview > Deployment.**

Step 2.   Click the **Specific Nodes** radio button.

Step 3.   Select all the nodes that need the service enabled.

Step 4.   Click **Save.**

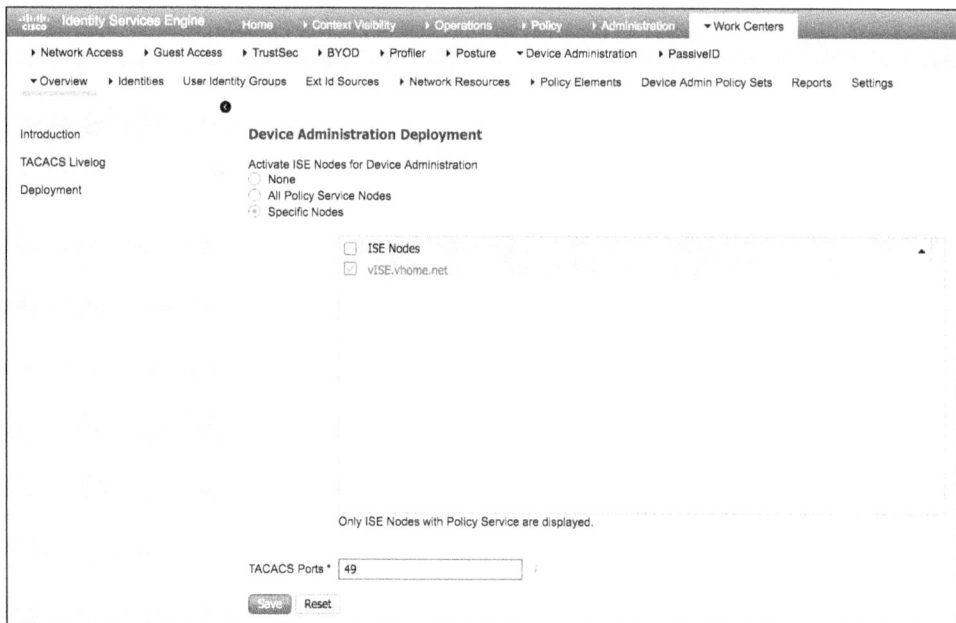

Figure 5-3   *Enabling TACACS+ Service on Multiple Nodes*

Adding TACACS+ Network Device

Before ISE can accept TACACS+ requests from a network device, it needs to know about the device and the shared secret. The shared secret is a key that the network device and ISE use to encrypt and decrypt all TACACS+ packets. The network device can be added in ISE by using the following steps:

Step 1.   Navigate to **Administration > Network Resources > Network Devices** or **Work Centers > Device Administration > Network Resources > Network Devices.**

Step 2.   Click **Add.**

Step 3.   In the Name field, type a name for the device, as shown in Figure 5-4.

Step 4.   In the IP field, type the IP address of the device. Alternatively, you can select **IP Range** from the drop-down list to the left of the IP field and enter an IP address range in the field. The range has to be written with a dash, such as 192.168.1.1-254.

Step 5.   Check the **TACACS+ Authentication Settings** check box.

Step 6.   In the Shared Secret field, type the shared secret.

Step 7.   Click **Submit**.

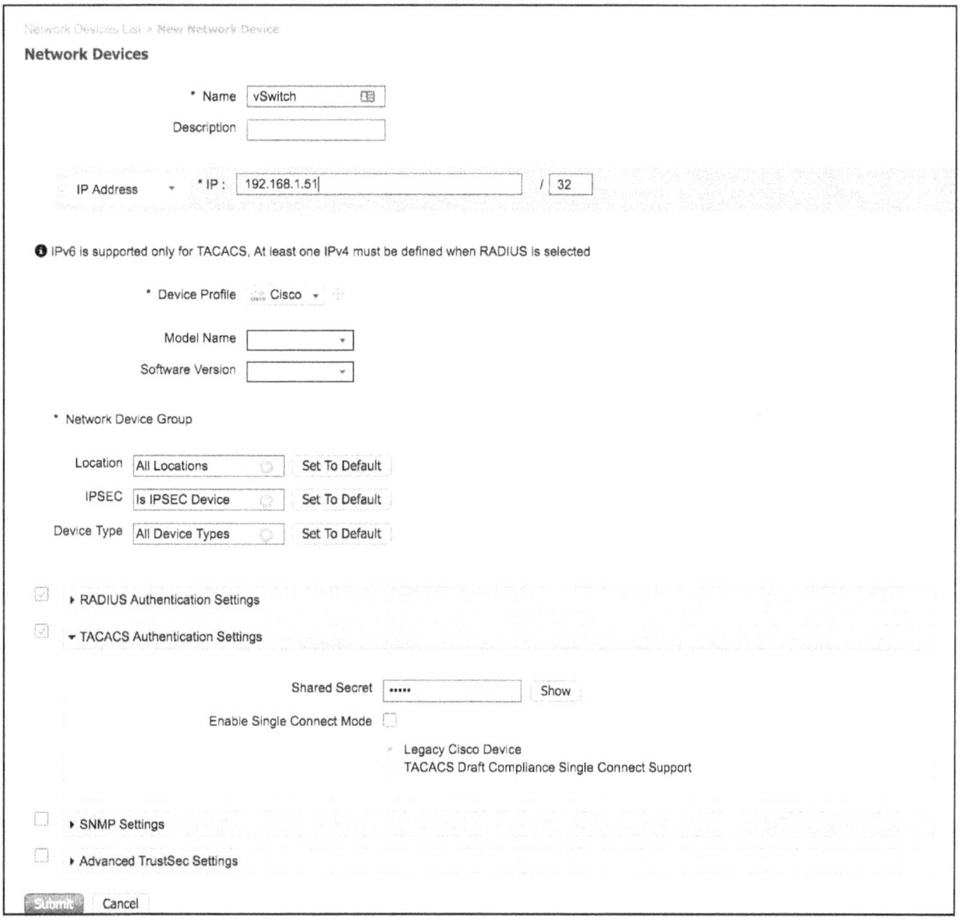

Figure 5-4   *Adding a TACACS+ Network Device in ISE*

You might have noticed that the steps required to add a TACACS+ network device are similar to those required to add a RADIUS network device. This is because ISE uses the same network device entry for both TACACS+ and RADIUS. You can enable both services for a network device, if required, as shown in Figure 5-4.

Creating TACACS+ Policy Elements

All authorization policies in ISE, whether for RADIUS or TACACS+, consist of two types of policy elements—Conditions and Results. *Conditions* are used to match specific sessions to a rule, and *Results* are what get applied to a session and define the actual attribute-value (AV) pairs sent to the network device.

The condition policy elements for RADIUS and TACACS+ are shared and can be used in policy sets for both protocols. Chapters 2 and 3 both discussed creating and using policy conditions, so we will not cover it here again, but the policy results for TACACS+ are different from those for RADIUS.

The policy elements for TACACS+ can only be created by navigating to **Work Centers > Device Administration > Policy Elements > Results**.

There are three types of policy elements that can be created and used for a TACACS+ policy:

- **Allowed Protocols:** The Allowed Protocols result is used in a TACACS+ authentication policy and defines which authentication protocols will be accepted by ISE. The TACACS+ result is much smaller than the RADIUS one and only accepts three protocols: PAP/ASCII, CHAP, and MS-CHAPv1. ISE provides a default result named Default Device Admin that has all the protocols enabled. Figure 5-5 shows an example Allowed Protocols result for TACACS+.

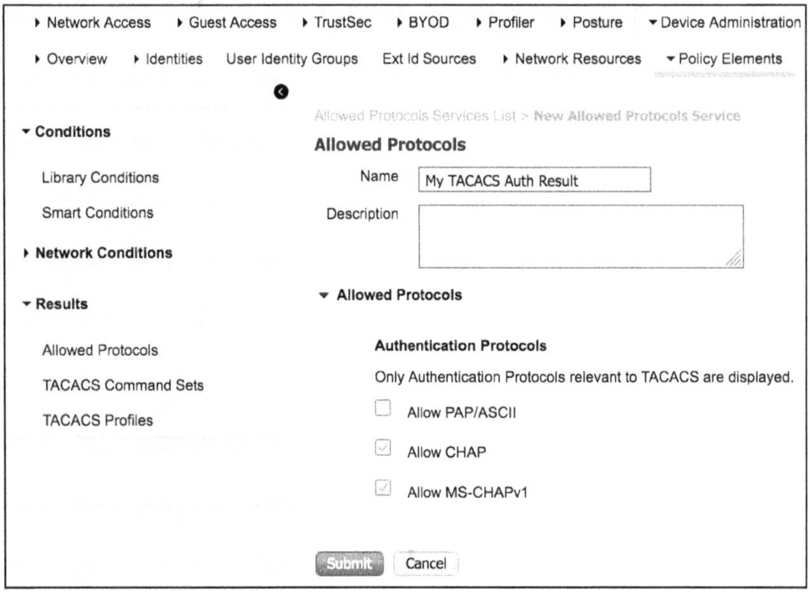

Figure 5-5   *Allowed Protocols Result for TACACS+*

■ **TACACS+ Profiles:** TACACS+ Profiles, also known as Shell Profiles, are used in authorization rules to specify the AV pairs that are sent to the network device in response to a login or EXEC authorization request. The AV pairs sent define the permissions that will be applied to the session. Common results that get applied to a session include permission to access the CLI, the privilege level that the user gets, and session or idle timeout values for the session.

Inside a TACACS+ profile, AV pairs can be specified either by using the provided templates or by specifying custom AV pairs. ISE provides templates for Cisco IOS devices (called Shell), Cisco WLC, and Cisco Nexus switches. For other Cisco and non-Cisco devices, you will need to manually enter the required attributes and their value. In the next few sections we will see specific examples of creating profiles and the usage of common attributes. Figure 5-6 shows an example TACACS+ profile created for a Cisco IOS device.

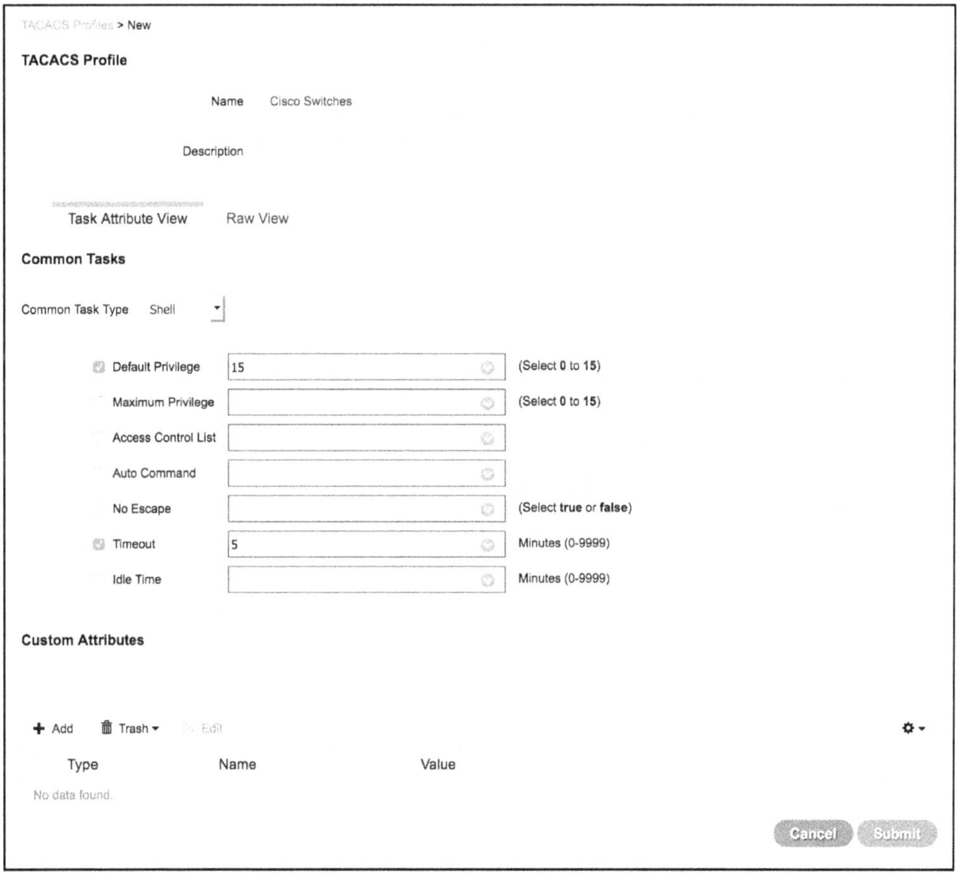

Figure 5-6 *TACACS+ Profile Result Policy Element*

■ **TACACS+ Command Sets:** Command sets are used in authorization policies to define the commands a user can or cannot use on a device. When command authorization is enabled on a network device, it requests ISE to authorize any command a user attempts to execute. Command sets are created as a list of permitted or denied commands. In the next few sections we'll discuss specific examples of command sets and how they are created. Figure 5-7 shows an example TACACS+ command set created to permit all commands except **configure** on an IOS device.

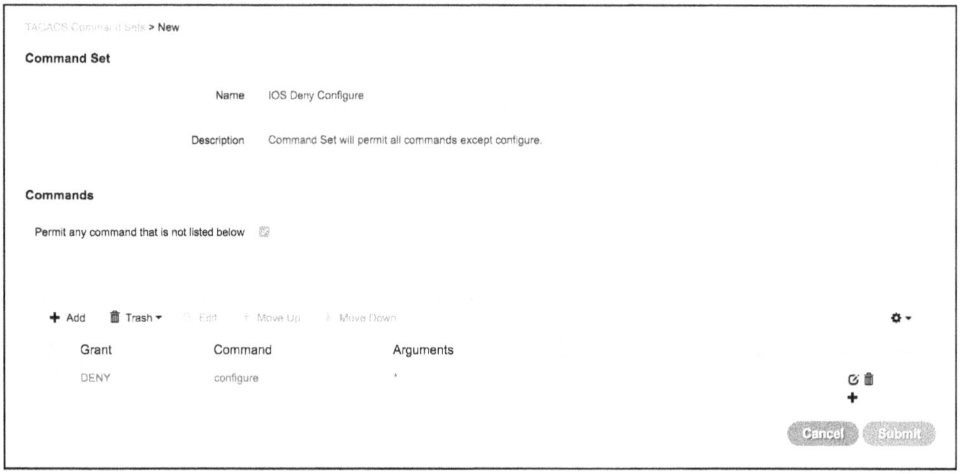

Figure 5-7   *TACACS+ Command Set Policy Element*

Create TACACS+ Policy Sets and Rules

As the previous chapters discussed, policy sets are what bring the various elements together to create the policies that apply to the authentication and authorization requests that ISE receives. TACACS+ policy sets are created very similarly to how RADIUS policy sets are created and also contain a set of authentication and authorization rules; however, they are created in a different section of the GUI and the authorization rules contain the policy elements we just discussed.

When a TACACS+ request is received, ISE first attempts to match a policy set, then an authentication rule OR authorization rule inside the set (remember, unlike a RADIUS request, TACACS+ will send different requests for authentication and authorization). The top-level conditions defined in the policy set allow ISE to match a request to a particular set. These top-level conditions are created in exactly the same way as those for RADIUS and use the same attributes.

TACACS+ policy sets (or as ISE calls them, *Device Admin policy sets*) can be accessed and created by navigating to **Work Center > Device Administration > Device Admin Policy Sets.**

Note   Although RADIUS can also be used for device administration AAA, the Cisco ISE interface associates all things TACACS+ to the term "Device Administration". Thus, be aware that TACACS+ policy sets exist under the Device Administration Work Center in ISE and RADIUS policy sets exist under the Policy menu even if a RADIUS policy set deals with Device Admin authentication, as we will discuss later in this chapter.

The steps to create Device Admin policy sets are exactly the same as those for creating RADIUS policy sets that were discussed in previous chapters. We will not discuss the steps here again, but Figure 5-8 shows a policy set condition that matches all devices that are part of the *Switch* Network Device Group (NDG) under the *Device Type* parent NDG. Figure 5-9 shows the policy set named *Cisco Switches* that uses this condition and the Default Device Admin *Allowed Authentication* result. With this policy set present, all requests that come from any device that is part of the *Switch* NDG in ISE will match this set and all protocols—PAP/ASCII, CHAP, and MS-CHAPv1—will be accepted.

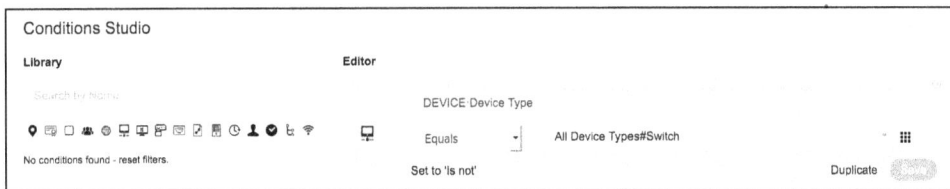

Figure 5-8   *Policy Set Condition*

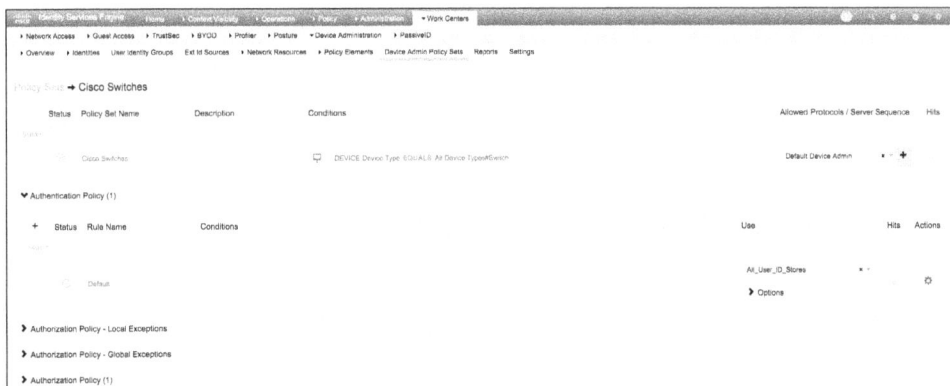

Figure 5-9   *Device Admin Policy Set*

Inside the policy set you will find the now familiar layout containing authentication and authorization policies. The Authentication Policy section should also be very familiar from previous chapters. The Default rule, as shown in Figure 5-10, checks all configured ID stores and can be modified to restrict the lookup to certain stores or store sequences.

If required, you can add more authentication rules based on conditions such as those used for RADIUS authentication policies.

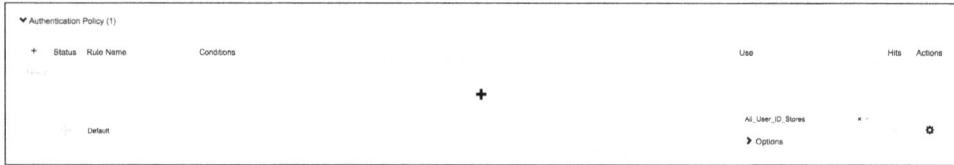

Figure 5-10   *Default Authentication Policy in Device Admin Policy Set*

The Authorization Policy section, though, is a little different from the one you are famil-iar with. Device Admin authorization policies use the same *Conditions* libraries or attri-butes and are created in the same way as conditions for RADIUS authorization rules, but the available *Results* are different. You will notice, as shown in Figure 5-11, that the two possible Results are Command Sets and Shell Profiles. These drop-down menus will let you select the policy elements we discussed earlier. It is not necessary to specify both the results for a rule.

Figure 5-11 shows an example of authorization rules for a Device Admin Policy Set. In the figure, the first rule applies the PermitAll default command set and the Cisco Switches Shell Profile that we created earlier to any user that belongs to the Domain Admins Active Directory group. This rule will allow any member of the Domain Admins group to log in to devices and execute any commands. The second rule, the Default rule, applies the IOS Deny Configure command set and the Cisco Switches Shell Profile that we created earlier to all other users. From Figure 5-7 you will remember that this com-mand set will permit all commands except the **configure** command.

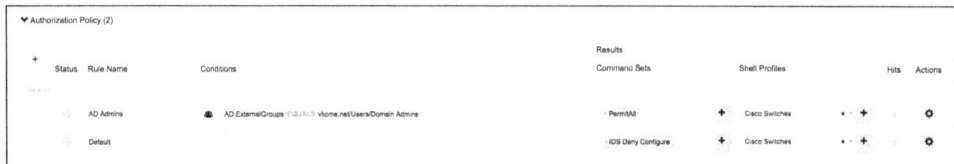

Figure 5-11   *Authorization Policy in a Device Admin Policy Set*

Now that you know the basics of configuring ISE for TACACS+-based authentication and authorization, the next three sections will look at specific examples of configuring Cisco network devices and ISE for TACACS+-based AAA.

TACACS+ with Cisco IOS Routers, Switches, and ISE

Chapter 2 of Volume I of this series discusses various privilege levels on an IOS device and methods to secure access to them. It also discusses methods to change the privilege levels of commands to make them accessible on lower privilege levels to allow role-based access. In this section, we will discuss how to secure access to the CLI and to configure role-based access control using TACACS+. On a Cisco IOS device, you can enable the following:

- Authentication, authorization, and accounting of login to user EXEC level

- Authentication and accounting when changing privilege levels with **enable** and **disable** commands

- Authorization and accounting of commands entered at privilege levels 0 to 15

- Authorization and accounting of commands entered in the *configuration* mode

Authenticating and Authorizing Login and Privilege Levels

There are two parts to configuring TACACS+-based AAA: the configuration of the device itself and the configuration on ISE. The first seven steps that follow outline how to configure the IOS device to start sending relevant requests to ISE. The next set of steps shows how to configure ISE, with relevant examples.

Step 1. By default, AAA function is disabled on IOS and all authentications and authorizations are based on configuration on the vty and console lines. As soon as you enable AAA, IOS will default to using local usernames and passwords instead of the line passwords. If you do not have a local username and password, immediately add one as follows to avoid being locked out of the device:

username *username* **password** *password*

If you need to switch back to using line passwords for, say, the console, you can do that using authentication method lists on the line as discussed below in Steps 5 and 6. In any case, ensure that you always have a local fallback to allow you to log in to the device in case ISE or communication to ISE fails.

Step 2. To start configuring IOS to use TACACS+ with ISE, enable AAA functions on IOS with the **aaa new-model** command.

Note Enabling **aaa new-model** will change the authentication method used to log in to the device. Unless a question in the CCIE lab specifically requests changing credentials or authentication methods, make sure the proctors can log in with the original credentials so that you avoid losing marks for any questions related to that device.

Step 3. After enabling AAA, you will need to add ISE as a TACACS+ server before configuring the actual AAA functions. In newer IOS codes (15.x and later), the TACACS+ server needs to be defined as an object, as shown in the following example:

```
Switch(config)# tacacs server myise
Switch(config-server-tacacs)# address 192.168.1.10
Switch(config-server-tacacs)# key mySecr3tK3y
```

In this example, *myise* is a name given to the object, the address is of an ISE Policy Service Node (PSN) where AAA requests will be sent, and the key is used to encrypt and decrypt the packets. The example shows the minimum required configuration, which is the address or hostname and the secret key. In addition to that, you can specify the port that the server is listening on and the timeout using **port** and **timeout** commands.

In older IOS versions, instead of defining the TACACS+ server as an object, you can define the server with a single command as follows:

```
Switch(config)# tacacs-server host 192.168.1.10 key cisco123!
```

Note   Make sure you practice the correct commands depending on the latest published IOS versions in the CCIE Security exam blueprint.

Irrespective of the method used, you can add multiple TACACS+ servers. All the servers added in this fashion form a group called *group TACACS+*. In effect, *group TACACS+* contains all TACACS+ servers defined on the device and in the order they were defined.

Step 4.   While the *group TACACS+* can be directly referenced in AAA commands, it is best to create a custom AAA server group for use. Doing so makes sure that the requests are being sent only to the intended servers. To create an AAA server group, you would enter the following:

```
Switch(config)# aaa group server tacacs+ ise-tacacs
Switch(config-sg-tacacs+)# server name myise
```

In this example, you are creating a new AAA group named *ise-tacacs* and declaring the servers that are part of the group with the **server** command. On newer IOS versions, you will need to use the **server name** command followed by the name of the TACACS+ server object that you created earlier. On older IOS versions, you will need to use the **server** *ip address* command to reference a TACACS+ server defined in the global configuration. The commands can be repeated to add multiple servers. The order in which the servers are added to the group will define the failover order starting from the first one defined. If you need to change the order, it is best to remove all the servers from the group using the **no server** command and re-add them in the required order.

Step 5.   To enable login authentication with TACACS+, IOS uses something called *method lists*. The simplest way to configure authentication is to use the default method list, as demonstrated here:

```
Switch(config)# aaa authentication login default group
ise-tacacs local
```

Here, the **aaa authentication login** command is used to define a default method list that will apply to all login requests, including those on the console line. The **group** parameter of the command is used to configure IOS to send authentication requests to a TACACS+ server group. In this example, the previously added *ise-tacacs* AAA server group is used. The last option, **local**, is added to provide a fallback to the local user database in case the TACACS+ server is not reachable.

Although the *default* method list is often sufficient, it is sometimes necessary to specify different method lists for different *lines*. For example, it may be prudent to configure the console to authenticate using line passwords always to provide a guaranteed access for emergency scenarios. To do so, a *named method list* can be defined and applied to specific lines, as demonstrated here:

```
Switch(config)# aaa authentication login consolelist line
Switch(config)# line console 0
Switch(config-line)# login authentication consolelist
Switch(config-line)# password my3merg3ncyp@ss
```

In this example, the **aaa authentication login** command is used to define a named method list called *consolelist* for authentication using the password defined in the line configuration. The method list is then applied to the *console line* using the **login authentication** command.

Step 6.   Using similar method lists, IOS can be configured to authorize login or EXEC sessions. The commands required to configure a default method list and a named method list are as follows:

```
Switch(config)# aaa authorization exec default group
ise-tacacs local
Switch(config)# aaa authorization exec consoleauthz none
Switch(config)# aaa authorization console
Switch(config)# line console 0
Switch(config-line)# authorization exec consoleauthz
Switch(config-line)# privilege level 15
```

As demonstrated here, the commands to create authorization method lists are similar to those used to create authentication method lists. In the named list *consoleauthz*, the example uses the method **none** because there is no specific option for line authorization. Also note the **aaa authorization console** command. This is used to enable authorization on the console. By default, authorization is disabled on the console. Strictly speaking, you can configure authentication and the privilege level on the console while leaving authorization disabled.

Step 7.   When a user logs in to IOS, they land at privilege level 1. To change to privilege level 15, they have to use the **enable** command and provide the enable password. The user can be taken to privilege level 15 directly if the TACACS+ server returns the privilege level during EXEC authorization, as will be discussed in the next few pages. If your security policy mandates an enable password, then IOS can be configured to authenticate the enable request also with a TACACS+ server, as demonstrated here:

```
SW2(config)# aaa authentication enable default group
ise-tacacs enable
```

In the preceding example, a default method list for enable authentication is configured to use TACACS+ and to failover to the locally configured enable password. IOS does not allow named method lists for enable authentication.

In the preceding steps, we enabled AAA on a Cisco IOS device and configured it to authenticate and authorize all administrative login sessions using TACACS+. We also configured a fallback local account as well as a line password-based authentication on the console line to allow emergency access if the device loses connection to the TACACS+ server. With the device now configured, it is time to configure ISE to respond to incoming requests. The previous sections discussed the various steps required to configure ISE but did not discuss specific steps to create appropriate *Shell Profiles*. That will be discussed here. For the purpose of understanding various options that ISE allows, we will use the following specific access requirements as examples:

■ Members of the *Network Admins* group should be able to log in to the device with privilege level 15.

■ Members of the *Network Ops* group should be able to log in to the device with privilege level 1.

The first step is to create Shell Profiles that will be used to give the two groups the required access. The following steps show how to create the required Shell Profiles:

Step 1.   Navigate to **Work Centers > Device Administration > Policy Elements > Results > TACACS Profiles**.

Step 2.   Click **Add**.

Step 3.   Enter **Network Admins Profile** in the Name field, as shown in Figure 5-12.

Step 4.   Check the **Default Privilege** check box and select **15** from the drop-down list.

Step 5.   Click **Submit**.

Step 6.   Click **Add**.

Step 7.   Enter **Network Ops Profile** in the Name field, as shown in Figure 5-13.

Step 8.   Check the **Default Privilege** check box and select **1** from the drop-down list.

Step 9.   Click **Submit**.

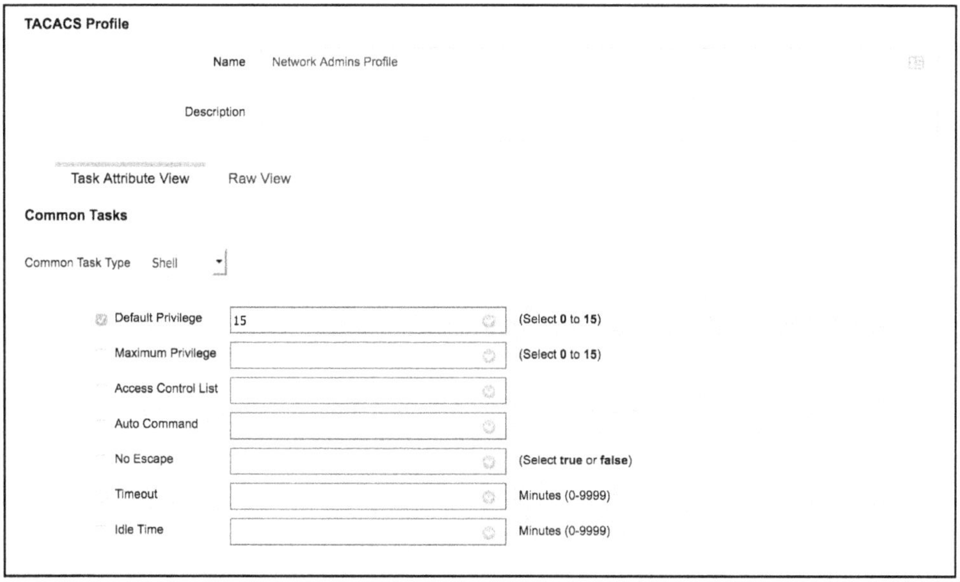

TACACS Profile

Name   Network Admins Profile

Description

Task Attribute View   Raw View

Common Tasks

Common Task Type   Shell   ▾

☑ Default Privilege	15	(Select **0** to **15**)
Maximum Privilege		(Select **0** to **15**)
Access Control List		
Auto Command		
No Escape		(Select **true** or **false**)
Timeout		Minutes (0-9999)
Idle Time		Minutes (0-9999)

Figure 5-12 *Network Admins Shell Profile*

TACACS Profile

Name   Network Ops Profile

Description

Task Attribute View   Raw View

Common Tasks

Common Task Type   Shell   ▾

☑ Default Privilege	1	(Select **0** to **15**)
Maximum Privilege		(Select **0** to **15**)
Access Control List		
Auto Command		
No Escape		(Select **true** or **false**)
Timeout		Minutes (0-9999)
Idle Time		Minutes (0-9999)

Figure 5-13 *Network Ops Shell Profile*

The next step in configuring ISE is to configure the authentication and authorization policies in a policy set. This example uses the Default policy set and creates two new rules in it. For authentication, this example uses the Internal Users database. The steps to configure the authentication policy are as follows:

Step 1.   Navigate to **Work Centers > Device Administration > Device Admin Policy Sets.**

Step 2.   Click **>** in the View column for the Default policy set.

Step 3.   Expand the **Authentication Policy** section.

Step 4.   From the drop-down list in the Use column, choose **Internal Users.**

Figure 5-14 shows the configured authentication policy.

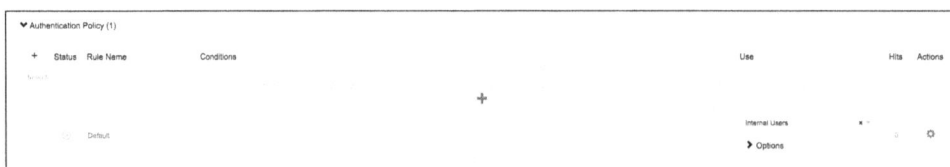

Figure 5-14   *Configuring an Authentication Policy*

After the authentication policy is configured, we need to add two authorization policies for our two example requirements. The steps to configure authorization policies are as follows:

Note   The *Network Admins* and *Network Ops* user groups were preconfigured for this example. If you are re-creating this example on your ISE, then create the groups by navigating to **Administration > Identity Management > Groups > User Identity Groups** before starting the steps that follow.

Step 1.   Expand the **Authorization Policy** section.

Step 2.   Click **+** above the Default policy.

Step 3.   Enter **Network Ops** in the Rule Name field.

Step 4.   Click **+** in the Conditions column.

Step 5.   Select the **Click to Add an Attribute** box.

Step 6.   Select the second icon, **Identity Groups.**

Step 7.   Select the **Identity Group - Name** attribute from the list.

Step 8.   Select **User Identity Groups:Network Ops** from the Choose From List Or Type drop-down list.

Step 9.   Click **Use.**

Step 10.   Select **Network Ops Profile** from the Shell Profiles drop-down list.

Step 11.   Click the **gear icon** at the end of the row and select **Insert New Row Above.**

Step 12.   Enter **Network Admins** as the name of the new rule.

Step 13.   Repeat Steps 4 to 7.

Step 14.   Select **User Identity Groups:Network Admins** from the Choose From List Or Type drop-down list.

Step 15.   Click **Use.**

Step 16.   Select **Network Admins Profile** from the Shell Profiles drop-down list.

Step 17.   Click **Save.**

Figure 5-15 shows the completed authorization policies.

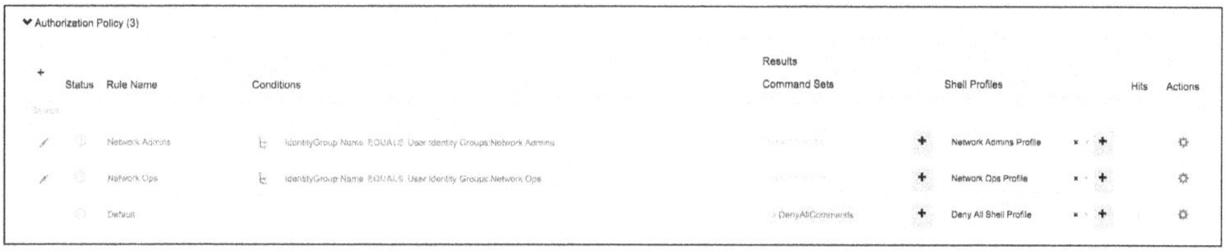

Figure 5-15   *Configuring Authorization Policies*

With these policies in place, any user belonging to the Network Admins and Network Ops groups in ISE will be able to log in to the IOS device and get privilege level 15 and 1, respectively.

Command Authorization

After configuring an IOS device and ISE for login authentication and authorization, an additional layer of security can be added by configuring command authorization. As already discussed, when command authorization is enabled, the IOS device will authorize all commands with ISE before executing them.

Command authorization is applied on a per privilege level basis on IOS. So, you will need to configure a command authorization method list for every privilege level that requires this enforcement. Generally, command authorization is configured on levels 0, 1, and 15. Custom privilege levels (2 to 14) are very useful when using local authorization on devices but are generally not used with command authorization because they create redundancy in functionality. Instead of creating custom levels, usually multiple command sets are used to limit available commands by role.

As with EXEC authorization, you can configure a default list that applies to all sessions or configure and apply named lists to the lines separately. The commands required to configure the *default* method list are as follows:

```
Switch(config)# aaa authorization commands 0 default group ise-tacacs
local
Switch(config)# aaa authorization commands 1 default group ise-tacacs
local
Switch(config)# aaa authorization commands 15 default group ise-tacacs
local
```

In this example, command authorization is enabled on privilege levels 0, 1, and 15 and the authorization requests will be sent to the server defined in the AAA server group *ise-tacacs*, which was created in an earlier example. The **local** keyword at the end of the commands configures a fallback to the local database if the ISE server cannot be reached.

One key point to note about the example is that while it enables command authorization on privilege level 15, IOS will not extend that to the configuration mode. To enable command authorization in the configuration mode (and all its submodes), add the **aaa authorization config-commands** command also.

If some lines such as console need to be exempted from command authorization, you can do so by using a named method list as shown in Example 5-1. In the example, a named method list *consoleca* is created and then applied to the console line.

Example 5-1   *Configuring Command Authorization with Default Lists*

```
Switch(config)# aaa authorization commands 0 consoleca none
Switch(config)# aaa authorization commands 1 consoleca none
Switch(config)# aaa authorization commands 15 consoleca none
Switch(config)# aaa authorization console
Switch(config)# line con 0
Switch(config-line)# authorization commands 0 consoleca
Switch(config-line)# authorization commands 1 consoleca
Switch(config-line)# authorization commands 15 consoleca
```

Now that the device is configured, it is time to configure ISE for command authorization. We discussed command sets briefly in previous sections, but we skipped the steps to create them, so we will cover them here. We will extend the *Network Admins* and *Network Ops* example to discuss the steps required to configure ISE for command authorization. For this example, we will use the following requirements:

■ Members of the *Network Admins* group should be able to log in to the device with privilege level 15 and execute all commands.

■ Members of the *Network Ops* group should be able to log in to the device with privilege level 1 and only execute **show** commands.

Because ISE is already configured with the correct authentication policy, authorization policy, and Shell Profiles, in the following steps we will configure the required command sets and apply them to the existing policies:

Step 1. Navigate to **Work Centers > Device Administration > Policy Elements > Results > TACACS Command Sets.**

Step 2. Click **Add.**

Step 3. Enter **Network Admin** in the Name field.

Step 4. Check **Permit any command that is not listed below.**

Step 5. Click **Submit.**

Step 6. Click **Add.**

Step 7. Enter **Network Ops** in the Name field.

Step 8. Click **Add.**

Step 9. Select **Permit** from the Grant drop-down list.

Step 10. Enter **show** in the Command field.

Step 11. Click the **check mark** next to the field.

Step 12. Repeat Steps 8 and 9.

Step 13. Enter **exit** in the Command field.

Step 14. Click the **check mark** next to the field.

Step 15. Click **Submit.**

Figure 5-16 and Figure 5-17 show the command sets created by these steps.

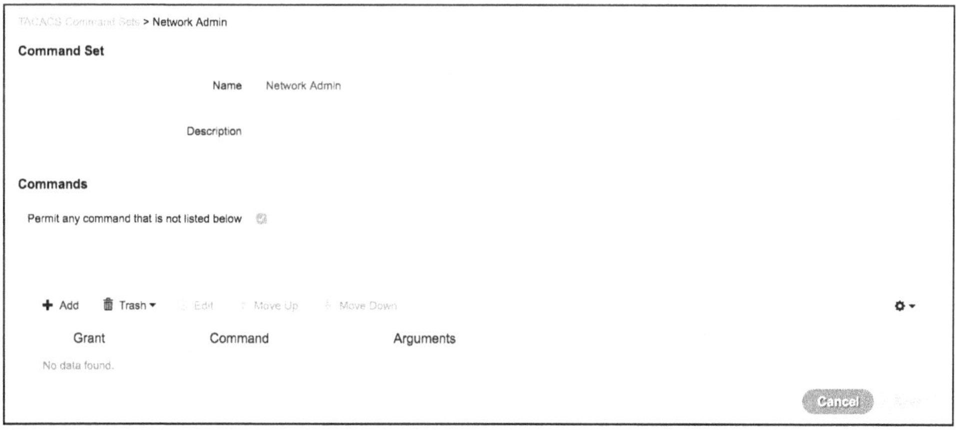

Figure 5-16 *Configuring Network Admin Command Set*

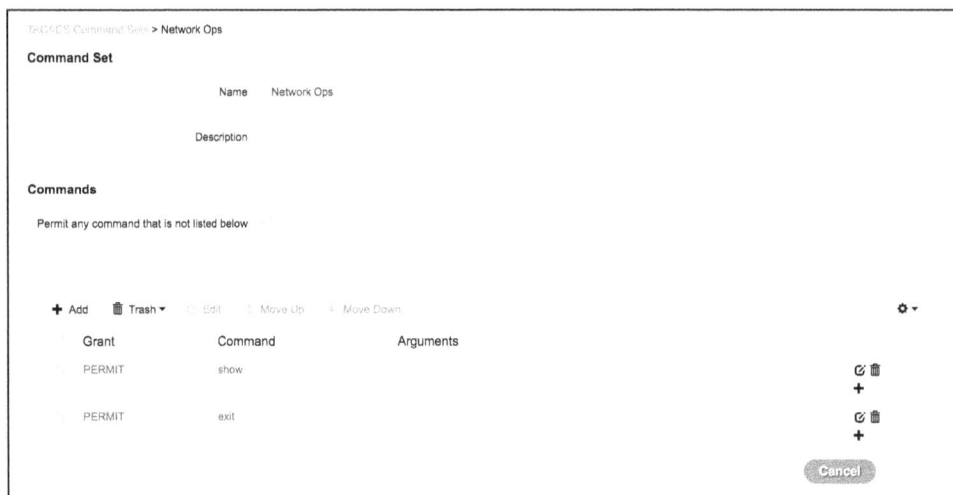

Figure 5-17   *Configuring Network Ops Command Set*

Note   Although the requirements did not explicitly ask for the **exit** command to be allowed for users in the *Network Ops* group, we added it because the users will need a way to log out of the device. Command authorization is all inclusive, so it requires authorization for all commands, including essential ones such as **exit**.

Now that we have created the command sets, we need to apply them to the appropriate policies. We will apply them to the policies created in the previous section, using the following steps:

Step 1.   Navigate to **Work Centers > Device Administration > Device Admin Policy Sets**.

Step 2.   Click **>** in the View column for the Default policy set.

Step 3.   Expand the **Authorization Policy** section.

Step 4.   Select **Network Admin** in the Command Sets drop-down list for the Network Admins rule.

Step 5.   Select **Network Ops** in the Command Sets drop-down list for the Network Ops rule.

Step 6.   Click **Save**.

The authorization policies will look as shown in Figure 5-18 after completing the preceding steps.

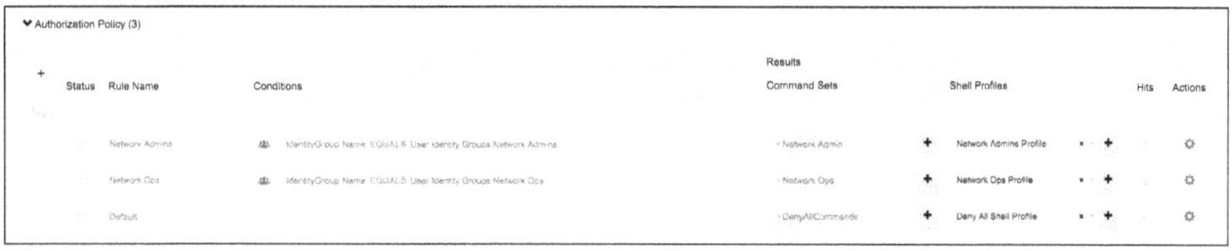

Figure 5-18 *Adding Command Sets to Authorization Rules*

Accounting

Although ISE does not require any configuration to accept accounting packets (as long as the network device has been added), IOS devices need to be specifically configured to enable accounting. The commands required to configure login and commands accounting are as follows:

```
SW2(config)# aaa accounting exec default start-stop group ise-tacacs
SW2(config)# aaa accounting commands 0 default start-stop group ise-tacacs
SW2(config)# aaa accounting commands 1 default start-stop group ise-tacacs
SW2(config)# aaa accounting commands 15 default start-stop group
ise-tacacs
```

As with authentication and authorization, the preceding example creates default method lists for accounting of EXEC sessions and all commands on privilege levels 0, 1, and 15. The method list uses the previously created TACACS+ AAA server group *ise-tacacs*. The **start-stop** option in the command tells IOS to send an accounting packet at the start and end of an event.

Verification

After configuring login authentication, EXEC authorization, and command authorization on IOS and ISE, it's finally time to make sure all of it works.

Note Because the authentication policies are configured to use the *Internal Users* database, make sure users exist in the *Network Admins and Network Ops* groups. Internal users can be added in ISE by navigating to **Administration > Identity Management > Identities > Users.**

Step 1. SSH to the device to test login authentication and EXEC authorization for a user in the *Network Admins* group:

```
vs-osx$ ssh netadmin@192.168.1.26
Password:
Switch# show privilege
Current privilege level is 15
Switch# exit
```

In the preceding output, notice that the user directly entered privilege level 15 after login; this means the Shell Profile works as intended. You can further verify this by looking at TACACS+ live logs at **Work Centers > Device Administration > Overview > TACACS Livelogs.** You will see something similar to what is shown in Figure 5-19.

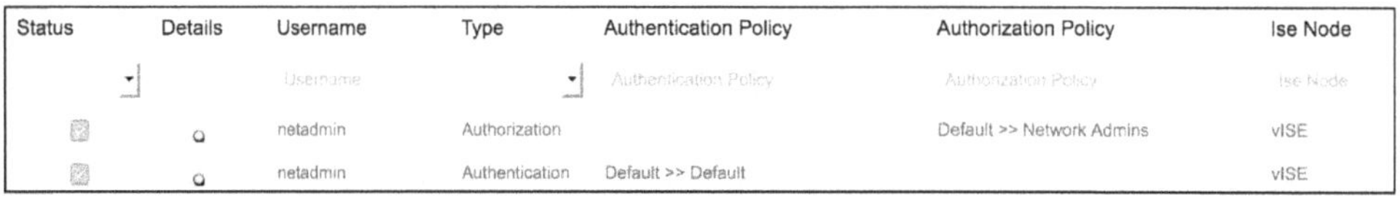

Status	Details	Username	Type	Authentication Policy	Authorization Policy	Ise Node
▾		Username	▾	Authentication Policy	Authorization Policy	Ise Node
☑	ℚ	netadmin	Authorization		Default >> Network Admins	vISE
☑	ℚ	netadmin	Authentication	Default >> Default		vISE

Figure 5-19 *TACACS+ Live Logs Showing Successful Authentication by Network Admin*

Step 2.   Repeat Step 1 with a user in the *Network Ops* group:

```
vs-osx$ ssh netops@192.168.1.26
Password:
Switch>show privilege
Current privilege level is 1
```

The preceding output validates that the user is able to log in and enters privilege level 1 as intended. Further verification can be seen in the TACACS+ Live logs as shown in Figure 5-20.

☑	ℚ	netops	Authorization		Default >> Network Ops	vISE
☑	ℚ	netops	Authentication	Default >> Default		vISE

Figure 5-20 *TACACS+ Live Logs Showing Successful Authentication by Network Ops*

Step 3.   Verify command authorization for a user in the *Network Ops* group:

```
vs-osx$ ssh netops@192.168.1.26
Password:
Switch>show version
Cisco IOS Software, C3560CX Software (C3560CX-UNIVERSALK9-M),
Version 15.2(4)E2, RELEASE SOFTWARE (fc2)
--truncated for brevity --
Switch>enable
Command authorization failed.
```

In the preceding output, you can see that the command authorization is working as intended because the user is able to execute **show** commands but not the **enable** command. Further verification can be seen in the TACACS+ live logs as shown in Figure 5-21. Notice the first line that shows the failure? That was generated for the failed command authorization of the **enable** command. Additional details can be verified by clicking the icon in the Details column, which opens a report as shown in Figure 5-22. On the report you can see the command that failed authorization.

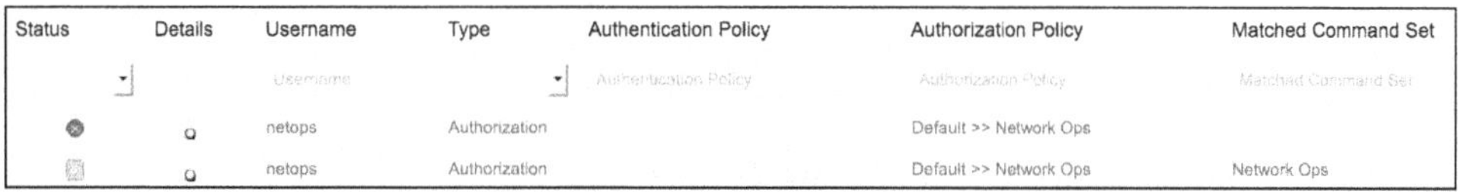

Status	Details	Username	Type	Authentication Policy	Authorization Policy	Matched Command Set
		Username		Authentication Policy	Authorization Policy	Matched Command Set
⊗	▢	netops	Authorization		Default >> Network Ops	
▢	▢	netops	Authorization		Default >> Network Ops	Network Ops

Figure 5-21 *TACACS+ Live Logs Showing Failed Command Authorization*

Overview

Request Type	Authorization
Status	Fail ◄───────────
Session Key	vISE/319315911/76465
Message Text	Failed-Attempt: Command Authorization failed
Username	netops
Authorization Policy	Default >> Network Ops
Shell Profile	
Matched Command Set	
Command From Device	enable ◄───────────

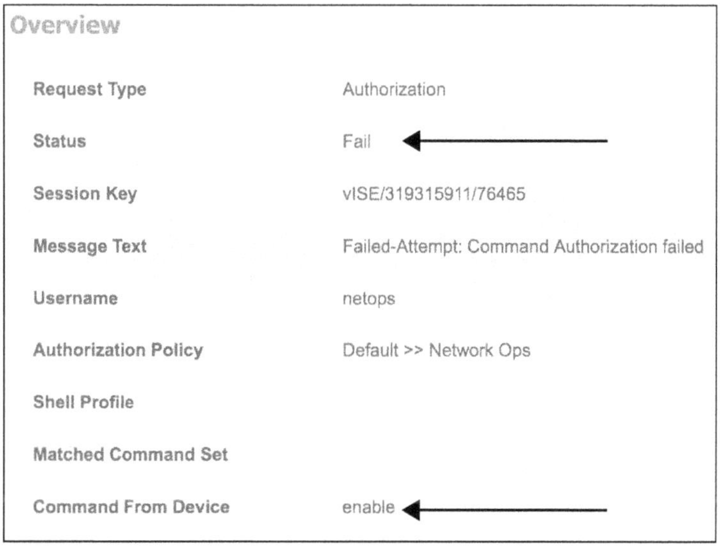

Figure 5-22 *TACACS+ Failure Details*

If things do not work as intended, then you can use the following **debug** commands on IOS to troubleshoot:

- **debug tacacs**
- **debug aaa authentication**
- **debug aaa authorization**
- **debug aaa accounting**

TACACS+ with Cisco ASA and ISE

As with IOS, the Cisco ASA can also be configured for TACACS+-based AAA. The AAA features supported on the ASA are exactly the same as the features supported on IOS, and they are configured in the same way but with different command syntax. The configuration required on the ASA can be broken down into the following steps:

Step 1. Add ISE as a TACACS+ server as demonstrated here:

```
vASA(config)# aaa-server ise-tacacs protocol tacacs+
vASA(config-aaa-server-group)# exit
vASA(config)# aaa-server ise-tacacs (inside) host
192.168.1.11
vASA(config-aaa-server-host)# key mys3cr3tK3y
vASA(config-aaa-server-host)# exit
```

In this example, the first instance of the **aaa-server** command defines a group named *ise-tacacs* that will use the TACACS+ protocol. The second instance of the **aaa-server** command adds the ISE PSN (192.168.1.11) to the group. You can use a hostname instead of an IP address as long as the name can be resolved. The **(inside)** parameter tells the ASA that the server can be reached via the *inside* interface. The **key** command defines the secret key used for encrypting and decrypting the TACACS+ packets.

Multiple TACACS+ servers can be added in the group by repeating the second **aaa-server** command. The order in which the servers are added is important because the ASA will try each server in sequence if it does not get a response. When a server does not respond, the ASA marks it as inactive, and when all servers in a group fail, the ASA will use the fallback method defined in an authentication or authorization method list for 10 minutes before attempting to reach the servers again. If no fallback is defined (a very bad idea!), the ASA will immediately reactivate all servers in the group and retry reaching them. This behavior can be changed to reactivate each failed server within 30 seconds of it being declared inactive by using the **reactivation-mode timed** command in the **aaa-server-group** mode.

Step 2. Enable authentication for the required login methods as shown here:

```
vASA(config)# aaa authentication ssh console ise-tacacs LOCAL
vASA(config)# aaa authentication telnet console ise-tacacs
LOCAL
vASA(config)# aaa authentication http console ise-tacacs
LOCAL
vASA(config)# aaa authentication serial console ise-tacacs
LOCAL
```

In this example, the ASA is configured to authenticate login events from SSH, Telnet (hopefully you are not using this!), console (serial), and HTTP using the previously defined *ise-tacacs* AAA server group.

Note   The **console** keyword in the preceding commands has no specific meaning in the command and should not be confused with the console port. The **serial** keyword refers to the console port.

Step 3.   Enable EXEC authorization with TACACS+ as shown here:

```
vASA(config)# aaa authorization exec authentication-server
auto-enable
```

The **auto-enable** option at the end of the **aaa authorization** command allows the user to log in directly to privilege level 15 if the Shell Profile returns that attribute. Without that option, any privilege level AV pair will be ignored by the ASA.

Note   The capability to allow a user to log in directly to privilege level 15 was one of the most requested AAA features for the PIX and ASA for years. This capability was not added in ASA until 9.2(1) code due to security concerns.

Step 4.   Enable command authorization on the ASA as shown here:

```
vASA(config)# aaa authorization command ise-tacacs LOCAL
```

Unlike IOS, the ASA requires a single command to enable command authorization on all privilege levels and configuration modes as shown in the preceding example. The **LOCAL** parameter in the command defines the fallback to the local database if all AAA servers in the group are inactive.

Step 5:   Enable accounting for EXEC sessions and commands as shown here:

```
vASA(config)# aaa accounting ssh console ise-tacacs
vASA(config)# aaa accounting telnet console ise-tacacs
vASA(config)# aaa accounting serial console ise-tacacs
vASA(config)# aaa accounting command ise-tacacs
```

In the preceding example, the first three commands enable accounting for login/EXEC sessions on SSH, Telnet, and console (serial) and the last command enables command accounting.

Now that the device is configured, you need to configure ISE to respond to the requests. The steps to configure ISE to respond to requests coming from the ASA are exactly the same as the steps to configure ISE to respond to requests from IOS. This includes adding the ASA as a network device, creating Shell Profiles and command sets, and creating authentication and authorization policies. Because these steps were covered in the previous sections, they will not be repeated here, but remember that the command sets used for authorizing requests from the ASA need to match the command syntax of the device. So, you might need to create separate policy set or authorization rules for the ASA.

For the purpose of this book, we will use the exact same configuration on ISE that we did for IOS—with the exception of adding the ASA as a network device. Figure 5-23 shows the same authorization policies as before. The reason why we can use the same command sets in this example is because these command sets were created to either permit everything or permit the **show** and **exit** commands that exist in the ASA also.

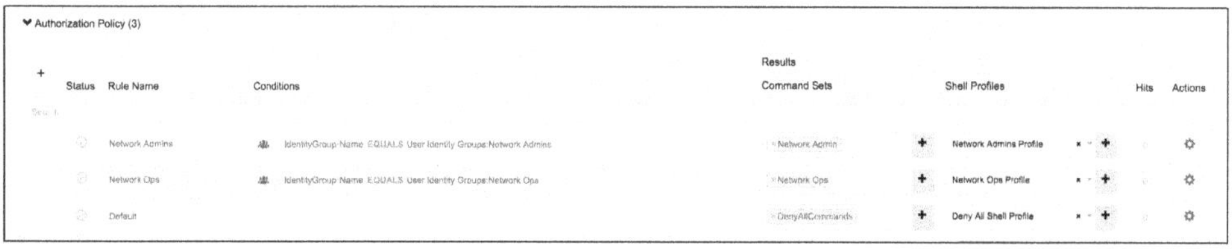

Figure 5-23   *Using IOS Authorization Policy for ASA on ISE*

The configuration on the ASA and ISE can be validated using steps similar to those used earlier:

```
Vs-osx$ ssh netops@192.168.1.22
netops@192.168.1.22's password:
User netops logged in to vASA
-snip-
vASA> ping 192.168.1.10
Command authorization failed
vASA> exit
Logoff
```

In this test, the netops user from the Network Ops group can log in and execute the **exit** command but not the **ping** command because that is not allowed by the command set. Figure 5-24 shows the logs from ISE that were generated from the authentication and authorization requests previously shown.

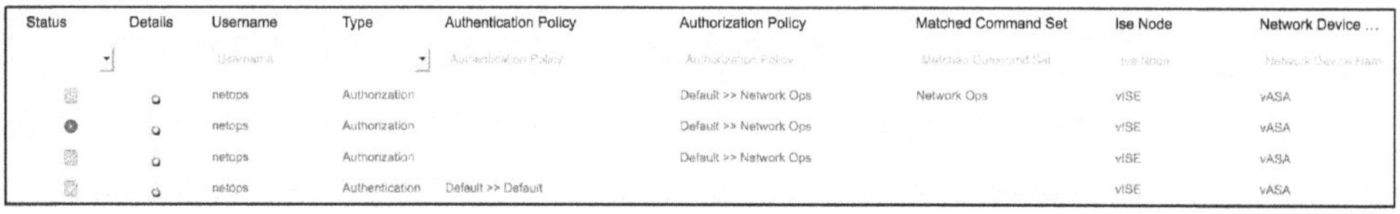

Figure 5-24   *ISE Logs for Authentication and Authorization Requests from ASA*

If things do not work as desired, then the following **debug** commands on the ASA can be useful:

- **debug tacacs**
- **debug aaa authentication**

- debug aaa authorization

- debug aaa accounting

TACACS+ with Cisco WLC and ISE

It is time to use everything you learned about configuring TACACS+ on ISE in the previous sections and apply this knowledge to your first GUI-based device—Cisco WLC. While most of the steps required to configure ISE are the same as before, the big difference lies in the Shell Profiles that are needed to authorize requests from the WLC.

The Cisco WLC supports both TACACS+ and RADIUS for administrative AAA, but using TACACS+ is easier because ISE provides templates for the WLC attributes in Shell Profiles.

Note   Another reason to use TACACS+ for the WLC is that the AV pairs that the WLC expects in a TACACS+ authorization response are far more intuitive than the ones that it expects in a RADIUS response.

The way the WLC implements AAA is a little different than IOS and the ASA. The WLC sends the usual authentication and authorization requests when a user attempts to log in, but the WLC expects the authorization response to contain a value for what is called a *role*. A role corresponds to the seven main menu items that exist on the WLC UI: Monitor, WLANs, Controller, Wireless, Security, Management, and Commands.

The value of **role** defines what menus the user will have write access to. An authorization response can contain multiple instances of the **role** attribute to provide write access to multiple menus.

In addition to the seven roles that correspond to the menu item names, the WLC also accepts an **ALL** or **Lobby** role. The **ALL** role will allow the user write access to all menu items. The **Lobby** role provides the user access to a special UI where guest users or whitelisted devices can be added. Irrespective of the role though, the user will have read access to the entire UI.

Note   Because the **Lobby** role provides access to a special UI, the user won't have access to the regular UI menus and won't be able to read the config either. This role is usually used to allow lobby ambassadors to create wireless guest users.

This can be equated to command authorization on IOS because the WLC enforces only the authorization or **role** during a write operation. Unlike IOS, though, the WLC does not send a command authorization request for each write request. It stores the authorized **role** information and enforces it throughout the session.

Another similarity between how the WLC enforces authorization and command authorization on IOS is that the WLC sends command accounting packets whenever the user makes a change to the configuration.

Note   When you make a change on the WLC GUI, it sends relevant commands to the CLI. Hence, for every change that is made in the GUI, the WLC will send command accounting for each command that it applies on the CLI.

Configuring the WLC

Configuring the WLC for administrative AAA with TACACS+ is a three-step process:

Step 1.   Add an ISE PSN as a TACACS+ authentication and authorization server on the WLC.

To add an authentication server, navigate to **Security > AAA > TACACS+ > Authentication** and click **New**. Enter the IP address of an ISE PSN and the shared secret key, as shown in Figure 5-25, and click **Apply**. This will automatically add this server as an authorization server also.

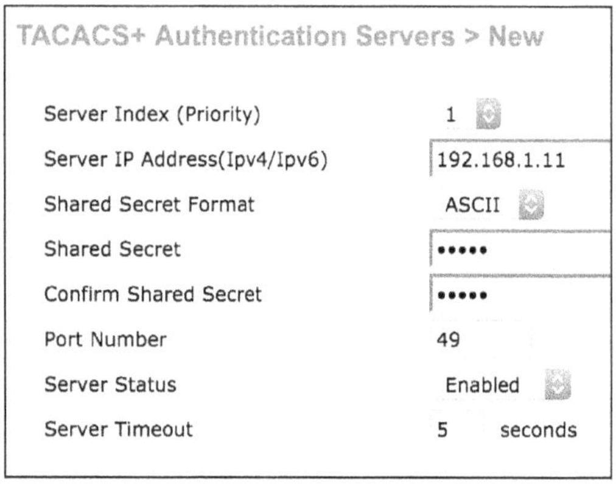

TACACS+ Authentication Servers > New	
Server Index (Priority)	1
Server IP Address(Ipv4/Ipv6)	192.168.1.11
Shared Secret Format	ASCII
Shared Secret	•••••
Confirm Shared Secret	•••••
Port Number	49
Server Status	Enabled
Server Timeout	5 seconds

Figure 5-25   *Adding TACACS+ Authentication Server on Cisco WLC*

Step 2.   Add an ISE PSN as a TACACS+ accounting server on the WLC.

To add an accounting server, navigate to **Security > AAA > TACACS+ > Accounting** and click **New**. Enter the IP address of an ISE PSN and the shared secret key, as shown in Figure 5-26, and click **Apply**.

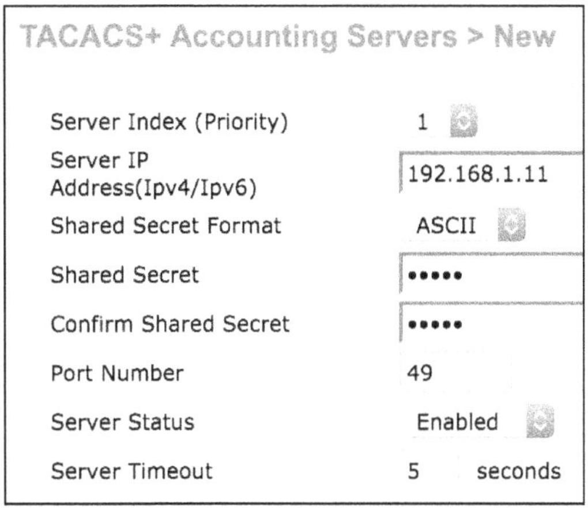

Figure 5-26 *Adding TACACS+ Accounting Server on Cisco WLC*

Step 3.   Configure the WLC to use TACACS+ for authentication.

To configure the WLC to use TACACS+ for authentication of administrative sessions, navigate to **Security > Priority Order > Management User.** On this page, select TACACS+ and use the directional buttons such that the right-side box has TACACS+ at the top followed by LOCAL, as shown in Figure 5-27.

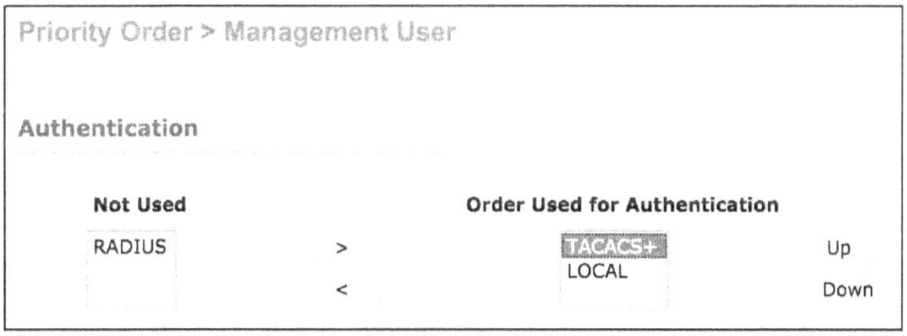

Figure 5-27 *Configuring WLC to Use TACACS+ for AAA*

Note   Make sure LOCAL is below TACACS+ in the right-side box. This will allow the WLC to use the local database if the TACACS+ servers are unreachable.

Configuring ISE

Configuring ISE to respond to TACACS+ requests from the WLC is also a three-step process:

Step 1.   Add the WLC as a network device.

Steps to add a network device in ISE were discussed earlier in the chapter so we will not repeat them here, but Figure 5-28 shows a WLC added as a TACACS+ server in ISE.

Note   Note that the Device Type is set to the WLC in Figure 5-28. This Network Device Group will be used when creating rules in Step 3. If you are following these steps to configure your ISE, create the WLC NDG under the Device Type NDG before adding the WLC as a network device.

Network Devices

* Name   vWLC

Description

IP Address   * IP :   192.168.1.16   /   32

ℹ IPv6 is supported only for TACACS, At least one IPv4 must be defined when RADIUS is selected

* Device Profile   Cisco

Model Name

Software Version

* Network Device Group

Location   All Locations   Set To Default

IPSEC   No   Set To Default

Device Type   WLC   Set To Default   ◄

▸ RADIUS Authentication Settings

▾ TACACS Authentication Settings   ◄

Shared Secret   •••••   Show   Retire   ◄

Enable Single Connect Mode ☐

○   Legacy Cisco Device
TACACS Draft Compliance Single Connect Support

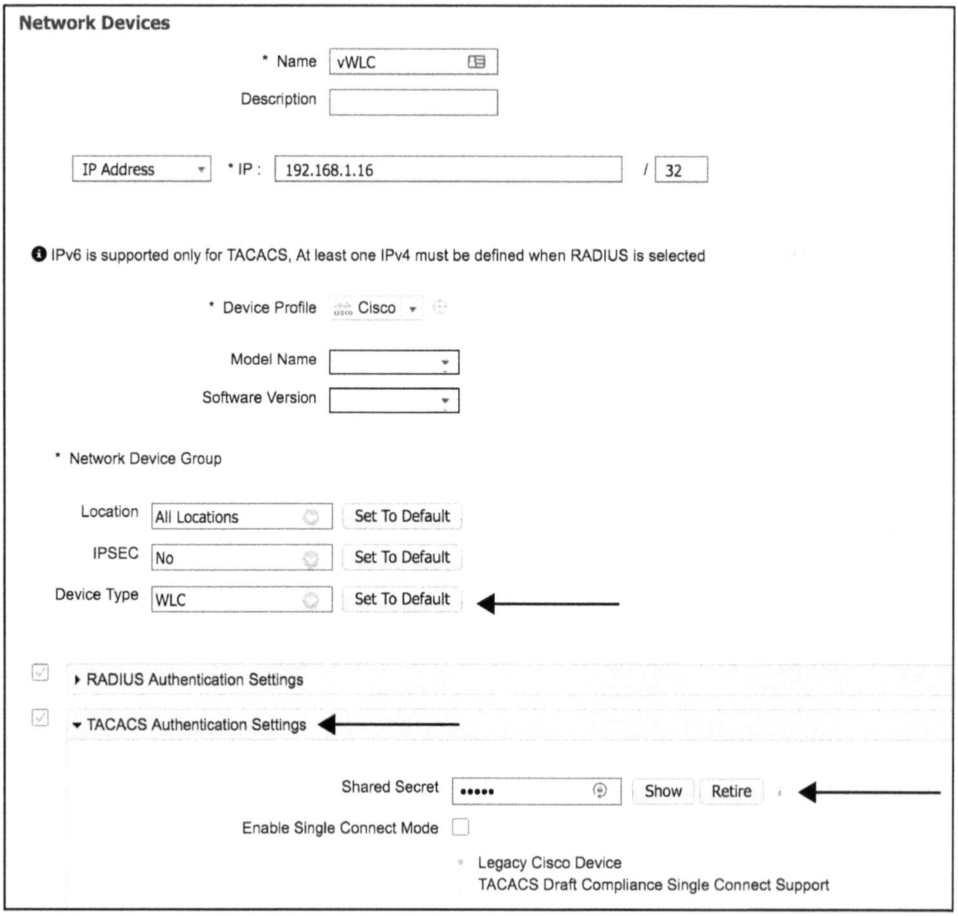

Figure 5-28   *WLC Added as Network Device in ISE*

Step 2.   Create Shell Profiles.

As discussed, Shell Profiles required for the WLC are different from those required for IOS or the ASA. For the purpose of this book, we will create two Shell Profiles: one for the Network Admins user group to allow them full access to the WLC, and one for the Network Ops user group to allow them access to the Monitoring menu only. These groups were created for previous examples.

To create the first Shell Profile, use the following steps:

a. Navigate to **Work Centers > Device Administration > Policy Elements > Results > TACACS Profiles**.

b. Click **Add**.

c. Enter **Network Admin WLC** in the Name field.

d. Select **WLC** from the Common Task Type drop-down list.

e. Click the **All** radio button.

f. Click **Save**.

Note   If you click the Raw View tab in the profile, you will notice the AV pair that will be sent is role1=ALL. This is the **role** AV pair that we discussed earlier.

Figure 5-29 shows the Shell Profile created by these steps.

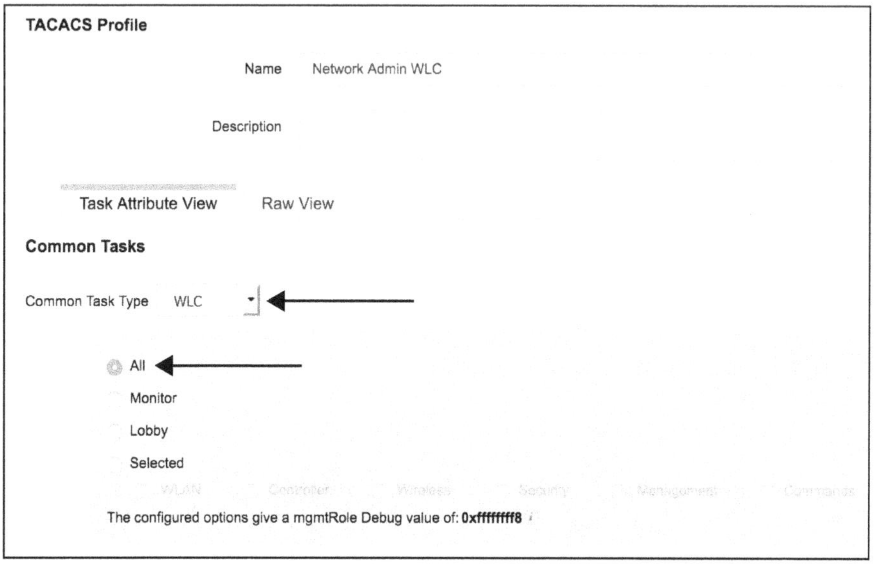

TACACS Profile

Name   Network Admin WLC

Description

Task Attribute View   Raw View

Common Tasks

Common Task Type   WLC

⊕ All

Monitor

Lobby

Selected

WLAN   Controller   Wireless   Security   Management   Commands

The configured options give a mgmtRole Debug value of: **0xffffffff8**

Figure 5-29   *Network Admin Shell Profile for WLC*

Similarly, the second Shell Profile can be created with the following steps:

a. Navigate to **Work Centers > Device Administration > Policy Elements > Results > TACACS Profiles.**

b. Click **Add.**

c. Enter **Network Ops WLC** in the Name field.

d. Select **WLC** from the Common Task Type drop-down list.

e. Click the **Monitor** radio button.

f. Click **Save.**

Note   If you click the Raw View tab in the profile, you will notice the AV pair that will be sent is role1=Monitor this time.

Figure 5-30 shows the Shell Profile created by these steps.

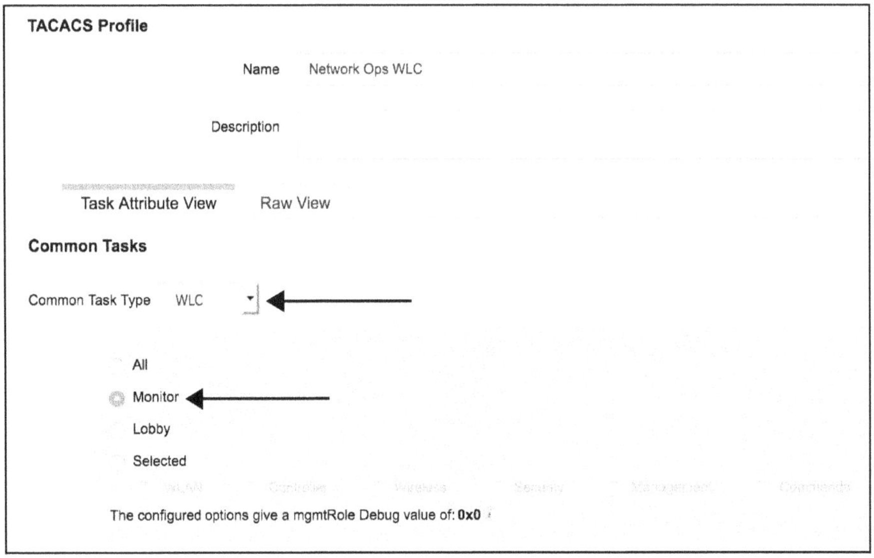

TACACS Profile

Name   Network Ops WLC

Description

Task Attribute View   Raw View

Common Tasks

Common Task Type   WLC

All

Monitor

Lobby

Selected

The configured options give a mgmtRole Debug value of: **0x0**

Figure 5-30   *Network Ops Shell Profile for WLC*

Step 3.   Create TACACS+ policy set, authentication policies, and authorization polices.

The steps to create TACACS+ policy set and authentication policies were discussed previously and will not be repeated here. When creating ISE policies, remember that the WLC will use a unique Shell Profile that cannot apply to other device types. Hence, you will need to either create a new policy set that matches requests from WLCs or create authorization rules that match those requests when using the Default policy set.

For example, if we want to use the Default policy set from our previous examples, we will need to add new authorization policies that match requests from the WLC. Because we want to create two policies—one for Network Admins and one for Network Ops—we will create two authorization policies using these steps:

a. Navigate to **Work Centers > Device Administration > Device Admin Policy Sets.**

b. Click **>** in the View column next for the Default policy.

c. Expand the **Authorization Policies** section.

d. Click the **gear icon** in the Actions column of the top rule.

e. Select **Insert New Row Above.**

f. Enter **Network Ops - WLC** in the Rule Name field.

g. Click **+** in the Conditions column.

h. Select **Click To Add Attribute** in the Editor section.

i. Select the fourth icon (Network device) in the window that opens.

j. Select the **Device Type** attribute.

k. Select **All Device Types#WLC** from the Attribute Value drop-down list.

l. Select **New** in the Editor section.

m. Select **Click To Add Attribute** in the Editor section.

n. Select the fourth icon (Identity group) in the window that opens.

o. Select the **Internal User:Identity Group** attribute.

p. Select **User Identity Groups:Network Ops** from the Attribute Value drop-down list.

q. Click **Use.**

r. Select **Network Ops WLC** from the Shell Profile drop-down list.

s. Click the **gear icon** in the last column of this new policy.

t. Select **Duplicate Above.**

u. Edit the name of the new rule to read **Network Admin - WLC.**

v. Select the **Conditions** column.

w. Delete the **User Identity Groups:Network Ops** selection in the Editor section.

x. Select **User Identity Groups:Network Admins** from the drop-down list.

y. Click **Use.**

> **z.** Select **Network Admin WLC** from the Shell Profile drop-down list.
>
> **aa.** Click **Save**.

Figure 5-31 shows the authorization rules created by the preceding steps. In the figure, note that the rules we created for IOS and the ASA still exist below the new rules created for the WLC. The Device Type condition in the new rules will match requests from any WLC in that NDG. All other requests will match the two old rules. In the new rules, one matches requests for users in the *Network Ops* identity group while the other matches the *Network Admins* identity group. Users belonging to the *Network Ops* group will get the **Monitor** role while those belonging to the *Network Admins* group will get the **All** role.

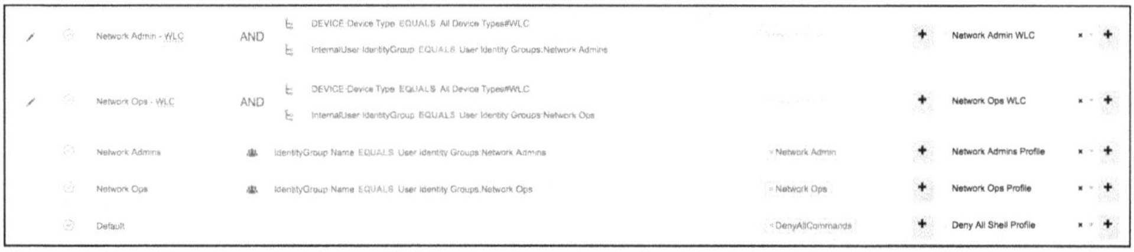

Figure 5-31 *Creating Authorization Policies for WLC in ISE*

Verification

Now that the WLC and ISE have been configured, it is time to verify the configuration. First, log in to the WLC with a user in the *Network Ops* group and click **Advanced** to bring up the main WLC menu. Navigate to **Commands > Reboot** and click **Save and Reboot**. Click **OK** on the prompt that appears. The WLC should display an "Authorization Failed. No sufficient privileges" error, as shown in Figure 5-32. This shows that the user in the *Network Ops* group does not have sufficient privileges to make any changes in the Commands menu. You will encounter the same error if you attempt to make changes in any other section.

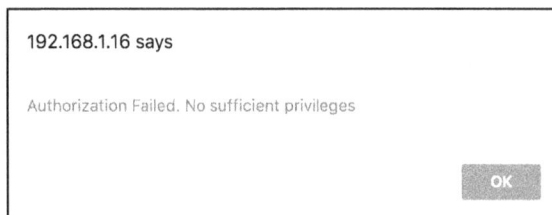

Figure 5-32 *Authorization Failed Message on WLC*

To further verify the configuration, log in to the WLC with a user in the *Network Admins* group and attempt to make any change. All changes should be accepted and applied by the WLC.

As a last verification step, navigate to **Operations > Reports > Device Administration > TACACS Command Accounting** on ISE. You will notice that any changes you made on the WLC are logged in this report as commands. Figure 5-33 shows an example.

① Username	Command	Command Arguments	ISE Node	Network Device Name
Username	Command	Command Arguments	ISE Node	Network Device Name
netadmin	snmp	version v3 enable	vISE	vWLC
netadmin	snmp	version v2c enable	vISE	vWLC
netadmin	snmp	version v1 disable	vISE	vWLC
netadmin	snmp	syscontact	vISE	vWLC
netadmin	snmp	syslocation USA	vISE	vWLC
netadmin	sysname	vWLC	vISE	vWLC

Figure 5-33 *ISE Command Accounting Report*

Using RADIUS for Device Administration

As discussed earlier, RADIUS also can be used for AAA of management sessions. Because RADIUS combines the authentication and authorization process, most devices that use RADIUS will require some form of a role or profile name to be sent in the authorization response. These roles often map to predefined policies, groups, or such on the device. We already saw an example of such authorization in the previous section with TACACS+ and the WLC where we configured ISE to send the **role** AV pair.

A large part of configuring RADIUS-based AAA for device administration is figuring out the configuration required on the network device and the AV pair it expects to enforce the desired access control. Every vendor implements this differently, so you may have to look for this information in device-specific guides or talk to the vendor's support team. Some vendors choose to use standard IETF-defined RADIUS attributes for this purpose, while others choose to use vendor-specific attributes. Cisco, for example, often uses vendor-specific attributes on most of its devices for RADIUS-based enforcement.

The ISE configuration, on the other hand, is relatively simple and requires everything that you are already familiar with—adding the device and creating authorization profiles, policy sets, authentication policies, and authorization policies.

In this section we will discuss two examples of using RADIUS for device administration. We will configure Cisco Firepower Management Center (FMC), Cisco Web Security Appliance (WSA), and Cisco Email Security Appliance (ESA) for RADIUS-based authentication with ISE.

RADIUS-Based Device Administration on Cisco FMC

Cisco FMC is one of the easiest devices to configure for RADIUS-based device administration AAA because it allows you to choose the AV pair that will be sent with authorization data. The FMC provides 11 predefined user roles, such as Administrator for full access, Access Admin for access to policies only, and Security Analyst (Read Only) for read-only access to events. The FMC also allows creation of custom roles, but the pre-defined roles are often enough.

When enabling authentication with RADIUS, you have to define the AV pair that maps to any of the roles. Generally, a standard RADIUS attribute such as Class (attribute 25) is used with a value that corresponds to the name of the role. When a user authenticates, the FMC will match the AV pairs in the RADIUS response to the configured values for the roles and apply the appropriate one. Based on the role granted, the FMC will only display the relevant menus on the UI.

In this section we will discuss the steps to configure the FMC and ISE for RADIUS authentication and role-based access. We will continue to use the *Network Admins* and *Network Ops* identity groups in ISE as examples for this section. The *Network Admins* group will be given full access to the FMC, while the *Network Ops* group will be given a read-only access to events.

Configuring the FMC

Configuring the FMC for RADIUS-based device administration access control requires adding the RADIUS server, defining the attribute mappings, and enabling external authentication. The steps to configure these are as follows:

Step 1. The FMC requires the RADIUS server to be added as an External Authentication Object. The object can be created as discussed in the steps that follow and shown in Figure 5-34:

a. In the FMC GUI, navigate to **System > Users > External Authentication**.

b. Click the **Add External Authentication Object** button.

c. Select **RADIUS** from the Authentication Method drop-down list.

d. Enter a name in the Name field.

e. Enter the hostname or IP address of an ISE PSN in the Host Name/IP Address field.

f. Enter the shared secret key in the RADIUS Secret Key field.

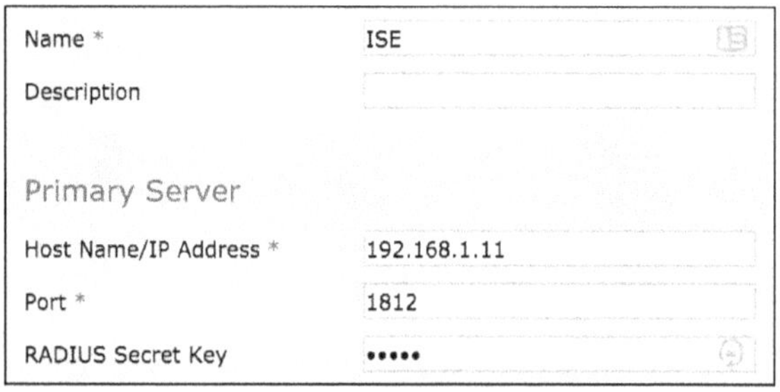

Name *	ISE
Description	
Primary Server	
Host Name/IP Address *	192.168.1.11
Port *	1812
RADIUS Secret Key	•••••

Figure 5-34 *Adding a RADIUS Object in FMC*

Step 2.   The External Authentication Object also needs to contain role-to-AV pair mappings. The object creation page contains a list of all available roles with a field next to each. You need to enter the AV pair that the FMC can expect for a role in the relevant field. For this example, we are using the RADIUS standard attribute Class with a value of the role name. We will only configure AV pairs for the Administrator and Security Analyst (Read Only) roles to match our example. The steps to configure them are provided in the steps that follow. Figure 5-35 also shows this configuration.

   a. Scroll down to the RADIUS-Specific Parameters section.

   b. In the Administrator field, type **Class=Administrator.**

   c. In the Security Analyst (Read Only) field, type **Class=SA-RO.**

   d. Click **Save.**

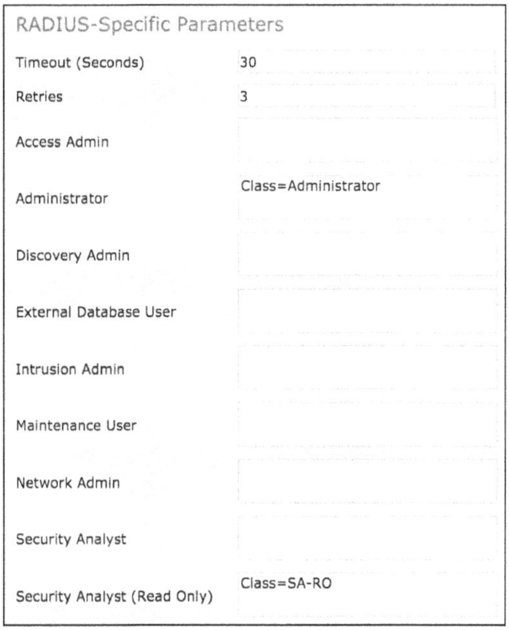

RADIUS-Specific Parameters	
Timeout (Seconds)	30
Retries	3
Access Admin	
Administrator	Class=Administrator
Discovery Admin	
External Database User	
Intrusion Admin	
Maintenance User	
Network Admin	
Security Analyst	
Security Analyst (Read Only)	Class=SA-RO

Figure 5-35   *Mapping AV Pairs to Roles in the RADIUS Object*

Note   You can select any RADIUS attribute to map to the roles. In this example, Class was selected because it can carry any string as a value and it is easy to configure ISE to send this attribute using one of the predefined options in an authorization profile. Another thing to note is that the example uses the value of SA-RO—an abbreviation instead of the whole name of the role. What this intends to show is that the value does not need to match the role name. Any attribute and value combination can be mapped to a role.

Step 3.   When the RADIUS object is created, it is disabled by default. The object needs to be enabled to allow the FMC to authenticate using RADIUS. Click the button in the Enabled column and then click **Save and Apply** to enable the object.

Configuring ISE

Because RADIUS policy sets, authentication policies, and authorization policies were extensively covered in the previous two chapters, we will not discuss those here again. Instead, this section discusses the authorization profiles that are needed to send the correct permissions to the FMC.

In response to an authentication request from the FMC, ISE needs to send only the attributes that were mapped to roles in the FMC. The authorization profiles will need to be configured to send the AV pair exactly as defined in the RADIUS object on the FMC. In our example, we used *Class=Administrator* and *Class=SA-RO* AV pairs to map to two roles. To create authorization profiles to send these AV pair, use the following steps:

Step 1.   In the ISE UI, navigate to **Policy > Policy Elements > Authorization > Authorization Profiles**.

Step 2.   Click **Add**.

Step 3.   Enter **Net Admins - Security Devices** in the Name field, as shown in Figure 5-36.

Step 4.   In the Common Tasks section, scroll down and check the **ASA VPN** check box.

Step 5.   Enter **Administrator** in the text box next to ASA VPN.

Note   The Common Task ASA VPN is used here because it maps to the Class attribute. If you look at the Attribute Details section, you will notice the *Class=Administrator* AV pair has been added. This is exactly what we need ISE to send to the FMC. Another way to send this attribute would be to select that attribute in the Advanced Attribute section and provide **Administrator** as its value. That will also result in the exact same thing.

Step 6.   Click **Save**.

Step 7.   Select the **Net Admins - Security Devices** profile.

Step 8.   Click **Duplicate**.

Step 9.   Edit the name of the profile to **Net Ops - Security Devices**, as shown in Figure 5-37.

Step 10.   Edit the value of the ASA VPN task to **SA-RO**.

Step 11.   Click **Save**.

Figures 5-36 and 5-37 show the two authorization profiles created by the preceding steps.

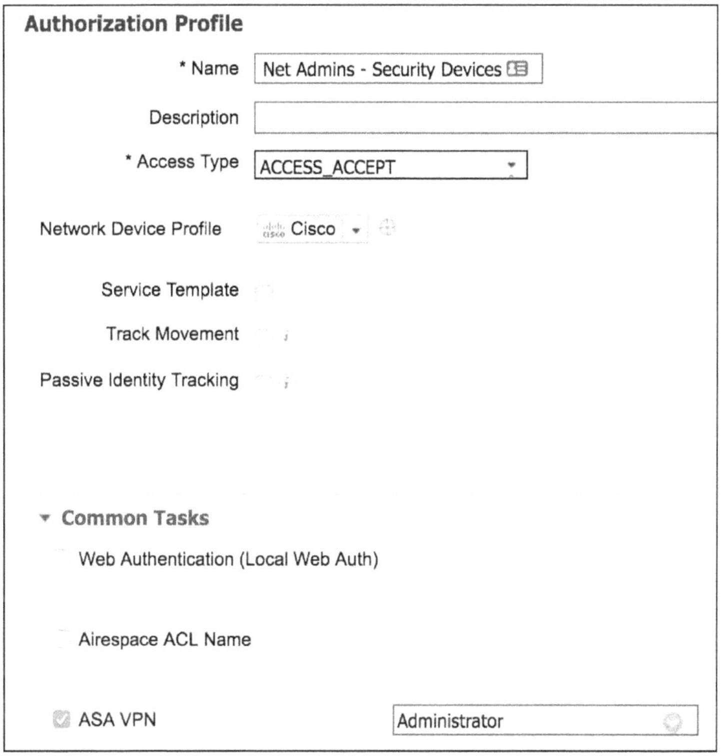

Authorization Profile

* Name	Net Admins - Security Devices
Description	
* Access Type	ACCESS_ACCEPT
Network Device Profile	Cisco
Service Template	
Track Movement	
Passive Identity Tracking	

▼ **Common Tasks**

Web Authentication (Local Web Auth)

Airespace ACL Name

☑ ASA VPN   Administrator

Figure 5-36   *Authorization Profile for Network Admins Group*

After creating the authorization profiles, they need to be applied to appropriate authorization policies. As mentioned earlier, we will not discuss the steps to create the policy set and configure authentication and authorization policies here again because they were covered in previous two chapters.

Figure 5-38 shows the policy set that will be used to verify configuration in the next section. This policy set matches requests coming from a device in the Security Devices NDG under the Device Type parent NDG and authenticates to the *Internal Users* database. (The FMC is added as a network device in the Security Devices NDG.) The authorization policies match on the user identity groups and apply the appropriate authorization policies.

Authorization Profile

* Name	Net Ops - Security Devices
Description	
* Access Type	ACCESS_ACCEPT
Network Device Profile	Cisco
Service Template	
Track Movement	
Passive Identity Tracking	

▾ **Common Tasks**

Web Authentication (Local Web Auth)

Airespace ACL Name

☑ ASA VPN   SA-RO

Figure 5-37 *Authorization Profile for Network Ops Group*

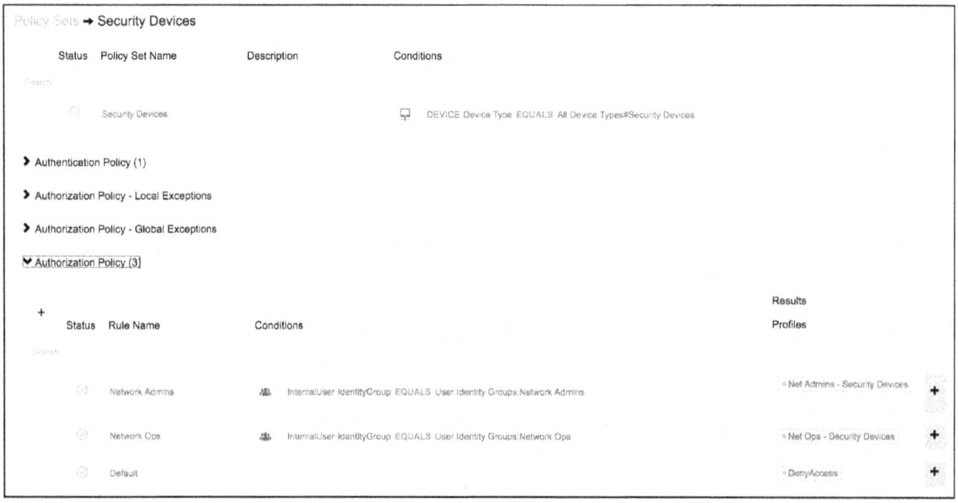

Policy Sets → Security Devices

Status	Policy Set Name	Description	Conditions
⊙	Security Devices		DEVICE Device Type EQUALS All Device Types#Security Devices

> Authentication Policy (1)

> Authorization Policy - Local Exceptions

> Authorization Policy - Global Exceptions

⌄ Authorization Policy (3)

	Status	Rule Name	Conditions	Results Profiles
	⊙	Network Admins	InternalUser IdentityGroup EQUALS User Identity Groups:Network Admins	Net Admins - Security Devices
	⊙	Network Ops	InternalUser IdentityGroup EQUALS User Identity Groups:Network Ops	Net Ops - Security Devices
	⊙	Default		DenyAccess

Figure 5-38 *Example Policy Set to Authenticate and Authorize Requests from FMC*

Verification

To verify the configuration, log in to the FMC UI with a user in the *Network Ops* group. You will notice that only the Overview and Analysis menus are available, as shown in Figure 5-39. This confirms that the *Security Analyst (Read Only)* role has been applied to the user as per the authorization profile.

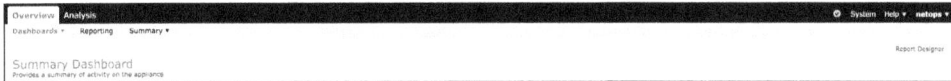

Figure 5-39   *Verifying Security Analyst (Read Only) Role on FMC*

Next, log in to the FMC with a user in the *Network Admins* group. This user should have access to all menus of the FMC and should be able to make any change in configuration.

RADIUS-Based Device Administration on Cisco WSA/ESA

Like the FMC, the Cisco WSA and ESA also support RADIUS-based device management access control and require RADIUS AV pairs to be mapped to locally defined roles in the RADIUS object. There are three key differences between the authentication and authorization implementation on the FMC and on the WSA and ESA:

- The WSA and ESA mandate the use of the RADIUS CLASS attribute, unlike the FMC that allows use of any attribute.

- The WSA and ESA have fixed roles and all users need to be mapped to one of the preexisting roles. The ESA has more predefined roles than the WSA.

- While the FMC hides menus based on the role applied, the WSA and ESA allow all roles to see most of the configuration. However, users with the Read-Only Operator role will not be able to commit changes.

Both the WSA and ESA are configured in exactly the same way, so this section will focus on the WSA and call out any differences that exist in the ESA.

In this section we will discuss the steps to configure the WSA and ISE for RADIUS authentication and role-based access. We will continue to use the *Network Admins* and *Network Ops* identity groups in ISE as examples. The *Network Admins* group will be given full access to the WSA, while the *Network Ops* group will be given read-only access to events.

Configuring the WSA

To configure the WSA for external authentication with RADIUS, use the following steps:

Step 1.   Navigate to **System Administration > Users.**

Step 2.   Click **Enable** in the External Authentication section.

Step 3.   Check the **Enable External Authentication** check box, as shown in Figure 5-40.

Step 4.   Select **RADIUS** from the Authentication Type drop-down list.

Step 5.   In the RADIUS Server Information section, enter the IP address or hostname of the ISE PSN.

Step 6.   In the same section, enter the shared secret key.

Step 7.   In the Group Mapping section, click the **Map Externally Authenticated Users To Multiple Local Roles** radio button.

Step 8.   In the same section, enter **Administrator** in the RADIUS CLASS Attribute field and select **Administrator** in the Role drop-down list.

Step 9.   In the same section, click **Add Row**.

Step 10. Enter **SA-RO** in the new RADIUS CLASS Attribute field and select **Read-Only Operator** from the drop-down list.

Step 11. Click **Submit**.

Step 12. Click **Commit Changes**.

Step 13. Click **Commit Changes** again on the next page.

Note   Remember that the value of the CLASS attribute does not need to match the name of the role. We used SA-RO for the Read-Only Operator role because that will allow us to reuse the authorization profiles that were created for the FMC earlier.

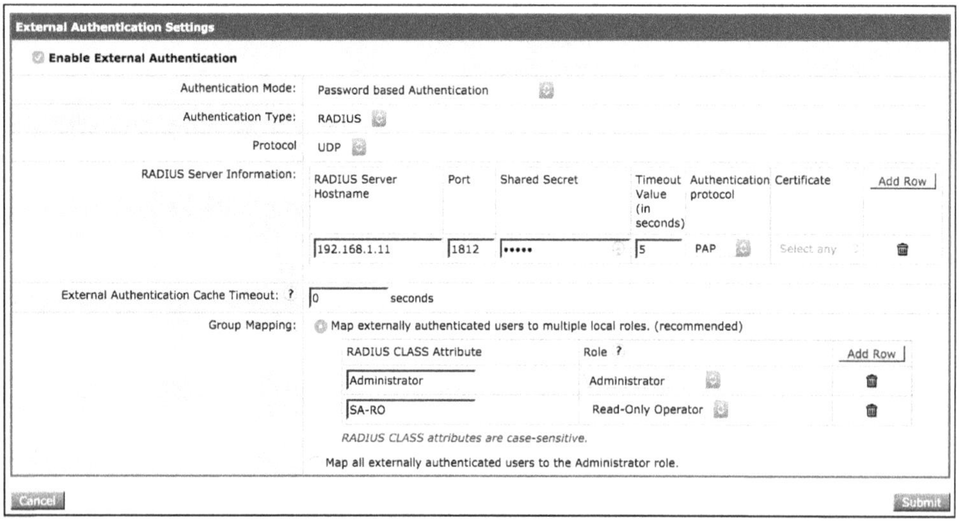

Figure 5-40   *Configuring WSA for External Authentication with RADIUS*

As soon as the changes are saved, the WSA will begin authenticating new requests to ISE. If the user is not found on ISE, it will fall back to the local users automatically.

Configuring ISE

Configuring ISE to authenticate requests from the WSA or ESA requires the usual steps of adding the device, creating authorization profiles, and creating authentication and authorization policies. By now, you should be very familiar with these steps from previous chapters.

You may have noticed when configuring the WSA that we used *Administrator* and *SA-RO* as values for the Class attribute to map to the Administrator and Read-Only Operator roles, respectively. The same attribute and values were used for the FMC. This allows us to use the authorization profiles and policy set that we used for the FMC to authenticate and authorize requests from the WSA and ESA. Refer back to Figures 5-36, 5-37, and 5-38 to review the authorization profiles and the policy set. The only thing we will need to do before testing is to add the WSA and ESA as network devices in ISE. Because the policy set shown in Figure 5-38 is matching on the *Security Devices* NDG, the WSA and ESA will need to be added to that NDG for this example.

Verification

To verify the configuration, log in to the WSA UI with a user in the *Network Ops* group. You will notice that if you make a configuration change and then attempt to commit it, the WSA throws an error as shown in Figure 5-41. This confirms that the *Read-Only Operator* role has been applied to the user as per the authorization profile.

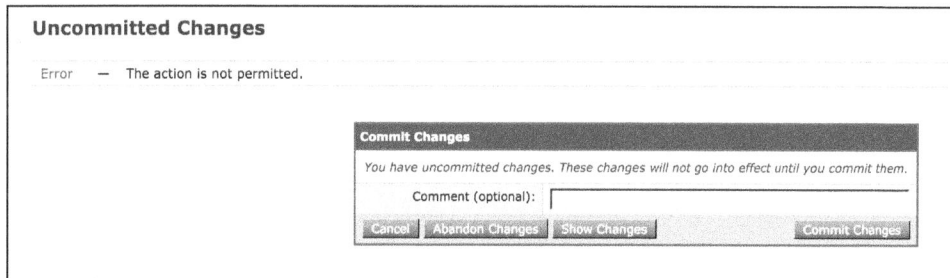

Uncommitted Changes

Error — The action is not permitted.

Commit Changes

You have uncommitted changes. These changes will not go into effect until you commit them.

Comment (optional):

Cancel   Abandon Changes   Show Changes   Commit Changes

Figure 5-41 *Read-Only Access Verification on WSA*

Next, log in to the WSA with a user in the *Network Admins* group. This user should have access to all menus of the FMC and should be able to make any changes in configuration and commit them.

Summary

Security of network devices is as important as the security of the network itself. Access to the network device should be strictly controlled and access should be tailored to the job role of the user. Most network devices allow centralized access management using RADIUS or TACACS+. The choice of protocol depends on what is supported on the device and the required security controls. If multiple authorization requests are needed within the same session, then TACACS+ should be the choice of protocol.

This chapter covered specific examples of configuring various devices such as Cisco IOS-based routers and switches, ASA, WLC, FMC, WSA, and ESA for AAA with ISE. You also learned how to create various policy elements and policies on ISE to respond to AAA requests from these devices.

Spread the Love!

Chapter 6

Sharing the Context

Because Cisco Identify Services Engine (ISE) is positioned to know exactly who and what is on the network at any given time, as well as assign different levels of access and context assignments with security group tags, it is the perfect security tool to be at the center of a security ecosystem.

There are so many tools that may exist within your "security toolbox": firewalls, next-generation firewalls (NGFWs), intrusion prevention systems (IPSs), NG-IPSs, security information and event management (SIEM) systems, secure web gateways, threat defense tools, vulnerability assessment scanners, mobile device managers, and more. Most of these tools do not know the identity of the user, only the identity of the endpoint. These other tools can be made even more valuable by integrating into a full security ecosystem with ISE.

Wouldn't the reporting in the SIEM be more valuable if it showed which user was involved in the security event, instead of only the IP address or MAC address? What about when your intrusion prevention tools or threat defense solutions identify malicious activity on the network? Wouldn't it be great if they could trigger something that would change the way the endpoint was treated on the network? With a single "trigger," the endpoint's level of network access could be changed, the endpoint's traffic could be inspected deeper as it passes through a Cisco Adaptive Security Appliance (ASA), the Cisco Web Security Appliance (WSA) can apply a different SSL decryption policy, and so much more.

You've already read about ISE integrating with mobile device managers (MDMs) and a little bit on how ISE can provide passive identities to ecosystem partners through technologies like pxGrid, but it can also provide the single point of policy control for threat containment and context setting.

The Many Integration Types of the Ecosystem

An *integration* might be ISE sharing data outbound, or it may be ISE steering traffic toward another solution. The integration method could be with ISE receiving information inbound for use within ISE's own network access policies, or even ISE brokering data exchange between other members of the security system.

MDM Integration

In Chapter 4, "Extending Network Access with ISE," you read about BYOD and the integration between ISE and mobile device management solutions. That integration is twofold: ISE provides the redirection to the MDM service for onboarding, but the MDM service is also able to provide "context-in" to ISE. In other words, the MDM service tells ISE about the mobile endpoints, the endpoint's compliance with the security policies set in the MDM (macro-level compliance), the status of encryption or pin lock, and more (micro-level compliance).

This integration uses a specific bidirectional application programming interface (API) between ISE and the MDM solution (cloud service or appliance). This API is unique and created just for MDM integration.

Note   Thanks to industry marketing, endpoint device management platforms may be referred to as Mobile Device Manager (MDM), Unified Endpoint Management (UEM) platforms, or even an Enterprise Mobility Management (EMM) platform. For the purposes of this book, the term MDM is leveraged to cover all the marketing acronyms referring to endpoint device managers.

Rapid Threat Containment

MDM is one of the first and most common integration types for ISE. In true Cisco marketing fashion, this next integration type, Rapid Threat Containment, has gone through several different names and marketing initiatives.

There was a feature added back in ISE 1.1 called *Endpoint Protection Services (EPS)*. EPS provided an API allowing other applications to initiate three actions against an endpoint based on IP address or MAC address:

- **Quarantine:** The quarantine action set the binary flag on the endpoint record to "true," added the endpoint to a list of quarantined endpoints, and allowed the administrator to create authorization policies that used that assignment to assign a different level of network access.

- **Unquarantine:** Removed the endpoint from the list of quarantined endpoints and cleared the binary flag.

- **Shutdown:** Was supposed to send a Change of Authorization (CoA) terminate to the network and shut down the port on the network switch.

Note   This option exists in the API, but it is not exposed to the policy and is therefore not usable.

Many of the first integrations with ISE used EPS, including the original integration with Lancope StealthWatch (now Cisco Stealthwatch), where an endpoint was quarantined from the StealthWatch user interface.

Figure 6-1 illustrates a flow with Stealthwatch initiating an EPS quarantine.

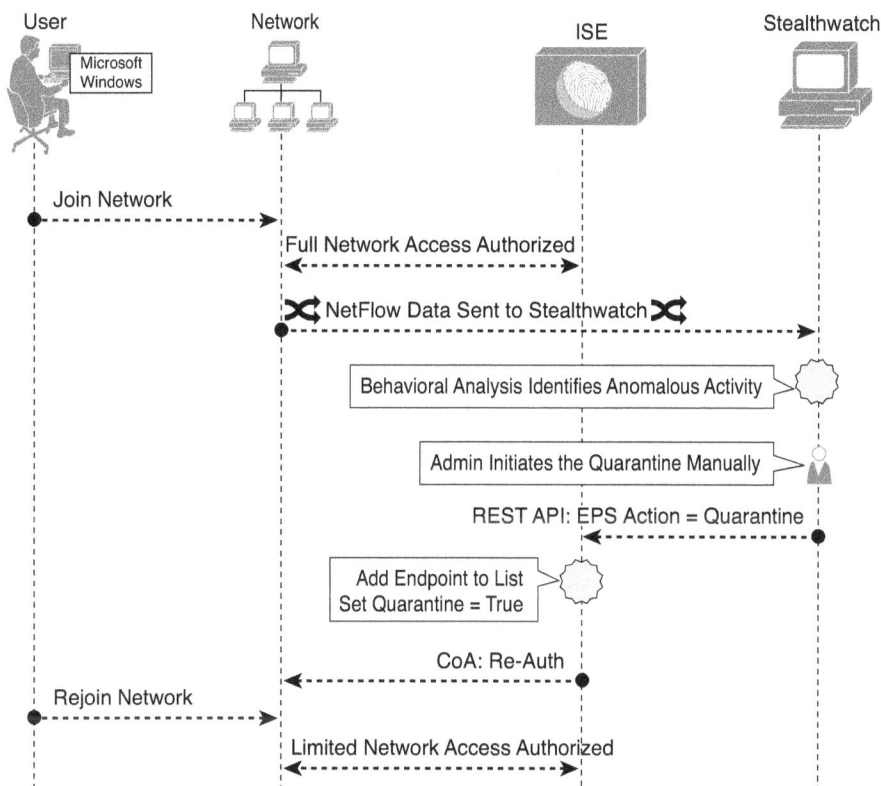

Figure 6-1   *Stealthwatch to ISE: EPS Quarantine*

The flow illustrated in Figure 6-1 shows an endpoint being admitted to the network with full access. The Stealthwatch admin initiates a quarantine, and Stealthwatch connects to ISE using the EPS REST API, telling ISE to quarantine the endpoint with the specific IP address.

ISE then adds the endpoint to the EPS list and sets the flag on the endpoint object and sends a CoA to the network.

When the new access request comes in, a rule created with the EPSStatus condition will be matched. Figure 6-2 shows that condition.

Figure 6-2   *EPSStatus Authorization Condition*

The resulting network authorization may provide for limited access, or even set a new Security Group Tag (SGT) that can be acted upon differently at miscellaneous points in the network, such as the Web Security Appliance.

Well, ultimately EPS was just too rigid. It provided for only a single actionable classification (Quarantine). More flexibility was needed to provide many different options, but also to be integrated into this new-fangled context-sharing technology that Cisco was creating named pxGrid. So, it needed to evolve into "EPS 2.0" or something like it.

So, ISE 1.3 introduced something new named Adaptive Network Control (ANC), which was a huge step forward by simply renaming EPS to ANC. Okay, hopefully the sarcasm was obvious there.

ISE 1.4 actually added new functionality to ANC. While still supporting the old EPS API calls for backward-compatibility purposes, it also added a new API with different labels available, including the ability to create your own label.

ISE refers to these labels as ANC "policies," but there is no policy to them whatsoever. An ANC policy is a tag or a label that gets assigned to an endpoint object and can be used in the authorization policy to invoke some action, such as changing the authorization level and assigning a new SGT.

Although you can add many different labels, there are only three choices for ANC policies: Quarantine, Shut Down, and Port Bounce—which determines the CoA type used when the label is applied to the endpoint.

To create an ANC policy (a.k.a. label), navigate to **Operations > Adaptive Network Control > Policy List** and click **Add**. Figure 6-3 shows the resulting page with the Action drop-down menu open.

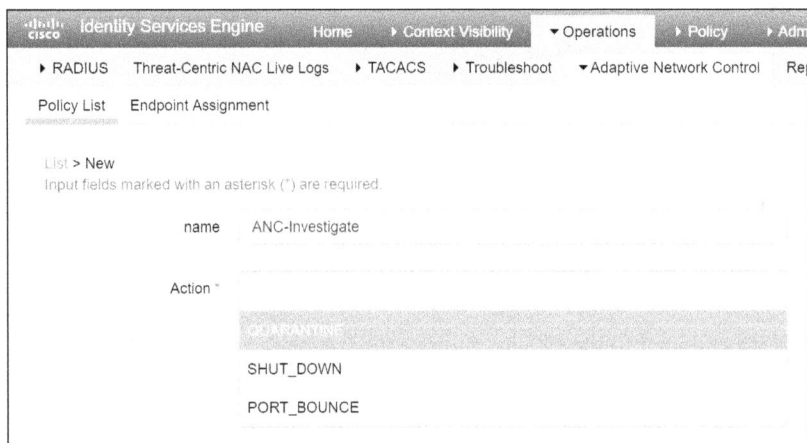

Figure 6-3   *Adding an ANC Policy*

You can create multiple ANC policies, and each policy may contain one or more actions. Each ANC policy can be associated to a different authorization. For example, you can end up with ANC policies such as:

- Investigate

- Phasers on Stun

- Eradicate

- Nuke from Orbit

In addition to a much more flexible approach to classification, or as Cisco's legendary Paul Forbes would call it, "flexible name spaces," ANC also integrates tightly with pxGrid, allowing pxGrid subscribers to trigger the ANC action within the pxGrid connection, not through the point API of the past.

So now you have Endpoint Protection Services which was renamed to Adaptive Network Control. Then Adaptive Network Control gets new functionality in ISE 1.4. Then Cisco security marketing gets involved and comes up with a new naming convention to refer to the entire integrated security system where any Cisco security product may take action through another Cisco security product.

That name is Rapid Threat Containment. You have solutions like: Rapid Threat Containment with Cisco Stealthwatch and the Identity Services Engine and Rapid Threat Containment with Cisco Firepower Management Center and Identity Services Engine.

While ISE is often the center of a security ecosystem, the Rapid Threat Containment portfolio includes more than just integrations with ISE. There are solutions like Rapid Threat Containment with Firepower Management Center and Cisco Stealthwatch, Firepower and Cisco Tetration, and many more. Actions taken using Cisco Threat Response are also part of the Rapid Threat Containment umbrella (no pun intended).

Crystal clear, right?

Cisco's platform eXchange Grid (pxGrid)

Now that you are thoroughly confused about the marketing term "Rapid Threat Containment", let's clear up one thing. Rapid Threat Containment may leverage pxGrid for the integration between two or more Cisco security products, but pxGrid is not a requirement. Many of those integrations are handled by API's or other connection types.

What is this pxGrid thing that we keep talking about?

pxGrid is Cisco's premier publish and subscribe (pub/sub) communication bus that was designed from the ground up to be a scalable, secure data sharing system.

Like most other next-generation AAA solutions, ISE originally started sharing information through the use of APIs. It was quickly recognized that point APIs would not scale to the level of data that needed to be shared and the scale of which it was requested.

Cisco went down the path of a pub/sub bus, similar to the way Cisco Unified Communications Manager (formerly known as Call Manager) and Cisco Jabber work. A *controller* keeps track of all the topics that exist. A *topic* is a list of information that is available. A topic might be session data of who and what is on the network, or it might be a list of vulnerable endpoints and the list of those vulnerabilities.

pxGrid participants can subscribe to any topic of interest and be notified when there is data to be retrieved. Those participants are known as *subscribers*. The true source of the data can be any other pxGrid participant, known as *publishers*. A publisher registers the topic with the controller, who performs the authorization for each subscriber to retrieve the data from the miscellaneous publishers.

Figure 6-4 shows the standard Cisco drawing that is often used to explain pxGrid. In this illustration, you see many different types of products, each of which has different information to publish and needs information from one of the other products.

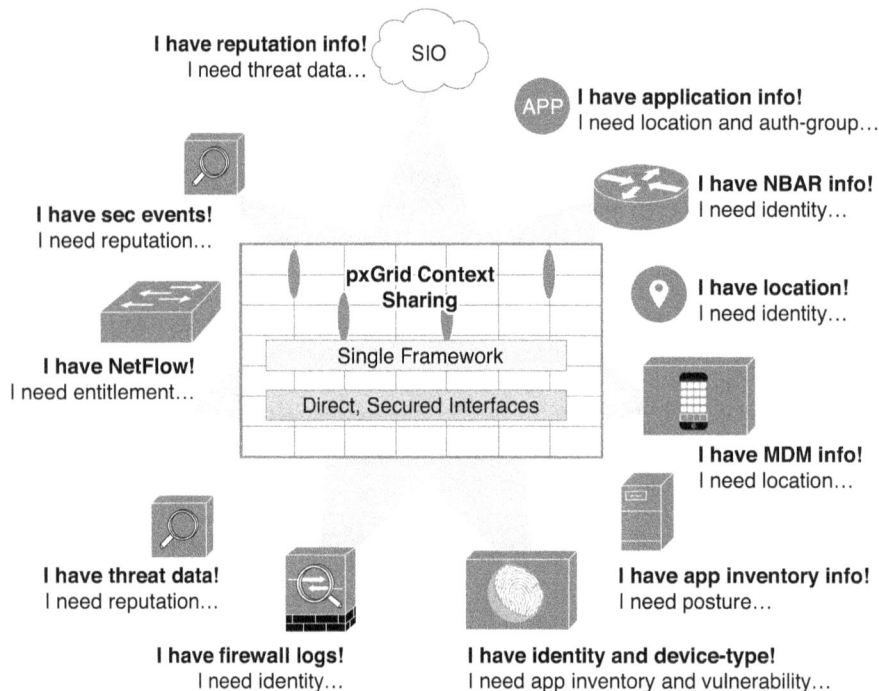

Figure 6-4   *Standard Cisco pxGrid Illustration*

pxGrid was initially added to ISE in version 1.3, so it's been around for a while now and has an ecosystem of partner applications that continue to grow at a very rapid pace.

ISE 2.2 made great strides in enhancing pxGrid. Most of the pxGrid-related enhancements are around ease of use, making it even easier to configure and maintain. ISE 2.2 also added more information into ISE's pxGrid topics for consumption by the subscribers. A specific example of additional information that was added to pxGrid topics in ISE version 2.2 is the list of groups that each active user is a member of; and that list was shared within the same topic(s) that was used in previous ISE versions, enabling backward compatibility seamlessly.

pxGrid in Depth

pxGrid version 1 was designed by extending the Extensible Messaging and Presence Protocol (XMPP), which is also the communication protocol used by Jabber. In fact, the pxGrid controller itself is a modified Jabber Extensible Communications Platform (XCP) server. (For more on XMPP, see https://xmpp.org.)

The XCP needs a client that knows how to communicate with it. Cisco DevNet partners can create applications that use the pxGrid common library (GCL) to join the pxGrid controller without having to write their own client from scratch.

Beginning in ISE version 2.3, ISE added a modernized WebSocket-based interface to pxGrid, to make it easier to integrate with. DevNet partners no longer are required to integrate a Java or C library into their application; they can use common Representational State Transfer (REST) connections instead.

No matter what the version, always remember that pxGrid is made up of three main components: a controller, publishers, and subscribers. Figure 6-5 is a basic drawing to illustrate this with products.

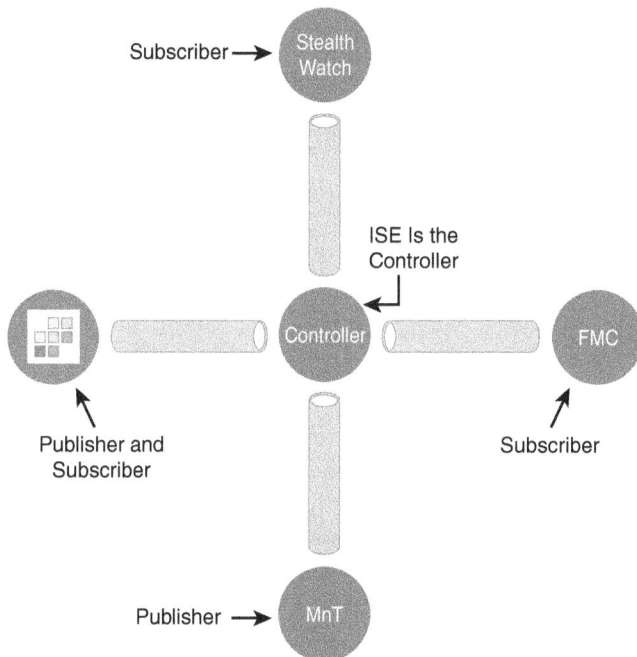

Figure 6-5 *Sample pxGrid Illustration*

pxGrid in Action

pxGrid uses secure communication between the participants, and therefore certificates are of great importance to the success and ease of your deployment. Every participant must trust the controller, and the controller must trust each of the participants.

Examining Figure 6-5 again, the Cisco Firepower Management Center (FMC) will need to speak to the pxGrid controller to learn of the topics that exist and who has published those topics, but then also speak directly to the MnT node to perform bulk downloads of the published session data. If the FMC were to trust the pxGrid controller's certificate but not the MnT's certificate, then the communication would ultimately fail.

Figure 6-6 illustrates this concept. You end up needing a full mesh of trust between pxGrid participants. Each participant must trust the controller as well as each other participant.

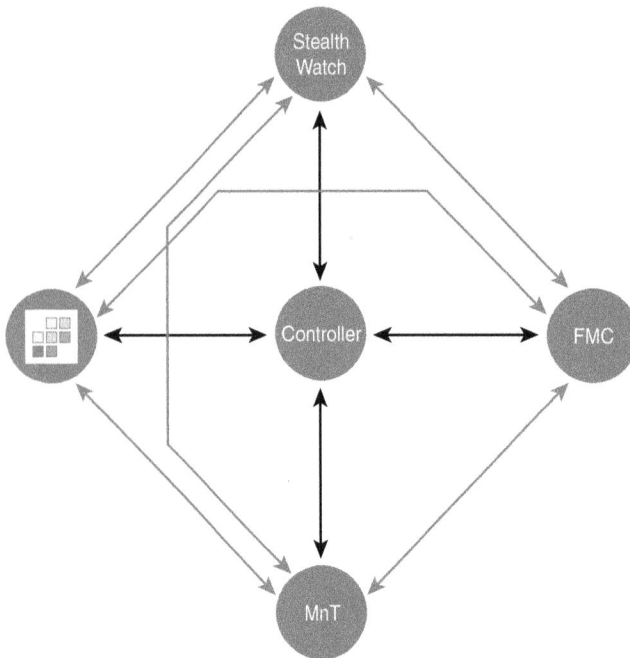

Figure 6-6 *Full Mesh of Trust*

Based on a lot of deployment experience, the resulting best practice is to always use the same certificate authority (CA) to issue the pxGrid certificates for each of the participants. To make that even easier, ISE's built-in CA was enhanced to issue pxGrid certificates in addition to endpoint certificates beginning with ISE version 2.1. In addition to the enhancement to the CA, APIs were added to automate the certificate enrollment from a pxGrid ecosystem partner—these are the exact same APIs and CA that Cisco's flagship DNA Center product uses to integrate with ISE.

Figure 6-7 illustrates a single CA issuing the certificates to all the participants.

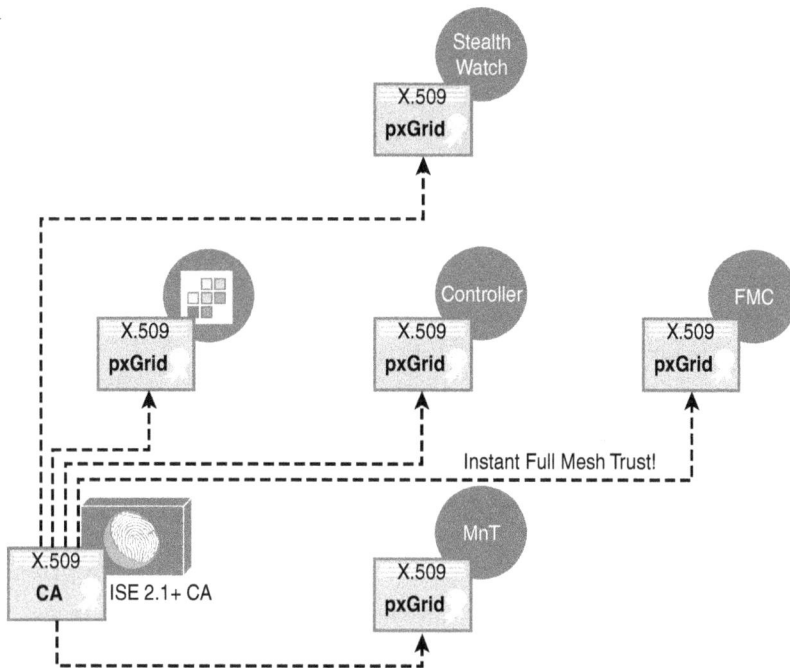

Figure 6-7 *ISE CA Issuing the pxGrid Certificates to All Participants*

Context-In

pxGrid not only shares context from ISE (referred to as *context-out*) but also is used for sharing information between external systems. As of ISE version 2.4, ISE is also able to receive information through pxGrid to help ISE with its own profiling policies. This is referred to as *context-in*.

In Chapter 3, "Beyond Basic Network Access Control," you learned about profiling and the different probes that ISE can use. One of those probes that was introduced in ISE version 2.4 is the pxGrid probe, which is used to learn profiling data about endpoints through pxGrid context-in.

The pxGrid profiling probe was first used with the Cisco Industrial Network Director (IND), which communicates with industrial switches and Internet of Things (IoT) security devices, collecting detailed information about the connected IoT devices.

IND v1.3 adds a pxGrid publisher interface to communicate IoT attributes to ISE, which are leveraged in profiling, as illustrated in Figure 6-8.

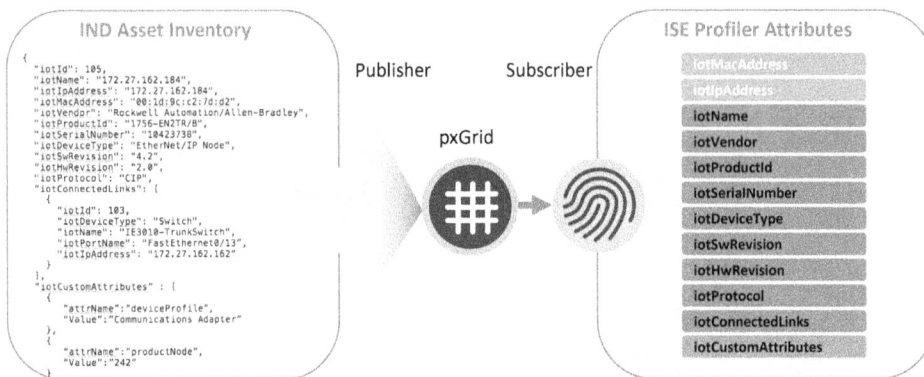

Figure 6-8 *Industrial Network Director Using ISE pxGrid Probe*

Configuring ISE for pxGrid

The pxGrid user interface is located under **Administration > pxGrid Services.** By default, the pxGrid services will not be enabled on any ISE node, and the following message will be displayed:

```
In order to navigate to the pxGrid Services page, pxGrid persona must
be enabled on at least one node in the ISE deployment. Please click on
this link to be redirected to the Deployment page.
```

You need to enable pxGrid on at least one of the policy services nodes in your deployment, but before enabling pxGrid on any of the ISE nodes in the deployment, it's best to ensure that each node in the ISE cube has a pxGrid certificate signed by the same certificate authority.

Beginning in ISE 2.2, each node's pxGrid certificate will be signed automatically by the internal CA. Naturally, you can replace that certificate with one from an external CA of your choosing, but the default certificate will use the internal CA in an attempt to simplify the setup and follow best practices. Truly, recommended practice dictates that you use the CA built into ISE for all pxGrid communications to keep things easy and working well. The steps are as follows:

Step 1.   Navigate to **Administration > System > Certificates**, as shown in Figure 6-9.

Step 2.   Select the pxGrid certificate of one of the nodes, by selecting the checkbook on the left end of the row.

Step 3.   Click **View.**

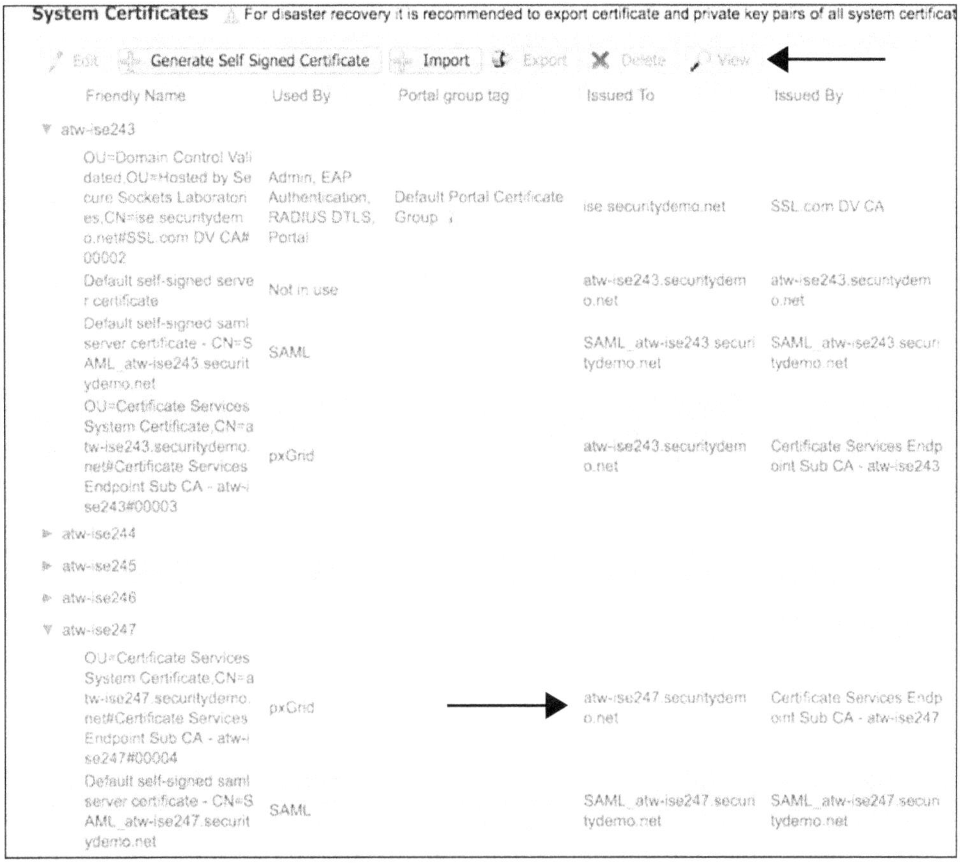

Figure 6-9 *Viewing a pxGrid Certificate*

Step 4.   Check that the root signer of the certificate is the primary PAN of the ISE cube (the root CA), as shown in Figure 6-10.

Once you're sure the certificates in use are all issued by the same PKI, then it's time to enable them. Experienced-based recommendation is to have a pxGrid certificate on every single node in the ISE deployment, even if the node will not run the pxGrid controller function.

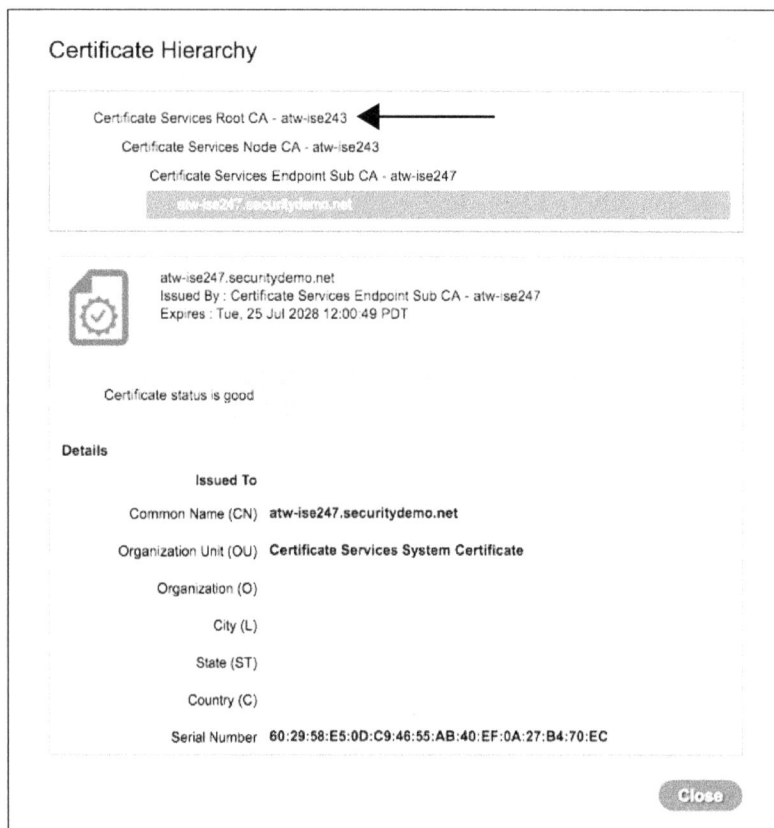

Figure 6-10 *Checking the Root Signer of Certificate in Certificate Hierarchy*

Note   Beginning in ISE version 2.2, all pxGrid communications occur within the secure pxGrid channel; in other words, all communication occurs leveraging the pxGrid certificate of the ISE node. In prior versions, all bulk downloads from the MnT node occurred using the admin certificate, not the pxGrid certificate. This caused many TAC cases and confusion and needed to change. If you are implementing pxGrid on any ISE version less than ISE 2.2, you must ensure that the participant trusts the issuing CA of the admin certificate as well as the pxGrid certificate.

To enable pxGrid on a PSN, follow these steps:

Step 1.   Navigate to **Administration > System > Deployment**.

Step 2.   The pxGrid controller function must run on a PSN. Select one of the PSNs from the list.

Step 3.   Check the **pxGrid** check box, as shown in Figure 6-11.

Step 4.   Click **Save**.

Figure 6-11   *Enabling the pxGrid Controller Function*

This enables the pxGrid controller function on the PSN. You may have up to two pxGrid controllers per ISE cube to provide redundancy.

Once the pxGrid services are all up and running, the PAN and MnT will automatically register and publish their respective topics into the grid, as shown in Figure 6-12.

Notice in Figure 6-12 the way the topics are listed under the pxGrid participant, as well as the role that node plays with the topic (Pub or Sub).

By default, only ISE nodes will be registered automatically; all others require approval, or they require you to enable auto-registration.

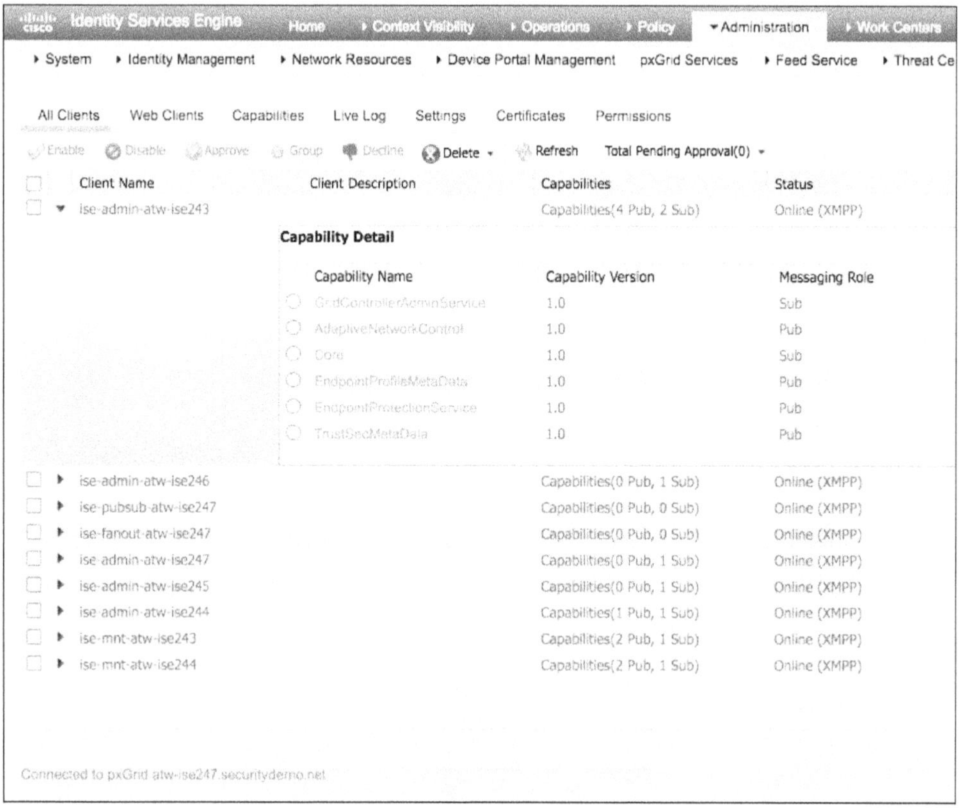

Figure 6-12   *Default pxGrid Services after Enabling*

Configuring pxGrid Participants

There are many different subscribers and publishers that can participate in the ecosystem with pxGrid. Each one will use the information in its own way, and the integration UI is bound to be unique per product, but the basic requirements and configuration steps will always remain the same:

Step 1.   Trust the ISE certificate authority.

Step 2.   Install a pxGrid certificate for its own identity.

Step 3.   Configure the IP or FQDN of the pxGrid controller.

For the most part, that is all that you really need to do on each participant. Some will make things easier than others. Let's take a look at configuring some of the main pxGrid participants: Cisco Firepower Management Center, Cisco Stealthwatch, and Cisco Web Security Appliance.

Configuring Firepower Management Center for Identity with pxGrid

The Cisco Firepower Management Center (FMC) is the enterprise-class device manager and security monitoring tool for Cisco's Firepower line of NGFWs and NGIPSs, described in detail in Chapter 5, "Next-Gen Firewalls," of *Integrated Security Technologies and Solutions -Volume I*, which also covers the Firepower Device Manger (FDM) used for individual device management.

The FMC has had pxGrid integration with ISE for a while, but version 6.2 added an even better integration, with the ability to use the TrustSec data independent of user identities. The FMC can use context information provided by pxGrid, such as endpoint profiles, TrustSec tags, and both passive and active user identities.

Much like the FMC, the FDM solution is also capable of integrating with ISE using pxGrid, but this section is only focused on the FMC integration.

The Firepower Management Center leverages pxGrid to learn the context of who and what is on the network and the mapping of those devices to IP addresses. However, the FMC leverages the LDAP-based realms to learn about what users and groups exist in Active Director for the creation of access policy.

We will begin by configuring the pxGrid integration, and then follow up with the realm configuration.

Configuring Firepower Management Center for pxGrid

Before configuring pxGrid on the FMC, generate a pxGrid certificate for the FMC to use. Beginning with ISE 2.2, an administrator can download the CA's certificates and generate certificates directly from the pxGrid Services user interface.

To generate a pxGrid certificate for the FMC:

Step 1.   Navigate to **Administration > pxGrid Services > Certificates**, as shown in Figure 6-13.

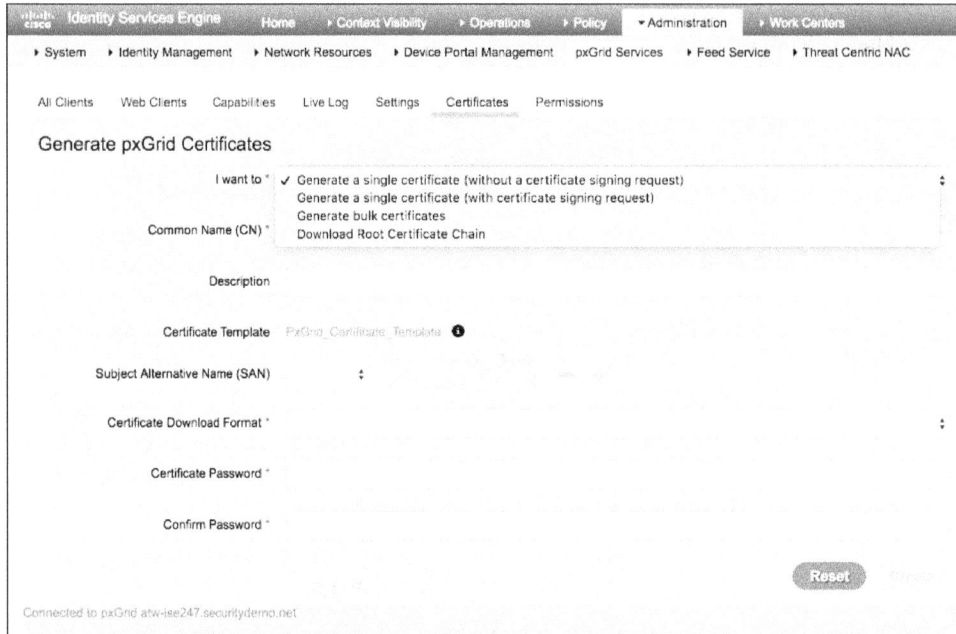

Figure 6-13   *Generating a pxGrid Certificate for the FMC*

Examining Figure 6-13, from this screen you can generate a single certificate, sign a certificate signing request (CSR), generate bulk certificates from a CSV file, or download the certificate authority chain for import into the trust store of the pxGrid participant. For the FMC, we need to generate a certificate-key pair.

Step 2.   Select **Generate a single certificate (without a certificate signing request)**.

Step 3.   In the Common Name (CN) field, enter a common name for the subject of your certificate.

The CN is normally the FQDN of the host (e.g., atw-fmc.securitydemo.net). However, a common practice is to add a prefix to your CN, such as *pxGrid-*, which will help you avoid installation errors that can sometimes occur when you try to install more than one certificate with the same FQDN.

Step 4.   In the Subject Alternative Name (SAN) spin box, add a SAN, if needed.

If you use anything other than the true FQDN for the device, then you need to enter a SAN in this field. Per RFC 6125, anytime you use a SAN, it must also contain the CN. Add an entry for the FQDN of the host. Adding a SAN for the IP address is helpful, just in case one of the pxGrid peers is sent to the host via the IP address instead of the FQDN.

Step 5.   In the Certificate Download Format spin box, choose **Certificate in Privacy Enhanced Electronic Mail (PEM) format, key in PKCS8 PEM format.**

All options will include the internal CA's certificates, for the entire PKI hierarchy. There is also an option to download it as a PKCS12 chain file, where the public certificate + private key + signing chain are all in a single file. For the FMC, the download format needs to be separate PEM files, not the PKCS12 chain.

Step 6.   In the Certificate Password field, add a password for the private key (and then confirm it).

ISE will never issue private keys without a password to encrypt the key.

Step 7.   Click **Create** and download the resulting ZIP file.

Figure 6-14 shows the completed certificate form, and Figure 6-15 shows the contents of the ZIP file.

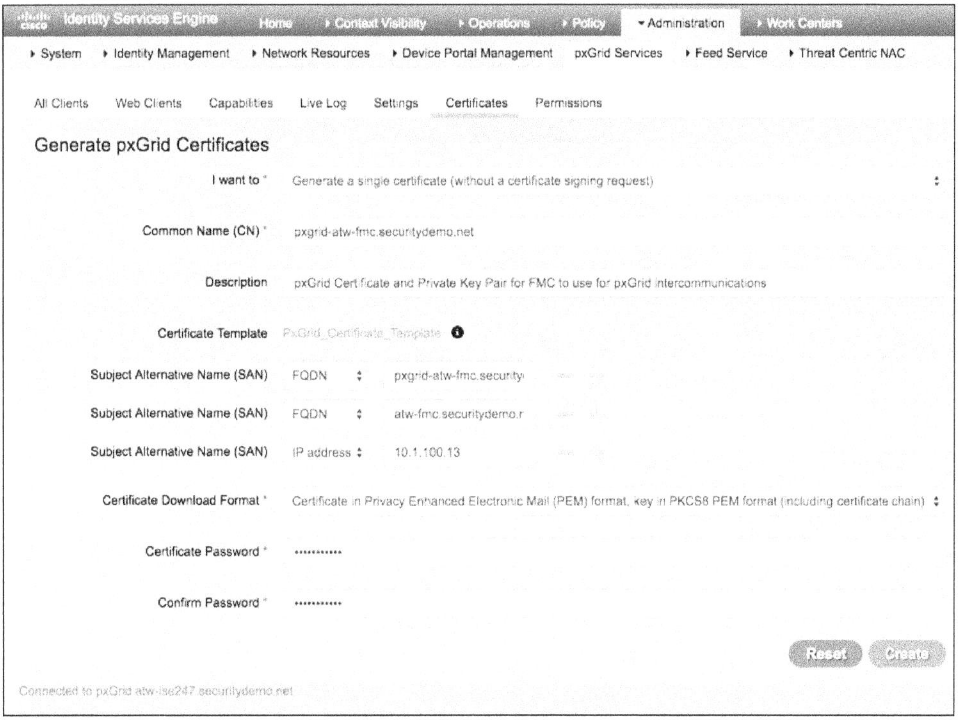

Figure 6-14   *Completed Certificate Form*

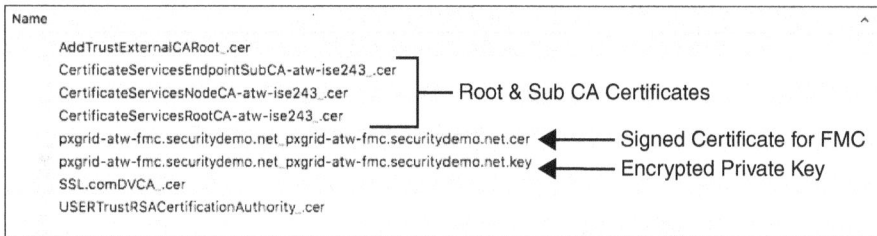

Figure 6-15   *Contents of the Resulting ZIP File*

Examining Figure 6-15, the ZIP file contains the signed certificate, the encrypted private key, and all the signing certificates in the PKI hierarchy for the issued certificate. Additionally, the signing certificates in the PKI hierarchy for the admin certificate are also included for good measure. Beginning with ISE 2.2, they should not be required, but are included in the ZIP file anyway.

Now you have all the required certificates and the private key for the FMC. To configure pxGrid on the FMC:

Step 1.   Navigate to **System > Integration > Identity Sources**, as shown in Figure 6-16.

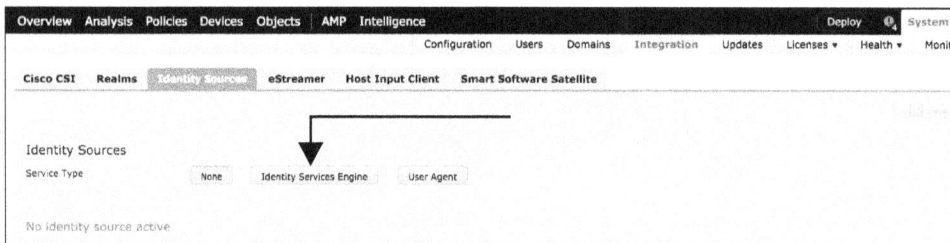

Figure 6-16   *FMC Identity Sources*

Step 2.   Click the **Identity Services Engine** button.

Step 3.   In the Primary Host Name/IP Address field, enter the FQDN or IP address of the primary pxGrid controller.

Step 4.   If there is a secondary controller, add its FQDN or IP address in the Secondary Host Name/IP Address field.

Step 5.   Click the green **+** button to the right of the pxGrid Server CA field to add the ISE root CA certificate.

This adds the root CA certificate to the list of trusted CAs in the FMC. In the Name field, give the certificate a name that makes sense to you, similar to what you see in Figure 6-17.

Step 6.   Click **Browse** and select the root CA certificate from the expanded ZIP file you downloaded earlier, as shown in Figure 6-17.

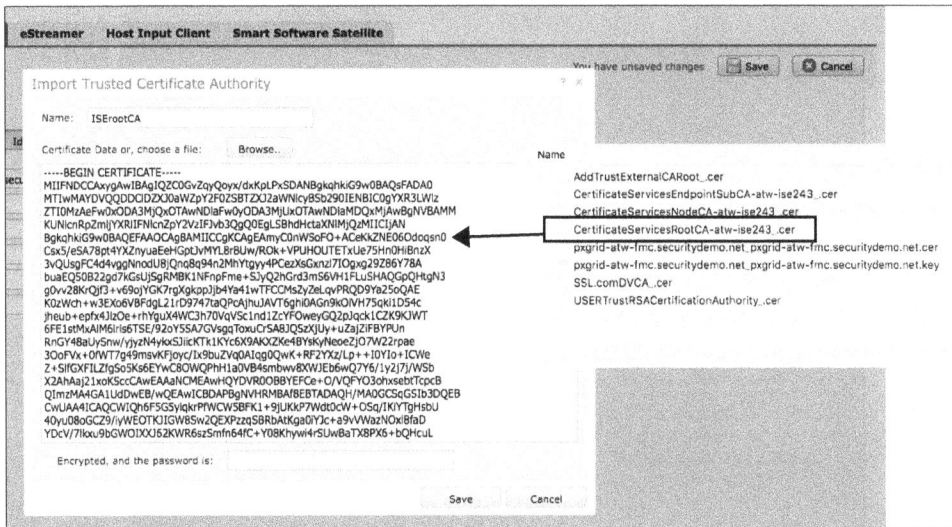

Figure 6-17   *Import Trusted Certificate Authority: ISE Root CA*

Step 7.   Click **Save**.

Step 8.   Ensure that the newly imported root CA certificate is listed in both the pxGrid Server CA and the MNT Server CA fields, as shown in Figure 6-19.

Note   The separate MnT certificate is there just in case you are not using a single CA for all pxGrid clients, but you now know that you should always use the same CA for all participants.

Step 9.   Add the signed certificate and private key for the FMC by clicking the green + button to the right of the FMC Server Certificate field.

This adds to the FMC the PEM-encoded certificate that was signed by ISE's endpoint CA and the encrypted private key. In the Name field, give the internal certificate a name that makes sense to you, similar to what you see in Figure 6-18.

Step 10.   Click **Browse** for Certificate Data and select the PEM certificate from the expanded ZIP file you downloaded earlier, as shown in Figure 6-18.

Step 11.   Click **Browse** for Key and select the PKCS8 key file from the expanded ZIP file you downloaded earlier, as shown in Figure 6-18.

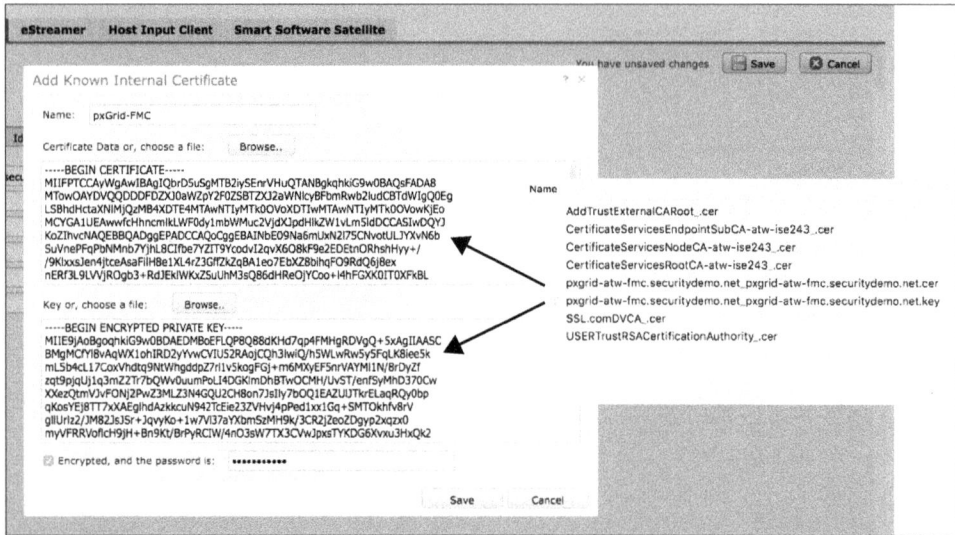

Figure 6-18 *Adding the Internal Certificate*

Step 12.   Click **Save** in the upper right corner of the screen. Figure 6-19 shows the completed form.

Figure 6-19 *Completed ISE Identity Source Form*

Step 13.   Click **Test** to verify a successful connection.

The test will most likely fail the first time you try unless ISE is configured to automatically approve new participants.

Step 14.   In the ISE UI, navigate to **Administration > pxGrid Services > Clients**.

If ISE is not configured to auto-approve participants, you need to accept the FMC's agent and test agent.

Step 15. Check the corresponding check box for the iseagent client for the FMC, as shown in Figure 6-20, and click **Approve**.

Step 16. Check the firesightisetest client check box and click **Approve**.

Figure 6-20 *pxGrid Clients*

Step 17. Return to the FMC UI and click **Test** to attempt the test again. This test should be successful.

Manually approving each and every pxGrid participant and their test accounts can be time consuming and somewhat confusing. Alternatively, you may enable the automatic approval of certificate-based accounts in the pxGrid Settings, as shown in Figure 6-21. Just remember to disable it again after you are finished.

Figure 6-21 *Enabling Automatic Approval of Certificate-Based Accounts in pxGrid Settings*

Note   The option in the pxGrid Settings to allow password-based account creation is an alternative to the certificate-based accounts that are shown in this chapter, where a password is leveraged instead and then tokens are assigned for authorization. At the time of writing, there are not any pxGrid client applications leveraging this account method. Also, in the Settings screen is a Test button to verify that pxGrid is working as expected within ISE. It is very useful for checking that ISE trusts its own certificates.

Configuring Realms for Identity in Access Rules

The FMC may download all the users and IP address bindings to its heart's content, but none of the data that is downloaded will be used in the policy until there is a realm configured to determine which groups and users to use in the firewall policies.

Realms leverage LDAP or LDAP/S to communicate to query the data from Active Directory. Within the FMC:

Step 1.   Navigate to **System > Integration > Realms**.

Step 2.   Click **New Realm**.

Step 3.   Provide a name for the realm and then choose **AD** from the Type drop-down list.

Step 4.   In the AD Primary Domain field, enter the IP address of the domain controller that the FMC should use to query AD.

Step 5.   In the AD Join Username field, provide a UPN (user principal name) for an AD user with enough permissions to join the FMC to the domain, such as administrator@securitydemo.net (used in this example).

Step 6.   In the AD Join Password field, enter the password for the AD user.

Step 7.   In the Directory Username field, provide a UPN for an AD user account for performing the LDAP queries, such as administrator@securitydemo.net.

Step 8.   In the Base DN field, enter the base distinguished name to begin the user account LDAP queries, such as ou=users,dc=securitydemo,dc=net.

Step 9.   Enter the base DN (distinguished name) to begin the group LDAP queries, such as ou=groups,dc=securitydemo,dc=net.

Hint   If you aren't getting the result you want, try backing up in the DN an extra level, such as dc=securitydemo,dc=net, which will then examine all organizational units (OUs).

Step 10.   Click OK.

Figure 6-22 shows the completed Add New Realm form.

Figure 6-22 *Completed Add New Realm Form*

After the realm has been created, you will need to add a "directory," which is another way of saying you need to add an LDAP server to perform the queries against.

Step 1. From the Realm configuration screen, click **Add directory**.

Step 2. In the Hostname/IP Address field, enter the IP address for the AD domain controller that the FMC should use for LDAP queries.

Step 3. In the Port field, enter the port for LDAP; **389** is the default port for unencrypted LDAP.

Step 4. If you are using secure LDAP, choose the encryption method and the certificate to trust.

Step 5. Click **OK**.

Figure 6-23 shows the completed directory entry.

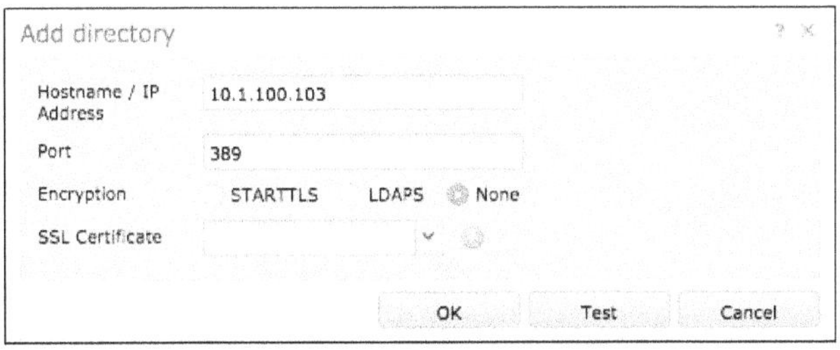

Figure 6-23 *Completed Directory Entry*

Now that the realm is configured along with an LDAP server, it is time to download users and groups for use in the policies:

Step 1.   Click the **User Download** tab.

Step 2.   Check the **Download users and groups** check box.

Step 3.   Select the interesting groups from the Available Groups list and use the **Add to Include** and **Add to Exclude** buttons to assign them for inclusion for use or exclusion from use within Firepower policies, as shown in Figure 6-24.

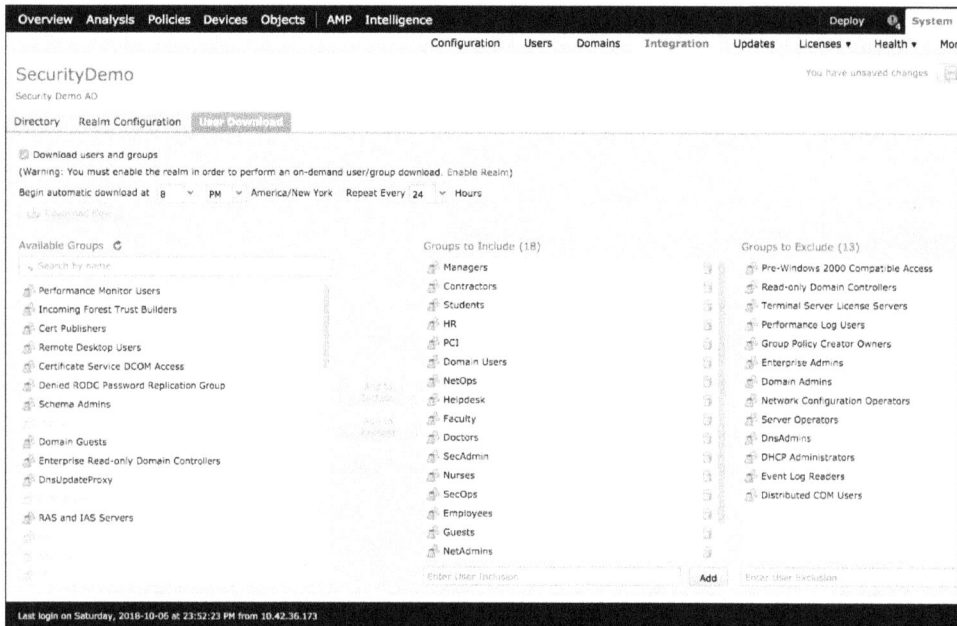

Figure 6-24   *Included and Excluded Groups*

Selective inclusion of AD groups is a key item for performance, as AD may have thousands of groups, most of which will not be relevant for identity policies in the firewalls, nor would it perform very well if all groups were candidates for identity rules.

Step 4.   Click **Save**.

Step 5.   **Enable** the Realm, as shown in Figure 6-25.

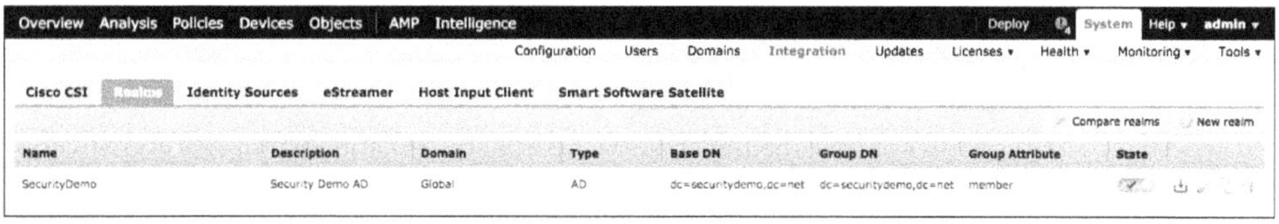

Figure 6-25 *Enabled Realm*

The realm is now fully configured for rule creation, along with the pxGrid integration for learning what IP addresses belong to which users and devices. Now you are ready to add identity information to the access policy rules in the FMC.

Configuring Firepower Access Rules with Context from pxGrid

Before you can add user identities or groups to the access-policy rule, you must first create an identity rule:

Step 1. Navigate to **Policies > Access Control > Identity**.

Step 2. Click **New Policy**.

Step 3. In the New Identity policy dialog box, shown in Figure 6-26, enter a name and, optionally, a description.

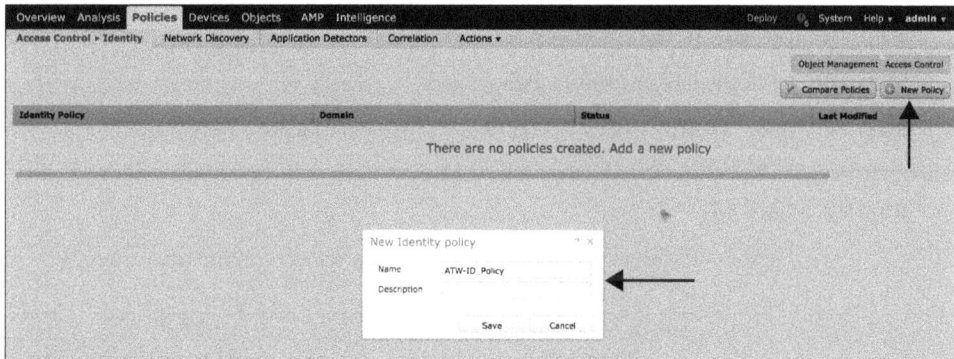

Step 4. Click **Save**.

Figure 6-26 *Creating a New Identity Policy*

Step 5. Click **Add Rule** to configure an identity rule.

Step 6. In the Name field, enter a name.

Step 7. Keep the Enabled check box checked.

Step 8. In the Action drop-down list, select **Passive Authentication**.

Step 9. Click the **Realm & Settings** tab.

Step 10.   From the Realm drop-down list, select your AD realm.

Step 11.   Click **Add**.

Figure 6-27 shows the new rule being added to the identity policy.

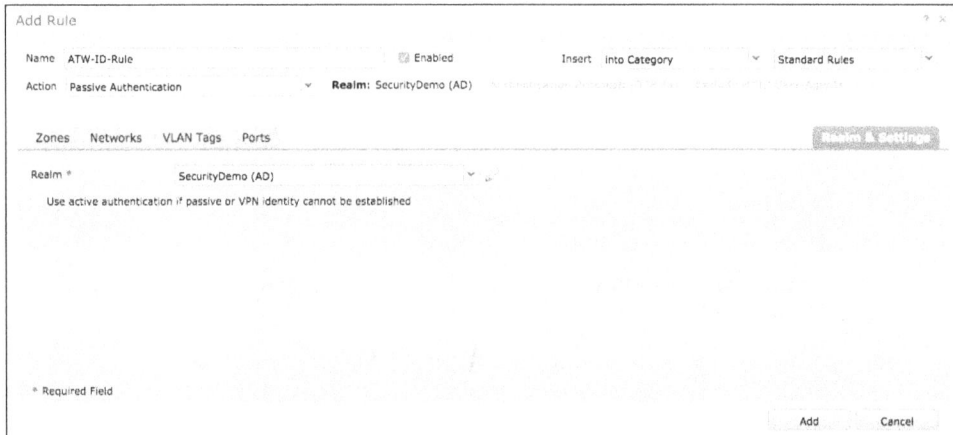

Figure 6-27   *Adding the Identity Rule to the Identity Policy*

Now that an identity policy has been created, you can attach it to the access policy.

Step 12.   Navigate to **Access Policy > Access Policy**.

Step 13.   Click the link in Identity Policy field.

Step 14.   In the Identity Policy dialog box, choose your identity policy from the drop-down list.

Step 15.   Click **OK**.

Figure 6-28 shows the identity policy being selected in the access policy.

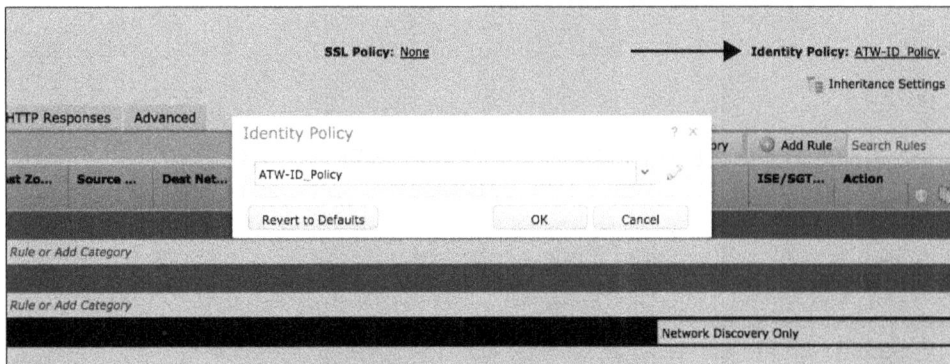

Figure 6-28   *Selecting the Identity Policy in the Access Policy*

Now that an identity policy has been attached to the access policy, you can add identities to the access rule.

Step 16. Navigate to **Access Policy > Access Policy**.

Step 17. Either click **Add Policy** to create a new policy or click **Edit** to add an existing policy.

Step 18. Click the **Users** tab.

Step 19. In the Available Realms column, select the realm you created.

Step 20. In the Available Users column, select the groups or users to match in this access rule.

Step 21. Click **Add to Rule** to transfer them to the Selected Users column.

Figure 6-29 shows the user group Employees being added to the access rule.

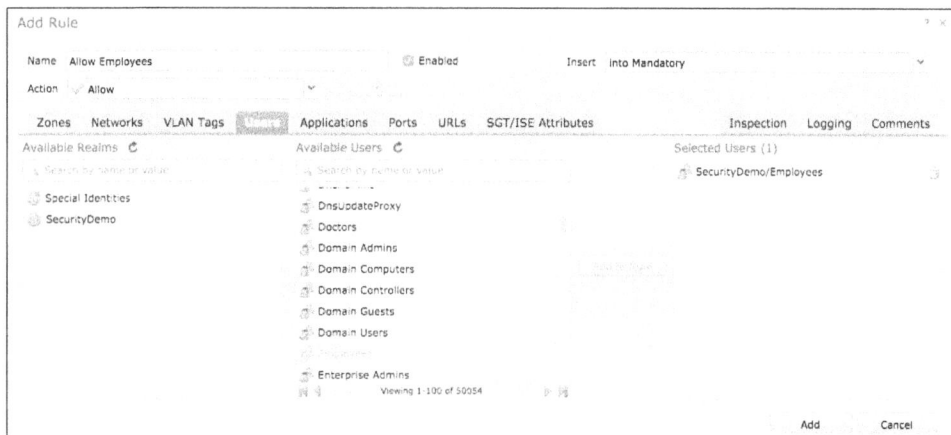

Figure 6-29 *Adding AD Groups to an Access Policy Rule*

Because we have integrated Firepower Management Center with ISE, we also have access to other bits of contextual data to build our policy on, such as endpoint profiles and TrustSec tags (also known as Scalable Group Tags or Security Group Tags).

Step 22. Click the **SGT/ISE Attributes** tab.

Step 23. In the Available Attributes column, select **Security Group Tag**.

Step 24. In the Available Metadata column, select one of the SGTs from ISE and click **Add to Rule**.

Figure 6-30 shows the SGT named Employees being added to the access rule.

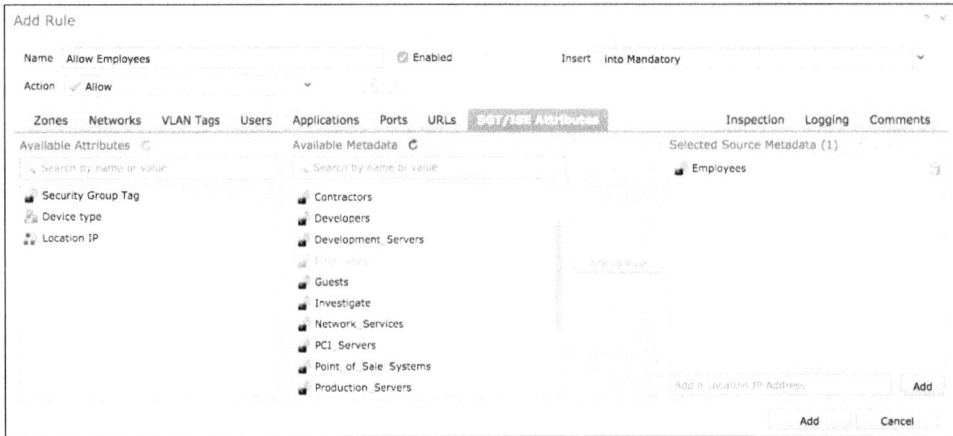

Figure 6-30 *Adding SGTs to an Access Policy Rule*

Step 25. In the Available Attributes column, select **Device Type.**

Step 26. In the Available Metadata column, select the endpoint profiles and click **Add to Rule** to add them to the policy.

Step 27. Click **Add** to save the access policy rule to the policy.

Step 28. Click **Save** to save the policy.

Figure 6-31 shows device type groups being added to the access rule.

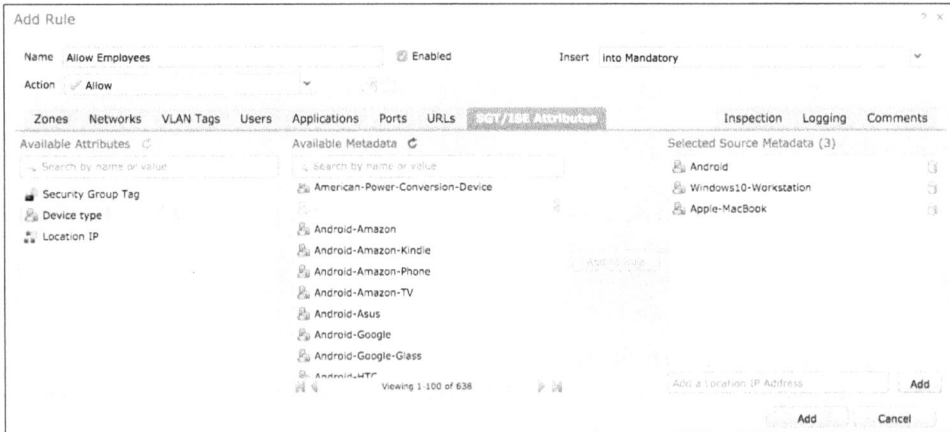

Figure 6-31 *Adding Endpoint Profiles to an Access Policy Rule*

Viewing Active Users

You've completed all the configuration steps for the identity integration with the FMC and ISE, but how do you know that the FMC is learning about the active and passive online users and devices?

Navigate to **Analysis > Users > Active Sessions** and you should start seeing domain logons, such as what you see in Figure 6-32.

Figure 6-32 shows the online users that ISE has learned about through either active or passive identity mappings. See Chapter 3, "Beyond Basic Network Access Control," for more on active versus passive identities.

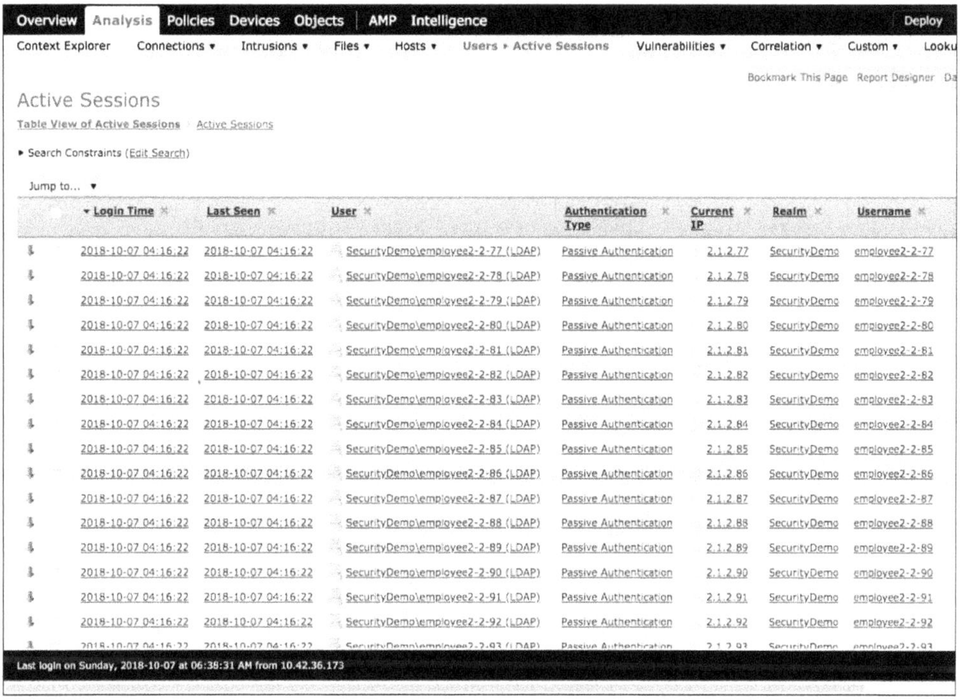

Figure 6-32 *Online Users Learned from ISE*

For the CLI-oriented CCIE or CCIE candidate, there is also a great way to see the user identities from the command line, **adi_cli session**, as shown in Example 6-1.

Example 6-1 *Viewing Online Users from the FMC CLI*

```
admin@atw-fmc:~$ sudo adi_cli session | more
input 'q' to quit
received realm information: operation REALM_DELETE_ALL, Null realm info
received realm information: operation REALM_ADD, realm name securitydemo.net, sh
ort name SECURITYDEMO, id 3
ADI is connected
received security group operation: DELETE ALL
received security group operation: ADD id: 92bb1950-8c01-11e6-996c-525400b48521
name: ANY fullyQualifiedName: Any Security Group tag: 65535
received security group operation: ADD id: 934557f0-8c01-11e6-996c-525400b48521
name: Auditors fullyQualifiedName: Auditor Security Group tag: 9
received security group operation: ADD id: 935d4cc0-8c01-11e6-996c-525400b48521
name: BYOD fullyQualifiedName: BYOD Security Group tag: 15
received security group operation: ADD id: 9370d4c0-8c01-11e6-996c-525400b48521
name: Contractors fullyQualifiedName: Contractor Security Group tag: 5
received security group operation: ADD id: 93837260-8c01-11e6-996c-525400b48521
name: Developers fullyQualifiedName: Developer Security Group tag: 8
received security group operation: ADD id: 9396d350-8c01-11e6-996c-525400b48521
```

Configuring Rapid Threat Containment with Firepower and ISE

Learning about the online users and endpoints is only one of the use cases when integrating the FMC with ISE. Another common use case of the integration is to act when a malicious activity has occurred, as you learned about in the "Rapid Threat Containment" section earlier in this chapter.

Figure 6-33 illustrates how the FMC works with correlation rules and remediation modules, to aid your understanding of how all the pieces fit together.

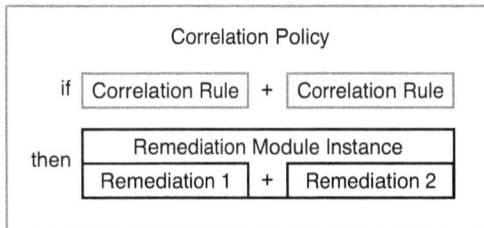

Figure 6-33 *Illustration of Correlation Policies and Components*

The parts that make up the response are as follows:

- **Correlation policy:** The policy construct that is made up of correlation rules and configured remediations.

■ **Correlation rule:** An individual rule housed inside of a correlation policy that is configured to look for one or more security events. There can be one or many correlation rules in each correlation policy.

■ **Remediation module:** Modules of the FMC that understand how to communicate to an external system; for example, the pxGrid module knows how to use EPS on ISE to quarantine endpoints.

■ **Remediation instance:** A specific instance of a remediation module, as there can be many instances, each with a different configuration.

■ **Remediation:** A specific action that is configured, such as quarantine. There can be many remediations in each instance of the remediation module.

The pxGrid mitigation module is built into the FMC, and that module can be used to take an EPS quarantine action when a correlation rule is triggered. Let's start by configuring the built-in pxGrid mitigation module:

Note   If you are following along only in the book, the following steps may seem a little strange. However, if you are following along with a live Firepower Management Center user interface, these steps will seem much more clear.

Step 1.   Navigate to **Policies > Actions > Remediation > Modules**, which brings you to the Installed Remediation Modules screen, as shown in Figure 6-34.

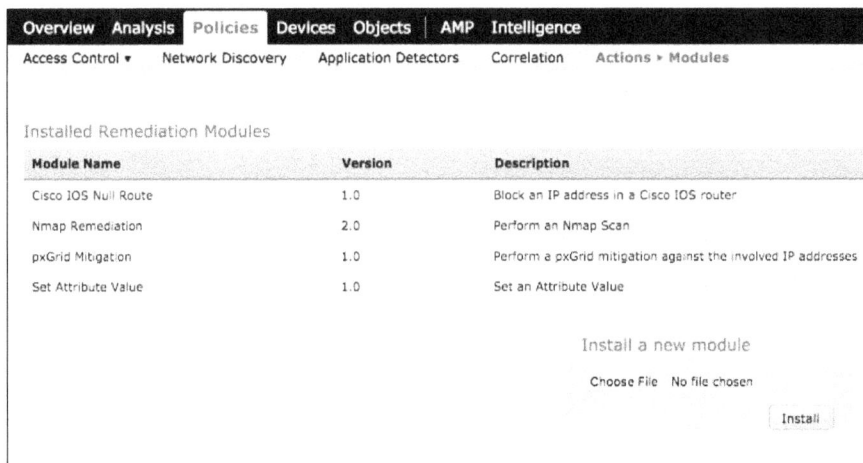

Overview	Analysis	Policies	Devices	Objects	AMP	Intelligence
Access Control ▾	Network Discovery	Application Detectors	Correlation	Actions ▸ Modules		

Installed Remediation Modules

Module Name	Version	Description
Cisco IOS Null Route	1.0	Block an IP address in a Cisco IOS router
Nmap Remediation	2.0	Perform an Nmap Scan
pxGrid Mitigation	1.0	Perform a pxGrid mitigation against the involved IP addresses
Set Attribute Value	1.0	Set an Attribute Value

Install a new module

Choose File   No file chosen

Install

Figure 6-34   *Remediation Modules*

Step 2.   Click the **magnifying glass icon** (not shown in Figure 6-34) at the right end of the pxGrid Mitigation module row.

Step 3.   Click **Add** to create a new instance of the module.

Step 4.   Provide a name for the instance and an optional description, as shown in Figure 6-35.

Step 5.   Click **Create**.

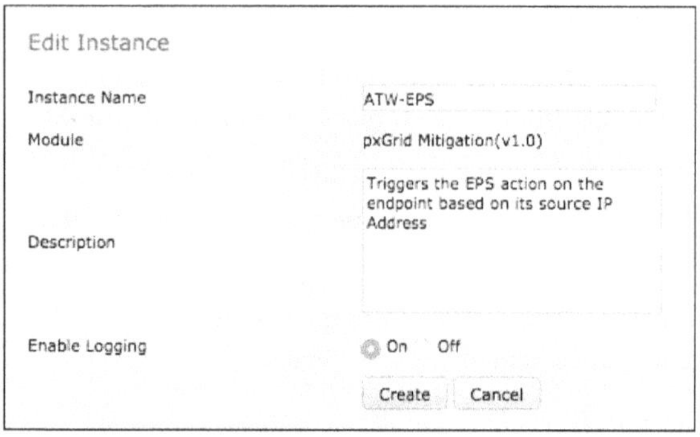

Edit Instance

Instance Name   ATW-EPS

Module   pxGrid Mitigation(v1.0)

Description   Triggers the EPS action on the
                       endpoint based on its source IP
                       Address

Enable Logging   ◉ On   Off

                       Create   Cancel

Figure 6-35   *Creating a New Instance of the pxGrid Mitigation Module*

Step 6.   Choose **Mitigate Source** in the Configured Remediations drop-down list, as shown in Figure 6-36.

Step 7.   Click **Create**.

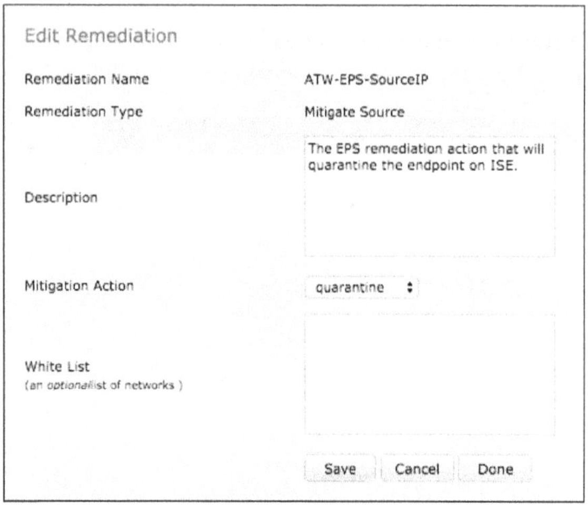

Edit Remediation

Remediation Name   ATW-EPS-SourceIP

Remediation Type   Mitigate Source

Description   The EPS remediation action that will
                       quarantine the endpoint on ISE.

Mitigation Action   quarantine ⬍

White List
(an optional list of networks)

                       Save   Cancel   Done

Figure 6-36   *Select Mitigate Source*

After clicking Create, you are brought automatically to the window where you create a remediation action for the module.

Step 8.   Provide a name for the remediation and an optional description, as shown in Figure 6-37.

Step 9.   Set the Mitigation Action to **quarantine**, as shown in Figure 6-36.

Step 10. Click **Create**.

Step 11. Click Save.

Step 12. Click Done.

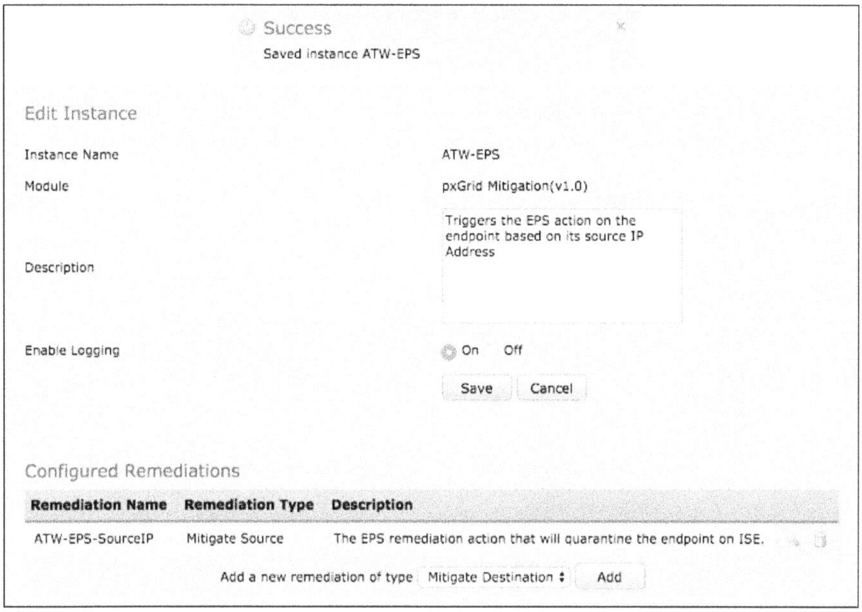

Figure 6-37 *Creating the Remediation*

Step 13. Click Save to save the module instance.

Figure 6-38 shows the completed instance of the pxGrid mitigation module.

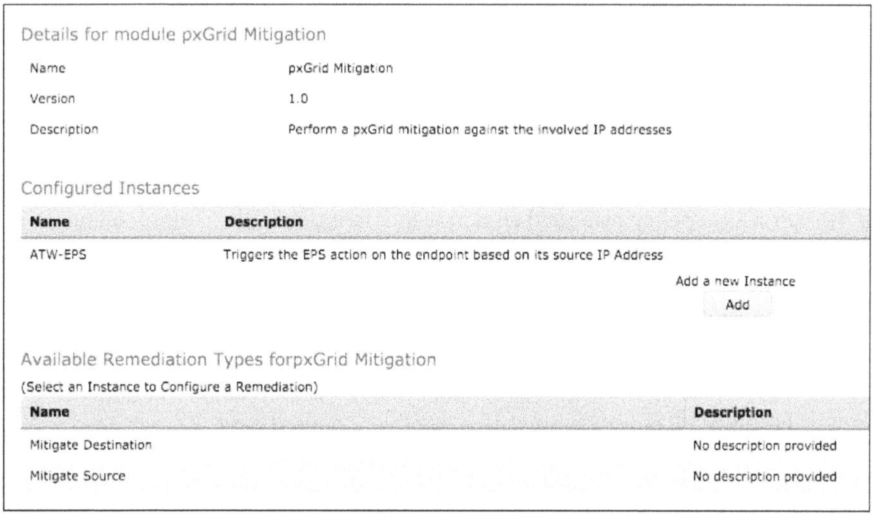

Figure 6-38 *Completed pxGrid Mitigation Module*

The remediation module is ready for use, so now we need to create a correlation rule that will use the remediation module whenever that correlation rule is matched.

Step 14. Navigate to **Policies > Correlation > Rule Management.**

Step 15. Click **Create Rule.**

Figure 6-39 shows a completed correlation rule that looks for an AMP for endpoints event where a cloud recalled file is unable to be quarantined.

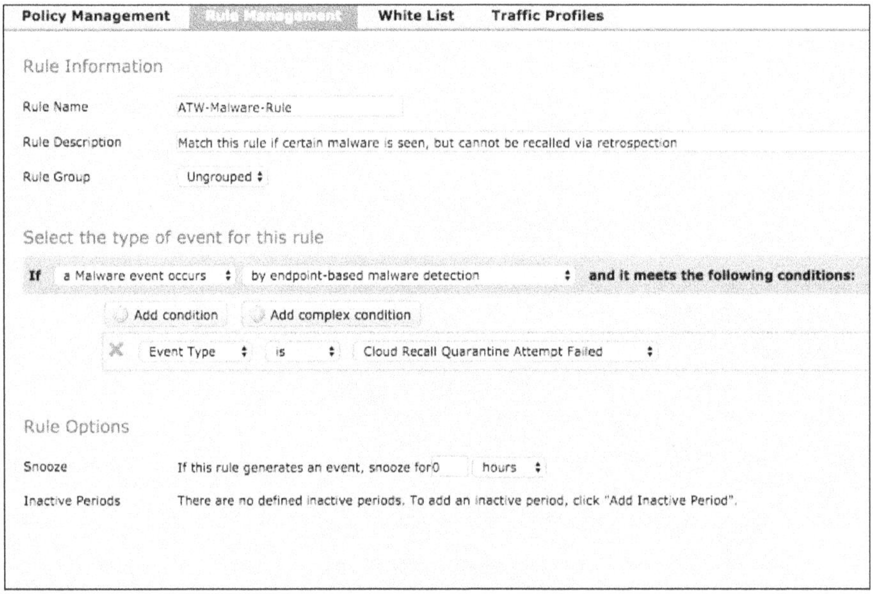

Figure 6-39 *Completed Correlation Rule*

Now that rule exists, we can add it to the correlation policy.

Step 16. Navigate to **Policies > Correlation > Policy Management.**

Step 17. Click **Create Policy.**

Step 18. Provide a policy name and an optional description in the corresponding fields.

Step 19. Click **Add Rules.**

Step 20. Select the correlation rule you created.

Figure 6-40 shows a correlation policy, with the correlation rule added; however, there is no remediation action configured yet.

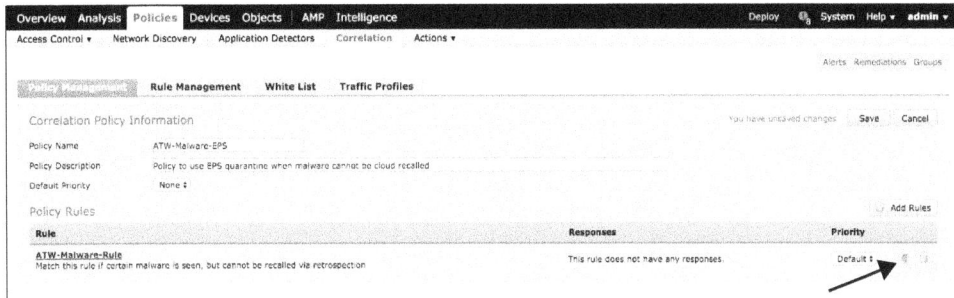

Figure 6-40 *Correlation Policy without a Remediation Action*

Let's add that remediation action.

Step 21. Click the response icon, pointed to in Figure 6-40.

Step 22. Assign the remediation action you created, as shown in Figure 6-41.

Step 23. Click **Update**.

Figure 6-41 *Assigning the Remediation Action*

Step 24. Click Save.

Step 25. Enable the policy, as shown in Figure 6-42.

Figure 6-42 *Final Policy, Enabled*

Configuring the Web Security Appliance for Identity with pxGrid

The Cisco Web Security Appliance (WSA) was one of the first pxGrid partner applications in the security ecosystem. The WSA may use pxGrid to ascertain both passive and active user identities, as well as TrustSec tags; however, at the time of writing, the WSA (version 11.5.1) is unable to combine Active Directory group membership with the identity information gathered from pxGrid, which means that TrustSec tagging is realistically the only scalable approach when using pxGrid.

Integrating the WSA and ISE with pxGrid

All pxGrid participants should be using certificates that are issued from the ISE internal CA. This is not a requirement, but it is certainly a best practice to ensure things always work optimally. So, before you continue to the following steps, create a certificate private-key pair, just like you did for the FMC in the "Configuring Firepower Management Center for pxGrid" section earlier in the chapter.

To configure pxGrid on the WSA, we will first add the ISE root certificates to the trusted certificate store:

Step 1.   Navigate to **Network > Certificate Management**.

Step 2.   Click **Manage Trusted Root Certificates**, as indicated in Figure 6-43.

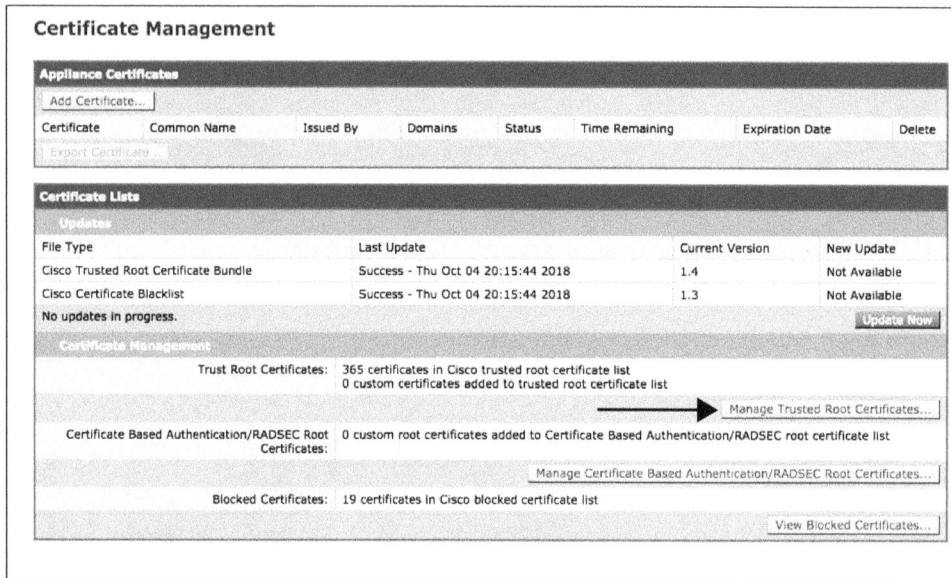

Figure 6-43   *Network > Certificate Management*

Step 3.   Click **Import**, as shown at the top of Figure 6-44.

Step 4.   Browse for each of the ISE CA certificates (Root, Node, and Endpoint) and click **Submit**, one at a time.

Step 5.   When all of the signing certificates are uploaded, click **Submit**, as indicated in Figure 6-44.

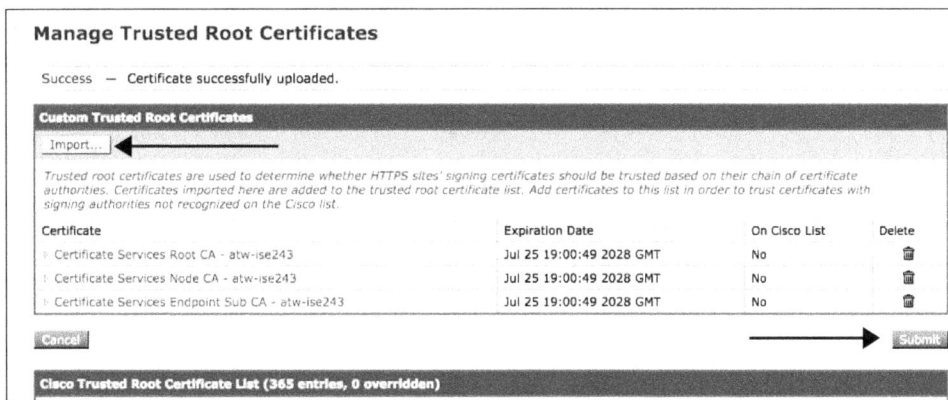

Manage Trusted Root Certificates

Success — Certificate successfully uploaded.

Custom Trusted Root Certificates

Import... ◄——————

Trusted root certificates are used to determine whether HTTPS sites' signing certificates should be trusted based on their chain of certificate authorities. Certificates imported here are added to the trusted root certificate list. Add certificates to this list in order to trust certificates with signing authorities not recognized on the Cisco list.

Certificate	Expiration Date	On Cisco List	Delete
Certificate Services Root CA - atw-ise243	Jul 25 19:00:49 2028 GMT	No	🗑
Certificate Services Node CA - atw-ise243	Jul 25 19:00:49 2028 GMT	No	🗑
Certificate Services Endpoint Sub CA - atw-ise243	Jul 25 19:00:49 2028 GMT	No	🗑

Cancel   ——————► Submit

Cisco Trusted Root Certificate List (365 entries, 0 overridden)

Figure 6-44   *Manage Trusted Root Certificates*

Step 6.   Click **Commit Changes** to save the WSA configuration.

Now that the ISE root certificates will be trusted, it is time to configure the WSA for pxGrid:

Step 1.   Navigate to **Network > Identification Services > Identity Services Engine**.

Step 2.   Click **Enable and Edit Settings**, as shown in Figure 6-45.

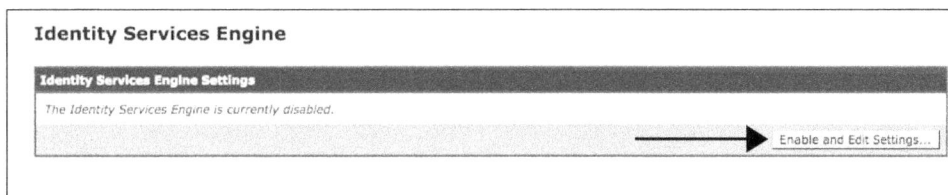

Identity Services Engine

Identity Services Engine Settings

The Identity Services Engine is currently disabled.

——————► Enable and Edit Settings...

Figure 6-45   *Identification Servers > Identity Services Engine*

In the Primary ISE pxGrid Node section:

Step 3.   In the Hostname or IPv4 address field, enter the FQDN for the primary pxGrid controller.

Step 4.   Click **Choose File** and select the ISE root CA certificate.

Step 5.   Click **Upload File**.

Figure 6-46 shows the completed Primary ISE pxGrid Node section.

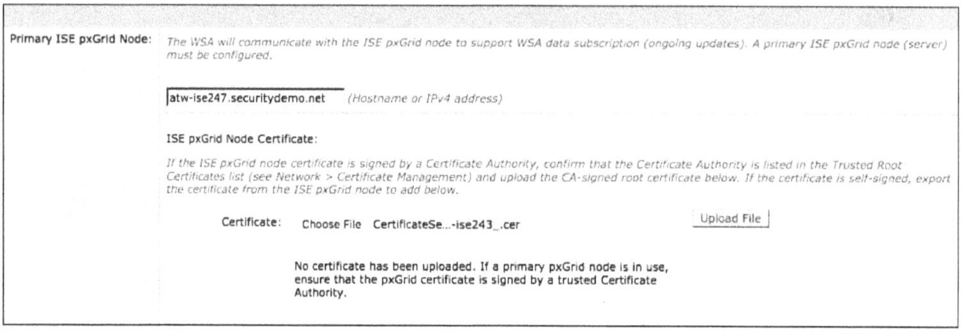

Figure 6-46   *Primary ISE pxGrid Node*

Step 6.   In the ISE Monitoring Node Admin Certificates section, click **Upload File** and upload the ISE root CA certificate for both the Primary and Secondary ISE Monitoring nodes.

Figure 6-47 shows the completed ISE Monitoring Node Admin Certificates section.

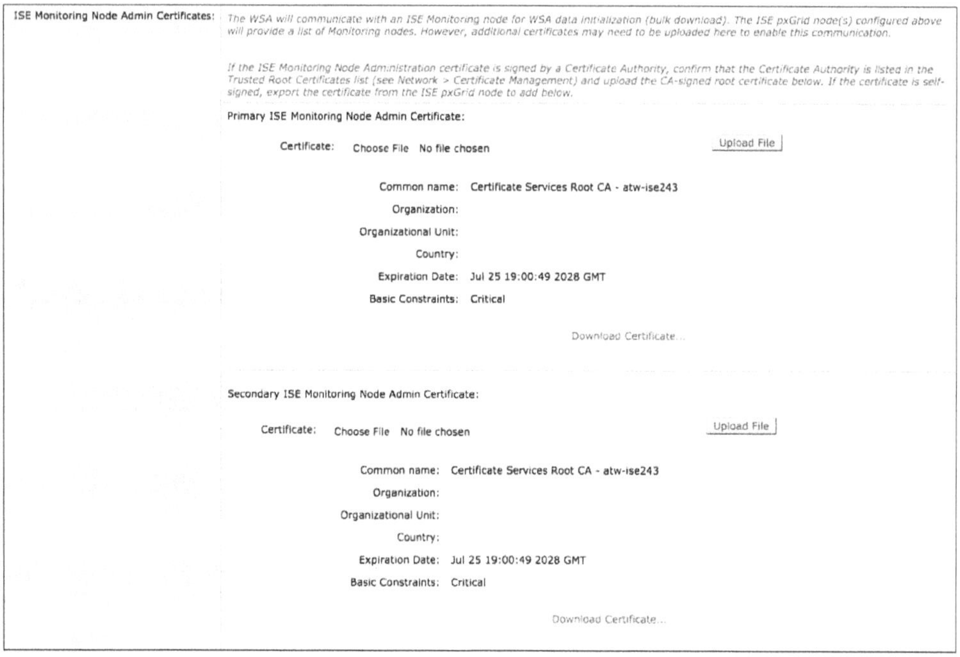

Figure 6-47   *ISE Monitoring Node Admin Certificates*

In the WSA Client Certificate Section:

Step 7.   Click **Use Uploaded Certificate and Key.**

Step 8.   Click **Choose File** in the Certificate field and select the WSA's certificate from the ISE CA.

Step 9. Click **Choose File** in the Key field and select the WSA's private key from the ISE CA.

Step 10. Check the **Key is Encrypted** check box.

Step 11. In the Password field, enter the password that you used to encrypt the key.

Step 12. Click **Upload Files.**

Figure 6-48 shows the WSA certificate and key selected and ready for upload.

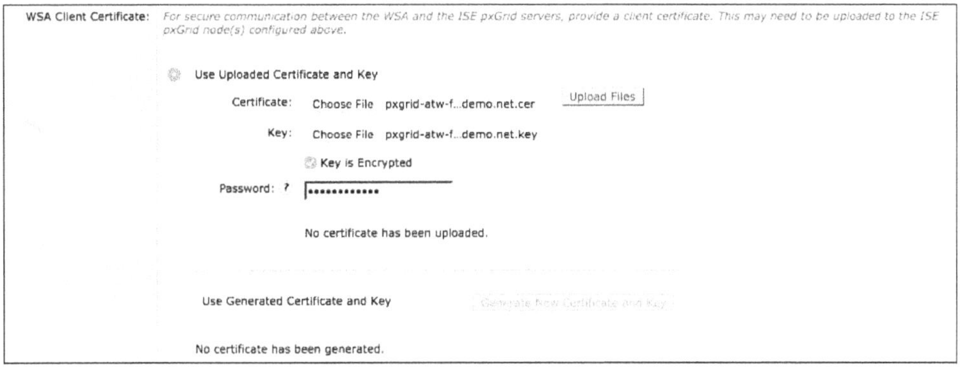

Figure 6-48 *WSA Client Certificate Section*

Step 13. Click **Submit** to complete the configuration.

Step 14. Click **Commit Changes** twice.

Step 15. To test the connection, click **Edit Settings.**

Step 16. Click **Start Test** at the bottom of the screen, as shown in Figure 6-49. If auto-approval is enabled, then the test should be successful. If it is not enabled, the test will fail until you manually approve the two WSA accounts on the pxGrid controller.

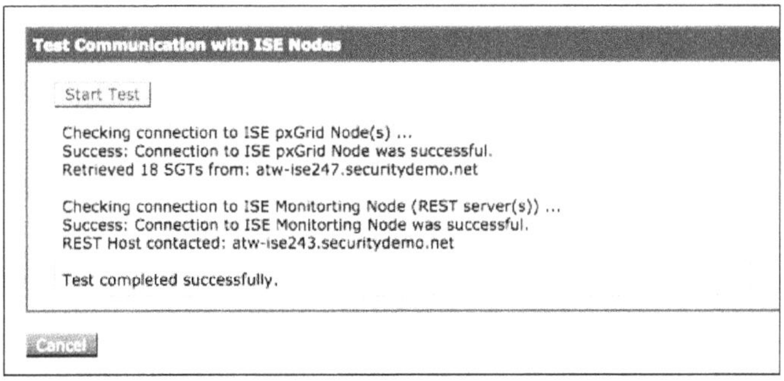

Figure 6-49 *Test Communication with ISE Nodes*

Example 6-2 shows an example of the test output.

Example 6-2   *Example Output for Testing Communication with ISE Nodes*

```
Checking DNS resolution of ISE pxGrid Node hostname(s) ...
Success: Resolved 'atw-ise247.securitydemo.net' address: 10.1.100.247

Validating WSA client certificate ...
Success: Certificate validation successful

Validating ISE pxGrid Node certificate(s) ...
Success: Certificate validation successful

Validating ISE Monitorting Node Admin certificate(s) ...
Success: Certificate validation successful

Checking connection to ISE pxGrid Node(s) ...
Success: Connection to ISE pxGrid Node was successful.
Retrieved 18 SGTs from: atw-ise247.securitydemo.net

Checking connection to ISE Monitorting Node (REST server(s)) ...
Success: Connection to ISE Monitorting Node was successful.
REST Host contacted: atw-ise243.securitydemo.net

Test completed successfully.
```

Configuring WSA Policies That Leverage the Data from ISE

Now that you have configured the WSA to work with ISE and to subscribe to the interesting pxGrid topics, it is time to configure policies. The first step is to create an identification profile:

Step 1.   Navigate to **Web Security Manager > Identification Profiles.**

Step 2.   Click **Add Identification Profile.**

Step 3.   In the Name field, provide a name for the profile.

Step 4.   In the User Identification Method section, in the Identification and Authentication spin box, select **Transparently identify users with ISE.**

Step 5.   Click **Submit.**

Step 6.   Click **Commit Changes** to save the WSA configuration.

Figure 6-50 shows the completed identification profile.

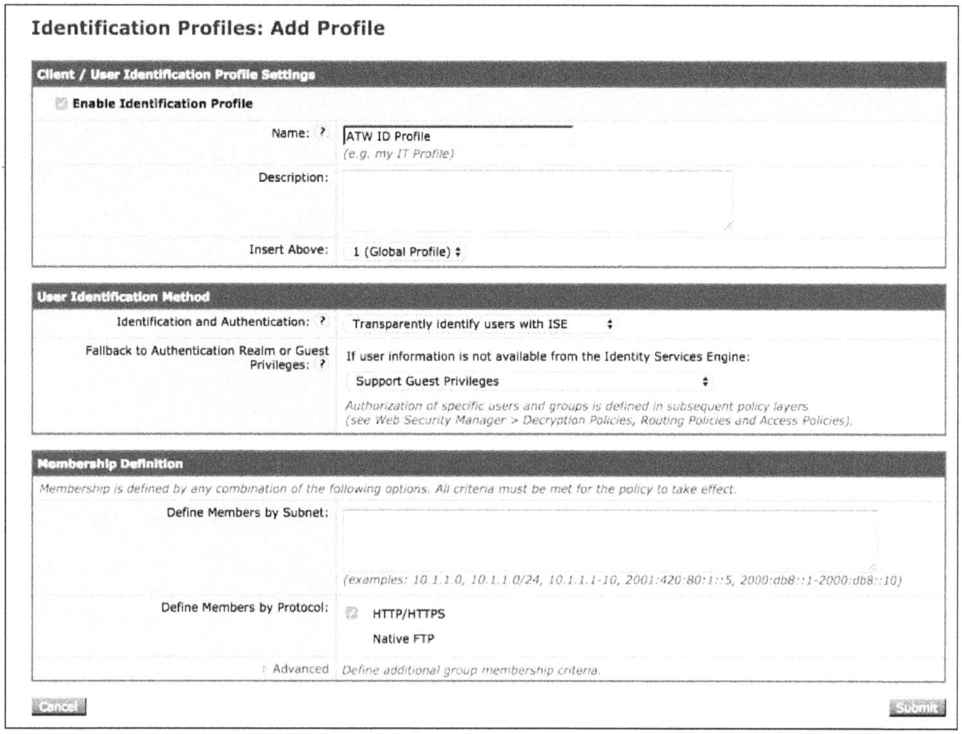

Identification Profiles: Add Profile

Client / User Identification Profile Settings

☑ **Enable Identification Profile**

Name: ?	ATW ID Profile
	(e.g. my IT Profile)
Description:	
Insert Above:	1 (Global Profile) ⇕

User Identification Method

Identification and Authentication: ?   Transparently identify users with ISE   ⇕

Fallback to Authentication Realm or Guest Privileges: ?   If user information is not available from the Identity Services Engine:

Support Guest Privileges   ⇕

Authorization of specific users and groups is defined in subsequent policy layers (see Web Security Manager > Decryption Policies, Routing Policies and Access Policies).

Membership Definition

Membership is defined by any combination of the following options. All criteria must be met for the policy to take effect.

Define Members by Subnet:

(examples: 10.1.1.0, 10.1.1.0/24, 10.1.1.1-10, 2001:420:80:1::5, 2000:db8::1-2000:db8::10)

Define Members by Protocol: ☑ HTTP/HTTPS
    Native FTP

▸ Advanced   *Define additional group membership criteria.*

Cancel   Submit

Figure 6-50 *Identification Profile*

To add an access policy leveraging security group tags from ISE:

Step 7. Navigate to **Web Security Manager > Access Policies.**

Step 8. Click **Add Policy.**

Step 9. In the Policy Name field, provide a name for the policy, as shown in Figure 6-51.

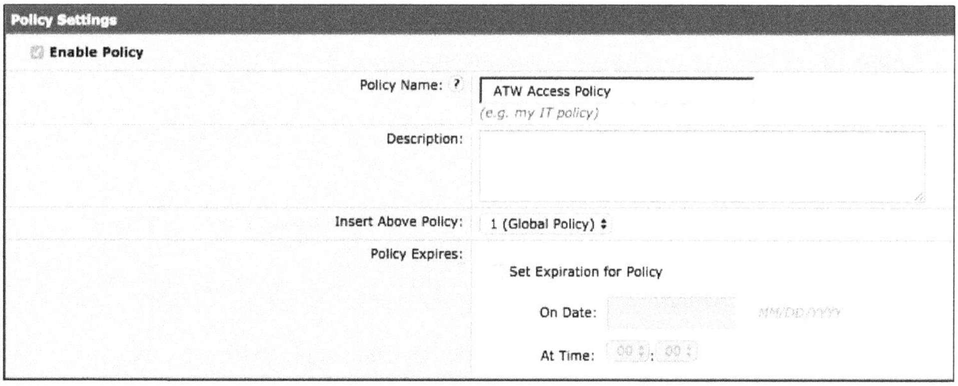

Policy Settings

☑ **Enable Policy**

Policy Name: ?	ATW Access Policy
	(e.g. my IT policy)
Description:	
Insert Above Policy:	1 (Global Policy) ⇕
Policy Expires:	Set Expiration for Policy
	On Date: _____ MM/DD/YYYY
	At Time: 00 ⇕ : 00 ⇕

Figure 6-51 *Naming the Access Policy*

Step 10.   In the Identification Profiles and Users section, choose **Select One or More Identification Profiles** in the top spin box.

Step 11.   In the Identification Profile column, choose the configured ID profile in the spin box.

Step 12.   In the Authorized Users and Groups column, click the **Selected Groups and Users** radio button.

Step 13.   Select SGTs in the ISE Secure Group Tags area directly below the radio button.

Step 14.   Click **Submit**.

Figure 6-52 shows the completed access policy that will apply to all users with the Employees SGT assigned.

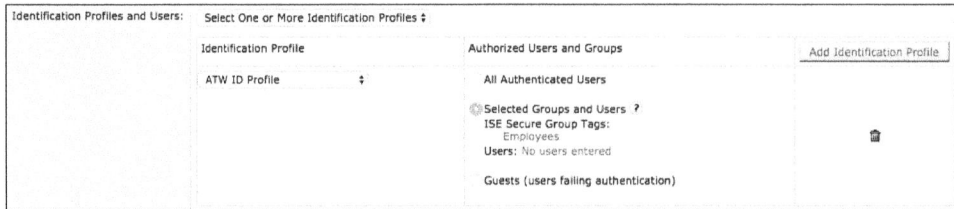

Identification Profiles and Users:	Select One or More Identification Profiles ⬍		
	Identification Profile	Authorized Users and Groups	Add Identification Profile
	ATW ID Profile ⬍	All Authenticated Users	
		⊙ Selected Groups and Users ? ISE Secure Group Tags: Employees **Users:** No users entered	🗑
		Guests (users failing authentication)	

Figure 6-52   *Access Policy with Employees SGT*

To add a decryption policy that will decrypt SSL traffic from users with a specific SGT:

Step 15.   Navigate to **Web Security Manager > Decryption Policies.**

Step 16.   Click **Add Policy.**

Step 17.   In the Policy Name field, provide a name for the policy.

Step 18.   In the Identification Profiles and Users section, choose **Select One or More Identification Profiles** in the top spin box.

Step 19.   In the Identification Profile column, choose the configured ID profile in the spin box.

Step 20.   In the Authorized Users and Groups column, click the **Selected Groups and Users** radio button.

Step 21.   Select SGTs in the ISE Secure Group Tags area directly below the radio button.

Step 22.   Click **Submit**.

Figure 6-53 shows the completed access policy that will apply to all users with the Investigate SGT assigned.

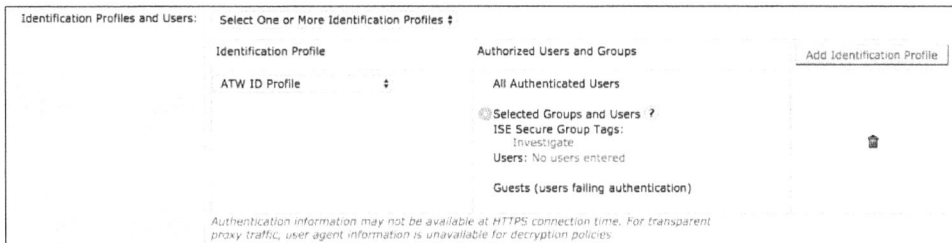

Identification Profiles and Users:	Select One or More Identification Profiles ‡

Figure 6-53 *Decryption Policy*

Integrating Stealthwatch and ISE for Identity and Rapid Threat Containment with pxGrid

For years, Cisco had a proven solution known as Cyber Threat Defense (CTD), the main components of which were Cisco ISE and a product called StealthWatch from Lancope. Lancope was acquired by Cisco in December of 2016, and Cisco proceeded to rebrand the product Cisco Stealthwatch. That's right, folks. Please don't capitalize that W, as Cisco branding would not be happy.

Regardless of what the product is called, what remains 100 percent true is that Stealthwatch is phenomenal at security analytics and visibility. It works primarily by analyzing NetFlow records from the network and providing analytics around the traffic, hosts, and other telemetry used to decorate the flows.

Why Integrate Stealthwatch and ISE?

Flow analysis itself is incredibly useful for pre- and post-attack analytics. Figure 6-54 shows a basic host report for a client PC in Stealthwatch before integrating it to ISE. This report is just a small taste of what Stealthwatch is able to provide to your security organization and security operations center (SOC) for incident response and alerting.

Beginning with version 6.9, Cisco Stealthwatch uses ISE as the primary source for learning passive and active user identities to merge into the flow records used for security analytics. The mechanisms used are exactly the same, whether it is full ISE or the ISE Passive Identity Connector (ISE-PIC), which provides only passive identities (see Chapter 3, "Beyond Basic Network Access Control," for more information on ISE and passive identity).

Just as with the WSA, the context provided to Stealthwatch can be much richer with full ISE and therefore provide more value by adding endpoint profiles and TrustSec data.

After integrating ISE, the flows will contain much more context about the hosts, including the logged-in user data. Figure 6-55 shows the populated Users & Sessions table after ISE integration.

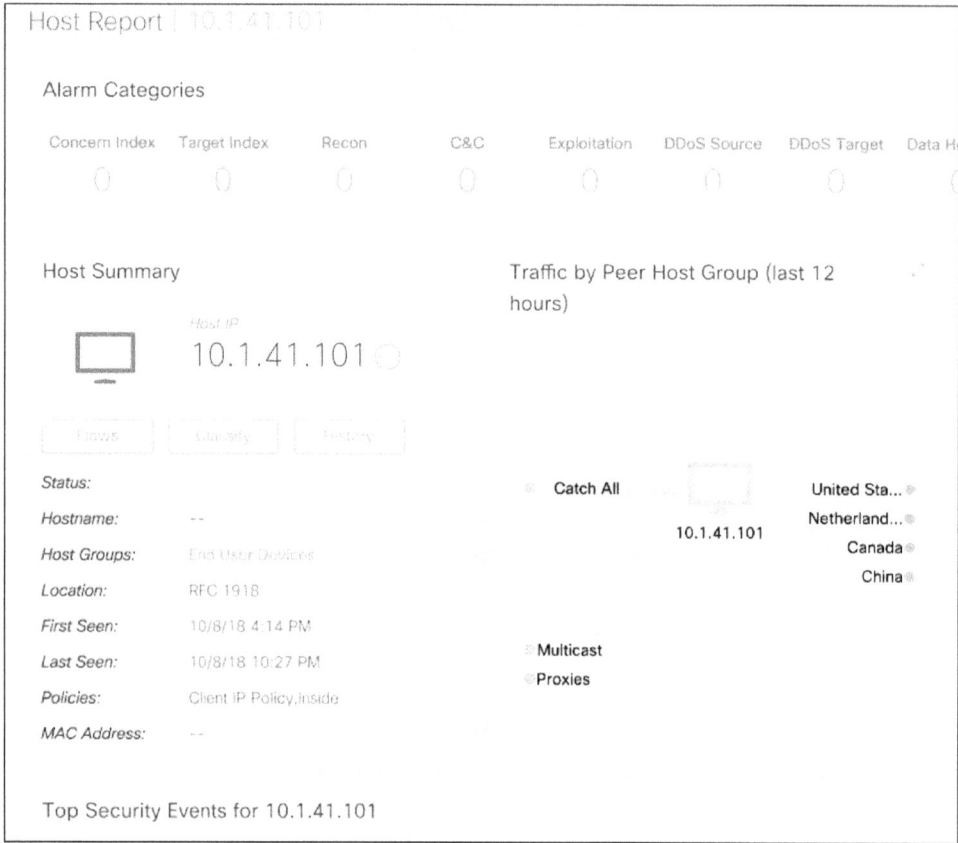

Figure 6-54   *Host Report—Pre-ISE Integration*

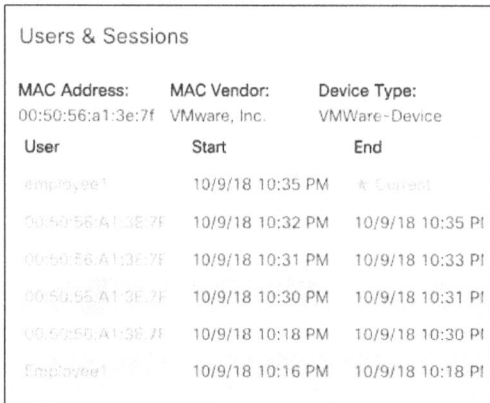

Figure 6-55   *Host Report—Post ISE-Integration*

Preparing Stealthwatch for pxGrid

To start configuring Stealthwatch for pxGrid, we will generate an "Additional TLS Identity" for the Stealthwatch Management Center (SMC); which is to say we will get a pxGrid certificate from ISE and install it on the SMC.

Unlike the FMC and the WSA, Stealthwatch uses the PKCS12 chain files instead of individual certificates. In other words, it requires the private key, signed certificate, and all the signing root certificates in a single encrypted file.

Note All steps in this book are for Cisco Stealthwatch version 7.0. To see the integration with version 6.x, check out *Cisco ISE for BYOD and Secure Unified Access, Second Edition* (Cisco Press, 2017).

Step 1. Click the **settings** cog in the upper-right corner and select **Central Management**, as shown in Figure 6-56.

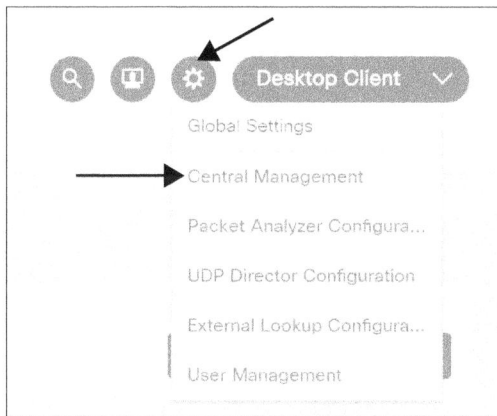

Figure 6-56 *Settings > Central Management*

Step 2. The Stealthwatch Central Management tab or window will open.

Step 3. In the Actions column, click the circle icon next to your Stealthwatch Management Center and click **Edit Appliance Configuration**, as shown in Figure 6-57.

Figure 6-57   *Choosing to Edit the Appliance Configuration*

Step 4.   Scroll down to the section titled Additional SSL/TLS Client Identities.

Step 5.   Click **Add New.**

Step 6.   Click **Generate CSR.**

Step 7.   In the Generate a CSR section, fill out the fields for the certificate signing request, as shown in Figure 6-58.

Step 8.   Click **Generate CSR**, as indicated in Figure 6-58.

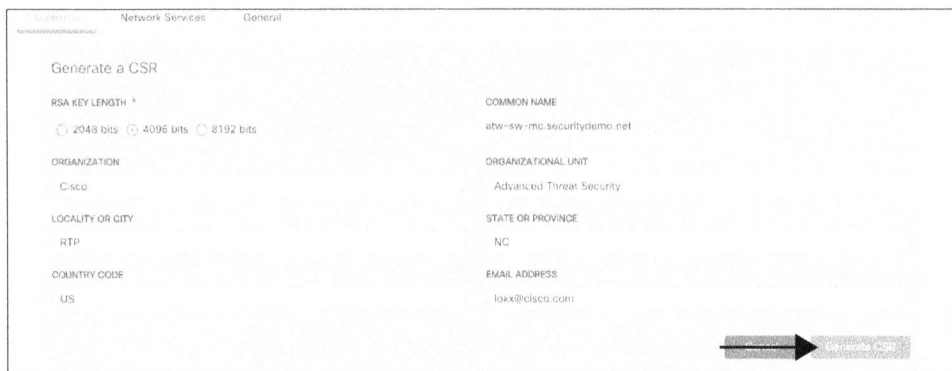

Figure 6-58   *Generating the CSR*

Step 9.   Save the resulting CSR file to a location where you can easily retrieve it.

Step 10.   Open the CSR in your favorite text editor.

Step 11.   Copy the contents of the CSR to your clipboard.

In the ISE user interface:

Step 12.   Navigate to **Administration > pxGrid Services > Certificates.**

Step 13. In the *I want to* spin box, select **Generate a single certificate (with certificate signing request)**.

Step 14. In the Certificate Download format spin box, choose **PKCS12 format (including certificate chain; one file for both the certificate chain and key)**.

Step 15. Enter and confirm a certificate password for the encrypted resulting file.

Step 16. Click **Create**.

Step 17. Save the resulting p12 file to a location where you can easily retrieve it.

Figure 6-59 shows the completed certificate generation screen in ISE.

Figure 6-59 *Generating the Certificate Chain for Stealthwatch*

Back in the Stealthwatch User Interface:

Step 18. In the **Friendly Name** field, enter a simplified name for the identity certificate.

Step 19. Click **Choose File** and select the downloaded p12 chain file.

Step 20. After the UI recognizes the chain file, the Bundle Password field appears; enter and confirm the bundle password.

Step 21. Click **Add Client Identity**.

Figure 6-60 shows the import of the PKCS certificate chain into Stealthwatch.

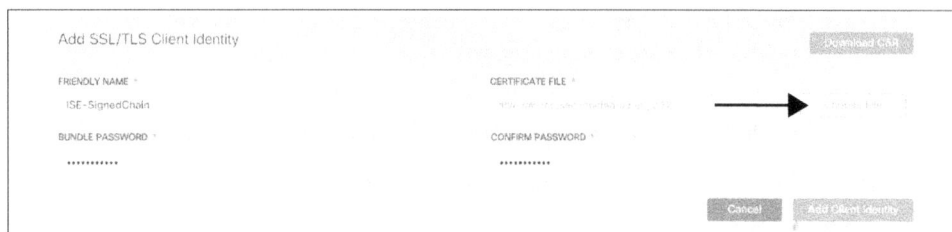

Figure 6-60 *Importing the Signed CSR Chain File*

Step 22. Click **Apply Changes** to save the new identity certificate.

Configuring Stealthwatch for ISE

Now that the pxGrid client identity certificate is imported to Stealthwatch, it is time to configure the ISE integration:

Step 1. On the main Stealthwatch screen, navigate to **Deploy > Cisco ISE Configuration**, as shown in Figure 6-61.

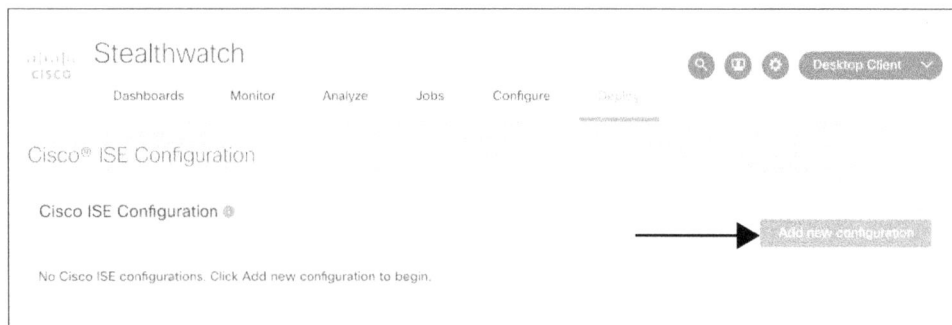

Figure 6-61 *Deploy > Cisco ISE Configuration*

Step 2. Click **Add new configuration.**

Step 3. In the Cluster Name field, enter a friendly name for the ISE cube.

Step 4. In the Certificate field, select the pxGrid certificate from the drop-down list.

Step 5. Enter the IP addresses for the primary and secondary pxGrid controllers.

Step 6. Create a username to uniquely identity Stealthwatch in the ISE pxGrid UI.

Step 7. Under Integration options, check the **Adaptive Network Control, Static SGT Classifications,** and **User sessions** check boxes.

Step 8. Click **Save.**

Figure 6-62 shows the completed Cisco ISE Configuration Setup screen.

Cisco ISE Configuration Setup

CLUSTER NAME:
ATW ISE Cube

CERTIFICATE:
ISE-SignedChain

PRIMARY PXGRID NODE: SECONDARY PXGRID NODE:
10.1.100.247

USER NAME:
atw-sw-mc

Integration options
☐ Adaptive Network Control
☐ Static SGT Classifications
☐ User sessions

Figure 6-62   *Configuring the pxGrid Connection*

After a bit of time, the Status indicator for the pxGrid connection should change from yellow to green to symbolize that the connection to pxGrid is up and running, as shown in Figure 6-63.

Cisco® ISE Configuration

Cisco ISE Configuration

Add new configuration

Cluster Name	Primary pxGrid Node	User Name	Status	Actions
ATW ISE Cube		atw-sw-mc	↻ ⬅	

Figure 6-63   *Connected Status for pxGrid Connection*

Figure 6-64 shows the final pxGrid clients screen, where you can see the FMC, WSA, and Stealthwatch clients in the list.

The integration is not only for providing telemetry to Stealthwatch; you can also act during an investigation in Stealthwatch for enforcement through ISE. Stealthwatch 7.0 uses Adaptive Network Control (ANC), whereas previous versions used EPS.

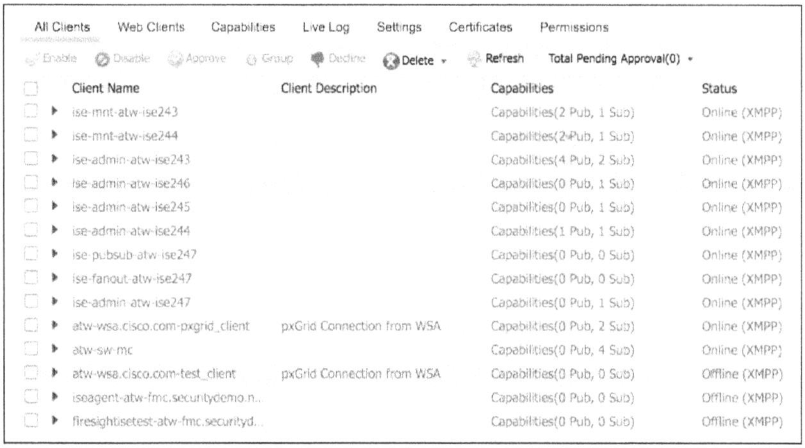

Figure 6-64   *Final pxGrid Clients Screen*

Unlike EPS, which had only two options (Quarantine & Unquarantine), ANC allows you to create many different labels of your choosing, for a variety of actions.

From the ISE user interface:

Step 1.   Navigate to **Operations > Adaptive Network Control > Policy List.**

Step 2.   Click **Add** to create a new label (called a policy).

Step 3.   In the Name field, give the policy a name, such as Investigate.

Step 4.   In the Action drop-down list, choose the type of CoA that ISE will issue: SHUT_DOWN, PORT_BOUNCE, or QUARANTINE).

Step 5.   Click **Save.**

Figure 6-65 shows two configured ANC labels.

Figure 6-65   *ANC Labels*

After your labels exist, you can include them as conditions in your authorization rules, as shown in Figure 6-66.

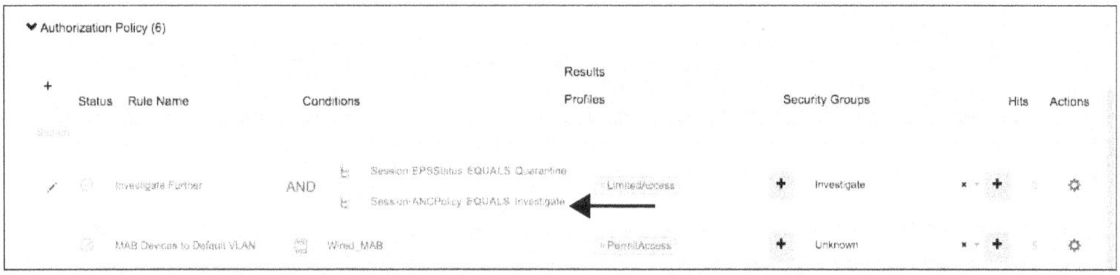

Figure 6-66 *ANC Labels in the Authorization Policy*

Now when something looks awry during an incident response, you can assign the ANC label to a host right in the Stealthwatch interface and have ISE take action.

From the Stealthwatch user interface:

Step 1.   Click **Edit** for ISE ANC Policy, as shown in Figure 6-67.

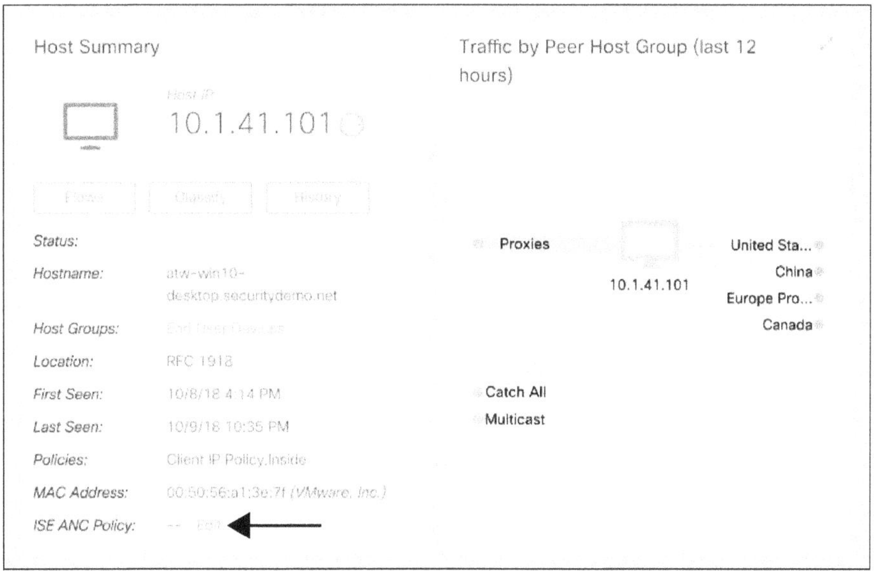

Figure 6-67 *Editing the ISE ANC Policy*

Step 2.   In the Applying ANC policy screen, select your chosen label from the ANC Policy drop-down list, as shown in Figure 6-68.

Step 3.   Click **Save**.

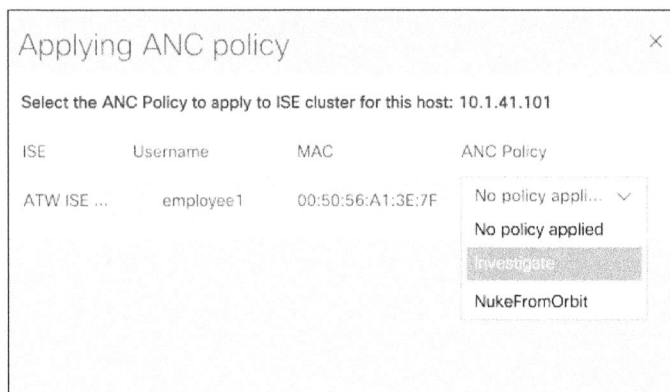

Figure 6-68 *Assigning ISE ANC Policy*

Summary

In this chapter, you learned about the many different ways of sharing context out of ISE to other security solutions, about Rapid Threat Containment, and about the Platform Exchange Grid (pxGrid). In addition to sharing context from ISE to other systems, ISE is able to learn contextual data from those systems as well, creating a true symbiotic ecosystem.

You integrated Firepower with ISE and Active Directory for identity-based firewalling and Rapid Threat Containment using endpoint protection services (EPS). You integrated the Web Security Appliance and Stealthwatch for pxGrid integration with ISE to enhance their capabilities as well.

Chapter 7

APIs in Cisco Security

This chapter provides the details of the Cisco security product portfolio's application programming interfaces (APIs). This chapter will explore these APIs and how to work with them. You will learn about the APIs available in Firepower Management Center (FMC), Identity Services Engine (ISE), Advanced Malware Protection (AMP), Threat Grid, and Umbrella.

APIs 101

An API is a set of subroutine definitions, protocols, and tools for building application software. An API may be for a web-based system, operating system, database system, computer hardware, or software library. Documentation for the API is usually provided by the manufacturer to facilitate usage. A good API makes it easier to develop a program or application by providing all the building blocks, which are then put together by the programmer. In the realm of APIs, organizations are putting more emphasis on security professionals' use of APIs to accomplish use cases to improve operations and incident response. Organizations can use APIs to collect and correlate the data their analysts need to look at every day, and to build custom and repeatable actions that save analysts time and money.

Many organizations want to automate incident handling because it has become a labor-intensive repetitive task for them. Other companies need to orchestrate provisioning of policy, threat hunting, and data-enrichment tasks to get ahead of a huge volume of threats. Knowing the benefits and available capabilities within an organization's security architecture is the first step to prioritizing API usage and integration use cases.

The following represent some of the top reasons organizations use APIs with their security products:

- **Orchestration of configuration changes:** Ever wonder how large organizations deal with changing policies on thousands of devices? APIs can support orchestration of changes to one or many devices, which could include use cases such as policy changes when deploying new applications or infrastructure.

- **Context sharing:** Is it time consuming to gather information accurately and prioritize events without more context? Context sharing gives security devices information about who the user is, what device type they are using, and the vulnerability and risk of the device and user. This allows analysts and operators to have an actionable picture of an event to respond quicker. For example, an organization could share vulnerability scanner data with the Firepower Next-Generation Intrusion Prevention System (NGIPS) so events can be prioritized based on whether the target is vulnerable or not.

- **Security or threat intelligence sharing:** Many organizations want to augment built-in intelligence feeds from manufacturers because of internal or external compliance requirements. Some organization have partnerships with public- or private-sector organizations that provide additional intelligence or internally created customized intelligence based on their observed threats. Many products provide APIs or native features to allow for utilization of outside threat intelligence for prevention or detection of threats.

- **Threat or incident response automation:** The goal of automation is to reduce mean time to respond (MTTR) and free security analysts to focus on high-priority incidents by automating manual tasks such as automatic remediation, creating tickets, or notifying interested parties. Solutions such as rapid threat containment allow for events or incidents to trigger a quarantine of a system to reduce risk or stop a threat. APIs enable organizations to customize and create their own automated threat response.

APIs are also used to integrate disparate point products in an architecture. Cisco has invested heavily in recent years to create a supported integrated architecture. Figure 7-1 illustrates some of the most common integrations in the Cisco Security Architecture. While these integrations are extremely beneficial, some organizations have other products or custom-built software they would like to use to integrate to create automation or orchestration. For this reason, the rest of the chapter after this introductory section will explore the APIs offered by Cisco security products to perform custom integrations.

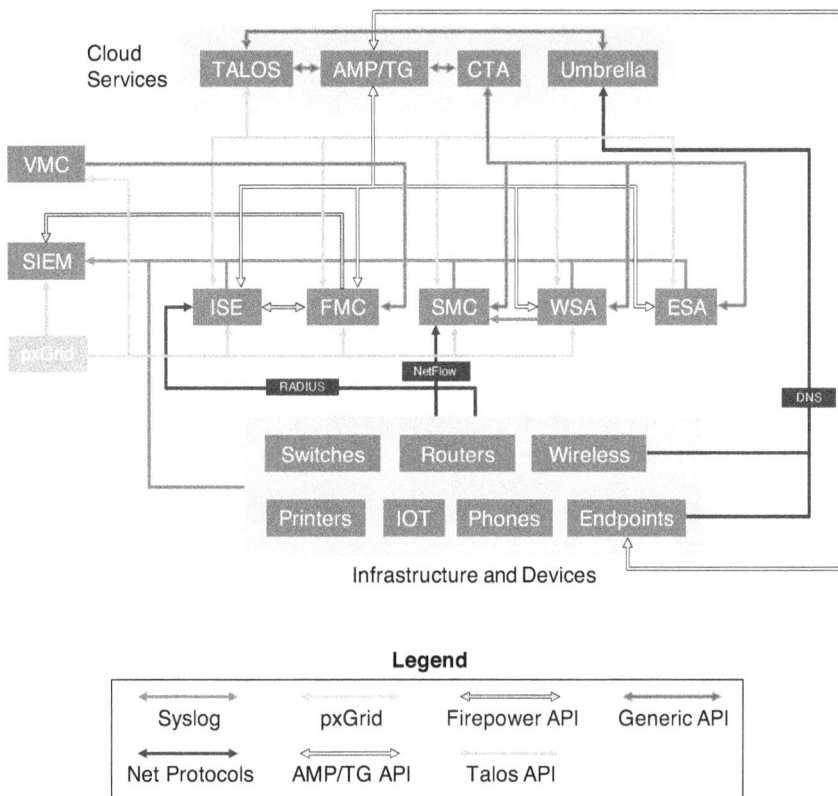

Figure 7-1 *Cisco Security Products Using APIs for Integration*

RESTful APIs

A RESTful API is an API that uses HTTP requests to get, put, post, and delete data. Based on Representational State Transfer (REST) technology, which is an architectural style and approach to communications often used in web services deployments, HTTP RESTful APIs are used in many network and security device APIs, including most of the Cisco security products.

The following represents some of the HTTP requests types and their purpose:

- **GET:** Used to retrieve an object
- **POST:** Used to create a new object
- **PUT:** Used to modify or replace an object
- **DELETE:** Used to delete an object
- **PATCH:** Used to partially modify an object

Note   Each of these methods should be passed with the API call to tell the server what to do.

Authentication is optional but is typically required by most security products. Authorization of API access is certainly a good idea when allowing potentially damaging commands like PUT or DELETE.

Working with APIs

After you understand the product and its API capabilities, getting started is easy. Most RESTful APIs can be accessed with basic HTTP clients, such as curl or wget. Example 7-1 is a curl request to the Umbrella Investigate API checking for the classification of a site.

Example 7-1   *Investigate API Request Using curl*

```
    curl --include --header "Authorization: Bearer <YourToken>" \
    "https://investigate.api.umbrella.com/url/gllpdbbbqdqb.biz/classifiers"
The response when running this request will include the following:
    {
"securityCategories":[
"Command and Control",
"Malware"
],
            "attacks":[
"Tinba"
            ],
"threatTypes":[
"Trojan"
]
}
```

There are many tools available to help make it easier to craft and work with API requests. One popular tool is Postman, an API development and debugging tool that is free for individual and small projects. Postman can run on Windows, macOS, or Linux and can help beginners test API requests and view the responses. Figure 7-2 illustrates the same curl request using Postman.

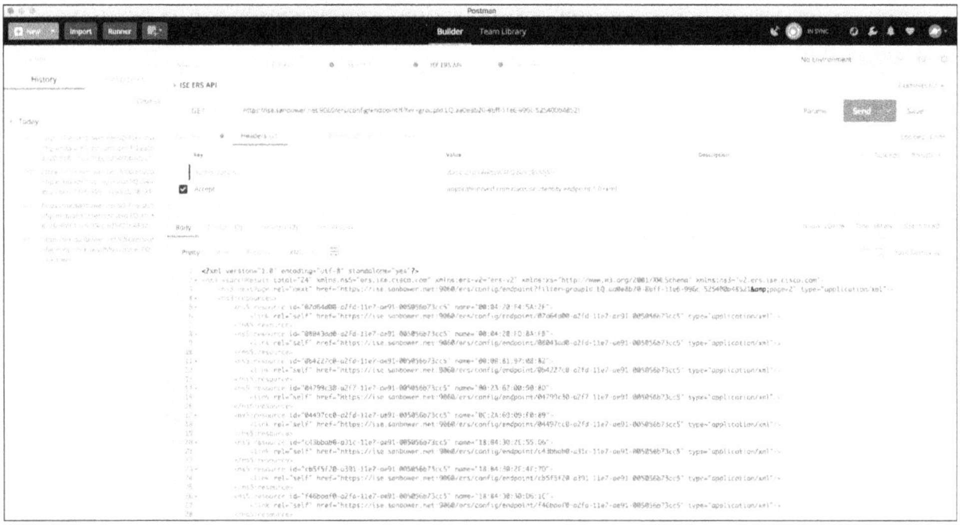

Figure 7-2   *Using Postman for API Requests*

An additional benefit of using tools such as Postman is their capability to generate code that can be used in another programming language. Figure 7-3 shows some of the available languages that are supported in Postman.

Figure 7-3   *Creating Code Snippets in Postman*

Most organizations will create applications, scripts, or programs based on the staff's experience and language of preference, such as Perl, Python, Java, C++, etc.

Cisco DevNet

Cisco DevNet, launched in 2014, is Cisco's developer program to help developers and IT professionals who want to write applications and develop integrations with Cisco products, platforms, and APIs. Cisco DevNet includes Cisco's products in software-defined networking (SDN), security, cloud, data center, Internet of Things (IoT), collaboration, and open source software development. The DevNet site also provides learning and sandbox environments for those trying to learn coding and testing apps.

DevNet also contains a community where developers can share their creations. DevNet also attends and hosts many developer events, such as hackathons and coding camps. It's easy to start learning the latest Cisco APIs and technologies with guided Learning Tracks, and it's free!

To get started, browse to https://developer.cisco.com. If you're just getting started or need a programming refresher, the Learning Labs will help you get started with tutorials covering REST APIs, Python, JavaScript, and other programming technologies and concepts. Figure 7-4 shows the "Introduction to DevNet" Learning Lab.

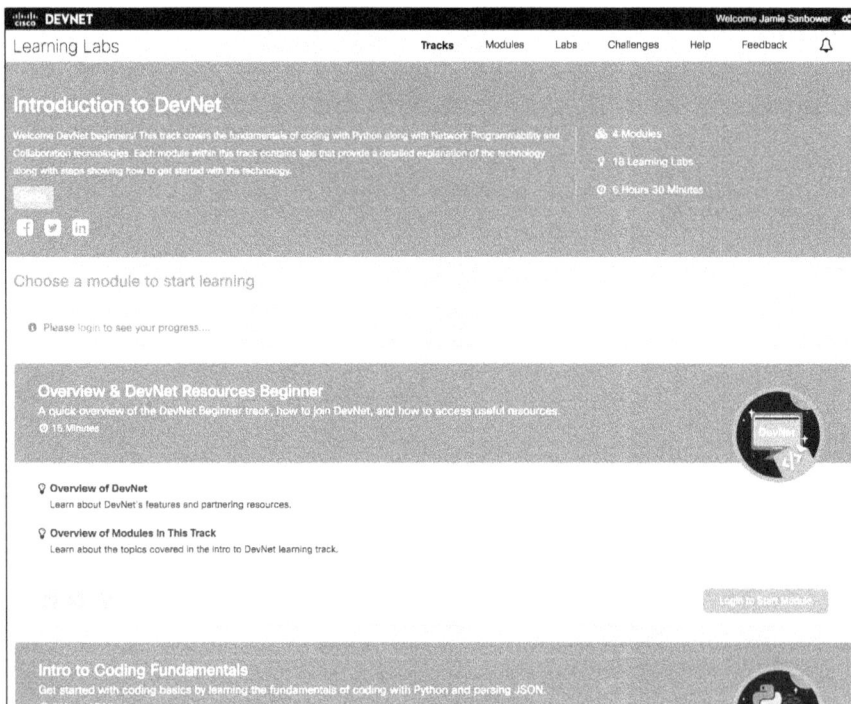

Figure 7-4 *Introduction to DevNet Learning Lab*

Firepower Management Center APIs

Firepower Management Center (FMC) provides complete and unified management over firewalls, application control, intrusion prevention, URL filtering, and advanced malware protection. It can help administrators to easily go from managing firewalls to controlling applications to investigating and remediating malware attacks. For more information on the FMC, NGFW, and NGIPS, please refer to *Integrated Security Technologies and Solutions: Volume I.*

FMC REST API for Configuration

Before release of FMC 6.1, the FMC could only be accessed via a web-based GUI. FMC 6.1 included the first set of REST APIs to access some of the most desired features of the FMC. The main motivation behind providing these APIs was to allow organizations a way to integrate custom applications with the FMC. If you have certain configuration workflows using the FMC GUI, REST APIs can enable workflow automation. Figure 7-5 illustrates how an application talking to the FMC can be used to orchestrate Firepower Threat Defense (FTD) and Firepower sensors.

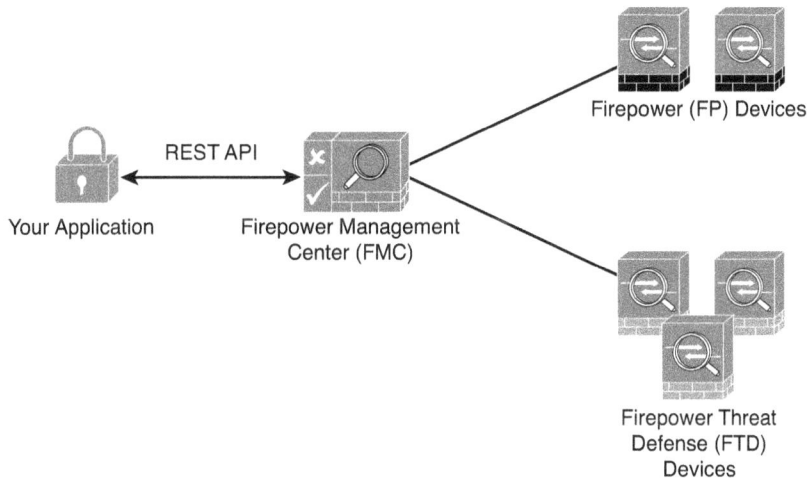

Figure 7-5 *REST API Application with FMC*

To use the FMC REST API, go to **System > Configuration > REST API Preferences** and make sure that the REST API is enabled on the FMC. Once enabled, you can access the API Explorer by going to **https://<FMC IP OR DNS NAME>/api/api-explorer** to review the types of requests and responses available. The REST API relies on the same authentication as the FMC UI. Each function in the REST API maps to permissions in the FMC. You can log in to the API Explorer using any account on the FMC, but you will only be able to perform the functions for which the account has permissions. Figure 7-6 shows how the API Explorer can be used to get all network objects from the FMC.

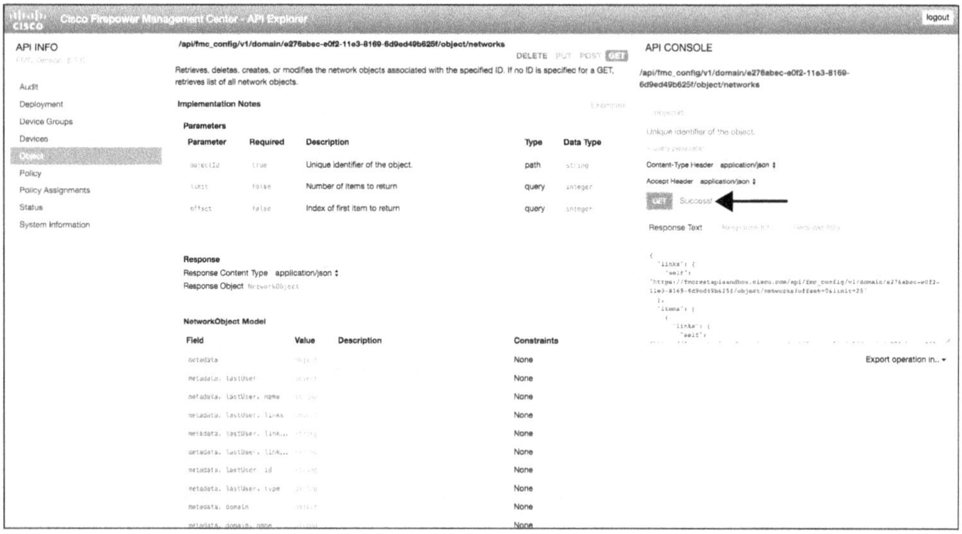

Figure 7-6 *FMC API Explorer*

The Export Operation button in the API Explorer can be used to save the displayed method example as a Python or Perl script file. This script can be used to make that REST call and can be integrated into an application. This is meant primarily as an educational and bootstrapping tool.

The following represents some of the popular use cases of the FMC's REST API:

■ **Adding a device:** Allows administrators to add new devices to the FMC

■ **Object management:** Allows adding, modifying, and deletion of objects and object groups for network, port, security zones, interface groups, application filter, VLAN tag, geolocation, URL, variable set, network/DNS/URL security intelligence lists/feeds, and file lists

■ **Access control policy configuration:** Enables administrators to add, modify, or delete rules, along with assigning policies to different Firepower devices

Firepower System Remediation API

The Firepower System remediation API allows organizations to create remediations that the FMC can automatically launch when conditions on the network violate the associated correlation policy. A remediation is the response the software program executes to mitigate the detected condition. For example, you can block traffic at a router on the source or destination IP address, or initiate a host nmap scan to assess the host status. If multiple rules in a policy trigger, the FMC can launch responses for each rule.

A remediation module is the package of files that is installed on the FMC to perform the remediation or response. The remediation daemon launches the remediation and passes the correlation event data and instance-specific parameters to your remediation program. It also accepts return codes from the remediation program. The FMC uses the return codes for status are displayed under **Analysis > Correlation > Correlation Events.**

The remediation program launches a set of instances of the remediation when the associated policy rule triggers. Each instance targets a particular network device. You create instances on the Instance Detail page of the Firepower Management Center web interface. For each instance, you provide the necessary instance-specific configuration details such as IP address and password of the target device.

The FMC web interface allows you to define and activate your correlation policies and associate them with remediations. When a policy violation occurs, the remediation subsystem passes the name of the remediation and the event data specified in the module template configuration file to the remediation daemon. Figure 7-7 illustrates how the correlation policy passes remediation type and policy event data to the remediation daemon, which then passes the data to the remediation module.

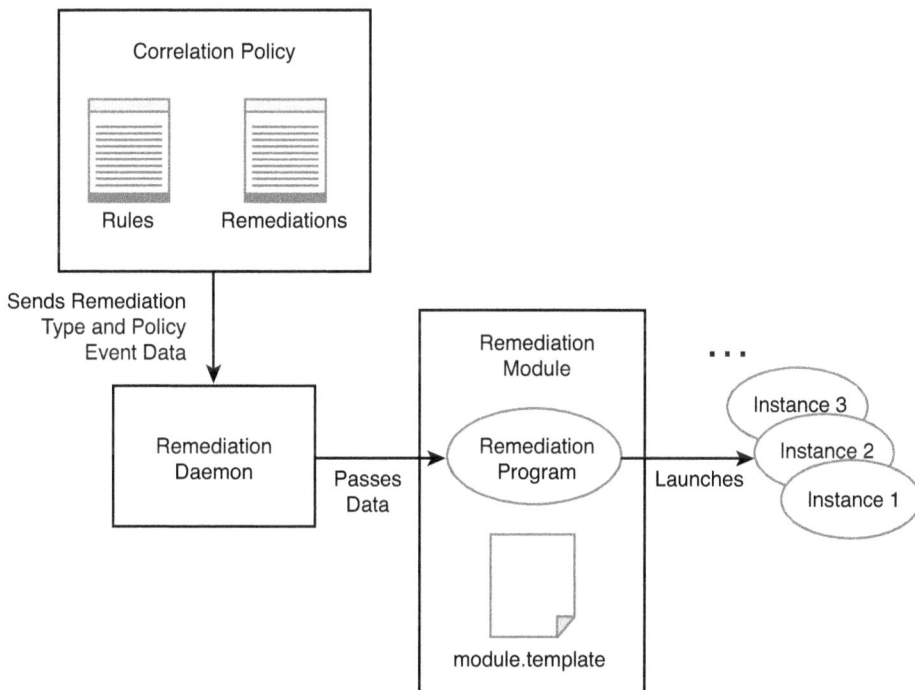

Figure 7-7   *FMC Remediation Data Flow*

The FMC contains four built-in remediation modules, as shown in Figure 7-8. One remediation module supported by Cisco that can be downloaded from Cisco Connection Online (CCO), www.cisco.com, and installed using the Install a New Module dialog box on the FMC is the Application Policy Infrastructure Controller (APIC) FMC Remediation Module. This module allows for the FMC to use APIC API to micro-segment servers, by changing the Endpoint Group (EPG) with Application Centric Infrastructure (ACI), if an event or threat is seen by the FMC. For example, if a server connects to a known command and control (C2) server, the FMC can tell APIC to change the EPG from "Web-Server" to a micro-segmented EPG (uSeg EPG) of "Web-Server-Quarantine," which would only allow the server to communicate internally.

Figure 7-8 *FMC Built-In Remediation Modules*

As discussed in Chapter 5, "Sharing the Context," the Cisco Rapid Threat Containment (RTC) solution automatically quarantines infected or risky endpoints and reduces risk. RTC uses the Firepower System Remediation API to set the quarantine status of a host in Identity Services Engine (ISE) using the pxGrid Mitigation remediation module. Quarantine, which is typically synonymous with isolation, can be defined by an administrator and is normally implemented differently depending on the organization's policy. Some organizations will use a quarantine to only allow Internet access and no internal or intranet access, whereas others will only allow internal access and no Internet access. The point being a quarantine does not have to be complete isolation and can be defined by an organization.

An organization can also create its own remediation modules to integrate the FMC with another product that hasn't already been created by Cisco. To illustrate, let's take a custom use case of changing a group for a device running Advanced Malware Protection (AMP) for Endpoints (AMP4E). These actions are the main functions your custom remediation program must implement. Figure 7-9 shows that when the FMC sees a threat, definable in the correlation policy, it will check to see if the computer has AMP for Endpoints installed by querying the AMP4E cloud API (discussed later in the section

"Advanced Malware Protection APIs") for the computer ID of the IP address the threat came from. Then, it will check for the group ID of the group used for quarantine that was defined in the instance configuration. Finally, it will tell AMP4E to put that computer into the designated group. This is a useful way of automating the moving of a computer from Audit mode to Protect mode.

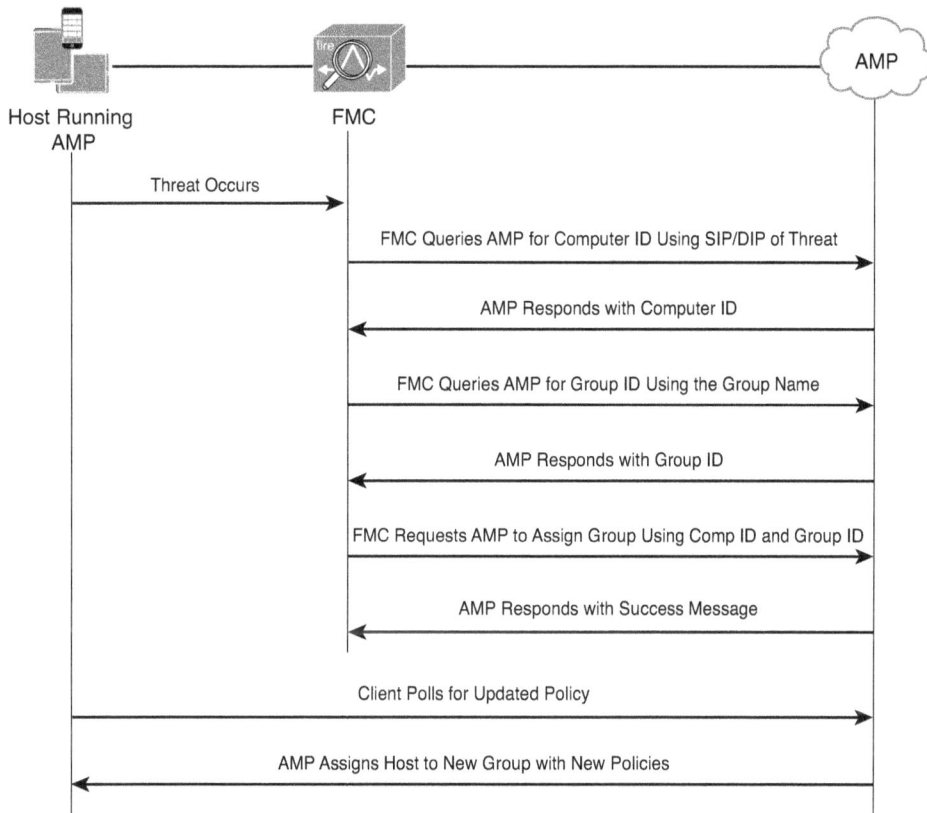

Figure 7-9   *FMC Custom AMP4E Remediation Module*

The first step in creating a custom remediation module is to create a module.template file, which is the module configuration file. It defines required event data, required information to collect in the web interface when users create instances, and other essential setup parameters. Figure 7-10 illustrates a module.template file for our AMP remediation module. It includes settings for the AMP API Client ID, API Key, the group, and a whitelist.

```
1      <?xml version="1.0" encoding="utf-8" ?>
2    ▼ <module name="AMP">
3    ▼   <global_config>
4          <display_name>AMP Remediation</display_name>
5          <description>Change AMP Computer Group by IP addresses using AMP Cloud</description>
6          <version>0.99.1</version>
7          <binary>amp.pl</binary>
8    ⌐   </global_config>
9    ▼   <config_template online_help="topic://EditInstance">
10   ▼     <string>
11            <name>user_name</name>
12            <display_name>API Client ID</display_name>
13   ⌐     </string>
14   ▼     <password>
15            <name>login_password</name>
16            <display_name>API Key</display_name>
17   ⌐     </password>
18   ▼     <string>
19            <name>group_name</name>
20            <display_name>Group Used as Quarantine</display_name>
21   ⌐     </string>
22   ▼     <boolean>
23            <name>logging</name>
24            <display_name>SYSLOG Logging</display_name>
25            <default_value>true</default_value>
26   ⌐     </boolean>
27   ▼     <list required="false">
28            <name>whitelist</name>
29            <display_name>White List</display_name>
30   ▼       <item_type>
31              <network_li/>
32   ⌐       </item_type>
33   ⌐     </list>
34   ⌐   </config_template>
35   ▼   <remediation_type name="quarantine_src">
36          <display_name>Quarantine Source IP</display_name>
37          <description>Quarantine the Source IP of an event</description>
38   ▼     <policy_event_data>
39            <pe_item>src_ip_addr</pe_item>
40            <pe_item>policy_id</pe_item>
41            <pe_item>rule_id</pe_item>
42            <pe_item>sig_id</pe_item>
43   ⌐     </policy_event_data>
44   ⌐   </remediation_type>
45   ▼   <remediation_type name="quarantine_dst">
46          <display_name>Quarantine Destination IP</display_name>
47          <description>Quarantine the Destination IP of an event</description>
48   ▼     <policy_event_data>
49            <pe_item>dest_ip_addr</pe_item>
50            <pe_item>policy_id</pe_item>
51            <pe_item>rule_id</pe_item>
52            <pe_item>sig_id</pe_item>
53   ⌐     </policy_event_data>
54   ⌐   </remediation_type>
55   ⌐ </module>
56
```

Figure 7-10   *Remediation module.template File*

Next, the main application should be created, which should perform the following:

■ **Load instance configuration:** The FMC creates an instance.conf file in the folder with the executing remediation program. The configuration information should be parsed from the config file into variables for use in the rest of the program.

- **Get parameters from policy:** The FMC passes the remediation type, IP address that should be remediated, the compliance policy and rule that called the remediation, and the signature ID if it was an intrusion event that called the remediation.

- **Whitelist check:** Optionally, your program should be able to check to see if the IP address should not be remediated based on the whitelist configured in the instance.

- **Main program:** Performs the tasks required for the remediation to occur.

- **Error checking:** The API allows for error handling and status updates from the remediation module to ensure everything completed correctly.

Once the main program is created, the remediation API requires that you package your remediation modules, the program, its dependencies, and the module.template file into a gzipped tar file. Figure 7-11 shows a working directory with all the required files for the AMP remediation module. The main program in amp.pl and its dependencies are in the directory along with the module.template file.

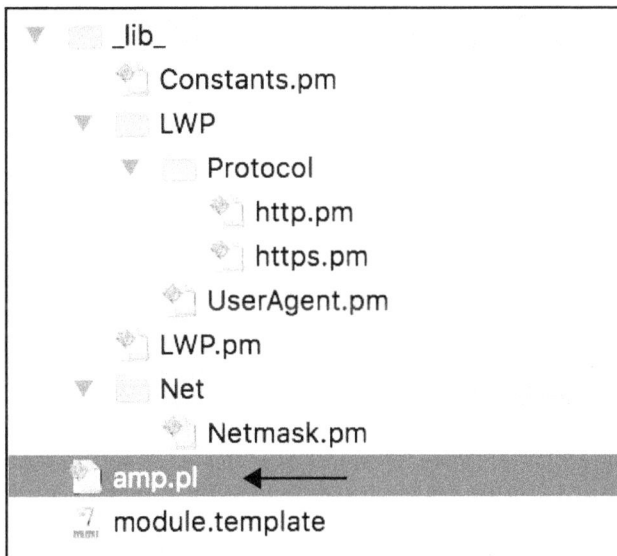

Figure 7-11 *Remediation Module Files before gzip*

After packaging, the module can be uploaded to the FMC and an instance can be configured under **Policies > Actions > Remediations > Instances**, as shown in Figure 7-12. Notice how the module.template file tells the FMC what to ask administrators for on the instance configuration.

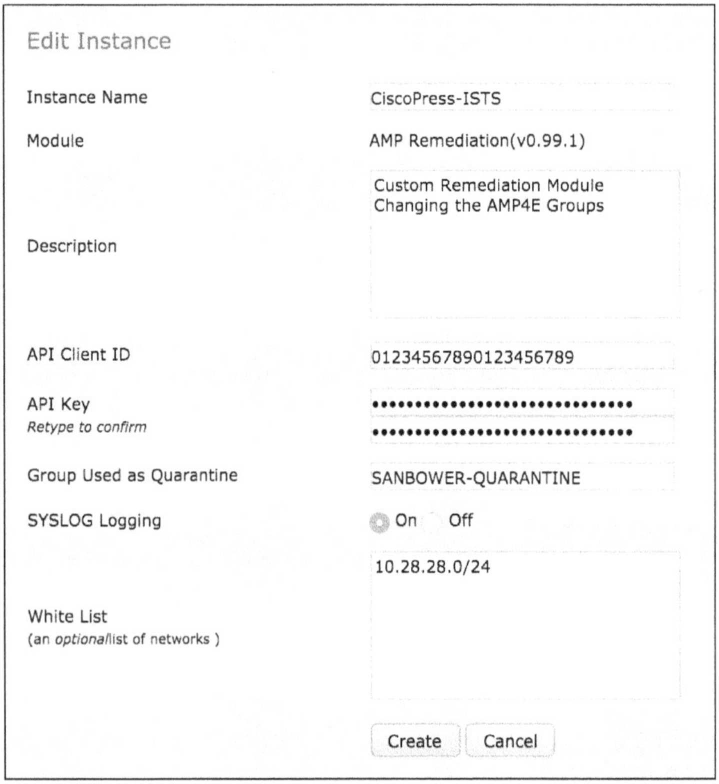

Edit Instance

Instance Name	CiscoPress-ISTS
Module	AMP Remediation(v0.99.1)
Description	Custom Remediation Module Changing the AMP4E Groups
API Client ID	01234567890123456789
API Key	••••••••••••••••••••••••••••••
Retype to confirm	••••••••••••••••••••••••••••••
Group Used as Quarantine	SANBOWER-QUARANTINE
SYSLOG Logging	On Off
White List (an *optional*list of networks)	10.28.28.0/24

Create   Cancel

Figure 7-12 *Remediation Module Instance Configuration*

Then a remediation type should be added on the same instance configuration. This example allows administrators to choose whether they want to quarantine based on the source or destination of an event. The goal would be to match the remediation type with the type of event. For example, if the correlation rule is matching connections to malware or C2 systems, then a source-based remediation would need to be used. If an attacker targeted a server that matched an IPS event, then destination-based remediation would be required.

Once remediations are added, correlation rules and policies can be added under **Policies > Correlation.**

Note   To test and review the entirety of the example code, please see https://github.com/ QuiLoxx/ATS-APIs/tree/master/amp4e/jsanbowe_AMP-RTC.

The remediation API gives organizations endless possibilities in how they automate and orchestrate responses to threats and events.

FMC Host Input API

The Firepower Management Center provides a Host Input API for importing data from other sources on your network to augment the monitored host information. Contextual awareness and host profiles are covered in detail in Chapter 6, "Next-Gen Intrusion Detection and Prevention," of *Integrated Security Technologies and Solutions: Volume I*. If you are setting up a new FMC, you might want to make sure that all the computers listed in your asset management software exist in the network map. You could export the host data from the asset management application, format the results into an appropriately formatted text file, and import the host data using the host input import tool. If the asset management system includes operating system information for each host, you can set up a third-party product map for the asset management system and map each third-party operating system label to the corresponding Cisco label. You can set that map before you run the import, and the system will associate the appropriate Cisco operating system definition with each host.

There are two ways to use the Host Input API to submit network map information: by running the nmimport tool on the FMC, or by using a remote client. In either case, you specify the network map details in a text file with comma-separated values (CSV format).

One example would be to export AMP4E vulnerability data and import into the FMC using the Host Input API. To allow remote use of the Host Input API, the FMC must be configured with a new identity source. Figure 7-13 shows configuration of a new identity source under **Policies > Network Discovery > Edit OS and Identity Sources > Add Source.**

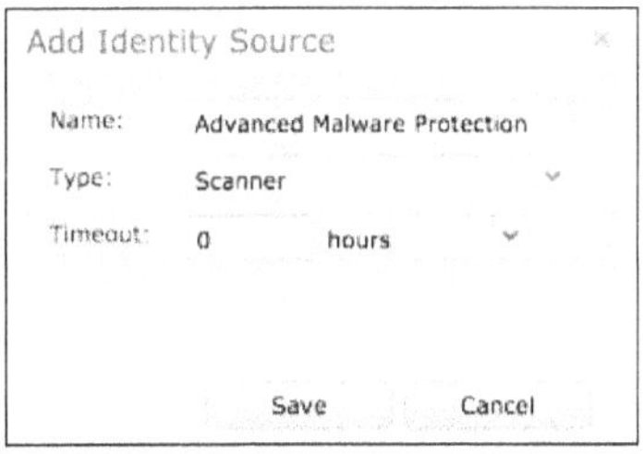

Figure 7-13 *FMC Add Identity Source*

A new host input client must be added under **System > Integration > Host Input Client > Create Client.** Figure 7-14 illustrates adding the new client. After adding the host, the certificate must be downloaded and placed on the client running the host input script.

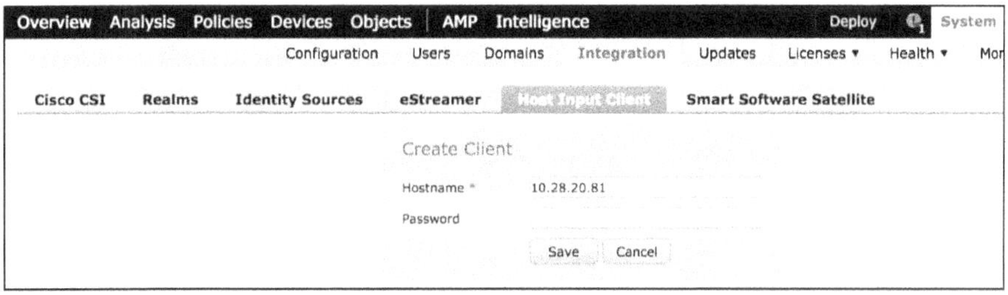

Figure 7-14 *FMC Add Host Input Source*

After setup has been completed on the FMC, the Python script amphost2csv.py can be run to take vulnerabilities that AMP4E has learned about and use the Host Input API to import them into the FMC. Scripts like this example can be scheduled using tools like cron or other similar tools. Figure 7-15 shows the vulnerabilities from AMP found on **Analysis > Vulnerabilities > Third-Party Vulnerabilities**.

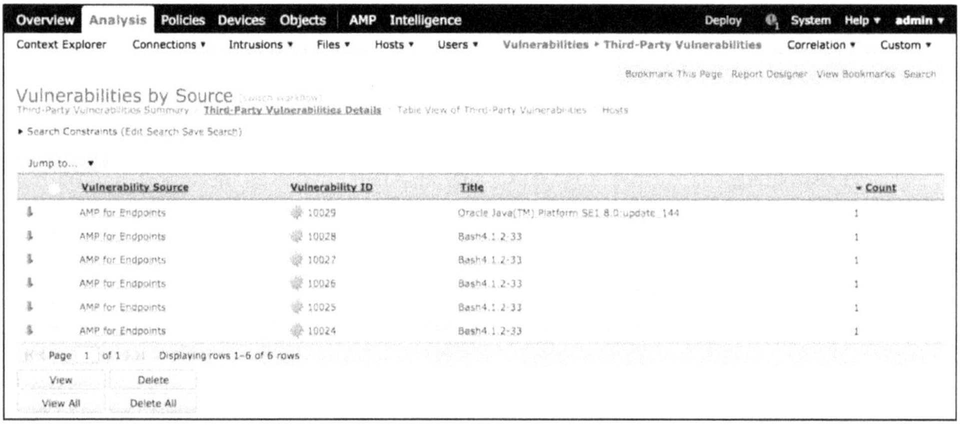

Figure 7-15   *FMC Vulnerabilities Learned from AMP*

Note   To test and review the entirety of the example code, please see https://github.com/QuiLoxx/ATS-APIs.

FMC Database Access API

The FMC Database Access API allows you to query intrusion, discovery, user activity, correlation, connection, vulnerability, and application and URL statistics database tables using a third-party client that supports JDBC SSL connections. Organizations can use an industry-standard reporting tool such as Crystal Reports, Actuate BIRT, or JasperSoft iReport to design and submit queries. A custom application could also be used to query. For example, you can build a servlet to report intrusion and discovery event data periodically or refresh an alert dashboard.

Note   Keep in mind that querying the FMC database reduces available appliance resources and should be used cautiously.

To configure access to the FMC database, perform the following steps:

Step 1. Create a user account and assign it permission to access the database. This permission can be granted by assigning the account the system-provided user role of External Database User.

Step 2. Enable access by going to **System > Configuration > External Database Access > Allow External Database Access.**

Step 3. Add an IP address or fully qualified domain name (FQDN) access control entry.

Step 4. Download the JDBC driver and certificate.

Querying the database requires knowledge of how to construct and execute SELECT statements on single tables and on multiple tables using join conditions. The following query duplicates the Drilldown of Event, Priority, and Classification view in the Events By Priority and Classification workflow. If you have not changed the default Intrusion Events workflow in your user preferences, this is the first page you see when you select **Analysis > Intrusion Events** on the FMC:

```
SELECT rule_message, priority, rule_classification, count(*) as Count
FROM intrusion_event
WHERE reviewed="0" GROUP BY rule_message, priority,
rule_classification
ORDER BY Count
DESCLIMIT 0, 25;
```

FMC eStreamer API

The Firepower System Event Streamer (eStreamer) uses a message-oriented protocol to stream events and host profile information to an application. The application can request event and host profile data from the FMC, and intrusion event data only from a managed device. The client application initiates the data stream by submitting request messages, which specify the data to be sent, and then controls the message flow from the FMC or managed device after streaming begins.

Many security information and event management (SIEM) systems use eStreamer to integrate with the FMC. The setup of eStreamer for third-party or custom applications is the same. To configure eStreamer, navigate to **System > Integration > eStreamer** and click **Create Client**. Add the IP address of the SIEM or custom application server and, optionally, add a password. Click **Save** and then download the certificate to be used by the client.

While on this same screen in the FMC, check the boxes for the events you would like to send via eStreamer and then click **Save**. Figure 7-16 illustrates all the available options for events with eStreamer.

Figure 7-16 *FMC eStreamer Events Configuration*

After setup on the FMC, supported SIEMs can be integrated or a custom application can connect. To help get started, an eStreamer Perl reference client is available for download on CCO, along with other FMC downloads.

Identity Services Engine APIs

Cisco ISE provides complete network access control (NAC) including authentication, profiling, bring your own device (BYOD), guest services, and posture assessment. For more information on ISE, please refer to Chapters 1–4. APIs in ISE allow organizations to automate repetitive tasks, orchestrate policy changes, or integrate third-party systems, such as IT inventory or visitor management systems.

ISE Monitoring REST API

The Monitoring REST API allows organizations to gather session- and node-specific information by querying monitoring ISE nodes. Monitoring REST API calls allow administrators to locate, monitor, and accumulate important real-time, session-based information stored in individual endpoints in a network. The real-time, session-based information that is gathered can help administrators understand Cisco ISE operations and assist in diagnosing conditions or issues. It can also be used to troubleshoot error conditions or an activity or behavior that might be affecting monitoring operations.

The Monitoring API includes session management, which allows administrators to query session counts, session lists, and individual session details, and to remove sessions. A simple example would be to query the active session count:

Request:
```
curl -k https://<USER>:<PASSWORD>@<ISEMnTNODE/admin/API/mnt/Session/
ActiveCount
```
Response:
```
<?xml version="1.0" encoding="UTF-8" standalone="yes"?>
<sessionCount><count>50805</count></sessionCount>
```

The Monitoring API also includes calls for troubleshooting use cases, including retrieving ISE node information, failure reasons information, and authentication/authorization status. The following example shows querying for ISE version information:

Request:
```
curl -k https://<USER>:<PASSWORD>@<ISEMnTNODE>/admin/API/mnt/Version
```
Response:
```
<?xml version="1.0" encoding="UTF-8" standalone="yes"?>
<product name="Cisco Identity Services Engine">
<version>2.3.0.298</version>
<type_of_node>1</type_of_node>
</product>
```

The Monitoring API can also be used for Change of Authorization (CoA). COA enables administrators to send session reauthentication and session disconnect commands such as the following:

Request:
```
curl -k
https://<USER>:<PW>@<ISEMnT>/admin/API/mnt/CoA/
Reauth/<AuthServer>/<MAC>/1
```
Response:
```
<?xml version="1.0" encoding="UTF-8" standalone="yes"?>
<remoteCoA requestType="reauth">
<results>true</results>
</remoteCoA>
```

ISE External RESTful Services API

The ISE External RESTful Services (ERS) API is designed to allow external clients to perform create, read, update, and delete (CRUD) operations on ISE resources. It is based on the HTTPS protocol and REST methodology and uses TCP port 9060. ERS must be enabled manually to start testing. Go to **Administration > System > Settings > ERS Settings** and click the **Enable ERS for Read/Write** radio button, as shown in Figure 7-17.

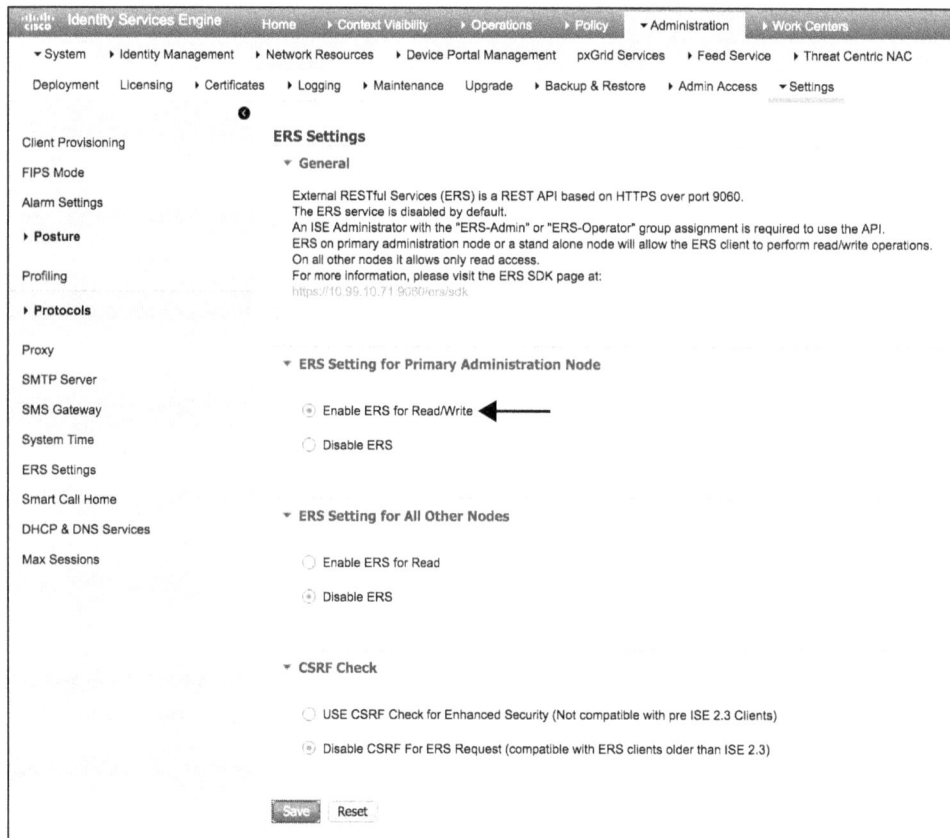

Figure 7-17 *Enable ISE ERS API*

After enabling the ERS API, access must be enabled on per-user basis. Users must be a part of one of the following groups and must be authenticated against the credentials stored in the Cisco ISE internal database:

■ **External RESTful Services Admin:** Full access to all ERS APIs (GET, POST, DELETE, PUT). This user can create, read, update, and delete ERS API requests.

■ **External RESTful Services Operator:** Read-only access (GET request only).

To get started, visit the ERS online software development kit (SDK) by visiting the following URL: https://<ISE-ADMIN-NODE>:9060/ers/sdk. Figure 7-18 illustrates the SDK and how it can be used to learn how to use the API.

External RESTful Services (ERS) Online SDK

> Quick Reference

ISE 2.0 Release Notes
ISE 2.1 Release Notes
ISE 2.2 Release Notes
ISE 2.3 Release Notes
ANC Endpoint
ANC Policy
Active Directory
Admin User
Advanced Customization Global Set
Allowed Protocols
Authorization Profile
BYOD Portal
Certificate Template
Clear Threats and vulnerabilities
Downloadable ACL
Egress Matrix Cell
End Point
End Point Certificates
EndPoints Identity Group
External Radius Server
Guest Location
Guest Smtp Notification Configurati
Guest Ssid
Guest Type
Guest User
Hotspot Portal
IP To SGT Mapping
IP To SGT Mapping Group
ISE Service Information
Identity Group
Identity Sequence
Internal User
My Device Portal
Native Supplicant Profile
Network Device
Network Device Group
Node Details
PSN Node Details with Radius Servi
Portal
Portal Theme

> Developer Resources

ANC Endpoint

- Overview
- Resource definition
- Revision History
- Get-By-Id
- clear
- apply
- Get-All
- Get Version
- Bulk Request
- Monitor Bulk Status

Overview

Adaptive Network Control (ANC) provides the ability to create network endpoint authorization controls based on ANC policies.

Please note that these examples are not meant to be used as is because they have references to DB data. You should treat it as a basic template and edit it before sending to server.

Back to top

Resource definition

Attribute	Type	Required	Default value	Description
name	String	Yes		Resource name
id	String	Yes		Resourse UUID
description	String	No		
macAddress	String	Yes		MAC address of the endpoint

Figure 7-18   *ISE ERS Online SDK*

The ERS API includes many different functions to allow organizations to automate and orchestrate important use cases. The following are some of the more popular functions available via the ERS API:

- **Guest management:** Create, read, update, delete, and search for guest users

- **Endpoint management:** Create, read, update, delete, and search for endpoints

- **Adaptive Network Control (ANC):** Create network endpoint authorization controls based on ANC policies

- **Network and policy configuration:** Allows for CRUD operations on common configuration items, such network access devices, TrustSec, authorization profiles, downloadable access control lists (dACLs), and so on

Similar to the Monitoring API, basic testing of the ERS API can be done using curl. Some of the API calls require additional data fields and input. For example, to add a new network access user using the ERS API, the administrator must include the username and password:

```
Request:
curl -k --include --header 'Content-Type:application/json' --header
'Accept: application/json' -user <ersadmin>:<erspw> --request POST
https://<ISE IP>:9060/ers/config/internaluser  --data '
{
            "InternalUser" : {
                    "name" : "jamie",
                    "password" : "C1sco12345",
                    "changePassword" : false
            }
}'
Response:
HTTP/1.1 201 Created
```

Many different use cases can be automated via the ERS API, and many organizations have already created custom scripts or applications to interface with it.

Advanced Malware Protection APIs

AMP for Endpoints is a next-generation endpoint security solution focused on detecting and preventing threats. AMP for Endpoints provides complete protection against the most advanced attacks. Not only will AMP prevent breaches and block malware at the point of entry, but it will also rapidly detect, contain, and remediate advanced threats if they evade front-line defenses and get inside. For more information on AMP, please refer to Chapter 10, "Protecting Against Advanced Malware," of *Integrated Security Technologies and Solutions: Volume I.*

The AMP API includes many different functions to allow organizations to automate and orchestrate important use cases. The following are some of the more popular functions available via the AMP API:

■ **Computers:** Allows for querying for a list of computers with agents deployed on them. You can use parameters to narrow the search by IP address or hostname. The trajectory associated with a particular computer can also be queried, which provides a list of all activities similar to the device trajectory on the AMP for Endpoints web console.

■ **Endpoint groups:** Create, read, update, delete, and search for groups. Provides basic information about groups in your organization. Allows applications to move endpoints to different groups.

■ **Events and event streaming:** View/get events, trajectory info, and details about events. This enables you to search all computers across your organization for any events or activities associated with a file or network operation, and returns computers matching that criteria.

■ **Files and policy:** Create, read, update, and delete files, file lists, and simple custom detections.

To get started using the AMP API, go to **Accounts > API Credentials**. The API Credentials page allows you to add and remove API credentials for specific scripts or applications. Click **New API Credential**, as shown in Figure 7-19, to generate an API Key for your application.

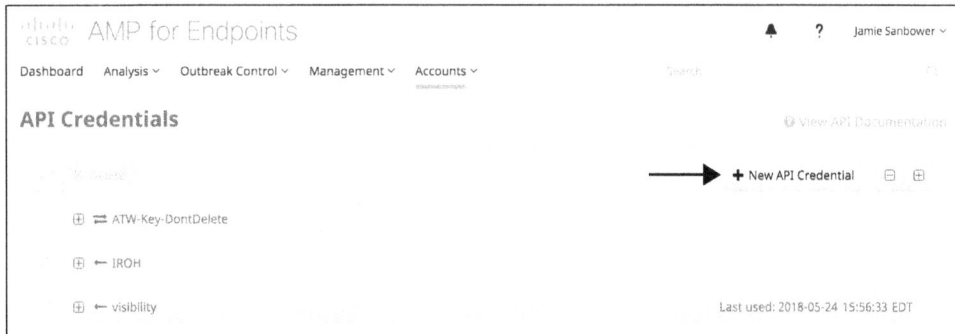

Figure 7-19 *AMP API Credentials*

Enter the name of the application or script for reference purposes and assign a scope of read-only or read and write permissions. You can also select to allow the API credential access to command-line capture data. Figure 7-20 illustrates the configuration of the new credential, and Figure 7-21 shows the resulting API Client ID and API Key that will be used to interact with the AMP API.

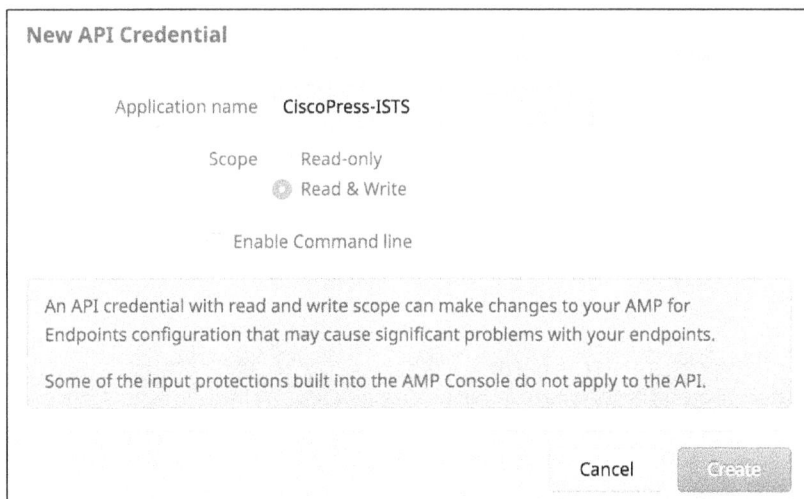

Figure 7-20 *Creating a New AMP API Credential*

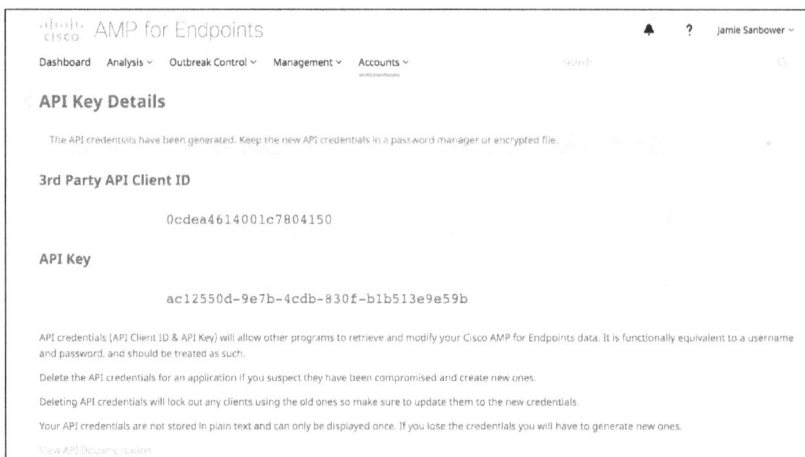

Figure 7-21 *AMP API Client ID and API Key*

After an API Client ID and Key have been generated, a simple request can be performed to test a query. In the following example, a query is used to gather information about a computer based on an IP address:

Request:
```
curl -s -k -X GET -H 'accept: application/json' -H 'content-type:
application/json' \
--compressed -H 'Accept-Encoding: gzip, deflate' -u <apiclientid>:
<apikey> \
'https://api.amp.cisco.com/v1/computers?internal_ip=<ip>'
```
Response:
```
{ "version":"v1.2.0", "metadata":{
     "links":{"self":"https://api.amp.cisco.com/v1/computers?internal_
ip=10.28.200.103"},
     "results":{
        "total":1,
        "current_item_count":1,
        "index":0,
        "items_per_page":500
     }},
   "data":[
     {
        "connector_guid":"e6face26-3d0f-4e13-b192-7855bdbb58f3",
        "hostname":"Cayden's MacBook Pro",
        "active":true,
        "links":{
   "computer":"https://api.amp.cisco.com/v1/computers/e6face26-3d0f-
4e13-b192-7855bdbb58f3",
   "trajectory":"https://api.amp.cisco.com/v1/computers/e6face26-3d0f-
4e13-b192-7855bdbb58f3/trajectory",
```

```
"group":"https://api.amp.cisco.com/v1/groups/9d08284d-d7f6-4549-9386-
1524a937a1ac" },
        "connector_version":"1.7.0.593",
        "operating_system":"OS X 10.13.4",
        "internal_ips":[  "10.28.200.103"],
        "external_ip":"100.64.28.28",
        "group_guid":"9d08284d-d7f6-4549-9386-1524a937a1ac",
        "install_date":"2018-03-31T21:07:01Z",
        "network_addresses":[
            {
                "mac":"a4:5e:60:e9:f8:7d",
                "ip":"10.28.200.103"
            }],
        "policy":{
            "guid":"201ed2ef-97a7-453e-9e8a-d6237dd71866",
            "name":"Initial FireAMP Mac Policy"
        }}]}
```

The results from the query not only give relative information about the computer, but also give links to other key information such as group or device trajectory information. If the application follows the links, those additional details could be useful in providing a security analyst relative information.

The AMP API also allows group changes for computers. For example, an organization might want to automate the moving of a computer from Audit mode to Protect mode. In the following example, the computer ID retrieved from the last query along with a known group ID will be used to set a new group assignment using a PUT request:

Request:
```
curl -s -k -X PATCH -H 'accept: application/json' -H 'content-type:
application/json' \
-H 'content-length: 53' --compressed -H 'Accept-Encoding: gzip,
deflate' \
-d '{"group_guid":"<group_ID>"}' -u <apiclientid>:<apikey>  \
'https://api.amp.cisco.com/v1/computers/<computer_ID>'
```
Response:
```
{  "version":"v1.2.0", "metadata":{
        "links":{
            "self":"https://api.amp.cisco.com/v1/computers/e6face26-3d0f-
4e13-b192-7855bdbb58f3"}},
    "data":{
        "connector_guid":"e6face26-3d0f-4e13-b192-7855bdbb58f3",
        "hostname":"Cayden's MacBook Pro",
        "active":true,
        "links":{
            "computer":"https://api.amp.cisco.com/v1/computers/e6face26-
3d0f-4e13-b192-7855bdbb58f3",
            "trajectory":"https://api.amp.cisco.com/v1/computers/
e6face26-3d0f-4e13-b192-7855bdbb58f3/trajectory",
```

```
        "group":"https://api.amp.cisco.com/v1/groups/d052af4c-a5f0-
4e38-8721-60ff3106e5e8"
      },
      "connector_version":"1.7.0.593",
      "operating_system":"OS X 10.13.4",
      "internal_ips":[
        "10.28.200.103"
      ],
      "external_ip":"71.47.255.162",
      "group_guid":"d052af4c-a5f0-4e38-8721-60ff3106e5e8",
      "install_date":"2018-03-31T21:07:01Z",
      "network_addresses":[  {
          "mac":"a4:5e:60:e9:f8:7d",
          "ip":"10.28.200.103"
        },{
          "mac":"4a:00:00:f2:a1:60",
          "ip":""
        },{
          "mac":"4a:00:00:f2:a1:61",
          "ip":""}],
      "policy":{
        "guid":"201ed2ef-97a7-453e-9e8a-d6237dd71866",
        "name":"Initial FireAMP Mac Policy"
      }}}
```

The successful move is audited through the AMP web console and can be found by going to **Accounts > Audit Log**. Figure 7-22 shows the computer being moved to a new group by user "API client."

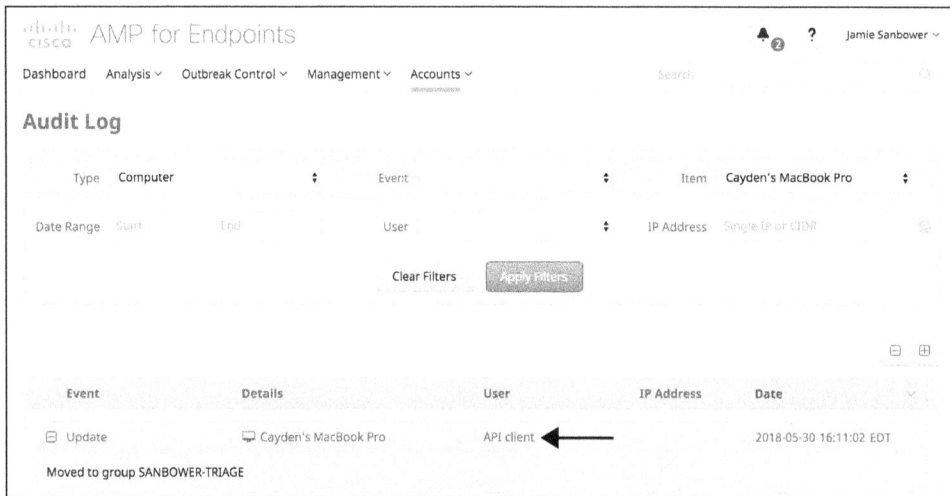

Figure 7-22 *AMP Moving Computer Groups via API*

Threat Grid APIs

Cisco Threat Grid combines advanced sandboxing with threat intelligence into one unified solution to protect organizations from malware. It helps administrators understand what malware is doing, or attempting to do, how large a threat it poses, and how to defend against it. Threat Grid rapidly analyzes files and suspicious behavior across your environment. For more information on Threat Grid, please refer to Chapter 10 of *Integrated Security Technologies and Solutions: Volume I.*

The Threat Grid API allows organizations to submit samples, view results, and search for specific file information. Most look at the API as a way to integrate custom or third-party applications with Threat Grid for malware analysis of files. To get started using the Threat Grid API, go to **User > Details**. The API Key can be found or generated on the page, as shown in Figure 7-23. The API rate limits associated with the user can be found on the same page. For example, the current user can submit up to 50 samples per 1 day. This means that the script, application, or integration using the API should limit submissions to those limits.

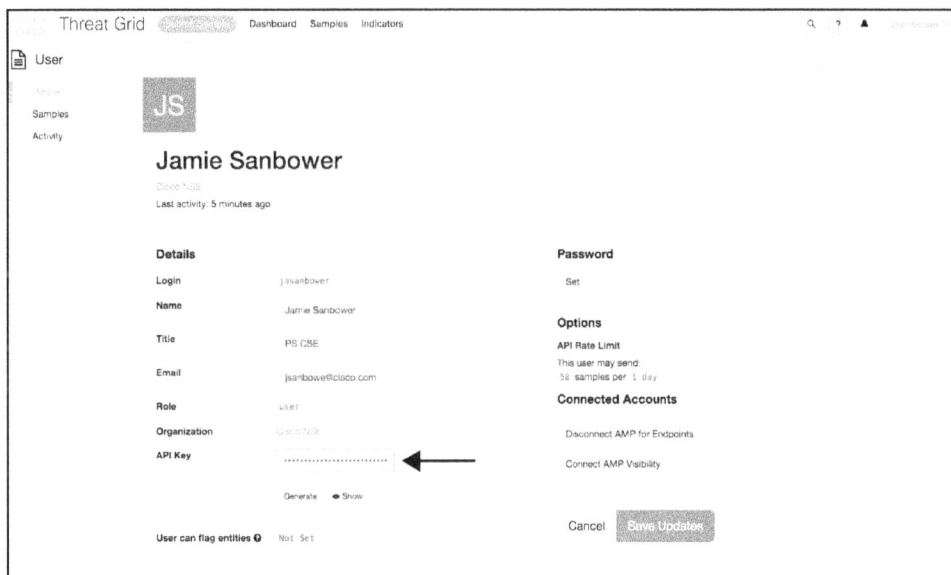

Figure 7-23 *Threat Grid API Key*

The following is an example using curl to submit a custom file to Threat Grid:

```
curl -XPOST -F "sample=@sample.docx" -F "api_key=YOURAPIKEYEHERE"
https://panacea.threatgrid.com/api/v2/samples
```
Request:
```
curl -XPOST -F "sample=@wannacry.exe" -F "api_key=<apikey>" \
https://panacea.threatgrid.com/api/v2/samples
```

Response:
```
{"api_version":2,"id":7322455,"data":{
"tags":[],
"md5":"84c82835a5d21bbcf75a61706d8ab549","vm":null,"submission_
id":524117927,
"state":"wait","login":"jasanbower",
"sha1":"5ff465afaabcbf0150d1a3ab2c2e74f3a4426467",
"filename":"wannacry.exe",
"status":"pending",
"submitted_at":"2018-05-30T21:27:25Z","id":"1ffa74226a06e11bd93392b3f9
0b1cf3"
,"sha256":"ed01ebfbc9eb5bbea545af4d01bf5f1071661840480439c6e5babe8e080
e41aa","os":""}}
```

After submitting a sample to Threat Grid, Threat Grid will run it in its sandbox and, by default, will take 5 to 10 minutes to provide results. The results can also be checked on via API using the sample ID or SHA of the file. The following example shows a sample request and response that could be used to check the summary of threat on the previous submission. This file is indeed very bad, with a threat score of 100.

Request:
```
curl -X GET -F "api_key=<apikey>" \
https://panacea.threatgrid.com/api/v2/samples/<sample_id>/threats
```
Response:
```
{ "api_version":2, "id":3799800,
    "data":{ "count":40, "max-confidence":100,"max-severity":100,
      "bis":[
          "antivirus-flagged-artifact",
          "pe-encrypted-section",
          "file-attribute-modification",
          "windows-util-cacls-everyonefull",
          "pe-header-timestamp-null",
          "wmic-shadowcopy-delete",
          "listening-port-opened",
          "pe-filename-mismatch",
          "modified-executable",
          "process-uses-localhost-traffic",
          "created-executable-in-user-dir",
          "malware-ransomware-wanacryptor",
          "antivirus-service-flagged-artifact",
          "pe-header-timestamp-prior",
          "desktop-wallpaper-modified",
          "artifact-exec-extension-obfuscation",
          "bcdedit-disable-recovery",
          "pe-tls-callback",
          "recycler-exe-artifact",
          "modified-file-in-user-dir",
```

```
        "registry-modification-reg",
        "windows-util-attrib-hide",
        "modified-file-on-usb",
        "file-pending-delete",
        "malware-generic-ransomware-backup-del",
        "recycler-exe-creation",
        "firefox-password-manager-local-database-access",
        "process-long-cmdline",
        "cmd-exe-file-execution",
        "registry-autorun-key-modified",
        "startup-folder-modification",
        "network-snort-sensitive-data",
        "malware-known-trojan-av",
        "document-decoy-dropped",
        "recycler-file-creation",
        "malware-generic-ransomware",
        "command-deleted-shadow-copy",
        "malware-generic-ransomware-entropy",
        "pe-uses-armadillo",
        "bcdedit-ignore-failure"
    ],
    "score":100,
    "sample":"1ffa74226a06e11bd93392b3f90b1cf3"
}}
```

Umbrella APIs

Cisco Umbrella is a solution, delivered from the cloud, that blocks malicious destinations using Domain Name System (DNS). Umbrella has the intelligence to see attacks before the application connection occurs. Umbrella is often considered a first line of defense in an organization's security architecture. In real time, all Internet activity across an organization is logged, categorized by threat and content, and then blocked when necessary. Umbrella can stop threats before a malware file is downloaded or before an IP connection over any port or any protocol is even established. For more information on Umbrella, please refer to Chapter 9, "Umbrella and the Secure Internet Gateway," of *Integrated Security Technologies and Solutions: Volume I.*

Umbrella provides multiple APIs to allow for common use cases. The following are the different available APIs for integration into applications or scripts:

- **Enforcement API:** Add, remove, and list custom blacklisted domains. Allows organizations to add their own domain blacklists to Umbrella for blocking.

- **Network Device Registration API:** Allows vendors to integrate their network devices with Umbrella. This API is used by devices such as Cisco Integrated Services Routers (ISR), Cisco Wireless LAN Controllers (WLC), and others.

■ **Investigate API:** Check the security status and get global security intelligence about a domain, IP address, or subset of domains.

Like other APIs, to get started with the Enforcement API, you must get an API Key by going to **Policies > Integrations** and clicking the Add (+) button. Figure 7-24 illustrates adding a new Integration.

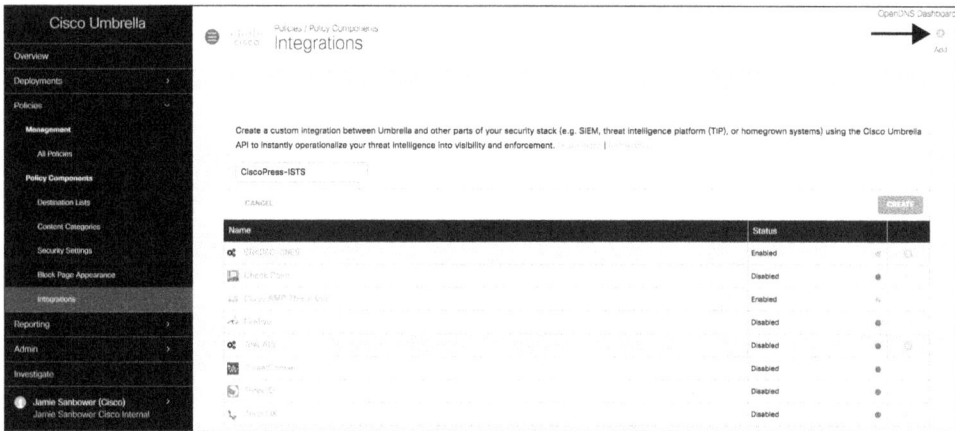

Figure 7-24   *Umbrella Add Integration*

After clicking Create, the integration must be enabled and saved. As a result, the API Key will be provided, as shown in Figure 7-25.

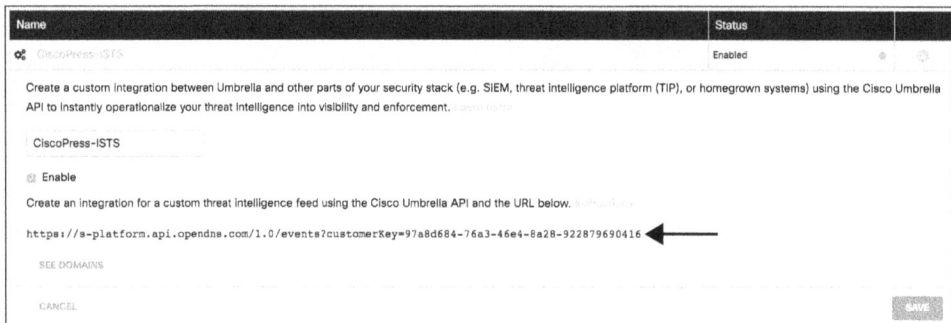

Figure 7-25   *Umbrella Enforcement API Key*

This is also the page that can be used to verify the full lists of domains submitted to the white/blacklist. The following is an example of how to submit a domain using the Enforcement API:

Request:
```
curl 'https://s-platform.api.opendns.com/1.0/events?customerKey=
<customer-api-key>\
-v -X POST -H 'Content-Type: application/json' \
```

```
-d '[{
   "alertTime": "2013-02-08T11:14:26.0Z",
   "deviceId": "ba6a59f4-e692-4724-ba36-c28132c761de",
   "deviceVersion": "13.7a",
   "dstDomain": "internetbadguys.com",
   "dstUrl": "http://internetbadguys.com/a-bad-url",
   "eventTime": "2013-02-08T09:30:26.0Z",
   "protocolVersion": "1.0a",
   "providerName": "CiscoPress-ISTS"
}]'
```
Response:
```
{"id":"125bd578,17b6,47f9,bf98-ef4687687158"}
```

Figure 7-26 illustrates the destination list with the newly updated blacklisted domain. To enforce the list, go to **Policies > Policy Components > Security Settings > Integrations** and select the newly created integration.

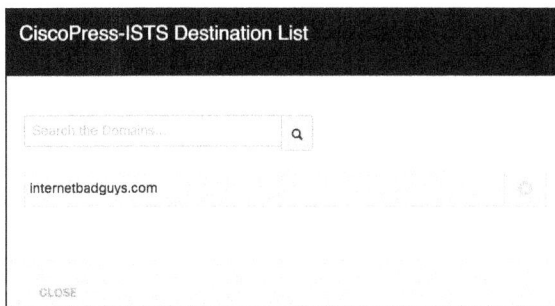

Figure 7-26 *Umbrella Enforcement API Domains*

Summary

In this chapter, you learned about the APIs available in the Cisco Security Architecture. You examined how to set up and interact with the APIs and were introduced to the most popular use cases. You saw examples using curl, which could easily be reproduced in your programming language of choice.

References

"Application Programming Interface," https://en.wikipedia.org/wiki/Application_programming_interface

"Cisco DevNet," https://en.wikipedia.org/wiki/Cisco_DevNet

"Firepower Management Center REST API Quick Start Guide, Version 6.2.3," https://www.cisco.com/c/en/us/td/docs/security/firepower/623/api/REST/Firepower_Management_Center_REST_API_Quick_Start_Guide_623/About_the_Firepower_REST_API.html

"Firepower System Remediation API Guide, Version 6.0," https://www.cisco.com/c/en/us/td/docs/security/firepower/60/api/remediation/FireSIGHT-System-Remediation-API-Guide.html

"Firepower System Host Input API Guide, Version 6.0," https://www.cisco.com/c/en/us/td/docs/security/firepower/60/api/host-input/HostInputAPIGuide/Intro.html

"Firepower System Database Access Guide, Version 6.2," https://www.cisco.com/c/en/us/td/docs/security/firepower/620/api/db-access/Database_Access.html

"Firepower System Event Streamer Integration Guide, Version 6.2.3," https://www.cisco.com/c/en/us/td/docs/security/firepower/623/api/eStreamer/EventStreamerIntegrationGuide_623.html

"Cisco AMP for Endpoints API," https://api-docs.amp.cisco.com/

"Getting Started with Threat Grid APIs," https://panacea.threatgrid.com/doc/main/api-getting-started.html

Part III

c28889775343d1ed91b

Chapter 8

Security Connectivity

Cryptography is nothing new. One of the earliest forms of cryptography was found to be used in the ancient writings of hieroglyphics in Egypt around 1900 BCE. At the basic level, cryptography is the use of codes and ciphers to hide the plaintext of a message in a manner that it can be deciphered only with the use of a key. Cryptography can be as rudimentary as a scytale, a strip of leather or paper wrapped around a pole and engraved with the message. When the strip is straight, the message is obfuscated from anyone who sees it in its travels to the intended recipient and can be decrypted only with the key, which in this case is the carrier of the message knowing the diameter of the pole around which to rewrap the strip for the recipient to read the message. Obviously, cryptography has come a long way since the days of hieroglyphics and scytales. In this chapter, we will review the components and functions of today's cryptographic mechanisms for network security as well as their use in securing the message while it is in transit across the network.

Hashing, Ciphers, Cryptography, and PKI

Today's cryptographic capabilities are vast and many. You have likely heard of DES, 3DES, AES, DH, IKEv1, IKEv2, SSL, TLS, ECC, and more. All cryptography, with the exception of hashing, is the function of taking a plaintext message and converting it to ciphertext with a key, for purposes of storage or for transport to a trusted party for decryption. As security has become paramount in most networks today, the need for stronger cryptographic mechanisms has resulted in many new ways to convert that plaintext to ciphertext. This section covers the common cryptographic mechanisms and their function that you will need to know for the CCIE exams.

Hashing

Hashes are an integral part of securing data transport and storage. Hashes are commonly used for protecting passwords, ensuring file integrity, digital signatures, and more. *Hashing* is the function of taking data in any form, size, or length and providing a fixed-length output string of characters or digest value. Depending on the hashing algorithm used, it will always output the exact same length of characters no matter what the input. Also important is that any change to the input data, even down to a single 0 being changed to a 1, will significantly change the hash output.

Note   Although a hash output may look like ciphertext, it is not encryption. Hashing is commonly referred to as one-way encryption. Hashing is irreversible and you cannot, no matter how hard you try, regenerate the plaintext from only the hash.

Two important items for hashes is that they should be able to generate the hash quickly and they should not be subject to *collision*, which occurs when two different file inputs could generate the same hash output.

Some of the more popular hashing algorithms are as follows:

- **SHA1:** Secure Hash Algorithm 1 has a digest value length of 160 bits. SHA1 is rather old and has been found to be vulnerable to collision attacks and thus has been replaced by SHA2 in many cases.

- **SHA2:** Secure Hash Algorithm 2 is a group of hash functions that have different input byte size options. There are six digest value lengths of 224, 256, 384, 512, 512/224, and 512/256 bits.

- **MD5:** Ron Rivest developed MD5. You may know his name from the popular RSA public key cryptography algorithm named after him and his co-inventors, Adi Shamir and Leonard Adleman. MD5 takes in multiples of 512 bits of data and produces a 128-bit message digest. Due to the short message digest, MD5 has been found to be vulnerable to collision attacks.

Let's take a look at some examples of hashing. First, we will use MD5 to hash "Cisco CCIE":

```
echo Cisco CCIE | md5
2034eaac75b4810aaa529aa2074c3c14
```

As you can see, the MD5 algorithm took the text output and created the message digest unique to that string. But what happens if we change just one character of the string and run it again? Let's try "Cisco CC1E":

```
echo Cisco CC1E | md5
c81fb446da8942502dcdf1ad9b657d90
```

The output hash from that text is completely different, as you can see. Now let's see what a SHA256 function will do with the same string as the first example:

```
echo Cisco CCIE | shasum -a 256
baa03c5f1608953de43bc65215bc321827c929b32c4671fd0d572006bc00e6a9
```

The output using SHA256 gives us a much longer unique output. The longer message digest allows us to gain some collision resistance.

As mentioned at the beginning of this section, hashing can also help us ensure file integrity, which is especially useful when downloading files from the Internet. A lot of malicious attacks and malware compromises have been traced back to malicious file downloads by end users of what seemed to be legitimate software. As an example of the role of hashing in downloading from the Internet, let's look at the Cisco.com software download portal. We are going to download the latest Identity Services Engine patch for version 2.3.0 and validate its integrity after download.

Figure 8-1 shows the Cisco Software Download page for ISE Release 2.3.0 and the checksums for the software package.

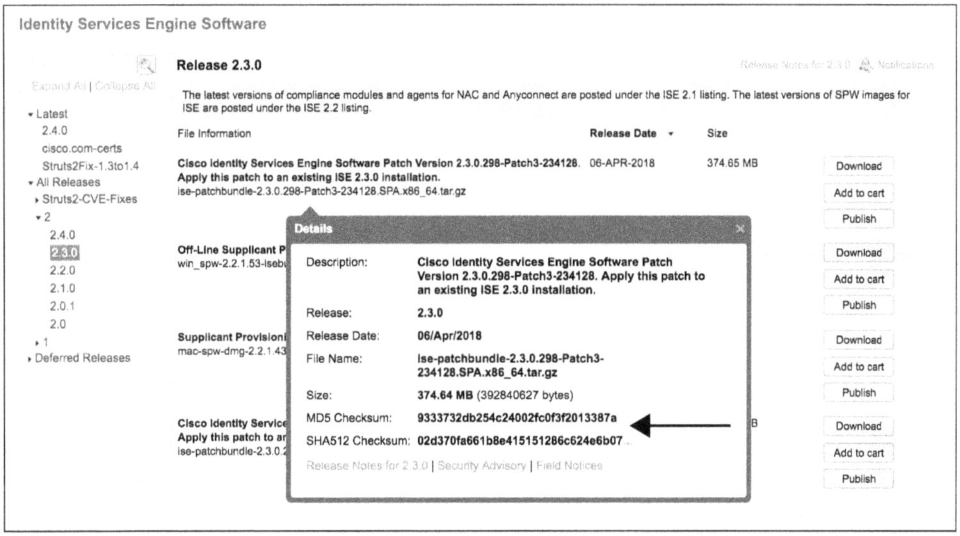

Figure 8-1   *Checksums for Cisco Software Download*

As you can see, Cisco provides both an MD5 checksum and a SHA512 checksum for the file so the end user can validate that the file they have downloaded matches and has not been corrupted or maliciously modified in transit to their workstation. Let's check the file after download:

```
md5 ise-patchbundle-2.3.0.298-Patch3-234128.SPA.x86_64.tar.gz
9333732db254c24002fc0f3f2013387a
```

As you can see, the MD5 hash matches the one shown on Cisco.com, so you can be sure that the patch file is *exactly* the same as the file that is tested and hosted on the server.

Note   The same MD5 algorithm was run against a 375-MB file and the resulting hash was the exact same length output as the previous example with the simple "Cisco CCIE" text string.

Cipher Types

A *cipher* is a method for encrypting and subsequently decrypting messages. You may have also heard ciphers referred to as *encryption algorithms*. There are two types of ciphers in use on today's networks, block ciphers and stream ciphers.

Block Ciphers

Block ciphers are the practice of encrypting and decrypting plaintext using a fixed size of bits of data. The cipher in use dictates the sizes of these blocks, such as 64, 128, 192, and 256 bits of data. Most mainstream symmetric ciphers are block ciphers, such as the DES, 3DES, AES, and Blowfish encryption algorithms.

Figure 8-2 shows a representation of how block ciphers encrypt data.

Figure 8-2   *Block Cipher Flow*

Stream Ciphers

Stream ciphers differ from block ciphers in the fact that they encrypt data one bit at a time versus in blocks of bits. Stream ciphers also leverage a key, but that key is used in conjunction with a pseudorandom generator to create a stream of pseudorandom bits for encrypting the plaintext. The most common stream cipher in use today is RC4, which is commonly used in WEP and WPA for wireless authentication.

Figure 8-3 shows a representation of how stream ciphers encrypt and decrypt data.

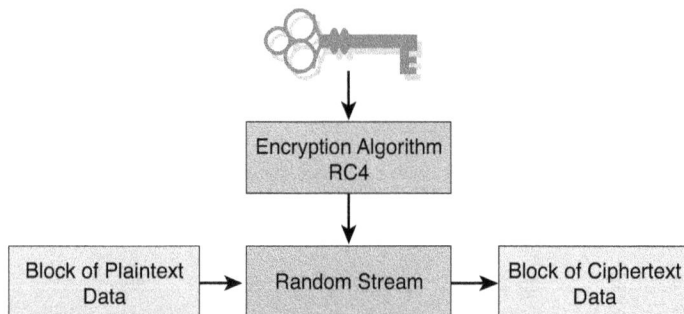

Figure 8-3   *Stream Cipher Flow*

Encryption Schemes

Block ciphers and stream ciphers are useless without the keys used to encode the ciphertext. How those keys are used breaks down into two categories: symmetric encryption and asymmetric encryption.

Symmetric Encryption

The opening of this chapter mentioned the scytale, a ciphertext generated by wrapping a strip of material around a pole. Although rudimentary, it is an example of a symmetric encryption scheme. The same size pole must be used to encrypt and decrypt the message. Symmetric encryption uses the same key to convert plaintext to and from ciphertext. Many of the ciphers, such as DES, 3DES, RC4, RC5, RC6, and AES, are also symmetric encryption schemes as well.

One of the primary challenges of symmetric encryption is that the key must be known by both the sender and the receiver of the message. The transport of that key could compromise the message if the key and message fall into the wrong hands. Shortly we will talk about secure key exchange mechanisms that work to protect the key to ensure the message integrity is maintained.

Figure 8-4 shows an example of a key use in symmetric encryption.

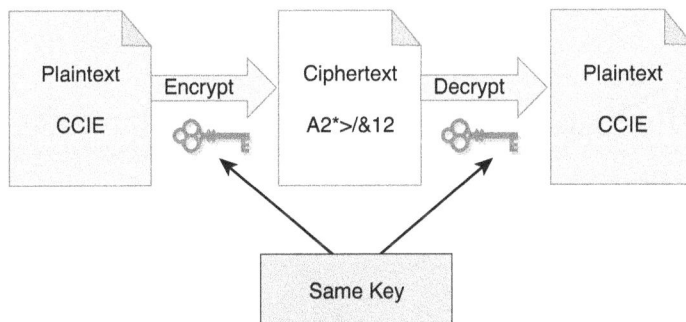

Figure 8-4   *Symmetric Encryption*

Asymmetric Encryption

A newer encryption scheme that also uses keys is asymmetric encryption, also commonly called public key cryptography. Asymmetric encryption leverages two keys, versus the one key used in symmetric encryption. These keys are called the *public and private key pair*. As the name implies, the public key can be shared with any party with which the key owner wishes to encrypt traffic. The private key, on the other hand, is just that, private. Private keys are commonly protected with a password, and the pair owner can dictate who or what devices have access to the key for encryption. When a process or application wants to encrypt traffic using public key cryptography, the sender will encrypt the traffic using the public key of the recipient. Once encrypted, the traffic can only be decrypted by the private key that matches the public key. When that user wishes to respond, if the original sender does not use public key cryptography, then they can encrypt the traffic with their private key, which can be decrypted by the public key, or if the user does have a public key, they can use the same process as was used for them to receive the message but with the original sender's public key.

Note Just like symmetric encryption, if the private key is compromised, then the security of the asymmetric encryption is at risk. The private key should be protected with utmost care.

Figure 8-5 shows an example of key use in asymmetric encryption.

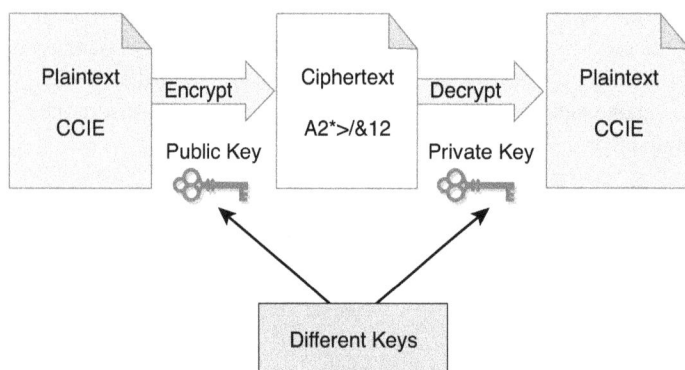

Figure 8-5 *Asymmetric Encryption*

The Keys to the Kingdom

We have been talking a lot about keys and how integral they are to encryption and protecting data. Something that you don't want to do is lose your keys! Losing your keys to the car is one thing. Losing the keys to your privacy and data is much worse, especially if they are the keys to your company's or nation's secrets. One of the challenges with encryption and cryptography is that it involves building connections over the Internet. The Internet is public and there are many actors on the Internet whose goal is to steal your data. What this means is that we must have a method for exchanging and transporting keys between trusted hosts and systems and a protocol for establishing a secure communications channel.

Authentication Mechanisms

So, you might be thinking, what are these keys? Keys can come in many forms and are sometimes even dynamically generated and formed from some other piece of information. Authentication provides a function to validate that something is valid or trusted, such as a peer to establish secure communications. We will now cover the common authentication methods that you will see covered in the CCIE exam.

Preshared Key

A preshared key (PSK) is the simplest of keys. You probably have used PSK in your daily life for wireless networks, codes for doors and garages, and so on. The PSK is set by the administrator and distributed to all the users who might need to use the key for access. The key is considered valid by any system that has been configured to validate it no matter who enters the code. This trust-based distribution of the key is one of the flaws of using PSKs. In many IT systems, the PSK will be hashed for obscurity, but that doesn't stop the person who knows the key from sharing it with others.

Some improvements have been made recently with Identity PSK (IPSK) in which a wireless network allows a single PSK SSID to have individual PSKs for each device session. Identity PSK eliminates the issues with unauthorized key sharing by directly associating a PSK with a MAC address in an external authentication server. IPSK leverages the use of AAA and RADIUS running on a server such as ISE, as previously covered in Chapters 1 through 3.

Username and Password

Another form of authentication that you should be very familiar with is the username and password (UN/PW) combination. This method of authentication is used daily by millions of people around the world for logins to workstations, websites, remote access VPNs, and more. Although a UN/PW is more unique than a PSK and more like using IPSK, it still falls to the same fate as PSKs regarding unauthorized use of the password by another person or device. With so many systems using a UN/PW for login verification, many people have a hard time keeping all of them straight. Some people resort to writing their UN/PWs on notes and storing them under their keyboard or keeping them in password books in their desk drawer, which presents the problem of someone else finding them and using them for malicious intent.

One-Time Password and Tokens

With PSKs and UN/PWs being commonly stolen and used for attacks or theft, the IT security industry developed another authentication option to increase security of logins. One-time passwords (OTPs) and/or authentication tokens have proven to be successful and are still widely used today for secure logins for functions such as network device CLI access and banking websites. A one-time password, as the name implies, is a password that is good for one use within a specific time period. OTPs are very often combined with the users' regular login passwords. This is commonly achieved with a hardware or software token that is time synchronized with a server and generates a new password on a regular timed interval using a mathematical algorithm based on the previous password or a challenge/counter.

With so many people in the world owning a smartphone these days, many companies have started using a software application on those devices as the OTP token for the end user. Companies such as Google, Apple, Paypal, RSA, and more offer OTP services to their customers for a higher level of security login authentication.

X509 PKI and Certificates

The final authentication mechanism that we will cover is certificate-based authentication or Public Key Infrastructure (PKI) and the X509 standard. PKI is more than just a certificate and key; it is an entire system with specific roles, procedures, and policies around the creation, distribution/revocation, use, storage, and management of digital certificates. The PKI system is designed to associate a certificate with a person, website, or system and provide a rigorous validation mechanism to ensure that the connection is authenticated and secure.

One of the benefits of PKI is that each certificate that is issued is bound to a person or system that is requesting it. Commonly, the private key that is bound to the identity certificate is not exportable from the system in which the client made the request for/from and is password protected. Smartcards are one exception because the certificate is issued to a chip embedded in a card that can be used on multiple systems. With smartcards, the private key is further protected by a pin that only the card holder knows to unlock the key for use by the application.

The following are the primary roles of the systems in PKI:

- **Certificate authority (CA):** PKI starts with a CA. The CA is the trusted root of the PKI that signs all certificates and maintains the status of each certificate through its lifecycle. For the certificates issued in the PKI system to be trusted, the CA must be trusted by others looking to secure data with systems signed by that CA. The CA has its own public key and private key that constitute its certificate. With the trust of the PKI system relying on the trust of the CA, the private key of the CA must be secured with utmost care. Commonly in a large PKI environment, the CA will be kept offline so as to protect the server from compromise and the theft of the CA's private key.

- **Registration authority (RA):** The RA is commonly a subordinate root of the CA and its primary role is to validate and issue certificates to the requesting user or system. The RA receives the request and passes it to the CA, which forwards it to a certificate server that generates the certificate and delivers it to the requestor.

- **Validation authority (VA):** The VA is the component within the PKI that is used for systems outside of the PKI to validate the certificate. There are two primary validation methods: Certification Revocation Lists (CRLs) and the Online Certificate Status Protocol (OCSP). A CRL offers HTTP or LDAP protocols for download of the CRL. Systems trying to validate the certificate validity can download the CRL and evaluate certificates presented to it against the list to ensure its status. OCSP is served over HTTP and, instead of being a list, is a direct query mechanism for certificate validation. (Both methods are described further in the "Certificate Revocation" section a bit later in the chapter.)

Figure 8-6 shows an example flow of a basic PKI for an encrypted exchange between two users.

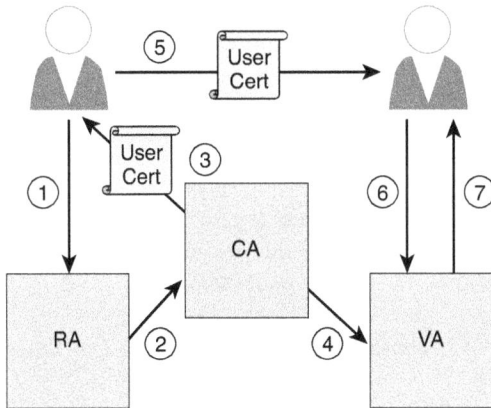

Figure 8-6 *Public Key Infrastructure*

The steps are as follows:

1. User1 requests a certificate from the RA.

2. The RA authenticates the requesting user and forwards the request to the issuing CA or certificate server.

3. The certificate server issues the certificate for the user and the user installs the certificate and private key on his or her device/system.

4. The CA notifies the VA of the status of the certificate.

5. User1 starts a PKI-authenticated session with User2.

6. User2 receives User1's public key of the certificate and validates its status with the VA.

7. The VA responds to User2 with the certificate status and User2 takes action based on the VA response.

Certificate Trust Relationship

The trust that comes with certificates is an important thing to understand for the exam as well as for the work you'll be doing after you get your CCIE number. There are a few important terms to understand:

- **Root CA:** The beginning of the trust chain.

- **Intermediate CA:** A certificate authority that is signed by the root CA and signs end-system certificates on behalf of the root CA.

As mentioned, there is always a root CA in every PKI implementation. This CA is the root of trust for all certificates issued to that organization and its customers. The root CA might not be the only CA in the infrastructure though, and as previously stated, many root CAs are kept offline, which means a new player comes into the game, called the *subordinate CA* or *intermediate CA*. The sub CA's certificate is signed by the root and is capable of all of the signing capabilities like the root; however, is not the top of the trust chain. Again, maintaining the security of the root CA's certificate key is paramount, and if it's compromised, all the certificates signed by that root are inherently compromised.

Becoming a trusted root CA is not a small task. Most major certificate issuers like Verisign, Comodo, GoDaddy, GeoTrust, and more have gone through the work and requirements of becoming trusted CAs and subsequently are published as such in all major browsers and operating systems. These root CAs typically have multiple signing intermediate CAs issuing to their customers certificates that are then being used by millions of users on the Internet every day.

Figure 8-7 shows the certificate trust relationship for Cisco.com. You can see that the root CA is QuoVadis Root CA 2 and the intermediate CA is HydrantID SSL ICA G2. The www.cisco.com certificate is the web server certificate and the end of the chain of trust.

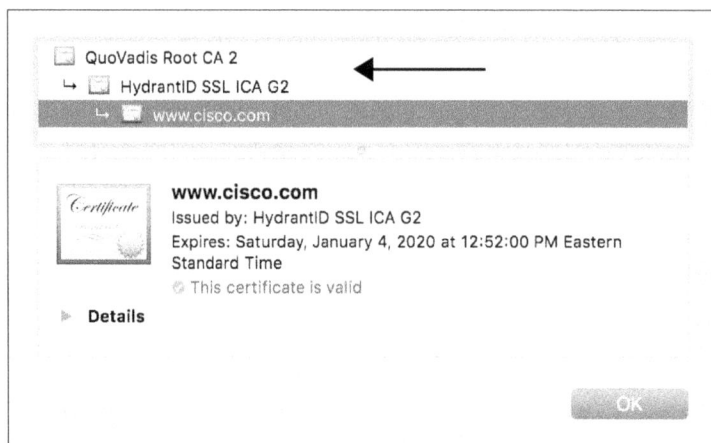

Figure 8-7   *Certificate Trust Relationship*

Certificate Lifecycle Expiration and Revocation

So now that we have covered extensively how a PKI is fashioned in an enterprise, it's now important to briefly cover the three major phases in the lifecycle of certificates: issue, expire, and revoke. We have already covered how certificates are issued extensively, so we will jump right into the expire and revoke phases, which are also relevant for your CCIE exams.

The process of certificate validation is commonly equated to the process of obtaining a U.S. driver's license or passport. Both of these forms of identification are issued by trusted parties—a U.S. state government for the driver's license and the U.S. Department of State for the passport. We will refer to these forms of ID as we continue the discussion of certificates.

Certificate Expiration

Both driver's licenses and passports have an issue date and expiration date printed on them along with a barcode or chip for electronic validation. Similarly, certificates have an issue/validity start date and time and an expiration/validity end date and time. These dates and times are very important in certificate-based protocols because the certificate can be used only during the time window specified. This is a good point to bring up that proper and synchronized Network Time Protocol (NTP) in your lab is *very* critical because otherwise failures might occur due to validity of the certificate not being started yet or already over. If you have ever let your driver's license or passport expire, you know that these dates are absolute and, no matter the reason, once the expiration date has passed, the license or passport is no longer valid to be used as identification. This same rule applies to certificates.

Figure 8-8 shows and example start and end dates and times for the www.cisco.com web server certificate.

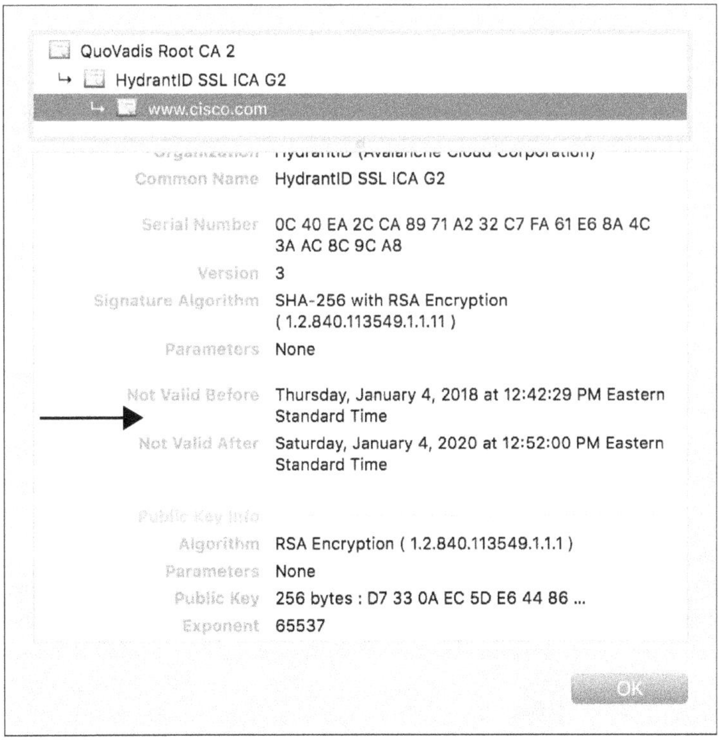

QuoVadis Root CA 2
    ↳ HydrantID SSL ICA G2
        ↳ www.cisco.com

Organization	HydrantID (Avalanche Cloud Corporation)
Common Name	HydrantID SSL ICA G2
Serial Number	0C 40 EA 2C CA 89 71 A2 32 C7 FA 61 E6 8A 4C 3A AC 8C 9C A8
Version	3
Signature Algorithm	SHA-256 with RSA Encryption (1.2.840.113549.1.1.11)
Parameters	None
Not Valid Before	Thursday, January 4, 2018 at 12:42:29 PM Eastern Standard Time
Not Valid After	Saturday, January 4, 2020 at 12:52:00 PM Eastern Standard Time
Public Key Info	
Algorithm	RSA Encryption (1.2.840.113549.1.1.1)
Parameters	None
Public Key	256 bytes : D7 33 0A EC 5D E6 44 86 ...
Exponent	65537

OK

Figure 8-8 *Certificate Validity*

You can also check validity dates for certificates on Cisco IOS using the **show crypto pki certificates** command, as demonstrated in Example 8-1.

Example 8-1   *Certificate Validity*

```
SVCRTR-2921#sh crypto pki certificates
CA Certificate
  **Output omitted **
  Validity Date:
    start date: 22:25:55 EST Jun 17 2015
    end   date: 22:35:55 EST Jun 17 2025
```

Certificate Revocation

Now that we have covered the issue and expire phases, let's talk about the revoke phase. *Certificate revocation* is when a certificate is deemed no longer valid for use even though the expiration date has not passed at the time of revocation. This commonly happens when a certificate key is compromised or when a person has left a company or, worse, has been terminated. Returning to the driver's license example, if a licensed driver is a repeat offender on the roads, such as multiple citations for driving while intoxicated or for continually and blatantly ignoring the rules of the road, that driver may have their license revoked by the state that issued it. When that happens, the license is no longer valid, even if the expiration date has not been reached. The driver may still hold the physical license card, but if they get pulled over again after their license was revoked, the police officer will discover via their onboard computer that the license has been revoked and will likely give the driver a new set of bracelets and a nice ride to the big house for driving with a revoked license. Similarly, if a certificate is revoked, although you may still have the electronic certificate and key on your system, it will not be valid when checked against the revocation lists from your issuer and you will be denied access (sans the shiny new bracelets).

As briefly mentioned in the discussion of PKI, there are two ways that certificate revocation is checked:

- **Certificate Revocation List (CRL):** This is basically a signed list that the CA publishes on a website that can be read by authentication servers. The file is periodically downloaded and stored locally on the authentication server, and when a certificate is being authenticated, the server examines the CRL to see if the client's certificate has been revoked already. A CRL could be compared to a police officer having a printed list of suspended/revoked driver's licenses in his or her squad car.

- **Online Certificate Status Protocol (OCSP):** This is the preferred method for revocation checks in most environments today, because it provides updates in near real time. OCSP enables the authentication server to send a real-time request (such as an HTTP web request) to the service running on the CA or another device and check the status of the certificate in near real time. OCSP could be compared to a police officer scanning the barcode on a driver's license via a computer in the squad car to determine whether the license is listed in the DMV's database of suspended/revoked licenses.

We have now covered everything that you will need to know for PKI in the exams. It is strongly recommended that you set up and play with certificates in the lab. Use of certificates is a commonly misunderstood topic, and deep knowledge of the operation and interdependencies of the PKI system is a valuable tool in today's secure networks.

Security Protocols

The next step is to discuss the protocols that leverage the ciphers, hashing, keys, and PKI to establish secure communications over the network. The options are vast and many, so we are going to focus on the protocols and their function that you need to know for the CCIE exam. Chapters 9, "Infrastructure VPN" & 10, "Remote Access VPN" will cover the details of configuration, so this section describes the protocols' use and operation at a topical level.

IPsec

When establishing a secure communications channel between peers, the most common method is to use the framework of open standards called *IPsec*. IPsec provides data confidentiality, data integrity, and data authentication between the initiators and responders of data flows. IPsec can be used in multiple types of encryption scenarios such as LAN-to-LAN, host-to-host, and host-to-LAN tunneling. IPsec leverages the Internet Key Exchange (IKE) mechanism to generate the keys used for authentication of peers and encryption of data.

IKEv1

Internet Key Exchange (IKE) versions 1 and 2 are protocols used in the IPsec suite of protocols to establish a security association (SA) over the network. First, we will cover IKEv1. IKEv1 has two phases that you should be very familiar with for the CCIE exam.

Phase 1

The main purpose of this phase is to authenticate the peers and establish a secure channel using ISAKMP for Phase 2 negotiations. (See the "ISAKMP" section later in the chapter for more details about this protocol.) The following items are completed during Phase 1:

- Secure the identity and authenticate the two peers

- Negotiate an acceptable and matching encryption, hashing policy to protect the IKE exchange

- Generate secret keys between the peers using an authenticated Diffie-Hellman (DH) exchange

This establishes a secure tunnel for Phase 2 negotiation.

Phase 1 can operate in two modes based on configuration and requirements of security on the tunnels:

- **Main Mode:** This mode consists of three bidirectional exchanges between the peers to negotiate the SA:

  - **Step 1.** The peers communicate their acceptable algorithms and hashing that will be used to secure the IKE communications. The peers must match on the algorithm and hashing decision, and commonly the IKE configuration will have multiple acceptable policies defined.

  - **Step 2.** Diffie-Hellman key exchange is used to generate shared secret keying material between the peers, which is then used to generate shared keys. This process also enables the clients to pass nonces or random numbers that are exchanged, signed, and returned to validate and prove the peer identity.

  - **Step 3.** The peer identities are validated via the peer IP address being represented in encrypted form.

- **Aggressive Mode:** This mode of IKE negotiation basically just combines more information into fewer exchanges between the peers. In the first exchange, the IKE proposal, Diffie-Hellman public key, nonce, and identity packet are all sent by the initiator to the other peer. The receiving peer simply validates and accepts (if acceptable) and responds with everything that is needed to complete the exchange. The initiator confirms the exchange and the SAs are established. The weakness with Aggressive Mode is that a sniffer can capture information, such as peer identity, in the clear as it is exchanged before a secure channel is established. Aggressive Mode is, however, faster than Main Mode negotiation.

The end result of Phase 1 is matching ISAKMP SAs between the peers for protecting subsequent communications such as IPsec SA negotiation in Phase 2. The Phase 1 ISAKMP SAs have a lifetime in seconds or kilobytes, and at the end of the lifetime, actions such as rekeying or termination will take place depending on the active condition of the peer tunnel needs.

Figure 8-9 shows a simplified flow of IKE Phase 1.

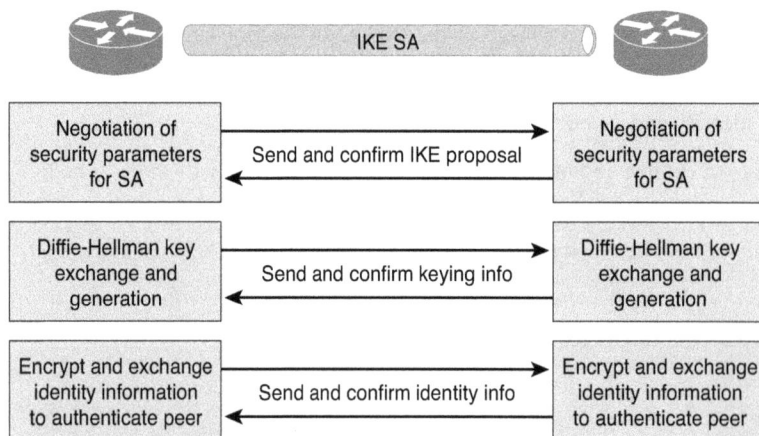

Figure 8-9 *IKE Phase 1 Negotiation*

Phase 2

Now that Phase 1 is complete, the IKE process moves on to Phase 2 in which the outcome is negotiated and established IPsec SAs for the IPsec tunnel. During Phase 2 the following functions are performed:

- Using the protection of the IKE, Phase 2 negotiates the parameters of the IPsec SA.

- Establishment of the IPsec security association.

- The Phase 2 IPsec SAs periodically renegotiate the SA to maintain security.

- An additional Diffie-Hellman exchange can also be performed during Phase 2.

Just like Phase 1 has modes, Phase 2 does as well, but it has only one mode, called Quick Mode. During the Quick Mode process, the following parameters are exchanged, negotiated, and established:

- Exchange of the IPsec policy.

- Generation and negotiation of a derived shared secret for keying.

- A nonce is exchanged to prevent replay attacks and bogus SAs.

- The IPsec SA is established.

The same Quick Mode process is repeated if the tunnel needs to be renegotiated when the lifetime expires. Quick Mode uses the Diffie-Hellman keying material from Phase 1 to create the shared key in Phase 2.

PFS

Perfect Forward Secrecy (PFS) can be specified in the IPsec policy. If specified, then Phase 2 will use Diffie-Hellman during each Quick Mode exchanged to create new keying material. The goal of this function is to create a greater resistance to crypto attacks and maintain the privacy of the tunnels. One downside of using PFS on IPsec tunnels is that the DH exchange is CPU intensive and may impact performance of the platform during negotiation.

After Phase 2 successfully completes, the endpoints have been established and can exchange data across an IPsec protected tunnel based on all the negotiated parameters set during the IKE process. The last item to cover here is the lifetime of the tunnel. Not all tunnels are needed at all times and won't need to be held up when not in use. There are many ways that a tunnel can be terminated. Manual deletion is pretty obvious, so we will move on to the other two common teardown reasons—lifetime based on time or number of transmitted bytes. When the SAs terminate, all of the associated keys are also discarded and will have to be rebuilt upon the next establishment of the SA.

IKEv2

Now that you understand IKEv1, let's look at how it compares to IKEv2. Table 8-1 highlights some of the major differences, which we will subsequently cover. For the full details of the benefits and advantages of IKEv2 over IKEv1, it would be good to reference the details in RFC 4306.

Table 8-1   *IKEv1/IKEv2 Comparison*

IKEv1	IKEv2
Exchange Modes	
Main Mode Aggressive Mode	Quick Mode
Messages Exchanged Before IPsec SA Established	
Main Mode: nine Aggressive Mode: six	As few as four messages total
Supported Authentication Methods	
Public Key Pre-Shared Secret Key RSA Certificate (RSA-SIG)	Pre-Shared Secret Key RSA Certificate (RSA-SIG) Elliptic Curve Digital Signature Certificate (ECDSA-SIG)
X-AUTH/Mode Config *Both peers must use the same* *authentication method.*	Extensible Authentication Protocol (EAP) *Asymmetric authentication is* *supported.*

IKEv2 does not have a clearly defined Phase 1 and 2 processing order, though you may encounter descriptions of IKEv2 that attribute the first two messages to a Phase 1 and the remaining to a Phase 2 when trying to explain the protocol process in comparison with IKEv1. The IKEv2 process is variable, and at minimum the initiator and responder will exchange a minimum of four messages; however, this could go up to as many as 30 or more messages depending on the number of SAs needed, EAP attributes in use, or authentication mechanisms in use for the tunnel. Figure 8-10 illustrates the IKEv2 establishment process, highlighting where the transition from cleartext to encrypted exchange is executed.

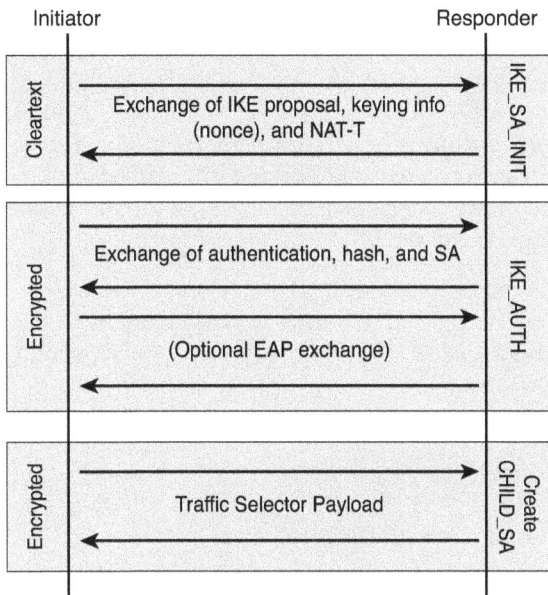

Figure 8-10 *IKEv2 Negotiation*

As mentioned, you may encounter the "Phase" terminology from IKEv1 in descriptions of IKEv2. If you do, for the sake of sanity, the mapping is as follows:

IKEv1	IKEv2
Phase 1	IKE_SA_INIT and IKE_AUTH
Phase 2	Creation of CHILD_SA

The first step, which is similar to IKEv1, is the IKE SA initialization phase. Also, as with IKEv1, the following data is exchanged and negotiated in the clear for IKEv2:

- Security association proposal

- Encryption algorithm proposal

- Hashing algorithm proposal

- Diffie-Hellman keys and nonce exchange

This SA initialization process consists of two of the four messages: the message from the initiator to the responder and the response from the responder to the initiator. Once the proposals are exchanged and agreed upon by both parties, the systems will generate a shared key that is used to encrypt and authenticate the communications in the next few messages.

One of the issues with this process is the amount of data that is included in the IKE_SA_INIT messages versus its IKEv1 counterpart. This results in a large processing impact on the responder; therefore, DoS attacks become a concern if an attacker sends a large number of IKEv2 requests from spoofed addresses. IKEv2 recommends an optional cookie function to prevent such attacks. If a threshold of incomplete sessions is reached, IKEv2 will stop processing incoming requests on the responder and will respond to the initiator with a cookie. The initiator must resend the initialization request with the cookie attached to begin the process with the responder.

Next, the initiator and responder will send the two remaining messages over the IKE SA that was established during exchange of the first two messages to create the first Child SA, which is similar to the IPsec SA established in IKEv1. Through these two messages, the initiator and responder will exchange the following:

■ Identity information

■ Certificate or authentication key

■ Traffic Selector Payload describing the initial Child SA to create

If additional Child SAs are needed after the initial IKEv2 negotiation has been completed, the initiator and responder will exchange two messages with the nonce, key exchange, and Traffic Selector Payload. This same process is used for IKE SA and Child SA rekeys.

The Bits and Pieces

Now that we have covered the foundations of secure tunneling via IPsec and IKE, we should also cover a few protocols that were mentioned previously and a few new concepts that should be understood before we get into configurations.

Diffie-Hellman

Diffie-Hellman key exchange, published in 1976, has been mentioned a few times in the IKE discussion in regard to key exchange. The protocol, conceptualized by Ralph Merkle and named after Whitfield Diffie and Martin Hellman, removed the need for physical exchange of keys to establish secure encrypted communications between two systems. DH was one of the first public-key protocols used for securely exchanging cryptographic keys over a public channel, which keys can then be used to encrypt the following data using a symmetric key cipher. DH is widely used today, as you will see throughout Chapter 9, "Infrastructure VPN."

All that being said, DH is not perfect and has been found to have security issues with the use of the lower groups because their key size is not sufficient to protect sensitive information. Cisco recommends avoiding groups 1, 2, and 5 and instead using groups 14 and higher.

Table 8-2 shows the DH groups and corresponding key size.

Table 8-2   *DH Groups, Key Sizes, and Recommendations*

Group	Key Size	Recommendation
Group 1	768-bit modulus	Do not use
Group 2	1024-bit modulus	Do not use
Group 5	1536-bit modulus	Do not use
Group 14	2048-bit modulus	Minimum acceptable
Group 19	256-bit elliptic curve	Recommended
Group 20	384-bit elliptic curve	Next-gen encryption
Group 21	521-bit elliptic curve	Next-gen encryption
Group 24	2048-bit modulus with 256-bit prime order subgroup	Next-gen encryption

ISAKMP

Internet Security Association and Key Management Protocol (ISAKMP) is exactly as its name suggests: it defines the process and procedure for authenticating and establishing SAs between peers. We have not mentioned ISAKMP directly much in this chapter as IKE is the implementation of ISAKMP. ISAKMP does not define key exchange but rather is the framework for establishing, modifying, and deleting SAs.

Transport Mode, Tunnel Mode, AH, and ESP

IPsec supports two modes of encryption that can be used for data payload transit:

- **Transport mode:** Encrypts the data payload only and does not modify the packet header. Transport mode is commonly used for gateway communications. Because it does not change the packet header. it cannot be used on public-routed networks when RFC 1918 addresses are in use.

- **Tunnel mode:** Encrypts the original data payload and header. It is commonly used as the default on VPNs because the device doing the encryption is not the data payload originator. Tunnel mode also allows for RFC 1918 address traversal across a public network because the header is concealed by the VPN gateway's IP header.

IPsec also defines two packet formats:

- **Authentication Header (AH):** Provides integrity by preventing insertion attacks or modification of any of the header fields that shouldn't be changed in transit of the payload. AH can also authenticate the packets to ensure the payload is from the expected source security device. AH can be used alone or in conjunction with ESP.

- **Encapsulating Security Payload (ESP):** Adds confidentiality to AH's authentication and integrity. ESP technically also does its own form of authentication, for the IP payload only and not the header. ESP is the function of encrypting the data payload and authenticating.

Both AH and ESP offer replay protection as well.

SSL, TLS, and DTLS

Secure Sockets Layer (SSL) and Transport Layer Security (TLS) should likely be terms that you are well familiar with if you have used any electronic device to connect to the Internet. TLS is the replacement for the deprecated SSL and is used for securing communications between two hosts, just like IPsec, but it is done at the application layer versus IP. From this point on, we refer primarily to TLS because SSL is deprecated.

TLS uses TCP and has three primary functions on connections between a client and server:

- **Privacy/confidentiality:** Keys are generated between the client and server during the session standup before any data is transmitted.

- **Identity/authentication:** The identity is verified, typically the server's identity, using PKI as discussed earlier in this chapter. Have you ever gotten one of the pesky "site is unsecure" messages when trying to access a secure site? This is why! It means TLS cannot properly identify the server due to a certificate issue.

- **Reliability:** Reliability is maintained by using a message authentication code that is transmitted with each packet to detect loss or change to the packet during its trip to or from the client.

Once again, as we covered very early in this chapter, keys and ciphers come into play. The client and server in a TLS communication must exchange or agree on a key and cipher to be used for encryption and decryption of the transmitted data. As mentioned previously, SSL was very limited in the keys that could be used to the point where SSL 2.0 only supported RSA certificates. TLS 1.2 has greatly expanded on that support to include keys such as Elliptic Curve Diffie-Hellman (TLS_ECDH) and TLS Pre-Shared Key (TLS_PSK).

Datagram Transport Layer Security (DTLS) is also of note as it is the implementation of TLS over UDP. DTLS is commonly implemented when there is a need for TLS security but the application is time or delay sensitive and should not be affected by packet reordering, loss of datagram, or flow control.

For the CCIE exam, you will not need to know much about SSL/TLS with regard to its use in web browsing and security, but rather how SSL/TLS is used for VPN communication between routers, firewalls, and endpoints. Most Cisco documentation still refers to SSL as the defining term to separate it from IPsec, but the reality is that TLS is in use over legacy SSL.

Virtual Private Networks

As you likely already know, a virtual private network (VPN) is an extension of a private network across a public network or medium. This section briefly introduces the multiple types of VPNs that you may encounter in the CCIE exams. The capabilities, configuration, and troubleshooting will be covered in Chapter 9 for infrastructure VPNs and Chapter 10 for remote access VPNs.

OK, now that we have gotten through all the nitty-gritty details of crypto, ciphers, hashing, IKE, security associations, and more, we can now cover how that can all be put to use in practice, which is what your lab will primarily focus on. In the rest of this chapter, we will cover the theory and function of different VPN solutions and how they operate (again, configurations will be covered in Chapters 9 and 10).

IPsec

IPsec can be used for LAN-to-LAN, client-based remote access, and other secure communication connections. As briefly mentioned in the IKE section, the end result of an IKE exchange is an IPsec SA. What we didn't cover during the IKE portion was what causes the IKE and IPsec SA to kick off and start negotiation of tunneling traffic. Figure 8-11 illustrates a basic example of an IPsec tunnel.

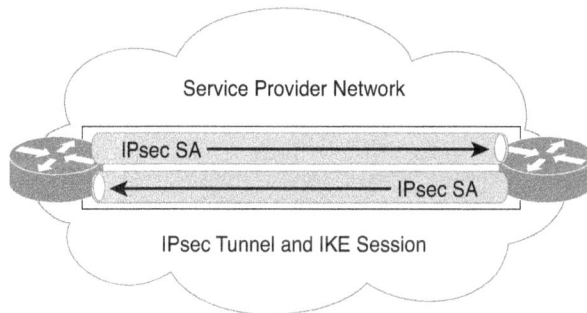

Figure 8-11   *IPsec VPN SAs*

With IPsec you define the traffic that is to be protected between two IPsec peers by using access lists and applying them to interfaces using *crypto map sets*. Within the crypto map sets you define the "interesting traffic" based on source and destination and, optionally, port and protocol. The access list you use works differently than standard access lists where you are permitting and denying traffic to transit the interface. Instead, you are classifying the traffic that is to be encrypted/decrypted between the two IPsec peers.

The *crypto map* can contain multiple entries, all with different peers, access lists, and transform sets (the definitions of the encryption parameters will be covered in Chapter 9). The crypto map is defined with sequence numbers that set the order in which traffic is analyzed and ties the peer, ACL, and transforms together for use. Best practice is to use the most specific/important mapping at the top of your crypto map, followed by all others. After you build the crypto map to your preference, you apply it to the interface that will be used to connect to the remote peer.

IPsec peers can have multiple SAs established between them at one time, and one peer can have multiple SAs with multiple IPsec peers at a single point in time. You can also even have multiple IPsec tunnels between two peers with differing authentication and encryption settings. When new traffic enters the IPsec peer, it is analyzed against the crypto map. If an SA does not exist for the source and destination addresses in the flow, then the peer kicks off IKE to establish a new IPsec SA if **ipsec-isakmp** is defined on the crypto map. If IKE is used to establish the SA, then it is kept up and rekeyed until the tunnel is torn down manually, by timeout, or by another teardown configuration on the tunnel. You can also configure **ipsec-manual**, which requires the SA to exist for IPsec to use for protection of the traffic; otherwise, the traffic will be dropped. We will cover both of these options in Chapter 9.

It is important to note that IPsec and its functions are the foundation of many newer VPN solutions that are available today and thus you should understand IPsec very well as a CCIE Security candidate. Much of Chapter 10 will cover the configuration, manipulation, verification, and troubleshooting of IPsec on its own and as part of VPN solutions that you will encounter in the written and lab exams.

DMVPN

Dynamic Multipoint VPN (DMVPN) is a solution that leverages IPsec as well as some other technology to enable enterprises to establish a secure connection in a hub-and-spoke network or spoke-to-spoke network easily and effectively. One of the challenges in the past when building these types of networks was the need to use leased-line or hardline services such as frame-relay and others, which can be very costly. Large, classic IPsec VPN networks needed the ability to scale and provide dynamic connection mechanisms to allow multiple sites to connect seamlessly but still securely. One of the downfalls of using IPsec alone without DMVPN, or the other solutions we will cover, is that you are limited to building IPsec associations on a point-to-point basis, which in a medium to large network can quickly become hard to manage. Before the availability of solutions such as DMVPN, many IT departments would build a hub-and-spoke design with IPsec to limit the need to buy leased lines between the spokes, in the interest of saving money and simplifying configuration. DMVPN and other solutions have greatly improved on the limitations of classic IPsec to allow simple and adaptable networks.

Enterprise networks using DMVPN now have the freedom of using the public Internet and DMVPN's dynamic tunneling capabilities along with IPsec to create a less-expensive hub-and-spoke topology, or it can even emulate a full mesh of leased lines between the hub and spokes. All of the spokes in a DMVPN network are configured to connect to the hub and, when interesting traffic calls for it, each spoke can connect directly to another spoke as well. DMVPN in a full mesh allows the network to adapt and scale to the needs of the traffic without imposing extra load on the hub router/s to process encrypted traffic going from spoke-to-spoke because the spokes can talk directly. Let's go into some of the details of the solution now.

DMVPN uses two primary technologies. First is Multipoint GRE (mGRE) with IPsec, which allows the routers in the solution to establish multiple GRE tunnels using only one configured tunnel interface. One of the challenges of non-multipoint GRE was that each tunnel interface was its own network and required dedicated IP addressing for the hub and spoke peering. mGRE removes that requirement, and in a DMVPN network, the mGRE tunnel interface on the hub and spokes creates one large non-broadcast multiple-access (NBMA) network. An NBMA network is one in which multiple hosts are attached to a single network but data is sent only directly from one host to another over a switched fabric or virtual circuit such as the mGRE tunnel.

The second primary technology that DMVPN uses is the Next Hop Resolution Protocol (NHRP), which can be seen as being similar to ARP on Ethernet. The hub router must always know the mapping of the NBMA address to the tunnel address of all spokes for which it is the next-hop server (NHS) in the topology. NHRP enables the device to map the tunnel IP addresses with an NBMA IP address. The hub in the DMVPN network will be able to resolve the mapping of all the next-hop addresses for all members of the DMVPN network.

When designing and implementing DMVPN, another important thing to consider is the routing protocol. Although routing protocols are outside the scope of this book, you should have a handle on them if you are studying for a CCIE exam:

- **Open Shortest Path First (OSPF):** Although functional, OSPF would suffer from scalability in larger networks because the DMVPN cloud is a single large subnet requiring all devices to be in a single OSPF area.

- **On-Demand Routing (ODR):** Also functional, but it advertises all connected networks over the tunnel, which would cause recursive routing issues. Although this could be solved with route filters, that would greatly add to the configuration complexity, which is what we are trying to avoid with DMVPN.

- **Routing Information Protocol (RIP):** Used in DMVPN enterprise networks today. RIP does require the disabling of split horizon.

- **Enhanced Interior Gateway Routing Protocol (EIGRP):** The most commonly used and recommended protocol for DMVPN networks. EIGRP also has to have split horizon disabled to function on the DMVPN network.

- **Border Gateway Protocol (BGP):** Another viable option, but certain precautions must be taken depending on whether you select interior BGP (iBGP) or exterior BGP (eBGP) and how you break down the autonomous systems, or the use of route reflectors using a single autonomous system, and configurations such as *allowas-in* to manipulate the defaults of the protocol's behavior.

This chapter and the configurations in the next chapter will only address the use of EIGRP.

Now that you know some basic terms and their functions within DMVPN, the next important topic is the different deployment types of DMVPN, which are called phases (yeah, that's a bit confusing in conjunction with IKEv1!):

- **Phase 1:** This can be deployed only as a hub-and-spoke tunnel deployment. In this deployment the hub is configured with an mGRE tunnel interface and the spokes have point-to-point GRE tunnel interface configurations. All traffic, including inter-spoke traffic, must traverse the hub.

- **Phase 2**: As mentioned previously, hub-and-spoke designs can impose additional load on the hub because it needs to process encrypted traffic that is simply traversing it during spoke-to-spoke flows. Phase 2 improves on Phase 1 by establishing a mechanism for spokes to build dynamic spoke-to-spoke tunnels on demand. Spokes in this deployment type have mGRE tunnel interfaces and learn of their peer spoke addresses and specific downstream routes through the use of a routing protocol.

- **Phase 3**: This phase is very similar to Phase 2, but the routing table must have the spoke address and all specific downstream routes propagated to all other spokes. This means that the hub cannot use summarization of routes in the routing protocol. This is where **nhrp redirect** and **nhrp shortcut** come into play. The hub uses NHRP redirect messages to inform the spoke of a more effective path to the spoke's network and the spoke will accept the "shortcut" and build the dynamic tunnel to the peer spoke.

In Figure 8-12, you can see that the foundation of the DMVPN design is a hub-and-spoke network. The dotted lines depict the abilities that are added with Phases 2 and 3 for spoke-to-spoke communication.

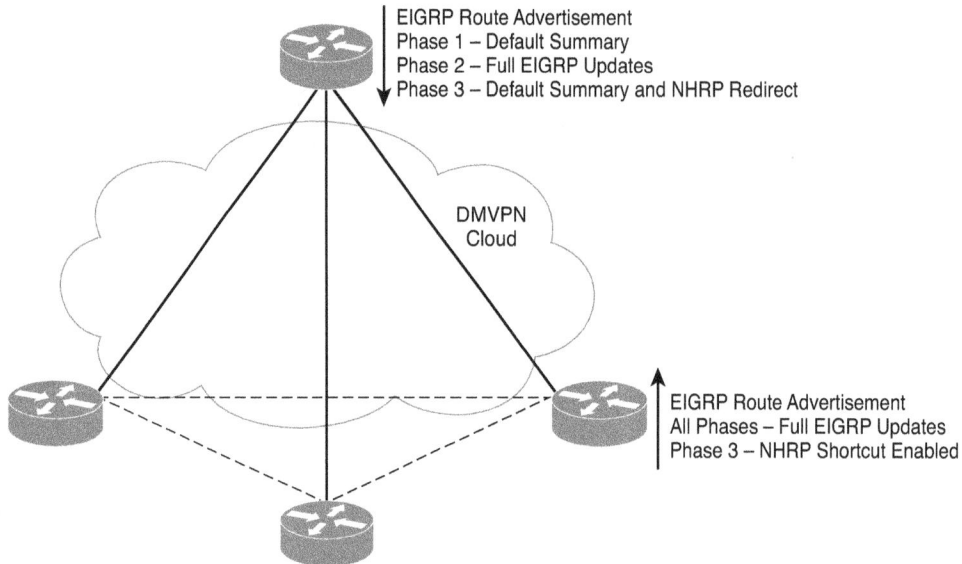

Figure 8-12   *Basic DMVPN Design with Phases*

DMVPN has multiple design options that can be used based on the use case needed for the network you are deploying on: single-hub; dual-hub, single-cloud; dual-hub, dual-cloud; etc. Network resiliency rules the day when it comes to which deployment method to choose. We will cover a few of the options for single- and dual-hub/cloud designs in Chapter 9.

The last aspect of DMVPN to cover is the tunnel protection used for encryption of the traffic between the hubs and spokes. Although tunnel protection is advised, it is not required with DMVPN. When tunnel protection is needed, DMVPN is primarily used with IKEv1. That being said, DMVPN can also be used with IKEv2; however, there is a better option called *FlexVPN* (you may also hear it called *DMVPN Phase 4!*).

FlexVPN

As the parenthetical reference to "DMVPN Phase 4" at the end of the prior section indicates, FlexVPN has a lot of similarities to DMVPN—but with some improvements, of course; otherwise, why would Cisco rename it completely? FlexVPN is most commonly deployed on routers and firewalls but also allows for client-based VPN tunnels, which DMVPN does not. Let's cover what you need to know about FlexVPN for the CCIE exams.

One of the biggest differences with FlexVPN over DMVPN is the interfaces used for the tunnel connections. As discussed, DMVPN uses mGRE and P2P GRE tunnel interfaces. FlexVPN uses static P2P interfaces for spoke-to-hub connections or virtual access interfaces for spoke-to-hub and spoke-to-spoke connections. The use of virtual access interfaces gives us great flexibility and enables us to see interface configurations for each tunnel versus the one mGRE configuration that applies to all tunnels.

The next noteworthy difference is that IPsec is a major part of the FlexVPN configuration, whereas with DMVPN it is optional. IKEv2 is the default key management protocol used for tunnel establishment and protection, and it also allows a dramatic simplification of NHRP. In addition, there is no longer a need for spokes to register with the hub. FlexVPN also has only one "phase" or mode of operation for NHRP, NHRP redirect/shortcut, and routing protocols. As for the routing protocols to use, again EIGRP and BGP are the most commonly used IGPs in networks today.

Figure 8-13 shows a sample diagram of a FlexVPN design: dual-hub, single-cloud with failover.

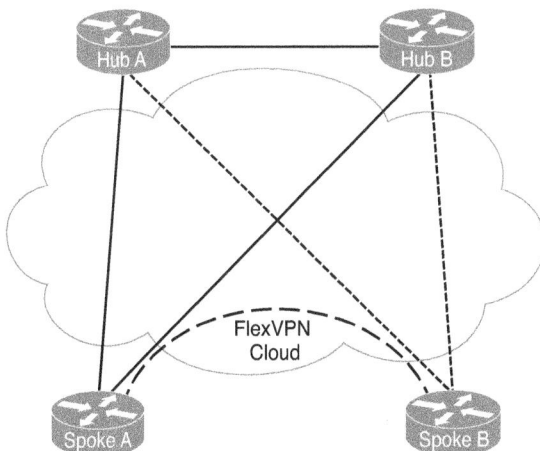

Figure 8-13 *FlexVPN Dual-Hub, Single-Cloud Design*

Finally, design choice, very much like for DMVPN, all depends on the resiliency requirements of the network. Single-cloud and dual-cloud designs are both still options here and have their own benefits and challenges for scalability, flexibility, complexity, and maintenance.

GETVPN

One of the benefits of all the previously described IPsec, DMVPN, and FlexVPN solutions is that they can be used over public Internet services for connectivity across multiple branches and offices without the need for dedicated links from service providers. Dedicated link services used to come at a significant price, but that has decreased over the years, making them more obtainable for most enterprise customers. One of the functions that is missing on dedicated link services is data protection, which these VPN solutions can provide. The X factor that has come into play is that, while the price of those circuits was dropping, government regulations and industry standards regarding data privacy have become mandatory. Unless you have been living under a rock, you must have heard of the Health Insurance Portability and Accountability Act (HIPAA), Gramm-Leach-Bliley Act (GBLA), and Payment Card Industry Data Security Standard (PCI DSS). All of these government regulations and industry standards mandate encryption of data in transit even when transiting a private network.

We have covered multiple solutions that can handle this problem; however, all of them to this point have been point-to-point. You might be saying, "But wait, what about DMVPN's spoke-to-spoke function with NHRP redirect/shortcut that you just told us about?" Well, although DMVPN and FlexVPN do provide functions to simulate a full mesh of tunnels, the spoke-to-spoke tunnels are only on-demand and terminate after they are not in use any longer until triggered again with "interesting traffic." DMVPN also overlays additional routing within the tunnel, which increases complexity and hardware requirements.

Cisco Group Encrypted Transport VPN (GETVPN) implements a trusted group of devices called group members (GMs) that share a common security association called the group SA. This in turn allows any device that is a group member to decrypt traffic from any other group member. It also allows the encrypted traffic to flow from the originator to the destination using the routing protocol that is already being used on the private WAN by using tunnel header preservation where the data is encrypted but the original source and destination remain intact. The functions of this group SA, GM relationship, and tunnel header preservation allow GETVPN to be "tunnel-less."

The integral piece of GETVPN is Group Domain of Interpretation (GDOI), which is a group key management protocol that provides the GMs a set of cryptographic keys and policies for the processing of traffic that must be protected. Once again, IKE Phase 1 enters the game to protect the GDOI protocol as group members connect to the network, providing the keys and policies. GDOI uses IKE on UDP 848. GDOI implements two keys, a key encryption key (KEK) for the control plane and a traffic encryption key (TEK) for the data plane.

Where do these keys come from? The key server (KS), of course. The key server is a Cisco IOS device running on the network that creates and maintains the KEK and TEK for all the GMs. The KS is also responsible for the configuration of all the encryption policies, such as defining interesting traffic, encryption protocols, security association parameters, and rekey timers. When a GM connects and authenticates to the KS using IKE Phase 1, it then downloads the policies and the keys for GETVPN functionality.

One important note on the policies of GETVPN is the definition of "interesting traffic." In traditional IPsec, we define ACLs that are specific to networks owned by the router and in the direction that traffic would flow, such as **permit 10.99.1.0/24 to 10.99.2.0/24**, and the other side of the tunnel would have the same ACL in the inverse. In GETVPN, the KS distributes the ACL to every GM that connects to the GETVPN network; therefore, the GM may or may not own networks defined in the ACL. It is recommended to keep the ACL as simple as possible. For example, if all GMs in the network own a network in the 10.0.0.0/8 IP address space, then the ACL on the KS should be exactly that: **permit 10.0.0.0/8 to 10.0.0.0/8**. Best practice is to summarize as much as possible. The KS being an integral part of GETVPN means that it is a dedicated device service and cannot be a GM as well in the GETVPN network.

We briefly mentioned the GM before, but for completeness let's make sure its role is clearly defined. The GM is a Cisco IOS device that is responsible for data plane traffic encryption and decryption. The only configuration on the GM is the necessary items for IKE Phase 1 and KS/Group information. As previously stated, the GM downloads all of the keys and policies from the KS and away its goes. But what if you have a specific GM that is a little different than the rest? Well, there is the ability to make local exceptions/overrides from the KS policy for these corner cases without having to define them in the global policy for all devices.

The group SA is a key benefit of GETVPN and allows for all GMs to encrypt and decrypt traffic from any other member in the group. The removal of the IPsec policy and tunnels between peers greatly reduces load on the GMs. That statement does not come without limitations, of course. GETVPN is limited to up to 100 ACL permit statements in a group to define interesting traffic. Each permit statement creates two SAs, and the max in a group is 200. Again, the best practice is to summarize as much as possible, and using policies where the source and destination are the same IP range maximizes the ability of GETVPN.

Keys, keys, keys! If this chapter hasn't driven home the importance of keys yet, then here's another reminder. GETVPN heavily relies on keys, and because we are encrypting a lot of traffic across a private network with regulations in play, the keys are even more important here. Also of importance is keeping the network passing traffic, right? This is where the rekey process and COOP KSs come into play. The KS is responsible for refreshing the keys and getting them to the GMs. This process must take place before the existing keys expire and must have some sort of fault tolerance. There are two ways to do the rekey process with GETVPN: unicast and multicast.

The unicast rekey process begins with the KS generating a rekey message and sending it to every registered GM. When the GM receives the message, it sends an ACK to the KS notifying the KS that the GM is active. If the KS does not receive an ACK from the GM it can be configured to retransmit the rekey message up to three times before it removes the GM from the list of active members. Once the rekey message is process the GM and KS will negotiate the rekey and traffic will continue to flow uninterrupted.

The multicast rekey process assumes that you already have a functional multicast configuration in the network, and it is almost the same as the unicast method, with two small changes. First, the rekey message is sent to a multicast group address that is predefined in the configuration and that each GM has joined during the registration process. Secondly, there is no ACK mechanism because it is multicast. The multicast rekey process removes the need for the KS to maintain a list of active GMs and takes the same amount of processing whether you have one GM or thousands.

Well, those are all good and fine rekey mechanisms as long as the GM receives the rekey message. What happens if the rekey message is not seen by the GM? When the current IPsec SA is 60 seconds from expiring, the GM will attempt to reregister with an ordered set of KSs. If successful, the GM will rekey and generate a new SA for uninterrupted traffic processing. If the KS is unreachable by the GM, it will try three more times every 10 seconds. If the preferred KS is still unreachable, the GM will try the next KS in the list 20 seconds before the IPsec SA expires. If both reregistration attempts are unsuccessful, traffic will be dropped when the exiting SA expires until reachability is restored to the KS and a registration can be successfully completed.

You can probably see how important the KS is to the GETVPN topology. Just having one KS is a great idea, right? Not in this lifetime, except maybe in a lab! That being said, GETVPN supports multiple KSs, called cooperative (COOP) KSs, for fault tolerance. The GM is configured in an ordered list with the KSs. The first KS in the list is contacted first by that GM. COOP is configured in each GDOI group, so a KS can COOP with different KSs for different groups and can be a COOP member in multiple groups. When COOP is configured on the KS and it boots, it assumes a secondary role until the election process is completed. All of the KSs in the COOP have a priority, and the KS with the highest priority is elected as the primary KS for the group. The primary KS is the KS that will distribute policies and keys to the GMs for that group. A GM can register to any of the KSs of the COOP, but again only the primary KS will send the rekey messages to the GMs. The primary KS will also periodically synchronize with the other members of the COOP. If a secondary KS does not hear an update from the primary KS in the COOP, the secondary KS will try to contact the primary KS. If that contact fails, the COOP reelection is started and a new primary KS is elected. In GETVPN you can have up to eight COOP KSs; while that seems high it can be common for large networks to handle the number of registrations handled at one time in the case of network failure.

GETVPN also employs a time-based anti-replay function to thwart denial of service attacks on the network.

Figure 8-14 shows an example of the components of a GETVPN network and the functions we covered thus far.

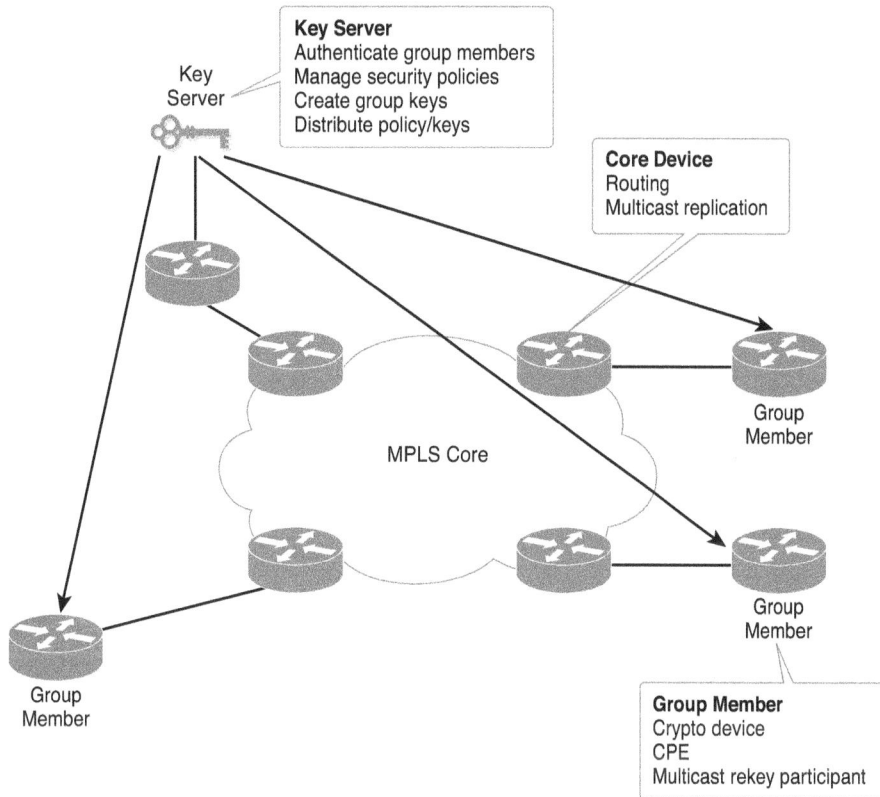

Figure 8-14 *GETVPN Components*

SSL Remote Access VPN

We have covered several VPN solutions thus far, but only a few support today's mobile workforce. Although some of us may think that it's cool and hip to walk around with a router under our arm as we travel from place to place, it isn't practical, which has led to solutions for remote access VPNs. IPsec and FlexVPN do offer the capability for remote access in addition to LAN-to-LAN VPNs and can be very useful for that, but some security policies and network restrictions would limit or outright block the ports and protocols needed to establish those VPN connections. Your author personally has encountered hotels and guest networks that blocked protocol 50 and 51 and UDP port

500, making the IPsec VPN service useless on those networks. SSL VPN was the fix for this. The use of a common port and protocol that is used for basic secure web-browsing (SSL/TLS) enables the use of a VPN basically anywhere that you can access the Internet.

The function of SSL RAVPN is rather quite simple. It operates just like a secure website and follows all of the rules set forth in the PKI section of this chapter regarding certificates and their use for securing connections between a host and a server. SSL RAVPN has two primary methods of operation, either browser based or client based. The choice of which method to use really depends on the policy of the VPN provider and what is needed for ease of use. Most browser-based SSL VPN use cases fit into scenarios where a user needs access to a secure portal or web resource at the main site, and that is all. A client-based solution can be just as limited, but can also provide a full tunnel of connectivity, giving the end user the sense that their workstation is connected directly to the corporate office network.

For Cisco, the solutions that are tied to this are WebVPN and Cisco AnyConnect Secure Mobility Client. WebVPN is a function on the Cisco ASA platform that allows the administrator to set up a secure portal providing multiple types of web applications and smart tunnels to the authenticated user. Differing portals can be set for differing user groups to customize the experience. On the flip side is the client-based experience where AnyConnect is the key player. The AnyConnect Client is capable of establishing IPsec- and SSL-based VPN connections in either a full-tunnel or split-tunnel mode. AnyConnect also adds the ability to perform things such as client posture assessment with either the ASA or Cisco ISE. AnyConnect also has many other modules that are covered extensively in other chapters of this volume as well as Volume 1 of this book series.

More information, including configuration and setup of remote access VPNs, will be covered in Chapter 10.

Layer 2 Encryption: IEEE 802.1AE/MACsec

Although it is not really a VPN technology, 802.1AE/MACsec is a method of encrypting traffic in transit between two devices that functions similarly to IPsec and the other solutions we have discussed thus far. As traffic throughput and speed requirements have risen over the years, the need for high-speed encryption has risen as well. IPsec and other VPN solutions have fit the bill for many customers to date however as these speed requirements rise it has also become the bottleneck of traffic between two peers. MACsec was built to fit the bill of this requirement. Another issue that arose with VPN solutions is the ability to look into the inner packets on trusted devices for things like QoS prioritization, policy routing, and filtering. MACsec leverages hop-by-hop encryption, meaning that the traffic is encrypted only on the wire between to MACsec peers and otherwise is in the clear while being processed by the device in the traffic flow. MACsec also leverages the ASIC on the line card or interface of the device to perform the encryption and decryption, versus having to offload to a crypto engine as with IPsec. Figure 8-15 illustrates how MACsec processes traffic transiting the device.

Figure 8-15 *MACsec Hop-by-Hop Encryption*

MACsec is based on the Ethernet frame format; however, an additional 16-byte MACsec Security Tag field and a 16-byte Integrity Check Value field are added, and the source/destination MAC addresses remain the same. This means that all devices in the flow of the MACsec communications must support MACsec for these fields to be used and secure the traffic. MACsec provides authentication using Galois Method Authentication Code (GMAC) or authenticated encryption using Galois/Counter Mode Advanced Encryption Standard (AES-GCM). Figure 8-16 illustrates the MACsec frame format and the contents of the MACsec tag.

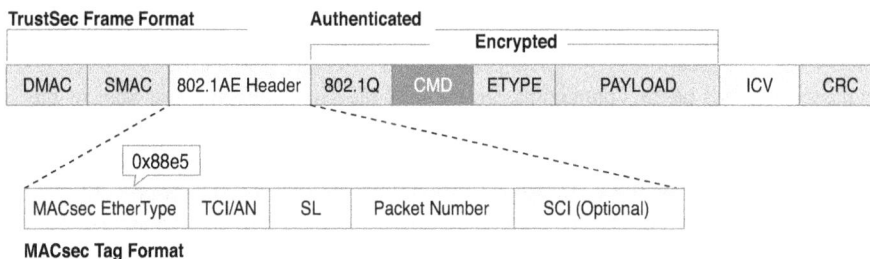

Figure 8-16 *MACsec Frame Format*

The MACsec Security Tag fields are as follows:

■ **MACsec EtherType (first 2 octets):** Set to 0x88e5, designating the frame as a MACsec frame

■ **TCI/AN (3rd octet):** Tag Control Information/Association Number field that designates the version number if confidentiality or integrity is used on its own

■ **SL (4th octet):** Short Length field that designates the length of the encrypted data

■ **Packet Number (octets 5–8):** Indicates the packet number for replay protection and building of the initialization vector

■ **SCI (octets 9–16):** Secure Channel Identifier used for classification of the connection to virtual port

Currently MACsec offers two mechanisms for keying: Security Association Protocol (SAP), which is Cisco proprietary, and MAC Security Key Agreement (MKA). These two keying mechanisms are used in differing connection types or modes of operation requiring MACsec protection.

MACsec has two methods of operation:

- **Downlink MACsec:** The use of MACsec to create an authenticated/encrypted link between a switch and the downstream connected host. This means that the switch must support MACsec and the endpoint must be running a client capable of MACsec, such as the AnyConnect Client. Downlink MACsec enables the operator to secure traffic across standard copper connections without the need to worry about snooping on the wire, which commonly resulted in implementation of fiber to the desktop. Downlink MACsec leverages MKA for its keying mechanism.

- **Uplink MACsec:** The use of authentication/encryption on the links between two devices such as switches and routers. The uplink MACsec association between two devices can be established manually via configuration or dynamically using Network Device Admission Control (NDAC). NDAC uses 802.1X for authenticating devices and their links to the network before allowing traffic to pass and be protected by MACsec. Uplink MACsec can use SAP or MKA (WAN MACsec) for building security associations to other devices.

So now that you know the common scenarios for MACsec, it is important to understand how it is implemented in the network. When setting up MACsec, it is important to remember that this technology will pass packets only after the association is secured and trusted by both ends of the connection. Downlink MACsec to the end host on a switch protects all frames from that host. If you don't set up MACsec correctly on the host or switch, you might end up with some angry end users. Luckily for us Downlink MACsec has some options to allow for a smooth migration with the **macsec access-control** command. The operators under this command are **must-secure** and **should-secure**. Understanding of the English language should make it pretty clear what those two options do for the end client. Recommended procedure is to start with **should-secure** and end with **must-secure**. This configuration is also dynamically configurable in a Cisco ISE 802.1X–enabled network where you have the ability to dynamically assign the MACsec behavior based on the context of the device's connection.

On the flip side, Uplink MACsec can be a little more intrusive and has more potential for locking yourself out. MACsec on the uplinks can be configured manually or with NDAC, as discussed previously. When configuring manually, it is important that you have secondary connectivity to the device for configuration or you run the risk of losing access if the configuration is not successful in establishing the MACsec connection appropriately.

There are a couple of items to note for NDAC. NDAC uses 802.1X on the switches to authenticate network devices into the trusted domain. There are a couple roles very similar to classic endpoint 802.1X; however, there is no endpoint as it is another network device:

- **Supplicant:** The unauthenticated switch that is attempting to connect to the trusted domain.

- **Authentication server:** The server that validates the credential of the supplicant device and allows it into the trusted domain. This is a Cisco book, so that will be Cisco ISE in this case.

- **Authenticator:** A network device that is already on the network and part of the trusted domain. This device will be the intermediary between the supplicant and the authentication server.

There is one more role within the NDAC process, which is the *seed device*. This device is commonly the first device that was added to the network as the root of the trusted domain. This device is responsible validation of the device into the trusted domain above and beyond the basic authentication that takes place by the authenticator. The biggest difference between a seed device and a non-seed device is that the seed device has the configuration of the ISE servers in its configuration, whereas the non-seed device gets the list of servers from the seed device upon registration into the trusted domain. Non-seed devices should only be the last leg of the switching fabric in your networks. Chapter 9 covers the configuration aspects of manual and NDAC MACsec for both Uplink and Downlink connections. Figure 8-17 shows an example of an NDAC trusted domain.

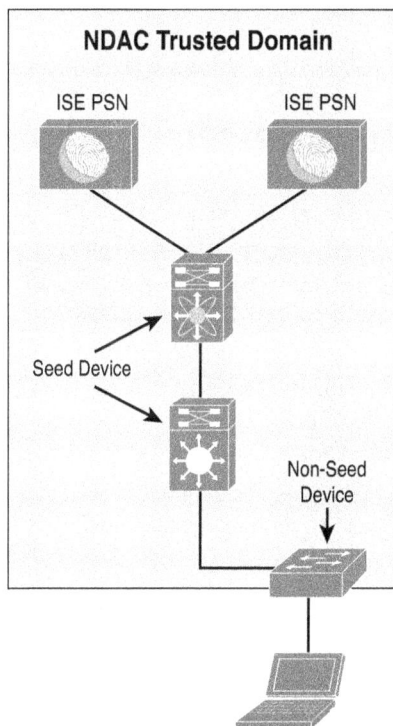

Figure 8-17 *NDAC Trusted Domain*

Summary

This chapter covered the foundations of secure connectivity. We have traveled from the days of old with scytale ciphers to cryptography, IKE, IPsec, dynamic VPN solutions, and link layer encryption with MACsec. Understanding these concepts and technologies is paramount to succeeding on the written and lab exams. By this time, you should have sufficient knowledge of how each of those items work to apply it to the relevant configurations for each technology, which will be covered in the next few chapters.

References

Security for VPNs with IPsec Configuration Guide, Cisco IOS Release 15M&T, https://www.cisco.com/c/en/us/td/docs/ios-xml/ios/sec_conn_vpnips/configuration/15-mt/sec-sec-for-vpns-w-ipsec-15-mt-book/sec-cfg-vpn-ipsec.html

Introduction to Cisco IPsec Technology, https://www.cisco.com/c/en/us/td/docs/net_mgmt/vpn_solutions_center/2-0/ip_security/provisioning/guide/IPsecPG1.html#wp1030249

Wikipedia entry for Transport Layer Security, https://en.wikipedia.org/wiki/Transport_Layer_Security

FlexVPN HA Dual Hub Configuration Example, https://www.cisco.com/c/en/us/support/docs/security/flexvpn/118888-configure-flexvpn-00.html

DMVP: The Phases In-Depth, https://learningnetwork.cisco.com/blogs/vip-perspectives/2017/02/15/dmvpn-the-phases-in-depth

Cisco IOS FlexVPN Data Sheet, https://www.cisco.com/c/en/us/products/collateral/routers/asr-1000-series-aggregation-services-routers/data_sheet_c78-704277.html

Scalable DMVPN Design and Implementation Guide, https://www.cisco.com/c/dam/en/us/products/collateral/security/dynamic-multipoint-vpn-dmvpn/dmvpn_design_guide.pdf

Group Encrypted Transport VPN (GETVPN) Design and Implementation Guide: https://www.cisco.com/c/dam/en/us/products/collateral/security/group-encrypted-transport-vpn/GETVPN_DIG_version_2_0_External.pdf

Cisco IOS GETVPN Solution Deployment Guide, https://www.cisco.com/c/en/us/products/collateral/security/group-encrypted-transport-vpn/deployment_guide_c07_554713.html

Cisco Site-to-Site VPN Technologies Comparison, https://www.cisco.com/c/dam/en/us/products/collateral/ios-nx-os-software/enterprise-class-teleworker-ect-solution/prod_brochure0900aecd80582078.pdf

Cisco AnyConnect Secure Mobility Client At a Glance, https://www.cisco.com/c/dam/en/us/products/collateral/security/anyconnect-secure-mobility-client/at_a_glance_c45-578609.pdf

Cisco TrustSec3.0 How-To Guide: Introduction to MACSec and NDAC Guide, https://www.cisco.com/c/dam/en/us/solutions/collateral/enterprise/design-zone-security/how_to_intro_macsec_ndac_guide.pdf

Catalyst 3750-X and 3560-X Software Configuration Guide, Release 15.0(1)SE, https://www.cisco.com/c/en/us/td/docs/switches/lan/catalyst3750x_3560x/software/release/15-0_1_se/configuration/guide/3750xcg/swmacsec.html

Innovations in Ethernet Encryption (802.1AE – MACsec) for Securing High Speed (1–100GE) WAN Deployments White Paper, https://www.cisco.com/c/en/us/products/collateral/ios-nx-os-software/identity-based-networking-services/white-paper-c11-737544.html

Chapter 9

Infrastructure VPN

This chapter covers the configuration, verification, and troubleshooting of the infrastructure VPN components discussed in Chapter 8, "Security Connectivity." We will cover the VPN technologies in the same order as they were discussed in Chapter 8 and cover the multitude of options under each one. During this chapter, make sure to note the keywords that distinguish one option from the other in each configuration; you will need to pay attention to these keywords during your CCIE written and lab exams to determine the answers correctly.

All of the lab configuration that you will see in this chapter are done with Cisco Virtual Internet Routing Lab (VIRL). VIRL is a great tool to use for preparations to take the CCIE lab exam. As described on the VIRL website (http://virl.cisco.com), VIRL enables you to do the following:

- Build highly accurate models of existing or planned networks.

- Design, configure, and operate networks using authentic versions of Cisco's network operating systems.

- Build using common platforms like IOSv, IOSv Layer-2, IOS-XRv, NX-OSv, CSR1000v, and ASAv, all of which are included.

- Integrate third-party virtual machines, appliances, VNFs, and servers.

- Connect real and virtual networks to form high-fidelity development and test environments.

- Design and test anywhere—VIRL is portable!

Without further delay, let's get started with basic IPsec using IKEv1 and IKEv2.

IPsec with IKEv1

Starting with basic IKEv1 allows us to clearly see the configurations for each section of IKE that is used throughout most of the infrastructure VPN technologies that we will cover. First, we will start with a configuration of two simple routers running a tunnel with preshared keys (PSKs) to encrypt the communications between networks local to them, as depicted in Figure 9-1.

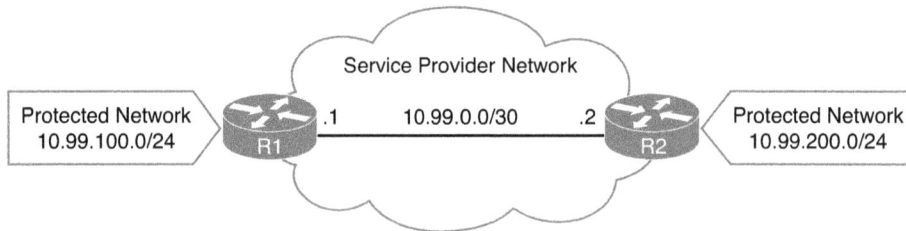

Figure 9-1   *Basic IOS IPsec Network*

The first step is to configure the ISAKMP policy for our Phase 1 authentication and negotiation, as demonstrated in Example 9-1.

Example 9-1   *IKEv1 ISAKMP Policy*

```
R1
crypto isakmp policy 10
 encr aes
 authentication pre-share
 group 14
 exit
crypto isakmp key cisco123 address 10.99.0.2

R2 <Same ISAKMP Policy>
crypto isakmp key cisco123 address 10.99.0.1
```

One important thing to note here is the priority number of 10 assigned to the ISAKMP policy. When you have multiple IKE policies on an initiating peer, it will negotiate with the responder to find a common policy between them. This policy is negotiated in order from lowest to highest number as defined when configured.

By default, Cisco IOS will use Main Mode instead of Aggressive Mode for ISAKMP establishment. If you want to use Aggressive Mode, remove the **crypto isakmp key** configuration and use the configuration shown in Example 9-2.

Example 9-2 *IKEv1 ISAKMP Aggressive Mode*

```
no crypto isakmp key cisco123 address 10.99.0.2
crypto isakmp peer address 10.99.0.2
 set aggressive-mode password cisco123
 set aggressive-mode client-endpoint ipv4-address 10.99.0.2
```

The next step is to define the interesting traffic that will start the IKE process. For this we will use an extended ACL as demonstrated in Example 9-3.

Example 9-3 *IKEv1 Interesting Traffic ACL*

```
R1
access-list 100 remark Interesting Traffic
access-list 100 permit ip 10.99.100.0 0.0.0.255 10.99.200.0 0.0.0.255
!
R2
access-list 100 remark Interesting Traffic
access-list 100 permit ip 10.99.200.0 0.0.0.255 10.99.100.0 0.0.0.255
```

Always make sure that you check, double-check, and triple-check your ACLs! They should mirror each other on both sides of the tunnel.

Next is to define our transform set, which is our Phase 2 negotiation and the establishment of the IPsec SA. This is also where we define if the tunnel should use the Transport mode or Tunnel mode of protection for the interesting traffic. The transform set must match between the peers for the IPsec SA to establish, as demonstrated in Example 9-4.

Example 9-4 *IKEv1 Transform Set*

```
R1
crypto ipsec transform-set TRANSFORMSET ah-sha512-hmac esp-aes esp-sha512-hmac
 mode tunnel
!
<R2 configured the same>
```

Here we have defined the algorithms to use for the authentication header and the payload encryption. Later when we validate the IPsec, we will see the algorithms referenced under the SAs.

The final piece, before we test, is to put all the pieces together in a crypto map and associate it to an interface, as demonstrated in Example 9-5. Be mindful of the interface that you are attaching the crypto map to as there might be more configuration or other devices to validate before spinning up the tunnel. Is NAT running on the crypto map interface? Does the router have routes to the network that will be encrypted? Is there a firewall or ACL in the path of the two peers that is blocking ISAKMP/IPsec ports or all UDP traffic? These are all things to keep in mind.

Example 9-5 *IKEv1 Crypto Map*

```
R1
crypto map CRYPTOMAP 10 ipsec-isakmp
 set peer 10.99.0.2
 set transform-set TRANSFORMSET
 match address 100
 exit
interface gig 0/1
 crypto map CRYPTOMAP
!
R2
crypto map CRYPTOMAP 10 ipsec-isakmp
 set peer 10.99.0.1
 set transform-set TRANSFORMSET
 match address 100
 exit
interface gig 0/1
 crypto map CRYPTOMAP
```

So far we have completed all the necessary configuration for one point-to-point tunnel protecting traffic between R1 and R2. To test our configurations, we need to start communication from either host sourcing from and destined to the networks defined in the interesting traffic ACL. Using ping shows that the first ping times out as the tunnels are negotiated and the subsequent pings succeed, as demonstrated in Example 9-6.

Example 9-6 *IKEv1 Tunnel Establishment*

```
R1#ping 10.99.200.1 source 10.99.100.1
Type escape sequence to abort.
Sending 5, 100-byte ICMP Echos to 10.99.200.1, timeout is 2 seconds:
Packet sent with a source address of 10.99.100.1
.!!!!
Success rate is 80 percent (4/5), round-trip min/avg/max = 1/1/2 ms
R1#
```

Next we can validate each of the phases with the following commands, as demonstrated in Example 9-7:

- **Phase 1—show crypto isakmp sa detail:** Shows peer IP addresses, negotiation encryption, hash, and Diffie-Hellman group with status

- **Phase 2—show crypto ipsec sa:** Shows interface, local and remote protected networks, packet counters, AH/ESP SA details, and SA lifetime

Example 9-7   *IKEv1 Validation*

```
R1#sh crypto isakmp sa detail
<omitted>
IPv4 Crypto ISAKMP SA
C-id  Local           Remote          I-VRF  Status Encr Hash  Auth DH Lifetime
  Cap.

1002  10.99.0.1       10.99.0.2              ACTIVE aes  sha    psk  14 23:58:06
        Engine-id:Conn-id =  SW:2
<omitted>

R1#sh crypto ipsec sa
interface: GigabitEthernet0/1
    Crypto map tag: CRYPTOMAP, local addr 10.99.0.1

  protected vrf: (none)
  local  ident (addr/mask/prot/port): (10.99.100.0/255.255.255.0/0/0)
  remote ident (addr/mask/prot/port): (10.99.200.0/255.255.255.0/0/0)
  current_peer 10.99.0.2 port 500
    PERMIT, flags={origin_is_acl,}
   #pkts encaps: 4, #pkts encrypt: 4, #pkts digest: 4
   #pkts decaps: 4, #pkts decrypt: 4, #pkts verify: 4
<omitted>
R1#
```

Now let's take a look at some of the debugs and how to troubleshoot the connection. The two debug commands for Cisco IOS are the following:

▪ **Phase 1: debug crypto isakmp**

▪ **Phase 2: debug crypto ipsec**

When we look at the output of these debugs, we can see that it clearly gives us detailed information on the status and steps taken as the tunnels establish, as illustrated in Example 9-8. This will come in handy when we break it to see how the router tells us that there is a problem.

Example 9-8   *IKEv1 Debug*

```
*Aug 27 15:07:07.412: ISAKMP: (0):Created a peer struct for 10.99.0.2, peer port 500
…
*Aug 27 15:07:07.412: ISAKMP: (0):local port 500, remote port 500
! Here we see the peer establishment and ports in use for ISAKMP.
*Aug 27 15:07:07.413: ISAKMP: (0):Can not start Aggressive mode, trying Main mode.
*Aug 27 15:07:07.413: ISAKMP: (0):found peer pre-shared key matching 10.99.0.2
```

```
*Aug 27 15:07:07.413: ISAKMP: (0):Old State = IKE_READY  New State = IKE_I_MM1
*Aug 27 15:07:07.413: ISAKMP: (0):beginning Main Mode exchange
*Aug 27 15:07:07.415: ISAKMP: (0):Scanning profiles for xauth ...
*Aug 27 15:07:07.415: ISAKMP: (0):Checking ISAKMP transform 1 against priority
  10 policy
*Aug 27 15:07:07.415: ISAKMP: (0):     encryption AES-CBC
*Aug 27 15:07:07.415: ISAKMP: (0):     keylength of 128
*Aug 27 15:07:07.415: ISAKMP: (0):     hash SHA
*Aug 27 15:07:07.415: ISAKMP: (0):     default group 14
*Aug 27 15:07:07.415: ISAKMP: (0):     auth pre-share
*Aug 27 15:07:07.415: ISAKMP: (0):     life type in seconds
*Aug 27 15:07:07.416: ISAKMP: (0):atts are acceptable. Next payload is 0
*Aug 27 15:07:07.416: ISAKMP: (0):Acceptable atts:actual life: 0
*Aug 27 15:07:07.416: ISAKMP: (0):Acceptable atts:life: 0
*Aug 27 15:07:07.416: ISAKMP: (0):Fill atts in sa vpi_length:4
*Aug 27 15:07:07.416: ISAKMP: (0):Fill atts in sa life_in_seconds:86400
*Aug 27 15:07:07.416: ISAKMP: (0):Returning Actual lifetime: 86400
*Aug 27 15:07:07.416: ISAKMP: (0):Started lifetime timer: 86400.
```

Next is the mode decision, and as you can see, Main Mode is selected because the configuration for Aggressive Mode was not done. You can also see the state change from IKE_READY to IKE_I_MM1, indicating the first of six messages in Main Mode exchange is about to be sent. The validation of the PSK and negotiation of the ISAKMP transform set policy are now completed. The remainder of the debug continues through the ISAKMP process and then hands off to the IPsec SA process. A good working configuration is likely not what you will encounter in the lab, so let's take a few common errors and see how the debugs can help us out.

The first common error is a mismatched PSK or invalid certificates. This will be indicated by a tunnel failing to establish and the debug trying to retransmit MM_KEY_EXCH until the retry limit is hit, as demonstrated in Example 9-9.

Example 9-9 *IKEv1 Mismatched Authentication Error*

```
*Aug 27 15:43:43.164: ISAKMP-ERROR: (1006):deleting SA reason "Death by
  retransmission P1" state (R) MM_KEY_EXCH (peer 10.99.0.2)
```

The next common error occurs if the peers do not have an ISAKMP policy that matches. For this let's change the DH group that is acceptable in the policy on R1 from group 14 to group 19 and initiate the tunnel from R2. Thankfully, the debug is pretty clear for this error and we can see what was offered by R2 to validate, as Example 9-10 demonstrates.

Example 9-10 *IKEv1 Mismatched ISAKMP Policy*

```
R1#show crypto isakmp policy
Global IKE policy
Protection suite of priority 10
        encryption algorithm:   AES - Advanced Encryption Standard (128 bit keys).
        hash algorithm:         Secure Hash Standard
        authentication method:  Pre-Shared Key
        Diffie-Hellman group:   #19 (256 bit)
        lifetime:               86400 seconds, no volume limit
R1#
*Aug 27 15:50:23.217: ISAKMP: (0):Checking ISAKMP transform 1 against priority
  10 policy
*Aug 27 15:50:23.217: ISAKMP: (0):      encryption AES-CBC
*Aug 27 15:50:23.217: ISAKMP: (0):      keylength of 128
*Aug 27 15:50:23.217: ISAKMP: (0):      hash SHA
*Aug 27 15:50:23.217: ISAKMP: (0):      default group 14
*Aug 27 15:50:23.217: ISAKMP: (0):      auth pre-share
*Aug 27 15:50:23.217: ISAKMP: (0):      life type in seconds
*Aug 27 15:50:23.217: ISAKMP:        life duration (VPI) of  0x0 0x1 0x51 0x80
*Aug 27 15:50:23.217: ISAKMP-ERROR: (0):Diffie-Hellman group offered does not match
  policy!
*Aug 27 15:50:23.218: ISAKMP-ERROR: (0):atts are not acceptable. Next payload is 0
*Aug 27 15:50:23.218: ISAKMP-ERROR: (0):no offers accepted!
*Aug 27 15:50:23.218: ISAKMP-ERROR: (0):phase 1 SA policy not acceptable! (local
  10.99.0.1 remote 10.99.0.2)
```

On the IPsec side, there are a couple of common errors to look for as well. Remember the advice to triple-check the crypto ACL defining the interesting traffic? If it is incorrect and not matching, the tunnels won't come up. Also check your routing and traffic path. Commonly, you will see a mismatch in encaps and decaps counters in the **show crypto ipsec sa** output, as shown in Example 9-11, if routing is not sending the traffic back through the tunnel or in some cases being blocked by a firewall on the return.

Example 9-11 *IPsec One-Way Encryption*

```
R1#show crypto ipsec sa
…omitted
  protected vrf: (none)
  local  ident (addr/mask/prot/port): (10.99.200.0/255.255.255.0/0/0)
  remote ident (addr/mask/prot/port): (10.99.101.0/255.255.255.0/0/0)
  current_peer 10.99.0.1 port 500
    PERMIT, flags={origin_is_acl,}
   #pkts encaps: 4, #pkts encrypt: 4, #pkts digest: 4
   #pkts decaps: 9, #pkts decrypt: 9, #pkts verify: 9
```

Those were just a few examples to show you how debugs and **show** commands can help you identify the problem. Set up and play with this in your lab as you will likely encounter a configuration that is not correct in the lab, and using debugs can quickly and efficiently point you in the right direction.

Example 9-12 is the same configuration with minor encryption changes but using an ASA as R1 versus the Cisco IOS device that we were using previously.

Example 9-12 *IKEv1 ASA Configuration*

```
object-group network local-network
 network-object 10.99.100.0 255.255.255.0
object-group network remote-network
 network-object 10.99.200.0 255.255.255.0
access-list ipsec-vpn extended permit ip object-group local-network object-group
  remote-network
crypto ipsec ikev1 transform-set TRANSFORMSET esp-aes esp-sha-hmac
crypto ipsec security-association pmtu-aging infinite
crypto map outside-map 10 match address ipsec-vpn
crypto map outside-map 10 set peer 10.99.0.2
crypto map outside-map 10 set ikev1 transform-set TRANSFORMSET
crypto map outside-map interface outside
crypto ikev1 enable outside
crypto ikev1 policy 10
 authentication pre-share
 encryption aes
 hash sha
 group 5
 lifetime 86400
tunnel-group 10.99.0.2 type ipsec-l2l
tunnel-group 10.99.0.2 ipsec-attributes
 ikev1 pre-shared-key cisco123
```

IPsec with IKEv2

Now for our configuration of IKEv2, we'll change things up a little bit to get some exposure across the platforms and solutions. In this example, we're going to build an IKEv2 IPsec tunnel between a Cisco IOS router and an ASA firewall. For authentication, instead of PSK, we will deploy a second router to act as an IOS CA server to issue and validate certificates to the peers. Finally, with certificates being reliant on time synchronization, the CA server will also act as our NTP server.

Figure 9-2 illustrates the network that we will use for this configuration.

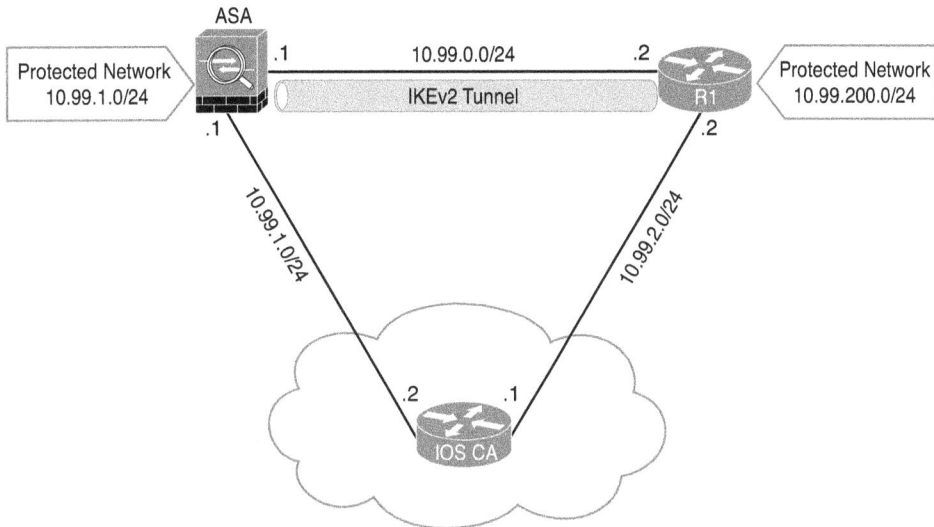

Figure 9-2 *IKEv2 IPsec with ASA and Router Using PKI from IOS CA Server*

We will start with the Cisco IOS NTP and CA configuration. When building in the lab or during your actual exam, ensure that you have time correct and your CA configuration correct, because you cannot change many settings after it is started and the CA certificate is generated. See the configuration and the inline notes in Example 9-13.

During your actual lab exam, if there is *any* NTP configuration to do (we cannot stress this enough), that is the first task you want to tackle. NTP synchronization can take some time (and it will feel like an eternity when you are on the clock in the lab!).

Example 9-13 *IKEv2 NTP and IOS CA Server Configuration*

```
! Set the time
clock timezone EST -5
clock summer-time EDT recurring
!
show clock
*17:29:24.096 EDT Mon Aug 27 2018
!
! Enable NTP
ntp trusted-key 1
ntp master 1
!
! Enable HTTP server for SCEP enrollment
ip http server
no ip http secure-server
!
```

```
! Set domain name
ip domain-name CCIE.LAB
!
! Set up CA server and parameters
crypto pki server ios-ca
 database archive pkcs12 password cisco123
 issuer-name CN=IOS-CA.CCIE.LAB
 grant auto
 lifetime certificate 10
 lifetime ca-certificate 30
 cdp-url http://10.99.3.1/ios-cdp.ios-ca.crl
 eku server-auth ipsec-end-system ipsec-tunnel ipsec-user
!
! Start the CA server
IOS-CA(cs-server)#shutdown
IOS-CA(cs-server)#no shutdown
%Some server settings cannot be changed after CA certificate generation.
% Generating 1024 bit RSA keys, keys will be non-exportable...
% Certificate Server enabled.
!
! After the CA is enabled, the following trustpoint is generated automatically in
! the configuration
!   crypto pki trustpoint ios-ca
!     revocation-check crl
!     rsakeypair ios-ca
!
! Verify the CA server certificate is a CA certificate and the Validity Date is
! valid with the current time on the router
IOS-CA#show clock
17:55:57.010 EDT Mon Aug 27 2018
IOS-CA#show crypto pki certificates
CA Certificate
  Status: Available
  Certificate Serial Number (hex): 01
  Certificate Usage: Signature
  Issuer:
    cn=IOS-CA.CCIE.LAB
  Subject:
    cn=IOS-CA.CCIE.LAB
  Validity Date:
    start date: 17:45:15 EDT Aug 27 2018
    end   date: 17:45:15 EDT Sep 26 2018
  Associated Trustpoints: ios-ca
```

Everything looks good here on the CA and NTP master. The next step before we start with IKEv2 configurations is to get a certificate on the ASA and R1 as well as get their clocks synchronized with the master, as Example 9-14 demonstrates.

Example 9-14 *IKEv2 Peer NTP Synchronization and Certificate SCEP Enrollment*

```
! Set the domain name
domain-name CCIE.LAB
!
! Set timezone
clock timezone EST -5
clock summer-time EDT recurring
!
! Configure NTP
ntp server 10.99.3.1
ntp trusted-key 1
!
! Validate NTP
show ntp status
Clock is synchronized, stratum 2, reference is 10.99.3.1
…omitted
!
! Create a private key
crypto key generate rsa label ios-ca modulus 2048
!
! Create the trustpoint
crypto ca trustpoint ios-ca
 enrollment url http://10.99.3.1:80
 fqdn ASA.CCIE.LAB
 keypair ios-ca
 crl configure
!
! Authenticate the CA certificate
crypto ca authenticate ios-ca

INFO: Certificate has the following attributes:
Fingerprint:     78e847c2 a101df1c 5c070286 212b38e1
Do you accept this certificate? [yes/no]: yes

Trustpoint CA certificate accepted.
!
! Enroll the device for a certificate
crypto ca enroll ios-ca
% Start certificate enrollment ..
% The fully-qualified domain name in the certificate will be: ASA.CCIE.LAB
% Include the device serial number in the subject name? [yes/no]: no
```

```
Request certificate from CA? [yes/no]: yes
% Certificate request sent to Certificate Authority
The certificate has been granted by CA!
!
! Validate the certificates on the device
ASA(config)#show crypto ca certificates
Certificate
  Status: Available
  Certificate Serial Number: 03
  Certificate Usage: General Purpose
  Public Key Type: RSA (2048 bits)
  Signature Algorithm: MD5 with RSA Encryption
  Issuer Name:
    cn=IOS-CA.CCIE.LAB
  Subject Name:
    hostname=ASA.CCIE.LAB
  CRL Distribution Points:
    [1]  http://10.99.3.1/ios-cdp.ios-ca.crl
  Validity Date:
    start date: 18:10:16 EDT Aug 27 2018
    end   date: 18:10:16 EDT Sep 6 2018
  Storage: config
  Associated Trustpoints: ios-ca

CA Certificate
  Status: Available
  Certificate Serial Number: 01
  Certificate Usage: Signature
  Public Key Type: RSA (1024 bits)
  Signature Algorithm: MD5 with RSA Encryption
  Issuer Name:
    cn=IOS-CA.CCIE.LAB
  Subject Name:
    cn=IOS-CA.CCIE.LAB
  Validity Date:
    start date: 17:45:15 EDT Aug 27 2018
    end   date: 17:45:15 EDT Sep 26 2018
  Storage: config
  Associated Trustpoints: ios-ca
! For brevity only the commands for the router are listed below.
ip domain-name CCIE.LAB
clock timezone EST -5
clock summer-time EDT recurring
ntp server 10.99.3.1
```

```
ntp trusted-key 1
crypto key generate rsa label ios-ca modulus 2048
crypto pki trustpoint ios-ca
 enrollment url http://10.99.3.1:80
 usage ike
 fqdn R1.CCIE.LAB
 revocation-check none
 rsakeypair ios-ca
 eku request server-auth
crypto pki authenticate ios-ca
crypto pki enroll ios-ca
show crypto pki certificates
```

Now that we have our peers synchronized with NTP and have certificates issued to them from a trusted CA, we can put in our IKEv2 configurations, as demonstrated in Example 9-15.

Example 9-15 *IKEv2 Configuration for ASA and IOS*

```
! Define the access list for interesting traffic
access-list CRYPTOACL extended permit ip 10.99.1.0 255.255.255.0 10.99.200.0
  255.255.255.0
!
! Define the IKEv1 proposals
crypto ipsec ikev2 ipsec-proposal AES256
 protocol esp encryption aes-256
 protocol esp integrity sha-1 md5
crypto ipsec ikev2 ipsec-proposal DES
 protocol esp encryption des
 protocol esp integrity sha-1 md5
!
! Set the peer, proposal, and trustpoint in the crypto map
crypto ipsec security-association pmtu-aging infinite
crypto map outside-map 1 match address CRYPTOACL
crypto map outside-map 1 set pfs
crypto map outside-map 1 set peer 10.99.0.2
crypto map outside-map 1 set ikev2 ipsec-proposal DES AES256
crypto map outside-map 1 set trustpoint ios-ca chain
crypto map outside-map interface outside
!
! By default the ASA will use the Certificate DN for identity for certificate
! authentication. In this example we will be using the IP address instead.
crypto isakmp identity address
!
```

```
! Configure the IKEv2 policy
crypto ikev2 policy 1
 encryption aes-256
 integrity sha
 group 14 5 2
 prf sha
 lifetime seconds 86400
!
! Enable IKEv2 on the outside interface
crypto ikev2 enable outside
!
! Configure the group policy specifying to use IKEv2 with the peer
group-policy IKEv2POLICY internal
group-policy IKEv2POLICY attributes
 vpn-idle-timeout 30
 vpn-tunnel-protocol ikev2
!
!  Build the peer tunnel-group and associate the group policy
tunnel-group 10.99.0.2 general-attributes
 default-group-policy IKEv2POLICY
!
! Finally configure the IPsec attributes for the peer. As you can see IKEv2 gives
! us the ability to configure differing authentication for either side of the
! tunnel, although we are using the same method in this example.
tunnel-group 10.99.0.2 ipsec-attributes
 peer-id-validate nocheck
 ikev2 remote-authentication certificate
 ikev2 local-authentication certificate ios-ca

! Again, on the router side much of the same just in a different syntax
crypto ikev2 proposal IKEv2PROPOSAL
 encryption aes-cbc-256
 integrity sha1
 group 14 5 2
!
crypto ikev2 policy IKEv2POLICY
 match address local 10.99.0.2
 proposal IKEv2PROPOSAL
!
crypto ikev2 profile IKEv2PROFILE
 description IKEv2 Profile
 match address local 10.99.0.2
 match identity remote address 10.99.0.1 255.255.255.255
 authentication remote rsa-sig
```

```
 authentication local rsa-sig
 pki trustpoint ios-ca
 no crypto ikev2 http-url cert
!
crypto ipsec transform-set TRANSFORMSET esp-aes 256 esp-sha-hmac
 mode tunnel
!
crypto map CRYPTOMAP 1 ipsec-isakmp
 set peer 10.99.0.1
 set transform-set TRANSFORMSET
 set pfs group2
 set ikev2-profile IKEv2PROFILE
 match address 100
!
access-list 100 permit ip 10.99.200.0 0.0.0.255 10.99.1.0 0.0.0.255
```

Now let's test the connection and tunnel establishment. To do this, we will start a ping from the R1 device destined to the IOS CA interface connected to the ASA. Just like before, we will see the first attempt fail as the tunnel establishes and the remainder will be sent encrypted through the tunnel. Let's take a look at some of the commands to validate, shown in Example 9-16.

Example 9-16 *IKEv2 Validation*

```
R1#ping 10.99.1.2 source 10.99.200.1
Type escape sequence to abort.
Sending 5, 100-byte ICMP Echos to 10.99.1.2, timeout is 2 seconds:
Packet sent with a source address of 10.99.200.1
.!!!!
Success rate is 80 percent (4/5), round-trip min/avg/max = 2/2/3 ms
R1#
! Using the "show crypto ikev2 sa" command we can see the negotiated encryption
! and hashes along with the authentication and verification types.
R1#sh crypto ikev2 sa
 IPv4 Crypto IKEv2  SA

Tunnel-id Local                 Remote              fvrf/ivrf          Status
1       10.99.0.2/500           10.99.0.1/500       none/none          READY
      Encr: AES-CBC, keysize: 256, PRF: SHA1, Hash: SHA96, DH Grp:14, Auth sign:
   RSA, Auth verify: RSA
      Life/Active Time: 86400/6 sec


! Next we can validate the IPsec tunnel with the following command and see the
! traffic is being encapsulated and decapsulated appropriately.
```

```
R1#sh crypto ipsec sa

interface: GigabitEthernet0/1
    Crypto map tag: CRYPTOMAP, local addr 10.99.0.2

  protected vrf: (none)
  local  ident (addr/mask/prot/port): (10.99.200.0/255.255.255.0/0/0)
  remote ident (addr/mask/prot/port): (10.99.1.0/255.255.255.0/0/0)
  current_peer 10.99.0.1 port 500
    PERMIT, flags={origin_is_acl,}
   #pkts encaps: 4, #pkts encrypt: 4, #pkts digest: 4
   #pkts decaps: 4, #pkts decrypt: 4, #pkts verify: 4
...omitted
R1#
```

Well, that was a lot of data about IKEv1 and IKEv2, right? These examples are only to get you started and in no way are all-inclusive. Think about the other items that might come into play in the lab, such as NAT on the ASA requiring you to do exclusions for the tunneled traffic. Or routing, which can commonly mess with a lot of VPN functions. If traffic isn't flowing to hit the crypto maps, then the tunnel will not establish; you will have one-way traffic or, worse, traffic bypassing the VPN, which will cost you points! Also, don't forget about dynamic addressing. Work with the baseline provided here and think about how the initiator and responder may be different in multiple scenarios and try it out in VIRL or a lab of your choice.

It cannot be stressed enough that you should try out in the lab all the configurations in this chapter. The best way to learn something is to play with it, break it, and identify how to diagnose the problem. Working in the lab and potentially creating impossible scenarios can enable you to learn why they are "impossible" and how to identify the pitfalls and avoid doing it again. On another note, building these things out in the lab helps commit these configurations to memory. Going into the lab knowing how to do each of these configurations from memory, and quickly will give you more time to work on the problems that you will encounter. This enables you to sit down, see the task at hand, and quickly identify the problem or execute on the configuration.

Enough with the boring point-to-point VPNs; let's move on to some of the more fun dynamic solutions that enable us to scale with ease and cut down on configuration.

EzVPN

A VPN solution that we didn't talk about explicitly in Chapter 8 is Cisco IOS Easy VPN (EzVPN). That is because EzVPN is really just another way of deploying IPsec with IKEv1 or IKEv2; however, with EzVPN the security policy is dictated from a central hub site to each of the spokes. This allows you, the administrator, to ensure that the remote clients have up-to-date policy before tunnel establishment and a single point of configuration management.

During this example, we will also introduce a couple more things into the mix, dynamic routing being the first. With EzVPN, enabling multiple spokes to connect without the need for modification on the hub to have a dynamic routing protocol running makes the administration that much easier. Just imagine having to go and add static routes for hundreds or even thousands of spokes as they join. Secondly, with dynamic routing comes redistribution. You might want everything to go through the tunnel, but you might *not* want that. We will introduce route maps and filters into the configuration, so the routing table is populated only with the routes you want. For authentication, we will use a preshared key for the group and username/password (UN/PW) for the XAUTH authentication process. Finally, we are going to use IPsec Virtual Tunnel Interfaces (VTIs) during this configuration. This feature simplifies the configuration of the multiple GRE tunnels that need to be stood up and protected by IPsec in a multiple-spoke environment. VTIs allow us to define configuration directly on the IPsec tunnel interfaces instead of on the physical interface.

Figure 9-3 illustrates the network that we will use for this configuration.

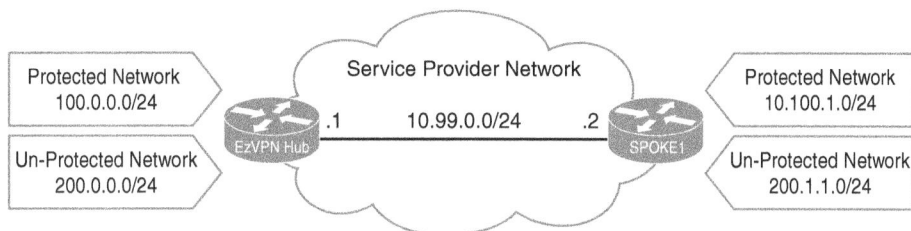

Figure 9-3 *EzVPN Dynamic VTI with Split Tunnel and Dynamic Routing*

Starting with our hub, let's get into some configuration in Example 9-17.

Example 9-17 *EzVPN Hub Configuration*

```
! Here we will be configuring our authentication mechanism that will be used for
! the XAUTH process of validating the spoke. As you can see it leverages AAA on
! the router. We will be using the local database in this example but RADIUS
! could also be an option here as well.
aaa new-model
aaa authentication login EZVPNAAA local
aaa authorization network EZVPNAAA local
!
username cisco password cisco123
!
! Next is the ISAKMP policy as we have done before with IPsec with IKEv1&2.
crypto isakmp policy 100
 encryption 3des
 hash md5
```

```
 authentication pre-share
 group 2
!
! With EzVPN the client or spoke will be getting a dynamically assigned IP from
! the hub for the tunnel interface. We configure that pool here.
crypto isakmp client configuration address-pool local ez
ip local pool ez 10.99.254.10 10.99.254.20
!
! Define the Split Tunnel ACL
ip access-list extended SPLITACL
 permit ip host 100.0.0.1 host 100.1.1.1
!
! Now this is an expansion on the regular ISAKMP configuration that we did
! before. Here we are building a client group with a password and assigning the
! pool we just created.
crypto isakmp client configuration group EZVPN_GP
 key cisco
 pool ez
 acl SPLITACL
 save-password
!
! The VTI in this example is tied to the below interface as mentioned. We are
! using IP unnumbered to mirror its IP and still enable tunnel establishment
! across the peers in the VPN.
interface Virtual-Template1 type tunnel
 ip unnumbered GigabitEthernet0/1
 tunnel source GigabitEthernet0/1
 tunnel mode ipsec ipv4
 tunnel protection ipsec profile EZVPN_PROF
!
! Now we build a ISAKMP profile where the authentication is set along with group
! mapping. Also here is where we first reference the VTI which we will configure
! later.
crypto isakmp profile IKMP_PROFILE
 match identity group EZVPN_GP
 client authentication list EZVPNAAA
 isakmp authorization list EZVPNAAA
 client configuration address respond
 client configuration group EZVPN_GP
 Virtual-Template 1
!
! Transform set just like IPsec P2P tunnels
crypto ipsec transform-set 3DES_MD5 esp-3des esp-md5-hmac
 mode tunnel
!
```

```
! Now the IPsec profile is where we tie the transform set to the ISAKMP profile.
crypto ipsec profile EZVPN_PROF
 set transform-set 3DES_MD5
 set isakmp-profile IKMP_PROFILE
!
! Important note here is the use of Reverse Route Injection, or RRI. If the
! network upstream from the hub needs updates in the routing table to ensure a
! proper traffic path back to the spoke, then this is very important to the
! network. The VPN hub device will insert the pool address as a static route in
! its own routing table and then can redistribute it based on configuration of
! your routing process. Also note the ability to add tags to the route to allow
! filtering or route manipulation if desired.
 set reverse-route tag 1
!
! Loopback simulation networks. Note that loopback 1 will be the only network
! that gets put through the tunnel per our ACL.
interface Loopback0
 ip address 10.99.100.1 255.255.255.255
interface Loopback1
 ip address 100.0.0.1 255.255.255.255
!
! This is the interface that the tunnel will be established through, but there
! is no crypto map or other IPsec configuration on it. This is because we are
! using VTIs.
interface GigabitEthernet0/1
 ip address 10.99.0.1 255.255.255.0
!
! Last is our routing. Here we are using EIGRP and filtering one of the loopbacks
! from the spokes using a route-map & prefix-list.
ip prefix-list LOOPBACK seq 5 permit 10.99.100.1/32
!
route-map DENYLOOPBACK deny 10
 match ip address prefix-list LOOPBACK
 route-map DENYLOOPBACK permit 20
!
router eigrp 10
 network 10.99.0.0 0.0.0.255
 redistribute connected route-map DENYLOOPBACK
```

Our hub configuration is complete. Now we can move on to a spoke/client node. The one thing to notice with the client node is that there is no encryption, hash, or protocols defined in the configuration in Example 9-18. The client node will retrieve and negotiate these items based on the hub configuration.

Example 9-18 *EzVPN Client Configuration*

```
! This first section is the only EzVPN configuration needed on the client side of
! the connection. As you can see it specifies the group and client authentication
! parameters and the hub IP. Also important is the "connect ACL" which is our
! interesting traffic ACL in the case of EzVPN. The client can operate and turn
! up or down the tunnel based on traffic needs using this configuration.
! Connection can also be set to automatic or manual driven based on the
! requirement.
crypto ipsec client ezvpn EZVPN_CLIENT
 connect acl SPLITACL
 group EZVPN_GP key cisco
 mode client
 peer 10.99.0.1
 username cisco password cisco123
 xauth userid mode local
!
! Loopback simulation networks. The 100 network is how we will trigger the EzVPN
! to come up. Important to notice here is the inside designation given to the
! Loopback1 interface. This tells the router to NAT/PAT the traffic
! from this interface to the "physical interface or the" VTI dynamic address
  received from the hub.
interface Loopback0
 ip address 10.99.200.1 255.255.255.255
interface Loopback1
 ip address 100.1.1.1 255.255.255.255
 crypto ipsec client ezvpn EZVPN_CLIENT inside
!
! On the client side the IPsec is configured directly on the interface in this
! example. This is considered Legacy EzVPN configuration. The client can instead
! use a VTI mapped to the inside interface. That method is called Enhanced EzVPN
! configuration.
interface GigabitEthernet0/1
 ip address 10.99.0.2 255.255.255.0
 duplex auto
 speed auto
 crypto ipsec client ezvpn EZVPN_CLIENT outside
!
! Finally, our routing and filtering configuration for the client
router eigrp 10
 network 10.99.0.0 0.0.0.255
 redistribute connected route-map DENYLOOPBACK
!
ip access-list extended SPLITACL
 permit ip host 100.1.1.1 host 100.0.0.1
!
```

```
ip prefix-list LOOPBACK seq 5 permit 10.99.200.1/32
!
route-map DENYLOOPBACK deny 10
 match ip address prefix-list LOOPBACK
route-map DENYLOOPBACK permit 20
```

And now we are ready to test and validate the configuration.

On the spoke/client side we can run an EzVPN-specific **show** command, as demonstrated in Example 9-19.

Example 9-19 *EzVPN Client Validation Tunnel Down*

```
SPOKE1#sh crypto ipsec client ezvpn
Easy VPN Remote Phase: 8


Tunnel name : EZVPN_CLIENT
Inside interface list: Loopback1
Outside interface: GigabitEthernet0/1
Easy VPN connect ACL checking active
Connect : ACL based with access-list SPLITACL
Current State: CONNECT_REQUIRED
Last Event: CONN_DOWN
Save Password: Allowed
Current EzVPN Peer: 10.99.0.1


SPOKE1#
```

As you can see, this gives us an easy-to-read output of all of the client configuration parameters. It also gives us the status of the tunnel. Let's go ahead and trigger the ACL and get the tunnel up to see how it changes, as shown in Example 9-20.

Example 9-20 *EzVPN Client Validation Tunnel Up*

```
SPOKE1#100.0.0.1 source 100.1.1.1
Type escape sequence to abort.
Sending 5, 100-byte ICMP Echos to 100.0.0.1, timeout is 2 seconds:
Packet sent with a source address of 100.1.1.1
!!!!!
Success rate is 100 percent (5/5), round-trip min/avg/max = 2/2/3 ms
SPOKE1#
SPOKE1#sh crypto ipsec client ezvpn
Easy VPN Remote Phase: 8
```

```
Tunnel name : EZVPN_CLIENT
Inside interface list: Loopback1
Outside interface: GigabitEthernet0/1
Connect : ACL based with access-list SPLITACL
Current State: IPSEC_ACTIVE
Last Event: SOCKET_UP
Address: 10.99.254.12 (applied on Loopback10000)
Mask: 255.255.255.255
Save Password: Allowed
Split Tunnel List: 1
        Address    : 100.0.0.1
        Mask       : 255.255.255.255
        Protocol   : 0x0
        Source Port: 0
        Dest Port  : 0
Current EzVPN Peer: 10.99.0.1

SPOKE1#
```

We can also use the commands we looked at previously, such as **show crypto isakmp sa** and **show crypto ipsec sa**, to look into the details of the SAs on both sides.

Once the session is established, on the hub we can run the **show crypto session** command to see a quick summary of the session, as demonstrated in Example 9-21.

Example 9-21   *EzVPN Hub Validation Tunnel Up*

```
EzVPN-HUB#sh crypto session
Crypto session current status

Interface: Virtual-Access1
Username: cisco
Profile: CRYPTO_MAP
Group: EZVPN_GP
Assigned address: 10.99.254.12
Session status: UP-ACTIVE
Peer: 10.99.0.2 port 500
  Session ID: 0
  IKEv1 SA: local 10.99.0.1/500 remote 10.99.0.2/500 Active
  IPSEC FLOW: permit ip 0.0.0.0/0.0.0.0 host 10.99.254.12
        Active SAs: 2, origin: crypto map

EzVPN-HUB#
```

Keeping in mind the importance of the "inside" and "outside" designations on the interfaces of the client, let's take a look at the hub with **debug ip icmp** turned on to see what the traffic comes in as, as shown in Example 9-22.

Example 9-22 *EzVPN Hub ICMP Debug*

```
! On the spoke we will send a ping through the tunnel sourced from the EzVPN
! inside interface.
SPOKE1#ping 100.0.0.1 source 100.1.1.1
Type escape sequence to abort.
Sending 5, 100-byte ICMP Echos to 100.0.0.1, timeout is 2 seconds:
Packet sent with a source address of 100.1.1.1
!!!!!
Success rate is 100 percent (5/5), round-trip min/avg/max = 1/2/3 ms
SPOKE1#
!
!
! Now look at what came in on the hub.
EzVPN-HUB#debug ip icmp
ICMP packet debugging is on
EzVPN-HUB#
*Aug 29 22:02:58.055: ICMP: echo reply sent, src 100.0.0.1, dst 10.99.254.12,
  topology BASE, dscp 0 topoid 0
*Aug 29 22:02:58.057: ICMP: echo reply sent, src 100.0.0.1, dst 10.99.254.12,
  topology BASE, dscp 0 topoid 0
*Aug 29 22:02:58.059: ICMP: echo reply sent, src 100.0.0.1, dst 10.99.254.12,
  topology BASE, dscp 0 topoid 0
*Aug 29 22:02:58.061: ICMP: echo reply sent, src 100.0.0.1, dst 10.99.254.12,
  topology BASE, dscp 0 topoid 0
*Aug 29 22:02:58.063: ICMP: echo reply sent, src 100.0.0.1, dst 10.99.254.12,
  topology BASE, dscp 0 topoid 0
EzVPN-HUB#
```

As you can see, the hub is sending responses to the ICMP packets but not to the IP that we sourced it from on the client! The destination shown here is the dynamic interface, or IPsec tunnel IP address, created on the client with an IP address from the pool from the hub.

Have fun with this configuration. Stand up a second client and see how it works with dynamic routing and so forth.

Let's get into some even more interesting configurations with even more dynamic configurations and flexibility. Enter DMVPN!

DMVPN

As discussed in the previous chapter, DMVPN offers tons of flexibility and configuration options depending on the desired traffic flow. We will cover the configuration and validation of all three phases of DMVPN as well as introduce some new configuration options that can be used with DMVPN and the other VPN technologies as well.

Starting with Phase 1 DMVPN, you should remember that this phase is a hub-and-spoke-only design and no static or dynamic tunnels are built between the peers. We will be using a multipoint GRE interface on the hub only and will introduce the concept of front door VRFs (fVRFs) for the tunnel and physical linkage to the DMVPN cloud. We're also going to integrate the use of keyrings for the preshared key instead of straight ISAKMP key configuration. Keyrings can pose some tricky situations if not used correctly and thought through: incorrect order, multiple matches in different keyrings, and so on. In this example, we are using a simple "match any" rule, which is the least tricky of the scenarios for keyrings!

Figure 9-4 illustrates the network that we will use for this configuration.

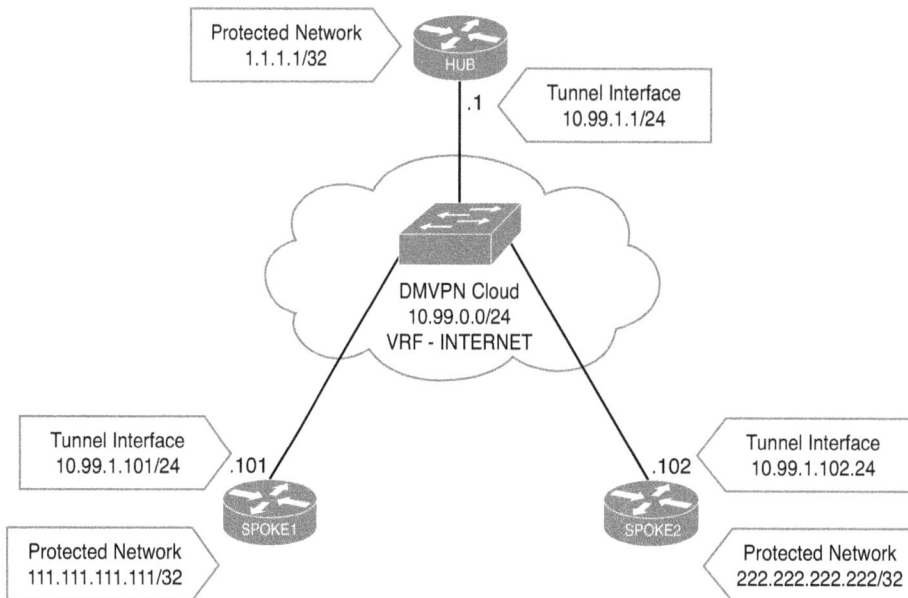

Figure 9-4   *Phase 1 DMVPN Example*

First, we need to build out our INTERNET VRF on all of the devices, as shown in Example 9-23.

Example 9-23 *VRF Configuration*

```
ip vrf INTERNET
 rd 100:1
```

Repeat this configuration on SPOKE1 and SPOKE2 as well.

Next is our keyring, which will also be configured the same on all devices (see Example 9-24). If you want to be more specific with the actual IP address or subnet for the preshared key, you can! Also note the VRF specification. You must specify the VRF to use if not using the default routing table. You will see debugs showing "no matching pre-shared key" errors if you misconfigure this.

Example 9-24 *Crypto Keyrings*

```
crypto keyring DMVPN-KEYRING vrf INTERNET
 pre-shared-key address 0.0.0.0 0.0.0.0 key cisco123
```

Next is our ISAKMP policy and IPsec transform set. As you can see in Example 9-25, there's nothing new here other than the VRF specification on the address match in the ISAKMP profile. This must be configured on all devices.

Example 9-25 *ISAKMP and Transform Set*

```
crypto isakmp policy 10
 encryption aes 256
 authentication pre-share
 group 2
!
crypto isakmp profile DMVPN
 keyring DMVPN-KEYRING
 match identity address 0.0.0.0 INTERNET
!
crypto ipsec transform-set AES256/SHA/TUNNEL esp-aes 256 esp-sha-hmac
 mode tunnel
```

Before we get to the tunnel interface, let's configure the INTERNET VRF Interface IP address and the loopback interface for testing. Also, we will use EIGRP for routing, as shown in Example 9-26.

Example 9-26 *DMVPN Hub Interface Configuration*

```
DMVPN-HUB1(config)#interface Loopback0
DMVPN-HUB1(config-if)#ip address 1.1.1.1 255.255.255.255
!
DMVPN-HUB1(config-if)#interface GigabitEthernet0/1
DMVPN-HUB1(config-if)#ip vrf forwarding INTERNET
```

```
DMVPN-HUB1(config-if)#ip address 10.99.0.1 255.255.255.0
!
DMVPN-HUB1(config-if)#router eigrp 10
DMVPN-HUB1(config-router)#network 1.1.1.1 0.0.0.0
DMVPN-HUB1(config-router)#network 10.99.1.0 0.0.0.255
DMVPN-HUB1(config-router)#redistribute static
DMVPN-HUB1(config-router)#passive-interface Loopback0
```

Finally, on the hub, we need to configure the tunnel interface that will be used for the DMVPN connection to all of the spokes, as demonstrated in Example 9-27. See the inline notes for the details of each line of configuration.

Example 9-27 *DMVPN Hub Tunnel Interface*

```
interface Tunnel0
 ip address 10.99.1.1 255.255.255.0
 no ip redirects
! Statically setting the MTU of the interface to 1360 prevents additional
! fragmentation. You can also do this via setting mtu to 1400 and using the "ip
! tcp adjust-mss 1360" commands.
 ip mtu 1360
! Disabling Split-Horizon for EIGRP enables the hub to retransmit routes learned
! from the peers to the other peers. Since all the routes are being learned
! through the tunnel interface, EIGRP will not advertise routes learned from an
! interface back out the same interface.
 no ip split-horizon eigrp 10
! The next three lines are the Next Hop Resolution Protocol (NHRP) configuration.
! Authentication and multicast are pretty straightforward. The network-id is a
! locally significant value that defines the NHRP domain to the router. When a
! router is a participant in two different DMVPN clouds this should be different.
! It is commonly recommended to keep this value the same on all peers in the same
! DMVPN cloud.
 ip nhrp authentication cisco
 ip nhrp map multicast dynamic
 ip nhrp network-id 23
! Last is our tunnel configuration. Notice the VRF specification here telling the
! router that the tunnel will use source of G0/1 and it is in the VRF INTERNET.
! Finally, is the multipoint designation for the hub, tunnel key, and the IPsec
! protection profile.
 tunnel source GigabitEthernet0/1
 tunnel mode gre multipoint
 tunnel key 12345
 tunnel vrf INTERNET
 tunnel protection ipsec profile DMVPN-PROFILE
```

Now on to the spokes. Much of the configuration for the spoke is identical to the hub, with the obvious exception of IP addressing and a small change on the tunnel interface, as you can see in Example 9-28.

Example 9-28 *DMVPN Spoke Configuration*

```
ip vrf INTERNET
 rd 100:1
!
crypto keyring DMVPN-KEYRING vrf INTERNET
 pre-shared-key address 0.0.0.0 0.0.0.0 key cisco123
!
crypto isakmp policy 10
 encr aes 256
 authentication pre-share
 group 2
!
crypto isakmp profile DMVPN
 keyring DMVPN-KEYRING
 match identity address 0.0.0.0 INTERNET
!
crypto ipsec transform-set AES256/SHA/TUNNEL esp-aes 256 esp-sha-hmac
 mode tunnel
!
crypto ipsec profile DMVPN-PROFILE
 set transform-set AES256/SHA/TUNNEL
 set isakmp-profile DMVPN
!
interface Loopback0
 ip address 111.111.111.111 255.255.255.255
!
interface GigabitEthernet0/1
 ip vrf forwarding INTERNET
 ip address 10.99.0.101 255.255.255.0
!
router eigrp 10
 network 10.99.1.0 0.0.0.255
 network 111.111.111.111 0.0.0.0
 passive-interface Loopback0
!
interface Tunnel0
 ip address 10.99.1.101 255.255.255.0
 ip mtu 1360
 ip nhrp authentication cisco
! Under the tunnel interface on the spokes we have to map the hub tunnel
```

```
! interface and physical interface together. This instructs the router that for
! NHRP messages to the hub IP should really be sent to the physical IP.
 ip nhrp map 10.99.1.1 10.99.0.1
! The same rule as above is configured below for multicast traffic.
 ip nhrp map multicast 10.99.0.1
 ip nhrp network-id 23
 ip nhrp nhs 10.99.1.1
 tunnel source GigabitEthernet0/1
! In Phase 1 DMVPN the spokes are statically assigned with a tunnel destination
! of the hub.
 tunnel destination 10.99.0.1
 tunnel key 12345
 tunnel vrf INTERNET
 tunnel protection ipsec profile DMVPN-PROFILE
```

So now you can replicate this configuration onto as many spokes as you need. One thing you won't see here is a crypto ACL. DMVPN creates a tunnel for all traffic across the tunnel interface, as you'll see when we look at the routing in the lab.

Now we can take a look at our **show** commands to validate the configuration and tunnel establishment. The first item to look at is the hub and spokes with a **show dmvpn** command to see our peers established, as the output in Example 9-29 shows.

Example 9-29   *DMVPN Hub/Spoke show dmvpn Verification*

```
DMVPN-HUB1#sh dmvpn
Legend: Attrb --> S - Static, D - Dynamic, I - Incomplete
        N - NATed, L - Local, X - No Socket
        T1 - Route Installed, T2 - Nexthop-override
        C - CTS Capable
        # Ent --> Number of NHRP entries with same NBMA peer
        NHS Status: E --> Expecting Replies, R --> Responding, W --> Waiting
        UpDn Time --> Up or Down Time for a Tunnel
==========================================================================


Interface: Tunnel0, IPv4 NHRP Details
Type:Hub, NHRP Peers:2,

 # Ent   Peer NBMA Addr Peer Tunnel Add State  UpDn Tm Attrb
 ----- --------------- --------------- ----- -------- -----
     1 10.99.0.101         10.99.1.101    UP 00:03:08      D
     1 10.99.0.102         10.99.1.102    UP 00:02:47      D

DMVPN-HUB1#
!
```

```
DMVPN-SPOKE1#sh dmvpn
Legend: Attrb --> S - Static, D - Dynamic, I - Incomplete
        N - NATed, L - Local, X - No Socket
        T1 - Route Installed, T2 - Nexthop-override
        C - CTS Capable
        # Ent --> Number of NHRP entries with same NBMA peer
        NHS Status: E --> Expecting Replies, R --> Responding, W --> Waiting
        UpDn Time --> Up or Down Time for a Tunnel
==========================================================================

Interface: Tunnel0, IPv4 NHRP Details
Type:Spoke, NHRP Peers:1,

 # Ent  Peer NBMA Addr Peer Tunnel Add State  UpDn Tm Attrb
 ----- --------------- --------------- ----- -------- -----
     1 10.99.0.1               10.99.1.1    UP 00:04:41      S

DMVPN-SPOKE1#
```

As you can see, our tunnel is up on the hub with the two peers, and the "D" attribute shows that these are dynamic peer relationships. On the spoke we only see a peer of the hub with the Static attribute checked.

The next item to check is our NHRP database with the **show ip nhrp** command, as Example 9-30 demonstrates. With Phase 1 the next hop will always be the hub, but you will see how this changes as we progress through Phases 2 and 3.

Example 9-30   *DMVPN NHRP Verification*

```
DMVPN-HUB1#show ip nhrp
10.99.1.101/32 via 10.99.1.101
   Tunnel0 created 00:08:34, expire 01:51:50
   Type: dynamic, Flags: unique registered nhop
   NBMA address: 10.99.0.101
10.99.1.102/32 via 10.99.1.102
   Tunnel0 created 00:08:14, expire 01:52:34
   Type: dynamic, Flags: unique registered nhop
   NBMA address: 10.99.0.102
DMVPN-HUB1#
!
DMVPN-SPOKE1#sh ip nhrp
10.99.1.1/32 via 10.99.1.1
   Tunnel0 created 3d15h, never expire
   Type: static, Flags:
   NBMA address: 10.99.0.1
DMVPN-SPOKE1#
```

In the NHRP commands you can see the NHRP protocol mapping the tunnel address to the NBMA physical address for proper operation of the tunnel.

DMVPN Phase 1

Now let's take a look at the routing and packet flow with DMVPN Phase 1, as shown in Example 9-31. On the hub we see two peers with their respective loopback advertised into the routing table. From the hub, the next hop of the loopback on the respective router is the tunnel address of the peers. You can also see a default route (to null 0 in this lab example) on the hub that we will redistribute to the peers as well.

Example 9-31 *DMVPN Hub Routing Verification*

```
DMVPN-HUB1#sh ip eigrp neighbors
EIGRP-IPv4 Neighbors for AS(10)
H   Address                 Interface            Hold Uptime    SRTT   RTO  Q  Seq
                                                 (sec)          (ms)        Cnt Num
1   10.99.1.102             Tu0                   12 00:11:19    3   1362   0  12
0   10.99.1.101             Tu0                   11 00:11:37    1   1362   0  13
DMVPN-HUB1#sh ip route
…omitted
Gateway of last resort is 0.0.0.0 to network 0.0.0.0

S*    0.0.0.0/0 is directly connected, Null0
      1.0.0.0/32 is subnetted, 1 subnets
C        1.1.1.1 is directly connected, Loopback0
      10.0.0.0/8 is variably subnetted, 2 subnets, 2 masks
C        10.99.1.0/24 is directly connected, Tunnel0
L        10.99.1.1/32 is directly connected, Tunnel0
      111.0.0.0/32 is subnetted, 1 subnets
D        111.111.111.111 [90/27008000] via 10.99.1.101, 00:11:40, Tunnel0
      222.222.222.0/32 is subnetted, 1 subnets
D        222.222.222.222 [90/27008000] via 10.99.1.102, 00:11:22, Tunnel0
DMVPN-HUB1#
```

Note that in this routing table you do not see the physical address interface of Gig0/1. That is because we have isolated that interface into the INTERNET VRF. This allows the routing table to be kept "clean," with only local routes specific to the DMVPN network being shown in the global routing table. A **show ip route vrf INTERNET** command will show you the VRF routing table and can be manipulated separately from the DMVPN routes.

Next, a **show ip route** command on the spoke will highlight the Phase 1 hub-and-spoke design, as Example 9-32 demonstrates.

Example 9-32 *DMVPN Spoke Routing Verification*

```
DMVPN-SPOKE1#sh ip route
...omitted
Gateway of last resort is 10.99.1.1 to network 0.0.0.0

D*EX  0.0.0.0/0 [170/26880000] via 10.99.1.1, 00:16:44, Tunnel0
       1.0.0.0/32 is subnetted, 1 subnets
D         1.1.1.1 [90/27008000] via 10.99.1.1, 00:16:44, Tunnel0
       10.0.0.0/8 is variably subnetted, 2 subnets, 2 masks
C         10.99.1.0/24 is directly connected, Tunnel0
L         10.99.1.101/32 is directly connected, Tunnel0
       111.0.0.0/32 is subnetted, 1 subnets
C         111.111.111.111 is directly connected, Loopback0
       222.222.222.0/32 is subnetted, 1 subnets
D         222.222.222.222 [90/28288000] via 10.99.1.1, 00:16:27, Tunnel0
DMVPN-SPOKE1#
```

On the spoke we can see our static default route from the hub is redistributed into the spoke's routing table as well as the loopback addresses from the hub and the second spoke. Notice the next hop of the 222.222.222.222 address from SPOKE2. Now we can verify the path taken with Phase 1 using a **traceroute** from SPOKE1 to SPOKE2, as demonstrated in Example 9-33.

Example 9-33 *DMVPN Spoke-to-Spoke Trace Route*

```
DMVPN-SPOKE1#traceroute 222.222.222.222
Type escape sequence to abort.
Tracing the route to 222.222.222.222
VRF info: (vrf in name/id, vrf out name/id)
  1 10.99.1.1 4 msec 3 msec 3 msec
  2 10.99.1.102 4 msec 4 msec 4 msec
DMVPN-SPOKE1#
```

We can see the hub-and-spoke design here as SPOKE1 sent the traffic to the hub and then down to the other spoke.

Another option you may see or chose to use in a hub-and-spoke design with EIGRP is the **summary-address** command (we will see this in Phase 3 later in this chapter). Just keep in mind that this will remove the more specific routes from the peer routing tables and should be used with caution when using Phase 2 DMVPN because it can prevent the routers from establishing spoke-to-spoke tunnels if done incorrectly.

That's it for Phase 1 DMVPN, and there really are not a whole lot of changes configuration-wise to get to Phases 2 and 3 from here. Now let's review how the configuration and the traffic flow changes with Phase 2.

DMVPN Phase 2

For DMVPN Phase 2, all that we need to change in our current configuration is the tunnel mode on the spokes and a small routing tweak on the hub. Contrary to Phase 1, this configuration will allow the routers to build dynamic spoke-to-spoke tunnels based on traffic needs. The tunnel to the hub(s) will be persistent. Now we will make our configuration changes and test as demonstrated in Example 9-34.

Example 9-34   *DMVPN Phase 2 Tunnel Interface Changes*

```
interface Tunnel0
 no tunnel destination 10.99.0.1
 tunnel mode gre multipoint
```

We will also need to make one change on the HUB1 router for the EIGRP process. By default, the router will insert its IP address as the next hop on the updates sent to the peers. This is why we saw the 222 network reachable via HUB1 on Phase 1 DMVPN. In Phase 2 DMVPN we want the spokes to see the tunnel interface IP address as the next hop for the remote networks. To do this we need to disable next-hop-self on the hub's tunnel interface, as shown in Example 9-35.

Example 9-35   *DMVPN Phase 2 Hub EIGRP Configuration*

```
interface tunnel0
 no ip next-hop-self eigrp 10
```

After these changes are complete, the first item is to look at the routing table specifically for the route to the loopback on our other spoke router, as demonstrated in Example 9-36.

Example 9-36   *DMVPN Phase 2 Spoke Routing Verification*

```
DMVPN-SPOKE1#sh ip route
…omitted
D       222.222.222.222 [90/28288000] via 10.99.1.102, 00:06:19, Tunnel0
DMVPN-SPOKE1#
```

A **show ip nhrp** command and a **show dmvpn** command will also look exactly the same until you decide to send traffic from SPOKE1 to SPOKE2.

Before we do that, though, let's look a little deeper into the CEF tables of the route to the peer. If we look at the adjacency table for the peers' tunnel interface, as shown in Example 9-37, we see that it shows as incomplete.

Example 9-37 *DMVPN Phase 2 Spoke CEF Adjacency*

```
DMVPN-SPOKE1#show adjacency 10.99.1.102
Protocol Interface            Address
IP      Tunnel0               10.99.1.102(5) (incomplete)
DMVPN-SPOKE1#
```

In order for the adjacency to be complete and build the GRE tunnel to the peer, it needs to know the non-broadcast multiaccess (NBMA) address of the peer. Because the adjacency is incomplete, the router will perform a punt to the CPU to resolve the NBMA address, and we can see that in the **show ip cef** command as Example 9-38 demonstrates.

Example 9-38 *DMVPN Phase 2 Spoke CEF Punt*

```
DMVPN-SPOKE1#sh ip cef 10.99.1.102 internal
10.99.1.0/24, epoch 0, flags [att, cnn, cover, deagg], RIB[C], refcnt 5,
  per-destination sharing
…omitted
connected to Tunnel0, punt
  output chain:
    punt
DMVPN-SPOKE1#
```

Because the two peers have never communicated previously and the CEF table is punting the routes to that IP address to the CPU, it causes SPOKE1 to send an NHRP resolution request to the hub for SPOKE2's NBMA address. The hub will forward this request to SPOKE2 and SPOKE2 will respond directly to SPOKE1. While all this is happening, SPOKE1 does not want to drop any packets, so it forwards the traffic to the hub. We can see the result of this in our initial communication being done with **traceroute**, as Example 9-39 demonstrates.

Example 9-39 *DMVPN Phase 2 Spoke-to-Spoke Trace Route*

```
! Initial traceroute
DMVPN-SPOKE1#traceroute 222.222.222.222
Type escape sequence to abort.
Tracing the route to 222.222.222.222
VRF info: (vrf in name/id, vrf out name/id)
  1 10.99.1.1 3 msec 3 msec 2 msec
  2 10.99.1.102 4 msec 3 msec 0 msec
!
! Traceroute after NHRP spoke resolution and tunnel establishment
DMVPN-SPOKE1#traceroute 222.222.222.222
Type escape sequence to abort.
Tracing the route to 222.222.222.222
VRF info: (vrf in name/id, vrf out name/id)
  1 10.99.1.102 2 msec 3 msec 0 msec
DMVPN-SPOKE1#
```

Finally, we can verify using our **show** commands for DMVPN and NHRP to see the status and resolution results, as Example 9-40 demonstrates.

Example 9-40 *DMVPN Phase 2 Spoke DMVPN and NHRP Verification*

```
DMVPN-SPOKE1#show dmvpn
…omitted
Interface: Tunnel0, IPv4 NHRP Details
Type:Spoke, NHRP Peers:2,

 # Ent  Peer NBMA Addr Peer Tunnel Add State  UpDn Tm Attrb
 ----- --------------- --------------- ----- -------- -----
     1 10.99.0.1               10.99.1.1    UP 00:17:54      S
     1 10.99.0.102          10.99.1.102    UP 00:06:15      D
!
DMVPN-SPOKE1#show ip nhrp
10.99.1.1/32 via 10.99.1.1
   Tunnel0 created 00:28:29, never expire
   Type: static, Flags: used
   NBMA address: 10.99.0.1
10.99.1.102/32 via 10.99.1.102
   Tunnel0 created 00:06:30, expire 01:53:39
   Type: dynamic, Flags: router used nhop
   NBMA address: 10.99.0.102
DMVPN-SPOKE1#
```

Now you may be saying, "That's all fine and good, but what if I don't want to have all the routes from all of my spokes populated in the other spokes' routing tables?" Maybe you have thousands of spokes running on small IOS platforms and that would just be a monstrous routing table to have on each and every spoke in the environment. This is where Phase 3 DMVPN comes into play.

DMVPN Phase 3

Phase 3 DMVPN is designed for the hub to only advertise a summary address to the spokes, and only when there is a better route to the destination network will the hub tell the spoke about it. This is done using an NHRP Traffic Indication message to signal the spoke that a better path exists. To do this, we will make a few small configuration changes.

On the hub, as promised earlier, we will change over to using a summary address on the tunnel interface, as Example 9-41 demonstrates.

Example 9-41 *DMVPN Phase 3 Hub NHRP Redirect and Summary Address*

```
interface tunnel 0
! NHRP Redirect is configured on the hub instructing it to send the NHRP traffic
! indication message if a better route exists.
 ip nhrp redirect
! Summary Address is configured to cut down the routing table size on the spokes.
 ip summary-address eigrp 10 0.0.0.0 0.0.0.0
```

On the spokes, we need to also add a configuration for the Phase 3 changes, as shown in Example 9-42. We can also review the new routing table while we are there.

Example 9-42 *DMVPN Phase 3 Hub NHRP Shortcut and Routing Verification*

```
DMVPN-SPOKE1(config)#interface tunnel 0
DMVPN-SPOKE1(config-if)#ip nhrp shortcut
DMVPN-SPOKE1(config-if)#end
DMVPN-SPOKE1#show ip route
Gateway of last resort is 10.99.1.1 to network 0.0.0.0

D*     0.0.0.0/0 [90/27008000] via 10.99.1.1, 00:01:04, Tunnel0
       10.0.0.0/8 is variably subnetted, 2 subnets, 2 masks
C         10.99.1.0/24 is directly connected, Tunnel0
L         10.99.1.101/32 is directly connected, Tunnel0
       111.0.0.0/32 is subnetted, 1 subnets
C         111.111.111.111 is directly connected, Loopback0
DMVPN-SPOKE1#
```

We will configure the **ip nhrp shortcut** command on all remaining spoke routers. As we can see on SPOKE1, the routing table is now receiving only a default summary address from the hub. It has no idea about the 222 network behind SPOKE2 or even the existence of SPOKE2 itself. If we start a trace route from SPOKE1 to the SPOKE2 loopback 222.222.222.222, we will see that the initial data path is again through the hub (see Example 9-43). That said, with a **debug nhrp packet** command we can see a Traffic Indication message from the hub directing the spoke to build a tunnel to SPOKE2.

Example 9-43 *DMVPN Phase 3 Trace Route and NHRP Redirect*

```
DMVPN-SPOKE1#debug nhrp packet
DMVPN-SPOKE1#traceroute 222.222.222.222
Type escape sequence to abort.
Tracing the route to 222.222.222.222
VRF info: (vrf in name/id, vrf out name/id)
  1 10.99.1.1 3 msec 3 msec 2 msec
  2 10.99.1.102 4 msec 3 msec 0 msec
```

```
! Debug output
*Sep  3 20:22:01.768: NHRP: Receive Traffic Indication via Tunnel0 vrf global(0x0),
  packet size: 97
... omitted
*Sep  3 20:22:01.768:   (M) traffic code: redirect(0)
... omitted
*Sep  3 20:22:01.795:        client NBMA: 10.99.0.102
*Sep  3 20:22:01.795:        client protocol: 10.99.1.102


DMVPN-SPOKE1#traceroute 222.222.222.222
Type escape sequence to abort.
Tracing the route to 222.222.222.222
VRF info: (vrf in name/id, vrf out name/id)
  1 10.99.1.102 4 msec 3 msec 0 msec
DMVPN-SPOKE1#
```

As we can see, the route went in the direction we expected initially, and the spoke received the redirect from the hub. A following **traceroute** shows the data now going directly through the dynamic tunnel established with the SPOKE2 router.

Now we need to take a look at the routing table and the **show** command previously used for verification. In the routing table, shown in Example 9-44, we see two new routes on the spoke that are designated with the "H" code, indicating that they were learned via NHRP.

Example 9-44 *DMVPN Phase 3 NHRP Routes Verification*

```
DMVPN-SPOKE1#sh ip route
Codes: L - local, C - connected, S - static, R - RIP, M - mobile, B - BGP
... omitted
       o - ODR, P - periodic downloaded static route, H - NHRP, l - LISP
...omitted
H        10.99.1.102/32 is directly connected, 00:11:52, Tunnel0
H        222.222.222.222 [250/255] via 10.99.1.102, 00:11:52, Tunnel0
DMVPN-SPOKE1#
```

A quick view of the **show dmvpn** and **show ip nhrp** output will also show us the dynamic tunnel and the NHRP mappings that were performed based on the NHRP Traffic Indication message from the hub, as Example 9-45 demonstrates.

Example 9-45 *DMVPN Phase 3 DMVPN and NHRP Verification*

```
DMVPN-SPOKE1#show ip nhrp
...omitted
10.99.1.102/32 via 10.99.1.102
...omitted
  NBMA address: 10.99.0.102
```

```
222.222.222.222/32 via 10.99.1.102
…omitted
   NBMA address: 10.99.0.102
!
DMVPN-SPOKE1#show dmvpn
Legend: Attrb --> S - Static, D - Dynamic, I - Incomplete
        N - NATed, L - Local, X - No Socket
        T1 - Route Installed, T2 - Nexthop-override
…omitted
 # Ent  Peer NBMA Addr Peer Tunnel Add State  UpDn Tm Attrb
 ----- --------------- --------------- ----- -------- -----
     1 10.99.0.1            10.99.1.1   UP 04:26:11     S
     2 10.99.0.102      10.99.1.102   UP 00:15:51    DT1
                        10.99.1.102   UP 00:15:51    DT1

DMVPN-SPOKE1#
```

Success! We have now covered all three phases of DMVPN configuration and their functions.

Dual-Hub DMVPN

One thing we have not covered yet is the scenario with two hubs. Everyone wants redundancy, right? Because DMVPN is an always-on connection with dynamic routing to the hub, routing is really what controls the traffic flow. Adding a hub is a relatively simple configuration step, and we will cover that quickly with our completed DMVPN Phase 3 configuration that we have up now.

Starting with HUB2 you will only need to replicate the configuration from HUB1 with the new IP addressing for the second hub. On the spoke side there are simply three commands to add for NHRP under the tunnel interface to get the second hub set up in the DMVPN network. See the new tunnel configuration in the output in Example 9-46.

Example 9-46 *DMVPN Phase 3 Dual-Hub Configuration*

```
DMVPN-SPOKE1#sh run int tunn0
…omitted
interface Tunnel0
 ip address 10.99.1.101 255.255.255.0
 no ip redirects
 ip mtu 1360
 ip nhrp authentication cisco
 ip nhrp map 10.99.1.1 10.99.0.1
 ip nhrp map multicast 10.99.0.1
 ip nhrp map 10.99.1.2 10.99.0.2
```

```
ip nhrp map multicast 10.99.0.2
ip nhrp network-id 23
ip nhrp nhs 10.99.1.1
ip nhrp nhs 10.99.1.2
ip nhrp shortcut
tunnel source GigabitEthernet0/1
tunnel mode gre multipoint
tunnel key 12345
tunnel vrf INTERNET
tunnel protection ipsec profile DMVPN-PROFILE
end

DMVPN-SPOKE1#
```

We have now completed the configuration for all three phases of DMVPN and multiple different configuration options that you may encounter in your lab scenarios. Configure, play, break, and commit to memory these things and you will have success in your adventure to becoming a Security CCIE. But wait! We're not done with all the VPNs that you may see. Recall that in Chapter 8 we discussed a Phase 4 of DMVPN called FlexVPN. It's now time to dig into that technology and its configuration.

FlexVPN

In Chapter 8 we talked about the benefits of FlexVPN and its use in networks today. As part of the configuration example in this section, we will utilize some new concepts once again to ensure that you see all the potential of the solution along with the variables that you may encounter in the CCIE exams.

We will start with a simple example of a FlexVPN configuration for connection between an IOS router and an ASA firewall. After that we will cover a more advanced dual-hub FlexVPN design using Virtual-Templates and BGP routing overlay.

The FlexVPN configuration will look very similar; however, we should recap what is similar and what makes FlexVPN different from DMVPN:

- Both DMVPN and FlexVPN use NHRP for spoke-to-spoke dynamic tunnel generation. That said, however, the spokes do not register NHRP to the hub. NHRP is only used for spoke resolution.

- Both solutions use tunnel interfaces, but under FlexVPN the tunnels are point-to-point versus using multipoint interfaces on the spokes as in DMVPN Phases 2 and 3.

Now we can get into some configuration starting with a basic ASA to IOS FlexVPN lab. Figure 9-5 illustrates the FlexVPN network we will be configuring in this section.

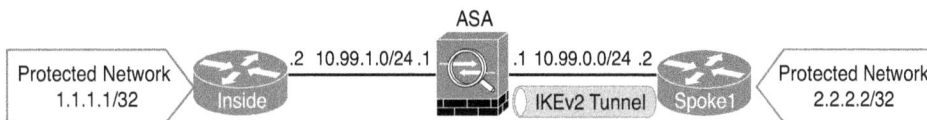

Figure 9-5 *FlexVPN with ASA and IOS*

First, we will set up our INSIDE router, which will be used to test the reachability across the VPN tunnel, as Example 9-47 demonstrates.

Example 9-47 *FlexVPN INSIDE Router Configuration*

```
interface Loopback1
 ip address 1.1.1.1 255.255.255.255
!
interface GigabitEthernet0/1
 ip address 10.99.1.2 255.255.255.0
!
router eigrp 1
 network 1.1.1.1 0.0.0.0
 network 10.99.1.0 0.0.0.255
```

That's pretty simple, as we are not doing any crypto on that router. Now let's configure the ASA! For Example 9-48, we are going to use PSK authentication with mismatched keys.

Example 9-48 *FlexVPN ASA Configuration*

```
! Define the interfaces and the routing protocol of EIGRP
interface GigabitEthernet0/0
 nameif outside
 security-level 0
 ip address 10.99.0.1 255.255.255.0
!
interface GigabitEthernet0/1
 nameif inside
 security-level 100
 ip address 10.99.1.1 255.255.255.0
!
router eigrp 1
 network 10.99.0.0 255.255.255.0
 network 10.99.1.0 255.255.255.0
! Define the interesting traffic that will be sent through the tunnel
access-list 100 extended permit ip host 1.1.1.1 host 2.2.2.2
! Define the IPsec proposal
```

```
crypto ipsec ikev2 ipsec-proposal IKEv2PROP
 protocol esp encryption aes-gcm
 protocol esp integrity null
! Define the crypto map
crypto ipsec security-association pmtu-aging infinite
crypto map outside 10 match address 100
crypto map outside 10 set peer 10.99.0.2
crypto map outside 10 set ikev2 ipsec-proposal IKEv2PROP
crypto map outside interface outside
! Define the IKEv2 Policy parameters
crypto ikev2 policy 10
 encryption aes
 integrity sha256
 group 19
 prf sha256
 lifetime seconds 86400
! Define our tunnel group
tunnel-group 10.99.0.2 type ipsec-l2l
tunnel-group 10.99.0.2 ipsec-attributes
! Note the difference of the PSKs. For the ASA it will send "cisco321" to the
! router and expect "cisco123" as the PSK from the router.
 ikev2 remote-authentication pre-shared-key cisco123
 ikev2 local-authentication pre-shared-key cisco321
! Enable IKEv2 on the outside interface
crypto ikev2 enable outside
```

Next is our VPN peer router configuration (see Example 9-49). We will use a Virtual-Template interface on the router side. Recall from the earlier "EzVPN" section that VTIs are useful for things such as QoS and tunnel-specific configurations that will get replicated to each established tunnel, and are very useful in dynamic tunnel environments.

Example 9-49 *FlexVPN SPOKE1 Configuration*

```
! Define the interfaces and the routing protocol of EIGRP
interface Loopback1
 ip address 2.2.2.2 255.255.255.255
!
interface Loopback2
 ip address 3.3.3.3 255.255.255.255
!
interface GigabitEthernet0/1
 ip address 10.99.0.2 255.255.255.0
!
router eigrp 1
 network 2.2.2.2 0.0.0.0
 network 10.99.0.0 0.0.0.255
```

```
! Define the IPsec transform set/proposal
crypto ipsec transform-set ESP_GCM esp-gcm
 mode transport
! Define the IKEv2 proposal
crypto ikev2 proposal default
 encryption aes-cbc-128
 integrity sha256
 group 19
! Define the IKEv2 profile
crypto ikev2 profile default
 match address local interface GigabitEthernet0/1
 match identity remote address 10.99.0.1 255.255.255.255
 authentication local pre-share key cisco123
 authentication remote pre-share key cisco321
 Virtual-Template 1
! Define the IPsec profile
crypto ipsec profile default
 set transform-set ESP_GCM
 set pfs group19
 set ikev2-profile default
! Configure the VTI tunnel interface
interface Virtual-Template1 type tunnel
 ip unnumbered GigabitEthernet0/1
 tunnel source GigabitEthernet0/1
 tunnel mode ipsec ipv4
 tunnel protection ipsec profile default
```

Now we can validate our tunnel! For the tunnel to establish we will do a **ping** from the INSIDE router sourced from the 1.1.1.1 loopback destined to the 2.2.2.2 address on the SPOKE1 router, as Example 9-50 demonstrates.

Example 9-50   *FlexVPN Verification Ping*

```
INSIDE#ping 2.2.2.2 source lo1
Type escape sequence to abort.
Sending 5, 100-byte ICMP Echos to 2.2.2.2, timeout is 2 seconds:
Packet sent with a source address of 1.1.1.1
.!!!!
Success rate is 80 percent (4/5), round-trip min/avg/max = 3/3/3 ms
INSIDE#
```

As you can see, we get what is expected. The first ping drops while the tunnel establishes and then the remainder of the pings go through the tunnel.

What we will see on the router is important and an integral part of how FlexVPN works. The Virtual-Template interface is just that—a "template." When the system is instructed via the crypto assignment of the **Virtual-Template 1** command, it actually creates a whole new interface label, called the Virtual-Access interface. This is the interface in which the traffic actually flows between the devices.

A look at the commands in Example 9-51 shows this behavior.

Example 9-51   *FlexVPN IOS Virtual Access Interface*

```
! Here we can see the Virtual-Access1 interface is active and in the Up/Up state.
SPOKE1#sh ip interface brief
Interface               IP-Address      OK? Method Status                Protocol
GigabitEthernet0/0      unassigned      YES NVRAM  administratively down down
GigabitEthernet0/1      10.99.0.2       YES NVRAM  up                    up
Loopback1               2.2.2.2         YES NVRAM  up                    up
Loopback2               3.3.3.3         YES NVRAM  up                    up
Virtual-Access1         10.99.0.2       YES unset  up                    up
Virtual-Template1       10.99.0.2       YES unset  up                    down
SPOKE1#
! You can see the configuration of the interface using the derived-config show
! option. As you can see it is a direct copy of the Virtual-Template interface
! that we configured earlier.
SPOKE1#sh derived-config interface Virtual-Access 1
…omitted
interface Virtual-Access1
 ip unnumbered GigabitEthernet0/1
 tunnel source GigabitEthernet0/1
 tunnel mode ipsec ipv4
 tunnel destination 10.99.0.1
 tunnel protection ipsec profile default
 no tunnel protection ipsec initiate
end
! Lastly if we look at the routing table we will see the route to the originating
! network of the ping is inserted as a static route reachable via the Virtual-
! Access1 interface.
SPOKE1#sh ip route
…omitted
      1.0.0.0/32 is subnetted, 1 subnets
S        1.1.1.1 is directly connected, Virtual-Access1
…omitted
SPOKE1#
```

On the ASA we can use a verification command that we didn't use earlier in the section covering classic IKE/IPsec. The **show vpn-sessiondb detail l2l** command provides nice and easy-to-read output of the tunnel status and the IKEv2 and IPsec encryption and hashing details, as Example 9-52 demonstrates.

Example 9-52   *FlexVPN ASA Verification*

```
ASAv#sh vpn-sessiondb detail l2l

Session Type: LAN-to-LAN Detailed

Connection  : 10.99.0.2
Index       : 10                    IP Addr      : 10.99.0.2
Protocol    : IKEv2 IPsec
Encryption  : IKEv2: (1)AES128  IPsec: (1)AES-GCM-128
Hashing     : IKEv2: (1)SHA256  IPsec: (1)none
Bytes Tx    : 400                   Bytes Rx     : 400
Login Time  : 22:29:03 UTC Thu Sep 6 2018
Duration    : 0h:03m:07s

IKEv2 Tunnels: 1
IPsec Tunnels: 1

IKEv2:
  Tunnel ID    : 10.1
  UDP Src Port : 500               UDP Dst Port : 500
  Rem Auth Mode: preSharedKeys
  Loc Auth Mode: preSharedKeys
  Encryption   : AES128            Hashing      : SHA256
  Rekey Int (T): 86400 Seconds     Rekey Left(T): 86213 Seconds
  PRF          : SHA256            D/H Group    : 19
  Filter Name  :

IPsec:
  Tunnel ID    : 10.2
  Local Addr   : 1.1.1.1/255.255.255.255/0/0
  Remote Addr  : 2.2.2.2/255.255.255.255/0/0
  Encryption   : AES-GCM-128       Hashing      : none
  Encapsulation: Tunnel
  Rekey Int (T): 28800 Seconds     Rekey Left(T): 28612 Seconds
  Rekey Int (D): 4608000 K-Bytes   Rekey Left(D): 4608000 K-Bytes
  Idle Time Out: 30 Minutes        Idle TO Left : 26 Minutes
  Bytes Tx     : 400               Bytes Rx     : 400
  Pkts Tx      : 4                 Pkts Rx      : 4

ASAv#
```

This command provides great detail on the ASA to validate all of our configuration and that traffic is in fact going through the tunnel, including byte and packet count!

Now how about that 3.3.3.3 loopback that we also have on the spoke? Is it reachable? Example 9-53 shows the results.

Example 9-53   *FlexVPN Traffic Problem with Using Crypto Map ACLs on ASA*

```
INSIDE#sh ip route
…omitted
3.0.0.0/32 is subnetted, 1 subnets
D        3.3.3.3 [90/131072] via 10.99.1.1, 00:22:46, GigabitEthernet0/1
…omitted
INSIDE#ping 3.3.3.3 source lo1
Type escape sequence to abort.
Sending 5, 100-byte ICMP Echos to 3.3.3.3, timeout is 2 seconds:
Packet sent with a source address of 1.1.1.1
.....
Success rate is 0 percent (0/5)
INSIDE#
```

As you can see, we have a route for the network through EIGRP but it is not reachable due to the limitation of using an ACL in our crypto map on the ASA. How can we fix this? We could add a new ACL entry for every network that would need to be accessed through the VPN. Then we have just another ACL to manage. We could also be more generic with the ACL statements, but wouldn't it be easier to just not have an ACL at all? Since ASA version 9.7.1, there has been support for VTI on the ASA too. Using the VTI on ASA does away with the need for static crypto map access lists. Let's see how the configuration and function changes with the ASA running a VTI in our design, as shown in Example 9-54.

Example 9-54   *FlexVPN ASA VTI Changes*

```
! First we will remove the ACL and the crypto map from the outside interface.
no access-list 100 extended permit ip host 1.1.1.1 host 2.2.2.2
no crypto map outside 10 match address 100
no crypto map outside 10 set peer 10.99.0.2
no crypto map outside 10 set ikev2 ipsec-proposal IKEv2PROP
no crypto map outside interface outside
! Next we build out the IPsec profile setting the IPsec proposal that used to be !
  on the crypto map statement.
crypto ipsec profile default
 set ikev2 ipsec-proposal IKEv2PROP
 set pfs group19
 set security-association lifetime seconds 86400
```

```
! Next is the tunnel interface. As you can see all of the commands that used to
! be in the crypto map statements have now been moved into the tunnel interface
! and IPsec profile with the exception of the ACL.
interface Tunnel0
 nameif vti
 ip address 10.99.2.1 255.255.255.0
 tunnel source interface outside
 tunnel destination 10.99.0.2
 tunnel mode ipsec ipv4
 tunnel protection ipsec profile default
! One challenge is dynamic routing over the tunnel. Currently the ASA does not
! support EIGRP over the tunnel interface even with static neighbors. In light of
! that let's do a little BGP configuration! Notice that we are building our
! neighbor statements based on the tunnel IP of the peer. This will keep our
! tunnel established and ensure the routes point through the tunnel for the
! remote networks.
router bgp 1
 bgp log-neighbor-changes
 address-family ipv4 unicast
  neighbor 10.99.2.2 remote-as 1
  neighbor 10.99.2.2 activate
  neighbor 10.99.2.2 next-hop-self
  network 10.99.2.0 mask 255.255.255.0
  bgp redistribute-internal
  redistribute eigrp 1
  no auto-summary
  no synchronization
 exit-address-family
! Since we are now running BGP with the SPOKE1 router over the tunnel interface,
! we are going to remove the network statement for the physical interface and
! redistribute BGP into the EIGRP process.
router eigrp 1
 default-metric 1000 10 255 1 1500
 no network 10.99.0.1 255.255.255.0
 redistribute bgp 1
```

We are not done just yet because we need to make the corresponding changes on the router. With the ASA now running the VTI interface method, we will remove the Virtual-Template configuration from the router and use a matching tunnel interface instead, as Example 9-55 demonstrates. This changes this example from being a FlexVPN example to an IKEv2 with ASA VTI example, but it's good to cover here anyway.

Example 9-55 *ASA VTI Peer Router Changes*

```
! First we remove the Virtual-Template configurations
crypto ikev2 profile default
 no Virtual-Template 1
!
no interface Virtual-Template 1
! Now we build out our tunnel interface on the router
interface Tunnel0
 ip address 10.99.2.2 255.255.255.0
 tunnel source GigabitEthernet0/1
 tunnel mode ipsec ipv4
 tunnel destination 10.99.0.1
 tunnel protection ipsec profile default
! Last we will build out the BGP configuration
router bgp 1
 bgp log-neighbor-changes
 network 10.99.2.0 mask 255.255.255.0
 redistribute connected
 neighbor 10.99.2.1 remote-as 1
```

Now to verify our configuration. Because we are using the VTI on the ASA and static tunnel on the router, there is no longer a need to initiate interesting traffic. The tunnel will be established with an Any-to-Any IPsec relationship. We will start with the **show vpn-sessiondb detail l2l** command again on the ASA, as Example 9-56 demonstrates.

Example 9-56 *ASA VTI Validation*

```
ASAv#sh vpn-sessiondb detail l2l

Session Type: LAN-to-LAN Detailed

Connection   : 10.99.0.2
Index        : 6                    IP Addr     : 10.99.0.2
Protocol     : IKEv2 IPsec
Encryption   : IKEv2: (1)AES128   IPsec: (1)AES-GCM-128
Hashing      : IKEv2: (1)SHA256   IPsec: (1)none
Bytes Tx     : 9426                 Bytes Rx    : 14766
Login Time   : 11:36:46 UTC Fri Sep 7 2018
Duration     : 0h:51m:48s


IKEv2 Tunnels: 1
IPsec Tunnels: 1
```

```
IKEv2:
  Tunnel ID    : 6.1
  UDP Src Port : 500              UDP Dst Port : 500
  Rem Auth Mode: preSharedKeys
  Loc Auth Mode: preSharedKeys
  Encryption   : AES128          Hashing      : SHA256
  Rekey Int (T): 86400 Seconds   Rekey Left(T): 83292 Seconds
  PRF          : SHA256          D/H Group    : 19
  Filter Name  :


IPsec:
  Tunnel ID    : 6.2
  Local Addr   : 0.0.0.0/0.0.0.0/0/0
  Remote Addr  : 0.0.0.0/0.0.0.0/0/0
  Encryption   : AES-GCM-128     Hashing      : none
  Encapsulation: Tunnel          PFS Group    : 19
  Rekey Int (T): 86400 Seconds   Rekey Left(T): 83291 Seconds
  Rekey Int (D): 4608000 K-Bytes Rekey Left(D): 4607986 K-Bytes
  Idle Time Out: 0 Minutes       Idle TO Left : 0 Minutes
  Bytes Tx     : 9426            Bytes Rx     : 14766
  Pkts Tx      : 157             Pkts Rx      : 175


ASAv#
```

As you can see, the tunnel is up and passing traffic. Let's have a look at the INSIDE router's routing table again and try our previously failed ping to confirm that we are done, as shown in Example 9-57.

Example 9-57 *ASA VTI INSIDE Router Routing and Ping Test*

```
INSIDE#sh ip route
…omitted
! We now see the route as an external route due to the redistribution of BGP into
! EIGRP.
      3.0.0.0/32 is subnetted, 1 subnets
D EX    3.3.3.3 [170/2562816] via 10.99.1.1, 00:52:06, GigabitEthernet0/1
…omitted
INSIDE#ping 3.3.3.3 source 1.1.1.1
Type escape sequence to abort.
Sending 5, 100-byte ICMP Echos to 3.3.3.3, timeout is 2 seconds:
Packet sent with a source address of 1.1.1.1
!!!!!
Success rate is 100 percent (5/5), round-trip min/avg/max = 2/2/3 ms
INSIDE#
```

Success! We have now completed the configuration of ASA FlexVPN with an IOS router and ASA IKEv2 with VTI.

Now let's look at a bit more complex network with multiple hubs and spokes using FlexVPN and NHRP's function within the network. Figure 9-6 shows the network that we will use for this example.

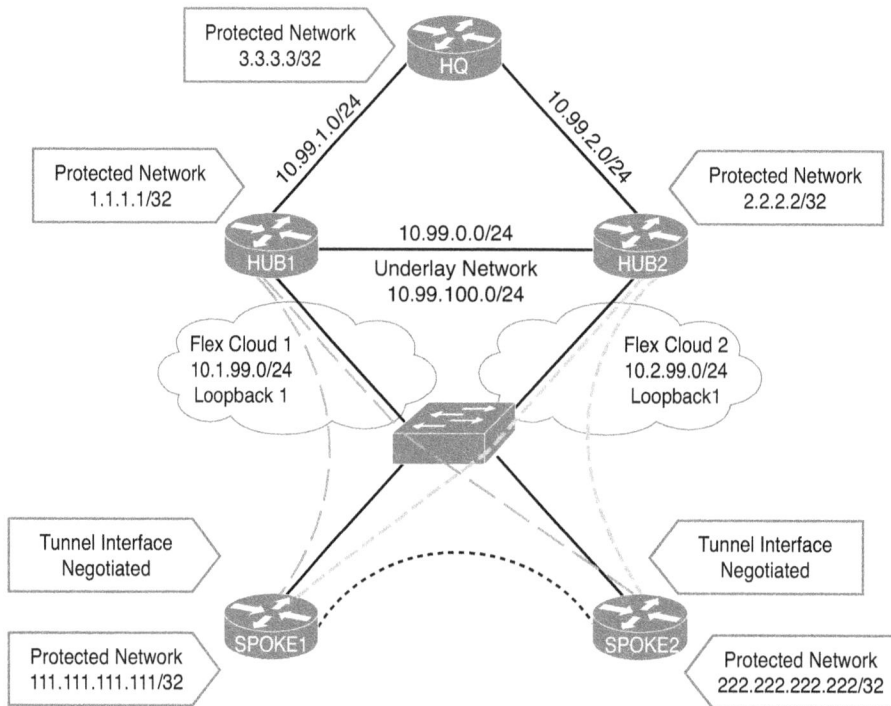

Figure 9-6   *FlexVPN Dual-Hub Network*

Reviewing the diagram, you can see that we have two hubs that are operating their own FlexVPN cloud. Behind the hubs there is an internal HQ router that is advertising the internal protected networks. On the FlexVPN clouds we have two spokes that are physically single connected to the network but logically connected over FlexVPN to both clouds. All of the peers are sharing overlay routes via BGP and the two hubs are interconnected for fault tolerance of the cloud connections to the spokes. Finally, the main benefit of FlexVPN, similarly to DMVPN, is our dynamic peering between the spokes via NHRP and Virtual-Template/access interfaces.

Example 9-58 shows the configuration.

Example 9-58 *FlexVPN Dual-Hub, Dual-Cloud Configurations*

```
Hub 1
! Starting off with the interface configuration. Note the description on each
! interface for its function.
interface GigabitEthernet0/1
 description Underlay Network Interface
 ip address 10.99.100.1 255.255.255.0
!
interface GigabitEthernet0/2
 description Hub to Hub Failover Link
 ip address 10.99.0.1 255.255.255.0
 bfd interval 50 min_rx 50 multiplier 5
!
interface GigabitEthernet0/3
 description Connection to HQ Router
 ip address 10.99.1.1 255.255.255.0
!
interface Loopback0
 description Protected Loopback Interface
 ip address 1.1.1.1 255.255.255.255
!
interface Loopback1
 description FlexVPN Overlay Tunnel Interface/IP
 ip address 10.1.99.1 255.255.255.0
!
! On all of the spokes we will build the Virtual-Template interfaces to negotiate
! the IP address with the peer. This pool is where the IPs will be pulled from
! for each spoke that registers to the FlexVPN cloud.
ip local pool SPOKES 10.1.99.100 10.1.99.200
!
! Build the IKEv2 Configuration Exchange policy by assigning the pool and
! instruct the routing process to build a route through the Virtual-Access
! interface to the dynamically assigned address
crypto ikev2 authorization policy default
 pool SPOKES
 route set interface
!
! Build the IKEv2 profile for the spokes
crypto ikev2 profile default
 match identity remote any
 authentication local pre-share key cisco
 authentication remote pre-share key cisco
```

```
 aaa authorization group psk list default default
 Virtual-Template 1
!
! GRE tunnel for connection to second hub. This is required for fault tolerance
! of the spoke-to-spoke tunnels to work in all failure scenarios. BFD echo, or
! same source and destination, configuration is to ignore/avoid Traffic
! Indication messages sent by the second hub.
interface Tunnel0
 ip unnumbered GigabitEthernet0/2
 ip nhrp network-id 1
 ip nhrp redirect
 bfd interval 50 min_rx 50 multiplier 3
 no bfd echo
 tunnel source GigabitEthernet0/2
 tunnel destination 10.99.0.2
!
! Build the Virtual-Template interface. This will be used to build the Virtual-
! Access interfaces that will build the tunnels.
interface Virtual-Template1 type tunnel
 ip unnumbered Loopback1
 ip nhrp network-id 1
 ip nhrp redirect
 tunnel protection ipsec profile default
!
! EGIRP peering configuration with HQ router
router eigrp 1
 network 10.99.1.0 0.0.0.255
 redistribute bgp 1 metric 100 1 1 1 1
!
! Build the BGP Overlay routing process
router bgp 1
 bgp log-neighbor-changes
! Dynamic Peer-Groups are used for the spokes since the addresses are dynamically
! assigned from the pool of addresses.
 bgp listen range 10.1.99.0/24 peer-group SPOKES
 timers bgp 15 30
 neighbor SPOKES peer-group
 neighbor SPOKES remote-as 1
! Static peering with Hub 2 including BFD to track hub status and route failover
 neighbor 10.99.0.2 remote-as 1
 neighbor 10.99.0.2 fall-over bfd
!
address-family ipv4
  network 0.0.0.0
 redistribute connected
```

```
  redistribute static
  redistribute eigrp 1
  neighbor SPOKES activate
  neighbor SPOKES route-reflector-client
  neighbor SPOKES next-hop-self all
  neighbor 10.99.0.2 activate
  neighbor 10.99.0.2 route-reflector-client
exit-address-family
!
! Hub 2 configuration follows the same configuration as Hub 1 but with its
! respective IP addressing based on Figure 9-6.
```

Now that the hubs are complete, we can build the spokes. On the spokes, there will be two static point-to-point tunnels to the hubs and a Virtual-Template for dynamic spoke-to-spoke tunnels. We will also filter BGP route advertisements to just the default.

Let's take a look at the configuration in Example 9-59.

Example 9-59   *FlexVPN Dual-Hub, Dual-Cloud Spoke Configurations*

```
SPOKE1
! Interface configuration
interface GigabitEthernet0/1
 description Underlay Network Interface
 ip address 10.99.100.101 255.255.255.0
!
interface Loopback0
 description Loopback Simulation and Dynamic Tunnel Interface
 ip address 111.111.111.111 255.255.255.255
!
! Crypto configuration to match the hubs
crypto ikev2 authorization policy default
 route set interface
!
crypto ikev2 profile default
 match identity remote any
 authentication local pre-share key cisco
 authentication remote pre-share key cisco
! Spokes will use Dead Peer Detection to tear down the tunnels if needed.
 dpd 10 2 on-demand
 aaa authorization group psk list default default
!
! Tunnel interface to Hub 1 FlexVPN Cloud
interface Tunnel0
 ip address negotiated
 ip nhrp network-id 1
```

```
 ip nhrp shortcut Virtual-Template 1
 tunnel source GigabitEthernet0/1
 tunnel destination 10.99.100.1
 tunnel protection ipsec profile default
!
! Tunnel interface to Hub 2 FlexVPN Cloud
interface Tunnel1
 ip address negotiated
 ip nhrp network-id 1
 ip nhrp shortcut Virtual-Template 1
 tunnel source GigabitEthernet0/1
 tunnel destination 10.99.100.2
 tunnel protection ipsec profile default
!
! Virtual-Template interface for dynamic spoke-to-spoke tunnels
interface Virtual-Template1 type tunnel
 ip unnumbered Loopback0
 ip nhrp network-id 1
 ip nhrp shortcut Virtual-Template 1
 tunnel protection ipsec profile default
!
! Prefix list and route map to filter BGP to only allow the default route
ip prefix-list default-only seq 5 permit 0.0.0.0/0
!
route-map DEFAULT permit 10
 match ip address prefix-list default-only
!
! BGP process configuration
router bgp 1
bgp log-neighbor-changes
timers bgp 15 30
neighbor 10.1.99.1 remote-as 1
neighbor 10.2.99.1 remote-as 1
!
address-family ipv4
  network 10.99.100.0
  redistribute connected
  neighbor 10.1.99.1 activate
  neighbor 10.1.99.1 route-map DEFAULT in
  neighbor 10.2.99.1 activate
  neighbor 10.2.99.1 route-map DEFAULT in
exit-address-family
!
! SPOKE2 configuration follows the same configuration as SPOKE1 but with its
! respective IP addressing based on Figure 9-6.
```

To verify the configurations on the IKE and IPsec level, you use the commands that we have covered previously in this chapter, so we will not do that again here. We will, however, look at the results of our configuration specific to the new functions leveraged by FlexVPN.

The first item to look at is our hubs and their new Virtual-Access interfaces that were generated when the tunnels established with the spokes. To do this we will use the **show interface Virtual-Access 1** command, as Example 9-60 demonstrates.

Example 9-60   *FlexVPN Hub Virtual Access Interface Verification*

```
! First a "show ip interfaces brief" will show the two virtual access interfaces
! from the peering with the spokes.
HUB1#sh ip int brief
…omitted
Virtual-Access1          10.1.99.1        YES unset  up                  up
Virtual-Access2          10.1.99.1        YES unset  up                  up
Virtual-Template1        10.1.99.1        YES unset  up                  down
!
! The show interfaces command verifies our peer, IPsec protection, and that
! traffic is indeed traversing the tunnels.
HUB1#sh interfaces Virtual-Access 1
Virtual-Access1 is up, line protocol is up
  Hardware is Virtual Access interface
  Interface is unnumbered. Using address of Loopback1 (10.1.99.1)
...omitted
  Encapsulation TUNNEL
  Tunnel vaccess, cloned from Virtual-Template1
…omitted
  Tunnel source 10.99.100.1, destination 10.99.100.101
  Tunnel protocol/transport GRE/IP
…omitted
  Tunnel protection via IPSec (profile "default")
…omitted
     818 packets input, 60266 bytes, 0 no buffer
     818 packets output, 60741 bytes, 0 underruns
!
! Also, a "show ip local pool" will show that 2 addresses have been assigned from
! Hub 1 to the spokes.
HUB1#sh ip local pool

Pool                    Begin            End             Free  In use  Blocked
SPOKES                  10.1.99.100      10.1.99.200      99     2       0
```

Next we look at the spokes. Example 9-61 shows the SPOKE1 device's interfaces and routing table.

Example 9-61 *FlexVPN Spoke Routing and Interface Verification*

```
SPOKE1#sh ip route
…omitted
Gateway of last resort is 10.1.99.1 to network 0.0.0.0

B*      0.0.0.0/0 [200/0] via 10.1.99.1, 18:22:05
        10.0.0.0/8 is variably subnetted, 6 subnets, 2 masks
S          10.1.99.1/32 is directly connected, Tunnel0
C          10.1.99.101/32 is directly connected, Tunnel0
S          10.2.99.1/32 is directly connected, Tunnel1
C          10.2.99.100/32 is directly connected, Tunnel1
C          10.99.100.0/24 is directly connected, GigabitEthernet0/1
L          10.99.100.101/32 is directly connected, GigabitEthernet0/1
        111.0.0.0/32 is subnetted, 1 subnets
C          111.111.111.111 is directly connected, Loopback0
! As you can see our route map and prefix list have filtered the routes from the
! hubs down to just the default route.
SPOKE1#sh ip int brief
GigabitEthernet0/1        10.99.100.101   YES NVRAM  up                    up
Loopback0                 111.111.111.111 YES NVRAM  up                    up
Tunnel0                   10.1.99.101     YES NVRAM  up                    up
Tunnel1                   10.2.99.100     YES NVRAM  up                    up
Virtual-Template1         111.111.111.111 YES unset  up                    down
SPOKE1#
```

We can see under the **show interfaces** command that the two tunnel interfaces are up to each hub. The IP addresses of these interfaces were assigned to the spoke via the hub address pool. What we don't see here is the Virtual-Access interface in use yet. The Virtual-Access interface will not be active until we generate traffic to the other spoke.

Now we can ping our SPOKE2 loopback from SPOKE1 to initiate the dynamic NHRP tunnel from spoke-to-spoke, as Example 9-62 demonstrates.

Example 9-62 *FlexVPN Spoke-to-Spoke Tunnel Verification*

```
SPOKE1#ping 222.222.222.222 source 111.111.111.111
Type escape sequence to abort.
Sending 5, 100-byte ICMP Echos to 222.222.222.222, timeout is 2 seconds:
Packet sent with a source address of 111.111.111.111
!!!!!
Success rate is 100 percent (5/5), round-trip min/avg/max = 4/6/13 ms
```

```
! As you can see no packets were dropped during the establishment of the tunnel
! using FlexVPN! This FlexVPN configuration will route the packets normally
! through the hubs until the dynamic tunnel completes and the routes are
! installed in the routing table of the peers.
! Looking at the interfaces on the router we can see that a new Virtual-Access
! interface is now active based off the Virtual-Template.
SPOKE1#sh ip int brief
…omitted
Virtual-Access1            111.111.111.111 YES unset  up                     up
Virtual-Template1          111.111.111.111 YES unset  up                     down
!
! If we look at the details of the Virtual-Access interface we can see the
! pertinent tunnel information.
SPOKE1#sh int Virtual-Access 1
Virtual-Access1 is up, line protocol is up
  Hardware is Virtual Access interface
  Interface is unnumbered. Using address of Loopback0 (111.111.111.111)
…omitted
  Tunnel vaccess, cloned from Virtual-Template1
…omitted
Tunnel source 10.99.100.101, destination 10.99.100.102
…omitted
  Tunnel protection via IPSec (profile "default")
…omitted
!
! Now we take a look at the routing table and see how NHRP and the "set route
! interface" commands affected it. What we see is an NHRP route for the tunnel 1
! interface of SPOKE2. Secondly, we see a Static next hop override route for the
! SPOKE2 loopback.
SPOKE1#sh ip route
…omitted
       + - replicated route, % - next hop override, p - overrides from PfR

Gateway of last resort is 10.1.99.1 to network 0.0.0.0

B*    0.0.0.0/0 [200/0] via 10.1.99.1, 18:25:20
      10.0.0.0/8 is variably subnetted, 7 subnets, 2 masks
S        10.1.99.1/32 is directly connected, Tunnel0
H        10.1.99.100/32 [250/255] via 10.1.99.100, 00:00:23, Virtual-Access1
C        10.1.99.101/32 is directly connected, Tunnel0
S        10.2.99.1/32 is directly connected, Tunnel1
C        10.2.99.100/32 is directly connected, Tunnel1
C        10.99.100.0/24 is directly connected, GigabitEthernet0/1
L        10.99.100.101/32 is directly connected, GigabitEthernet0/1
```

```
       111.0.0.0/32 is subnetted, 1 subnets
C         111.111.111.111 is directly connected, Loopback0
       222.222.222.0/32 is subnetted, 1 subnets
S  %     222.222.222.222 is directly connected, Virtual-Access1
SPOKE1#
```

That's it! FlexVPN has many ways of being used for infrastructure VPNs, and we've only broken the ice. Take a look at Cisco.com for many more examples of FlexVPN and all its permutations, including AnyConnect-based clients.

GETVPN

It's now time to get into our last infrastructure VPN configuration with GETVPN. GETVPN should be used only on private WAN/LAN networks that need encryption; it should not be used over public Internet links. As introduced in Chapter 8, GETVPN leverages a key server (KS) to have a central location of policy and encryption keys for traffic protection. The routers that do the encryption in GETVPN are called group members (GMs) and they authenticate and register with the key server(s) to get the policy for the network. In this example, we will build out a network with three remote spokes and a data center router all acting as GMs and encrypting traffic from their respective hosts and servers. We will also implement two key servers (KSs), one as the primary and one as the secondary. More commonly, the deployment of multiple key servers is called Cooperative KS, in which you can have up to eight in a single GETVPN network; however, more than four is seldom required. Figure 9-7 illustrates the GETVPN network that we will configure in this section.

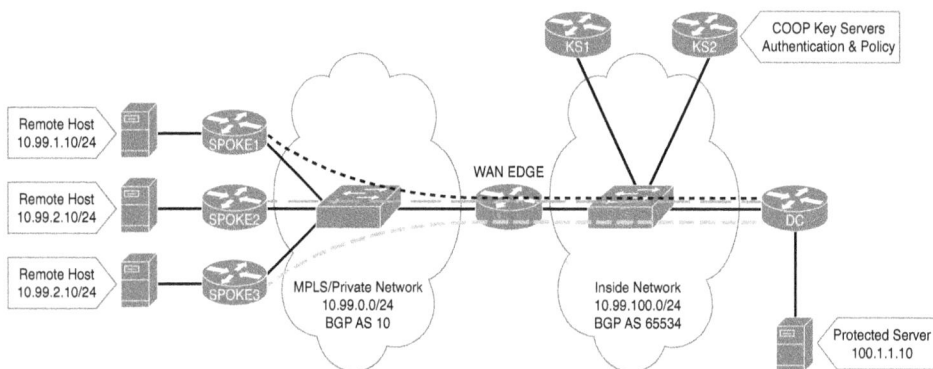

Figure 9-7   *GETVPN with COOP KS*

We will start with the key server configuration, shown in Example 9-63, because it is what dictates policy to the GMs. We will also configure the items needed to start our COOP KS pair.

Example 9-63 *GETVPN Primary Key Server*

```
! First is the interface and routing configuration with the other nodes inside
! the MPLS/Private WAN/LAN edge router.
interface GigabitEthernet0/1
 ip address 10.99.100.3 255.255.255.0
!
router bgp 65534
 bgp log-neighbor-changes
 network 10.99.100.0 mask 255.255.255.0
 neighbor 10.99.100.1 remote-as 65534
 neighbor 10.99.100.2 remote-as 65534
 neighbor 10.99.100.4 remote-as 65534
 neighbor 10.99.100.5 remote-as 65534
!
! Next is to build out the ACL to be used for encryption between the GMs. It is
! recommended to make this ACL as generic as possible via supernetting or a
! permit any as shown below. GETVPN only supports ACLs with 100 ACEs or less.
! When deciding to use a permit any statement make sure that you exclude
! protocols needed for connectivity and management of the remote device. As you
! can see below we are excluding items such as bgp, isakmp, ssh, and more.
ip access-list extended GETVPN-ENCR
 deny    esp any any
 deny    tcp any eq tacacs any
 deny    tcp any any eq 22
 deny    tcp any eq 22 any
 deny    tcp any any eq bgp
 deny    tcp any eq bgp any
 deny    pim any 224.0.0.0 0.0.0.255
 deny    udp any eq isakmp any eq isakmp
 permit ip any any
!
! Basic ISAKMP policy
crypto isakmp policy 10
 encr aes
 authentication pre-share
 group 19
!
! As mentioned previously the GMs and COOP KSs will have to authenticate to the
! KS. This is done over ISAKMP so we need to have the key and address for the GMs
! entered here.
crypto isakmp key cisco123 address 10.99.100.1
crypto isakmp key cisco123 address 10.99.100.4
crypto isakmp key cisco123 address 10.99.0.101
crypto isakmp key cisco123 address 10.99.0.102
```

```
crypto isakmp key cisco123 address 10.99.0.103
!
! Basic transform set
crypto ipsec transform-set ESP-AES esp-aes esp-sha-hmac
 mode tunnel
!
! IPsec profile with SA lifetime to match the rekey when time-based antireplay is
! enabled
crypto ipsec profile GETVPN-GDOI
 set security-association lifetime seconds 7200
 set transform-set ESP-AES
!
! We will need a RSA key generated on the key servers that is the same across all
! servers in the network. To do this we will need to generate an exportable key
! on the primary KS and export and import it into all the remaining key
! servers.
crypto key generate rsa general-keys label GETVPN modulus 2048 exportable
!
! Next is to build GDOI Group. Here we set a common group ID number of 12345 and
! set the rekey key to use and set it to use unicast for rekey communications.
crypto gdoi group GETVPN
 identity number 12345
 server local
  rekey authentication mypubkey rsa GETVPN
  rekey transport unicast
!
! Here under the IPsec SA settings of the group we set the interesting traffic
! ACL, IPsec profile, and the anti-replay settings.
  sa ipsec 1
   profile GETVPN-GDOI
   match address ipv4 GETVPN-ENCR
   replay time window-size 5
   no tag
  address ipv4 10.99.100.3
!
! Lastly is the COOP KS settings. Here you can see that we have set a priority
! for the local KS (1-255), as well as the peer KS addresses. When a KS initially
! boots it will boot into a secondary state and begin an election with the other
! KS peers based on priority.
  redundancy
   local priority 100
   peer address ipv4 10.99.100.4
```

The COOP key servers will receive the same configuration with the changed IP addresses to pair up with the primary KS and any others in the design.

Next is to configure the GMs. In Example 9-64, we have four GMs that all receive the same configuration.

Example 9-64   *GETVPN Group Member Configuration*

```
! The GM only needs a few crypto and GDOI group items to be operational. First is !
  the ISAKMP policy used for authentication and registration with the KSs.
crypto isakmp policy 10
 encr aes
 group 19
 authentication pre-share
!
! All KS IPs and their associated keys should be entered in the configuration.
crypto isakmp key cisco123 address 10.99.100.3
crypto isakmp key cisco123 address 10.99.100.4
!
! GDOI Group name and ID number to match the KS along with the KS IP address
crypto gdoi group GETVPN
 identity number 12345
 server address ipv4 10.99.100.3
 server address ipv4 10.99.100.4
!
! Crypto map setting the GDOI group for connecting to the KSs
crypto map GETVPN-MAP 10 gdoi
 set group GETVPN
!
! Finally setting the crypto map on the MPLS/Private network interface
interface G0/1
 ip address 10.99.0.XXX 255.255.255.0
 crypto map GETVPN-MAP
```

After setting the configuration on all of the remaining GMs, we are now ready to validate that we have a functional GETVPN network.

First on the key servers we will validate the KS status and the registered group members, as shown in Example 9-65.

Example 9-65   *GETVPN Key Server Configuration and GM Status Validation*

```
! The "show crypto gdoi ks" command gives us a good picture of the configured
! settings such as Group Identity, ACL, number of GMs registered, and COOP KS
! status.
KS1#sh crypto gdoi ks
Total group members registered to this box: 4
```

```
Key Server Information For Group GETVPN:
    Group Name            : GETVPN
    Re-auth on new CRL    : Disabled
    Group Identity        : 12345
    Group Type            : GDOI (ISAKMP)
    Group Members         : 4
    Rekey Acknowledgement Cfg: Cisco
    IPSec SA Direction    : Both
    IP D3P Window         : Disabled
    CKM status            : Disabled
    ACL Configured:
        access-list GETVPN-ENCR
    Redundancy            : Configured
        Local Address     : 10.99.100.3
        Local Priority    : 100
        Local KS Status   : Alive
        Local KS Role     : Primary
        Local KS Version  : 1.0.18


!
! The "show crypto gdoi ks members summary" shows us the status and registered IP
! of the GMs along with their rekey status. For a more detailed view of each
! member run the command without the "summary" operator.
KS1#sh crypto gdoi ks members summary

Group Member Information :

Group Name: GETVPN, ID: 12345, Group Members: 4
Key Server ID: 10.99.100.3, GMDB state: LOCAL, Group Members: 4
  Member ID      Version      Rekey sent      Rekey Ack missed
  10.99.0.101    1.0.17          16               0
  10.99.0.102    1.0.17          16               0
  10.99.0.103    1.0.17          16               0
  10.99.100.1    1.0.17          16               0

Key Server ID: 10.99.100.4, GMDB state: REDUNDANT, Group Members: 0
  Member ID      Version      Rekey sent      Rekey Ack missed
KS1#
```

We can also see the details of the key encryption key (KEK), traffic encryption key (TEK), and ACL with the **show** commands in Example 9-66.

Example 9-66   *GETVPN Key Server Policy and ACL Validation*

```
! The "show crypto gdoi ks policy" gives a nice view of the KEK and TEK policy
! with their timeouts and other information.
KS1#sh crypto gdoi ks policy
Key Server Policy:
For group GETVPN (handle: 2147483650) server 10.99.100.3 (handle: 2147483650):

  # of teks : 1  Seq num : 16
  KEK POLICY (transport type : Unicast)
    spi : 0x6A4E995EDF4E4A310594BAE9FD75B16B
    management alg    : disabled    encrypt alg       : 3DES
    crypto iv length  : 8           key size          : 24
    orig life(sec)    : 86400       remaining life(sec): 21756
    time to rekey (sec): 21531
    sig hash algorithm : enabled    sig key length    : 294
    sig size          : 256
    sig key name      : GETVPN
    acknowledgement   : Cisco


  TEK POLICY (encaps : ENCAPS_TUNNEL)
    spi               : 0x60137A99
    access-list       : GETVPN-ENCR
    CKM rekey epoch   : N/A (disabled)
    transform         : esp-aes esp-sha-hmac
    alg key size      : 16          sig key size      : 20
    orig life(sec)    : 7200        remaining life(sec)  : 4847
    tek life(sec)     : 7200        elapsed time(sec)    : 2353
    override life (sec): 0          antireplay window size: 5
    time to rekey (sec): 4101


  Replay Value 152497.84 secs
For group GETVPN (handle: 2147483650) server 10.99.100.4 (handle: 2147483651):

! The "show gdoi ks acl" is a good command to use to validate the ACL that is
! being applied to the GMs.
KS1#sh crypto gdoi ks ac
KS1#sh crypto gdoi ks acl
Group Name: GETVPN
 Configured ACL:
   access-list GETVPN-ENCR  deny esp any any
   access-list GETVPN-ENCR  deny tcp any port = 49 any
   access-list GETVPN-ENCR  deny tcp any any port = 22
   access-list GETVPN-ENCR  deny tcp any port = 22 any
   access-list GETVPN-ENCR  deny tcp any any port = 179
```

```
access-list GETVPN-ENCR  deny tcp any port = 179 any
access-list GETVPN-ENCR  deny pim any 224.0.0.0 0.0.0.255
access-list GETVPN-ENCR  deny udp any port = 500 any port = 500
access-list GETVPN-ENCR  permit ip any any

KS1
```

Finally, to verify the GMs and their encryption of traffic, we will evaluate the commands and their output, as demonstrated in Example 9-67.

Example 9-67 *GETVPN GM Validation*

```
! On the spoke we can get all the information we need displayed with the "show
! crypto gdoi detail" command.
SPOKE1#sh crypto gdoi detail
GROUP INFORMATION

    Group Name            : GETVPN
    Group Identity        : 12345
    Group Type            : GDOI (ISAKMP)
    Crypto Path           : ipv4
    Key Management Path   : ipv4
    Rekeys received       : 20
    IPSec SA Direction    : Both

     Group Server list    : 10.99.100.3
                            10.99.100.4


Group Member Information For Group GETVPN:
    IPSec SA Direction    : Both
    ACL Received From KS  : gdoi_group_GETVPN_temp_acl

    Group member          : 10.99.0.101     vrf: None
       Local addr/port    : 10.99.0.101/848
       Remote addr/port   : 10.99.100.3/848
       fvrf/ivrf          : None/None
       Version            : 1.0.17
       Registration status : Registered
       Registered with    : 10.99.100.3
       Re-registers in    : 4172 sec
       Succeeded registration: 8
       Attempted registration: 8
       Last rekey from    : 10.99.100.3
       Last rekey seq num : 16
```

```
        Unicast rekey received: 20
        Rekey ACKs sent        : 20
        Rekey Rcvd(hh:mm:ss)   : 00:44:16
        DP Error Monitoring    : OFF
        IPSEC init reg executed    : 0
        IPSEC init reg postponed   : 0
        Active TEK Number      : 1
        SA Track (OID/status) : disabled

        allowable rekey cipher: any
        allowable rekey hash  : any
        allowable transformtag: any ESP

    Rekeys cumulative
        Total received         : 20
        After latest register  : 7
        Rekey Acks sents       : 20

  ACL Downloaded From KS 10.99.100.3:
    access-list    deny esp any any
    access-list    deny tcp any port = 49 any
    access-list    deny tcp any any port = 22
    access-list    deny tcp any port = 22 any
    access-list    deny tcp any any port = 179
    access-list    deny tcp any port = 179 any
    access-list    deny pim any 224.0.0.0 0.0.0.255
    access-list    deny udp any port = 500 any port = 500
    access-list    permit ip any any

KEK POLICY:
    Rekey Transport Type     : Unicast
    Lifetime (secs)          : 21453
    Encrypt Algorithm        : 3DES
    Key Size                 : 192
    Sig Hash Algorithm       : HMAC_AUTH_SHA
    Sig Key Length (bits)    : 2352

TEK POLICY for the current KS-Policy ACEs Downloaded:
  GigabitEthernet0/1:
    IPsec SA:
        spi: 0x60137A99(1611889305)
        KGS: Disabled
        transform: esp-aes esp-sha-hmac
        sa timing:remaining key lifetime (sec): (4544)
```

```
        Anti-Replay(Time Based) : 5 sec interval
        tag method : disabled
        alg key size: 16 (bytes)
        sig key size: 20 (bytes)
        encaps: ENCAPS_TUNNEL
...omitted
!
! Lastly to verify traffic is flowing through the tunnel we can look at the "sh
! crypto ipsec sa" output.
SPOKE1#show crypto ipsec sa

interface: GigabitEthernet0/1
    Crypto map tag: GETVPN-MAP, local addr 10.99.0.101

   protected vrf: (none)
   local  ident (addr/mask/prot/port): (0.0.0.0/0.0.0.0/0/0)
   remote ident (addr/mask/prot/port): (0.0.0.0/0.0.0.0/0/0)
   Group: GETVPN
   current_peer 0.0.0.0 port 848
     PERMIT, flags={}
    #pkts encaps: 150690, #pkts encrypt: 150690, #pkts digest: 150690
    #pkts decaps: 150690, #pkts decrypt: 150690, #pkts verify: 150690
    #pkts compressed: 0, #pkts decompressed: 0
    #pkts not compressed: 0, #pkts compr. failed: 0
    #pkts not decompressed: 0, #pkts decompress failed: 0
    #send errors 0, #recv errors 0

     local crypto endpt.: 10.99.0.101, remote crypto endpt.: 0.0.0.0
     plaintext mtu 1426, path mtu 1500, ip mtu 1500, ip mtu idb GigabitEthernet0/1
     current outbound spi: 0x60137A99(1611889305)
     PFS (Y/N): N, DH group: none
```

With that we have completed the configuration review of GETVPN and all of the infrastructure VPNs discussed in Chapter 8.

Again, make sure that you experiment with these configurations and different scenarios such as fVRF and iVRF, different routing protocols, devices such as ASAs in the traffic path between encrypting routers, NAT, and more. Committing these configurations to memory as well is a great help in the exams. Being able to quickly identify issues because you know what should be there is much faster than trying to reference documentation during the exam.

Summary

In this chapter, you reviewed and verified the configuration of multiple infrastructure VPN technologies. From routers to ASAs and more, there are many permutations of each of these solutions, but we tried to cover the ones you are most likely to encounter in the exams. You saw a common thread of ISAKMP, IKE, and IPsec configurations throughout, as these are the baseline used for all of the VPN solutions you will encounter.

References

FlexVPN HA Dual Hub Configuration Example, https://www.cisco.com/c/en/us/support/docs/security/flexvpn/118888-configure-flexvpn-00.html

Scalable DMVPN Design and Implementation Guide, https://www.cisco.com/c/dam/en/us/products/collateral/security/dynamic-multipoint-vpn-dmvpn/dmvpn_design_guide.pdf

Group Encrypted Transport VPN (GETVPN) Design and Implementation Guide, https://www.cisco.com/c/dam/en/us/products/collateral/security/group-encrypted-transport-vpn/GETVPN_DIG_version_1_0_External.pdf

Chapter 10

Remote Access VPN

This chapter provides the details of remote access virtual private networks (RAVPN) as it relates to client-based and clientless VPNs. This chapter explores the different types of VPN headends and some example configurations. You will learn how to configure IPsec and SSL remote access VPNs on Cisco Adaptive Security Appliance (ASA) firewalls, Cisco Firepower Threat Defense (FTD), and Cisco IOS–based routers.

Remote Access VPN Overview

RAVPN enables users to connect to an organization's headquarters, network, or resources through a secure connection over a network such as the Internet, enabling employees (or contractors) to work from anywhere, anytime, on an organization laptop or personal device. RAVPN provides a consistent user experience across devices, both on and off premises, without creating a headache for IT teams. Figure 10-1 illustrates the vast user, location, and connectivity options RAVPN allows.

The goal of RAVPN is to provide highly reliable connectivity for all the approved users and endpoints across the corporate network, regardless of location, so that they can be as productive as possible from anywhere and at any time. It should also provide IT teams with visibility into what and who is accessing the network. Finally, a mobile security solution should offer comprehensive, always-on protection for every user and device in your network.

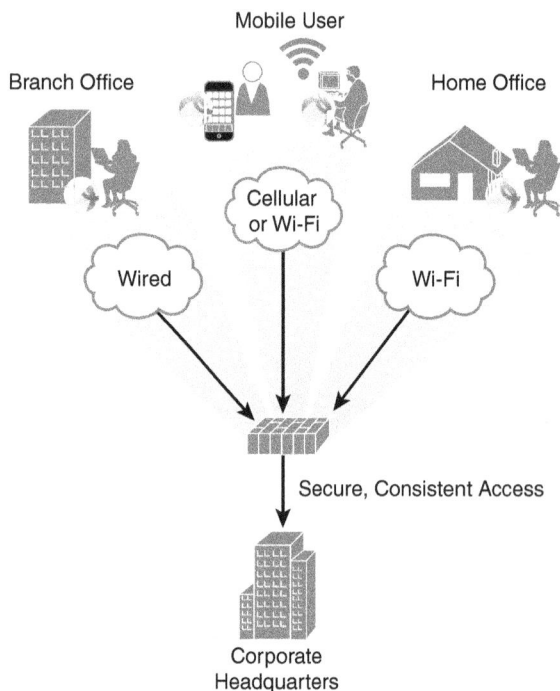

Figure 10-1   *RAVPN Overview*

There are many different remote access use cases, which highlight the variety of end-user groups, connectivity options, and devices that must be met by a VPN secure remote access deployment. The following represents the most popular remote access use cases:

■ **Mobile worker:** An employee who connects from home or on the road and requires full virtual network access to work efficiently. A typical scenario is that a user starts work in the morning at home, then puts their laptop on standby and leaves for work, uses their smartphone during the commute time to check email, stops in a café and uses the laptop over a Wi-Fi hotspot to finish an urgent task, then drives to the office and connects the endpoints directly to the corporate network. At the time of writing, this is the most popular use case.

■ **Teleworker:** An employee who works from home and requires consistent connectivity and performance as if working in the organization's office. While RAVPN is a popular option for the teleworker, other virtual office solutions, including site-to-site VPNs, are also common.

■ **Disaster recovery:** An emergency situation, where a high number of regular employees need to work remotely, without necessarily having been provided with a corporate endpoint for full VPN client access. Business continuity is key to many businesses, and is even outlined in some legislation mandates (COOP). This scenario may occur, for instance, when a natural catastrophe, a pandemic, a national threat, or a local network outage occurs. Corporate employees would benefit from clientless VPN access to essential work tools and resources such as Microsoft Outlook Web Access (OWA), Remote Desktop Protocol (RDP), and Citrix presentation server tools. By enabling such access, the corporation ensures that its key business functions are resilient, and maintains its productivity.

- **Business partner:** The partner needs only limited access to a few applications and/or to a specific work load or service. Such users typically use their own (partner) company's laptop to access the resources. The device is unmanaged and, as a result, support concerns are complex.

- **Contractors:** Access requirements vary greatly by type of contractor. Devices might be managed or unmanaged. Access should be limited to only the services required to do the job/contract hired for.

Clientless versus Client-Based VPNs

A clientless SSL VPN refers to a secure web portal where a user can access internal resources and launch web-based plug-ins. A clientless SSL VPN creates a secure, remote access VPN tunnel to an ASA using a web browser without requiring a software or hardware client. It provides secure and easy access to a broad range of web resources and both web-enabled and legacy applications from almost any device that can connect to the Internet via HTTP. A clientless VPN is a great option for contractors, business partners, or disaster recovery use cases, where the machine connecting cannot be fully trusted to be "on the network" but requires access to certain applications. Especially for unmanaged devices, the clientless option can save IT teams from having to support a client installation on devices it does not control. Figure 10-2 shows the clientless portal that users use to connect to resources.

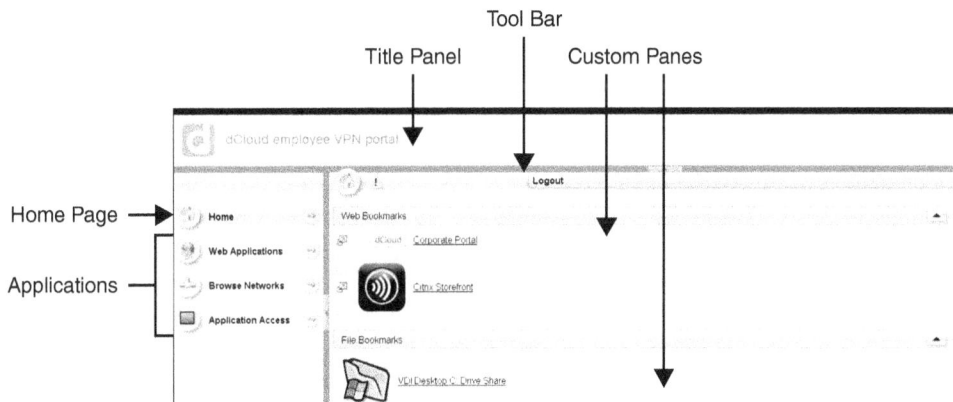

Figure 10-2 *Clientless SSL VPN Portal*

Note Clientless features may depend on the OS, browser version, browser plug-ins, and endpoint security settings.

Client-based RAVPNs are IPsec or SSL VPNs using a thick or mobile client, such as Cisco AnyConnect Secure Mobility Client, to connect to a VPN headend, such as an ASA, FTD, or an IOS-based router. Chapter 8, "Secure Connectivity," provides additional background on IPsec, Transport Layer Security (TLS), and Datagram Transport Layer Security (DTLS). These types of VPNs are typically used for mobile and teleworker use cases because they provide access just like a user is in the office and allow administrators to enforce granular policies.

Cisco AnyConnect Secure Mobility Client

The Cisco AnyConnect Secure Mobility Client provides secure SSL and IPsec/IKEv2 connections for client-based VPN users. AnyConnect has been installed on over 100 million endpoints in the world. AnyConnect is a unified agent that combines many different enterprise security services. The following summarizes the different services or modules that can be installed with AnyConnect:

- **VPN Client:** A range of access features from very basic VPN access to Cisco IOS-based headends to more sophisticated policy-driven access to Cisco ASAs or FTD.

- **Network Visibility Module:** Collects rich flow context from an endpoint on or off premises and provides visibility into network-connected devices and user behaviors when coupled with a Cisco solution such as Stealthwatch or a third-party solution such as Splunk.

- **Network Access Manager:** 802.1X connection manager with a range of access control capabilities such as validating users and devices in a single transaction, via eap-chaining, when used in conjunction with Cisco Wired and Wireless Infrastructure and Cisco Identity Services Engine.

- **ISE Posture Assessment:** Provides endpoint posture checks across wired, wireless, and VPN networks when combined with Cisco Identity Services Engine.

- **Umbrella Roaming Security:** Provides DNS-layer security when no VPN is active, and a Cisco Umbrella subscription adds Intelligent Proxy and IP Layer Enforcement features, both on- and off-network.

- **Web Security:** Redirects web traffic for inspection services and browsing controls when combined with Cisco Cloud Web Services.

- **Advanced Malware Protection (AMP) Enabler:** Enables the distribution of AMP for endpoint to remote users and/or endpoints to help detect and stop advanced threats.

- **AnyConnect Diagnostic and Reporting Tool (DART):** Used to collect data for troubleshooting AnyConnect installation and connection problems. DART assembles the logs, status, and diagnostic information for Cisco Technical Assistance Center (TAC) analysis.

Figure 10-3 illustrates the AnyConnect Secure Mobility Client running on Windows with multiple modules. For additional details on other AnyConnect modules, please refer to the latest release of *Cisco AnyConnect Secure Mobility Client Administrator Guide*.

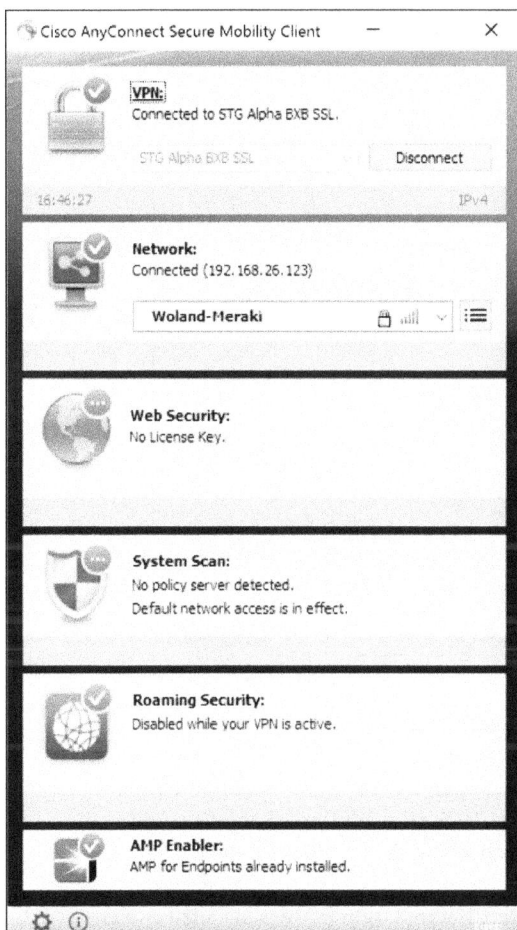

Figure 10-3   *AnyConnect Secure Mobility Client Modules*

AnyConnect Profile Editor

AnyConnect profiles are created and used as configuration files, instructing the VPN client of all the administrator-defined end-user requirements and authentication policies on endpoints. The AnyConnect Profile Editor can be used to create and configure one or more profiles. AnyConnect includes the Profile Editor as part of the Cisco Adaptive Security Device Manager (ASDM) software and as a standalone Windows program. When predeploying the client, you use the standalone profile editors to create profiles for the VPN service and other modules that you deploy to computers using your software management system or other options discussed in this section.

To install the standalone profile editor, download from cisco.com, run the installer and select which types of profile editors you wish to use, as shown in Figure 10-4.

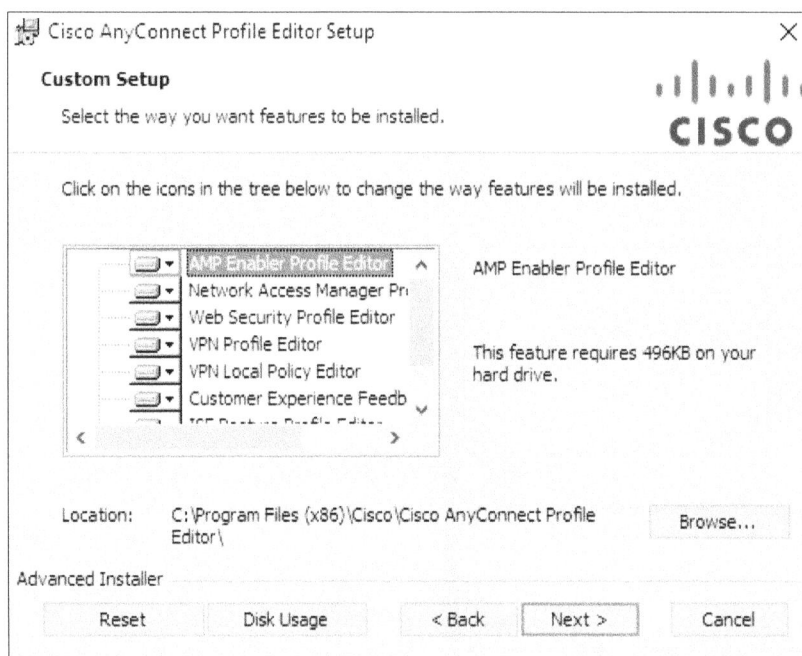

Figure 10-4   *AnyConnect Profile Editor Setup*

To create a new AnyConnect VPN profile, open the VPN profile editor. On the Preferences (Part 1) page, shown in Figure 10-5, you will find some of the optional client connection settings. For example, checking the **Use Start Before Login** check box allows users to establish their VPN connection to the enterprise infrastructure before logging in to Windows. When Start Before Login (SBL) is installed and enabled, clicking the Network Connection button launches the AnyConnect VPN. SBL is available on Windows systems only. SBL is required for organizations that need the PC to have access to the network prior to Windows login—for example, if the PC doesn't allow cached credentials, a user has network-mapped drives, or a login script needs to run.

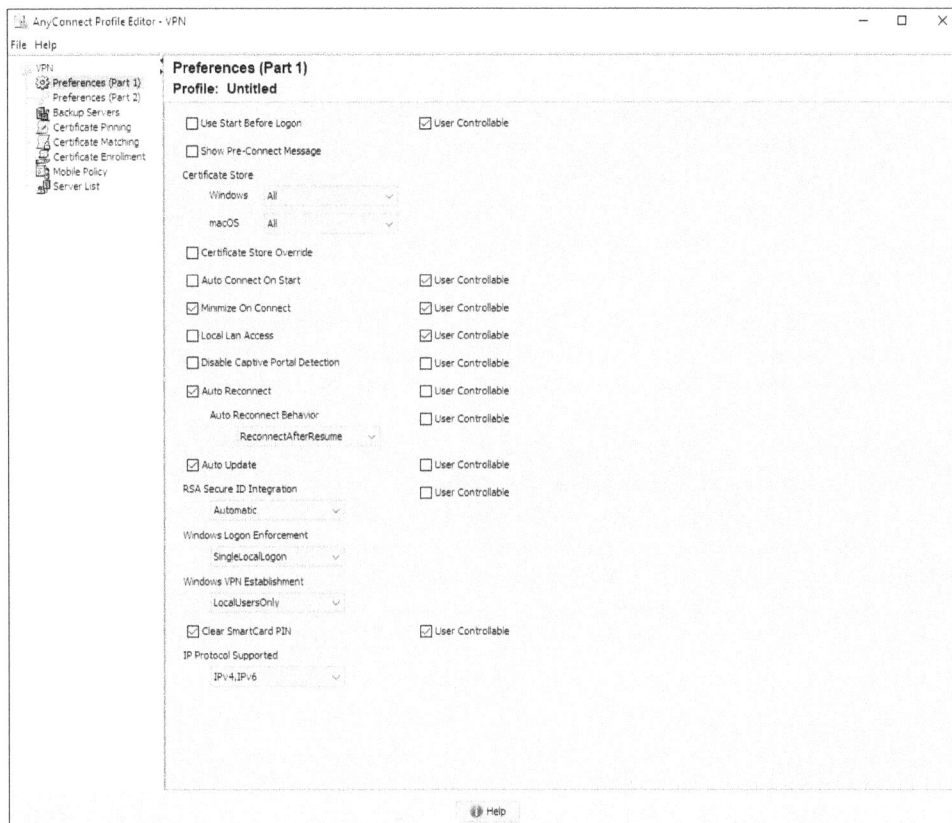

Figure 10-5   *AnyConnect VPN Profile Preferences Part 1*

The certificate store settings control which certificate store(s) AnyConnect uses for storing and reading certificates. The VPN gateway—for example, ASA, FTD, or IOS—must be configured accordingly and dictates to the client which one of the multiple certificate authentication combinations is acceptable for a particular VPN connection. The configuration can be set for the profile to use two user certificates or one machine and one user certificate.

The "Auto-Reconnect" settings, help enable session persistence, which is an important feature to create a seamless end-user experience. When users are roaming between wired, wireless, and cellular networks, auto-reconnect allows them to reconnect without reauthentication. This allows for a continuous connection experience when transitioning from location to another.

Click **Preferences (Part 2)** in the left navigation pane to configure additional desirable features, as shown in Figure 10-6.

Checking the **Optimal Gateway Selection** check box helps with deployments by having AnyConnect identify and select which headend device is best for connection or reconnection based on the round-trip time (RTT), minimizing latency for Internet traffic without user intervention. Optimal Gateway Selection (OGS) is not a security feature, and it performs no load balancing. Administrators control the activation and deactivation of OGS and specify whether end users may control the feature themselves. OGS cannot operate with Always-On VPN turned on (via the Always On check box) and unless certificates are used. Also, users may have to re-enter their credentials when transitioning to a different VPN headend.

Checking the **Automatic VPN Policy** check box enables Trusted Network Detection (TND), allowing AnyConnect to automatically manage when to start or stop a VPN connection according to the Trusted Network Policy and Untrusted Network Policy settings. TND is supported only on Windows and macOS. Setting an Automatic VPN Policy does not prevent users from manually controlling a VPN connection. This feature is very popular because it allows administrators to ensure devices automatically connect when out of the office and disconnect after connecting to the organization's network. TND provides a seamless, simple user experience that ensures the user has the same access on or off the network, providing the sense "I am always at work." Also, by connecting users into the corporate network, administrators can provide increased security by using all of the enterprise security features and tools, such as a Next-Generation Firewall (NGFW) or web proxy.

If the Always On check box is checked, Always-On VPN determines whether AnyConnect automatically connects to the VPN when the user logs in to a computer running one of the supported Windows or macOS operating systems. Administrators can set the Always-On VPN parameter in group policies and dynamic access policies on the VPN headend to override the client/AnyConnect setting by specifying exceptions according to the matching criteria used to assign the policy. Organizations can decide whether or not to allow VPN disconnect (via the Allow VPN Disconnect check box) and, if allowed, choose a connection failure policy. For example, the connect failure policy could ensure the client device cannot access the Internet if the VPN is unavailable. The purpose of this type of setting is to help protect corporate assets from network threats when resources in the private network responsible for protecting the endpoint are unavailable.

Note It is highly recommended that organizations follow a phased approach if enforcing a connection failure policy. For example, first deploy Always-On VPN with a connect failure open policy and survey users for the frequency with which AnyConnect does not connect seamlessly. Then deploy a small pilot deployment of a connect failure closed policy among early-adopter users and solicit their feedback. As you deploy a connect failure closed policy, be sure to educate the VPN users about the network access limitation as well as the advantages of a connect failure closed policy.

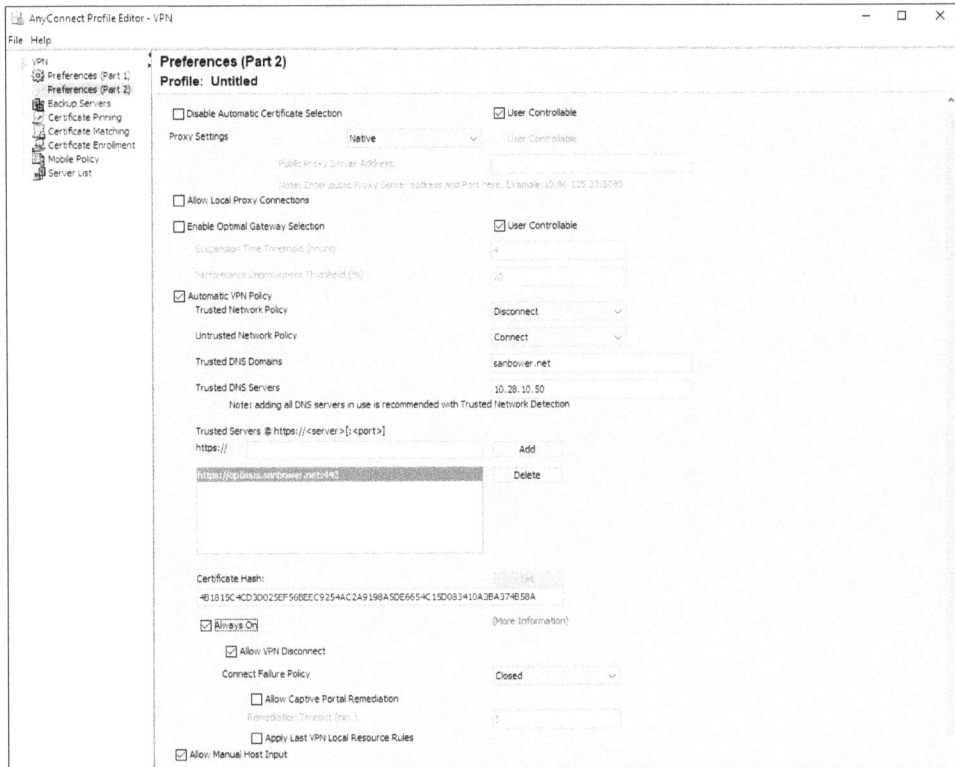

Figure 10-6   *AnyConnect VPN Profile Preferences Part 2*

The final step is to configure the AnyConnect VPN Trusted Servers list. It consists of hostname and host address pairs identifying the secure gateways that your VPN users will connect to. The hostname can be an alias, a fully qualified domain name (FQDN), or an IP address. The hosts added to the Trusted Servers list display in the Connect to drop-down list in the AnyConnect GUI. The user can then select from the drop-down list to initiate a VPN connection. The host at the top of the list is the default server, and appears first in the GUI drop-down list. If the user selects an alternate server from the list, the selected server becomes the new default server.

Once you add a server to the server list, you can click **Server List** in the navigation pane to view its details and edit or delete the server entry, as shown in Figure 10-7.

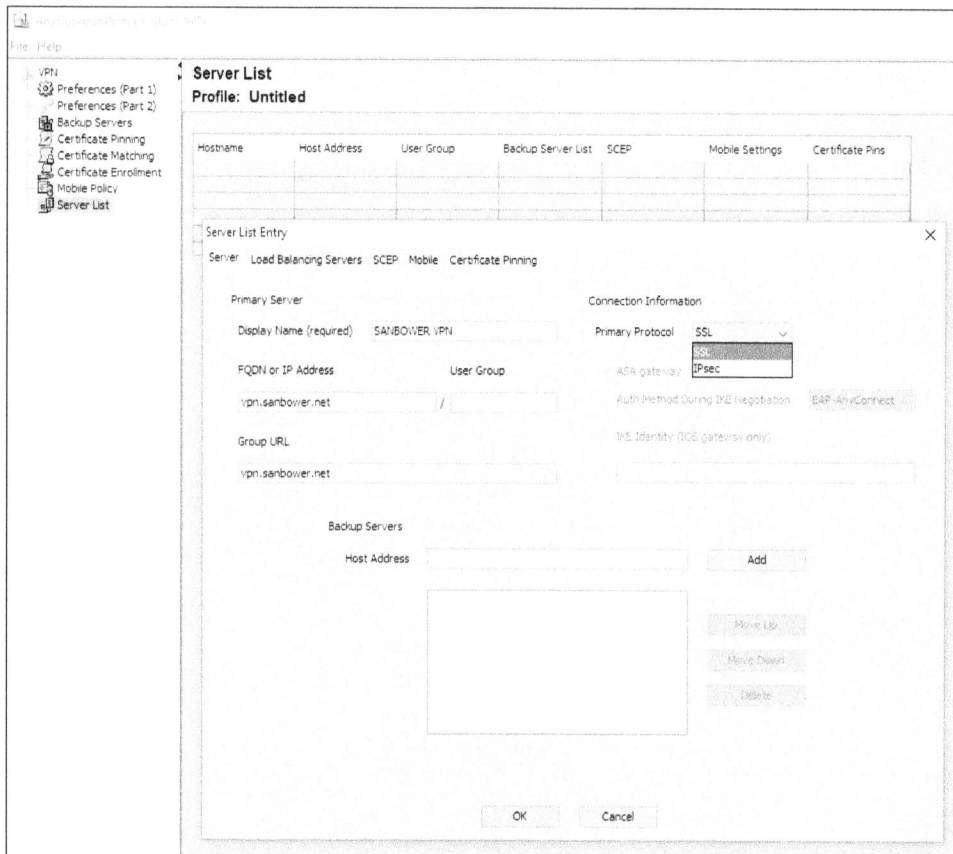

Figure 10-7 *AnyConnect VPN Profile Server List*

Deploying AnyConnect

After creating configuration profiles, AnyConnect needs to be deployed to endpoints. The following represents the supported operating systems that AnyConnect can be installed on at the time of writing (AnyConnect 4.6):

- **PC**

  - **Windows:** Windows 10, 8.1, 8, and 7 running on x86 (32-bit) and x64 (64-bit)

  - **macOS** 10.14, 10.13, 10.12, and 10.11

  - **Linux Red Hat:** 7 and 6 (64-bit)

  - **Ubuntu:** 18.04 (LTS), 16.04 (LTS), and 14.04 (LTS) (all 64-bit)

- **Mobile**

  - iOS

  - Android

  - Windows Phone

  - Google Chrome OS

  - BlackBerry

Some might say that deploying a new software client is the most complicated step of a VPN deployment, because it typically requires interaction with desktop or helpdesk teams to ensure consistent support across an enterprise. AnyConnect offers diverse methods of deploying the agent to allow organizations to deploy in a manner best suited to their needs. The following are the most common ways of deploying AnyConnect to an organization's devices:

- **Web deployment (installed from a browser):** Requires administrative privileges, and the headend offering the client should be a trusted site with a trusted SSL certificate. The AnyConnect package is loaded on the headend, which is either an ASA or FTD firewall or an ISE server. When the user connects to a VPN headend or to ISE, AnyConnect is deployed to the client.

  - **VPN headend:** Deploy AnyConnect software and profiles from ASA and/or FTD web deployment at time of VPN access across range of user roles. The user connects to the AnyConnect clientless portal on the headend device and selects to download AnyConnect. The user downloads the AnyConnect Downloader. The AnyConnect Downloader downloads the client, installs the client, and starts a VPN connection.

  - **Identity Services Engine (ISE):** Deploy AnyConnect using web redirect for wired or wireless users connecting to the enterprise network. The user connects to the network access device (NAD), such as a wireless controller or switch. The NAD authorizes the user and redirects the user to the ISE portal. The AnyConnect Downloader is installed on the client to manage the package extraction and installation, but does not start a VPN connection.

- **Predeployment:** New installations and upgrades are done either by the end user or by using an enterprise software management system (SMS).

  - **Enterprise Software Management Systems:** Software management tools such as Microsoft System Center Configuration Manager (SCCM) can be used to automate AnyConnect client and profile installation.

  - **App stores:** Mobile users install directly from respective app stores (iPhone/iPad via iTunes, Android via Google Play, etc.).

■ **Manual installation:** Users manually download and install using OS-specific AnyConnect installers. An AnyConnect file archive is manually distributed, with installation instructions for the user. File archive formats are ZIP for Windows, DMG for macOS, and gzip for Linux.

For predeployments, the AnyConnect profile that is created through the editor should be saved alongside the respective module. The following lists the locations where the VPN profiles should be saved by operating system:

■ **Windows:** %ProgramData%\Cisco\Cisco AnyConnect Secure Mobility Client\ Profile

■ **macOS:** /opt/cisco/anyconnect/profile

■ **Linux:** /opt/cisco/anyconnect/profile

Client-Based Remote Access VPN

Now that you have seen how to configure AnyConnect client settings, this section is all about configuring a VPN headend to support clients to connect. Client-based RAVPN allows for computers and mobile devices to establish an IP-based tunnel, either IPsec or SSL, to communicate with the corporate network.

RAVPN with ASA

The ASA is one of the most popular and feature-rich VPN headends available. The ASA makes it easy to build your first remote access VPN using the ASA Device Manager (ASDM). Simply open the ASDM and select **Wizards > VPN Wizards > AnyConnect VPN Wizard.** The AnyConnect VPN Connection Setup Wizard walks you through the required configuration steps and the many different options for connectivity and policy.

Figure 10-8 illustrates Step 2 of the AnyConnect VPN Wizard, which is to create a VPN connection profile and assign an interface. A connection profile consists of a set of records that determines tunnel connection policies, including identifying the group policy for a specific connection. When using the ASA CLI, connection profiles are configured using **tunnel-group** commands.

Step 3 of the wizard is to define which VPN protocols are to be used. AnyConnect terminating on an ASA supports both SSL and IPsec VPN tunnels. (Chapter 8 discusses the different protocols in greater detail.) The device certificate will be used to identify the ASA to the remote access clients. Recommended practice dictates that you use a publicly signed certificate, so that clients will trust the ASA's identity and not show an error or warning on connection establishment. If self-signed certificates are used, all clients should have the certificate imported into their trusted store manually or via an enterprise software manager. The wizard makes adding or selecting an identity certificate, signed with RSA or Elliptic Curve Digital Signature Algorithm (ECDSA), simple, as shown in Figure 10-9. ECDSA is used only for IPsec connections.

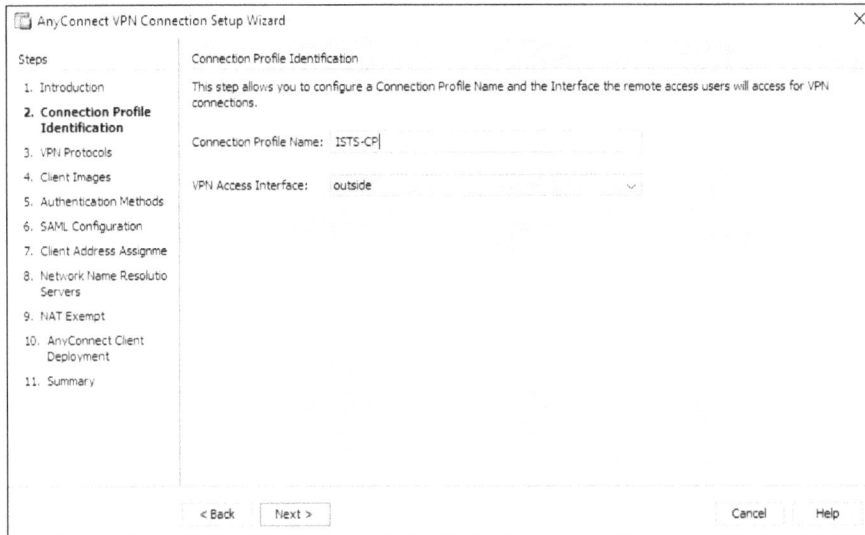

Figure 10-8 *AnyConnect VPN Wizard: Connection Profile*

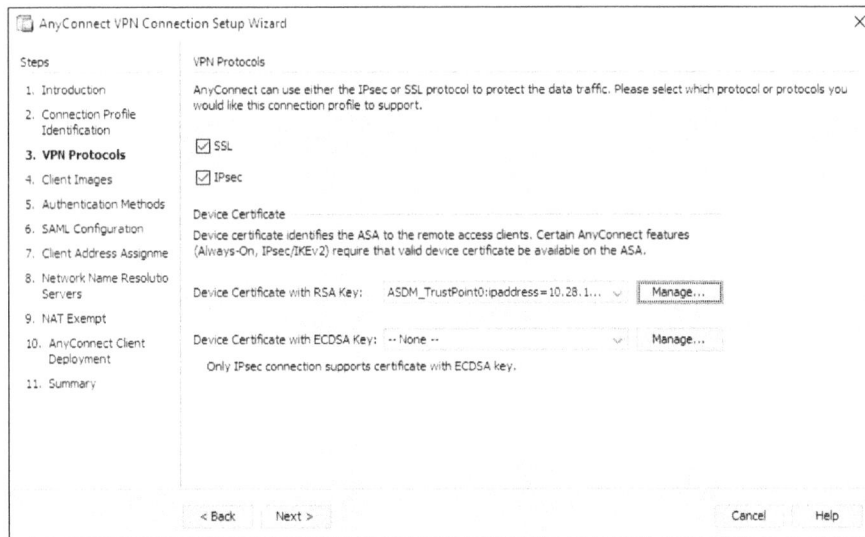

Figure 10-9 *AnyConnect VPN Wizard: Protocols and Certificate*

In Step 4 of the wizard, you should upload AnyConnect client images to the ASA to offer web deployment, as discussed in the previous section. The ASA allows for multiple images to be uploaded and regular expressions to match the target operating system for the image. Figure 10-10 illustrates two AnyConnect 4.6 packages being added to the ASA and matched to their respective client OS.

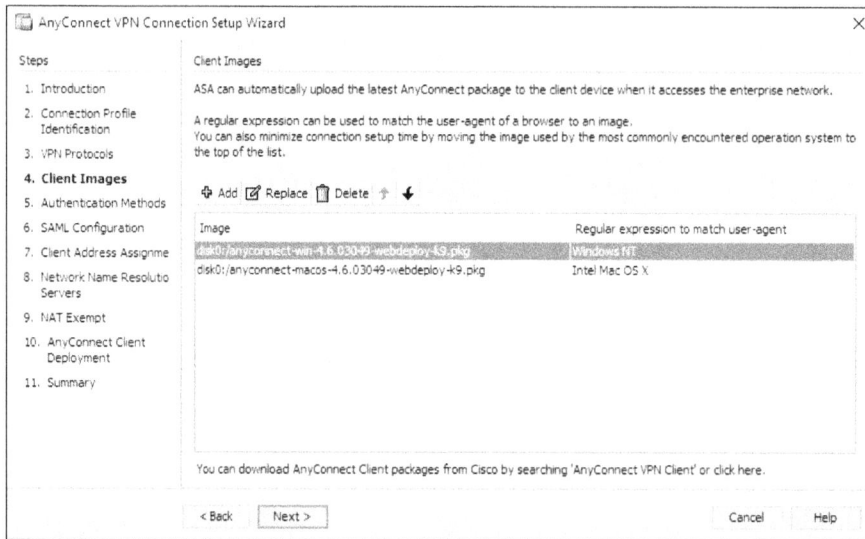

Figure 10-10 *AnyConnect VPN Wizard: Client Images*

In Step 5 of the wizard, authentication of VPN users can be configured to utilize the local user database on the ASA or to reference an external authentication source, such as RADIUS, LDAP, etc. Figure 10-11 shows the selection of LOCAL and the ability to add additional local users inside the wizard.

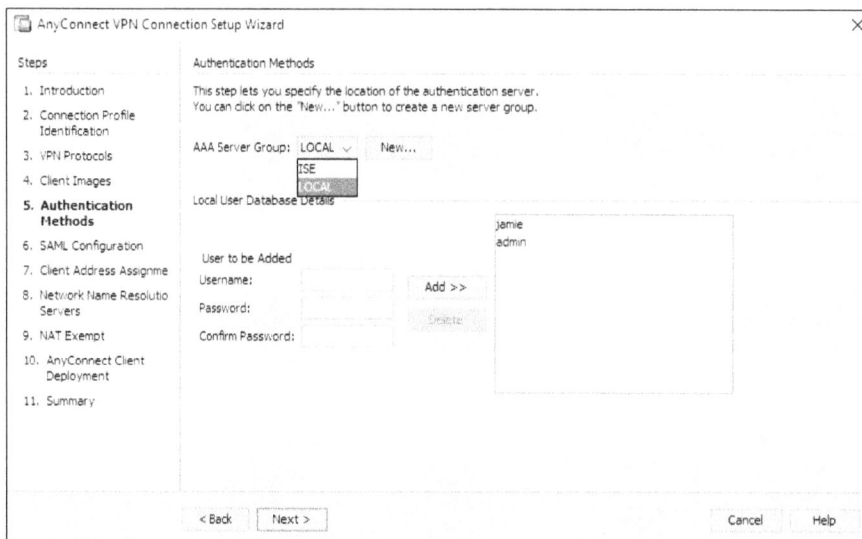

Figure 10-11 *AnyConnect VPN Wizard: Authentication Methods*

Step 6 of the wizard enables you to configure Security Assertion Markup Language (SAML) authentication. SAML supports browser-based authentication with AnyConnect. If a user is already SAML authenticated and attempts to connect with AnyConnect, single sign-on (SSO) will occur. If a user authenticates via SAML to the ASA, then SSO occurs when the user accesses other web sites.

Step 7 is VPN IP address pool assignment, as shown in Figure 10-12. Both IPv4 and IPv6 can be used for address assignment of VPN clients. VPN pools need to be added to existing routing outside of the VPN wizard. Reverse route injection (RRI) is one option that can be used to populate the routing table of an internal router for remote VPN client sessions. RRI is the ability to automatically insert static routes in the routing process for those networks and hosts protected by a remote tunnel endpoint. To configure RRI via CLI, enable it on the dynamic crypto map: **crypto dynamic-map outside_map 65535 set reverse-route.**

Note   Most VPN headends have a default route pointing toward the Internet to be able to route to clients connected to the Internet. If the connecting clients should use a different default, which is common in deployments, you can add the **tunneled** keyword to the **route** command (for example, **route inside 0.0.0.0 0.0.0.0 10.28.20.1 tunneled**) to route VPN clients to the internal network.

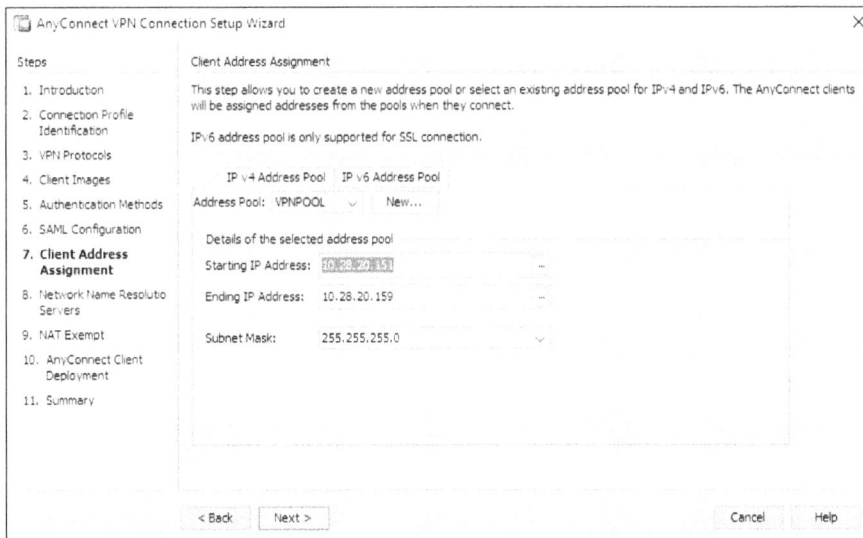

Figure 10-12   *AnyConnect VPN Wizard: Client Address Assignment*

Step 8 of the wizard enables you to enter DNS servers, WINS servers, and a domain name. This allows the clients to resolve internal resources using corporate resolution versus their local connections resolvers.

Next, in Step 9, you need to configure NAT exemption for traffic destined for VPN devices, as shown in Figure 10-13. Forgetting about required NAT configuration is a common mistake and can lead to traffic not passing between the remote access client and the corporate network. Another scenario to contemplate is where the client is sending all traffic through the tunnel and Internet access is provided through the same firewall. This type of scenario requires a NAT configuration to be added to allow communication from VPN users to the Internet interface, sometimes on the same interface and termed *hair-pinning*.

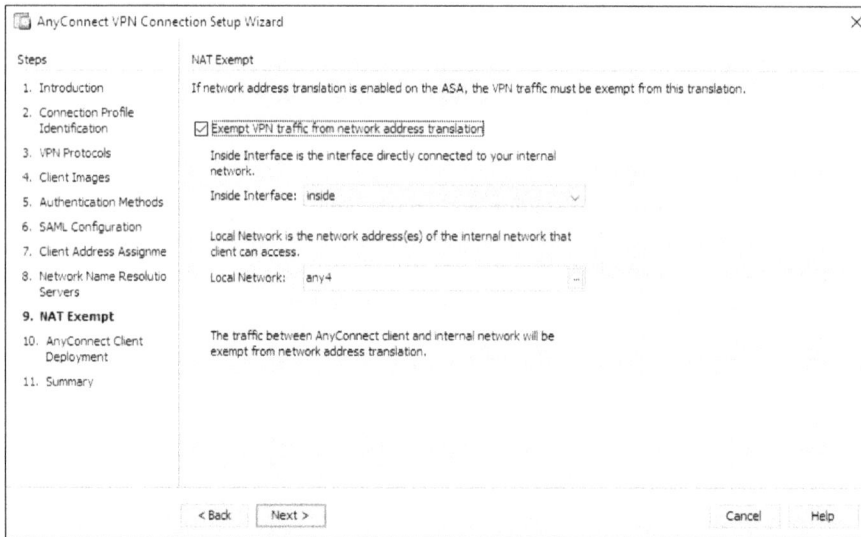

Figure 10-13   *AnyConnect VPN Wizard: NAT Exemption*

As mentioned in the "Deploying AnyConnect" section above, Step 9 offers web deployment from the ASA to remote users via a web portal. Step 10, summarizes the selections throughout the wizard and allows for completion. After completing the wizard, you should perform a connection test with AnyConnect, the goal being to make sure authentication, session establishment, address assignment, and traffic forwarding occur. To verify client connectivity through the ASDM, go to **Monitoring > VPN > VPN Statistics > Sessions**. Figure 10-14 shows the connection details on a test session. Similar information can be retrieved via the CLI by issuing **show vpn-sessiondb detail anyconnect**.

For those who like to work with the CLI, Example 10-1 shows the CLI representation of the configuration applied via the wizard. This is easily retrieved when the ASDM preferences are set up to "Preview commands before sending them to the device," which can be done by going to **Tools > Preferences > General tab**.

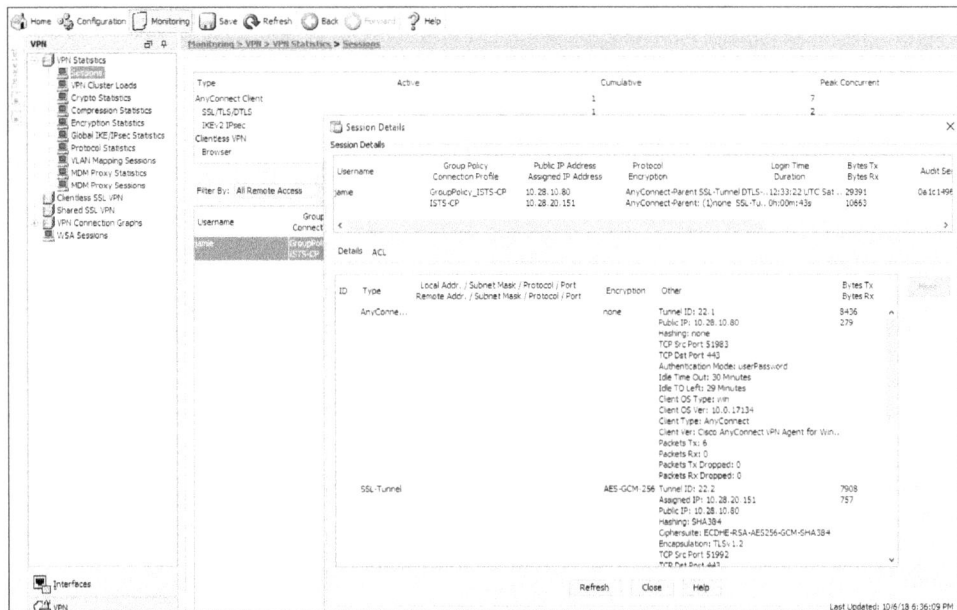

Figure 10-14 *RAVPN ASA VPN Monitoring*

Example 10-1 *CLI Representation of RAVPN with AnyConnect on an ASA Configuration Applied via the Wizard*

```
ip local pool VPNPOOL 10.28.20.151-10.28.20.159 mask 255.255.255.0
!
object network NETWORK_OBJ_10.28.20.144_28
 subnet 10.28.20.144 255.255.255.240
!
nat (inside,outside) source static any any destination static NETWORK_
  OBJ_10.28.20.144_28 NETWORK_OBJ_10.28.20.144_28 no-proxy-arp
!
access-list VPNST standard permit 10.28.20.0 255.255.255.0
!
aaa-server ISE protocol radius
aaa-server ISE (inside) host 10.28.20.200
 timeout 5
 key *****
!
crypto ipsec ikev2 ipsec-proposal 3DES
 protocol esp encryption 3des
 protocol esp integrity sha-1 md5
```

```
crypto ipsec ikev2 ipsec-proposal AES
 protocol esp encryption aes
 protocol esp integrity sha-1 md5
crypto ipsec ikev2 ipsec-proposal AES256
 protocol esp encryption aes-256
 protocol esp integrity sha-1 md5
crypto ipsec security-association pmtu-aging infinite
!
crypto dynamic-map SYSTEM_DEFAULT_CRYPTO_MAP 65535 set ikev2 ipsec-proposal AES256
  AES 3DES
crypto map outside_map 65535 ipsec-isakmp dynamic SYSTEM_DEFAULT_CRYPTO_MAP
crypto map outside_map interface outside
!
crypto ca trustpoint ASDM_TrustPoint0
 enrollment self
 fqdn CP-VPN-ASA.sanbower.net
 subject-name CN=CP-VPN-ASA
 ip-address 10.28.15.150
 keypair VPN
 crl configure
crypto ca trustpool policy
 auto-import
crypto ca certificate chain ASDM_TrustPoint0
 certificate 04f8b55b
  !!!! CUT FOR BREVITY
  quit
!
!
crypto ikev2 policy 1
 encryption aes-256
 integrity sha
 group 5 2
 prf sha
 lifetime seconds 86400
crypto ikev2 policy 20
 encryption aes
 integrity sha
 group 5 2
 prf sha
 lifetime seconds 86400
crypto ikev2 policy 30
 encryption 3des
 integrity sha
```

```
 group 5 2
 prf sha
 lifetime seconds 86400
!
!
crypto ikev2 enable outside client-services port 443
crypto ikev2 remote-access trustpoint ASDM_TrustPoint0
!
ssl trust-point ASDM_TrustPoint0 outside
!
webvpn
 enable outside
 anyconnect image disk0:/anyconnect-win-4.6.03049-webdeploy-k9.pkg 1 regex "Windows
  NT"
 anyconnect image disk0:/anyconnect-macos-4.6.03049-webdeploy-k9.pkg 2 regex "Intel
  Mac OS X"
 anyconnect profiles ISTS-CP_client_profile disk0:/ISTS-CP_client_profile.xml
 anyconnect profiles Test disk0:/test.xml
 anyconnect enable
 tunnel-group-list enable
 cache
  disable
 error-recovery disable
group-policy GroupPolicy_ISTS-CP internal
group-policy GroupPolicy_ISTS-CP attributes
 wins-server none
 dns-server value 10.28.10.50
 vpn-tunnel-protocol ikev2 ssl-client
 default-domain value sanbower.net
 webvpn
  anyconnect profiles value ISTS-CP_client_profile type user
!
dynamic-access-policy-record DfltAccessPolicy
!                 '
tunnel-group ISTS-CP type remote-access
tunnel-group ISTS-CP general-attributes
 address-pool VPNPOOL
 default-group-policy GroupPolicy_ISTS-CP
tunnel-group ISTS-CP webvpn-attributes
 group-alias ISTS-CP enable
```

Group Policies

Groups and users are core concepts in managing the security of RAVPN. They specify attributes that determine connection parameters, access control, and other configuration essentials. As users connect, they get their connection attributes from group policies.

To streamline the configuration task, the ASA provides a default group policy, DfltGrpPolicy. The default group policy provides settings that are likely to be common for many users. When adding a new group policy, it can "inherit" parameters from the default group policy.

Technically, an organization could grant identical rights to all VPN users, then all users could simply use the default group policy, but RAVPNs rarely work that way. For example, you might allow an IT group to access one part of a private network, an executive to access another part, and an HR group to access other parts. In addition, you might allow specific users within IT to access systems that other IT users cannot access. Configuring group policies is one way to achieve this level of control.

To configure group policies, go to **Configuration > Remote Access VPN > Network (Client) Access > Group Policies and select a policy and click "edit"** as shown in Figure 10-15.

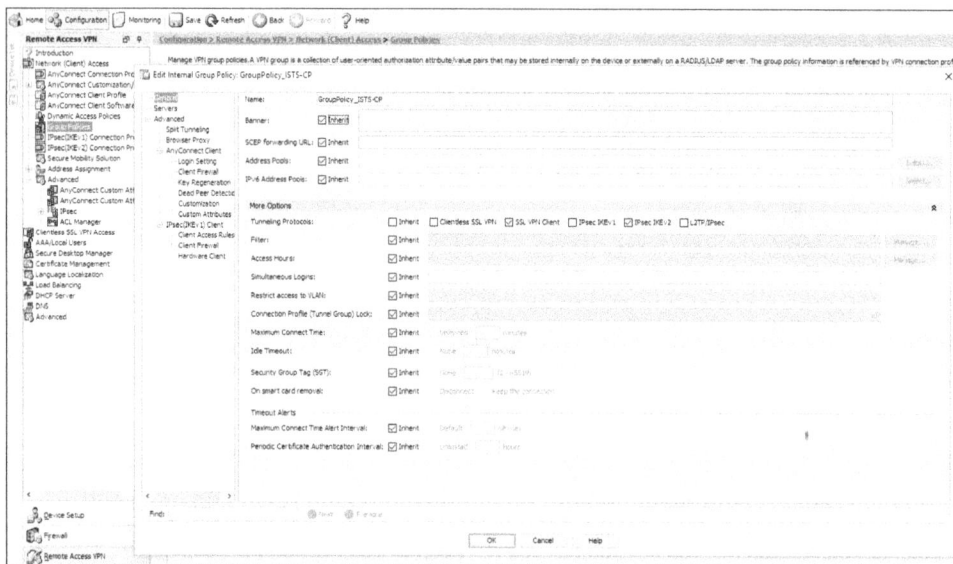

Figure 10-15 *RAVPN Group Policies*

Organizations can use group policies to give users the correct level of access. Some of the options shown in Figure 10-15 that can be used to limit the level of access include the following:

■ **Filter:** Specify which access control list to use for an IPv4 or an IPv6 connection, or whether to inherit the value from the default group policy. Filters consist of rules that determine whether to allow or reject tunneled data packets coming through the ASA, based on criteria such as source address, destination address, and protocol.

■ **Restrict access to VLAN:** Also called "VLAN mapping," this parameter specifies the egress VLAN interface for sessions to which this group policy applies. The ASA forwards all traffic from this group to the selected VLAN. Use this attribute to assign a VLAN to the group policy to simplify access control. Assigning a value to this attribute is an alternative to using ACLs to filter traffic on a session but could be used in conjunction with a filter ACL. VLAN mapping is useful if the internal network already has other forms of segmentation using VLANs.

■ **Security Group Tag (SGT):** Enter the numerical value of the SGT tag that will be assigned to VPN users connecting with this group policy. SGTs, as discussed in detail in Chapter 4, "Extending Network Access with ISE," can integrate with other enforcement devices, such as routers, switches, and firewalls.

Note When using Identity Services Engine (ISE) for authentication or authorization, downloadable ACLs (dACLs) can be returned and used on a per-session basis. This can be helpful when you have multiple VPN headends with centralized policy defined on ISE or ACS.

Split tunneling directs some of the AnyConnect network traffic through the VPN tunnel (encrypted) and other network traffic outside the VPN tunnel (unencrypted or "in the clear"). Organizations sometimes choose to use split tunneling to alleviate the bandwidth requirements at the central site. With split tunneling disabled, all Internet traffic will be forced through the tunnel, requiring the organization to support the bandwidth requirements of its local and remote users.

Split tunneling is configured by navigating to **Advanced > Split Tunneling** and creating a split tunneling policy, configuring an access control list for that policy, and adding the split tunnel policy to a group policy. When the group policy is sent to the client, that client uses the ACLs in the split tunneling policy to decide where to direct network traffic. Figure 10-16 illustrates a split tunneling policy only requiring tunneling of the traffic defined in the "VPNST" ACL.

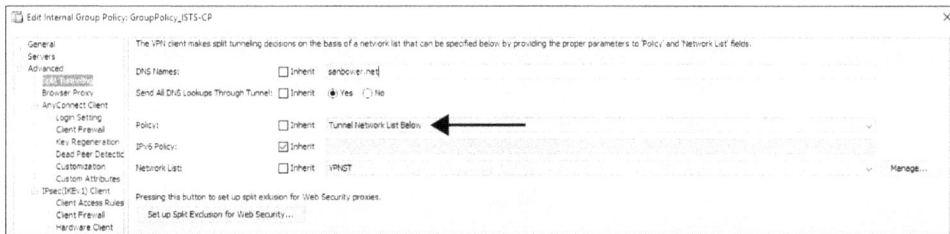

Figure 10-16 *Configuring Split Tunneling*

Example 10-2 shows the CLI configuration of split tunneling.

Example 10-2   *Split Tunneling CLI Configuration*

```
group-policy GroupPolicy_ISTS-CP attributes
        split-tunnel-policy   tunnelspecified
        split-tunnel-network-list value VPNST
        split-dns value sanbower.net
        split-tunnel-all-dns enable
```

As an administrator, after you understand the options and benefits of group policies, you must plan to assign sessions to a group policy through one of the following methods:

- **Static connection profile:** A connection profile identifies the group policy for a specific connection. With this method, multiple connection profiles—for example, a different connection profile for accounting and then for HR—can be used to assign the policy required. The following shows a CLI example of statically assigning a group policy to a tunnel group:

```
tunnel-group HR general-attributes
default-group-policy HR
```

Note   If a user is assigned a group policy, statically or dynamically, as shown in this list, the user assignment will override the static assignment configured via the connection profile.

- **Static local user assignment:** Each local user on the ASA can have a group policy assigned. If the VPN is using the local user database for authentication, this is a valid option for assigning a group policy.

```
username accounting1 attributes
vpn-group-policy ACCOUNTING
```

- **Dynamic assignment via RADIUS authentication or authorization:** RADIUS class attribute (25) can be used to define the group policy for the ASA. Any standard RADIUS server can return the class attribute in the Access-Accept message. In ISE, the class attribute is shown as "ASA VPN" in the Common Tasks section under the authorization profile. Figure 10-17 illustrates the ISE authorization profile created to assign "HR" group policy to sessions matching the authorization rule.

- **Dynamic assignment via LDAP attribute map:** This method matches LDAP groups to ASA group policies. The following example shows mapping an attribute map matching employees and contractors and assigning the respective group policy:

```
ldap attribute-map ISTS-MAP
  map-name memberOf IETF-Radius-Class
  map-value memberOf CN=Employees,CN=Users,DC=sanbower,DC=net,Empl
  oyees
```

```
map-value memberOf CN=Contractors,CN=Users,DC=sanbower,DC=net
Contractors
aaa-server ISTS_LDAP_SRV_GRP (inside) host 10.28.10.50
ldap-attribute-map ISTS-MAP
```

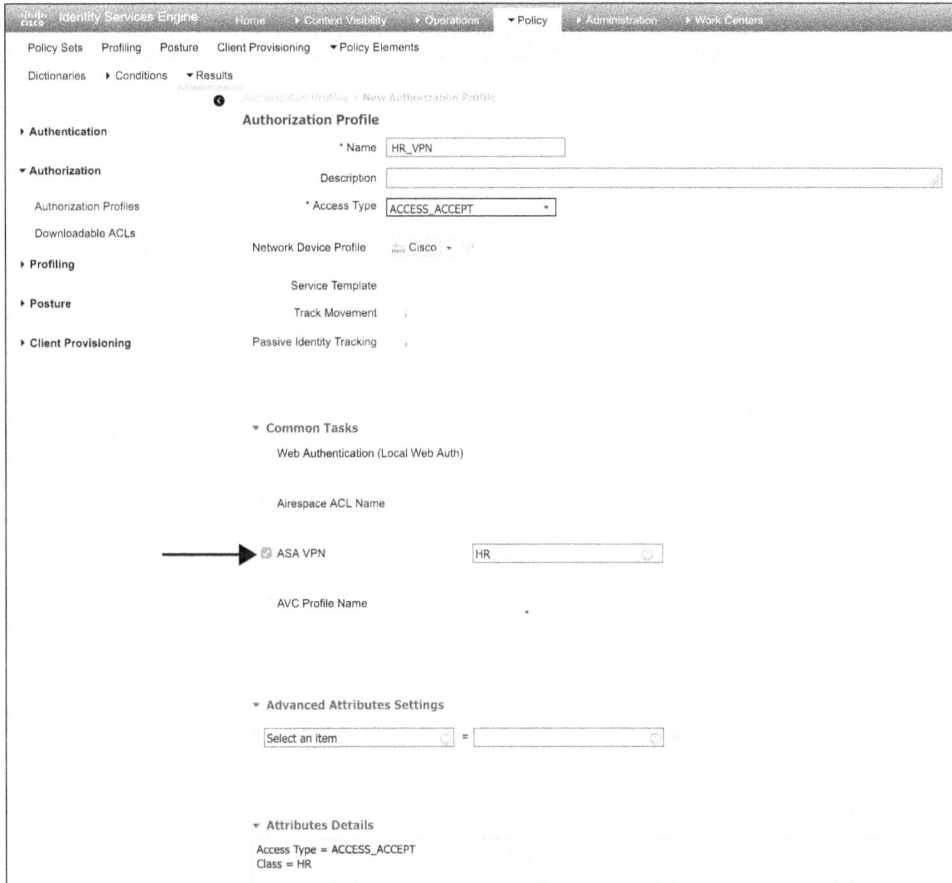

Figure 10-17   *ISE Authorization Profile Assigning ASA Group Policy*

Dynamic Access Policies

The Dynamic Access Policies (DAP) are a collection of access control attributes associated with a specific tunnel or access session. The DAP is dynamically generated by selecting and/or aggregating attributes from one or more DAP records. The DAP records are selected based on the endpoint security information of the remote device and/or the AAA authorization information of the authenticated user.

Note The Host Scan module must be installed on the ASA before configuring DAP endpoint attributes that require posture assessment. Posture assessment is covered in the next section.

The DAP will be generated and then applied to the user's tunnel or session. It supports session establishment applications by providing access policy attributes that are dynamically generated by the DAP, including access method (for example, you can force clientless VPN for certain sessions with defined attributes), ACLs, and clientless features, such as URL lists, bookmarks, and port forwarding lists.

Figure 10-18 provides an example of matching HR users through RADIUS class attribute (25) and matching the operating system version coming from AnyConnect (apple-ios) and, as a result, applying an ACL to the session.

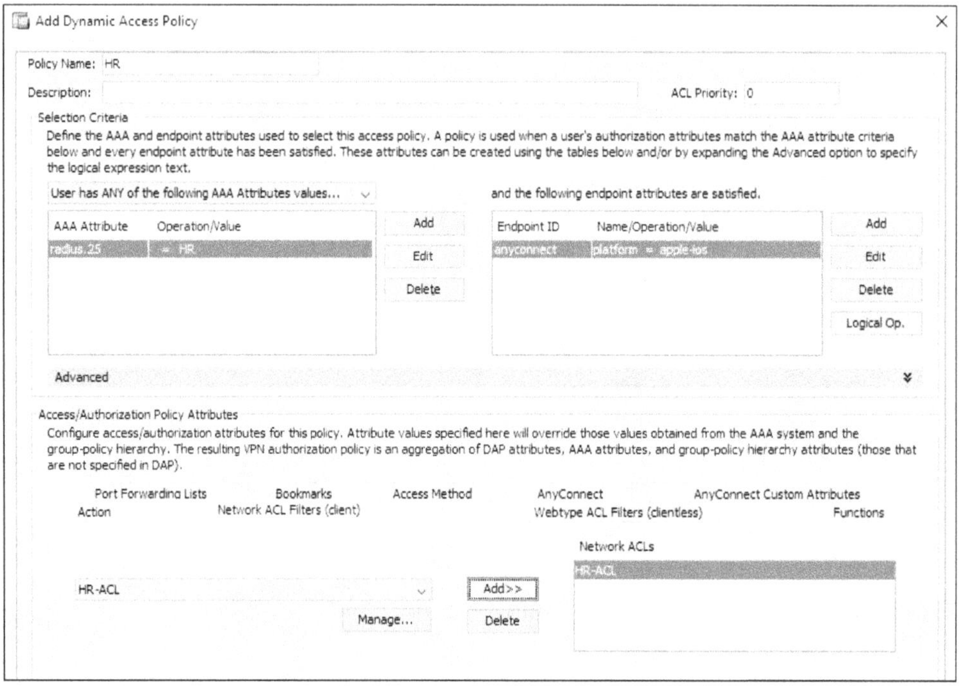

Figure 10-18 *DAP Example*

The DAP can be used in lieu of or in combination with group policies. As shown in the example, the DAP can also assign a subset of the attributes that are also available within group policies. The biggest difference is that the DAP allows for granular attribute matching, whereas group policy is limited in assignment.

Posture Assessment

The AnyConnect Secure Mobility Client offers a VPN Posture (HostScan) Module and an ISE Posture Module. Both enable AnyConnect to assess an endpoint's compliance for things such as anti-virus, anti-spyware, and firewall software installed on the host. An administrator can then restrict network access until the endpoint is in compliance or can provide different levels of access for different levels of compliance.

VPN Posture is bundled with a hostscan package, hostscan_version.pkg, which is the application that gathers the details of which operating system, anti-virus, anti-spyware, and software are installed on the host. ISE Posture deploys one client when accessing ISE-controlled networks, rather than deploying both AnyConnect and the NAC agent. ISE Posture and HostScan are modules you can choose to install as an additional security component into the AnyConnect agent.

ISE Posture performs a client-side evaluation. The client receives the posture requirement policy from the headend ISE server, performs the posture data collection, compares the results against the policy, and sends the assessment results back to ISE. Even though ISE actually determines whether or not the endpoint is compliant, it relies on the endpoint's own evaluation of the policy.

In contrast, HostScan performs server-side evaluation where the ASA asks only for a list of endpoint attributes, such as operating system, IP address, registry entries, local certificates, and filenames, and they are returned by HostScan. Based on the result of the policy's evaluation, organizations can control which hosts are allowed to create a remote access connection to the VPN headend.

Deploying posture with ISE requires the same configuration steps performed for wired and wireless deployments. The details are discussed and demonstrated in Chapter 4. With that said, the ASA needs to be configured to interact with ISE correctly. Starting with ASA 9.2, an ISE inline posture node is not required. RADIUS Change of Authorization (CoA), as defined in RFC 5176, is natively supported and is the recommended deployment method. To configure integration with ISE Posture on the ASA for VPN, a redirect ACL, dynamic authorization, and interim accounting updates must be configured, as shown in Example 10-3.

Example 10-3 *Redirect ACL, Dynamic Authorization, and Interim Accounting Update Configuration for ISE Posture Integration with ASA for VPN*

```
access-list redirect extended deny udp any any eq domain
access-list redirect extended deny ip any host 10.28.20.200
access-list redirect extended deny icmp any any
access-list redirect extended permit tcp any any eq www
!
aaa-server ISE protocol radius
 authorize-only
 interim-accounting-update periodic 1
```

```
 dynamic-authorization
!
aaa-server ISE (inside) host 10.28.20.200
 key ISTS
!
tunnel-group RA general-attributes
 authentication-server-group ISE
 accounting-server-group ISE
```

After configuration on the ASA, the following steps occur when a VPN user connects and the ASA uses ISE for posture:

1. The remote user uses Cisco AnyConnect for VPN access to the ASA.

2. The ASA sends a RADIUS Access-Request for that user to ISE.

3. ISE authenticates the user successfully. As a result, the authorization profile is returned. ISE sends a RADIUS Access-Accept with the following attributes:

   ■ **url-redirect-acl=redirect:** This is the ACL name that is defined locally on the ASA, which decides which traffic should be redirected to ISE.

   ■ **url-redirect=https://ise.sanbower.net:8443/guestportal/gateway?sessionId=xx &action=cpp:** This is the URL to which the remote user should be redirected. The DNS servers that are assigned to the RAVPN users must be able to resolve the FQDN that is returned in the redirect URL.

4. The ASA sends a RADIUS Accounting-Request start packet and receives a response. This is needed in order to send all the details regarding the session to ISE. These details include the session_id, external IP address of the VPN client, and the IP address of the ASA.

5. Assuming the client already has the ISE Posture Module provisioned with AnyConnect, when the traffic from the ISE Posture Agent matches the locally defined ACL (redirect), it is redirected to the correct ISE Policy Services Node (PSN).

6. The ISE Posture Module automatically performs specific checks through scans.

7. When the ISE PSN receives the posture report from the agent, it processes the authorization rules once again. This time, the posture result is known and another rule is hit. It sends a RADIUS CoA packet containing the correct authorization based on whether the user is compliant or non-compliant. dACLs, group policy, or named ACLs can all be used to apply the correct policy.

8. The ASA removes the redirection and applies the correct level of authorization based on the information passed from ISE.

For organizations that aren't using ISE, the ASA can leverage the AnyConnect posture module to perform scans. ASA integrates the HostScan/Posture features into the dynamic access policies (DAP). Depending on the configuration, the ASA uses one or more endpoint attribute values in combination with optional AAA attribute values as conditions for assigning the DAP. The HostScan features supported by the endpoint attributes of DAPs include OS detection, policies, basic results, and endpoint assessment.

You can specify a single attribute or combine attributes that form the conditions required to assign a DAP to a session. The DAP provides network access at the level that is appropriate for the endpoint AAA attribute value. The ASA applies a DAP when all of its configured endpoint criteria are satisfied.

To get started using ASA HostScan, you must upload the pkg file to the ASA's flash memory and enable it in the configuration, as shown in Figure 10-19.

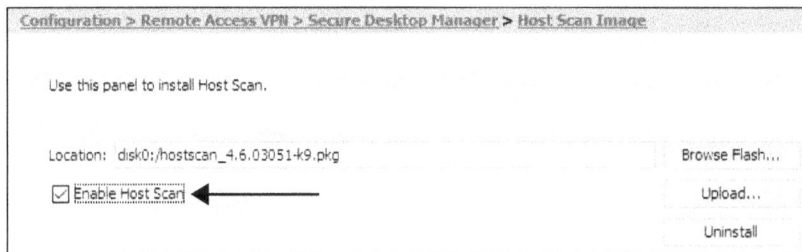

Figure 10-19 *Enabling ASA HostScan*

You can also perform the task using the CLI:

```
webvpn
        hostscan image disk0:/hostscan_4.6.03051-k9.pkg
        hostscan enable
```

All scans must be defined in the ASDM by going to **Secure Desktop Manager > Host Scan.** Figure 10-20 illustrates a file scan for c:\test.txt and shows how to add additional registry, file, and process scans that can be used in DAPs.

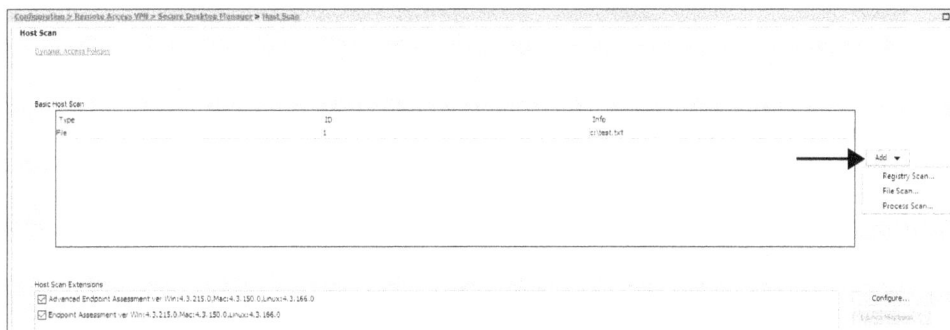

Figure 10-20 *ASA HostScan Checks*

Once file, process, and registry scans have been defined, they can be used in the DAP. Additional checks for anti-virus, anti-malware, firewall, etc. can be configured under the DAP by selecting a policy and clicking on edit. Figure 10-21 shows a policy that checks for corporate compliance.

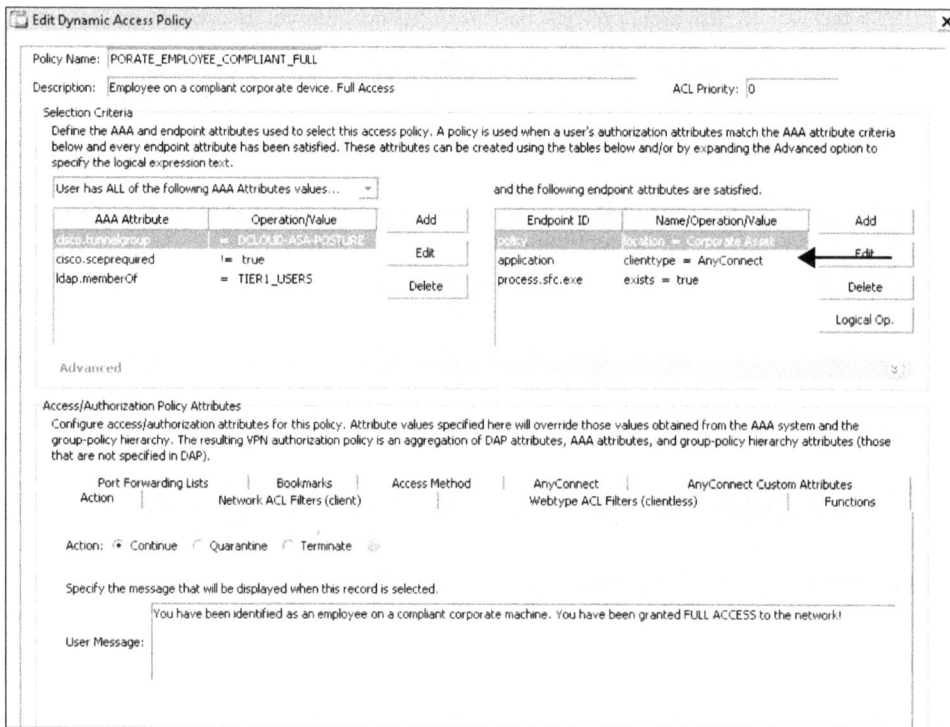

Figure 10-21   *ASA HostScan Using a DAP*

RAVPN with Firepower Threat Defense

Starting with Firepower Threat Defense (FTD) version 6.2, FTD now supports remote access VPN functionality. Although FTD supports IKEv2 and SSL VPN tunnels, it does not support all VPN features, including, for example, Always-On, Trusted Network Detection (TND) and Start Before Logon (SBL). For the latest list of supported features, please consult the FTD release notes at Cisco.com.

Use the Remote Access VPN Policy Wizard in the Firepower Management Center (FMC) to quickly and easily set up SSL and/or IPsec remote access VPNs with basic capabilities. Then, enhance the policy configuration if desired and deploy it to your FTD devices.

In order to go through the remote access wizard in the FMC, the administrator must first follow these steps:

Step 1.   **Certificate:** Create a certificate to use for server identification by going to **Objects > Object Management > PKI > Cert Enrollment** and clicking **Add Cert Enrollment.** Figure 10-22 shows an example of creating a self-signed certificate.

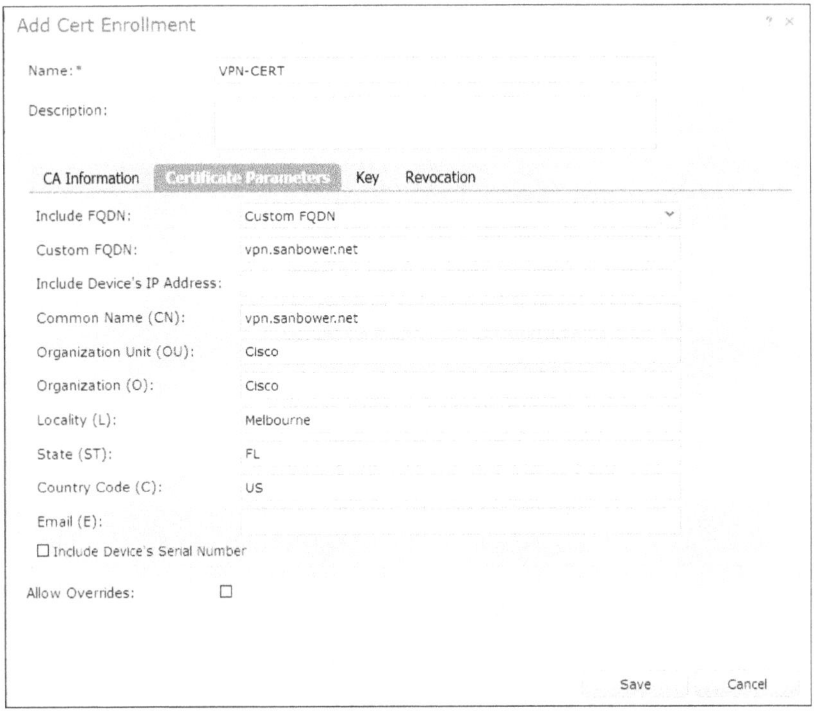

Figure 10-22   *Creating a Certificate in the FMC*

Note   While self-signed certificates can work in labs, trusted public certificate authority signed certificates are recommended and highly encouraged for production environments.

Step 2.   **Authentication server:** Configure a RADIUS or LDAP server for user authentication. On the FTD platform, the local user database *cannot* be used, so a RADIUS or LDAP server is required for user authentication. To add an LDAP server, go to **System > Integration > Realms > Add Realm.** To configure RADIUS, go to **Objects > Object Management > RADIUS Server Group > Add RADIUS Server Group,** as shown in Figure 10-23.

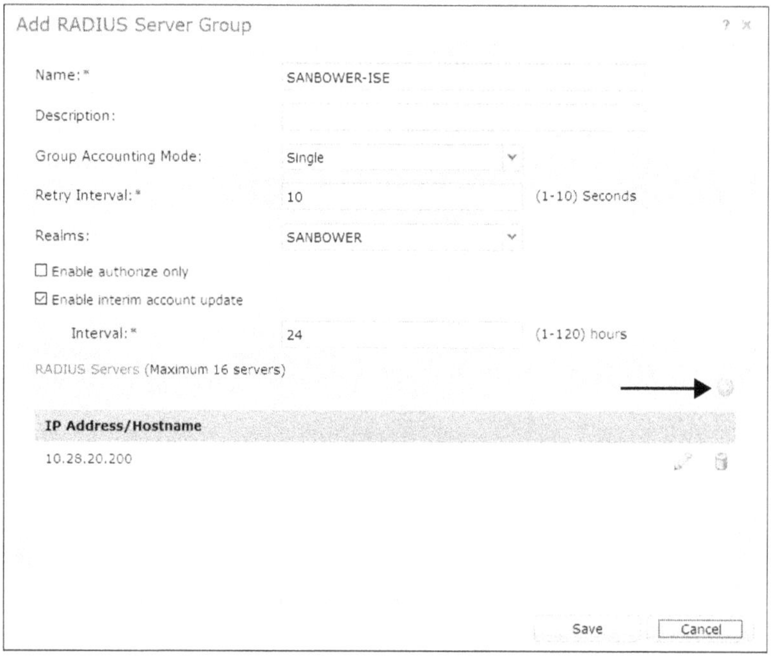

Figure 10-23 *FMC Add RADIUS Server*

Step 3. **VPN pool:** Create an IPv4 pool of addresses for VPN users by going to **Objects > Object Management > Address Pools > Add IPv4 Pools**, as illustrated in Figure 10-24. You can also create and use an IPv6 pool by choosing **Address Pools > Add IPv6 Pools** instead.

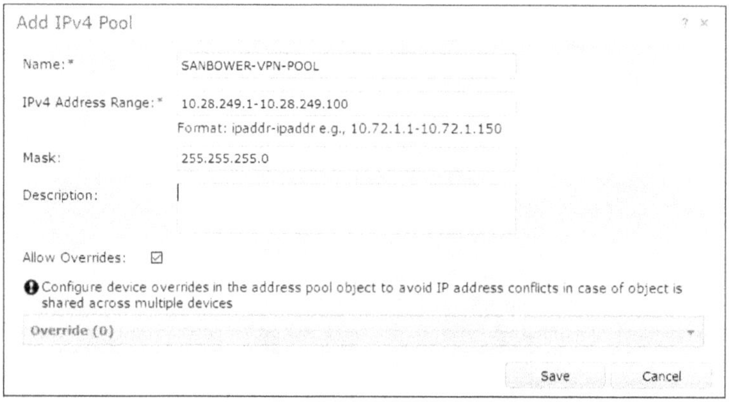

Figure 10-24 *Adding a VPN Pool in the FMC*

Step 4. **VPN profile:** Using the standalone AnyConnect Profile Editor (discussed earlier in the chapter), create an XML configuration for VPN that can be uploaded alongside the VPN client images.

Step 5.   **VPN client images:** AnyConnect images must be uploaded to the FMC for the different platforms that are planned to connect to remote access VPN. Download the pkg files from the Cisco Download site, then go to **Objects > Object Management > VPN > AnyConnect File > Add AnyConnect File** to add them to the FMC. Figure 10-25 demonstrates adding a macOS AnyConnect package.

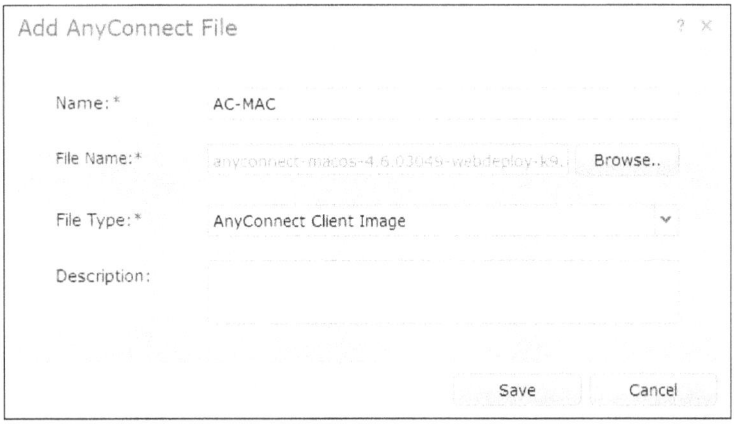

Figure 10-25   *Adding an AnyConnect Package to the FMC*

Step 6.   Once those prerequisites are met, go to **Devices > VPN > Remote Access > Add a new configuration** to launch the Remote Access VPN Policy Wizard, as shown in Figure 10-26. Give the profile a descriptive name, select the target FTD device, and specify SSL and/or IPsec-IKEv2.

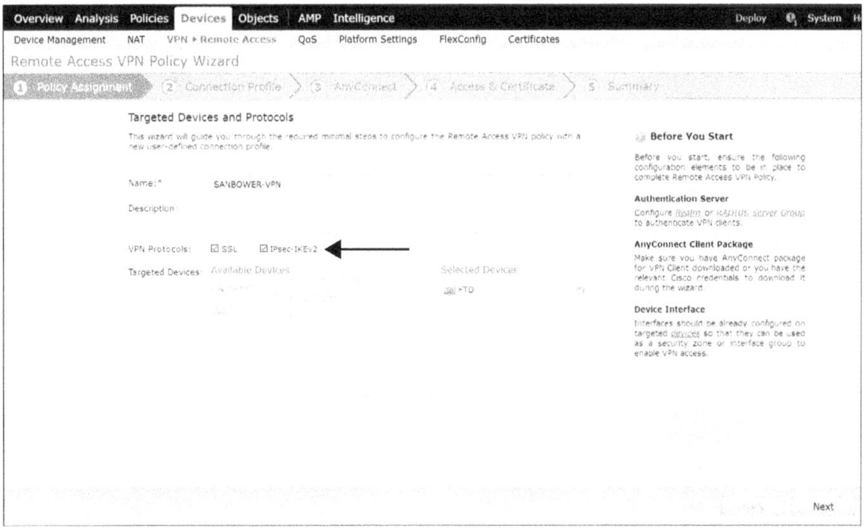

Figure 10-26   *FMC RAVPN Policy Wizard: Policy Assignment*

Step 7.   In Step 2 of the wizard, select the authentication method and servers. By default, **AAA Only** is selected in the Authentication Method drop-down list (see Figure 10-27) and you can select the preconfigured RADIUS or LDAP server.

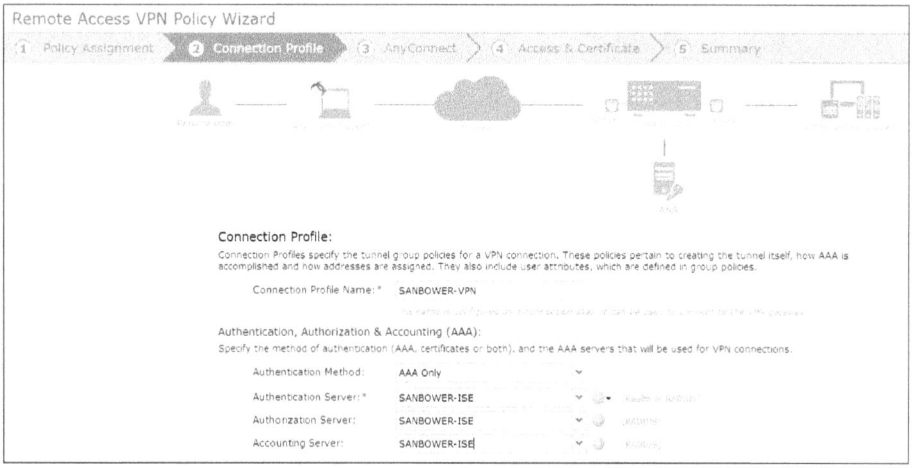

Figure 10-27   *FMC RAVPN Policy Wizard: Connection Profile Configuration*

As an alternative, you can choose **Client Certificate Only** from the Authentication Method drop-down list if the user should be authenticated using a client certificate. The client certificate must be configured on VPN client endpoints. When deploying with certificates, RADIUS or LDAP can be used to determine authorization information, such as Active Directory group or RADIUS class/group policy. Double authentication is also supported by selecting **Client Certificate & AAA.**

Step 8.   The connection profile also needs to reference the IP pool created earlier. Figure 10-28 illustrates the selection of the pool. You can modify the default group policy or create a new one. To create a new group policy, click the **+** symbol, referenced in Figure 10-28.

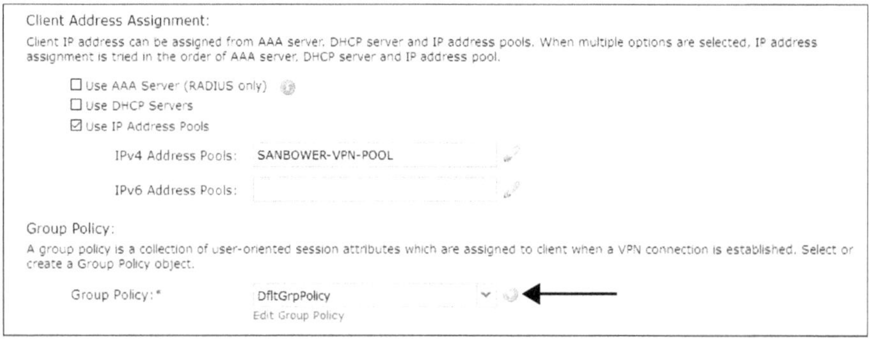

Figure 10-28   *FMC RAVPN Policy Wizard: VPN Pool and Group Policy Configuration*

Group policies in FTD contain a limited version of what is available in ASA. The items that do exist, such as VPN protocols, IP address pools, DNS, traffic filter, and so on, behave the same as with the ASA. Figure 10-29 shows assigning a split-tunneling configuration that will only include certain subnets, configured in an access list, to be sent over the VPN and encrypted.

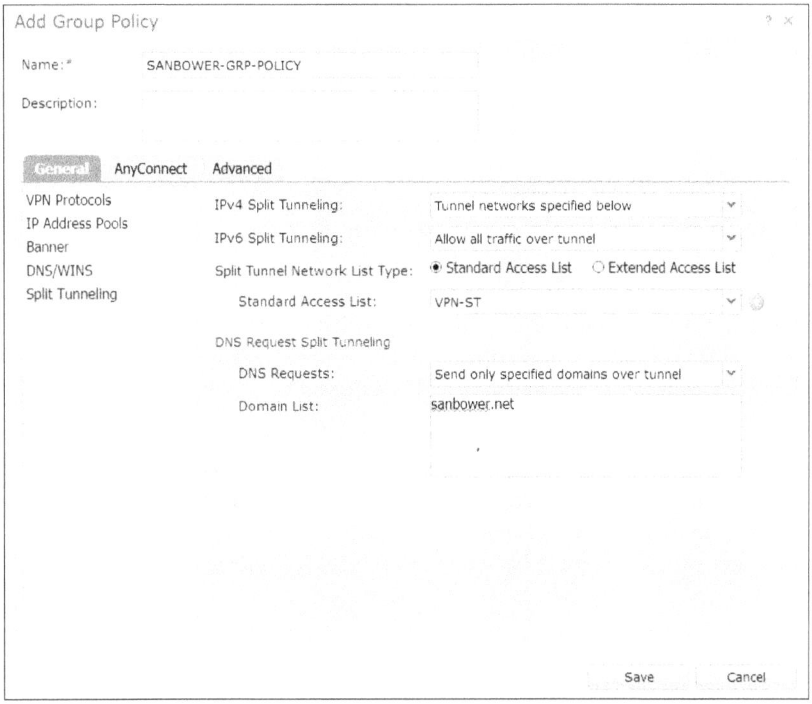

Figure 10-29 *FMC Remote Access VPN Policy Wizard: New Group Policy Configuration*

Step 9.   Step 3 of the wizard is to reference the previously uploaded AnyConnect clients. This allows remote users to enter the IP address of an FTD interface configured to accept VPN connections in their browser to download and install the AnyConnect client and profile. The FTD device delivers the AnyConnect package that matches the OS of the remote computer. After downloading, the client installs and establishes a secure connection. In the case of a previously installed client, when the user authenticates, the Firepower Threat Defense device examines the revision of the client and upgrades the client as necessary.

The Firepower Management Center determines the type of OS by using the file package name. In case the user renamed the file without indicating the OS information, the valid OS type must be selected from the drop-down list. Figure 10-30 shows the Windows and macOS images selected for the remote access VPN.

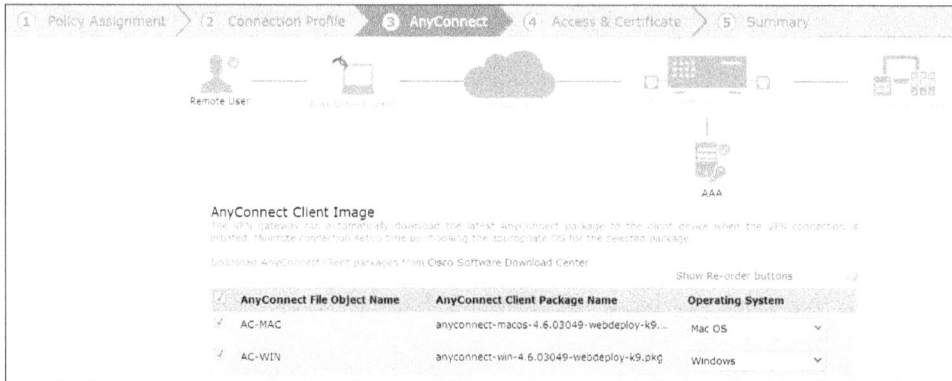

Figure 10-30 *FMC Remote Access VPN Policy Wizard: AnyConnect Client Image Configuration*

Step 10. In Step 4 of the wizard, inform the FMC which interface VPN services should be enabled on and which certificate should be used. Figure 10-31 illustrates the configuration of the interface and certificate.

Note By default, Datagram Transport Layer Security (DTLS) is also enabled on the interface. As described in Chapter 8, DTLS is a communications protocol that provides TLS security for UDP applications. DTLS, which uses UDP port 443, should be used. If the client cannot use DTLS, it will fall back to TLS (TCP 443) communications.

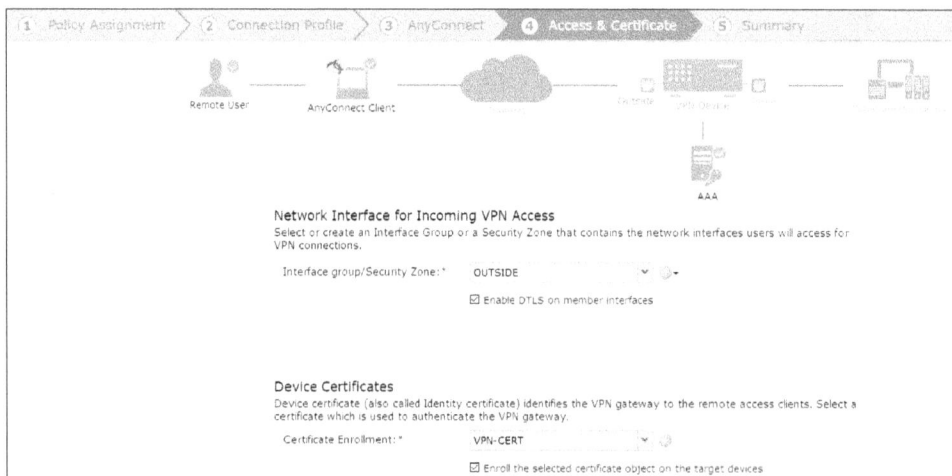

Figure 10-31 *FMC Remote Access VPN Policy Wizard: Access and Certificate Configuration*

Step 11. After reviewing the wizard's summary in Step 5 (see Figure 10-32), click **Finish** to save the configuration. The configuration will *not* be deployed to the FTD device(s) until a deployment process (clicking **Deploy**) is completed.

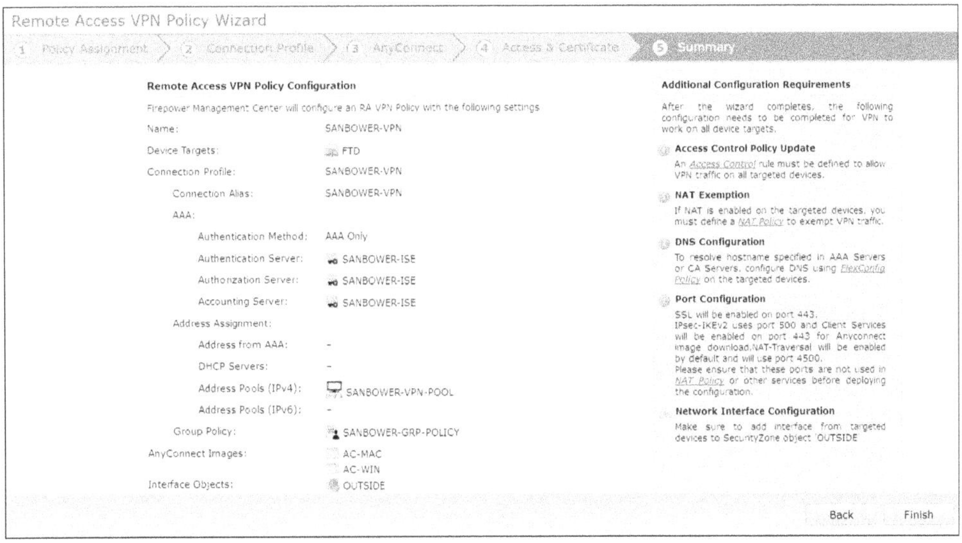

Figure 10-32 *FMC Remote Access VPN Policy Wizard: Summary*

Step 12. Although the VPN has been configured correctly, there are some additional steps you should take to enable FTD to properly forward traffic for the VPN clients that connect. The first step is to determine whether VPN user traffic should be allowed implicitly or individual firewall rules are explicitly added to the access control policy (ACP). If the organization would like to bypass ACP for decrypted traffic, then go to **Devices > VPN > Remote Access > Edit Profile > Access Interfaces** and check the **Bypass Access Control policy for decrypted traffic (sysopt permit-vpn)** check box, as illustrated in Figure 10-33. This will allow all decrypted traffic to be forwarded without ACP evaluation.

Step 13. If Network Address Translation (NAT) is in use on the FTD device terminating the VPN, in order for communication to take place between the organization's network and remote users, a NAT rule must be added to ensure NAT doesn't happen between the inside users and the VPN users. Figure 10-34 shows a rule that will match traffic from the inside network to the VPN pool and preserve the source and destination. To configure a NAT rule, go to **Devices > NAT > Edit Policy > Add Rule.**

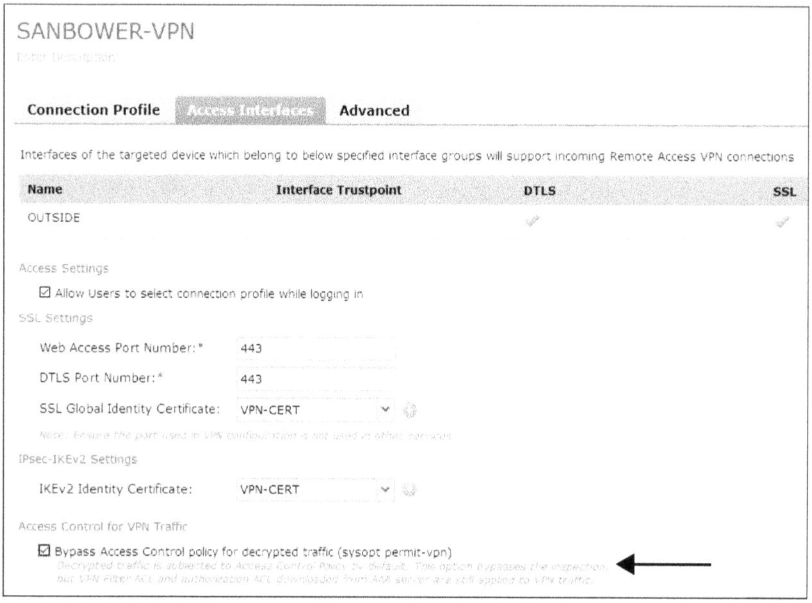

Figure 10-33 *Enabling Access Control for VPN Traffic*

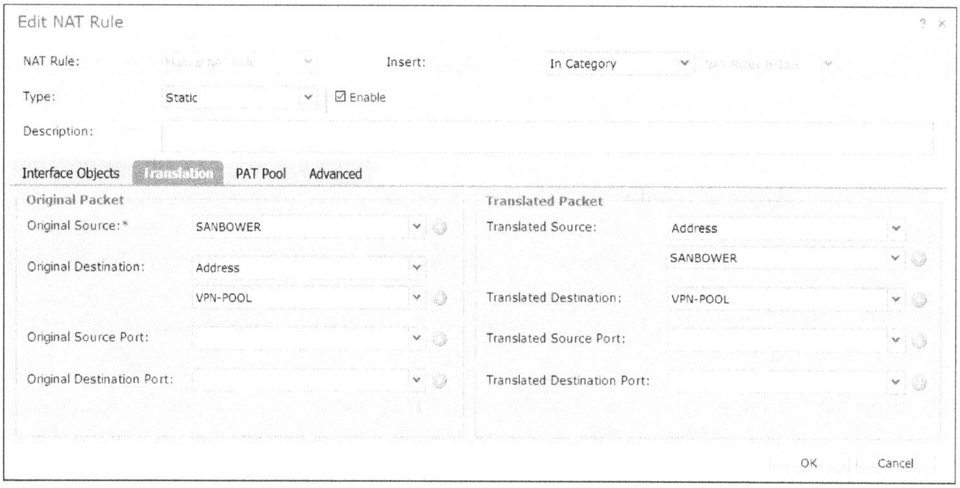

Figure 10-34 *Adding a NAT Rule to Exempt VPN Traffic*

Step 14. The last optional configuration step is to ensure all routing on FTD is configured to work appropriately. For example, any networks that need to be reachable from the VPN connection need to be in FTD's routing table. Similarly,
to the ASA, a "tunneled" route can be added to direct all VPN clients to a
different default next hop. Routing is configured by going to **Devices > Device**

Management and editing the FTD device. Routing is configured under the "Routing" tab. Either static or dynamic routing may be used to ensure the VPN pool is reachable.

Step 15. After completing configuration, you can test the VPN by launching a browser and going to the FQDN that matches the certificate name. Figure 10-35 shows the default page after login to allow a user to download AnyConnect for their operating system. Both the client and profile will be installed, allowing for tunnel establishment via AnyConnect.

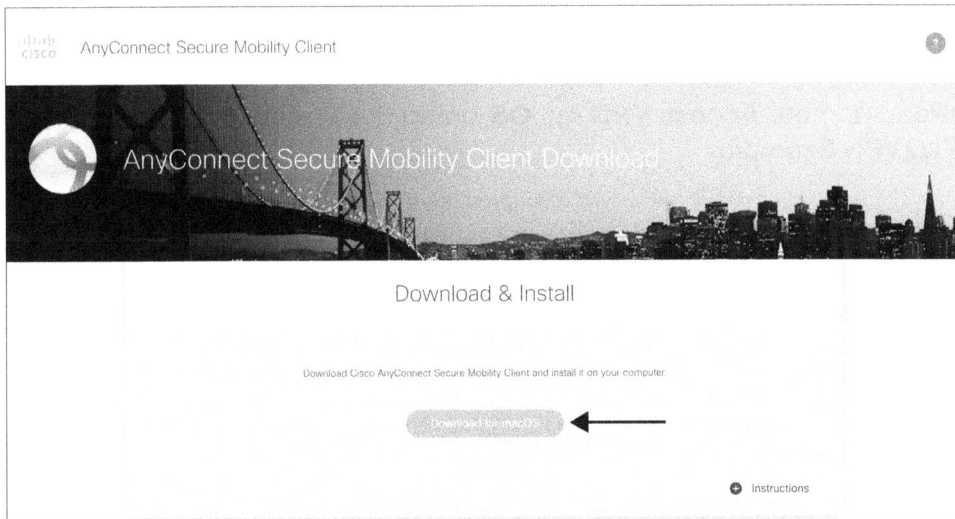

Figure 10-35 *FTD RAVPN Web Download of AnyConnect*

Step 16. After devices are connected, go to **Analysis > Users > Active Sessions** to view and filter all VPN connected sessions. Figure 10-36 illustrates an active session for VPN Authentication.

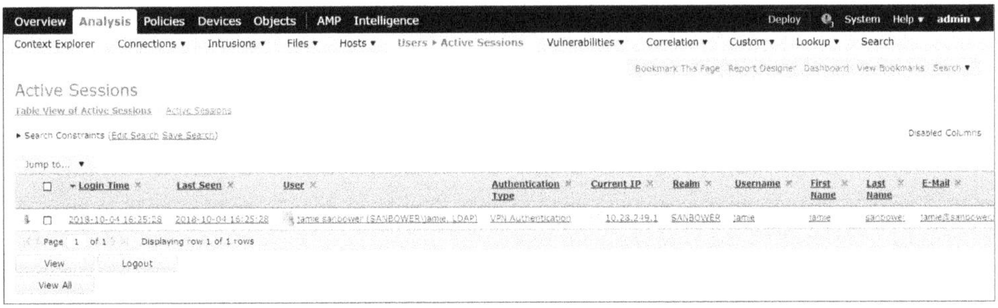

Figure 10-36 *Monitoring Active Remote Access VPN Session on the FMC*

RAVPN with Routers

RAVPN can be deployed on Cisco IOS and IOS-XE devices to allow for remote users to connect through a router-based VPN headend. Although very uncommon and typically deployed for limited-use cases, routers support IKEv1 and IKEv2 IPsec and SSL VPN termination—typically used for backup connections to smaller sites or by organizations that do not have a firewall for RAVPN.

Greenfield deployments, that is, deploying a new VPN, should use FlexVPN CLI structure for all IPsec configurations. EzVPN is the predecessor to FlexVPN and is used to configure IKEv1. The same structure of configuration will be created using FlexVPN for remote access as was shown in Chapter 9 for site-to-site.

IPsec Remote Access VPN on IOS Using IKEv2 with FlexVPN Example

The following example shows the configuration of an IPsec IKEv2 VPN on a Cloud Services Router (CSR) using AnyConnect Secure Mobility Client as the software client.

The first thing the router needs prior to configuring RAVPN is an identity certificate. For FlexVPN, using self-signed certificates is not supported. Although it is recommended that organizations get a publicly signed certificate for production deployments, in this example we will use the IOS CA to generate a certificate for the router.

The following steps configure the IOS CA and generate an identity certificate for the FlexVPN server.

Step 1.   Generate RSA keys for the CA server:

```
crypto key generate rsa label ROOT-CA modulus 2048
```

Note   The time and timezone should be set or synchronized to an NTP server before the CA server can be enabled.

Step 2.   Generate RSA keys for the identity certificate:

```
crypto key generate rsa label CSR modulus 2048
```

Step 3.   Configure the certificate authority by enabling HTTP server services and defining the CA service:

```
ip http server
crypto pki server ROOT-CA
   issuer-name cn=ROOT-CA.sanbower.net
   hash sha256
   lifetime certificate 1095
  lifetime ca-certificate 3650
  eku server-auth
  no shutdown
```

Step 4. Configure the trustpoint used for the identity certificate:

```
crypto pki trustpoint CSR-TP
 enrollment url http://10.28.20.150:80
 fqdn none
 subject-name cn=csr.sanbower.net
 revocation-check none
 rsakeypair CSR
```

Step 5. Authenticate the CA:

```
crypto pki authenticate CSR-TP
% Do you accept this certificate? [yes/no]: yes
Trustpoint CA certificate accepted.
```

Step 6. Enroll the router to the CA:

```
crypto pki enroll CSR-TP
% Start certificate enrollment ..
% Create a challenge password. You will need to verbally
provide this
    password to the CA Administrator in order to revoke your
certificate.
    For security reasons your password will not be saved in
the configuration.
    Please make a note of it.

Password:
Re-enter password:

% The subject name in the certificate will include: cn=csr.
sanbower.net
% The fully-qualified domain name will not be included in the
certificate
% Include the router serial number in the subject name? [yes/
no]: no
% Include an IP address in the subject name? [no]: no
Request certificate from CA? [yes/no]: yes
% Certificate request sent to Certificate Authority
```

Step 7. Grant the certificate using proper ReqID, which can be found by issuing **show crypto pki server ROOT-CA requests:**

```
crypto pki server ROOT-CA grant 1
```

Once the router has a certificate, authentication, authorization, and accounting (AAA) should be configured to be referenced in the FlexVPN configurations. In this example, ISE will be used as the RADIUS server. One benefit of using ISE in this instance is that ISE can provide posture assessment support for clients connecting. This is possible because the IOS/IOS-XE routers support RADIUS CoA, which is used to reauthorize an endpoint after ISE completes compliance or posture checking.

To enable AAA globally:

```
aaa new-model
```

To add ISE RADIUS Server Groups configuration:

```
aaa group server radius ISE
   server-private 10.28.20.200 key Cisco123
```

To add ISE Change of Authorization configuration:

```
aaa server radius dynamic-author
  client 10.28.20.200 server-key Cisco123
     server-key Cisco123
     auth-type any
```

Next, add AAA lists to the configuration, which will be referenced later in the configuration:

```
aaa authentication login VPNAUTHC group ISE
aaa authorization network VPNAUTHZ local
aaa accounting network VPNACCT start-stop group ISE
aaa accounting update newinfo
```

A VPN IP pool needs to be added to be used for address assignment of connecting endpoints. The VPN pool requires routing advertisement, which is outside the scope of this example:

```
ip local pool VPNPOOL 192.168.10.10 192.168.10.20
```

An IKEv2 authorization policy needs to be defined. The authorization policy defines the local authorization policy and contains local and/or remote attributes. Local attributes, for example, VPN routing and forwarding (VRF) and the QoS policy, are applied locally. Remote attributes, such as IP address pool, subnet mask, and DNS, are pushed to the peer via the configuration mode.

```
crypto ikev2 authorization policy VPN-POLICY
   pool VPNPOOL
   dns 10.28.10.50
   netmask 255.255.255.0
   def-domain sanbower.net
```

The IKEv2 profile is a repository of non-negotiable parameters of the IKE SA, such as local or remote identities and AAA methods and services that are available to authenticated peers that match the profile:

```
crypto ikev2 profile VPN-PROFILE
  match identity remote key-id sanbower.net
```

```
identity local dn
authentication local rsa-sig
authentication remote eap query-identity
pki trustpoint CSR-TP
dpd 60 2 on-demand
aaa authentication eap VPNAUTHC
aaa authorization group eap list VPNAUTHZ VPN-POLICY
aaa authorization user eap cached
aaa accounting eap VPNACCT
virtual-template 10
```

The IPsec transform set defines the data encryption, data authentication, and the encapsulation mode:

```
crypto ipsec transform-set VPN-TS esp-aes esp-sha-hmac
  mode tunnel
```

The IPsec profile will tie together the transform set and the IKEv2 profile:

```
crypto ipsec profile VPN-IPSEC-PROFILE
    set transform-set VPN-TS
    set ikev2-profile VPN-PROFILE
```

Finally, the virtual template referenced in the IKEv2 profile needs the IPsec profile assigned along with IP address and tunnel information. The Virtual Template feature provides a generic service that can be used to apply predefined interface configurations (virtual template interfaces) in creating and freeing virtual access interfaces dynamically, as needed:

```
interface Virtual-Template10 type tunnel
    ip unnumbered GigabitEthernet2
    tunnel mode ipsec ipv4
    tunnel protection ipsec profile VPN-IPSEC-PROFILE
```

To configure AnyConnect to connect to the router, an AnyConnect configuration profile must be configured to specify the Auth Method During IKE Negotiation. When connecting to an IOS VPN Headend, IKE Identity containing a group or domain as the client identity should be supplied. This field must match the "identity remote key-id" that is configured in the IKEv2 profile. The client sends the string as the ID_GROUP type IDi payload. By default, the string is *$AnyConnectClient$*. Figure 10-37 illustrates adding a server to the AnyConnect Profile Editor that will connect to the example IKEv2 profile previously defined.

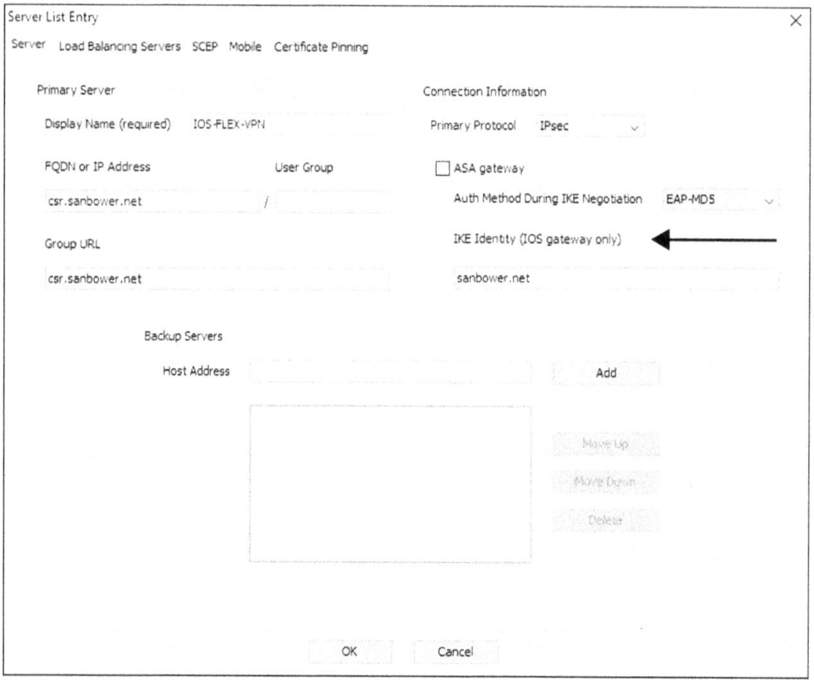

Figure 10-37 *AnyConnect Profile Editor: Adding IOS FlexVPN Server*

Once the configuration is created, the AnyConnect Profile Editor will save the output in XML format. Example 10-4 shows the output of the server entry in XML.

Example 10-4 *AnyConnect XML Profile Server Entry*

```
<ServerList>
    <HostEntry>
        <HostName>IOS-FLEX-VPN</HostName>
        <HostAddress>csr.sanbower.net</HostAddress>
        <PrimaryProtocol>IPsec
            <StandardAuthenticationOnly>true
                <AuthMethodDuringIKENegotiation>EAP-MD5</AuthMethodDuringIKENe-
gotiation>
                <IKEIdentity>sanbower.net</IKEIdentity>
            </StandardAuthenticationOnly>
        </PrimaryProtocol>
    </HostEntry>
</ServerList>
```

Once connected to the VPN, the commands in Example 10-5 enable you to validate the connection on the router.

Example 10-5 *IOS Validation of VPN Session*

```
CSR#show crypto session detail
Crypto session current status
Code: C - IKE Configuration mode, D - Dead Peer Detection
K - Keepalives, N - NAT-traversal, T - cTCP encapsulation
X - IKE Extended Authentication, F - IKE Fragmentation
R - IKE Auto Reconnect, U - IKE Dynamic Route Update
S - SIP VPN

Interface: Virtual-Access1
Profile: VPN-PROFILE
Uptime: 00:04:32
Session status: UP-ACTIVE
Peer: 10.28.128.176 port 54361 fvrf: (none) ivrf: (none)
      Phase1_id: sanbower.net
      Desc: (none)
  Session ID: 4
  IKEv2 SA: local 10.28.10.151/4500 remote 10.28.128.176/54361 Active
        Capabilities:DNX connid:1 lifetime:23:55:28
  IPSEC FLOW: permit ip 0.0.0.0/0.0.0.0 host 192.168.10.10
       Active SAs: 2, origin: crypto map
       Inbound:  #pkts dec'ed 1840 drop 0 life (KB/Sec) 4607776/3327
       Outbound: #pkts enc'ed 294 drop 0 life (KB/Sec) 4607977/3327


CSR#show crypto ikev2 sa detail
 IPv4 Crypto IKEv2  SA

Tunnel-id Local                  Remote             fvrf/ivrf          Status
1        10.28.10.151/4500     10.28.128.176/54361   none/none          READY
      Encr: AES-CBC, keysize: 256, PRF: SHA512, Hash: SHA512, DH Grp:21, Auth sign:
  RSA, Auth verify: EAP
      Life/Active Time: 86400/300 sec
      CE id: 1002, Session-id: 1
      Status Description: Negotiation done
      Local spi: D93A1C9731230528       Remote spi: 58DBA8D20D26F75D
      Local id: cn=csr.sanbower.net
      Remote id: sanbower.net
      Remote EAP id: jamie
      Local req msg id:  0              Remote req msg id:  15
      Local next msg id: 0              Remote next msg id: 15
      Local req queued:  0              Remote req queued:  15
      Local window:      5              Remote window:      1
      DPD configured for 60 seconds, retry 2
      Fragmentation not  configured.
```

```
Dynamic Route Update: disabled
Extended Authentication configured.
NAT-T is detected  outside
Cisco Trust Security SGT is disabled
Assigned host addr: 192.168.10.10
Initiator of SA : No
```

Clientless Remote Access VPN

Clientless SSL VPN, also referred to as WebVPN, enables end users to securely access resources on an organization's network from anywhere using an SSL-enabled web browser. The user first authenticates with a clientless SSL VPN gateway, which then allows the user to access preconfigured network resources. Clientless remote access VPNs are popular for use cases where the organization does not manage the connecting user's device, typically because the IT support team does not want to support installing a thick VPN client on the machine. Disaster recovery, business partners, and contractor connectivity are all good examples of use cases that benefit from clientless remote access VPN deployments.

Clientless VPNs can allow access to the following:

- Internal websites
- Web-enabled applications
- NT/Active Directory or other file shares
- Microsoft Outlook on the web
- Application access (smart tunnel or port forwarding access to other TCP-based applications)

Clientless SSL VPN uses the Secure Sockets Layer protocol and its successor, Transport Layer Security (SSL/TLS), to provide the secure connection between remote users and specific, supported internal resources that are configured as an internal server.

Although some IOS router versions support clientless features, the ASA firewall is the only viable headend that should be used for client remote access VPN deployments.

The administrator provides access to resources by users of clientless SSL VPN sessions on a group basis. Users have no direct access to resources on the internal network. The ASA recognizes connections that must be proxied, and the HTTP server interacts with the authentication subsystem to authenticate users. The ASA will proxy all of the connections coming from the clients, with a few minor exceptions, such as port forwarding and smart tunnels.

There are five major steps to configuring clientless RAVPN on the ASA:

Step 1.   Configure the identity certificate that will be used by the ASA.

Step 2.   Enable the WebVPN service on an ASA interface.

Step 3.   Create a list of servers and/or Uniform Resource Locator (URL) for WebVPN access.

Step 4.   Create a group policy for WebVPN users.

Step 5.   Apply the new group policy to a tunnel group.

To simplify these steps, open the ASDM and select **Wizards > VPN Wizards > Clientless SSL VPN Wizard**. The wizard walks you through all the required configuration steps. Figure 10-38 illustrates Step 1 of the wizard.

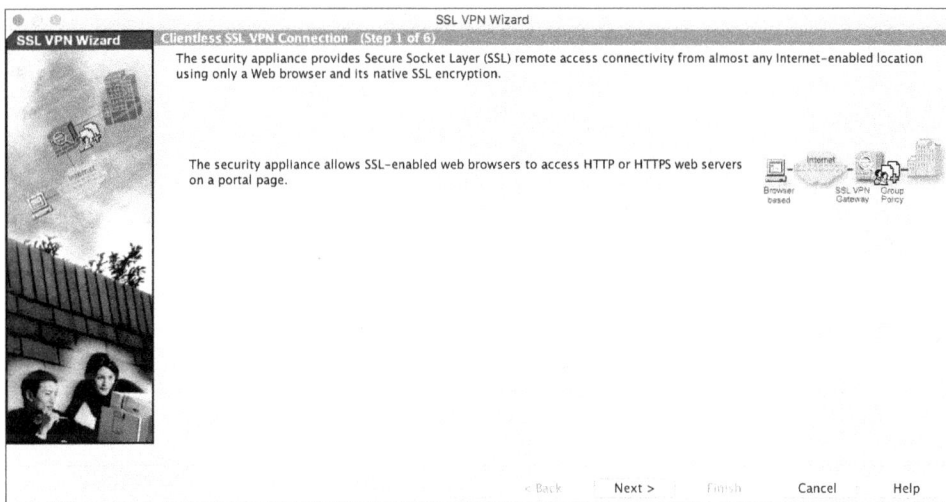

Figure 10-38   *ASA Clientless SSL VPN Wizard: Overview*

Click **Next** and complete Step 2 of the wizard by providing a connection profile name and specifying which interface the VPN service should run on, typically the outside interface, as shown in Figure 10-39. Like any web server using HTTPS, the server requires a certificate to perform SSL/TLS. For production, publicly signed certificates are highly recommended. For an example or a lab, a self-signed certificate is fine. If there are multiple VPNs or groups, a user must either connect to a group URL/alias or select the correct alias via a drop-down list on the login page. Similarly to client-based VPNs, connection profiles map to group policies, so having multiple connection profiles is one method to provide differentiated access to resources.

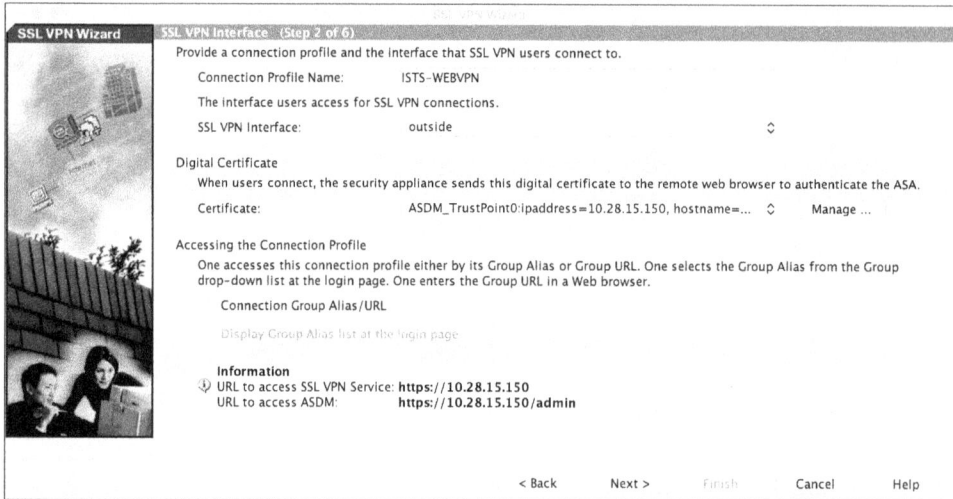

Figure 10-39 *ASA Clientless SSL VPN Wizard: VPN Profile and Interface Configuration*

Clientless SSL VPN allows user authentication using the ASA's local database or an AAA server, such as ISE, ACS, or LDAP. Figure 10-40 shows selection of the local database and a few users added.

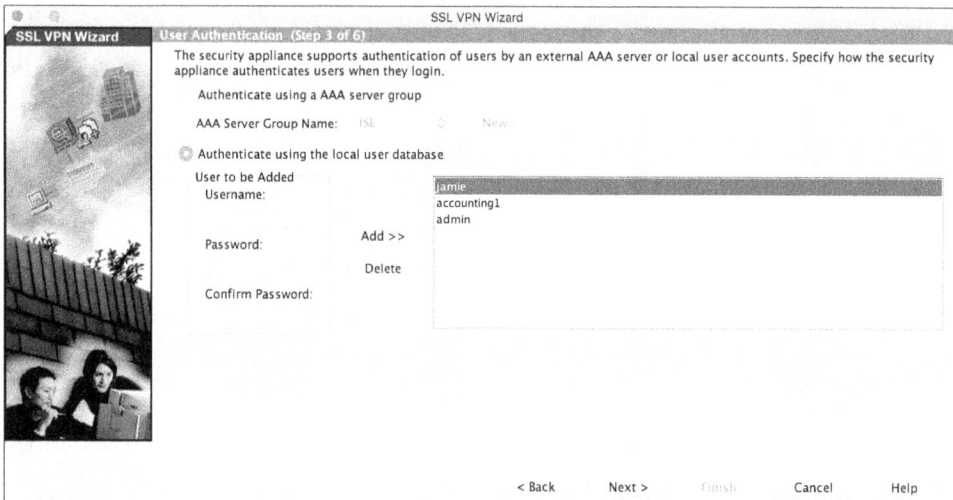

Figure 10-40 *ASA Clientless SSL VPN Wizard: User Authentication*

Step 4 of the wizard allows you to either create a new group policy or select an existing group policy as a default for the connection profile. Assigning group policies via authentication is done exactly the same way for clientless SSL VPN, as shown previously in the "RAVPN with ASA" section.

Step 5 of the wizard enables you to define bookmarks for the WebVPN. Bookmarks are just like those you probably use with a browser, such as Firefox or Chrome—saved locations that can be easily accessed. The wizard allows use of the bookmarks panel to configure lists of servers and URLs for access over clientless SSL VPN. To create a new bookmark list, click manage next to the drop-down list of bookmarks in Step 5 of the wizard and then click "Add". When creating a bookmark, the ASA will prompt you to specify what type of bookmark it is. Figure 10-41 represents the three types of bookmarks. The different types allow for additional levels of automation of single sign-on (SSO) to applications. This can include configurations that achieve SSO by posting authentication data to a custom form on a web application.

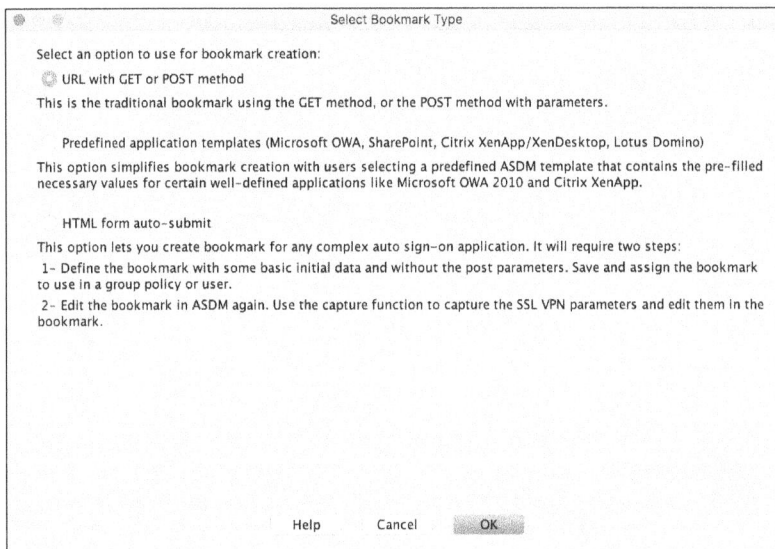

Figure 10-41   *ASA Clientless SSL VPN Wizard: Bookmark Type*

Figure 10-42 shows an example of a traditional bookmark being created for Common Internet File System (CIFS) File Share.

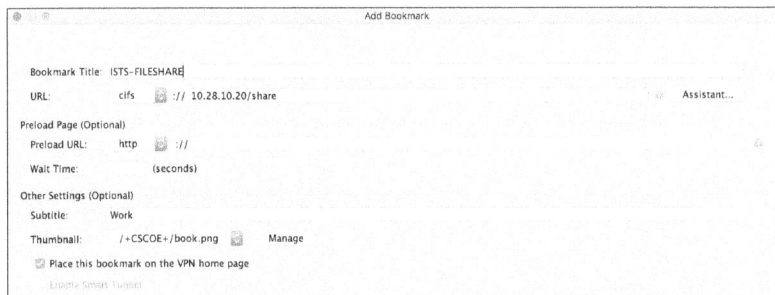

Figure 10-42   *ASA Clientless SSL VPN Wizard: Bookmark Creation*

Once all the appropriate bookmarks are added to the list, you can reorder and search through the bookmarks, as shown in Figure 10-43. Outside of the VPN Wizard, organizations can assign the bookmark list to one or more policies using group policies, dynamic access policies, or both. Each policy can have only one bookmark list.

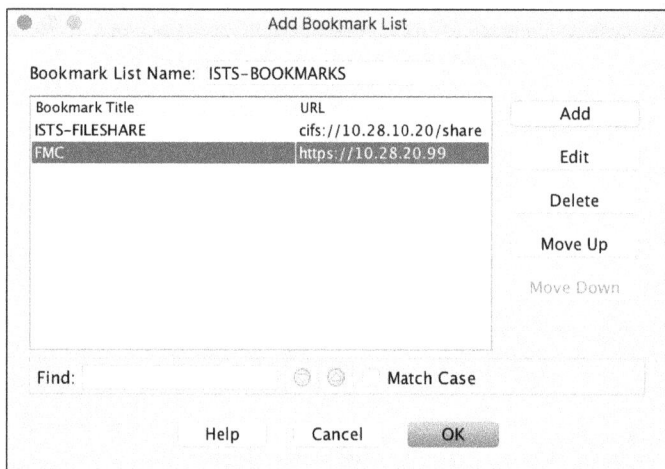

Figure 10-43   *ASA Clientless SSL VPN Wizard: Bookmark List*

Note   Configuring bookmarks does not prevent the user from visiting fraudulent sites or sites that violate an organization's policy. In addition to assigning a bookmark list, it is recommended to apply a web ACL to the policies, group, or DAP, to control access to traffic flows. Another alternative is to switch off URL entry on these policies to prevent user confusion over what is accessible.

Figure 10-44 shows the selection of the created bookmark list within Step 5 of the wizard. After clicking **Next**, you can review and submit the configuration settings to the ASA. Some configuration items completed in the wizard do not have a CLI equivalent, hence the use of the ASDM solely. For example, the bookmarks are converted from the ASDM to .xml lists that are imported as web content into the ASA.

Once finished, clients can connect through a web browser to the ASA. A login screen, like the one shown in Figure 10-45, is presented asking for group information and credentials. After the initial login, the user will be presented with a home page, as shown in Figure 10-46.

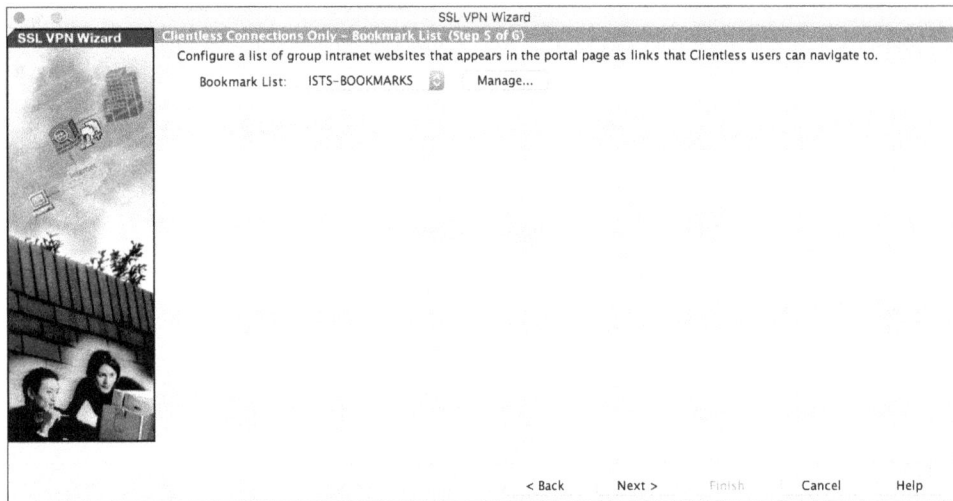

Figure 10-44   *ASA Clientless SSL VPN Wizard – Bookmark List Selection*

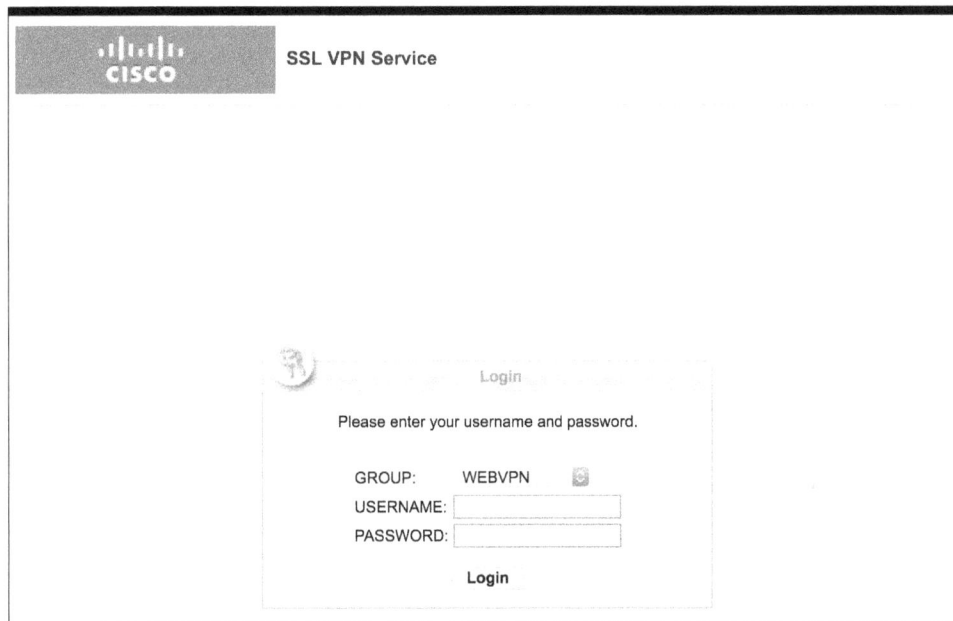

Figure 10-45   *ASA Clientless SSL VPN Login Screen*

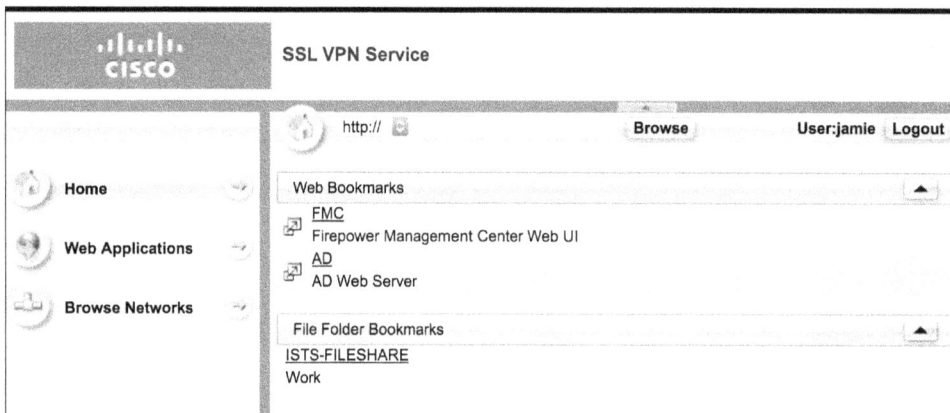

Figure 10-46   *ASA Clientless SSL VPN Home Page*

After getting the basics going, modifying the created group policy or creating a new one is probably the most common configuration step. In the ASDM, go to **Configuration > Remote Access VPN > Clientless SSL VPN Access > Group Policies** to add or edit a group policy. Figure 10-47 shows the portal configuration of the group policy, where everything from URL entry to smart tunnels can be configured on a per-group basis.

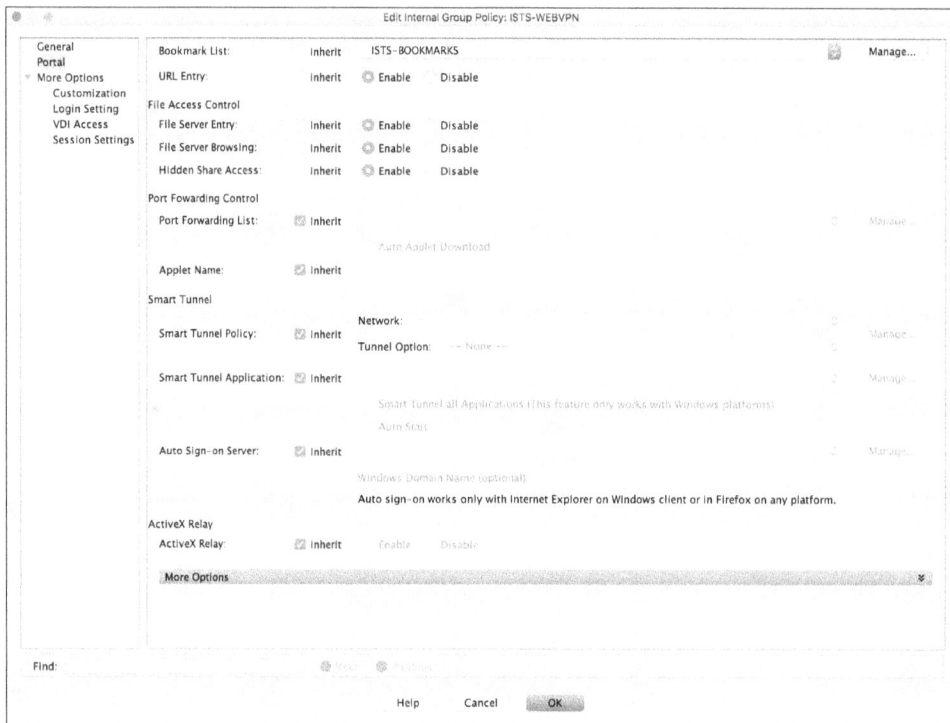

Figure 10-47   *ASA Clientless SSL VPN Group Policy Customization*

While clientless SSL VPN offers many different advanced features to customize the end-user experience, the list that follows represents the most commonly implemented features:

■ **Smart tunnels:** A connection between a TCP-based application and a private site, using a clientless (browser-based) SSL VPN session with the ASA as a proxy server. Smart tunnels use a Java applet to forward the traffic to the ASA. Microsoft Outlook is an example of an application that can be configured via smart tunnels to allow direct communication through the ASA. In this example, the user would be able to synchronize email with Microsoft Exchange even though the user is not directly connected to the network. Figure 10-48 shows the creation of a smart-tunnel app, which is performed by going to **Configuration > Remote Access VPN > Clientless SSL VPN Access > Portal > Smart Tunnels** and adding a new application list.

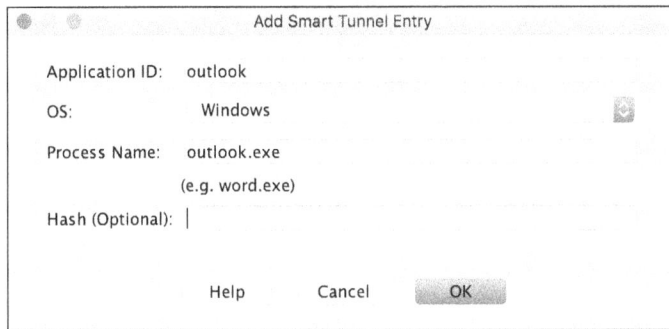

Figure 10-48 *ASA Clientless SSL VPN Smart Tunnels*

■ **Port forwarding:** Port forwarding lets users access TCP-based applications over a clientless SSL VPN connection. Port forwarding requires local administrative privileges on the client machine. Port forwarding is a legacy technology superseded by smart tunnels. In function, port forwarding accomplishes the same thing as smart tunnels, allowing access directly to services via proxying on the ASA, but it is accomplished differently. In port forwarding, to allow access to the exchange server, a local port would be opened (e.g., TCP 10443) which would map to the server's port 443.

■ **Virtual desktop support:** The ASA supports connections to Citrix and VMware VDI servers. This allows users to log in remotely to a desktop and work like they normally would on a machine inside the organization.

■ **Plug-ins:** A browser plug-in is a separate program that a web browser invokes to perform a dedicated function, such as connect a client to a server within the browser window. The ASA allows organizations to import plug-ins for download to remote browsers in clientless SSL VPN sessions. Examples of plug-ins include a Telnet/SSH plug-in or a Remote Desktop Protocol (RDP) plug-in.

■ **Dynamic Access Policies (DAP):** The DAP can be used to assign web ACLs, bookmarks, and functions based on AAA information or endpoint attributes. The DAP was covered in detail earlier in the chapter in the "Client-Based VPN" section.

■ **Portal customization:** The logon, portal, and logout pages can be customized to enhance and brand the clientless SSL VPN user experience. An organization can either modify the existing templates, including font, colors, text, logos, and so forth, or import an entirely custom HTML page. Figure 10-49 illustrates customizing the Title Panel.

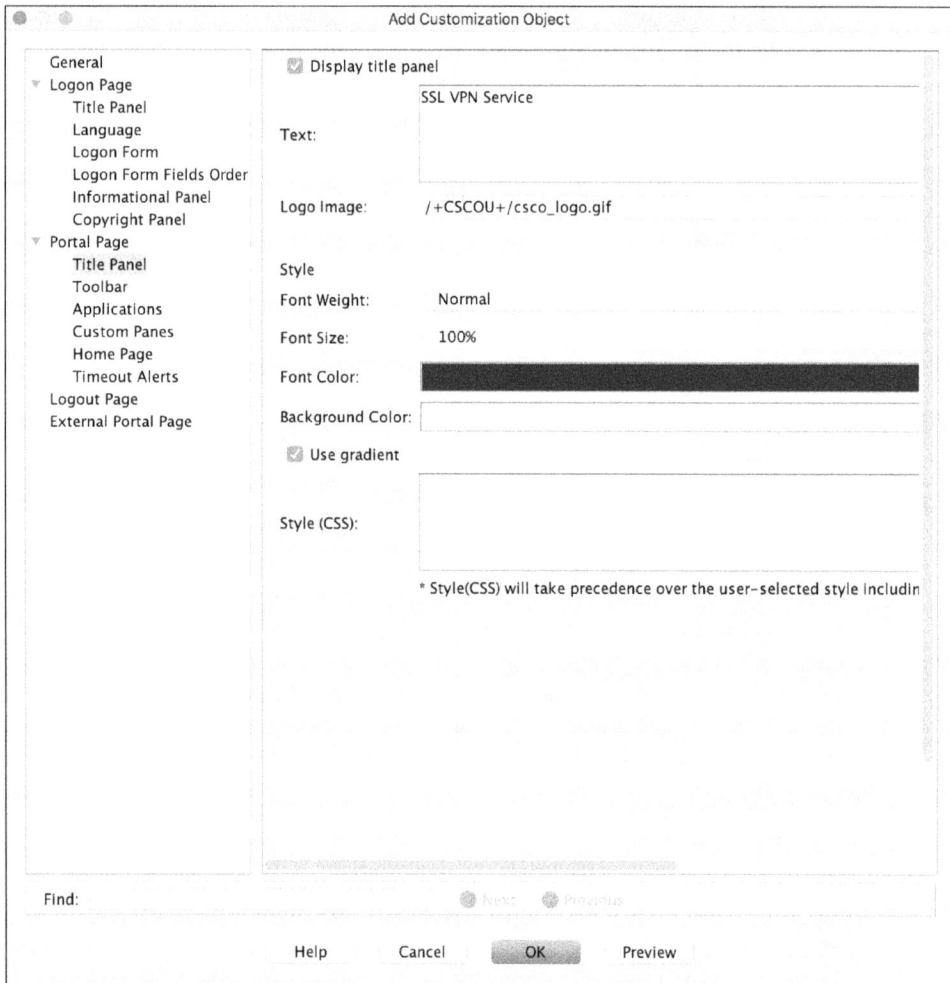

Figure 10-49 *ASA Clientless SSL VPN Portal Customization*

Summary

In this chapter, you learned about client-based and clientless remote access VPNs. You examined the different headends available for VPNs, including ASA, FTD, and IOS. You found out how to integrate posture assessment into VPN deployments. Finally, you reviewed some step-by-step example configurations that can help get you started.

References

ASDM Book 3: Cisco ASA Series VPN ASDM Configuration Guide, 7.9, https://www. cisco.com/c/en/us/td/docs/security/asa/asa99/asdm79/vpn/asdm-79-vpn-config.html

CLI Book 3: Cisco ASA Series VPN CLI Configuration Guide, 9.9, https://www.cisco. com/c/en/us/td/docs/security/asa/asa99/configuration/vpn/asa-99-vpn-config.html

AnyConnect Remote Access VPN configuration on FTD, https://www.cisco.com/c/en/ us/support/docs/network-management/remote-access/212424-anyconnect-remote-access-vpn-configurati.html

Remote Access VPNs for Firepower Threat Defense, https://www.cisco.com/c/en/us/td/ docs/security/firepower/623/configuration/guide/fpmc-config-guide-v623/firepower_ threat_defense_remote_access_vpns.pdf

Configure AnyConnect Secure Mobility Client with Split Tunneling on an ASA, https:// www.cisco.com/c/en/us/support/docs/security/anyconnect-secure-mobility-client/119006-configure-anyconnect-00.html

Cisco AnyConnect Secure Mobility Client Administrator Guide, Release 4.7, https:// www.cisco.com/c/en/us/td/docs/security/vpn_client/anyconnect/anyconnect47/ administration/guide/b_AnyConnect_Administrator_Guide_4-7.html

Cisco AnyConnect Secure Mobility Client: Configuration Examples and TechNotes, https://www.cisco.com/c/en/us/support/security/anyconnect-secure-mobility-client/ products-configuration-examples-list.html

ASA Version 9.2.1 VPN Posture with ISE Configuration Example, https://www. cisco.com/c/en/us/support/docs/security/adaptive-security-appliance-asa-software/117693-configure-ASA-00.html

Configure ISE Posture with FlexVPN, https://www.cisco.com/c/en/us/support/docs/ security/identity-services-engine/213400-configure-ise-posture-with-flexvpn.html

Part IV

The Red Pill

Chapter 11

Security Virtualization and Automation

This chapter will cover the concepts and practice of using virtualization and automation with respect to security in today's networks. Virtualization and automation can mean many things. The concept of using a hypervisor platform that can emulate the hardware equivalent is one type of virtualization that likely first comes to mind. As for automation, you might think of systems taking action based on a simple rule set over APIs or native integrations. This chapter will go well beyond those examples, as virtualization and automation mean much more in the networks operated today.

Cisco Virtual Solutions and Server Virtualization

For someone to say we don't offer a virtual option to a customer today would likely be met with a look of bewilderment by the customer or end user. The use of hypervisors and server virtualization has been around for quite some time and pretty much everything (there are some exceptions) can be virtualized on a platform such as VMware ESXi, Microsoft Hyper-V, KVM, and many more. Cisco security solutions strive to offer a virtual option across the board on all products.

Let's take a quick rundown of the virtual offerings that Cisco has in the portfolio:

- Adaptive Security Virtual Appliance (ASAv)

- Next-Generation Firewall Virtual (NGFWv)

- Identity Services Engine (ISE)

- Stealthwatch

- Email Security Virtual Appliance (ESAv)

- Web Security Virtual Appliance (WSAv)

- Many more...

Virtualizing systems in a hypervisor platform implies running multiple systems on a single host platform that runs the hypervisor software. These host platforms, such as the Cisco Unified Computing System (UCS), have the capability to have more processing power and memory on board than the typical server platform from the days of old. A single server running two, four, or more CPU sockets with 12+ processors per socket and over 1 terabyte of memory is not out of the question in a data center. Unless there is a super resource-hungry application or process running on the server, it doesn't make sense to only run one application on it. Hypervisors allow the system CPU and memory resources to be shared across multiple workloads running on that single server, thereby decreasing costs of multiple servers, power, HVAC, and more. Figure 11-1 illustrates the basic concept of virtualizing server platforms onto a single hypervisor host such as the UCS C240 M5.

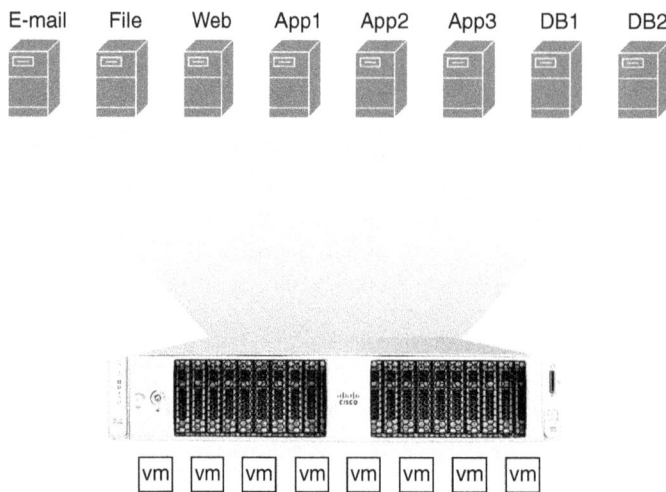

Figure 11-1   *Server Virtualization Basics*

There are some exceptions to the benefits of virtualization! What are they? Notice the word "shared" in the previous paragraph. This is where the first exception comes into play, which is the effect of shared resources on application stability and variable resource requirements. Many times, when analyzing how many workloads can be run on the hypervisor, the concept of shared resources is calculated in. Suppose you have 10 workloads that each need two CPUs and 4 GB of memory to install and run. Commonly, those workloads will not need *all* of the CPU and memory at the same point in time; therefore, instead of needing 20 CPUs and 40 GB of memory, you may be able to pare down the requirements to a shared 10 CPUs and 20 GB of memory that can be utilized when needed by all the workloads. What happens, however, when the workloads start seeing utilization that requires them to use all of those CPU and memory resources to process the requests of the application or service it is running? Well, you have a resource shortage and resource allocation collision. What if the workloads are sensitive database applications or user-facing security applications? The oversubscription of resources via poor capacity planning, a migration of workloads to oversubscribed hosts, or other issues can cause application instability and, in some cases, application failure such as corrupting a database. In the end, good capacity planning can prevent these issues from arising; however, some applications are just better off having their own hardware that isn't shared with any other workload.

Other exceptions that don't require as much description as above are application scale or capacity, such as number of supported active hosts using the virtual application or active VPN session terminations and more. Another exception is interface speed and throughput of the platform. Remember that a 100-GB interface might be capable with a hypervisor host platform; however, it is shared with the other workloads on that system. Always refer to the virtual system's datasheet to find these scale and throughput numbers for the system that you are looking at using. Because this is a security book, we will not dive deeper into server virtualization and capacity planning.

Now enough with the negatives and pitfalls that you might encounter with general server virtualization, let's take a look at the benefits. Looking at a few of the Cisco virtual solution options, we can review the benefits of each:

- Cisco ASAv
  - Has the same code and feature set as the physical platform with the exception of clustering and multiple context, including site-to-site, remote access, and clientless VPN. Do you need multiple context *and* virtual with the ASA? Deploy multiple instances of ASAv! The ability to spin up multiple ASAv instances gives you the option to deploy a dedicated firewall function per workload or group of workloads.
  - Using ASAv in the data center to protect workloads in conjunction with ASAs in your production network gives you uniform security across different network domains and a common configuration syntax.
  - Provides firewall functions for East-West traffic in the hypervisor that may never hit a physical firewall upstream in the network from the host.
  - Software-defined networking dynamic provisioning can be done when an SDN rule or contract requires firewall functions in between two workloads or external clients and the workload.
  - Offers scalable throughput options from 100-Mbps to 10-Gbps virtual appliances.
- Cisco Content Security Virtual Appliances: WSAv and ESAv
  - Web and email traffic is rather unpredictable these days, and using WSAv and ESAv gives administrators the ability to provision additional resources on the fly during peaks or just due to general growth.
  - No need to buy and ship appliances for additional content filtering.
  - Provided at no cost with an active Web or Email Security bundle.

■ Cisco NGFWv

■ Provides visibility and protection in the hypervisor by seeing the traffic that may never leave the host and being able to protect the workloads at the hypervisor level.

■ Provides required protection in the virtual environment in accordance with regulations such as PCI DSS and HIPAA.

■ Protects inadvertent security exposure to the workload.

■ Managed and monitored from the same FMC that can be managing the physical sensors at the Internet edge or elsewhere in the production network with a common policy throughout.

■ Like the ASAv and its physical counterpart, NGFWv has the same code and functions as the physical Firepower platforms.

Virtualization and Automation Solutions

As we proceed through the solutions and capabilities available, separating them into "virtual only" and "automation only" categories is rather difficult because the functions of the solutions leverage both categories to achieve the platform-specific task. For instance, virtualizing a firewall dynamically based on a contract or automatic policy application via dynamic group assignment kind of fits into both virtualization and automation. All that being said, we can dig into the technologies of interest.

Cisco Virtual Security Gateway

The Cisco Virtual Security Gateway (VSG) combined with the Cisco Nexus 1000V switch provides security for VM-to-VM or external-to-VM traffic. The VSG can be deployed in VMware vSphere, Microsoft Hyper-V, and KVM environments. For lack of a better term, the VSG is related to a firewall for traffic policy enforcement in the environment. The primary benefits of the VSG are as follows:

■ Dynamic (virtualization-aware) operation

■ Cisco Virtual Service Data Path (vPath)-aware enforcement

■ Operational simplicity

■ Efficient deployment

Let's dig a bit further into the first two of those benefits, starting with dynamic operation. The VSG working with the Nexus 1000V and vPath supports the requirements of dynamic virtualization. Security policy is broken down into trust zones and associated security profiles for the network tenants or business purpose. Cisco Prime Network Services Controller (NSC) defines the security profiles that are attached and bound to the Nexus 1000V port profiles within the Nexus 1000V Virtual Supervisor Module (VSM). The port profiles are then published into the hypervisor management platform for assignment to the virtual machine. When a new VM is built or migrated on the host, the administrator would assign the port profile to the VM's virtual Ethernet port, resulting in the security policy being applied as well. After initial build of the VM, no matter where that VM moves within the virtual environment, the policy stays with it. Administrators can also easily move the VM from one security zone to another, such as development to test network migration, by simply changing the port profile. The movement of a virtual work-load between hosts in the same deployment using vMotion or Hyper-V Live Migration events are also not impacted, and again the security will follow.

The other function where the VSG and the Nexus 1000V differ from physical network path insertion is with Cisco vPath. With vPath, the administrator can steer traffic from external sources or for VM-to-VM traffic to a virtual service node such as the VSG or others. As you can see in Figure 11-2, the traffic steering can be a simple one-step process or can include multiple redirections based on the policy. vPath provides a plat-form for dynamic service insertion on the fly via simple port profile/policy changes.

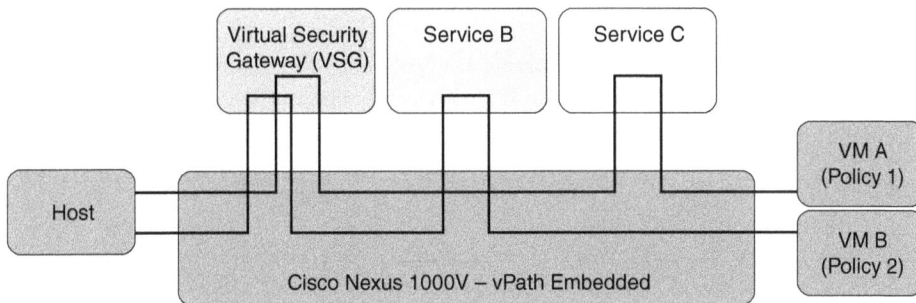

Figure 11-2   *vPath Virtual Service Node Insertion*

You might be thinking, "Why is this dynamic traffic steering function only available in the Nexus 1000V with the VSG?" Well, it isn't, and that leads us into our next topic of service function chaining with Network Service Header (NSH).

Service Function Chaining with Network Service Header

Even without knowing it, if you have implemented a network service, you have likely done service function chaining (SFC). Have you ever had to figure out how to design a firewall to fit into the Internet edge or data center edge? Layer 2 or Layer 3? Where should the IPS reside? Those very questions (and others) and the implementation of them via physical cabling, VLAN mapping, VRFs, PBR, or any other means of traffic control is essentially service function chaining. Now that you have that in mind, what happens when you want to add another service or remove one? You will likely have to deal with another outage and likely another change to the network topology.

What if you could insert services into (or remove them from) the traffic path of any flow or network just simply based on a configuration attribute? What if the firewall, IDS/IPS, Wide Area Application Service (WAAS), or other service didn't even have to be located in the traffic path at all? That's what the function of service chaining and NSH is intended to provide. Based on the successes of vPath, however, missing that same ability in physical networks and devices was the drive behind the development of NSH as the solution and proposal of NSH to the IETF, currently in draft, for standardization across more than just Cisco infrastructure.

NSH is often applied on ingress to the network between the packet or frame and the outer transport encapsulation such as GRE, VXLAN, MPLS, and more. Once inserted, the header data is analyzed against policy on the transport devices as it flows from source to destination. In this case, however, we have no reliance on the hypervisor or virtual Ethernet modules—everything is done natively by the network. NSH and the service path in which the traffic should be directed through the chain can be configured manually via the CLI or through a system such as the Cisco Application Policy Infrastructure Controller Enterprise Module (APIC-EM) or others to build the policy and push it to the network.

Figure 11-3 shows a service chain applying a simple policy for inbound and outbound traffic to the Internet with firewall and IPS where outbound traffic is only subject to the firewall policy and inbound traffic is subject to both the firewall and IPS policy.

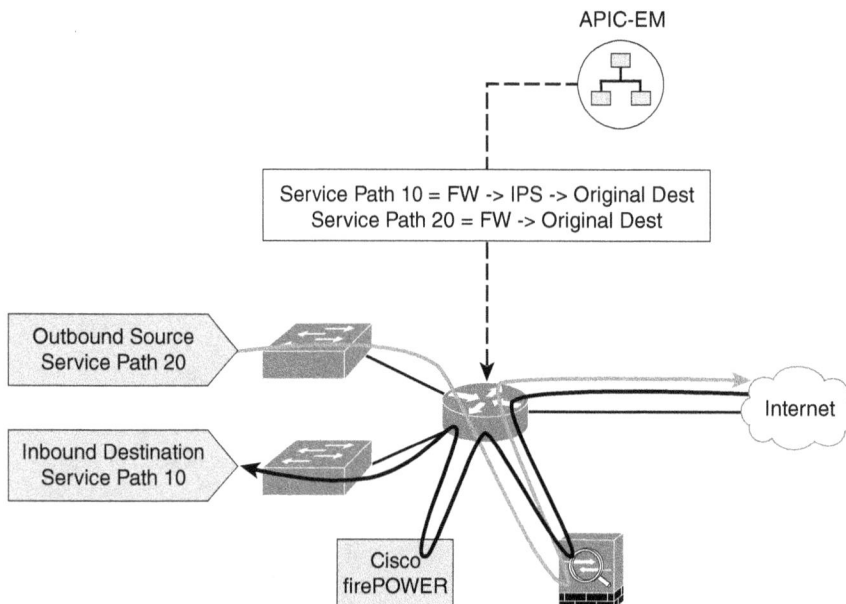

Figure 11-3 *NSH Service Chaining*

Example 11-1 shows a CLI example for Figure 11-3, without the service function (firewall/IPS) definitions.

Example 11-1 *Service Chaining Policy CLI*

```
service-chain service-path 10
  service-index 255 service-function IPS
  service-index 254 service-function FW-INBOUND
  service-index 253 terminate
!
service-chain service-path 20
  service-index 255 service-function FW-OUTBOUND
  service-index 254 terminate
!
ip access-list extended PERMITALL
 permit ip any any
!
class-map match-all ALLTRAFFIC
 match access-group PERMITALL
!
policy-map type service-chain OUTBOUND
 class all-ip
  forward service-path 20 service-index 255
!
policy-map type service-chain INBOUND
 class all-ip
  forward service-path 10 service-index 255
!
interface GigabitEthernet0/1
 description Inside Router Interface
 service-policy type service-chain input OUTBOUND
!
interface GigabitEthernet0/2
 description Router WAN Interface
 service-policy type service-chain input INBOUND
```

Even with the simple configurations in Example 11-1, you should be able to see how powerful NSH and service chaining can be in production networks. Simple, automated, and effective security can be inserted and removed on the fly through simple configuration parameters versus through rigorous network topology changes.

Network Function Virtualization

So, the VSG and vPath are great for virtual networks and NSH is great for traffic direction in physical and virtual environments, but what about deployment time and the hardware it takes to get all of this done? Pretty much every network or even small-est branch that we deal with today has three to four physical devices to manage and secure—a router/firewall, switch, and hosts/servers (and don't forget wireless, as no one has time for cables to plug in anymore!). In some very small branch locations, this can all be done by one device, and has been for many years through companies that provide small all-in-one devices that are managed locally. Notice those last two words, *managed locally*! Once a company expands or decides to branch out, often a small router doing all those functions is no longer sufficient because it must be managed and monitored by a central IT department. For a long time now, that has meant that each site has a dedicated router, switch, firewall, and more running. For example, head to your local fast-food joint, look through the drive-through window and you will likely see the stack of gear hanging in a wall-mounted rack, and think, "Why would a single fast-food restaurant with seven to ten people working need a full 48-port Gigabit switch and dedicated router and firewall?" There is no simple answer other than that it's the standardized deployment of a manage-able solution by a central IT department.

There is a simpler solution that is the product of the growth of the server virtualization market. If we can virtualize servers, why can't we virtualize network infrastructure too? Well, we can! The network no longer needs to be hardware-based, because we have rede-fined the network with software. Cisco Enterprise Network Functions Virtualization (NFV) enables us to do that. Some of the benefits are as follows:

- Deploy changes or network services across multiple sites in minutes without hardware ordering or delivery

- Reduce the footprint of hardware in your sites, saving on power, reducing complexity, and freeing up physical space that is no longer needed

- Create new locations all at once and on demand

- Orchestrate all nodes from a central platform

With NFV you have the option to convert your physical infrastructure onto a platform such as Cisco UCS, Cisco 4000 Series Integrated Services Routers (ISR), or Cisco 5000 Enterprise Network Compute System (ENCS). Each of these platforms have their own benefits but we won't cover them here as this is a security-focused book. That being said, there is some security to talk about when it comes to NFV.

From this point forward let's assume that only the ENCS platform will be used for executing NFV in the network. The ENCS 5000 platform provides the network and security functions and capability to automate and orchestrate from Cisco Enterprise Service Automation (ESA) or directly on the ENCS device. When we look at security for a remote office where ENCS would fit in, one of the first items to think about is likely security. With ENCS, you can deploy and stitch an ASAv into the traffic path of the net-work at the branch edge. Looking at the ENCS console, you can see empty whitespace with solution icons at the top and WAN/LAN physical interface mappings. Building the network path and stitching is simply done by dragging the desired system, shown at the top of the screen, into the whitespace and connecting them as desired. Once completed, the network is deployed and the virtual instances are spun up as designed. Once deployed, configuration can be completed on the solutions deployed in the ENCS device. Figure 11-4 shows the ENCS console with a basic network built and deployed.

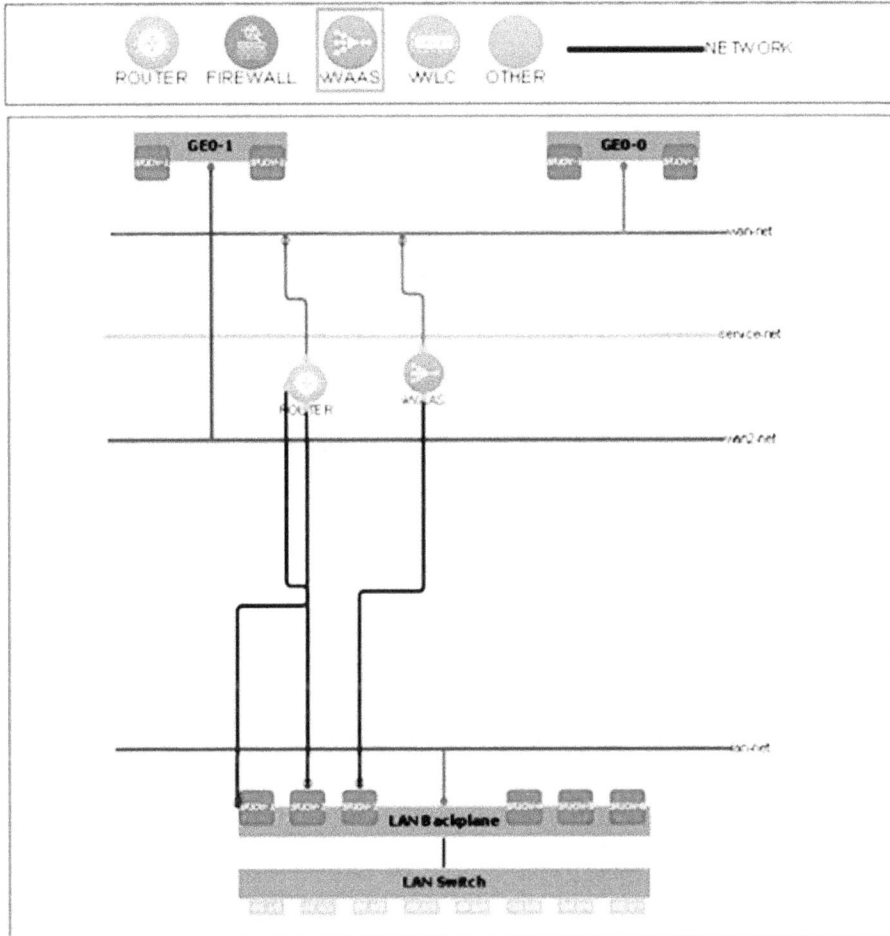

Figure 11-4   *Cisco ENCS VM Deployment*

Not only service providers but also enterprises can now leverage NFV and platforms such as ENCS to dynamically spin up and down remote offices as needed. In addition, the Cisco ESA platform supports zero-touch deployments based off templates and central control and monitoring.

Application Centric Infrastructure and Micro-Segmentation

Cisco Application Centric Infrastructure (ACI) provides network administrators the capability to integrate physical and virtual networks and workloads into a programmable fabric in the enterprise and data center. ACI leverages what is called the "network fabric," which combines all of the systems, such as routers and switches, into a single entity that is provisioned and monitored from a central station.

Cisco ACI transitions the classic three-tier network design of access, distribution, and core into what is called the spine-and-leaf topology. Figure 11-5 depicts an example of the ACI spine-and-leaf topology.

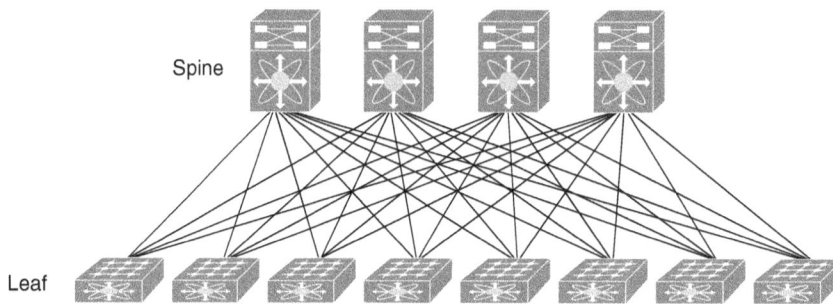

Figure 11-5   *Cisco ACI Spine-and-Leaf Topology*

As you can see in Figure 11-5, there are only two levels versus the three in the legacy design. The lower-tier leaf nodes are the access switches to connect to the servers or clients in the network. The spine nodes are the backbone of the network and interconnect to all leaf nodes in the topology. Traffic forwarding is done using random selection so that the traffic load is evenly distributed across all of the spine nodes in the design. Also important is that traffic has a consistent hop count to another node in the network (unless it is connected to the same leaf node) no matter where it is connected.

Once the spine-and-leaf design is completed, the next step of ACI is the concept of overlay networks. Before we dig into that, let's review a bit about the history of applications and networks. When initially designing networks, the idea of an application or system moving from one place to another was not a common use case, or even a scenario, when servers were the size of rooms. With that in mind, the IP address was not only the identity of the system but also the location. Since then, things have changed significantly— mobile systems, vMotion, dynamic service provisioning, and so forth have broken that mold into what we have today and, therefore, although the identity doesn't change, the location will. When we look at overlay networks, we need to separate the identity from the location. This is done by taking the original message from the system and its identity and encapsulating it with the location that it needs to be delivered to before forwarding it onto the network.

With ACI's spine-and-leaf architecture making all the nodes work together and look like a single physical switch, the concept of VLANs and forwarding using classic Layer 2 boundaries results in inefficient use of links and requires proper device placement in the design. When you think of large data centers and networks, the limitation of 4096 VLANs can be a factor as well. Another item of consideration is the movement of virtual workloads and requirements for Layer 2 adjacency for certain application functions such as replication or clustering. VXLAN is an industry-standard overlay that enables the extension of Layer 2 segments over Layer 3 architecture. This allows the network to expand and hosts to reside anywhere on the fabric without the risks or configuration complexity. As traffic enters the network, it is encapsulated into VXLAN packets and forwarded onto the destination. We could go on and on about other ACI topics, such as VXLAN Tunnel Endpoints (VTEP), VXLAN Instance ID (VNID), and the ton of other technology and acronyms associated with ACI and VXLAN, but they are not relevant to the Security CCIE topics. If you wish to dig deeper, check out *Deploying ACI: The Complete Guide to Planning, Configuring, and Managing Application Centric Infrastructure* (Cisco Press, 2018) by Frank Dagenhardt, Jose Moreno, and Bill Dufresne.

That said, there are some topics regarding ACI that are relevant to security and that you should know for the exams, including the following:

- Object models
- Device packages
- Application network profiles
- Endpoint groups
- Contracts
- Service graphs

Object Models

Similar to object-oriented programming, an object model provides the capability to make a change in one place that is reused in multiple places. With the legacy configuration methods of the CLI on Cisco IOS, IOS-XE, and more, the challenge of making changes sometimes resulted in connecting to multiple switches and routers to execute the same change. With ACI's object model, you can execute an ACL change that gets updated across the relevant devices in the infrastructure instantly. This model enables quick and effective change without the burden and overhead of manual CLI input across multiple platforms.

Device Packages

ACI device packages are importable packages that enable the ACI fabric to incorporate Layer 4 through Layer 7 devices into the packet flow seamlessly and include the capability to configure and monitor the L4–L7 device through the APIC controller. The device package consists of a configuration model formatted in XML and Python scripts for execution of the configuration on the device. Device packages are already written and enable the fabric to insert many types of device types into the flow, such as Cisco

ASA, FTD, Check Point, Palo Alto, A10, and more. You can also create your own device package if there is a function that you would like to insert that is not already available.

Figure 11-6 is a simple example device package operation with ACI.

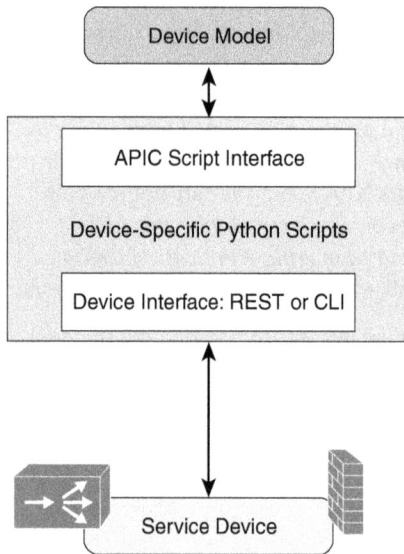

Figure 11-6 *Cisco ACI Device Package Operation*

Application Network Profiles

Application network profiles enable us to build a definition of how new devices in a particular network are set up and provisioned. Imagine a three-tier web, application, and database use case. In this scenario, we need to allow external web access into the fabric to the web tier, allow secure access from the web tier to the app tier with high priority, and finally allow secure app to DB communications. Using a profile, we can build a blueprint of what the packet flow should be and what devices should be inserted into the flow. For external access into the web server, we can insert the ASA with a secure firewall connection policy; the web tier to the app tier can have basic port filtering with QoS; and so on. This profile can then be reapplied to multiple servers with ease and automatic policy creation. Build, assign, deploy, and you're done.

Endpoint Groups

Now let's talk about the clients and servers that use the ACI fabric to communicate. ACI endpoint groups (EPGs) enable the logical grouping of application endpoints with complete separation from VLAN and IP addressing. By not having to rely on addressing for policy, ACI can use the relationship of two EPGs and the traffic that should be allowed between them as the policy. A few good ways to think about EPGs are as

Production, Development, and Test; or Web, Application, and Database. With ACI, all of the endpoints in these different EPGs can be in the same address space but have completely different policies applied because of their assignment to the EPG. Sounds a lot like TrustSec and Scalable/Security Group Tags from Chapter 4, right? That's because they are very similar, but SGTs are targeted more at user endpoints and ACI EPGs are used in the data center. That being said, user endpoint traffic goes into the data center and vice versa, in which case we can leverage the SGTs assigned on the LAN and EPG policy via integration of ISE with the APIC. ISE shares the SGT groups that are available in the TrustSec policy and the mapping is defined on the APIC as an external EPG. The APIC also shares the EPGs with ISE for TrustSec enforcement on ACI traffic that has left the fabric. As clients connect to the network, ISE shares the IP-to-SGT binding with APIC so that the appropriate EPG and associated contracts can be assigned as the client traffic enters the ACI fabric, and the same is done in reverse for server-to-client traffic out of the fabric. Figure 11-7 depicts how TrustSec tags can be mapped into EPGs with ACI.

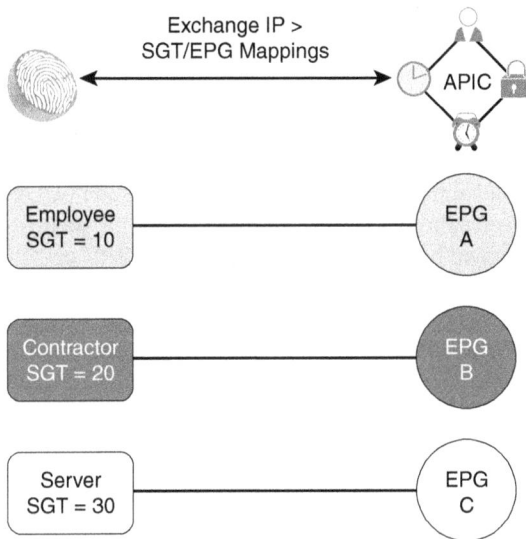

Figure 11-7   *Cisco TrustSec–ACI Policy Plane Integration*

Now that is a real segmentation story! Segmentation and micro-segmentation are achievable with ISE SGTs and ACI EPGs. Micro-segmentation is the primary function of those technologies. The ability to separate and control access in a zero-trust methodology along with the ability to not have to rely on VLANs or other methods of policy separation is why SGTs and EPGs are so important to understand. There is not much more to EPGs which is covered extensively in books dedicated to ACI such as, *Deploying ACI: The Complete Guide to Planning, Configuring, and Managing Application Centric Infrastructure*. How they are used for security, which we will cover next, is paramount to the function of ACI.

Contracts

Contracts! Scary word, right? When we think of contracts, we think of legally binding documents full of unintelligible statements that hold us responsible to take some action, make some payment, or some other obligation. With ACI, contracts are much less scary but follow the same principal: an agreement of permitted and enforceable action between two parties. Contracts are built between relational mappings of EPGs, such as web to app. The contracts follow the provider-consumer model where an EPG has services that an endpoint in another EPG wants to use. At the basic level, a contract is essentially an ACL with a source EPG, a destination EPG, and a service. ACI follows the hard-set rule of zero trust, meaning hosts within two different EPGs have zero ability to communicate without the explicit definition of a contract between them. There are a few protocol exceptions, such as EIGRP, OSPF, DHCP, and Multicast, that are allowed between EPGs without a contract. On the other side of that, all hosts within the same EPG can communicate without a contract.

Contracts can execute many functions directly with the fabric, such as permit, deny, mark (DSCP/CoS), and log. You can also redirect or copy traffic within the contract when service graphs are in use (which we will cover next). The contracts can also be enabled for reverse port filtering, where the provider and consumer can initiate the traffic specified in the contract filter without the other initiating first communication. In the previous discussion of application network profiles, contracts are what are assigned in the profile to filter the traffic from web to app and app to DB, for example. Contracts can be reused and shared all over the fabric as well. Without getting too deep out of the security aspects of ACI, contracts can be assigned to a scope of Global, Tennant, VRF, or Application profile to limit accessibility of the contract to others on the same fabric.

Service Graphs

The last item that we will cover with regard to security with ACI is service graphs. This topic was saved until last because service graphs build on everything we have covered thus far. Service graphs in ACI act very much like a service chain, covered earlier in this chapter. Using the service graph ACI can redirect traffic to a firewall, IPS, load balancer, and so on without the need for the security device to be in the traffic path or routing topology. There are three different management modes for the service graph that dictate how they use the network or device packages that are defined in the graph:

- **Network Policy Mode:** Also commonly called Unmanaged Mode, in this mode, the ACI fabric only manages the network portion or traffic flow within the graph. No configuration is pushed to the device type.

- **Service Policy Mode:** Also commonly called Managed Mode, in this mode, ACI configures the network and pushes the relevant configuration to the L4–L7 device using the device package.

- **Service Manager Mode:** This mode enables multiple administrators to define the policy separately and have it pushed to the fabric and L4–L7 device. For example, the security administrator would build the firewall policy and the network administrator would build the network policy and associate the L4–L7 policy with the network policy.

Now that you understand the different types of service graphs, we will look at how service graphs come into play with the traffic as it goes through a contract. In Figure 11-8 you can see a consumer EPG of External connecting to a provider EPG of WebServer. This relationship has a contract (ExternaltoWeb) associated to it that can be associated with Graph1, which inserts a firewall device, or Graph2, which inserts a load balancer, or Graph3, which has a sequence of firewall and load balancer. This contract can associate all traffic with one of the graphs or can even use a different graph for different Layer 4 relationships in the contract.

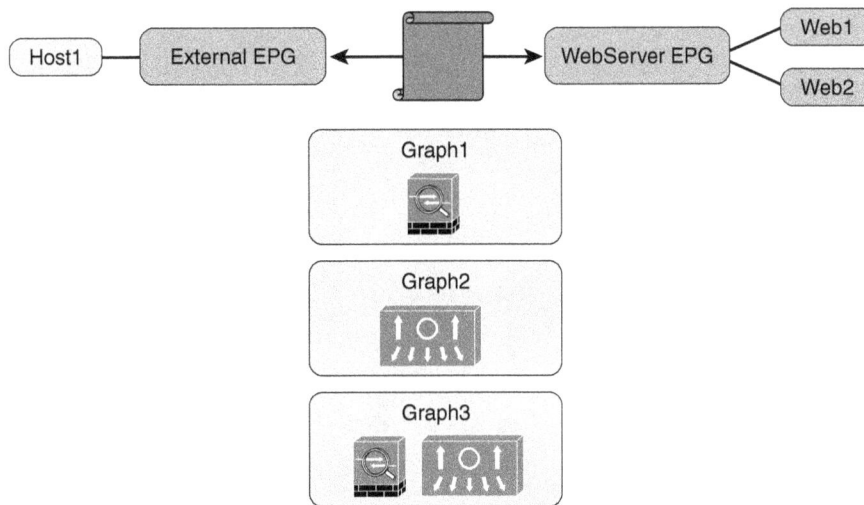

Figure 11-8 *Cisco ACI Service Graphs*

As you have seen throughout this section, there are a lot of tools in the ACI framework and the relationships between those pieces. Effective use, understanding, and implementation of those tools enables security practitioners to execute effective policy and micro-segmentation in the LAN and data center with ACI.

Summary

In this chapter, you learned about many different types of virtualization, from basic x86 server virtualization all the way to network virtualization and automation. Looking at technologies such as NFV and NSH may have you wondering how long the networks will look and function the way they do now. We also covered the security-centric concepts and introduction of ACI along with network segmentation and what products can achieve it. These topics are the result of technology evolution and growth to meet the needs of the network consumer. Today's networks are always evolving and becoming more agile and programmable, maybe to the point of working via voice commands in the future. As the need evolves, the network does the same, and keeping on top of emerging technology is a trait of a seasoned CCIE.

References

Service Graph Design with Cisco Application Centric Infrastructure White Paper, https://www.cisco.com/c/en/us/solutions/collateral/data-center-virtualization/application-centric-infrastructure/white-paper-c11-734298.html

Cisco Virtual Security Gateway, https://www.cisco.com/c/en/us/products/switches/virtual-security-gateway/index.html

Service Graph Design with Cisco Application Centric Infrastructure, https://www.cisco.com/c/en/us/solutions/collateral/data-center-virtualization/application-centric-infrastructure/white-paper-c11-734298.pdf

Index

Numbers

802.1AE, 470–473

802.1X, 199

authentication servers, 55

authenticators, 55

C3PL switch configuration, 95–96

Catalyst switch configuration, 79

components of, 54–56

EAP (Extensible Authentication Protocol)

authentication type identity stores, 61

types of, 57–61

EasyConnect as stepping-stone to, 183–186

MAB (MAC Authentication Bypass), 62–65

supplicants, 55

verification

with Cisco WLC (Wireless LAN Controller), 145–147

endpoint supplicant verification, 140

network access device verification, 140–145

overview of, 140

Web Authentication

CWA (Centralized Web Authentication), 69–71

LWA (Local Web Authentication), 66–69

overview of, 65–66

A

AAA (authentication, authorization, and accounting). *See also* device administration; network access control; policies; posture assessment; profiles

centralized, 307–308

commands, 73–74

concept of, 3–4

configuration, 197

credentials, 4

definition of, 4

protocols, 4–5

RADIUS (Remote Authentication Dial-In User Service)

accounting messages, 14–15

accounting servers, 119–120

authentication messages, 13–14

authentication servers, 118–119

D

E

H

J

K

L

M

Q-R

S

T

U

V

X-Y-Z